GIVE ME LIBERTY!

AN AMERICAN HISTORY

★

Brief Fifth Edition

GIVE ME LIBERTY!

AN AMERICAN HISTORY

★

Brief Fifth Edition

VOLUME 2: FROM 1865

ERIC FONER

W · W · NORTON & COMPANY
NEW YORK · LONDON

For my mother, Liza Foner (1909–2005), an accomplished artist who lived through most of the twentieth century and into the twenty-first

W. W. Norton & Company has been independent since its founding in 1923, when William Warder Norton and Mary D. Herter Norton first published lectures delivered at the People's Institute, the adult education division of New York City's Cooper Union. The firm soon expanded its program beyond the Institute, publishing books by celebrated academics from America and abroad. By midcentury, the two major pillars of Norton's publishing program—trade books and college texts—were firmly established. In the 1950s, the Norton family transferred control of the company to its employees, and today—with a staff of four hundred and a comparable number of trade, college, and professional titles published each year—W. W. Norton & Company stands as the largest and oldest publishing house owned wholly by its employees.

Editor: Steve Forman
Associate Editor: Scott Sugarman
Project Editors: Katie Callahan, Jennifer Barnhardt
Editorial Assistants: Travis Carr, Kelly Rafey
Managing Editor, College: Marian Johnson
Managing Editor, College Digital Media: Kim Yi
Production Manager: Sean Mintus
Media Editor: Laura Wilk
Associate Media Editor: Michelle Smith
Media Project Editor: Rachel Mayer
Media Assistant Editor: Chris Hillyer
Marketing Manager, History: Sarah England Bartley
Associate Design Director: Hope Miller Goodell
Designer: Chin-Yee Lai
Photo Editor: Stephanie Romeo
Permissions Manager: Megan Schindel
Permissions Specialist: Bethany Salminen
Composition: Jouve
Illustrations: Mapping Specialists, Ltd.
Manufacturing: Transcontinental

Permission to use copyrighted material is included on page A-105.

ISBN 978-0-393-60340-8

W. W. Norton & Company, Inc., 500 Fifth Avenue, New York, NY 10110-0017
wwnorton.com

W. W. Norton & Company Ltd., Castle House, 15 Carlisle Street, London W1D 3BS
2 3 4 5 6 7 8 9 0

ABOUT THE AUTHOR

ERIC FONER is DeWitt Clinton Professor of History at Columbia University, where he earned his B.A. and Ph.D. In his teaching and scholarship, he focuses on the Civil War and Reconstruction, slavery, and nineteenth-century America. Professor Foner's publications include *Free Soil, Free Labor, Free Men: The Ideology of the Republican Party before the Civil War*; *Tom Paine and Revolutionary America*; *Nothing but Freedom: Emancipation and Its Legacy*; *Reconstruction: America's Unfinished Revolution, 1863–1877*; *The Story of American Freedom; and Forever Free: The Story of Emancipation and Reconstruction*. His history of Reconstruction won the *Los Angeles Times* Book Award for History, the Bancroft Prize, and the Parkman Prize. He has served as president of the Organization of American Historians and the American Historical Association. In 2006 he received the Presidential Award for Outstanding Teaching from Columbia University. His most recent books are *The Fiery Trial: Abraham Lincoln and American Slavery*, winner of the Bancroft and Lincoln Prizes and the Pulitzer Prize for History, and *Gateway to Freedom: The Hidden History of the Underground Railroad*, winner of the New York Historical Society Book Prize.

CONTENTS

About the Author ... v

List of Maps, Tables, and Figures ... xvi

Preface ... xviii

Acknowledgements ... xxv

15. "WHAT IS FREEDOM?": RECONSTRUCTION, 1865-1877 ... 441

THE MEANING OF FREEDOM ... 443

Families in Freedom ... 443 ★ Church and School ... 444 ★ Political Freedom ... 444 ★ Land, Labor, and Freedom ... 445 ★ Masters without Slaves ... 445 ★ The Free Labor Vision ... 447 ★ The Freedmen's Bureau ... 447 ★ The Failure of Land Reform ... 448 ★ The White Farmer ... 449

Voices of Freedom: *From* Petition of Committee in Behalf of the Freedmen to Andrew Johnson (1865), and *From* A Sharecropping Contract (1866) ... 450

The Aftermath of Slavery ... 453

THE MAKING OF RADICAL RECONSTRUCTION ... 454

Andrew Johnson ... 454 ★ The Failure of Presidential Reconstruction ... 454 ★ The Black Codes ... 455 ★ The Radical Republicans ... 456 ★ The Origins of Civil Rights ... 456 ★ The Fourteenth Amendment ... 457 ★ The Reconstruction Act ... 458 ★ Impeachment and the Election of Grant ... 459 ★ The Fifteenth Amendment ... 460 ★ The "Great Constitutional Revolution" ... 460 ★ The Rights of Women ... 461

RADICAL RECONSTRUCTION IN THE SOUTH ... 462

"The Tocsin of Freedom" ... 462 ★ The Black Officeholder ... 464 ★ Carpetbaggers and Scalawags ... 464 ★ Southern Republicans in Power ... 465 ★ The Quest for Prosperity ... 465

THE OVERTHROW OF RECONSTRUCTION ... 466

Reconstruction's Opponents ... 466 ★ "A Reign of Terror" 467 The Liberal Republicans ... 469 ★ The North's Retreat ... 470 ★ The Triumph of the Redeemers ... 471 ★ The Disputed Election and Bargain of 1877 ... 472 ★ The End of Reconstruction ... 473

REVIEW ... 474

16. AMERICA'S GILDED AGE, 1870-1890 ... 475

THE SECOND INDUSTRIAL REVOLUTION ... 476

The Industrial Economy ... 477 ★ Railroads and the National Market ... 478 ★ The Spirit of Innovation ... 480 ★ Competition and Consolidation ... 480 ★ The Rise of Andrew Carnegie ... 481 ★ The Triumph of John D. Rockefeller ... 481 ★ Workers' Freedom in an Industrial Age ... 483

THE TRANSFORMATION OF THE WEST ... 484

A Diverse Region ... 484 ★ Farming in the Trans-Mississippi West ... 485 ★ The Cowboy and the Corporate West ... 487 ★ The Chinese Presence ... 487 ★ Conflict on the Mormon Frontier ... 489 ★ The Subjugation of the Plains Indians ... 490 ★ "Let Me Be a Free Man" ... 491 ★ Remaking Indian Life ... 492 ★ The Dawes Act and Wounded Knee ... 492 ★ Settler Societies and Global Wests ... 493

Voices of Freedom: *From* Speech of Chief Joseph of the Nez Percé Indians, in Washington, D.C. (1879), and *From* Letter by Saum Song Bo, *American Missionary* (October 1885) ... 494

Myth, Reality, and the Wild West ... 497

POLITICS IN A GILDED AGE ... 497

The Corruption of Politics ... 498 ★ The Politics of Dead Center ... 499 ★ Government and the Economy ... 500 ★ Reform Legislation ... 500 ★ Political Conflict in the States ... 501

FREEDOM IN THE GILDED AGE ... 502

The Social Problem ... 502 ★ Social Darwinism in America ... 502 ★ Liberty of Contract and the Courts ... 503

LABOR AND THE REPUBLIC ... 505

"The Overwhelming Labor Question" ... 505 ★ The Knights of Labor and the "Conditions Essential to Liberty" ... 505 ★ Middle-Class Reformers ... 506 ★ Protestants and Moral Reform ... 507 ★ A Social Gospel ... 508 ★ The Haymarket Affair ... 509 ★ Labor and Politics ... 509

REVIEW ... 511

17. FREEDOM'S BOUNDARIES, AT HOME AND ABROAD, 1890-1900 ... 512

THE POPULIST CHALLENGE ... 514

The Farmers' Revolt ... 514 ★ The People's Party ... 515 ★ The Populist Platform ... 516 ★ The Populist Coalition ... 517 ★ The Government and Labor ... 517 ★ Populism and Labor ... 518 ★ Bryan and Free Silver ... 519 ★ The Campaign of 1896 ... 520

THE SEGREGATED SOUTH ... 521

The Redeemers in Power ... 521 ★ The Failure of the New South Dream ... 521 ★ Black Life in the South ... 522 ★ The Kansas Exodus ... 522 ★ The Decline of Black Politics ... 523 ★ The Elimination of Black Voting ... 524 ★ The Law of Segregation ... 525 ★ The Rise of Lynching ... 526 ★ Politics, Religion, and Memory ... 527

REDRAWING THE BOUNDARIES ... 528

The New Immigration and the New Nativism ... 528 ★ Chinese Exclusion and Chinese Rights ... 529 ★ The Emergence of Booker T. Washington ... 531 ★ The Rise of the AFL ... 531 ★ The Women's Era ... 532

BECOMING A WORLD POWER ... 533

The New Imperialism ... 533 ★ American Expansionism ... 534 ★ The Lure of Empire ... 534 ★ The "Splendid Little War" ... 535 ★ Roosevelt at

San Juan Hill ... 537 ★ An American Empire ... 537 ★ The Philippine War ... 539 ★ Citizens or Subjects? ... 539

Voices of Freedom: *From* Booker T. Washington, Address at the Atlanta Cotton Exposition (1895), and *From* W. E. B. Du Bois, "Of Mr. Booker T. Washington and Others" (1903) ... 540

Drawing the Global Color Line ... 543 ★ "Republic or Empire?" ... 544

REVIEW ... 545

18. THE PROGRESSIVE ERA, 1900-1916 ... 546

AN URBAN AGE AND A CONSUMER SOCIETY ... 548

Farms and Cities ... 548 ★ The Muckrakers ... 549 ★ Immigration as a Global Process ... 549 ★ The Immigrant Quest for Freedom ... 550 ★ Consumer Freedom ... 551 ★ The Working Woman ... 552 ★ The Rise of Fordism ... 553 ★ The Promise of Abundance ... 553

VARIETIES OF PROGRESSIVISM ... 554

Industrial Freedom ... 554 ★ The Socialist Presence and Eugene Debs ... 555 ★ AFL and IWW ... 556 ★ The New Immigrants on Strike ... 557

Voices of Freedom: *From* Charlotte Perkins Gilman, *Women and Economics* (1898), and *From* John Mitchell, "The Workingman's Conception of Industrial Liberty" (1910) ... 558

Labor and Civil Liberties ... 560 ★ The New Feminism ... 560 ★ The Birth-Control Movement ... 561 ★ Native American Progressivism ... 562

THE POLITICS OF PROGRESSIVISM ... 562

Effective Freedom ... 562 ★ State and Local Reforms ... 563 ★ Progressivism in the West ... 563 ★ Progressive Democracy ... 565 ★ Jane Addams and Hull House ... 566 ★ The Campaign for Woman Suffrage ... 567 ★ Maternalist Reform ... 567

THE PROGRESSIVE PRESIDENTS ... 570

Theodore Roosevelt ... 570 ★ John Muir and the Spirituality of Nature ... 571 ★ The Conservation Movement ... 572 ★ Taft in Office ... 572 ★ The Election of 1912 ... 573 ★ New Freedom and New Nationalism ... 574 ★ Wilson's First Term ... 575 ★ The Expanding Role of Government ... 576

REVIEW ... 577

19. SAFE FOR DEMOCRACY: THE UNITED STATES AND WORLD WAR I, 1916-1920 ... 578

AN ERA OF INTERVENTION ... 580

"I Took the Canal Zone" ... 580 ★ The Roosevelt Corollary ... 582 ★ Moral Imperialism ... 583 ★ Wilson and Mexico ... 583

AMERICA AND THE GREAT WAR ... 584

Neutrality and Preparedness ... 585 ★ The Road to War ... 586 ★ The Fourteen Points ... 587

THE WAR AT HOME ... 588

The Progressives' War ... 588 ★ The Wartime State ... 589 ★ The Propaganda War ... 589 ★ The Coming of Woman Suffrage ... 590 ★ Prohibition ... 591

Voices of Freedom: *From* Woodrow Wilson, War Message to Congress (1917), and *From* Eugene V. Debs, Speech to the Jury before Sentencing under the Espionage Act (1918) ... 592

Liberty in Wartime ... 594 ★ The Espionage and Sedition Acts ... 594 ★ Coercive Patriotism ... 595

WHO IS AN AMERICAN? ... 596

The "Race Problem" ... 596 ★ The Anti-German Crusade ... 597 ★ Toward Immigration Restriction ... 597 ★ Groups Apart: Mexicans and Asian-Americans ... 598 ★ The Color Line ... 598 ★ Roosevelt, Wilson, and Race ... 599 ★ W. E. B. Du Bois and the Revival of Black Protest ... 599 ★ Closing Ranks ... 600 ★ The Great Migration... 601 ★ Racial Violence, North and South ... 602 ★ The Rise of Garveyism ... 603

1919 ... 603

A Worldwide Upsurge ... 603 ★ Upheaval in America ... 604 ★ The Red Scare ... 604 ★ Wilson at Versailles ... 605 ★ The Wilsonian Moment ... 607 ★ The Seeds of Wars to Come ... 609 ★ The Treaty Debate ... 609

REVIEW ... 611

20. FROM BUSINESS CULTURE TO GREAT DEPRESSION: THE TWENTIES, 1920-1932 ... 612

THE BUSINESS OF AMERICA ... 614

A Decade of Prosperity ... 614 ★ A New Society ... 615 ★ The Limits of Prosperity ... 616 ★ The Farmers' Plight ... 616 ★ The Image of Business ... 617 ★ The Decline of Labor ... 618 ★ The Equal Rights Amendment ... 618 ★ Women's Freedom ... 619

BUSINESS AND GOVERNMENT ... 620

The Republican Era ... 621 ★ Corruption in Government ... 621 ★ The Election of 1924 ... 622 ★ Economic Diplomacy ... 622

THE BIRTH OF CIVIL LIBERTIES ... 623

A "Clear and Present Danger" ... 624 ★ The Court and Civil Liberties ... 624

THE CULTURE WARS ... 625

The Fundamentalist Revolt ... 625 ★ The Scopes Trial ... 627 ★ The Second Klan ... 628 ★ Closing the Golden Door ... 628 ★ Race and the Law ... 629 ★ Promoting Tolerance ... 631 ★ The Emergence of Harlem ... 631

Voices of Freedom: *From* Lucian W. Parrish, Speech in Congress on Immigration (1921), and *From* Majority Opinion, Justice James C. McReynolds, in *Meyer v. Nebraska* (1923) ... 632

The Harlem Renaissance ... 634

THE GREAT DEPRESSION ... 635

The Election of 1928 ... 635 ★ The Coming of the Depression ... 636 ★ Americans and the Depression ... 638 ★ Resignation and Protest ... 639 ★ Hoover's Response ... 640 ★ The Worsening Economic Outlook ... 640 ★ Freedom in the Modern World ... 641

REVIEW ... 642

21. THE NEW DEAL, 1932-1940 ... 643

THE FIRST NEW DEAL ... 645

FDR and the Election of 1932 ... 645 ★ The Coming of the New Deal ... 645 ★ The Banking Crisis ... 646 ★ The NRA ... 647 ★ Government Jobs ... 648 ★ Public-Works Projects ... 649 ★ The New Deal and Agriculture ... 650 ★ The New Deal and Housing ... 651 ★ The Court and the New Deal ... 652

THE GRASSROOTS REVOLT ... 652

Labor's Great Upheaval ... 652 ★ The Rise of the CIO ... 653 ★ Labor and Politics ... 654 ★ Voices of Protest ... 655 ★ Religion on the Radio ... 656

THE SECOND NEW DEAL ... 656

The WPA and the Wagner Act ... 657 ★ The American Welfare State: Social Security ... 658

A RECKONING WITH LIBERTY ... 659

Voices of Freedom: *From* Franklin D. Roosevelt, "Fireside Chat" (1934), and *From* John Steinbeck, *The Harvest Gypsies: On the Road to the Grapes of Wrath* (1938) ... 660

The Election of 1936 ... 662 ★ The Court Fight ... 662 ★ The End of the Second New Deal ... 663

THE LIMITS OF CHANGE ... 664

The New Deal and American Women ... 664 ★ The Southern Veto ... 665 ★ The Stigma of Welfare ... 666 ★ The Indian New Deal ... 666 ★ The New Deal and Mexican-Americans ... 667 ★ Last Hired, First Fired ... 667 ★ Federal Discrimination ... 669

A NEW CONCEPTION OF AMERICA ... 669

The Heyday of American Communism ... 670 ★ Redefining the People ... 670 ★ Challenging the Color Line ... 671 ★ Labor and Civil Liberties ... 672 ★ The End of the New Deal ... 673 ★ The New Deal in American History ... 674

REVIEW ... 675

22. FIGHTING FOR THE FOUR FREEDOMS: WORLD WAR II, 1941-1945 ... 676

FIGHTING WORLD WAR II ... 678

Good Neighbors ... 678 ★ The Road to War ... 679 ★ Isolationism ... 679 ★ War in Europe ... 680 ★ Toward Intervention ... 681 ★ Pearl Harbor ... 681 ★ The War in the Pacific ... 682 ★ The War in Europe ... 683

THE HOME FRONT ... 686

Mobilizing for War ... 686 ★ Business and the War ... 687 ★ Labor in Wartime ... 688 ★ Fighting for the Four Freedoms ... 688 ★ The Fifth Freedom ... 689 ★ Women at Work ... 690

VISIONS OF POSTWAR FREEDOM ... 691

Toward an American Century ... 691 ★ "The Way of Life of Free Men" ... 692 ★ *The Road to Serfdom* ... 693

THE AMERICAN DILEMMA ... 693

Patriotic Assimilation ... 694 ★ The *Bracero* Program ... 694 ★ Indians during the War ... 695

Voices of Freedom: *From* League of United Latin American Citizens, "World War II and Mexican Americans" (1945), and *From* Charles H. Wesley, "The Negro Has Always Wanted the Four Freedoms," in *What the Negro Wants* (1944) ... 696

Asian-Americans in Wartime ... 698 ★ Japanese-American Internment ... 698 ★ Blacks and the War ... 700 ★ Blacks and Military Service ... 701 ★ Birth of the Civil Rights Movement ... 701 ★ The Double-V ... 702 ★ The War and Race ... 702 ★ *An American Dilemma* ... 703 ★ Black Internationalism ... 704

THE END OF THE WAR ... 704

"The Most Terrible Weapon" ... 705 ★ The Dawn of the Atomic Age ... 705 ★ The Nature of the War ... 706 ★ Planning the Postwar World ... 707 ★ Yalta and Bretton Woods ... 707 ★ The United Nations ... 708 ★ Peace, but Not Harmony ... 708

REVIEW ... 710

23. THE UNITED STATES AND THE COLD WAR, 1945–1953 ... 711

ORIGINS OF THE COLD WAR ... 713

The Two Powers ... 713 ★ The Roots of Containment ... 713 ★ The Truman Doctrine ... 714 ★ The Marshall Plan ... 715 ★ The Reconstruction of Japan ... 716 ★ The Berlin Blockade and NATO ... 717 ★ The Growing Communist Challenge ... 717 ★ The Korean War ... 719 ★ Cold War Critics ... 721 ★ Imperialism and Decolonization ... 721

THE COLD WAR AND THE IDEA OF FREEDOM ... 722

Freedom and Totalitarianism ... 722 ★ The Rise of Human Rights ... 723 ★ Ambiguities of Human Rights ... 724

THE TRUMAN PRESIDENCY ... 724

The Fair Deal ... 724 ★ The Postwar Strike Wave ... 725 ★ The Republican Resurgence ... 725 ★ Postwar Civil Rights ... 726 ★ *To Secure These Rights* ... 727 ★ The Dixiecrat and Wallace Revolts ... 728

THE ANTICOMMUNIST CRUSADE ... 729

Loyalty and Disloyalty ... 730 ★ The Spy Trials ... 731 ★ McCarthy and McCarthyism ... 732 ★ The Atmosphere of Fear ... 733 ★ The Uses of Anticommunism ... 733

Voices of Freedom: *From* Joseph R. McCarthy, Speech at Wheeling (1950), and *From* Margaret Chase Smith, Speech in the Senate (1950) ... 734

Anticommunist Politics ... 736 ★ Cold War Civil Rights ... 737

REVIEW ... 739

24. AN AFFLUENT SOCIETY, 1953-1960 ... 740

THE GOLDEN AGE ... 742

A Changing Economy ... 743 ★ A Suburban Nation ... 743 ★ The Growth of the West ... 745 ★ The TV World ... 746 ★ Women at Work and at Home ... 746 ★ A Segregated Landscape ... 747 ★ The Divided Society ... 748 ★ Religion and Anticommunism ... 748 ★ Selling Free Enterprise ... 749 ★ The Libertarian Conservatives and the New Conservatives ... 749

THE EISENHOWER ERA ... 750

Ike and Nixon ... 750 ★ The 1952 Campaign ... 751 ★ Modern Republicanism ... 752 ★ The Social Contract ... 753 ★ Massive Retaliation ... 753 ★ Ike and the Russians ... 754 ★ The Emergence of the Third World ... 755 ★ Origins of the Vietnam War ... 756 ★ Mass Society and Its Critics ... 757 ★ Rebels without a Cause ... 758

THE FREEDOM MOVEMENT ... 759

Origins of the Movement ... 759 ★ The Legal Assault on Segregation ... 760 ★ The *Brown* Case ... 761 ★ The Montgomery Bus Boycott ... 762 ★ The Daybreak of Freedom ... 763 ★ The Leadership of King ... 764 ★ Massive Resistance ... 764 ★ Eisenhower and Civil Rights ... 765

Voices of Freedom: *From* Martin Luther King Jr., Speech at Montgomery, Alabama (December 5, 1955), and *From* The Southern Manifesto (1956) ... 766

THE ELECTION OF 1960 ... 768

Kennedy and Nixon ... 768 ★ The End of the 1950s ... 770

REVIEW ... 771

25. THE SIXTIES, 1960-1968 ... 772

THE CIVIL RIGHTS REVOLUTION ... 774

The Rising Tide of Protest ... 774 ★ Birmingham ... 775 ★ The March on Washington ... 776

THE KENNEDY YEARS ... 776

Kennedy and the World ... 777 ★ The Missile Crisis ... 777 ★ Kennedy and Civil Rights ... 778

LYNDON JOHNSON'S PRESIDENCY ... 779

The Civil Rights Act of 1964 ... 780 ★ Freedom Summer ... 780 ★ The 1964 Election ... 781 ★ The Conservative Sixties ... 782 ★ The Voting Rights Act ... 783 ★ Immigration Reform ... 784 ★ The Great Society ... 784 ★ The War on Poverty ... 785 ★ Freedom and Equality ... 785

THE CHANGING BLACK MOVEMENT ... 786

The Ghetto Uprisings ... 786 ★ Malcolm X ... 788 ★ The Rise of Black Power ... 788

VIETNAM AND THE NEW LEFT ... 789

Old and New Lefts ... 789 ★ The Fading Consensus ... 790 ★ America and Vietnam ... 791

Voices of Freedom: *From* Barry Goldwater, Speech at Republican National Convention (1964), and *From* Statement of Purpose, National Organization for Women (1966) ... 792

Lyndon Johnson's War ... 794 ★ The Antiwar Movement ... 796 ★ The Counterculture ... 796 ★ Personal Liberation and the Free Individual ... 797 ★ Faith and the Counterculture ... 797

THE NEW MOVEMENTS AND THE RIGHTS REVOLUTION ... 798

The Feminine Mystique ... 799 ★ Women's Liberation ... 799 ★ Personal Freedom ... 800 ★ Gay Liberation ... 800 ★ Latino Activism ... 801 ★ Red Power ... 801 ★ Environmentalism and the Consumer Movement ... 802 ★ The Rights Revolution ... 803 ★ The Right to Privacy ... 804

1968 ... 805

A Year of Turmoil ... 805 ★ The Global 1968 ... 806 ★ Nixon's Comeback ... 807 ★ The Legacy of the Sixties ... 807

REVIEW ... 808

26. THE TRIUMPH OF CONSERVATISM, 1969–1988 ... 809

PRESIDENT NIXON ... 810

Nixon's Domestic Policies ... 811 ★ Nixon and Welfare ... 811 ★ Nixon and Race ... 812 ★ The Burger Court ... 812 ★ The Continuing Sexual Revolution ... 813 ★ Nixon and Détente ... 814

VIETNAM AND WATERGATE ... 816

Nixon and Vietnam ... 816 ★ The End of the Vietnam War ... 817 ★ Watergate ... 818 ★ Nixon's Fall ... 818

THE END OF THE GOLDEN AGE ... 819

The Decline of Manufacturing ... 819 ★ Stagflation ... 821 ★ The Beleaguered Social Compact ... 821 ★ Ford as President ... 822 ★ The Carter Administration ... 823 ★ Carter and the Economic Crisis ... 823 ★ The Emergence of Human Rights Politics ... 824 ★ The Iran Crisis and Afghanistan ... 825

THE RISING TIDE OF CONSERVATISM ... 826

The Religious Right ... 827

Voices of Freedom: *From* Barry Commoner, *The Closing Circle* (1971), and *From* Richard E. Blakemore, Report on the Sagebrush Rebellion (1979) ... 828

The Battle over the Equal Rights Amendment ... 830 ★ The Abortion Controversy ... 831 ★ The Tax Revolt ... 832 ★ Conservatism in the West ... 832 ★ The Election of 1980 ... 833

THE REAGAN REVOLUTION ... 834

Reagan and American Freedom ... 834 ★ Reagan's Economic Policies ... 835 ★ Reagan and Labor ... 835 ★ The Problem of Inequality ... 836 ★ The Second Gilded Age ... 836 ★ Conservatives and Reagan ... 838 ★ Reagan and the Cold War ... 838 ★ The Iran-Contra Affair ... 840 ★

Reagan and Gorbachev ... 840 ★ Reagan's Legacy ... 841 ★ The Election of 1988 ... 841

REVIEW ... 842

27. FROM TRIUMPH TO TRAGEDY, 1989-2001 ... 843

THE POST-COLD WAR WORLD ... 845

A New World Order? ... 846 ★ The Gulf War ... 846 ★ Visions of America's Role ... 846 ★ The Election of Clinton ... 847 ★ Clinton in Office ... 848 ★ The "Freedom Revolution" ... 849 ★ Clinton's Political Strategy ... 849

Voices of Freedom: *From* Bill Clinton, Speech on Signing of NAFTA (1993), and *From* Global Exchange, Seattle, Declaration for Global Democracy (December 1999) ... 850

Clinton and World Affairs ... 852 ★ Human Rights ... 853

GLOBALIZATION AND ITS DISCONTENTS ... 854

The Computer Revolution ... 855 ★ The Stock Market Boom and Bust ... 856 ★ The Enron Syndrome ... 857 ★ Fruits of Deregulation ... 857 ★ Rising Inequality ... 858

CULTURE WARS ... 859

The Newest Immigrants ... 859 ★ The New Diversity ... 862 ★ The Changing Face of Black America ... 865 ★ The Spread of Imprisonment ... 866 ★ The Continuing Rights Revolution ... 867 ★ Native Americans in the New Century ... 868 ★ Multiculturalism ... 869 ★ Family Values in Retreat ... 870 ★ The Antigovernment Extreme ... 870

IMPEACHMENT AND THE ELECTION OF 2000 ... 871

The Impeachment of Clinton ... 872 ★ The Disputed Election ... 872 ★ A Challenged Democracy ... 873

THE ATTACKS OF SEPTEMBER 11 ... 874

REVIEW ... 876

28. A NEW CENTURY AND NEW CRISES ... 877

THE WAR ON TERROR ... 879

Bush before September 11 ... 879 ★ "They Hate Freedom" ... 879 ★ The Bush Doctrine ... 880 ★ The "Axis of Evil" ... 881

AN AMERICAN EMPIRE? ... 881

Confronting Iraq ... 881 ★ The Iraq War ... 882 ★ The World and the War ... 883

THE AFTERMATH OF SEPTEMBER 11 AT HOME ... 885

Security and Liberty ... 885 ★ The Power of the President ... 886 ★ The Torture Controversy ... 886 ★ The Economy under Bush ... 887

THE WINDS OF CHANGE ... 887

The 2004 Election ... 887 ★ Bush's Second Term ... 888 ★ Hurricane Katrina ... 888 ★ Battle over the Border ... 889 ★ Islam, America, and the "Clash of Civilizations" ... 890 ★ The Constitution and Liberty ... 891 ★ The Court and the President ... 892 ★ The Midterm Elections of 2006 ...

893 ★ The Housing Bubble ... 893 ★ The Great Recession ... 894 ★ "A Conspiracy against the Public" ... 895 ★ Bush and the Crisis ... 897 ★ The 2008 Campaign ... 897 ★ The Age of Obama? ... 898 ★ Obama's First Inauguration ... 898

OBAMA IN OFFICE ... 899

The Health-Care Debate ... 900 ★ Financial Reform ... 900 ★ The Problem of Inequality ... 901

Voices of Freedom: *From* Opinion of the Court in *Obergefell v. Hodges* (2015), and *From* Barack Obama, Eulogy at Emanuel African Methodist Episcopal Church (2015) ... 902

The Occupy Movement ... 904

THE OBAMA PRESIDENCY ... 906

Postracial America? ... 906 ★ Obama and the World ... 908 ★ The Republican Resurgence ... 910 ★ The 2012 Campaign ... 911

FREEDOM IN THE TWENTY-FIRST CENTURY ... 913

Exceptional America ... 913 ★ Learning from History ... 915

REVIEW ... 917

APPENDIX

DOCUMENTS

The Declaration of Independence (1776) ... A-2 ★ The Constitution of the United States (1787) ... A-5 ★ *From* George Washington's Farewell Address (1796) ... A-17 ★ The Seneca Falls Declaration of Sentiments and Resolutions (1848) ... A-22 ★ *From* Frederick Douglass's "What, to the Slave, Is the Fourth of July?" Speech (1852) ... A-25 ★ The Gettysburg Address (1863) ... A-29 ★ Abraham Lincoln's Second Inaugural Address (1865) ... A-30 ★ The Populist Platform of 1892 ... A-31 ★ Franklin D. Roosevelt's First Inaugural Address (1933) ... A-34 ★ *From* The Program for the March on Washington for Jobs and Freedom (1963) ... A-37 ★ Ronald Reagan's First Inaugural Address (1981) ... A-38 ★ Barack Obama's First Inaugural Address (2009) ... A-42

TABLES AND FIGURES

Presidential Elections ... A-46 ★ Admission of States ... A-54 ★ Population of the United States ... A-55

Historical Statistics of the United States:

Labor Force—Selected Characteristics Expressed as a Percentage of the Labor Force, 1800–2010 ... A-56 ★ Immigration, by Origin ... A-56 ★ Unemployment Rate, 1890–2015 ... A-57 ★ Union Membership as a Percentage of Nonagricultural Employment, 1880–2015 ... A-57 ★ Voter Participation in Presidential Elections, 1824–2016 ... A-57 ★ Birthrate, 1820–2015 ... A-57

SUGGESTED READING ... A-59

GLOSSARY ... A-73

CREDITS ... A-105

INDEX ... A-109

MAPS

CHAPTER 15

The Barrow Plantation . . . 446
Sharecropping in the South, 1880 . . . 452
The Presidential Election of 1868 . . . 460
Reconstruction in the South, 1867–1877 . . . 471
The Presidential Election of 1876 . . . 472

CHAPTER 16

The Railroad Network, 1880 . . . 479
The Industrial West . . . 488
Indian Reservations, ca. 1890 . . . 496
Political Stalemate, 1876–1892 . . . 499

CHAPTER 17

Populist Strength, 1892 . . . 516
The Presidential Election of 1896 . . . 520
The Spanish-American War: The
    Pacific . . . 536
The Spanish-American War: The
    Caribbean . . . 536
American Empire, 1898 . . . 542

CHAPTER 18

Socialist Towns and Cities, 1900–1920 . . . 556
The Presidential Election of 1912 . . . 576

CHAPTER 19

The United States in the Caribbean,
    1898–1941 . . . 581
World War I: The Western Front . . . 587
Europe in 1914 . . . 606
Europe in 1919 . . . 607

CHAPTER 20

The Presidential Election of 1928 . . . 636

CHAPTER 21

The Presidential Election of 1932 . . . 645
The Tennessee Valley Authority . . . 650

CHAPTER 22

World War II in the Pacific,
    1941–1945 . . . 683
World War II in Europe, 1942–1945 . . . 685
Japanese-American Internment,
    1942–1945 . . . 699

CHAPTER 23

Cold War Europe, 1956 . . . 718
The Korean War, 1950–1953 . . . 720
The Presidential Election of 1948 . . . 729

CHAPTER 24

The Interstate Highway System . . . 744
The Presidential Election of 1952 . . . 752
The Presidential Election of 1960 . . . 769

CHAPTER 25

The Presidential Election of 1964 . . . 782
The Vietnam War, 1964–1975 . . . 795

CHAPTER 26

The Presidential Election of 1980 . . . 833
The United States in the Caribbean and Central
    America, 1954–2004 . . . 839

CHAPTER 27

Eastern Europe after the
    Cold War . . . 845
Immigrant Populations in Cities and States, 1900
    and 2010 . . . 861
Origin of Largest Immigrant Populations by State,
    1910 and 2013 . . . 863
The Presidential Election of 2000 . . . 873

CHAPTER 28

U.S. Presence in the Middle East, 1947–
    2015 . . . 884
Percentage of Population Below the Poverty Line,
    2014 . . . 905
The Presidential Election of 2012 . . . 912

TABLES AND FIGURES

CHAPTER 16

Table 16.1 Indicators of Economic Change,
1870–1920 . . . 477

CHAPTER 17

Table 17.1 States with over 200 Lynchings,
1889–1918 . . . 526

CHAPTER 18

Table 18.1 Rise of the City, 1880–1920 . . . 549

Table 18.2 Immigrants and Their Children as
Percentage of Population, Ten Major Cities,
1920 . . . 550

Table 18.3 Percentage of Women 14 Years and
Older in the Labor Force . . . 552

Table 18.4 Percentage of Women Workers in
Various Occupations . . . 553

Table 18.5 Sales of Passenger Cars . . . 554

CHAPTER 19

Table 19.1 The Great Migration . . . 601

CHAPTER 20

Figure 20.1 Household Appliances,
1900–1930 . . . 615

Table 20.1 Selected Annual Immigration
Quotas under the 1924 Immigration
Act . . . 630

CHAPTER 21

Figure 21.1 The Building Boom and Its Collapse,
1919–1939 . . . 651

Figure 21.2 Unemployment, 1925–1945 . . . 663

CHAPTER 22

Table 22.1 Labor Union Membership . . . 688

CHAPTER 24

Figure 24.1 Real Gross Domestic Product per
Capita, 1790–2014 . . . 742

Figure 24.2 Average Daily Television Viewing,
1950–1970 . . . 746

Figure 24.3 The Baby Boom and Its
Decline . . . 747

CHAPTER 25

Figure 25.1 Percentage of Population below
Poverty Level, by Race, 1959–1969 . . . 786

CHAPTER 26

Figure 26.1 Median Age at First Marriage,
1947–1981 . . . 814

Table 26.1 The Misery Index, 1970–1980 . . . 820

Figure 26.2 Real Average Weekly Wages,
1955–1990 . . . 822

Figure 26.3 Changes in Families' Real Income,
1980–1990 . . . 836

CHAPTER 27

Table 27.1 Immigration to the United States,
1961–2010 . . . 860

Figure 27.1 The Projected Non-White
Majority: Racial and Ethnic
Breakdown . . . 865

Table 27.2 Home Ownership Rates by Group,
1970–2000 . . . 865

Figure 27.2 Change in Family Structure,
1970–2010 . . . 869

Figure 27.3 Median Ages of First Marriages,
1970–2010 . . . 870

Figure 27.4 Women in the Paid Workforce,
1940–2010 . . . 871

CHAPTER 28

Figure 28.1 Portrait of a Recession . . . 895

Figure 28.2 Income Inequality in the United
States, 1910–2010 . . . 904

PREFACE

Give Me Liberty! An American History is a survey of American history from the earliest days of European exploration and conquest of the New World to the first decades of the twenty-first century. It offers students a clear, concise narrative whose central theme is the changing contours of American freedom.

I am extremely gratified by the response to the first four editions of *Give Me Liberty!*, which have been used in survey courses at many hundreds of two- and four-year colleges and universities throughout the country. The comments I have received from instructors and students encourage me to think that *Give Me Liberty!* has worked well in their classrooms. Their comments have also included many valuable suggestions for revisions, which I greatly appreciate. These have ranged from corrections of typographical and factual errors to thoughts about subjects that needed more extensive treatment. In making revisions for this Fifth Edition, I have tried to take these suggestions into account. I have also incorporated the findings and insights of new scholarship that has appeared since the original edition was written.

The most significant changes in this Fifth Edition reflect my desire to integrate the history of the American West and especially the regions known as borderlands more fully into the narrative. In recent years these aspects of American history have been thriving areas of research and scholarship. Of course earlier editions of *Give Me Liberty!* have discussed these subjects, but in this edition their treatment has been deepened and expanded. I have also added notable works in these areas to many chapter bibliographies and lists of websites.

The definition of the West has changed enormously in the course of American history. In the colonial period, the area beyond the Appalachians—present-day Kentucky, Tennessee, and western Pennsylvania and New York—constituted the West. In the first half of the nineteenth century, the term referred to Ohio, Michigan, Alabama, and Mississippi. After the Civil War, the West came to mean the area beyond the Mississippi River. Today, it is sometimes used to refer mainly to the Pacific coast. But whatever its geographic locale, the West has been as much an idea as a place—an area beyond the frontier of settlement that promised newcomers new kinds of freedom, sometimes at the expense of the freedom of others, such as native inhabitants and migrant laborers. In this edition we follow Americans as they constructed their Wests, and debated the kinds of freedom they would enjoy there.

Borderlands is a more complex idea that has influenced much recent historical scholarship. Borders are lines dividing one country, region, or state from another. Crossing them often means becoming subject to different laws and customs, and enjoying different degrees of freedom. Borderlands are regions that exist on both sides of borders. They are fluid areas where people of different cultural and social backgrounds converge. At various points in American history, shifting borders have opened new opportunities and closed off others in the borderlands. Families living for decades or centuries in a region have suddenly found themselves divided by a newly created border but still living in a borderland that transcends the new division. This happened to Mexicans in modern-day California, Arizona, and New Mexico, for example, in 1848, when the treaty ending the Mexican-American War transferred the land that would become those states from Mexico to the United States.

Borderlands exist within the United States as well as at the boundaries with other countries. For example, in the period before the Civil War, the region straddling the Ohio River contained cultural commonalities that in some ways overrode the division there between free and slave states. The borderlands idea also challenges simple accounts of national development in which empires and colonies pave the way for territorial expansion and a future transcontinental nation. It enables us, for example, to move beyond the categories of conquest and subjugation in understanding how Native Americans and Europeans interacted over the early centuries of contact. This approach also provides a way of understanding how the people of Mexico and the United States interact today in the borderland region of the American Southwest, where many families have members on both sides of the boundary between the two countries.

Small changes relating to these themes may be found throughout the book. The major additions seeking to illuminate the history of the West and of borderlands are as follows:

Chapter 1 now introduces the idea of borderlands with a discussion of the areas where European empires and Indian groups interacted and where authority was fluid and fragile. Chapter 4 contains expanded treatment of the part of the Spanish empire now comprising the borderlands United States (Arizona, California, New Mexico, Texas, and Florida) and how Spain endeavored, with limited success, to consolidate its authority in these regions. In Chapter 6, a new subsection, "The American Revolution as a Borderlands Conflict," examines the impact on both Americans and Canadians of the creation, because of American independence, of a new national boundary separating what once had been two parts of the British empire. Chapter 8 continues this theme with a discussion of the borderlands aspects of the War of 1812. Chapter 9 discusses how a common culture came into being along the Ohio River in the early nineteenth century despite the existence of slavery on one side and free labor on the other. Chapter 13 expands the treatment of Texan independence from Mexico by discussing its impact on both Anglo and Mexican residents of this borderland region. Chapter 14 contains a new examination of the Civil War in the American West.

In Chapter 16, I have expanded the section on the industrial west with new discussions of logging and mining, and added a new subsection on the dissemination of a mythical image of the Wild West in the late nineteenth century. Chapter 17 contains an expanded discussion of Chinese immigrants in the West and the battle over exclusion and citizenship, a debate that centered on what kind of population should be allowed to inhabit the West and enjoy the opportunities the region offered. Chapter 18 examines Progressivism, countering conventional narratives that emphasize the origins of Progressive political reforms in eastern cities by relating how many, from woman suffrage to the initiative, referendum, and recall, emerged in Oregon, California, and other western states. Chapter 20 expands the treatment of western agriculture in the 1920s by highlighting the acceleration of agricultural mechanization in the region and the agricultural depression that preceded the general economic collapse of 1929 and after. In Chapter 22 we see the new employment opportunities for Mexican-American women in the war production factories that opened in the West. In Chapter 26, there is a new subsection on conservatism in the West and the Sagebrush Rebellion of the 1970s and 1980s. Chapter 27 returns to the borderlands theme by discussing the consequences of the creation, in the 1990s, of a free trade zone connecting the two sides of the Mexican-American border. And Chapters 27 and 28 now include expanded discussions of the southwestern borderland as a site of an acrimonious battle over immigration—legal and undocumented—involving the federal and state governments, private vigilantes, and continuing waves of people trying to cross into the United States. The contested borderland now extends many miles into the United States north of the boundary between the two nations, and southward well into Mexico and even Central America.

I have also added a number of new selections to Voices of Freedom, the paired excerpts from primary documents in each chapter. Some of the new documents reflect the stronger emphasis on the West and borderlands; others seek to sharpen the juxtaposition of divergent concepts of freedom at particular moments in American history. And this edition contains many new images—paintings, broadsides, photographs, and others—related to these themes.

Americans have always had a divided attitude toward history. On the one hand, they tend to be remarkably future-oriented, dismissing events of even the recent past as "ancient history" and sometimes seeing history as a burden to be overcome, a prison from which to escape. On the other hand, like many other peoples, Americans have always looked to history for a sense of personal or group identity and of national cohesiveness. This is why so many Americans devote time and energy to tracing their family trees and why they visit historical museums and National Park Service historical sites in ever-increasing numbers. My hope is that this book will convince readers with all degrees of interest that history does matter to them.

The novelist and essayist James Baldwin once observed that history "does not refer merely, or even principally, to the past. On the contrary, the great force of history comes from the fact that we carry it within us, . . . [that] history is literally present in all that we do." As Baldwin recognized, the force of history is evident in our own world. Especially in a political democracy like the United States, whose government is designed to rest on the consent of informed citizens, knowledge of the past is essential—not only for those of us whose profession is the teaching and writing of history, but for everyone. History, to be sure, does not offer simple lessons or immediate answers to current questions. Knowing the history of immigration to the United States, and all of the tensions, turmoil, and aspirations associated with it, for example, does not tell us what current immigration policy ought to be. But without that knowledge, we have no way of understanding which approaches have worked and which have not—essential information for the formulation of future public policy.

History, it has been said, is what the present chooses to remember about the past. Rather than a fixed collection of facts, or a group of interpretations that cannot be challenged, our understanding of history is constantly changing. There is nothing unusual in the fact that each generation rewrites history to meet its own needs, or that scholars disagree among themselves on basic questions like the causes of the Civil War or the reasons for the Great Depression. Precisely because each generation asks different questions of the past, each generation formulates different answers. The past thirty years have witnessed a remarkable expansion of the scope of historical study. The experiences of groups neglected by earlier scholars, including women, African-Americans, working people, and others, have received unprecedented attention from historians. New subfields—social history, cultural history, and family history among them—have taken their place alongside traditional political and diplomatic history.

Give Me Liberty! draws on this voluminous historical literature to present an up-to-date and inclusive account of the American past, paying due attention to the experience of diverse groups of Americans while in no way neglecting the events and processes Americans have experienced in common. It devotes serious attention to political, social, cultural, and economic history, and to their interconnections. The narrative brings together major events and prominent leaders with the many groups of ordinary people who make up American society. *Give Me Liberty!* has a rich cast of characters, from Thomas Jefferson to campaigners for woman suffrage, from Franklin D. Roosevelt to former slaves seeking to breathe meaning into emancipation during and after the Civil War.

Aimed at an audience of undergraduate students with little or no detailed knowledge of American history, *Give Me Liberty!* guides readers through the complexities of the subject without overwhelming them with excessive detail. The unifying theme of freedom that runs through the text gives shape to the narrative and integrates the numerous strands that make up the American experience. This approach builds on that of my earlier book, *The Story of American Freedom* (1998), although *Give Me Liberty!* places events and personalities in the foreground and is more geared to the structure of the introductory survey course.

Freedom, and the battles to define its meaning, have long been central to my own scholarship and undergraduate teaching, which focuses on the nineteenth century and especially the era of the Civil War and Reconstruction (1850–1877). This was a time when the future of slavery tore the nation apart and emancipation produced a national debate over what rights the former slaves, and all Americans, should enjoy as free citizens. I have found that attention to clashing definitions of freedom and the struggles of different groups to achieve freedom as they understood it offers a way of making sense of the bitter battles and vast transformations of that pivotal era. I believe that the same is true for American history as a whole.

No idea is more fundamental to Americans' sense of themselves as individuals and as a nation than freedom. The central term in our political language, freedom—or liberty, with which it is almost always used interchangeably—is deeply embedded in the record of our history and the language of everyday life. The Declaration of Independence lists liberty among mankind's inalienable rights; the Constitution announces its purpose as securing liberty's blessings. The United States fought the Civil War to bring about a new birth of freedom, World War II for the Four Freedoms, and the Cold War to defend the Free World. Americans' love of liberty has been represented by liberty poles, liberty caps, and statues of liberty, and acted out by burning stamps and burning draft cards, by running away from slavery, and by demonstrating for the right to vote. "Every man in the street, white, black, red, or yellow," wrote the educator and statesman Ralph Bunche in 1940, "knows that this is 'the land of the free' . . . 'the cradle of liberty.'"

The very universality of the idea of freedom, however, can be misleading. Freedom is not a fixed, timeless category with a single unchanging definition. Indeed, the history of the United States is, in part, a story of debates, disagreements, and struggles over freedom. Crises like the American Revolution, the Civil War, and the Cold War have permanently transformed the idea of freedom. So too have demands by various groups of Americans to enjoy greater freedom. The meaning of freedom has been constructed not only in congressional debates and political treatises, but on plantations and picket lines, in parlors and even bedrooms.

Over the course of our history, American freedom has been both a reality and a mythic ideal—a living truth for millions of Americans, a cruel mockery for others. For some, freedom has been what some scholars call a "habit of the heart," an ideal so taken for granted that it is lived out but rarely analyzed. For others, freedom is not a birthright but a distant goal that has inspired great sacrifice.

Give Me Liberty! draws attention to three dimensions of freedom that have been critical in American history: (1) the *meanings* of freedom; (2) the *social conditions* that make freedom possible; and (3) the *boundaries* of freedom that determine who is entitled to enjoy freedom and who is not. All have changed over time.

In the era of the American Revolution, for example, freedom was primarily a set of rights enjoyed in public activity—the right of a community to be governed by laws to which its representatives had consented and of individuals to engage in religious worship without governmental interference. In the nineteenth century, freedom came to be closely identified with each person's opportunity to develop to the fullest his or her innate talents. In the twentieth, the "ability to choose," in both public and private life, became perhaps the dominant understanding of freedom. This development was encouraged by the explosive growth of the consumer marketplace (a development that receives considerable attention in *Give Me Liberty!*), which offered Americans an unprecedented array of goods with which to satisfy their needs and desires. During the 1960s, a crucial chapter in the history of American freedom, the idea of personal freedom was extended into virtually every realm, from attire and "lifestyle" to relations between the sexes. Thus, over time, more and more areas of life have been drawn into Americans' debates about the meaning of freedom.

A second important dimension of freedom focuses on the social conditions necessary to allow freedom to flourish. What kinds of economic institutions and relationships best encourage individual freedom? In the colonial era and for more than a century after independence, the answer centered on economic autonomy, enshrined in the glorification of the independent small producer—the farmer, skilled craftsman, or shopkeeper—who did not have to depend on another person for his livelihood. As the industrial economy matured, new conceptions of economic freedom came to the fore: "liberty of contract" in the Gilded Age, "industrial freedom" (a say in corporate decision-making) in the Progressive era, economic security during the New Deal, and, more recently, the ability to enjoy mass consumption within a market economy.

The boundaries of freedom, the third dimension of this theme, have inspired some of the most intense struggles in American history. Although founded on the premise that liberty is an entitlement of all humanity, the United States for much of its history deprived many of its own people of freedom. Non-whites have rarely enjoyed the same access to freedom as white

Americans. The belief in equal opportunity as the birthright of all Americans has coexisted with persistent efforts to limit freedom by race, gender, and class and in other ways.

Less obvious, perhaps, is the fact that one person's freedom has frequently been linked to another's servitude. In the colonial era and nineteenth century, expanding freedom for many Americans rested on the lack of freedom—slavery, indentured servitude, the subordinate position of women—for others. By the same token, it has been through battles at the boundaries—the efforts of racial minorities, women, and others to secure greater freedom—that the meaning and experience of freedom have been deepened and the concept extended into new realms.

Time and again in American history, freedom has been transformed by the demands of excluded groups for inclusion. The idea of freedom as a universal birthright owes much both to abolitionists who sought to extend the blessings of liberty to blacks and to immigrant groups who insisted on full recognition as American citizens. The principle of equal protection of the law without regard to race, which became a central element of American freedom, arose from the antislavery struggle and the Civil War and was reinvigorated by the civil rights revolution of the 1960s, which called itself the "freedom movement." The battle for the right of free speech by labor radicals and birth-control advocates in the first part of the twentieth century helped to make civil liberties an essential element of freedom for all Americans.

Although concentrating on events within the United States, *Give Me Liberty!* also situates American history in the context of developments in other parts of the world. Many of the forces that shaped American history, including the international migration of peoples, the development of slavery, the spread of democracy, and the expansion of capitalism, were worldwide processes not confined to the United States. Today, American ideas, culture, and economic and military power exert unprecedented influence throughout the world. But beginning with the earliest days of settlement, when European empires competed to colonize North America and enrich themselves from its trade, American history cannot be understood in isolation from its global setting.

Freedom is the oldest of clichés and the most modern of aspirations. At various times in our history, it has served as the rallying cry of the powerless and as a justification of the status quo. Freedom helps to bind our culture together and exposes the contradictions between what America claims to be and what it sometimes has been. American history is not a narrative of continual progress toward greater and greater freedom. As the abolitionist Thomas Wentworth Higginson noted after the Civil War, "revolutions may go backward." Though freedom can be achieved, it may also be taken away. This happened, for example, when the equal rights granted to former slaves immediately after the Civil War were essentially nullified during the era of segregation. As was said in the eighteenth century, the price of freedom is eternal vigilance.

In the early twenty-first century, freedom continues to play a central role in American political and social life and thought. It is invoked by individuals and groups of all kinds, from critics of economic globalization to those who seek to secure American freedom at home and export it abroad. I hope that *Give Me Liberty!* will offer beginning students a clear account of the course of American history, and of its central theme, freedom, which today remains as varied, contentious, and ever-changing as America itself.

ACKNOWLEDGMENTS

All works of history are, to a considerable extent, collaborative books, in that every writer builds on the research and writing of previous scholars. This is especially true of a textbook that covers the entire American experience, over more than five centuries. My greatest debt is to the innumerable historians on whose work I have drawn in preparing this volume. The Suggested Reading list for each chapter offers only a brief introduction to the vast body of historical scholarship that has influenced and informed this book. More specifically, however, I wish to thank the following scholars, who generously read portions of this work and offered valuable comments, criticisms, and suggestions:

Joel Benson, Northwest Missouri State University
Lori Bramson, Clark College
Tonia Compton, Columbia College
Adam Costanzo, Texas A&M University
Carl Creasman Jr., Valencia College
Blake Ellis, Lone Star College–CyFair
Carla Falkner, Northeast Mississippi Community College
Van Forsyth, Clark College
Aram Goudsouzian, University of Memphis
Michael Harkins, Harper College
Sandra Harvey, Lone Star College–CyFair
Robert Hines, Palo Alto College
Traci Hodgson, Chemeketa Community College
Tamora Hoskisson, Salt Lake Community College
William Jackson, Salt Lake Community College
Alfred H. Jones, State College of Florida
David Kiracofe, Tidewater Community College
Brad Lookingbill, Columbia College
Jennifer Macias, Salt Lake Community College
Thomas Massey, Cape Fear Community College
Derek Maxfield, Genesee Community College
Marianne McKnight, Salt Lake Community College
Jonson Miller, Drexel University
Ted Moore, Salt Lake Community College
Robert Pierce, Foothills College
Ernst Pinjing, Minot State University
Harvey N. Plaunt, El Paso Community College

Steve Porter, University of Cincinnati

John Putman, San Diego State University

R. Lynn Rainard, Tidewater Community College

Nicole Ribianszky, Georgia Gwinnett College

Nancy Marie Robertson, Indiana University—Purdue University Indianapolis

John Shaw, Portland Community College

Danielle Swiontek, Santa Barbara Community College

Richard Trimble, Ocean County College

Alan Vangroll, Central Texas College

Eddie Weller, San Jacinto College

Andrew Wiese, San Diego State University

Matthew Zembo, Hudson Valley Community College

I am particularly grateful to my colleagues in the Columbia University Department of History: Pablo Piccato, for his advice on Latin American history; Evan Haefeli and Ellen Baker, who read and made many suggestions for improvements in their areas of expertise (colonial America and the history of the West, respectively); and Sarah Phillips, who offered advice on treating the history of the environment.

I am also deeply indebted to the graduate students at Columbia University's Department of History who helped with this project. For this edition, Michael "Mookie" Kideckel offered invaluable assistance in gathering material related to borderlands and Western history. For previous editions, Theresa Ventura assisted in locating material for new sections placing American history in a global context, April Holm did the same for new coverage of the history of American religion and debates over religious freedom, James Delbourgo conducted research for the chapters on the colonial era, and Beverly Gage did the same for the twentieth century. In addition, Daniel Freund provided all-around research assistance. Victoria Cain did a superb job of locating images. I also want to thank my colleagues Elizabeth Blackmar and Alan Brinkley for offering advice and encouragement throughout the writing of this book. I am also grateful to students who, while using the textbook, pointed out to me errors or omissions that I have corrected in this edition: Jordan Farr, Chris Jendry, Rafi Metz, Samuel Phillips-Cooper, Richard Sereyko, and David Whittle.

Many thanks to Joshua Brown, director of the American Social History Project, whose website, History Matters, lists innumerable online resources for the study of American history. Thanks also to the instructors who helped build our robust digital resource and ancillary package. The new InQuizitive for History was developed by Tonia M. Compton (Columbia College), Matt Zembo (Hudson Valley Community College), Jodie Steeley (Merced Community College District), Bill Polasky (Stillman Valley High School), and Ken Adler (Spring Valley High School). Our new History Skills Tutorials were created by Geri Hastings. The Coursepack was thoroughly updated by Beth Hunter (University of Alabama at Birmingham). Allison Faber (Texas A&M University) and Ben Williams (Texas A&M University) revised the Lecture PowerPoint slides. And our Test Bank and Instructor's Manual was revised to include new questions authored by Robert O'Brien (Lone Star College–CyFair) and Tamora M. Hoskisson (Salt Lake Community College).

At W. W. Norton & Company, Steve Forman was an ideal editor—patient, encouraging, and always ready to offer sage advice. I would also like to thank Steve's editorial assistants, Travis Carr and Kelly Rafey, and associate editor, Scott Sugarman, for their indispensable and always cheerful help on all aspects of the project; Ellen Lohman and Bob Byrne for their careful copyediting and proofreading work; Stephanie Romeo and Fay Torresyap for their resourceful attention to the illustrations program; Hope Miller Goodell and Chin-Yee Lai for their refinements of the book design; Leah Clark, Tiani Kennedy, and Debra Morton-Hoyt for splendid work on the covers for the Fifth Edition; Jennifer Barnhardt and Katie Callahan for keeping the many threads of the project aligned and then tying them together; Sean Mintus for his efficiency and care in book production; Laura Wilk for orchestrating the rich media package that accompanies the textbook; Jessica Brannon-Wranowsky for the terrific new web quizzes and outlines; Sarah England Bartley, Steve Dunn, and Mike Wright for their alert reads of the U.S. survey market and their hard work in helping establish *Give Me Liberty!* within it; and Drake McFeely, Roby Harrington, and Julia Reidhead for maintaining Norton as an independent, employee-owned publisher dedicated to excellence in its work.

Many students may have heard stories of how publishing companies alter the language and content of textbooks in an attempt to maximize sales and avoid alienating any potential reader. In this case, I can honestly say that W. W. Norton allowed me a free hand in writing the book and, apart from the usual editorial corrections, did not try to influence its content at all. For this I thank them, while I accept full responsibility for the interpretations presented and for any errors the book may contain. Since no book of this length can be entirely free of mistakes, I welcome readers to send me corrections at ef17@columbia.edu.

My greatest debt, as always, is to my family—my wife, Lynn Garafola, for her good-natured support while I was preoccupied by a project that consumed more than its fair share of my time and energy, and my daughter, Daria, who while a ninth and tenth grader read every chapter as it was written and offered invaluable suggestions about improving the book's clarity, logic, and grammar.

Eric Foner
New York City
July 2016

GIVE ME LIBERTY! DIGITAL RESOURCES FOR STUDENTS AND INSTRUCTORS

W. W. Norton offers a robust digital package to support teaching and learning with *Give Me Liberty!* These resources are designed to make students more effective textbook readers, while at the same time developing their critical thinking and history skills.

RESOURCES FOR STUDENTS

All resources are available through digital.wwnorton.com /givemeliberty5brv2 with the access card at the front of this text.

NORTON INQUIZITIVE FOR HISTORY

Norton InQuizitive for history is an adaptive quizzing tool that improves students' understanding of the themes and objectives from each chapter, while honing their critical-analysis skills with primary source, image, and map analysis questions. Students receive personalized quiz questions with detailed, guiding feedback on the topics in which they need the most help, while the engaging, gamelike elements motivate them as they learn.

HISTORY SKILLS TUTORIALS

The History Skills Tutorials feature three modules—Images, Documents, and Maps—to support students' development of the key skills needed for the history course. These tutorials feature videos of Eric Foner modeling the analysis process, followed by interactive questions that will challenge students to apply what they have learned.

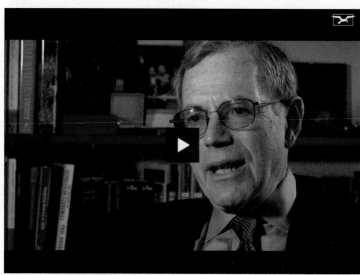

STUDENT SITE

The free and easy-to-use Student Site offers additional resources for students to use outside of class. Resources include interactive iMaps from each chapter, author videos, and a comprehensive Online Reader with a collection of historical longer works, primary sources, novellas, and biographies.

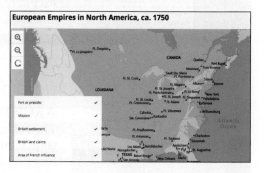

EBOOK

Free and included with new copies of the text, the **Norton Ebook Reader** provides an enhanced reading experience that works on all computers and mobile devices. Features include intuitive highlighting, note-taking, and bookmarking as well as pop-up definitions and enlargeable maps and art. Direct links to InQuizitive also appear in each chapter. Instructors can focus student reading by sharing notes with their classes, including embedded images and video. Reports on student and class-wide access and time on task allow instructors to monitor student reading and engagement.

RESOURCES FOR INSTRUCTORS

All resources are available through www.wwnorton.com /instructors.

NORTON COURSEPACKS

Easily add high-quality digital media to your online, hybrid, or lecture course—all at no cost to students. Norton's Coursepacks work within your existing Learning Management System and are ready to use and easy to customize. The coursepack offers a diverse collection of assignable and assessable resources: **Primary Source Exercises, Guided Reading Exercises, Review Quizzes, U.S. History Tours powered by Google Earth, Flashcards, Map Exercises**, and all of the resources from the **Student Site**.

NORTON AMERICAN HISTORY DIGITAL ARCHIVE

The Digital Archive offers roughly 2,000 additional primary source images, audio, and video files spanning American history that can be used in assignments and lecture presentations.

TEST BANK

The Test Bank is authored by Robert O'Brien, Lone Star College–CyFair, and Tamora M. Hoskisson, Salt Lake Community College, and contains more than 4,000 multiple-choice, true/false, short-answer, and essay questions.

INSTRUCTOR'S MANUAL

The Instructor's Manual contains detailed Chapter Summaries, Chapter Outlines, Suggested Discussion Questions, and Supplemental Web, Visual, and Print Resources.

LECTURE AND ART POWERPOINT SLIDES

The Lecture PowerPoint sets authored by Allison Faber, Texas A&M University, and Ben Williams, Texas A&M University, combine chapter review, art, and maps.

CHAPTER 15

"WHAT IS FREEDOM?"

★

RECONSTRUCTION, 1865-1877

1865	Special Field Order 15
	Freedmen's Bureau established
	Lincoln assassinated; Andrew Johnson becomes president
1865– 1867	Presidential Reconstruction
	Black Codes
1866	Civil Rights Bill
	Ku Klux Klan established
1867	Reconstruction Act of 1867
	Tenure of Office Act
1867– 1877	Radical Reconstruction
1868	Impeachment and trial of President Johnson
	Fourteenth Amendment ratified
1869	Inauguration of Ulysses S. Grant
1870	Hiram Revels, first black U.S. senator
	Fifteenth Amendment ratified
1870– 1871	Enforcement Acts
1872	Liberal Republicans established
1873	Colfax Massacre
	Slaughterhouse Cases
	National economic depression begins
1876	*United States v. Cruikshank*
1877	Bargain of 1877

The Shackle Broken—by the Genius of Freedom. This 1874 lithograph depicts Robert B. Elliott, a black congressman from South Carolina, delivering a celebrated speech supporting the bill that became the Civil Rights Act of 1875.

FOCUS
QUESTIONS

- *What visions of freedom did the former slaves and slaveholders pursue in the postwar South?*

- *What were the competing visions of Reconstruction?*

- *What were the social and political effects of Radical Reconstruction in the South?*

- *What were the main factors, in both the North and South, for the abandonment of Reconstruction?*

On the evening of January 12, 1865, less than a month after Union forces captured Savannah, Georgia, twenty leaders of the city's black community gathered for a discussion with General William T. Sherman and Secretary of War Edwin M. Stanton. The conversation revealed that the black leaders brought out of slavery a clear definition of freedom. Asked what he understood by slavery, Garrison Frazier, a Baptist minister chosen as the group's spokesman, responded that it meant one person's "receiving by irresistible power the work of another man, and not by his consent." Freedom he defined as "placing us where we could reap the fruit of our own labor, and take care of ourselves." The way to accomplish this was "to have land, and turn it and till it by our own labor."

Sherman's meeting with the black leaders foreshadowed some of the radical changes that would take place during the era known as Reconstruction (meaning, literally, the rebuilding of the shattered nation). In the years following the Civil War, former slaves and their white allies, North and South, would seek to redefine the meaning and boundaries of American freedom. Previously an entitlement of whites, freedom would be expanded to include black Americans. The laws and Constitution would be rewritten to guarantee African-Americans, for the first time in the nation's history, recognition as citizens and equality before the law. Black men would be granted the right to vote, ushering in a period of interracial democracy throughout the South. Black schools, churches, and other institutions would flourish, laying the foundation for the modern African-American community. Many of the advances of Reconstruction would prove temporary, swept away during a campaign of violence in the South and the North's retreat from the ideal of equality. But Reconstruction laid the foundation for future struggles to extend freedom to all Americans.

Four days after the meeting, Sherman responded to the black delegation by issuing Special Field Order 15. This set aside the Sea Islands and a large area along the South Carolina and Georgia coasts for the settlement of black families on forty-acre plots of land. He also offered them broken-down mules that the army could no longer use. In Sherman's order lay the origins of the phrase "forty acres and a mule," which would reverberate across the South in the next few years. Among the emancipated slaves, Sherman's order raised hopes that the end of slavery would be accompanied by the economic independence that they, like other Americans, believed essential to genuine freedom.

THE MEANING OF FREEDOM

"What is freedom?" asked Congressman James A. Garfield in 1865. "Is it the bare privilege of not being chained? If this is all, then freedom is a bitter mockery, a cruel delusion." Did freedom mean simply the absence of slavery, or did it imply other rights for the former slaves, and if so, which ones? Equal civil rights, the vote, ownership of property? During Reconstruction, freedom became a terrain of conflict, its substance open to different, often contradictory interpretations.

Conflicts over freedom

African-Americans' understanding of freedom was shaped by their experiences as slaves and their observation of the free society around them. To begin with, freedom meant escaping the numerous injustices of slavery—punishment by the lash, the separation of families, denial of access to education, the sexual exploitation of black women by their owners—and sharing in the rights and opportunities of American citizens. "If I cannot do like a white man," Henry Adams, an emancipated slave in Louisiana, told his former master in 1865, "I am not free."

Family Record, a lithograph marketed to former slaves after the Civil War, centers on an idealized portrait of a middle-class black family, with scenes of slavery and freedom.

Families in Freedom

With slavery dead, institutions that had existed before the war, like the black family, free blacks' churches and schools, and the secret slave church, were strengthened, expanded, and freed from white supervision. The family was central to the postemancipation black community. Former slaves made remarkable efforts to locate loved ones from whom they had been separated under slavery. One northern reporter in 1865 encountered a freedman who had walked more than 600 miles from Georgia to North Carolina, searching for the wife and children from whom he had been sold away before the war.

While freedom helped to stabilize family life, it also subtly altered relationships within the family. Immediately after the Civil War, planters complained that freedwomen had "withdrawn" from field labor and work as house servants. Many black women preferred to devote more time to their families than had been possible under slavery, and men considered it a badge of

Five Generations of a Black Family, an 1862 photograph that suggests the power of family ties among emancipated slaves.

Mother and Daughter Reading, Mt. Meigs, Alabama, an 1890 photograph by Rudolph Eickemeyer. During Reconstruction and for years thereafter, former slaves exhibited a deep desire for education, and learning took place outside of school as well as within.

honor to see their wives remain at home. Eventually, the dire poverty of the black community would compel a far higher proportion of black women than white women to go to work for wages.

Church and School

At the same time, blacks abandoned white-controlled religious institutions to create churches of their own. On the eve of the Civil War, 42,000 black Methodists worshiped in biracial South Carolina churches; by the end of Reconstruction, only 600 remained. As the major institution independent of white control, the church played a central role in the black community. A place of worship, it also housed schools, social events, and political gatherings. Black ministers came to play a major role in politics. Some 250 held public office during Reconstruction.

Another striking example of the freedpeople's quest for individual and community improvement was their desire for education. The thirst for learning sprang from many sources—a desire to read the Bible, the need to prepare for the economic marketplace, and the opportunity, which arose in 1867, to take part in politics. Blacks of all ages flocked to the schools established by northern missionary societies, the Freedmen's Bureau, and groups of ex-slaves themselves. Reconstruction also witnessed the creation of the nation's first black colleges, including Fisk University in Tennessee, Hampton Institute in Virginia, and Howard University in the nation's capital.

Political Freedom

In a society that had made political participation a core element of freedom, the right to vote inevitably became central to the former slaves' desire for empowerment and equality. As Frederick Douglass put it soon after the South's surrender in 1865, "Slavery is not abolished until the black man has the ballot." In a "monarchial government," Douglass explained, no "special" disgrace applied to those denied the right to vote. But in a democracy, "where universal suffrage is the rule," excluding any group meant branding them with "the stigma of inferiority."

Anything less than full citizenship, black spokesmen insisted, would betray the nation's democratic promise and the war's meaning. To demonstrate their patriotism, blacks throughout the South organized Fourth of July celebrations. For years after the Civil War, white southerners would

The First African Church, Richmond, as depicted in *Harper's Weekly*, June 27, 1874. The establishment of independent black churches was an enduring accomplishment of Reconstruction.

"shut themselves within doors" on Independence Day, as a white resident of Charleston recorded in her diary, while former slaves commemorated the holiday themselves.

Land, Labor, and Freedom

Like those of rural people throughout the world, former slaves' ideas of freedom were directly related to landownership. On the land they would develop independent communities free of white control. Many former slaves insisted that through their unpaid labor, they had acquired a right to the land. "The property which they hold," declared an Alabama black convention, "was nearly all earned by the sweat of *our* brows." In some parts of the South, blacks in 1865 seized property, insisting that it belonged to them.

Freedom and landownership

In its individual elements and much of its language, former slaves' definition of freedom resembled that of white Americans—self-ownership, family stability, religious liberty, political participation, and economic autonomy. But these elements combined to form a vision very much their own. For whites, freedom, no matter how defined, was a given, a birthright to be defended. For African-Americans, it was an open-ended process, a transformation of every aspect of their lives and of the society and culture that had sustained slavery in the first place. Although the freedpeople failed to achieve full freedom as they understood it, their definition did much to shape national debate during the turbulent era of Reconstruction.

Freedom's meaning for former slaves

Masters without Slaves

Most white southerners reacted to military defeat and emancipation with dismay, not only because of the widespread devastation but also because they must now submit to northern demands. "The demoralization is

The southern white reaction to emancipation

Two maps of the Barrow plantation illustrate the effects of emancipation on rural life in the South. In 1860, slaves lived in communal quarters near the owner's house. Twenty-one years later, former slaves working as sharecroppers lived scattered across the plantation and had their own church and school.

THE BARROW PLANTATION

1860

1881

Sabrina Dalton
Lizzie Dalton
Frank Maxey
Joe Bug   Jim Reid
Nancy Pope
Cane Pope
Church   School Gus Barrow Willis
                               Bryant
                     Lem Bryant Gin House
Lewis Watson
Reuben Barrow   Tom Wright
Omy Barrow   Ben Thomas   "Granny"
        Peter Tom   Landlord's
        Barrow Thomas   House
Milly Barrow   Handy Barrow
                      Old Isaac
Tom Tang   Calvin
            Parker   Branch Creek

Beckton Barrow   Swift's Fork

Lem
Douglas

Wright's Branch
Little River
Gin House
Slave
Quarters   Master's
            House
Branch Creek
Swift's Fork

complete," wrote a Georgia girl. "We are whipped, there is no doubt about it." The appalling loss of life, a disaster without parallel in the American experience, affected all classes of southerners. Nearly 260,000 men died for the Confederacy—more than one-fifth of the South's adult male white population. The wholesale destruction of work animals, farm buildings, and machinery ensured that economic revival would be slow and painful. In 1870, the value of property in the South, not counting that represented by slaves, was 30 percent lower than before the war.

Confederate deaths

Planter families faced profound changes in the war's aftermath. Many lost not only their slaves but also their life savings, which they had patriotically invested in now-worthless Confederate bonds. Some, whose slaves departed the plantation, for the first time found themselves compelled to do physical labor.

Planters

Southern planters sought to implement an understanding of freedom quite different from that of the former slaves. As they struggled to accept the reality of emancipation, most planters defined black freedom in the narrowest manner. As journalist Sidney Andrews discovered late in 1865, "The whites seem wholly unable to comprehend that freedom for the negro means the same thing as freedom for them."

Narrow understanding of freedom

The Free Labor Vision

Along with former slaves and former masters, the victorious Republican North tried to implement its own vision of freedom. Central to its definition was the antebellum principle of free labor, now further strengthened as a definition of the good society by the Union's triumph. In the free labor vision of a reconstructed South, emancipated blacks, enjoying the same opportunities for advancement as northern workers, would labor more productively than they had as slaves. At the same time, northern capital and migrants would energize the economy. The South would eventually come to resemble the "free society" of the North, complete with public schools, small towns, and independent farmers.

Free labor and the good society

With planters seeking to establish a labor system as close to slavery as possible, and former slaves demanding economic autonomy and access to land, a long period of conflict over the organization and control of labor followed on plantations throughout the South. It fell to **the Freedmen's Bureau**, an agency established by Congress in March 1865, to attempt to establish a working free labor system.

The Freedmen's Bureau

Under the direction of O. O. Howard, a graduate of Bowdoin College in Maine and a veteran of the Civil War, the bureau took on responsibilities that can only be described as daunting. The bureau was an experiment in government social policy that seems to belong more comfortably to the New Deal of the 1930s or the Great Society of the 1960s (see Chapters 21 and 25, respectively) than to nineteenth-century America. Bureau agents were supposed to establish schools, provide aid to the poor and aged, settle disputes between whites and blacks and among the freedpeople, and secure for former slaves and white Unionists equal treatment before the courts. "It is not . . . in your power to fulfill one-tenth of the expectations of those who framed the Bureau," General William T. Sherman wrote to Howard. "I fear you have Hercules' task."

The bureau lasted from 1865 to 1870. Even at its peak, there were fewer than

Winslow Homer's 1876 painting *A Visit from the Old Mistress* depicts an imaginary meeting between a southern white woman and her former slaves. Their stance and gaze suggest the tensions arising from the birth of a new social order. Homer places his subjects on an equal footing, yet maintains a space of separation between them. He exhibited the painting to acclaim at the Paris Universal Exposition in 1878.

The Freedmen's Bureau, an engraving from *Harper's Weekly*, July 25, 1868, depicts the bureau agent as a promoter of racial peace in the violent postwar South.

Achievements of the Freedmen's Bureau

1,000 agents in the entire South. Nonetheless, the bureau's achievements in some areas, notably education and health care, were striking. By 1869, nearly 3,000 schools, serving more than 150,000 pupils in the South, reported to the bureau. Bureau agents also ran hospitals established during the war and provided medical care and drugs to both black and white southerners.

The Failure of Land Reform

One provision of the law establishing the bureau gave it the authority to divide abandoned and confiscated land into forty-acre plots for rental and eventual sale to the former slaves. In the summer of 1865, however, President Andrew Johnson, who had succeeded Lincoln, ordered nearly all land in federal hands returned to its former owners. A series of confrontations followed, notably in South Carolina and Georgia, where the army forcibly evicted blacks who had settled on "Sherman land." When O. O. Howard, head of the Freedmen's Bureau, traveled to the Sea Islands to inform blacks of the new policy, he was greeted with disbelief and protest. A committee of former slaves drew up petitions to Howard and President Johnson. Land, the freedmen insisted, was essential to the meaning of freedom. Without it, they declared, "we have not bettered our condition" from the days of slavery—"you will see, this is not the condition of really free men."

Andrew Johnson and land reform

Because no land distribution took place, the vast majority of rural freedpeople remained poor and without property during Reconstruction.

They had no alternative but to work on white-owned plantations, often for their former owners. Far from being able to rise in the social scale through hard work, black men were largely confined to farm work, unskilled labor, and service jobs, and black women to positions in private homes as cooks and maids. The failure of land reform produced a deep sense of betrayal that survived among the former slaves and their descendants long after the end of Reconstruction. "No sir," Mary Gaffney, an elderly ex-slave, recalled in the 1930s, "we were not given a thing but freedom."

Out of the conflict on the plantations, new systems of labor emerged in the different regions of the South. **Sharecropping** came to dominate the Cotton Belt and much of the Tobacco Belt of Virginia and North Carolina. Sharecropping initially arose as a compromise between blacks' desire for land and planters' demand for labor discipline. The system allowed each black family to rent a part of a plantation, with the crop divided between worker and owner at the end of the year. Sharecropping guaranteed the planters a stable resident labor force. Former slaves preferred it to gang labor because it offered them the prospect of working without day-to-day white supervision. But as the years went on, sharecropping became more and more oppressive. Sharecroppers' economic opportunities were severely limited by a world market in which the price of farm products suffered a prolonged decline.

A nursemaid and her charge, from a daguerreotype around 1865.

Difficulties with sharecropping

The White Farmer

The plight of the small farmer was not confined to blacks in the postwar South. Wartime devastation set in motion a train of events that permanently altered the independent way of life of white yeomen, leading to what they considered a loss of freedom. To obtain supplies from merchants, farmers were forced to take up the growing of cotton and pledge a part of the crop as collateral (property the creditor can seize if a debt is not paid). This system became known as the **crop lien**. Since interest rates were extremely high and the price of cotton fell steadily, many farmers found themselves still in debt after marketing their portion of the crop at year's end. They had no choice but to continue to plant cotton to obtain new loans. By the mid-1870s, white farmers, who cultivated only 10 percent of the South's cotton crop in 1860, were growing 40 percent, and many who had owned their land had fallen into dependency as sharecroppers who now rented land owned by others.

The crop-lien system

Both black and white farmers found themselves caught in the sharecropping and crop-lien systems. The workings of sharecropping and the

The burden of debt

VOICES OF FREEDOM

From Petition of Committee in Behalf of the Freedmen to Andrew Johnson (1865)

In the summer of 1865, President Andrew Johnson ordered land that had been distributed to freed slaves in South Carolina and Georgia returned to its former owners. A committee of freedmen drafted a petition asking for the right to obtain land. Johnson did not, however, change his policy.

We the freedmen of Edisto Island, South Carolina, have learned from you through Major General O. O. Howard . . . with deep sorrow and painful hearts of the possibility of [the] government restoring these lands to the former owners. We are well aware of the many perplexing and trying questions that burden your mind, and therefore pray to god (the preserver of all, and who has through our late and beloved President [Lincoln's] proclamation and the war made us a free people) that he may guide you in making your decisions and give you that wisdom that cometh from above to settle these great and important questions for the best interests of the country and the colored race.

Here is where secession was born and nurtured. Here is where we have toiled nearly all our lives as slaves and treated like dumb driven cattle. This is our home, we have made these lands what they were, we are the only true and loyal people that were found in possession of these lands. We have been always ready to strike for liberty and humanity, yea to fight if need be to preserve this glorious Union. Shall not we who are freedmen and have always been true to this Union have the same rights as are enjoyed by others? . . . Are not our rights as a free people and good citizens of these United States to be considered before those who were found in rebellion against this good and just government? . . .

[Are] we who have been abused and oppressed for many long years not to be allowed the privilege of purchasing land but be subject to the will of these large land owners? God forbid. Land monopoly is injurious to the advancement of the course of freedom, and if government does not make some provision by which we as freedmen can obtain a homestead, we have not bettered our condition. . . .

We look to you . . . for protection and equal rights with the privilege of purchasing a homestead—a homestead right here in the heart of South Carolina.

From a Sharecropping Contract (1866)

Few former slaves were able to acquire land in the post–Civil War South. Most ended up as sharecroppers, working on white-owned land for a share of the crop at the end of the growing season. This contract, typical of thousands of others, originated in Tennessee. The laborers signed with an X, as they were illiterate.

Thomas J. Ross agrees to employ the Freedmen to plant and raise a crop on his Rosstown Plantation. . . . On the following Rules, Regulations and Remunerations.

The said Ross agrees to furnish the land to cultivate, and a sufficient number of mules & horses and feed them to make and house said crop and all necessary farming utensils to carry on the same and to give unto said Freedmen whose names appear below one half of all the cotton, corn and wheat that is raised on said place for the year 1866 after all the necessary expenses are deducted out that accrues on said crop. Outside of the Freedmen's labor in harvesting, carrying to market and selling the same the said Freedmen . . . covenant and agrees to and with said Thomas J. Ross that for and in consideration of one half of the crop before mentioned that they will plant, cultivate, and raise under the management control and Superintendence of said Ross, in good faith, a cotton, corn and oat crop under his management for the year 1866. And we the said Freedmen agrees to furnish ourselves & families in provisions, clothing, medicine and medical bills and all, and every kind of other expenses that we may incur on said plantation for the year 1866 free of charge to said Ross. Should the said Ross furnish us any of the above supplies or any other kind of expenses, during said year, [we] are to settle and pay him out of the net proceeds of our part of the crop the retail price of the county at time of sale or any price we may agree upon—The said Ross shall keep a regular book account, against each and every one or the head of every family to be adjusted and settled at the end of the year.

We furthermore bind ourselves to and with said Ross that we will do good work and labor ten hours a day on an average, winter and summer. . . . We further agree that we will lose all lost time, or pay at the rate of one dollar per day, rainy days excepted. In sickness and women lying in childbed are to lose the time and account for it to the other hands out of his or her part of the crop. . . .

We furthermore bind ourselves that we will obey the orders of said Ross in all things in carrying out and managing said crop for said year and be docked for disobedience . . . and are also responsible to said Ross if we carelessly, maliciously maltreat any of his stock for said year to said Ross for damages to be assessed out of our wages.

Samuel (X) Johnson, Thomas (X) Richard, Tinny (X) Fitch, Jessie (X) Simmons, Sophe (X) Pruden, Henry (X) Pruden, Frances (X) Pruden, Elijah (X) Smith.

QUESTIONS

1. *Why do the black petitioners believe that owning land is essential to the enjoyment of freedom?*

2. *In what ways does the contract limit the freedom of the laborers?*

3. *What do these documents suggest about competing definitions of black freedom in the aftermath of slavery?*

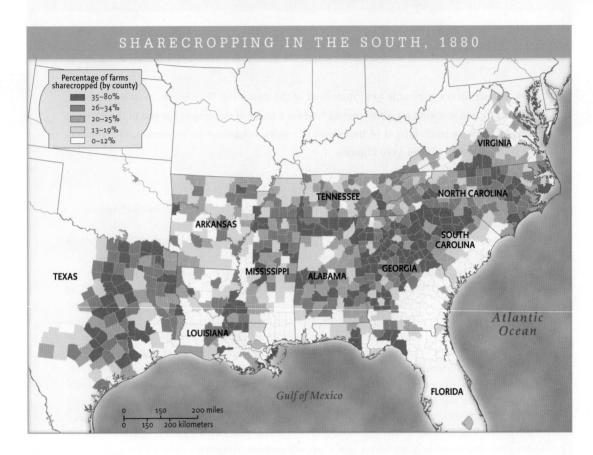

Percentage of farms
sharecropped (by county)
- 35–80%
- 26–34%
- 20–25%
- 13–19%
- 0–12%

VIRGINIA

TENNESSEE

NORTH CAROLINA

ARKANSAS

SOUTH CAROLINA

MISSISSIPPI   ALABAMA   GEORGIA

TEXAS

Atlantic Ocean

LOUISIANA

Gulf of Mexico   FLORIDA

0   150   200 miles

0   150   200 kilometers

By 1880, sharecropping had become the dominant form of agricultural labor in large parts of the South. The system involved both white and black farmers.

Growth of southern cities

crop-lien system are illustrated by the case of Matt Brown, a Mississippi farmer who borrowed money each year from a local merchant. He began 1892 with a debt of $226 held over from the previous year. By 1893, although he produced cotton worth $171, Brown's debt had increased to $402, because he had borrowed $33 for food, $29 for clothing, $173 for supplies, and $112 for other items. Brown never succeeded in getting out of debt. He died in 1905; the last entry under his name in the merchant's account book is a coffin.

Even as the rural South stagnated economically, southern cities experienced remarkable growth after the Civil War. As railroads penetrated the interior, they enabled merchants in market centers like Atlanta to trade directly with the North, bypassing coastal cities that had traditionally monopolized southern commerce. A new urban middle class of merchants, railroad promoters, and bankers reaped the benefits of the spread of cotton production in the postwar South.

The cotton depot at Guthrie, Texas. Bales of cotton have been loaded onto trains for shipment. After the Civil War, more and more white farmers began growing cotton to support their families, permanently altering their formerly self-sufficient way of life.

Aftermath of Slavery

The United States, of course, was not the only society to confront the problem of the transition from slavery to freedom. Indeed, many parallels exist between the debates during Reconstruction and struggles that followed slavery in other parts of the Western Hemisphere over the same issues of land, control of labor, and political power. Planters elsewhere held the same stereotypical views of black laborers as were voiced by their counterparts in the United States—former slaves were supposedly lazy and lacking in ambition, and thought that freedom meant an absence of labor.

Emancipation in the Western Hemisphere

For their part, former slaves throughout the hemisphere tried to carve out as much independence as possible, both in their daily lives and in their labor. In many places, the plantations either fell to pieces, as in Haiti, or continued operating with a new labor force composed of indentured servants from India and China, as in Jamaica, Trinidad, and British Guiana. Southern planters in the United States brought in a few Chinese laborers in an attempt to replace freedmen, but since the federal government opposed such efforts, the Chinese remained only a tiny proportion of the southern workforce.

Chinese laborers at work on a Louisiana plantation during Reconstruction.

But if struggles over land and labor united its post-emancipation experience with that of other societies, in one respect the United States was unique. Only in the United States were former slaves, within two years of the end of slavery, granted the right to vote and, thus, given a major share of political power. Few anticipated this development when the Civil War ended. It came about as the result of one of the greatest political crises of American history—the battle between President Andrew Johnson and Congress over Reconstruction. The struggle resulted in profound changes in the nature of citizenship, the structure of constitutional authority, and the meaning of American freedom.

Emancipation and the right to vote

THE MAKING OF RADICAL RECONSTRUCTION

Andrew Johnson

To Lincoln's successor, Andrew Johnson, fell the task of overseeing the restoration of the Union. Born in poverty in North Carolina, as a youth Johnson worked as a tailor's apprentice. Becoming a successful politician after moving to Tennessee, Johnson identified himself as the champion of his state's "honest yeomen" and a foe of large planters, whom he described as a "bloated, corrupted aristocracy." A strong defender of the Union, he became the only senator from a seceding state to remain at his post in Washington, D.C., when the Civil War began in 1861. When northern forces occupied Tennessee, Abraham Lincoln named him military governor. In 1864, Republicans nominated him to run for vice president as a symbol of the party's hope of extending its organization into the South.

Johnson's background

Outlook

In personality and outlook, Johnson proved unsuited for the responsibilities he shouldered after Lincoln's death. A lonely, stubborn man, he was intolerant of criticism and unable to compromise. He lacked Lincoln's political skills and keen sense of public opinion. Moreover, while Johnson had supported emancipation once Lincoln made it a goal of the war effort, he held deeply racist views. African-Americans, Johnson believed, had no role to play in Reconstruction.

The Failure of Presidential Reconstruction

A little over a month after Lee's surrender at Appomattox, and with Congress out of session until December, Johnson in May 1865 outlined his plan for reuniting the nation. He issued a series of proclamations that began the period of Presidential Reconstruction (1865–1867). Johnson offered a pardon (which restored political and property rights, except for slaves) to nearly all white southerners who took an oath of allegiance to the Union. He excluded Confederate leaders and wealthy planters whose prewar property had been valued at more than $20,000. Most of those exempted, however, soon received individual pardons from the president. Johnson also appointed provisional governors and ordered them to call state conventions, elected by whites alone, that would establish loyal governments in the South. Apart from the requirement that they abolish slavery, repudiate secession, and refuse to pay the Confederate debt—all unavoidable consequences of southern defeat—he granted the new governments a free hand in managing local affairs.

Johnson's program

The conduct of the southern governments elected under Johnson's program turned most of the Republican North against the president. By and large, white voters returned prominent Confederates and members of the old elite to power. Reports of violence directed against former slaves and northern visitors in the South further alarmed Republicans.

Republicans against Johnson

The Black Codes

But what aroused the most opposition to Johnson's Reconstruction policy were the **Black Codes**, laws passed by the new southern governments that attempted to regulate the lives of the former slaves. These laws granted blacks certain rights, such as legalized marriage, ownership of property, and limited access to the courts. But they denied them the rights to testify

Regulating former slaves

Selling a Freedman to Pay His Fine at Monticello, Florida, an engraving from *Frank Leslie's Illustrated Newspaper*, January 19, 1867. Under the Black Codes enacted by southern legislatures immediately after the Civil War, blacks convicted of "vagrancy"—often because they refused to sign contracts to work on plantations—were fined and, if unable to pay, auctioned off to work for the person who paid the fine.

against whites, to serve on juries or in state militias, or to vote. And in response to planters' demands that the freedpeople be required to work on the plantations, the Black Codes declared that those who failed to sign yearly labor contracts could be arrested and hired out to white landowners.

Reaction to Black Codes

Clearly, the death of slavery did not automatically mean the birth of freedom. But the Black Codes so completely violated free labor principles that they called forth a vigorous response from the Republican North. In general, few groups of rebels in history have been treated more leniently than the defeated Confederates. A handful of southern leaders were arrested, but most were quickly released. Only one was executed—Henry Wirz, the commander of Andersonville prison, where thousands of Union prisoners of war had died. Most of the Union army was swiftly demobilized. What motivated the North's turn against Johnson's policies was not a desire to "punish" the white South, but the inability of the South's political leaders to accept the reality of emancipation as evidenced by the Black Codes.

The Radical Republicans

When Congress assembled in December 1865, Johnson announced that with loyal governments functioning in all the southern states, the nation had been reunited. In response, Radical Republicans, who had grown increasingly disenchanted with Johnson during the summer and fall, called for the dissolution of these governments and the establishment of new ones with "rebels" excluded from power and black men guaranteed the right to vote. Radicals shared the conviction that Union victory created a golden opportunity to institutionalize the principle of equal rights for all, regardless of race.

The most prominent Radicals in Congress were Charles Sumner, a senator from Massachusetts, and Thaddeus Stevens, a lawyer and iron manufacturer who represented Pennsylvania in the House of Representatives. Before the Civil War, both had been outspoken foes of slavery and defenders of black rights. Stevens's most cherished aim was to confiscate the land of disloyal planters and divide it among former slaves and northern migrants to the South. But his plan to make "small independent landholders" of the former slaves proved too radical even for many of his Radical colleagues and failed to pass.

Thaddeus Stevens, leader of the Radical Republicans in the House of Representatives during Reconstruction.

The Origins of Civil Rights

With the South unrepresented, Republicans enjoyed an overwhelming majority in Congress. Most Republicans were moderates, not Radicals.

Moderates believed that Johnson's plan was flawed, but they desired to work with the president to modify it. They feared that neither northern nor southern whites would accept black suffrage. Moderates and Radicals joined in refusing to seat the southerners recently elected to Congress, but moderates broke with the Radicals by leaving the Johnson governments in place.

Radical Republicans vs. moderates

Early in 1866, Senator Lyman Trumbull of Illinois proposed two bills that reflected the moderates' belief that Johnson's policy required modification. The first extended the life of the Freedmen's Bureau, which had originally been established for only one year. The second, the **Civil Rights Bill of 1866**, was described by one congressman as "one of the most important bills ever presented to the House for its action." It defined all persons born in the United States as citizens and spelled out rights they were to enjoy without regard to race. Equality before the law was central to the measure—no longer could states enact laws like the Black Codes discriminating between white and black citizens. So were free labor values. According to the law, no state could deprive any citizen of the right to make contracts, bring lawsuits, or enjoy equal protection of one's person and property. These, said Trumbull, were the "fundamental rights belonging to every man as a free man." The bill made no mention of the right to vote for blacks. In constitutional terms, the Civil Rights Bill represented the first attempt to define in law the essence of freedom.

The Civil Rights Bill of 1866

To the surprise of Congress, Johnson vetoed both bills. Both, he said, would centralize power in the national government and deprive the states of the authority to regulate their own affairs. Moreover, he argued, blacks did not deserve the rights of citizenship. Congress failed by a single vote to muster the two-thirds majority necessary to override the veto of the Freedmen's Bureau Bill (although later in 1866, it did extend the bureau's life to 1870). But in April 1866, the Civil Rights Bill became the first major law in American history to be passed over a presidential veto.

The Fourteenth Amendment

Congress now proceeded to adopt its own plan of Reconstruction. In June, it approved and sent to the states for ratification the **Fourteenth Amendment**, which placed in the Constitution the principle of citizenship for all persons born in the United States, and which empowered the federal government to protect the rights of all Americans. The amendment prohibited the states from abridging the "privileges or immunities" of citizens or denying any person the "equal protection of the laws." This broad language opened the door for future Congresses and the federal courts to breathe meaning into the guarantee of legal equality.

President Andrew Johnson, in an 1868 lithograph by Currier and Ives. Because of Johnson's stubborn opposition to the congressional Reconstruction policy, one disgruntled citizen drew a crown on his head with the words, "I am King."

A Democratic Party broadside from the election of 1866 in Pennsylvania uses racist imagery to argue that government assistance aids lazy former slaves at the expense of hardworking whites.

A Democratic Party broadside from the election of 1866 in Pennsylvania uses racist imagery to argue that government assistance aids lazy former slaves at the expense of hardworking whites.

Black suffrage and political power

In a compromise between the radical and moderate positions on black suffrage, the amendment did not grant blacks the right to vote. But it did provide that if a state denied the vote to any group of men, that state's representation in Congress would be reduced. (This provision did not apply when states barred women from voting.) The abolition of slavery threatened to increase southern political power, since now all blacks, not merely three-fifths as in the case of slaves, would be counted in determining a state's representation in Congress. The Fourteenth Amendment offered the leaders of the white South a choice—allow black men to vote and keep their state's full representation in the House of Representatives, or limit the vote to whites and sacrifice part of their political power.

By writing into the Constitution the principle that equality before the law regardless of race is a fundamental right of all American citizens, the amendment made the most important change in that document since the adoption of the Bill of Rights.

The Reconstruction Act

Johnson's speaking tour

The Fourteenth Amendment became the central issue of the political campaign of 1866. Johnson embarked on a speaking tour of the North.

Denouncing his critics, the president made wild accusations that the Radicals were plotting to assassinate him. His behavior further undermined public support for his policies, as did riots that broke out in Memphis and New Orleans, in which white policemen and citizens killed dozens of blacks.

In the northern congressional elections that fall, Republicans opposed to Johnson's policies won a sweeping victory. Nonetheless, at the president's urging, every southern state but Tennessee refused to ratify the Fourteenth Amendment. The intransigence of Johnson and the bulk of the white South pushed moderate Republicans toward the Radicals. In March 1867, over Johnson's veto, Congress adopted the **Reconstruction Act**, which temporarily divided the South into five military districts and called for the creation of new state governments, with black men given the right to vote. Thus began the period of Radical Reconstruction, which lasted until 1877.

Radical Reconstruction

Impeachment and the Election of Grant

In March 1867, Congress adopted the **Tenure of Office Act**, barring the president from removing certain officeholders, including cabinet members, without the consent of the Senate. Johnson considered this an unconstitutional restriction on his authority. In February 1868, he removed Secretary of War Edwin M. Stanton, an ally of the Radicals. The House of Representatives responded by approving articles of **impeachment**—that is, it presented charges against Johnson to the Senate, which had to decide whether to remove him from office.

That spring, for the first time in American history, a president was placed on trial before the Senate for "high crimes and misdemeanors." By this point, virtually all Republicans considered Johnson a failure as president. But some moderates feared that conviction would damage the constitutional separation of powers between Congress and the executive. Johnson's lawyers assured moderate Republicans that, if acquitted, he would stop interfering with Reconstruction policy. The final tally was 35-19 to convict Johnson, one vote short of the two-thirds necessary to remove him. Seven Republicans had joined the Democrats in voting to acquit the president.

A few days after the vote, Republicans nominated Ulysses S. Grant, the Union's most prominent military

A Republican campaign poster from 1868 depicts Ulysses S. Grant and his running mate Henry Wilson not as a celebrated general and U.S. senator but as ordinary workingmen, embodiments of the dignity of free labor.

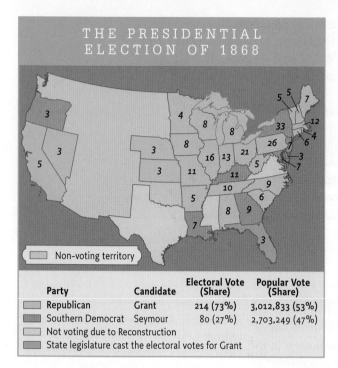

THE PRESIDENTIAL ELECTION OF 1868

Party	Candidate	Electoral Vote (Share)	Popular Vote (Share)
Republican	Grant	214 (73%)	3,012,833 (53%)
Southern Democrat	Seymour	80 (27%)	2,703,249 (47%)
Not voting due to Reconstruction			
State legislature cast the electoral votes for Grant			

Non-voting territory

hero, as their candidate for president. Grant's Democratic opponent was Horatio Seymour, the former governor of New York. Reconstruction became the central issue of the bitterly fought 1868 campaign. Democrats denounced Reconstruction as unconstitutional and condemned black suffrage as a violation of America's political traditions. They appealed openly to racism. Seymour's running mate, Francis P. Blair Jr., charged Republicans with placing the South under the rule of "a semibarbarous race" who longed to "subject the white women to their unbridled lust."

The Fifteenth Amendment

Race and voting rights

Grant won the election of 1868, although by a margin—300,000 of 6 million votes cast—that many Republicans found uncomfortably slim. The result led Congress to adopt the **Fifteenth Amendment**, which prohibited the federal and state governments from denying any citizen the right to vote because of race. Bitterly opposed by the Democratic Party, it was ratified in 1870.

Although the Fifteenth Amendment opened the door to suffrage restrictions not explicitly based on race—literacy tests, property qualifications, and poll taxes—and did not extend the right to vote to women, it marked the culmination of four decades of abolitionist agitation. "Nothing in all history," exclaimed veteran abolitionist William Lloyd Garrison, equaled "this wonderful, quiet, sudden transformation of four millions of human beings from . . . the auction-block to the ballot-box."

The "Great Constitutional Revolution"

Effects of Reconstruction Amendments

The laws and amendments of Reconstruction reflected the intersection of two products of the Civil War era—a newly empowered national state, and the idea of a national citizenry enjoying equality before the law. What Republican leader Carl Schurz called the "great Constitutional revolution" of Reconstruction transformed the federal system and with it, the language of freedom so central to American political culture.

Before the Civil War, American citizenship had been closely linked to race. But the laws and amendments of Reconstruction repudiated the idea that citizenship was an entitlement of whites alone. And, as one congressman noted, the amendments expanded the liberty of whites as well as blacks, including "the millions of people of foreign birth who will flock to our shores."

Race and citizenship

The new amendments also transformed the relationship between the federal government and the states. The Bill of Rights had linked civil liberties to the autonomy of the states. Its language—"Congress shall make no law"—reflected the belief that concentrated national power posed the greatest threat to freedom. The authors of the Reconstruction amendments assumed that rights required national power to enforce them. Rather than a threat to liberty, the federal government, in Charles Sumner's words, had become "the custodian of freedom."

The Reconstruction amendments transformed the Constitution from a document primarily concerned with federal-state relations and the rights of property into a vehicle through which members of vulnerable minorities could stake a claim to freedom and seek protection against misconduct by all levels of government. In the twentieth century, many of the Supreme Court's most important decisions expanding the rights of American citizens were based on the Fourteenth Amendment, perhaps most notably the 1954 *Brown* ruling that outlawed school segregation (see Chapter 24).

Constitutional significance

The Rights of Women

"The contest with the South that destroyed slavery," wrote the Philadelphia lawyer Sidney George Fisher in his diary, "has caused an immense increase in the popular passion for liberty and equality." But advocates of women's rights encountered the limits of the Reconstruction commitment to equality. Women activists saw Reconstruction as the moment to claim their own emancipation. The rewriting of the Constitution, declared suffrage leader Olympia Brown, offered the opportunity to sever the blessings of freedom from sex as well as race and to "bury the black man and the woman in the citizen."

Women and the limits of equality

Even Radical Republicans insisted that Reconstruction was the "Negro's hour" (the hour, that is, of the black male). The Fourteenth Amendment for the first time introduced the word "male" into the Constitution, in its clause penalizing a state for denying any group of men the right to vote. The Fifteenth Amendment outlawed discrimination in voting based on race but not gender. These measures produced a bitter split both

Voting rights

A Delegation of Advocates of Woman Suffrage Addressing the House Judiciary Committee, an engraving from *Frank Leslie's Illustrated Newspaper*, February 4, 1871. The group includes Elizabeth Cady Stanton, seated just to the right of the speaker, and Susan B. Anthony, at the table on the extreme right.

between feminists and Radical Republicans, and within feminist circles. Some leaders, like Elizabeth Cady Stanton and Susan B. Anthony, denounced their former abolitionist allies and moved to sever the women's rights movement from its earlier moorings in the antislavery tradition.

Thus, even as it rejected the racial definition of freedom that had emerged in the first half of the nineteenth century, Reconstruction left the gender boundary largely intact. When women tried to use the rewritten legal code and Constitution to claim equal rights, they found the courts unreceptive. Myra Bradwell invoked the idea of free labor in challenging an Illinois statute limiting the practice of law to men, but the Supreme Court in 1873 rebuffed her claim. Free labor principles, the justices declared, did not apply to women, since "the law of the Creator" had assigned them to "the domestic sphere."

Despite their limitations, the Fourteenth and Fifteenth Amendments and the Reconstruction Act of 1867 marked a radical departure in American history. The Reconstruction Act of 1867 inaugurated America's first real experiment in interracial democracy.

RADICAL RECONSTRUCTION IN THE SOUTH

"The Tocsin of Freedom"

Political action by African-Americans

Among the former slaves, the passage of the Reconstruction Act inspired an outburst of political organization. At mass political meetings—community gatherings attended by men, women, and children—African-Americans staked their claim to equal citizenship. Blacks, declared an Alabama meeting, deserved "exactly the same rights, privileges and immunities as are enjoyed by white men. We ask for nothing more and will be content with nothing less."

Registering to vote

Determined to exercise their new rights as citizens, thousands joined the Union League, an organization closely linked to the Republican Party, and the vast majority of eligible African-Americans registered

Electioneering at the South, an engraving from *Harper's Weekly*, July 25, 1868, depicts a speaker at a political meeting in the rural South. Women as well as men took part in these grassroots gatherings.

From the Plantation to the Senate, an 1883 lithograph celebrating African-American progress during Reconstruction. Among the black leaders pictured at the top are Reconstruction congressmen Benjamin S. Turner, Josiah T. Walls, and Joseph H. Rainey; Hiram Revels of Mississippi, the first African-American senator; religious leader Richard Allen; and abolitionists Frederick Douglass and William Wells Brown. At the center emancipated slaves work in the cotton fields, and below children attend school and a black family stands outside its home.

to vote. James K. Green, a former slave in Hale County, Alabama, and a League organizer, went on to serve eight years in the Alabama legislature. In the 1880s, Green looked back on his political career. Before the war, he declared, "I was entirely ignorant; I knew nothing more than to obey my master; and there were thousands of us in the same attitude. . . . But the tocsin [warning bell] of freedom sounded and knocked at the door and we walked out like free men and shouldered the responsibilities."

By 1870, all the former Confederate states had been re-admitted to the Union, and in a region where the Republican Party had not existed before the war, nearly all were under Republican control. Their new state constitutions, drafted in 1868 and 1869 by the first public bodies in American history with substantial black representation, marked a considerable improvement over those they replaced. The constitutions greatly expanded public responsibilities. They established the region's first state-funded systems of free public education, and they created new penitentiaries, orphan asylums, and homes for the insane. The constitutions guaranteed equality of civil and political rights and abolished practices of the antebellum era such as whipping as a punishment for crime, property qualifications for officeholding, and imprisonment for debt. A few states initially barred former Confederates from voting, but this policy was quickly abandoned by the new state governments.

The First Vote, an engraving from *Harper's Weekly*, November 16, 1867, depicts the first biracial elections in southern history. The voters represent key sources of the black political leadership that emerged during Reconstruction—the artisan carrying his tools, the well-dressed city person (probably free before the war), and the soldier.

The Black Officeholder

Throughout Reconstruction, black voters provided the bulk of the Republican Party's support. But African-Americans did not control Reconstruction politics, as their opponents frequently charged. The highest offices remained almost entirely in white hands, and only in South Carolina, where blacks made up 60 percent of the population, did they form a majority of the legislature. Nonetheless, the fact that some 2,000 African-Americans held public office during Reconstruction marked a fundamental shift of power in the South and a radical departure in American government.

African-Americans were represented at every level of government. Fourteen were elected to the national House of Representatives. Two blacks served in the U.S. Senate during Reconstruction, both representing Mississippi. Hiram Revels, who had been born free in North Carolina, in 1870 became the first black senator in American history. The second, Blanche K. Bruce, a former slave, was elected in 1875. At state and local levels, the presence of black officeholders and their white allies made a real difference in southern life, ensuring that blacks accused of crimes would be tried before juries of their peers and enforcing fairness in such aspects of local government as road repair, tax assessment, and poor relief.

Northerners and former slaves in office

In South Carolina and Louisiana, homes of the South's wealthiest and best-educated free black communities, most prominent Reconstruction officeholders had never experienced slavery. In addition, a number of black Reconstruction officials, like Pennsylvania-born Jonathan J. Wright, who served on the South Carolina Supreme Court, had come from the North after the Civil War. The majority, however, were former slaves who had established their leadership in the black community by serving in the Union army; working as ministers, teachers, or skilled craftsmen; or engaging in Union League organizing.

Carpetbaggers and Scalawags

White northerners in the South

The new southern governments also brought to power new groups of whites. Many Reconstruction officials were northerners who for one reason or another had made their homes in the South after the war. Their opponents dubbed them **carpetbaggers**, implying that they had packed all their belongings in a suitcase and left their homes in order to reap the spoils of office in the South. Some carpetbaggers were undoubtedly corrupt adventurers. The large majority, however, were former Union soldiers who decided to remain in the South when the war ended, before there was any prospect of going into politics.

Most white Republicans had been born in the South. Former Confederates reserved their greatest scorn for these **scalawags**, whom they considered traitors to their race and region. Some southern-born Republicans were men of stature and wealth, like James L. Alcorn, the owner of one of Mississippi's largest plantations and the state's first Republican governor. Most "scalawags," however, were non-slaveholding white farmers from the southern upcountry. Many had been wartime Unionists, and they now cooperated with the Republicans in order to prevent "rebels" from returning to power.

Southern Republicans in Power

In view of the daunting challenges they faced, the remarkable thing is not that Reconstruction governments in many respects failed, but how much they did accomplish. Perhaps their greatest achievement lay in establishing the South's first state-supported public schools. The new educational systems served both black and white children, although generally in schools segregated by race. Only in New Orleans were the public schools integrated during Reconstruction, and only in South Carolina did the state university admit black students (elsewhere, separate colleges were established). The new governments also pioneered civil rights legislation. Their laws made it illegal for railroads, hotels, and other institutions to discriminate on the basis of race. Enforcement varied considerably from locality to locality, but Reconstruction established for the first time at the state level a standard of equal citizenship and a recognition of blacks' right to a share of public services.

Republican governments also took steps to strengthen the position of rural laborers and promote the South's economic recovery. They passed laws to ensure that agricultural laborers and sharecroppers had the first claim on harvested crops, rather than merchants to whom the landowner owed money. South Carolina created a state Land Commission, which by 1876 had settled 14,000 black families and a few poor whites on their own farms.

The Quest for Prosperity

Rather than on land distribution, however, the Reconstruction governments pinned their hopes for southern economic growth and opportunity for African-Americans and poor whites alike on regional economic development.

A portrait of Hiram Revels, the first black U.S. senator, by Theodore Kaufmann, a German-born artist who emigrated to the United States in 1855. Lithograph copies sold widely in the North during Reconstruction. Frederick Douglass, commenting on the dignified image, noted that African-Americans "so often see ourselves described and painted as monkeys, that we think it a great piece of fortune to find an exception to this general rule."

Protecting rural laborers

Economic development during Reconstruction

A group of black students and their teacher in a picture taken by an amateur photographer, probably a Union army veteran, while touring Civil War battlefields.

Railroad construction

Railroad construction, they believed, was the key to transforming the South into a society of booming factories, bustling towns, and diversified agriculture. Every state during Reconstruction helped to finance railroad construction, and through tax reductions and other incentives tried to attract northern manufacturers to invest in the region. The program had mixed results. Economic development in general remained weak.

To their supporters, the governments of Radical Reconstruction presented a complex pattern of disappointment and accomplishment. A revitalized southern economy failed to materialize, and most African-Americans remained locked in poverty. On the other hand, biracial demo-

Biracial democracy

cratic government, a thing unknown in American history, for the first time functioned effectively in many parts of the South. The conservative elite that had dominated southern government from colonial times to 1867 found itself excluded from political power, while poor whites, newcomers from the North, and former slaves cast ballots, sat on juries, and enacted and administered laws. It is a measure of how far change had progressed that the reaction against Reconstruction proved so extreme.

THE OVERTHROW OF RECONSTRUCTION

Reconstruction's Opponents

The South's traditional leaders—planters, merchants, and Democratic politicians—bitterly opposed the new governments. "Intelligence, virtue,

Sources of opposition

and patriotism" in public life, declared a protest by prominent southern

Practical Illustration of the Virginia Constitution.

WHITE MAN THE BOTTOM RAIL.

MIXED SCHOOL SYSTEM.

NEGRO COURT AND JURY.

A cartoon from around 1870 illustrates a key theme of the racist opposition to Reconstruction—that blacks had forced themselves upon whites and gained domination over them. A black schoolteacher inflicts punishment on a white student in an integrated classroom, and a racially mixed jury judges a white defendant.

Democrats, had given way to "ignorance, stupidity, and vice." Corruption did exist during Reconstruction, but it was confined to no race, region, or party. The rapid growth of state budgets and the benefits to be gained from public aid led in some states to a scramble for influence that produced bribery, insider dealing, and a get-rich-quick atmosphere. Southern frauds, however, were dwarfed by those practiced in these years by the Whiskey Ring, which involved high officials of the Grant administration, and by New York's Tweed Ring, controlled by the Democrats, whose thefts ran into the tens of millions of dollars. (These are discussed in the next chapter.) The rising taxes needed to pay for schools and other new public facilities and to assist railroad development were another cause of opposition to Reconstruction. Many poor whites who had initially supported the Republican Party turned against it when it became clear that their economic situation was not improving.

Economic issues

The most basic reason for opposition to Reconstruction, however, was that most white southerners could not accept the idea of former slaves voting, holding office, and enjoying equality before the law. Opponents launched a campaign of violence in an effort to end Republican rule. Their actions posed a fundamental challenge both for Reconstruction governments in the South and for policymakers in Washington, D.C.

Social issues

"A Reign of Terror"

The Civil War ended in 1865, but violence remained widespread in large parts of the postwar South. In the early years of Reconstruction, violence was mostly local and unorganized. Blacks were assaulted and murdered for refusing to give way to whites on city sidewalks, using "insolent" language, challenging end-of-year contract settlements, and attempting to buy land. The violence that greeted the advent of Republican governments after 1867, however, was far more pervasive and more directly motivated by politics. In wide areas of the South, secret societies sprang up with the aim of preventing blacks from voting and destroying the organization of the Republican Party by assassinating local leaders and public officials.

The most notorious such organization was the **Ku Klux Klan**, which in effect served as a military arm of the Democratic Party in the South. From its founding in 1866 in Tennessee, the Klan was a terrorist organization. It committed some of the most brutal criminal acts in American history. In many counties throughout the South, it launched what one victim called a "reign of terror" against Republican leaders, black and white.

The Klan's victims included white Republicans, among them wartime Unionists and local officeholders, teachers, and party organizers. But African-Americans—local political leaders, those who managed to acquire land, and others who in one way or another defied the norms of white supremacy—bore the brunt of the violence. On occasion, violence escalated from assaults on individuals to mass terrorism and even local insurrections. The bloodiest act of violence during Reconstruction took place in Colfax, Louisiana, in 1873, where armed whites assaulted the town with a small cannon. Hundreds of former slaves were murdered, including fifty members of a black militia unit after they had surrendered.

In 1870 and 1871, Congress adopted three **Enforcement Acts**, outlawing terrorist societies and allowing the president to use the army against them. These laws continued the expansion of national authority during Reconstruction. In 1871, President Grant dispatched federal marshals, backed up by troops in some areas, to arrest hundreds of accused Klansmen. Many Klan leaders fled the South. After a series of well-publicized trials, the Klan went out of existence. In 1872, for the first time since before the Civil War, peace reigned in most of the former Confederacy.

A Prospective Scene in the City of Oaks, a cartoon in the September 1, 1868, issue of the *Independent Monitor*, a Democratic newspaper published in Tuscaloosa, Alabama. The cartoon sent a warning to the Reverend A. S. Lakin, who had moved from Ohio to become president of the University of Alabama, and Dr. N. B. Cloud, a southern-born Republican serving as Alabama's superintendent of public education. The Ku Klux Klan forced both men from their positions. While most of the Klan's victims were black, the two men pictured here are white.

The Liberal Republicans

Despite the Grant administration's effective response to Klan terrorism, the North's commitment to Reconstruction waned during the 1870s. Northerners increasingly felt that the South should be able to solve its own problems without constant interference from Washington. The federal government had freed the slaves, made them citizens, and given them the right to vote. Now, blacks should rely on their own resources, not demand further assistance.

Waning commitment in the North

In 1872, an influential group of Republicans, alienated by corruption within the Grant administration and believing that the growth of federal power during and after the war needed to be curtailed, formed their own party. They included Republican founders like Lyman Trumbull and prominent editors and journalists such as E. L. Godkin of *The Nation*. Calling themselves Liberal Republicans, they nominated Horace Greeley, editor of the *New York Tribune*, for president.

Liberal Republicans

Democratic criticisms of Reconstruction found a receptive audience among the Liberals. As in the North, they became convinced, the "best men" of the South had been excluded from power while "ignorant" voters controlled politics, producing corruption and misgovernment. Greeley had spent most of his career, first as a Whig and then as a Republican, denouncing the Democratic Party. But with the

Changes in graphic artist Thomas Nast's depiction of blacks in *Harper's Weekly* mirrored the evolution of Republican sentiment in the North. *And Not This Man?*, August 5, 1865, shows the black soldier as an upstanding citizen deserving of the vote. *Colored Rule in a Reconstructed (?) State*, March 14, 1874, suggests that Reconstruction legislatures had become travesties of democratic government.

A bankbook issued by the Freedman's Savings and Trust Company, a private corporation established by Congress to promote thrift among the former slaves. Black individuals, families, church groups, and civic organizations deposited nearly $2 million in branches scattered across the South. The bank failed in 1874 because of mismanagement, and thousands of depositors lost their savings.

Republican split presenting an opportunity to repair their political fortunes, Democratic leaders endorsed Greeley as their candidate. But many rank-and-file Democrats, unable to bring themselves to vote for Greeley, stayed at home on election day. As a result, Greeley suffered a devastating defeat by Grant, whose margin of more than 700,000 popular votes was the largest in a nineteenth-century presidential contest. But Greeley's campaign placed on the northern agenda the one issue on which the Liberal reformers and the Democrats could agree—a new policy toward the South.

The North's Retreat

The Liberal attack on Reconstruction, which continued after 1872, contributed to a resurgence of racism in the North. Journalist James S. Pike, a leading Greeley supporter, in 1874 published *The Prostrate State*, an influential account of a visit to South Carolina. The book depicted a state engulfed by political corruption, drained by governmental extravagance, and under the control of "a mass of black barbarism." Resurgent racism offered a convenient explanation for the alleged "failure" of Reconstruction. The solution, for many, was to restore leading whites to political power.

Other factors also weakened northern support for Reconstruction. In 1873, the country plunged into a severe economic depression. Distracted by economic problems, Republicans were in no mood to devote further attention to the South. The depression dealt the South a severe blow and further weakened the prospect that Republicans could revitalize the region's economy. Democrats made substantial gains throughout the nation in the elections of 1874. For the first time since the Civil War, their party took control of the House of Representatives. Before the new Congress met, the old one enacted a final piece of Reconstruction legislation, the **Civil Rights Act of 1875**. This outlawed racial discrimination in places of public accommodation like hotels and theaters. But it was clear that the northern public was retreating from Reconstruction.

The Supreme Court and Reconstruction

The Supreme Court whittled away at the guarantees of black rights Congress had adopted. In the *Slaughterhouse Cases* (1873), the justices ruled that the Fourteenth Amendment had not altered traditional federalism. Most of the rights of citizens, it declared, remained under state control. Three years later, in *United States v. Cruikshank*, the Court gutted

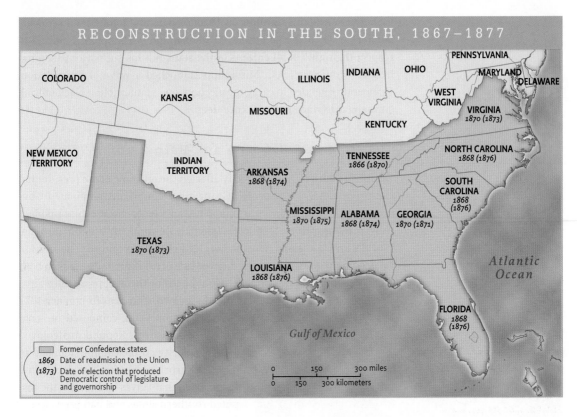

RECONSTRUCTION IN THE SOUTH, 1867–1877

the Enforcement Acts by throwing out the convictions of some of those responsible for the Colfax Massacre of 1873.

The Triumph of the Redeemers

By the mid-1870s, Reconstruction was clearly on the defensive. Democrats had already regained control of states with substantial white voting majorities such as Tennessee, North Carolina, and Texas. The victorious Democrats called themselves **Redeemers**, since they claimed to have "redeemed" the white South from corruption, misgovernment, and northern and black control.

Democratic victories at the polls

In those states where Reconstruction governments survived, violence again erupted. This time, the Grant administration showed no desire to intervene. In Mississippi, in 1875, armed Democrats destroyed ballot boxes and drove former slaves from the polls. The result was a Democratic landslide and the end of Reconstruction in Mississippi. Similar events

Return of violence

took place in South Carolina in 1876. Democrats nominated for governor former Confederate general Wade Hampton. Hampton promised to respect the rights of all citizens of the state, but his supporters, inspired by Democratic tactics in Mississippi, launched a wave of intimidation. Democrats intended to carry the election, one planter told a black official, "if we have to wade in blood knee-deep."

The Disputed Election and Bargain of 1877

Events in South Carolina directly affected the outcome of the presidential campaign of 1876. To succeed Grant, the Republicans nominated Governor Rutherford B. Hayes of Ohio. The Democrats chose as his opponent New York's governor, Samuel J. Tilden. By this time, only South Carolina, Florida, and Louisiana remained under Republican control. The election turned out to be so close that whoever captured these states—which both parties claimed to have carried—would become the next president.

Unable to resolve the impasse on its own, Congress in January 1877 appointed a fifteen-member Electoral Commission, composed of senators, representatives, and Supreme Court justices. Republicans enjoyed an 8-7 majority on the commission, and to no one's surprise, the members decided by that margin that Hayes had carried the disputed southern states and had been elected president.

Even as the commission deliberated, however, behind-the-scenes negotiations took place between leaders of the two parties. Hayes's representatives agreed to recognize Democratic control of the entire South and to avoid further intervention in local affairs. For their part, Democrats promised not to dispute Hayes's right to office and to respect the civil and political rights of blacks.

Thus was concluded the **Bargain of 1877**. Hayes became president and quickly ordered federal troops to stop guarding the state houses in Louisiana and South Carolina, allowing Democratic claimants to become governors. (Contrary to legend,

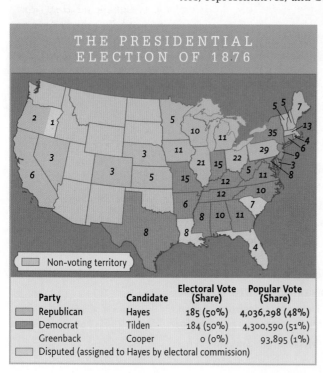

THE PRESIDENTIAL ELECTION OF 1876

Non-voting territory

Party		Candidate	Electoral Vote (Share)	Popular Vote (Share)
	Republican	Hayes	185 (50%)	4,036,298 (48%)
	Democrat	Tilden	184 (50%)	4,300,590 (51%)
	Greenback	Cooper	0 (0%)	93,895 (1%)
	Disputed (assigned to Hayes by electoral commission)			

Hayes did not remove the last soldiers from the South—he simply ordered them to return to their barracks.) The triumphant southern Democrats failed to live up to their pledge to recognize blacks as equal citizens.

The End of Reconstruction

As a historical process—the nation's adjustment to the destruction of slavery—Reconstruction continued well after 1877. Blacks continued to vote and, in some states, hold office into the 1890s. But as a distinct era of national history—when Republicans controlled much of the South, blacks exercised significant political power, and the federal government accepted the responsibility for protecting the fundamental rights of all American citizens—Reconstruction had come to an end. Despite its limitations, Reconstruction was a remarkable chapter in the story of American freedom. Nearly a century would pass before the nation again tried to bring equal rights to the descendants of slaves. The civil rights era of the 1950s and 1960s would sometimes be called the Second Reconstruction.

Is This a Republican Form of Government?, a cartoon by Thomas Nast in *Harper's Weekly*, September 2, 1876, illustrates his conviction that the overthrow of Reconstruction meant that the United States was not prepared to live up to its democratic ideals or protect the rights of black citizens threatened by violence.

CHAPTER REVIEW AND ONLINE RESOURCES

REVIEW QUESTIONS

1. In 1865, the former Confederate general Robert Richardson remarked that "the emancipated slaves own nothing, because nothing but freedom has been given to them." Explain whether this would be an accurate assessment of Reconstruction twelve years later.

2. The women's movement split into two separate national organizations in part because the Fifteenth Amendment did not give women the vote. Explain why the two groups split.

3. How did black families, churches, schools, and other institutions contribute to the development of African-American culture and political activism in this period?

4. Why did ownership of land and control of labor become major points of contention between former slaves and whites in the South?

5. By what methods did southern whites seek to limit African-American civil rights and liberties? How did the federal government respond?

6. How did the failure of land reform and continued poverty lead to new forms of servitude for both blacks and whites?

7. What caused the confrontation between President Johnson and Congress over Reconstruction policies?

8. What national issues and attitudes combined to bring an end to Reconstruction by 1877?

9. By 1877, how did the condition of former slaves in the United States compare with that of freedpeople around the globe?

KEY TERMS

the Freedmen's Bureau (p. 447)

sharecropping (p. 449)

crop lien (p. 449)

Black Codes (p. 455)

Civil Rights Bill of 1866 (p. 457)

Fourteenth Amendment (p. 457)

Reconstruction Act (p. 459)

Tenure of Office Act (p. 459)

impeachment (p. 459)

Fifteenth Amendment (p. 460)

carpetbaggers (p. 464)

scalawags (p. 465)

Ku Klux Klan (p. 468)

Enforcement Acts (p. 468)

Civil Rights Act of 1875 (p. 470)

Redeemers (p. 471)

Bargain of 1877 (p. 472)

Go to 🐰 INQUIZITIVE

To see what you know—and learn what you've missed—with personalized feedback along the way.

Visit the *Give Me Liberty!* **Student Site** for primary source documents and images, interactive maps, author videos featuring Eric Foner, and more.

CHAPTER 16

AMERICA'S GILDED AGE

★

1870–1890

1872	Crédit Mobilier Scandal
1873	Mark Twain and Charles Dudley Warner's *Gilded Age*
1876	Battle of the Little Bighorn
1877	Reconstruction ends
	Great Railroad Strike
1879	Henry George's *Progress and Poverty*
1883	Civil Service Act
	Railroads create time zones
1886	Knights of Labor's membership peaks
	Haymarket affair
1887	Interstate Commerce Commission created
	Dawes Act
1888	Edward Bellamy's *Looking Backward*
1890	Sherman Antitrust Act
	Jacob Riis's *How the Other Half Lives*
	Massacre at Wounded Knee
1894	Henry Demarest Lloyd's *Wealth against Commonwealth*
1895	*United States v. E. C. Knight Co.*
1899	Thorstein Veblen's *The Theory of the Leisure Class*
1905	*Lochner v. New York*

Across the Continent, a lithograph from 1868 by the British-born artist Frances F. Palmer, celebrates post–Civil War westward expansion as the spread of civilization—represented by the railroad, telegraph, school, church, and wagon trains—into a wilderness that appears totally uninhabited except for two Indians in the far distance and a herd of buffalo.

FOCUS QUESTIONS

- *What factors combined to make the United States a mature industrial society after the Civil War?*

- *How was the West transformed economically and socially in this period?*

- *Was the Gilded Age political system effective in meeting its goals?*

- *How did the economic development of the Gilded Age affect American freedom?*

- *How did reformers of the period approach the problems of an industrial society?*

An immense crowd gathered in New York Harbor on October 28, 1886, for the dedication of *Liberty Enlightening the World*, a fitting symbol for a nation now wholly free. The idea for the statue originated in 1865 with Édouard de Laboulaye, a French educator and the author of several books on the United States, as a response to the assassination of Abraham Lincoln. Measuring more than 150 feet from torch to toe and standing atop a huge pedestal, the edifice was the tallest man-made structure in the Western Hemisphere.

In time, the Statue of Liberty, as it came to be called, would become Americans' most revered national icon. For over a century it has stood as a symbol of freedom. The statue has welcomed millions of immigrants—the "huddled masses yearning to breathe free" celebrated in a poem by Emma Lazarus inscribed on its base in 1903. In the years since its dedication, the statue's familiar image has been reproduced by folk artists in every conceivable medium and has been used by advertisers to promote everything from cigarettes and lawn mowers to war bonds. It has become a powerful international symbol as well.

The year of the statue's dedication, 1886, also witnessed the "great upheaval," a wave of strikes and labor protests that touched every part of the nation. The 600 dignitaries (598 of them men) who gathered on what is now called Liberty Island for the dedication hoped the Statue of Liberty would inspire renewed devotion to the nation's political and economic system. But for all its grandeur, the statue could not conceal the deep social divisions and fears about the future of American freedom that accompanied the country's emergence as the world's leading industrial power. Crucial questions moved to the center stage of American public life during the 1870s and 1880s and remained there for decades to come: What are the social conditions that make freedom possible, and what role should the national government play in defining and protecting the liberty of its citizens?

THE SECOND INDUSTRIAL REVOLUTION

Roots of economic change

Between the end of the Civil War and the early twentieth century, the United States underwent one of the most rapid and profound economic revolutions any country has ever experienced. There were numerous causes for this explosive economic growth. The country enjoyed abundant natural resources, a growing supply of labor, an expanding market for manufactured goods, and the availability of capital for investment. In addition, the federal government actively promoted industrial and agricultural development. It enacted high tariffs that protected American industry from foreign competition, granted land to railroad companies to encourage construction, and used the army to remove Indians from western lands desired by farmers and mining companies.

Promoting development

The Industrial Economy

The rapid expansion of factory production, mining, and railroad construction in all parts of the country except the South signaled the transition from Lincoln's America—a world centered on the small farm and artisan workshop—to a mature industrial society. By 1913, the United States produced

A changing America

TABLE 16.1 Indicators of Economic Change, 1870–1920

	1870	1900	1920
Farms (millions)	2.7	5.7	6.4
Land in farms (million acres)	408	841	956
Wheat grown (million bushels)	254	599	843
Employment (millions)	14	28.5	44.5
In manufacturing (millions)	2.5	5.9	11.2
Percentage in workforce[a]			
Agricultural	52	38	27
Industry[b]	29	31	44
Trade, service, administration[c]	20	31	27
Railroad track (thousands of miles)	53	258	407
Steel produced (thousands of tons)	0.8	11.2	46
GNP (billions of dollars)	7.4	18.7	91.5
Per capita (in 1920 dollars)	371	707	920
Life expectancy at birth (years)	42	47	54

[a] Percentages are rounded and do not total 100

[b] Includes manufacturing, transportation, mining, construction

[c] Includes trade, finance, public administration

Forging the Shaft, a painting from the 1870s by the American artist John Ferguson Weir, depicts workers in a steel factory making a propeller shaft for an ocean liner. Weir illustrates both the dramatic power of the factory at a time when the United States was overtaking European countries in manufacturing, and the fact that industrial production still required hard physical labor.

Industrial growth

one-third of the world's industrial output—more than Great Britain, France, and Germany combined. By 1880, for the first time, the U.S. Census Bureau found a majority of the workforce engaged in non-farming jobs.

The traditional dream of economic independence seemed obsolete. By 1890, two-thirds of Americans worked for wages, rather than owning a farm, business, or craft shop. Drawn to factories by the promise of employment, a new working class emerged in these years. Between 1870 and 1920, almost 11 million Americans moved from farm to city, and another 25 million immigrants arrived from overseas.

The industrial Great Lakes region

Most manufacturing now took place in industrial cities. The heartland of what is sometimes called the "second industrial revolution" was the region around the Great Lakes, with its factories producing iron and steel, machinery, chemicals, and packaged foods. Pittsburgh had become the world's center of iron and steel manufacturing. Chicago, by 1900 the nation's second-largest city with 1.7 million inhabitants, was home to factories producing steel and farm machinery and giant stockyards where cattle were processed into meat products for shipment east in refrigerated rail cars.

Railroads and the National Market

The railroad made possible the second industrial revolution. Spurred by private investment and massive grants of land and money by federal, state, and local governments, the number of miles of railroad track in the United

Key role of railroads

THE RAILROAD NETWORK, 1880

States tripled between 1860 and 1880 and tripled again by 1920, opening vast new areas to commercial farming and creating a truly national market for manufactured goods. The railroads even reorganized time itself. In 1883, the major companies divided the nation into the four time zones still in use today.

By 1880, the transnational rail network made possible the creation of a truly national market for goods.

The growing population formed an ever-expanding market for the mass production, mass distribution, and mass marketing of goods, essential elements of a modern industrial economy. The spread of national brands like Ivory Soap and Quaker Oats symbolized the continuing integration of the economy. So did the growth of national chains, most prominently the Atlantic and Pacific Tea Company, better known as A & P grocery stores. Based in Chicago, the national mail-order firms Montgomery Ward and Sears, Roebuck & Co. sold clothing, jewelry, farm equipment, and numerous other goods to rural families throughout the country.

The rise of national brands

The Greatest Department Store on Earth, a cartoon from *Puck*, November 29, 1899, depicts Uncle Sam selling goods, mostly manufactured products, to the nations of the world. The search for markets overseas would be a recurring theme of twentieth-century American foreign policy.

The Spirit of Innovation

A remarkable series of technological innovations spurred rapid communication and economic growth. The opening of the Atlantic cable in 1866 made it possible to send electronic telegraph messages instantaneously between the United States and Europe. During the 1870s and 1880s, the telephone, typewriter, and handheld camera came into use.

Edison's innovations

Scientific breakthroughs poured forth from research laboratories in Menlo Park and West Orange, New Jersey, created by the era's greatest inventor, Thomas A. Edison. During the course of his life, Edison helped to establish entirely new industries that transformed private life, public entertainment, and economic activity. Among Edison's innovations were the phonograph, lightbulb, motion picture, and a system for generating

Electricity

and distributing electric power. The spread of electricity was essential to industrial and urban growth, providing a more reliable and flexible source of power than water or steam.

Competition and Consolidation

Economic growth was dramatic but highly volatile. The combination of a market flooded with goods and the federal monetary policies (discussed later) that removed money from the national economy led to a relentless

Deflation

fall in prices. The world economy suffered prolonged downturns in the 1870s and 1890s.

Businesses engaged in ruthless competition. Railroads and other companies tried various means of bringing order to the chaotic marketplace. They formed "pools" that divided up markets between supposedly competing firms and fixed prices. They established **trusts**—legal devices whereby the affairs of several rival companies were managed by a single director. Such efforts to coordinate the economic activities of independent companies generally proved short-lived.

To avoid cutthroat competition, more and more corporations battled to control entire industries. Between 1897 and 1904, some 4,000 firms fell by the wayside or were gobbled up by others. By the time the wave of mergers had been completed, giant corporations like U.S. Steel (created by financier J. P. Morgan in 1901 by combining eight large steel companies into the first billion-dollar economic enterprise), Standard Oil, and International Harvester (a manufacturer of agricultural machinery) dominated major parts of the economy.

The Electricity Building at the Chicago World's Fair of 1893, painted by Childe Hassam. The electric lighting at the fair astonished visitors and illustrated how electricity was changing the visual landscape.

The Rise of Andrew Carnegie

In an era without personal or corporate income taxes, some business leaders accumulated enormous fortunes and economic power. During the depression that began in 1873, Andrew Carnegie set out to establish a steel company that incorporated **vertical integration**—that is, one that controlled every phase of the business from raw materials to transportation, manufacturing, and distribution. By the 1890s, he dominated the steel industry and had accumulated a fortune worth hundreds of millions of dollars. Carnegie's complex of steel factories at Homestead, Pennsylvania, were the most technologically advanced in the world.

Vertical integration

Believing that the rich had a moral obligation to promote the advancement of society, Carnegie denounced the "worship of money" and distributed much of his wealth to various philanthropies, especially the creation of public libraries in towns throughout the country. But he ran his companies with a dictatorial hand. His factories operated nonstop, with two twelve-hour shifts every day of the year except the Fourth of July.

Philanthropy

The Triumph of John D. Rockefeller

If any single name became a byword for enormous wealth, it was John D. Rockefeller, who began his working career as a clerk for a Cleveland

Next!, a cartoon from the magazine *Puck*, September 7, 1904, depicts the Standard Oil Company as an octopus with tentacles wrapped around the copper, steel, and shipping industries, as well as a state house and Congress. One tentacle reaches for the White House.

A turn-of-the-century photograph of the Casino Grounds, Newport, Rhode Island, an exclusive country club for rich socialites of the Gilded Age.

merchant and rose to dominate the oil industry. He drove out rival firms through cutthroat competition, arranging secret deals with railroad companies, and fixing prices and production quotas. Rockefeller began with **horizontal expansion**—buying out competing oil refineries. Like Carnegie, he soon established a vertically integrated monopoly, which controlled the drilling, refining, storage, and distribution of oil. By the 1880s, his Standard Oil Company controlled 90 percent of the nation's oil industry. Like Carnegie, Rockefeller gave much of his fortune away, establishing foundations to promote education and medical research. And like Carnegie, he bitterly fought his employees' efforts to organize unions.

These and other industrial leaders inspired among ordinary Americans a combination of awe, admiration, and hostility. Depending on one's point of view, they were "captains of industry," whose energy and vision pushed the economy forward, or "**robber barons**," who wielded power without any accountability in an unregulated marketplace. Their dictatorial attitudes, unscrupulous methods, repressive labor policies, and exercise of power without any democratic control led to fears that they were undermining political and economic freedom. Concentrated wealth degraded the political process, declared Henry Demarest Lloyd in *Wealth against Commonwealth* (1894), an exposé of how Rockefeller's Standard Oil Company made a mockery of economic competition and political democracy by manipulating the market and bribing legislators. "Liberty and monopoly," Lloyd concluded, "cannot live together."

Workers' Freedom in an Industrial Age

Remarkable as it was, the country's economic growth distributed its benefits very unevenly. For a minority of workers, the rapidly expanding industrial system created new forms of freedom. In some industries, skilled workers commanded high wages and exercised considerable control over the production process. A worker's economic independence now rested on technical skill rather than ownership of one's own shop and tools as in earlier times. Through their union, skilled iron- and steelworkers fixed output quotas and controlled the training of apprentices in the technique of iron rolling. These workers often knew more about the details of production than their employers did.

Uneven distribution of wealth

For most workers, however, economic insecurity remained a basic fact of life. During the depressions of the 1870s and 1890s, millions of workers lost their jobs or were forced to accept reductions of pay. The "tramp" became a familiar figure on the social landscape as thousands of men took to the roads in search of work. Between 1880 and 1900, an average of 35,000 workers perished each year in factory and mine accidents, the highest rate in the industrial world. Much of the working class remained desperately poor and to survive needed income from all family members.

Baxter Street Court, 1890, one of numerous photographs by Jacob Riis depicting living conditions in New York City's slums.

By 1890, the richest 1 percent of Americans received the same total income as the bottom half of the population and owned more property than the remaining 99 percent. Many of the wealthiest Americans consciously pursued an aristocratic lifestyle, building palatial homes, attending exclusive social clubs, schools, and colleges, holding fancy-dress balls, and marrying into each other's families. In 1899, the economist and social historian Thorstein Veblen published *The Theory of the Leisure Class*, a devastating critique of an upper-class culture focused on "conspicuous consumption"—that is, spending money not on needed or even desired goods, but simply to demonstrate the possession of wealth.

At the same time much of the working class lived in desperate conditions. Jacob Riis, in *How the Other Half Lives* (1890), offered a shocking account of living conditions among the urban poor, complete with photographs of apartments in dark, airless, overcrowded tenement houses.

THE TRANSFORMATION OF THE WEST

Nowhere did capitalism penetrate more rapidly or dramatically than in the trans-Mississippi West, whose "vast, trackless spaces," as the poet Walt Whitman called them, were now absorbed into the expanding economy. At the close of the Civil War, the frontier of continuous white settlement did not extend far beyond the Mississippi River. To the west lay millions of acres of fertile and mineral-rich land roamed by giant herds of buffalo whose meat and hides provided food, clothing, and shelter for a population of more than 250,000 Indians.

The West as a place of opportunity

Ever since the beginning of colonial settlement in British North America, the West—a region whose definition shifted as the population expanded—had been seen as a place of opportunity for those seeking to improve their condition in life. From farmers moving into Ohio, Indiana, and Illinois in the decades after the American Revolution to prospectors who struck it rich in the California gold rush of the mid-nineteenth century, millions of Americans and immigrants from abroad found in the westward movement a path to economic opportunity. But the West was hardly a uniform paradise of small, independent farmers. Landlords, railroads, and mining companies in the West also utilized Mexican migrant and indentured labor, Chinese working on long-term contracts, and, until the end of the Civil War, African-American slaves.

A Diverse Region

The West, of course, was hardly a single area. West of the Mississippi River lay a variety of regions, all marked by remarkable physical beauty—the Great Plains, the Rocky Mountains, the desert of the Southwest, the Sierra Nevada, and the valleys and coastline of California and the Pacific Northwest. It would take many decades before individual settlers and corporate business enterprises penetrated all these areas. But the process was far advanced by the end of the nineteenth century.

Gradual development of the American West

The political and economic incorporation of the American West was part of a global process. In many parts of the world, indigenous inhabitants—the Zulu in South Africa, Aboriginal peoples in Australia,

American Indians—were pushed aside (often after fierce resistance) as centralizing governments brought large interior regions under their control. In the United States, the incorporation of the West required the active intervention of the federal government, which acquired Indian land by war and treaty, administered land sales, regulated territorial politics, and distributed land and money to farmers, railroads, and mining companies.

Western states used land donated by the federal government, in accordance with the Morrill Land Grant Act passed during the Civil War, to establish public universities. And, of course, the abolition of slavery by the Thirteenth Amendment decided the long contest over whether the West would be a society based on free or slave labor.

Newly created western territories such as Arizona, Idaho, Montana, and the Dakotas remained under federal control far longer than had been the pattern in the East. Many easterners were wary of granting statehood to the territories until white and non-Mormon settlers counterbalanced the large Latino and Mormon populations.

In the twentieth century, the construction of federally financed irrigation systems and dams would open large areas to commercial farming. The West would become known (not least to its own inhabitants) as a place of rugged individualism and sturdy independence. But, ironically, without active governmental assistance, the region could never have been settled and developed.

Having been granted millions of acres of land by the federal and state governments, railroads sought to encourage emigration to the West so they could sell real estate to settlers. This is a post–Civil War advertisement by a Texas railroad.

Farming in the Trans-Mississippi West

Even as sporadic Indian wars raged, settlers poured into the West. Territorial and state governments eager for population and railroad companies anxious to sell the immense tracts of land they had acquired from the government flooded European countries and eastern cities with promotional literature promising easy access to land. More land came into cultivation in the thirty years after the Civil War than in the previous two and a half centuries of American history. Hundreds of thousands of families acquired farms under the Homestead Act, and even more purchased land from speculators and from railroad companies. A new agricultural empire producing wheat and corn arose on the Middle Border (Minnesota, the Dakotas, Nebraska, and Kansas), whose population rose from 300,000 in 1860 to 5 million in 1900. The farmers were a diverse group, including native-born easterners, blacks

Agricultural development

escaping the post-Reconstruction South, and immigrants from Canada, Germany, Scandinavia, and Great Britain. In the late nineteenth century the most multicultural state in the Union was North Dakota.

Women and farming

Despite the promises of promotional pamphlets, farming on the Great Plains was not an easy task. Much of the burden fell on women. Farm families generally invested in the kinds of labor-saving machinery that would bring in cash, not machines that would ease women's burdens in the household (like the back-breaking task of doing laundry). A farm woman in Arizona described her morning chores in her diary: "Get up, turn out my chickens, draw a pail of water . . . make a fire, put potatoes to cook, brush and sweep half inch of dust off floor, feed three litters of chickens, then mix biscuits, get breakfast, milk, besides work in the house, and this morning had to go half mile after calves."

Family farms

Despite the emergence of a few **bonanza farms** that covered thousands of acres and employed large numbers of agricultural wage workers, family farms still dominated the trans-Mississippi West. Even small farmers, however, became increasingly oriented to national and international markets, specializing in the production of single crops for sale in faraway places. At the same time, railroads brought factory-made goods to rural people, replacing items previously produced in farmers' homes. Farm families became more and more dependent on loans to purchase land, machinery, and industrial products, and increasingly vulnerable to the ups and downs of prices for agricultural goods in the world market. Agriculture reflected how the international economy was becoming more integrated. The combination of economic depressions and expanding agricultural production in places like Argentina, Australia, and the American West pushed prices of farm products steadily downward. Small farmers throughout the world suffered severe difficulties in the last quarter of the nineteenth century. Many joined the migration to cities within their countries or the increasing international migration of labor.

The future of western farming ultimately lay with giant agricultural enterprises relying heavily on irrigation, chemicals, and machinery—investments far beyond the means of family farmers. A preview of the agricultural future was already evident in California, where, as far back as Spanish and Mexican days, landownership had been concentrated in

The family of David Hilton on their Nebraska homestead in 1887. The Hiltons insisted on being photographed with their organ, away from the modest sod house in which they lived, to better represent their aspiration for prosperity.

large units. In the late nineteenth century, California's giant fruit and vegetable farms, owned by corporations like the Southern Pacific Railroad, were tilled not by agricultural laborers who could expect to acquire land of their own, but by migrant laborers from China, the Philippines, Japan, and Mexico, who tramped from place to place following the ripening crops. In the 1870s, California's "wheat barons," who owned ranches of 30,000 or more acres, shipped their grain from San Francisco all the way to Great Britain, while large-scale growers in the new "Orange Empire" of the southern part of the state sent fruit east by rail, packaged in crates bedecked with images of an Edenic landscape filled with lush orchards.

In the late 1800s, California tried to attract immigrants by advertising its pleasant climate and the availability of land, although large-scale corporate farms were coming to dominate the state's agriculture.

The Cowboy and the Corporate West

The two decades following the Civil War also witnessed the golden age of the cattle kingdom. The Kansas Pacific Railroad's stations at Abilene, Dodge City, and Wichita, Kansas, became destinations for the fabled drives of millions of cattle from Texas. A collection of white, Mexican, and black men who conducted the cattle drives, the cowboys became symbols of a life of freedom on the open range. Their exploits would later serve as the theme of many a Hollywood movie, and their clothing inspired fashions that remain popular today. But there was nothing romantic about the life of the cowboys, most of whom were low-paid wage workers. (Texas cowboys even went on strike for higher pay in 1883.) The days of the long-distance cattle drive ended in the mid-1880s, as farmers enclosed more and more of the open range with barbed-wire fences, making it difficult to graze cattle on the grasslands of the Great Plains, and two terrible winters destroyed millions of cattle. When the industry recuperated, it was reorganized in large, enclosed ranches close to rail connections.

Cattle

The West was more than a farming empire. By 1890, a higher percentage of its population lived in cities than was the case in other regions. Large corporate enterprises appeared throughout the West. Western mining, from Michigan iron ore and copper to gold and silver in California, Nevada, and Colorado, fell under the sway of companies that mobilized eastern and European investment to introduce advanced technology. Gold and silver rushes took place in the Dakotas in 1876, Idaho in 1883, Colorado in the 1890s, and Alaska at the end of the century.

Western industries

The Chinese Presence

Chinese immigration, which had begun at the time of the California gold rush, continued in the postwar years. Before the Civil War, nearly all

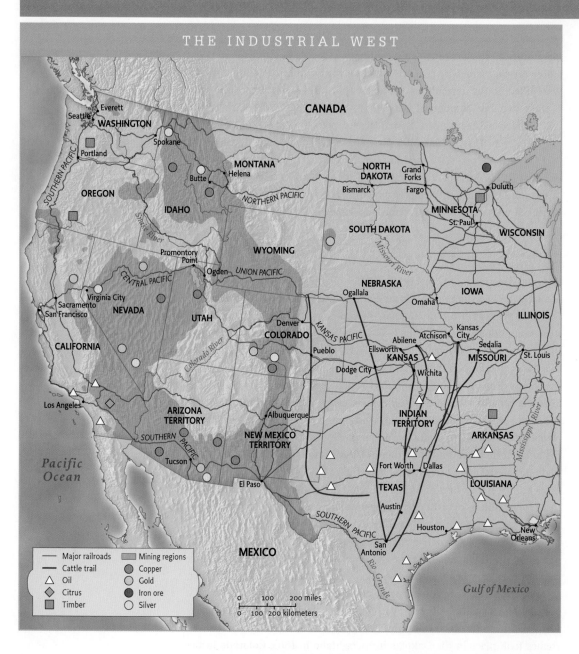

THE INDUSTRIAL WEST

Legend:
— Major railroads
— Cattle trail
△ Oil
◇ Citrus
▢ Timber

▢ Mining regions
● Copper
○ Gold
● Iron ore
○ Silver

0   100   200 miles
0 100 200 kilometers

Chinese immigration

Chinese newcomers had been unattached men, brought in by labor contractors to work in western gold fields, railroad construction, and factories. In the early 1870s, entire Chinese families began to immigrate. By 1880, 105,000 persons of Chinese descent lived in the United States. Three-quarters lived in California, where Chinese made up over half of the state's farm workers.

But Chinese immigrants could be found in mines in Idaho, Colorado, and Nevada, as domestic workers in urban households, and in factories producing cigars, clothing, and shoes in western cities. Many men had wives and children in China, and like members of other immigrant groups, they kept in touch by sending letters and money to their families at home and reading magazines aimed at emigrants that reported on local events in China.

A photograph of Denver, Colorado, in the early 1890s. Although generally thought of as a region of rural pioneers, the West, like the East, experienced rapid urbanization.

Conflict on the Mormon Frontier

The Mormons had moved to the Great Salt Lake Valley in the 1840s, hoping to practice their religion free of the persecution they had encountered in the East. They envisioned their community in Utah as the foundation of a great empire they called Deseret. Given the widespread unpopularity of Mormon polygamy and the close connection of church and state in Mormon theology, conflict with the growing numbers of non-Mormon settlers moving west became inevitable. When President James Buchanan removed the Mormon leader Brigham Young as Utah's territorial governor and Young refused to comply, federal troops entered the Salt Lake Valley, where they remained until the beginning of the Civil War. In 1857, during this time of tension, a group of Mormons attacked a wagon train of non-Mormon settlers traveling through Utah toward California. What came to be called the Mountain Meadows Massacre resulted in the death of all the adults and older children in the wagon train—over 100 persons. Nearly twenty years later, one leader of the assault was convicted of murder and executed.

Deseret community

Mountain Meadows Massacre

After the Civil War, Mormon leaders sought to avoid further antagonizing the federal government. In the 1880s, Utah banned the practice of polygamy (although the practice persists to this day among some fundamentalist Mormons living in isolated areas). But sporadic conflict

A family festival in San Juan, a town in southern California, around 1880. Long after the area was annexed to the United States, the Spanish-speaking residents continued their traditional religious and cultural practices.

Short-lived "peace policy"

continued between Mormon families, who spread out across the Southwest, and Native Americans as well as other settlers.

The Subjugation of the Plains Indians

The transcontinental railroad, a symbol of the reunited nation, brought tens of thousands of newcomers to the West and stimulated the expansion of farming, mining, and other enterprises. The incorporation of the West into the national economy spelled the doom of the Plains Indians and their world. Their lives had already undergone profound transformations. In the eighteenth century, the spread of horses, originally introduced by the Spanish, led to a wholesale shift from farming and hunting on foot to mounted hunting of buffalo.

Most migrants on the Oregon and California Trails before the Civil War encountered little hostility from Indians, often trading with them for food and supplies. But as settlers encroached on Indian lands, bloody conflict between the army and Plains tribes began in the 1850s and continued for decades.

In 1869, President Ulysses S. Grant announced a new "peace policy" in the West, but warfare soon resumed. Drawing on methods used to defeat the Confederacy, Civil War generals like Philip H. Sheridan set out

Albert Bierstadt's 1863 painting *The Rocky Mountains, Lander's Peak* depicts Indians as an integral part of the majestic landscape of the West.

This pencil-and-crayon drawing by a Cheyenne Indian from the 1880s depicts a Native American fighting two black members of the U.S. military. After the Civil War, black soldiers, whose presence was resented by many whites, in the North as well as the South, were reassigned to the West.

to destroy the foundations of the Indian economy—villages, horses, and especially the buffalo. Hunting by mounted Indians had already reduced the buffalo population—estimated at 30 million in 1800—but it was army campaigns and the depredations of hunters seeking buffalo hides that rendered the vast herds all but extinct.

The buffalo

"Let Me Be a Free Man"

The army's relentless attacks broke the power of one tribe after another. In 1877, troops commanded by former Freedmen's Bureau commissioner O. O. Howard pursued the Nez Percé Indians on a 1,700-mile chase across the Far West. The Nez Percé (whose name was given them by Lewis and Clark in 1805 and means "pierced nose" in French) were seeking to escape to Canada after fights with settlers who had encroached on tribal lands in Oregon and Idaho. After four months, Howard forced the Indians to surrender, and they were removed to Oklahoma.

The Nez Percé

Two years later, the Nez Percé leader, Chief Joseph, delivered a speech in Washington to a distinguished audience that included President Rutherford B. Hayes. Condemning the policy of confining Indians to reservations, Joseph adopted the language of freedom and equal rights before the law so powerfully reinforced by the Civil War and Reconstruction. "Treat all men alike," he pleaded. "Give them the same law. . . . Let me be a free man—free to travel, free to stop, free to work, free to trade where I choose, free to . . . think and talk and act for myself." Until his death in 1904, Joseph would unsuccessfully petition successive presidents for his people's right to return to their beloved Oregon homeland.

Chief Joseph

Indians occasionally managed to inflict costly delay and even defeat on army units. The most famous Indian victory took place in June 1876 at the **Battle of the Little Bighorn**, when General George A. Custer and his entire command of 250 men perished. The Sioux and Cheyenne warriors,

Indian victories

Chief Joseph of the Nez Percé, in a photograph possibly taken in Washington, D.C., in 1879, when he was part of an Indian delegation to the nation's capital.

led by Sitting Bull and Crazy Horse, were defending tribal land in the Black Hills of the Dakota Territory. Eventually the Sioux were worn down, partly because of the decimation of the buffalo, and relinquished their claim to the Black Hills.

Remaking Indian Life

"The life my people want is a life of freedom," Sitting Bull declared. The Indian idea of freedom, however, which centered on preserving their cultural and political autonomy and control of ancestral lands, conflicted with the interests and values of most white Americans.

In 1871, Congress eliminated the treaty system that dated back to the revolutionary era, by which the federal government negotiated agreements with Indians as if they were independent nations. The federal government also pressed forward with its assault on Indian culture. The Bureau of Indian Affairs established boarding schools where Indian children, removed from the "negative" influences of their parents and tribes, were dressed in non-Indian clothes, given new names, and educated in white ways.

The Dawes Act and Wounded Knee

The crucial step in attacking "tribalism" came in 1887 with the passage of the **Dawes Act**, named for Senator Henry L. Dawes of Massachusetts, chair of the Senate's Indian Affairs Committee. The act broke up the land of nearly all tribes into small parcels to be distributed to Indian families, with the remainder auctioned off to white purchasers. Indians who accepted the farms and "adopted the habits of civilized life" would become full-fledged American citizens. The policy proved to be a disaster, leading to the loss of much tribal land and the erosion of Indian cultural traditions. When the government made 2 million acres of Indian land available in Oklahoma, 50,000 white settlers poured into the territory to claim farms on the single day of April 22, 1889. Further land rushes followed in the 1890s. In the half century after the passage of the Dawes Act, Indians lost 86 million of the 138 million acres of land in their possession in 1887. Overall, according to one estimate, between 1776 and today, via the "right of discovery," treaties, executive orders, court decisions, and outright theft, the United States has acquired over 1.5 billion acres of land from Native Americans, an area twenty-five times as large as Great Britain.

Loss of tribal land

Some Indians sought solace in the **Ghost Dance**, a religious revitalization campaign. Its leaders foretold a day when whites would disappear, the buffalo would return, and Indians could once again practice their ancestral customs "free from misery, death, and disease." Large numbers of Indians gathered for days of singing, dancing, and religious observances. Fearing a general uprising, the government sent troops to the reservations. On December 29, 1890, soldiers opened fire on Ghost Dancers encamped near Wounded Knee Creek in South Dakota, killing between 150 and 200 Indians, mostly women and children. The Wounded Knee massacre was widely applauded in the press. An army court of inquiry essentially exonerated the troops and their commander, and twenty soldiers were later awarded the Medal of Honor, a recognition of exceptional heroism in battle, for their actions at Wounded Knee.

The **Wounded Knee massacre** marked the end of four centuries of armed conflict between the continent's native population and European settlers and their descendants. By 1900, the Indian population had fallen to 250,000, the lowest point in American history. Of that number, roughly 53,000 had become American citizens by accepting land allotments under the Dawes Act. The following year, Congress granted citizenship to 100,000 residents of Indian Territory (in present-day Oklahoma). The remainder would have to wait until 1919 (for those who fought in World War I) and 1924, when Congress made all Indians American citizens.

Between Two Worlds, a drawing produced in the 1870s by the Kiowa warrior Wohaw when he was a prisoner in Fort Marion, Florida. Wohaw depicts himself being torn between his traditional way of life, represented by the buffalo, and the culture whites were trying to force him to accept, symbolized by the steer and tiny farmhouse. Wohaw later returned to the West and served in the U.S. Army.

Settler Societies and Global Wests

The conquest of the American West was part of a global process whereby settlers moved boldly into the interior of regions in temperate climates around the world, bringing their familiar crops and livestock and establishing

One of the masterpieces of Native American art, this three-foot-long wood sculpture carved by a Lakota Sioux artist around 1870 honors a dead or wounded horse. It has a horsehair mane and tail and leather reins and bridle, and there are holes representing bullet wounds on the torso and red paint representing blood. The horse may be leaping from life to death.

VOICES OF FREEDOM

From Speech of Chief Joseph of the Nez Percé Indians, in Washington, D.C. (1879)

Chief Joseph, leader of the Nez Percé Indians, led his people on a 1,700-mile trek through the Far West in 1877 in an unsuccessful effort to escape to Canada. Two years later, he addressed an audience in Washington, D.C. that included President Rutherford B. Hayes, appealing for the freedom and equal rights enshrined in the law after the Civil War.

I have heard talk and talk, but nothing is done. Good words do not last long unless they amount to something. Words do not pay for my dead people. They do not pay for my country, now overrun by white men.... Good words will not get my people a home where they can live in peace and take care of themselves. I am tired of talk that comes to nothing. It makes my heart sick when I remember all the ... broken promises....

If the white man wants to live in peace with the Indian he can live in peace. There need be no trouble. Treat all men alike. Give them the same law. Give them all an even chance to live and grow. All men were made by the same Great Spirit Chief. They are all brothers. The earth is the mother of all people, and all people should have equal rights upon it. You might as well expect the rivers to run backward as that any man who was born a free man should be contented when penned up and denied liberty to go where he pleases....

When I think of our condition my heart is heavy. I see men of my race treated as outlaws and driven from country to country, or shot down like animals. I know that my race must change. We cannot hold our own with the white men as we are. We only ask an even chance to live as other men live....

Let me be a free man—free to travel, free to stop, free to work, free to trade where I choose, free to choose my own teachers, free to follow the religion of my fathers, free to think and talk and act for myself—and I will obey every law, or submit to the penalty.

From Letter by Saum Song Bo, *American Missionary* (October 1885)

During the 1880s, Chinese-Americans were subjected to discrimination in every phase of their lives. In 1882, Congress temporarily barred further immigration from China. In 1885, when funds were being raised to build a pedestal for the Statue of Liberty, Saum Song Bo, a Chinese-American writer, contrasted the celebration of liberty with the treatment of the Chinese.

A paper was presented to me yesterday for inspection, and I found it to be specially drawn up for subscription among my countrymen toward the Pedestal Fund of the . . . Statue of Liberty. . . . But the word liberty makes me think of the fact that this country is the land of liberty for men of all nations except the Chinese. I consider it as an insult to us Chinese to call on us to contribute toward building in this land a pedestal for a statue of Liberty. That statue represents Liberty holding a torch which lights the passage of those of all nations who come into this country. But are the Chinese allowed to come? As for the Chinese who are here, are they allowed to enjoy liberty as men of all other nationalities enjoy it? Are they allowed to go about everywhere free from the insults, abuses, assaults, wrongs, and injuries from which men of other nationalities are free? . . .

And this statue of Liberty is a gift from another people who do not love liberty for the Chinese. [To] the Annamese and Tonquinese Chinese [colonial subjects of the French empire in Indochina], . . . liberty is as dear as to the French. What right have the French to deprive them of their liberty?

Whether this statute against the Chinese or the statue to Liberty will be the most lasting monument to tell future ages of the liberty and greatness of this country, will be known only to future generations.

QUESTIONS

1. *What are Chief Joseph's complaints about the treatment of his people?*

2. *Why does Saum Song Bo believe that the Chinese do not enjoy liberty in the United States?*

3. *What are the similarities and differences in the definition of freedom in the two documents?*

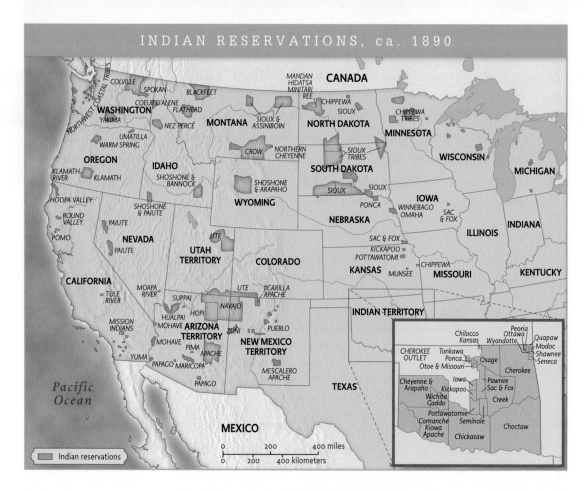

INDIAN RESERVATIONS, ca. 1890

Indian reservations

Pacific Ocean

0   200   400 miles
0   200   400 kilometers

By 1890, the vast majority of the remaining Indian population had been removed to reservations scattered across the western states.

Aboriginal peoples in Australia

mining and other industries. Countries such as Argentina, Australia, Canada, and New Zealand, as well as the United States, are often called "settler societies," because immigrants from overseas quickly outnumbered and displaced the original inhabitants—unlike in India and most parts of colonial Africa, where fewer Europeans ventured and those who did relied on the labor of the indigenous inhabitants.

In many settler societies, native peoples were subjected to cultural reconstruction similar to policies in the United States. In Australia, the government gathered the Aboriginal populations—their numbers devastated by disease—in "reserves" reminiscent of American Indian reservations. Australia went further than the United States in the forced assimilation of surviving Aboriginal peoples. The government removed large numbers of children from their families to be adopted by whites—a policy abandoned only in the 1970s.

Myth, Reality, and the Wild West

The West has long played many roles in Americans' national self-consciousness. It has been imagined as a place of individual freedom and unbridled opportunity for those dissatisfied with their lives in the East and as a future empire that would dominate the continent and the world. Even as farms, mines, and cities spread over the landscape in the post–Civil War years, a new image of the West began to circulate—the Wild West, a lawless place ruled by cowboys and Indians (two groups by this time vastly outnumbered by other westerners), and marked by gunfights, cattle drives, and stagecoach robberies.

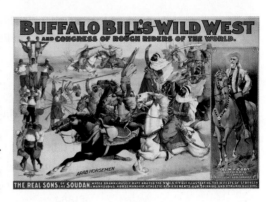

An advertisement for Buffalo Bill's Wild West Show, which brought an image of the West as a violent yet romantic place of gunfights, Indian rituals, and buffalo hunts to audiences in the East and Europe.

The image of a violent yet romantic frontier world would later become a staple of Hollywood movies. In the late nineteenth century, it was disseminated in vaudeville shows that achieved immense popularity. Although not the first, William "Buffalo Bill" Cody was the most important popularizer of this idea of the West. Buffalo Bill's Wild West Show included reenactments of battles with Indians (including Custer's Last Stand), buffalo hunts, Indian rituals, and feats by the sharpshooter Annie Oakley. The image of the Wild West also circulated in cheap popular books known as dime novels and sensational journalistic accounts.

Theater audiences and readers found fantasies of adventure in observing western violence from a safe distance and marveled at the skills of horseback riding, roping, and shooting on display. They imagined the West as a timeless place immune to the corruption of civilization, which offered a striking contrast to the increasingly sedentary lives of men in eastern cities. The real West—for example, the struggles of farm families— played no role in this depiction. The West's multiracial, multiethnic population also disappeared, although different groups added their own elements to the mythical West. Mexican-Americans, for example, made a folk hero of Gregorio Cortez, a Texas outlaw renowned for his ability to outwit pursuers.

The real West

POLITICS IN A GILDED AGE

The era from 1870 to 1890 is the only period of American history commonly known by a derogatory name—**the Gilded Age**, after the title of an 1873 novel by Mark Twain and Charles Dudley Warner. "Gilded" means covered with a layer of gold, but it also suggests that the glittering surface masks a core of little real value and is therefore deceptive.

The Corruption of Politics

As they had earlier in the nineteenth century, Americans during the Gilded Age saw their nation as an island of political democracy in a world still dominated by undemocratic governments. In Europe, only France and Switzerland enjoyed universal male suffrage. Even in Britain, most of the working class could not vote until the passage of the Reform Act of 1884.

Nonetheless, the power of the new corporations, seemingly immune to democratic control, raised disturbing questions for the American understanding of political freedom as popular self-government. Political corruption was rife. In Pennsylvania's legislature, the "third house" of railroad lobbyists was said to enjoy as much influence as the elected chambers. In the West, many lawmakers held stock or directorships in lumber companies and railroads that received public aid.

"Boss" Tweed of New York

Urban politics fell under the sway of corrupt political machines like New York's Tweed Ring, which plundered the city of tens of millions of dollars. "Boss" William M. Tweed's organization reached into every neighborhood. He won support from the city's immigrant poor by fashioning a kind of private welfare system that provided food, fuel, and jobs in

The Bosses of the Senate, a cartoon from *Puck*, January 23, 1889, shows well-fed monopolists towering over the obedient senators. Above them, a sign rewrites the closing words of Lincoln's Gettysburg Address: "This is the Senate of the Monopolists, by the Monopolists, and for the Monopolists."

hard times. A combination of political reformers and businessmen tired of paying tribute to the ring ousted Tweed in the early 1870s, although he remained popular among the city's poor, who considered him an urban Robin Hood.

At the national level, the most notorious example of corruption came to light during Grant's presidency. This was Crédit Mobilier, a corporation formed by an inner ring of Union Pacific Railroad stockholders to oversee the line's government-assisted construction. Essentially, it enabled the participants to sign contracts with themselves, at an exorbitant profit, to build the new line. The arrangement was protected by the distribution of stock to influential politicians.

The Crédit Mobilier scandal

The Politics of Dead Center

In national elections, party politics bore the powerful imprint of the Civil War. Republicans controlled the industrial North and Midwest and the agrarian West and were particularly strong among members of revivalist churches, Protestant immigrants, and blacks. Organizations of Union veterans formed a bulwark of Republican support. Every Republican candidate for president from 1868 to 1900 except James G. Blaine had fought in the Union army. By 1893, a lavish system of pensions for Union soldiers and their widows and children consumed more than 40 percent of the federal budget. Democrats, after 1877, dominated the South and did well among Catholic voters, especially Irish-Americans, in the nation's cities.

Republican strength

The parties were closely divided. In three of the five presidential elections between 1876 and 1892, the margin separating the major candidates was less than 1 percent of the popular vote. Twice, in 1876 and 1888, the candidate with an electoral-college majority trailed in the popular vote. Only for brief periods did the same party control the White House and both houses of Congress. More than once, Congress found itself paralyzed as important bills shuttled back and forth between House and Senate, and special sessions to complete legislation became

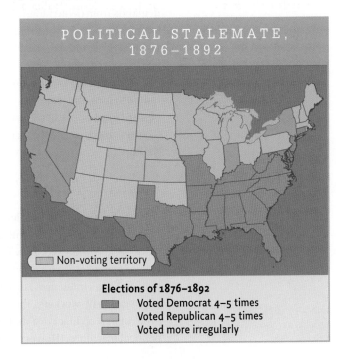

POLITICAL STALEMATE, 1876–1892

☐ Non-voting territory

Elections of 1876–1892
▨ Voted Democrat 4–5 times
▨ Voted Republican 4–5 times
▨ Voted more irregularly

This political cartoon from the 1884 presidential campaign depicts Republican nominee James G. Blaine as a champion of a high tariff that would protect American workers from cheap foreign labor. Blaine's attire is a reference to the nominating speech at the Republican convention by Robert G. Ingersoll, who referred to the candidate as a "plumed knight."

Favoring easterners

Civil Service Act of 1883

necessary. Gilded Age presidents made little effort to mobilize public opinion or extend executive leadership.

In some ways, though, American democracy in the Gilded Age seemed remarkably healthy. Elections were closely contested, party loyalty was intense, and 80 percent or more of eligible voters turned out to cast ballots.

Government and the Economy

The nation's political structure, however, proved ill equipped to deal with the problems created by the economy's rapid growth. Despite its expanded scope and powers arising from the Civil War, the federal government remained remarkably small by modern standards. The federal workforce in 1880 numbered 100,000 (today, it exceeds 2.5 million).

Nationally, both parties came under the control of powerful political managers with close ties to business interests. Republicans strongly supported a high tariff to protect American industry, and throughout the 1870s they pursued a fiscal policy based on reducing federal spending, repaying much of the national debt, and withdrawing greenbacks—the paper money issued by the Union during the Civil War—from circulation. Democrats opposed the high tariff, but the party's national leadership remained closely linked to New York bankers and financiers and resisted demands from debt-ridden agricultural areas for an increase in the money supply. In 1879, for the first time since the war, the United States returned to the **gold standard**—that is, paper currency became exchangeable for gold at a fixed rate.

Republican economic policies strongly favored the interests of eastern industrialists and bankers. These policies worked to the disadvantage of southern and western farmers, who had to pay a premium for manufactured goods while the prices they received for their produce steadily declined.

Reform Legislation

Gilded Age national politics did not entirely lack accomplishments. Inspired in part by President Garfield's assassination by a disappointed office seeker, the **Civil Service Act of 1883** created a merit system for federal employees, with appointment via competitive examinations rather than political influence. Although it applied at first to only 10 percent of government workers, the act marked the first step in establishing a professional civil service and removing officeholding from the hands of political machines. (However, since funds raised from political appointees had helped to finance the political parties, civil service reform had the unintended result of increasing politicians' dependence on donations from business interests.)

In 1887, in response to public outcries against railroad practices, Congress established the **Interstate Commerce Commission** (ICC) to ensure that the rates railroads charged farmers and merchants to transport their goods were "reasonable" and did not offer more favorable treatment to some shippers. The ICC was the first federal agency intended to regulate economic activity, but since it lacked the power to establish rates on its own—it could only sue companies in court—it had little impact on railroad practices. Three years later, Congress passed the **Sherman Antitrust Act**, which banned all combinations and practices that restrained free trade. But the language was so vague that the act proved almost impossible to enforce. Weak as they were, these laws helped to establish the precedent that the national government could regulate the economy to promote the public good.

A Republican campaign poster for Benjamin Harrison in the election of 1888 emphasizes the party's policy of protection, or a high tariff on imported manufactured goods, as benefiting industry, labor, and farmers.

Political Conflict in the States

At the state and local level the Gilded Age was an era of political ferment and conflict over the proper uses of governmental authority. In the immediate aftermath of the Civil War, state governments in the North, like those in the Reconstruction South, greatly expanded their responsibility for public health, welfare, and education, and cities invested heavily in public works such as park construction and improved water and gas services.

The policies of railroad companies produced a growing chorus of protest, especially in the West. Farmers and local merchants complained of excessively high freight rates, discrimination in favor of large producers and shippers, and high fees charged by railroad-controlled grain warehouses. Critics of the railroads came together in the Patrons of Husbandry, or Grange (1867), which moved to establish cooperatives for storing and marketing farm output in the hope of forcing the carriers "to take our produce at a fair price."

Criticism of railroad companies

At the same time, the labor movement, revitalized during the Civil War, demanded laws establishing eight hours as a legal day's work. Seven northern legislatures passed such laws, but since most lacked strong

Labor movement

means of enforcement they remained dead letters. Nevertheless, the efforts of workers, like those of farmers, inspired a far-reaching national debate.

FREEDOM IN THE GILDED AGE

The Social Problem

New social order

As the United States matured into an industrial economy, Americans struggled to make sense of the new social order. Debates over political economy engaged the attention of millions, reaching far beyond the tiny academic world into the public sphere inhabited by self-educated workingmen and farmers, reformers of all kinds, newspaper editors, and politicians. This broad public discussion produced thousands of books, pamphlets, and articles on such technical issues as land taxation and currency reform, as well as widespread debate over the social and ethical implications of economic change.

Social unrest

Many Americans sensed that something had gone wrong in the nation's social development. Talk of "better classes," "respectable classes," and "dangerous classes" dominated public discussion, and bitter labor strikes seemed to have become the rule. In 1881, the Massachusetts Bureau of Labor Statistics reported that virtually every worker it interviewed in Fall River, the nation's largest center of textile production, complained of overwork, poor housing, and tyrannical employers.

Freedom and equality disconnected

With factory workers living on the edge of poverty alongside a growing class of millionaires, it became increasingly difficult to view wage labor as a temporary resting place on the road to economic independence. Yet given the vast expansion of the nation's productive capacity, many Americans viewed the concentration of wealth as inevitable, natural, and justified by progress. By the turn of the century, advanced economics taught that wages were determined by the iron law of supply and demand and that wealth rightly flowed not to those who worked the hardest but to men with business skills and access to money. The close link between freedom and equality, forged in the Revolution and reinforced during the Civil War, appeared increasingly out of date.

Social Darwinism in America

The idea of the natural superiority of some groups to others, which before the Civil War had been invoked to justify slavery in an otherwise free society, now reemerged in the vocabulary of modern science to explain the success and failure of individuals and social classes. In 1859, the British scientist Charles Darwin published *On the Origin of Species*. One of the most influential works of science ever to appear, it expounded the theory of evolution whereby plant and animal species best suited to their environment took the place of those less able to adapt.

Charles Darwin

In a highly oversimplified form, language borrowed from Darwin, such as "natural selection," "the struggle for existence," and "the survival of the fittest," entered public discussion of social problems in the Gilded Age. According to what came to be called **Social Darwinism**, evolution was as natural a process in human society as in nature, and government must not interfere. Especially misguided, in this view, were efforts to uplift those at the bottom of the social order, such as laws regulating conditions of work or public assistance to the poor. The giant industrial corporation, Social Darwinists believed, had emerged because it was better adapted to its environment than earlier forms of enterprise. To restrict its operations by legislation would reduce society to a more primitive level.

The misapplication of Darwin's theory of evolution

Even the depressions of the 1870s and 1890s did not shake the widespread view that the poor were essentially responsible for their own fate. Failure to advance in society was widely thought to indicate a lack of character, an absence of self-reliance and determination in the face of adversity.

The era's most influential Social Darwinist was Yale professor William Graham Sumner. For Sumner, freedom required frank acceptance of inequality. Society faced two and only two alternatives: "liberty, inequality, survival of the fittest; not-liberty, equality, survival of the unfittest." Government, Sumner believed, existed only to protect "the property of men and the honor of women," not to upset social arrangements decreed by nature.

William Graham Sumner

Liberty of Contract and the Courts

The growing influence of Social Darwinism helped to popularize an idea that would be embraced by the business and professional classes in the last quarter of the nineteenth century—a "negative" definition of freedom as limited government and an unrestrained free market. Central to this social vision was the idea of contract. So long as labor relations were governed by contracts freely arrived at by independent individuals, neither the government nor unions had a right to interfere with working conditions, and Americans had no grounds to complain of a loss of freedom. Thus the principle of free labor, which originated as a celebration of the

A new idea of free labor

independent small producer in a society of broad equality and social harmony, was transformed into a defense of the unrestrained operations of the capitalist marketplace.

The courts and economic freedom

State and federal courts struck down state laws regulating economic enterprise as an interference with the right of the free laborer to choose his employment and working conditions, and of the entrepreneur to utilize his property as he saw fit. For decades, the courts viewed state regulation of business—especially laws establishing maximum hours of work and safe working conditions—as an insult to free labor.

The courts generally sided with business enterprises that complained of a loss of economic freedom. In 1885, the New York Court of Appeals invalidated a state law that prohibited the manufacture of cigars in tenement dwellings on the grounds that such legislation deprived the worker

Women and work

of the "liberty" to work "where he will." Although women still lacked political rights, they were increasingly understood to possess the same economic "liberty," defined in this way, as men. The Illinois Supreme Court in 1895 declared unconstitutional a state law that outlawed the production of garments in sweatshops and established a forty-eight-hour workweek for women and children. In 1895 in *United States v. E. C. Knight Co.*, the U.S.

E. C. Knight case

Supreme Court ruled that the Sherman Antitrust Act of 1890, which barred combinations in restraint of trade, could not be used to break up a sugar refining monopoly, because the Constitution empowered Congress to regulate commerce but not manufacturing. Their unwillingness to allow regulation of the economy, however, did not prevent the courts from acting to impede labor organization. The Sherman Act, intended to prevent business mergers that stifled competition, was used by judges primarily to issue injunctions prohibiting strikes on the grounds that they illegally interfered with the freedom of trade.

In a 1905 case that became almost as notorious as *Dred Scott*, the

Lochner v. New York

Supreme Court in *Lochner v. New York* voided a state law establishing ten hours per day or sixty per week as the maximum hours of work for bakers. By this time, the Court was invoking "liberty" in ways that could easily seem absurd. In one case, it overturned as a violation of "personal liberty" a Kansas law prohibiting "yellow-dog" contracts, which made nonmembership in a union a condition of employment. In another, it struck down state laws requiring payment of coal miners in money rather than paper usable only at company-owned stores. Workers, observed mine union leader John P. Mitchell, could not but feel that "they are being guaranteed the liberties they do not want and denied the liberty that is of real value to them."

LABOR AND THE REPUBLIC

"The Overwhelming Labor Question"

As Mitchell's remark suggests, public debate in the late nineteenth century, more than at almost any other moment in American history, divided along class lines. The shift from the slavery controversy to what one politician called "the overwhelming labor question" was dramatically illustrated in 1877, the year of both the end of Reconstruction and also the first national labor walkout—the **Great Railroad Strike**. When workers protesting a pay cut paralyzed rail traffic in much of the country, militia units tried to force them back to work. After troops fired on strikers in Pittsburgh, killing twenty people, workers responded by burning the city's railroad yards, destroying millions of dollars in property. General strikes paralyzed Chicago and St. Louis. The strike revealed both a strong sense of solidarity among workers and the close ties between the Republican Party and the new class of industrialists. President Rutherford B. Hayes, who a few months earlier had ordered federal troops in the South to end their involvement in local politics, ordered the army into the North. The workers, the president wrote in his diary, were "put down by force."

In the aftermath of 1877, the federal government constructed armories in major cities to ensure that troops would be on hand in the event of further labor difficulties. Henceforth, national power would be used not to protect beleaguered former slaves but to guarantee the rights of property.

> *Public debate divided along class lines*

> *Railroad strikes*

Ruins of the Pittsburgh Round House, a photograph published in the July 1895 issue of *Scribner's Magazine*, shows the widespread destruction of property during the Great Railroad Strike of July 1877.

The Knights of Labor and the "Conditions Essential to Liberty"

The 1880s witnessed a new wave of labor organizing. At its center stood the **Knights of Labor**, led by Terence V. Powderly. The Knights were the first group to try to organize unskilled workers as well as skilled, women alongside men, and blacks as well as whites (although even the Knights excluded the despised Asian immigrants on the West Coast). The group reached a peak membership of nearly 800,000 in 1886 and involved millions of workers in strikes, boycotts, political action, and educational and social activities.

Labor reformers of the Gilded Age put forward a wide array of programs, from the eight-hour day to public employment in hard times, currency reform, anarchism, socialism, and the creation of a vaguely defined

The Great Labor Parade of September 1, from *Frank Leslie's Illustrated Newspaper*, September 13, 1884. A placard illustrates how the labor movement identified Gilded Age employers with the Slave Power of the pre–Civil War era.

Social commentary in literature

Progress and Poverty

The Cooperative Commonwealth

"cooperative commonwealth." Labor raised the question whether meaningful freedom could exist in a situation of extreme economic inequality.

Middle-Class Reformers

Dissatisfaction with social conditions in the Gilded Age extended well beyond aggrieved workers. Alarmed by fear of class warfare and the growing power of concentrated capital, social thinkers offered numerous plans for change. In the last quarter of the century, more than 150 utopian or cataclysmic novels appeared, predicting that social conflict would end either in a new, harmonious social order or in total catastrophe.

Of the many books proposing more optimistic remedies for the unequal distribution of wealth, the most popular were *Progress and Poverty* (1879) by Henry George, *The Cooperative Commonwealth* (1884) by Laurence Gronlund, and Edward Bellamy's *Looking Backward* (1888). All three were among the century's greatest best-sellers, their extraordinary success testifying to what George called "a wide-spread consciousness . . . that there is something *radically* wrong in the present social organization." All three writers, though in very different ways, sought to reclaim an imagined golden age of social harmony and American freedom.

Progress and Poverty probably commanded more public attention than any book on economics in American history. Henry George began with a famous statement of "the problem" suggested by its title—the growth of "squalor and misery" alongside material progress. His solution was the **single tax**, which would replace other taxes with a levy on increases in the value of real estate. No one knows how many of Henry George's readers actually believed in this way of solving the nation's ills. But millions responded to his clear explanation of economic relationships and his stirring account of how the "social distress" long thought to be confined to the Old World had made its appearance in the New.

Quite different in outlook was *The Cooperative Commonwealth*, the first book to popularize socialist ideas for an American audience. Its author, Laurence Gronlund, was a lawyer who had emigrated from Denmark in

1867. Socialism—the belief that private control of economic enterprises should be replaced by government ownership in order to ensure a fairer distribution of the benefits of the wealth produced—became a major political force in western Europe in the late nineteenth century. In the United States, however, where access to private property was widely considered essential to individual freedom, socialist beliefs were largely confined to immigrants, whose writings, frequently in foreign languages, attracted little attention.

Gronlund began the process of socialism's Americanization. Whereas Karl Marx, the nineteenth century's most influential socialist theorist, had predicted that socialism would come into being via a working-class revolution, Gronlund portrayed it as the end result of a process of peaceful evolution, not violent upheaval. He thus made socialism seem more acceptable to middle-class Americans who desired an end to class conflict and the restoration of social harmony.

Edward Bellamy, author of the utopian novel *Looking Backward*.

Not until the early twentieth century would socialism become a significant presence in American public life. As Gronlund himself noted, the most important result of *The Cooperative Commonwealth* was to prepare an audience for Edward Bellamy's *Looking Backward*, which promoted socialist ideas while "ignoring that name" (Bellamy wrote of nationalism, not socialism). In *Looking Backward*, his main character alls asleep in the late nineteenth century only to awaken in the year 2000, in a world where cooperation has replaced class strife, "excessive individualism," and cutthroat competition. Freedom, Bellamy insisted, was a social condition resting on interdependence, not autonomy.

Looking Backward

The book inspired the creation of hundreds of nationalist clubs devoted to bringing into existence the world of 2000 and left a profound mark on a generation of reformers and intellectuals. Bellamy held out the hope of retaining the material abundance made possible by industrial capitalism while eliminating inequality.

Protestants and Moral Reform

Mainstream Protestants played a major role in seeking to stamp out sin during the Gilded Age. What one historian calls a "Christian lobby" promoted political solutions to what they saw as the moral problems raised by labor conflict and the growth of cities, and threats to religious faith by Darwinism and other scientific advances.

"Christian lobby"

Unlike the pre–Civil War period, when "moral suasion" was the preferred approach of many reformers, powerful national organizations like the Woman's Christian Temperance Union, National Reform Association, and Reform Bureau now campaigned for federal legislation that would "Christianize the government" by outlawing sinful behavior. Among the proposed targets were the consumption of alcohol, gambling, prostitution, polygamy, and birth control. In a striking departure from the prewar situation, southerners joined in the campaign for federal regulation of individual behavior, something whites in the region had strongly opposed before the Civil War, fearing it could lead to action against slavery. The key role played by the white South in the campaign for moral legislation helped earn the region a reputation as the Bible Belt—a place where political action revolved around religious principles. Although efforts to enact a national law requiring businesses to close on Sunday failed, the Christian lobby's efforts set the stage for later legislation such as the Mann Act of 1910, banning the transportation of women across state lines for immoral purposes (an effort to suppress prostitution), and Prohibition.

Legislation on morals

The Bible Belt

A Social Gospel

Most of the era's Protestant preachers concentrated on attacking individual sins like drinking and Sabbath-breaking and saw nothing immoral about the pursuit of riches. But the outlines of what came to be called the **Social Gospel** were taking shape in the writings of Walter Rauschenbusch, a Baptist minister in New York City; Washington Gladden, a Congregational clergyman in Columbus, Ohio; and others. They insisted that freedom and spiritual self-development required an equalization of wealth and power and that unbridled competition mocked the Christian ideal of brotherhood.

Rauschenbusch and Gladden

The Social Gospel movement originated as an effort to reform Protestant churches by expanding their appeal in poor urban neighborhoods and making them more attentive to the era's social ills. The movement's adherents established missions and relief programs in urban areas that attempted to alleviate poverty, combat child labor, and encourage the construction of better working-class housing. Within American Catholicism as well, a group of priests and bishops emerged who attempted to alter the church's traditional hostility to movements for social reform and its isolation from contemporary currents of social thought. With most of its parishioners working men and women, they argued, the church should lend its support to the labor movement.

Religion and social reform

The Haymarket Affair

The year of the dedication of the Statue of Liberty, 1886, also witnessed an unprecedented upsurge in labor activity. On May 1, 1886, some 350,000 workers in cities across the country demonstrated for an eight-hour day. Having originated in the United States, May 1, or May Day as it came to be called, soon became an annual date of parades, picnics, and protests, celebrated around the world by organized labor.

The first May Day

The most dramatic events of 1886 took place in Chicago, a city with a large and vibrant labor movement that brought together native-born and immigrant workers, whose outlooks ranged from immigrant social-ism and anarchism to American traditions of equality and anti-monopoly. On May 3, 1886, four strikers were killed by police. The next day, a rally was held in Haymarket Square to protest the killings. Near the end of the speeches, someone—whose identity has never been determined—threw a bomb into the crowd, killing a policeman. The panicked police opened fire, shooting several bystanders and a number of their own force. Soon after, police raided the offices of labor and radical groups and arrested their leaders. Employers took the opportunity presented by the **Haymarket Affair** to paint the labor movement as a dangerous and un-American force, prone to violence and controlled by foreign-born radicals. Eight anarchists were charged with plotting and carrying out the bomb-ing. Even though the evidence against them was extremely weak, a jury convicted the "Haymarket martyrs." Four were hanged, one committed suicide in prison, and the remaining three were imprisoned until John Peter Altgeld, a pro-labor governor of Illinois, commuted their sentences in 1893.

Haymarket protests

Seven of the eight men accused of plotting the Haymarket bomb-ing were foreign-born—six Germans and an English immigrant. The last was Albert Parsons, a native of Alabama who had served in the Confederate army in the Civil War, married a black woman, and edited a Republican newspaper in Texas during Reconstruction. Having sur-vived the Ku Klux Klan in Reconstruction Texas, Parsons perished on the Illinois gallows for a crime that he, like the other "Haymarket martyrs," did not commit.

Labor and Politics

The Haymarket affair took place amid an outburst of independent labor political activity. In Kansas City, for example, a coalition of black and Irish-American workers and middle-class voters elected Tom Hanna as mayor.

Independent labor political activity

The Hercules of Labor saving his Country.

In this pro-labor cartoon from 1888, a workingman rescues liberty from the stranglehold of monopolies and the pro-business major parties.

He proceeded to side with unions rather than employers in industrial disputes.

The most celebrated labor campaign took place in New York City, where in 1886, somewhat to his own surprise, Henry George found himself thrust into the role of labor's candidate for mayor. George's aim in running was to bring attention to the single tax on land. The labor leaders who organized the United Labor Party had more immediate goals in mind, especially stopping the courts from barring strikes and jailing unionists for conspiracy. A few days after the dedication of the Statue of Liberty, New Yorkers flocked to the polls to elect their mayor. Nearly 70,000 voted for George, who finished second, eclipsing the total of the Republican candidate, Theodore Roosevelt, and coming close to defeating Democrat Abram Hewitt.

The events of 1886 suggested that labor might be on the verge of establishing itself as a permanent political force. In fact, that year marked the high point of the Knights of Labor. Facing increasing employer hostility and linked by employers and the press to the violence and radicalism associated with the Haymarket events, the Knights soon declined. The major parties, moreover, proved remarkably resourceful in appealing to labor voters.

In the early twentieth century, reformers would turn to new ways of addressing the social conditions of freedom and new means of increasing ordinary Americans' political and economic liberty. But before this, in the 1890s, the nation would face its gravest crisis since the Civil War, and the boundaries of freedom would once again be redrawn.

CHAPTER REVIEW AND ONLINE RESOURCES

REVIEW QUESTIONS

1. *The American economy thrived because of federal involvement, not the lack of it. How did the federal government actively promote industrial and agricultural development in this period?*

2. *Why were railroads so important to America's second industrial revolution? What events demonstrate their influence on society and politics as well as the economy?*

3. *Why did organized efforts of farmers, workers, and local reformers largely fail to achieve substantive change in the Gilded Age?*

4. *Describe the involvement of American family farmers in the global economy after 1870 and its effects on their independence.*

5. *How did American political leaders seek to remake Indians and change the ways they lived?*

6. *How do the ideas of Henry George, Edward Bellamy, and other authors conflict with Social Darwinism?*

7. *How did social reformers such as Edward Bellamy, Henry George, and advocates of the Social Gospel movement conceive of liberty and freedom differently than the proponents of the liberty of contract ideal and laissez-faire?*

8. *In what ways did the West provide a "safety valve" for the problems in the industrial East? In what ways did it reveal some of the same problems?*

KEY TERMS

trusts (p. 481)

vertical integration (p. 481)

horizontal expansion (p. 482)

robber barons (p. 482)

bonanza farms (p. 486)

Battle of the Little Bighorn (p. 491)

Dawes Act (p. 492)

Ghost Dance (p. 492)

Wounded Knee massacre (p. 493)

the Gilded Age (p. 497)

gold standard (p. 500)

Civil Service Act of 1883 (p. 500)

Interstate Commerce Commission (p. 501)

Sherman Antitrust Act (p. 501)

Social Darwinism (p. 503)

Great Railroad Strike (p. 505)

Knights of Labor (p. 505)

single tax (p. 506)

Social Gospel (p. 508)

Haymarket Affair (p. 509)

Go to INQUIZITIVE

To see what you know—and learn what you've missed—with personalized feedback along the way.

Visit the *Give Me Liberty!* **Student Site** for primary source documents and images, interactive maps, author videos featuring Eric Foner, and more.

1867   Alaska purchased

1874   Woman's Christian Temperance Union founded

1879–1880   Kansas Exodus

1882   Chinese Exclusion Act

1883   *Civil Rights Cases*

1886   American Federation of Labor established

1890   National American Woman Suffrage Association organized

         Alfred T. Mahan's *The Influence of Sea Power upon History*

1892   Homestead Strike

         Populist Party organized

1893   Hawaii's Queen Liliuokalani overthrown

         Economic depression begins

1894   Coxey's Army marches to Washington

         Pullman Strike

         Immigration Restriction League established

1895   Booker T. Washington's Atlanta speech

1896   *Plessy v. Ferguson*

         The National Association of Colored Women established

1897   William McKinley inaugurated president

1898   Spanish-American War

1899–1903   Philippine War

1900   Gold Standard Act

1901–1904   Insular Cases

CHAPTER 17

FREEDOM'S BOUNDARIES, AT HOME AND ABROAD

★

1890–1900

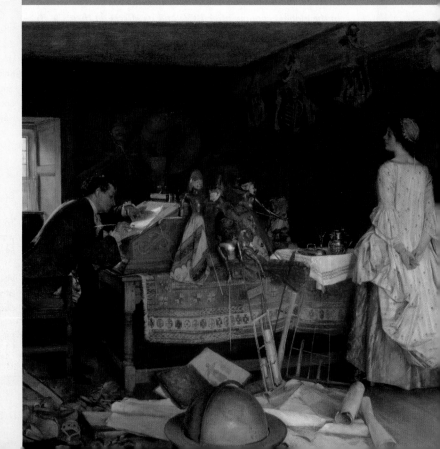

Painted in 1899 by the American artist Francis Davis Millet soon after his return from Asia, where he served as a newspaper correspondent during the Spanish-American War, *The Expansionist* depicts a well-dressed couple in a parlor filled with maps of the world and goods and mementos from Asia. In the wake of the emergence of the United States as the ruler of an overseas empire, it suggests that manifest destiny involves not just territorial expansion but acquiring the spoils of travel and war.

One of the most popular songs of 1892 bore the title "Father Was Killed by a Pinkerton Man." It was inspired by an incident during a bitter strike at Andrew Carnegie's steelworks at Homestead, Pennsylvania, the nineteenth century's most widely publicized confrontation between labor and capital.

Homestead's twelve steel mills were the most profitable and technologically advanced in the world. The union contract gave the Amalgamated Association a considerable say in their operation, including the right to approve the hiring of new workers and to regulate the pace of work. In 1892, Carnegie and Henry Clay Frick, his local supervisor, decided to operate the plant on a nonunion basis. Henceforth, only workers who agreed not to join the union could work at Homestead. In response, the workers blockaded the steelworks and mobilized support from the local community. The battle memorialized in song took place on July 6, 1892, when armed strikers confronted 300 private policemen from the Pinkerton Detective Agency. Seven workers and three Pinkerton agents were killed, and the Pinkertons were forced to retreat. Four days later, the governor of Pennsylvania dispatched 8,000 militiamen to open the complex on management's terms. In the end, the Amalgamated Association was destroyed.

Homestead demonstrated that neither a powerful union nor public opinion could influence the conduct of the largest corporations. Moreover, two American ideas of freedom collided at Homestead—the employers' definition, based on the idea that property rights, unrestrained by union rules or public regulation, sustained the public good; and the workers' conception, which stressed economic security and independence from what they considered the "tyranny" of employers. During the 1890s, many Americans came to believe that they were being denied economic independence and democratic self-government, long central to the popular understanding of freedom.

Millions of farmers joined the Populist movement in an attempt to reverse their declining economic prospects and to rescue the government from what they saw as control by powerful corporate interests. The 1890s witnessed the imposition of a new racial system in the South that locked African-Americans into the status of second-class citizenship, denying them many of the freedoms white Americans took for granted. Increasing immigration produced heated debates over whether the country should reconsider its traditional self-definition as a refuge for foreigners seeking greater

FOCUS QUESTIONS

- *What were the origins and the significance of Populism?*

- *How did the liberties of blacks after 1877 give way to legal segregation across the South?*

- *In what ways did the boundaries of American freedom grow narrower in this period?*

- *How did the United States emerge as an imperial power in the 1890s?*

Andrew Carnegie's ironworks at Homestead, Pennsylvania.

freedom on American shores. At the end of the 1890s, in the Spanish-American War, the United States for the first time acquired overseas possessions and found itself ruling over subject peoples from Puerto Rico to the Philippines. Was the democratic republic, many Americans wondered, becoming an empire like those of Europe? Rarely has the country experienced at one time so many debates over both the meaning of freedom and freedom's boundaries.

THE POPULIST CHALLENGE

The Farmers' Revolt

Even as labor unrest crested, a different kind of uprising was ripening in the South and the trans-Mississippi West, a response to falling agricultural prices and growing economic dependency in rural areas. In the South, the sharecropping system, discussed in Chapter 15, locked millions of tenant farmers, white and black, into perpetual poverty. The interruption of cotton exports during the Civil War had led to the rapid expansion of production in India, Egypt, and Brazil. The glut of cotton on the world market led to declining prices, throwing millions of small farmers deep into debt and threatening them with the loss of their land. In the West, farmers who had mortgaged their property to purchase seed, fertilizer, and equipment faced the prospect of losing their farms when unable to repay their bank loans. Farmers increasingly believed that their plight derived from the high freight rates charged by railroad companies, excessive interest rates for loans from merchants and bankers, and the fiscal policies of the federal government (discussed in the previous chapter) that reduced the supply of money and helped to push down farm prices.

Causes of unrest

Through the Farmers' Alliance, the largest citizens' movement of the nineteenth century, farmers sought to remedy their condition. Founded in Texas in the late 1870s, the Alliance spread to forty-three states by 1890. The Alliance proposed that the federal government establish warehouses where farmers could store their crops until they were sold. Using the crops as collateral, the government would then issue loans to farmers at low interest rates, thereby ending their dependence on bankers and merchants. Since it would have to be enacted by Congress, the "subtreasury plan," as this proposal was called, led the Alliance into politics.

The Farmers' Alliance

The People's Party

In the early 1890s, the Alliance evolved into the People's Party (or **Populists**), the era's greatest political insurgency. Attempting to speak for all "producing classes," the party did not just appeal to farmers. It achieved some of its greatest successes in states like Colorado and Idaho, where it won the support of miners and industrial workers. But its major base lay in the cotton and wheat belts of the South and West.

Populist organizing

The Populists embarked on a remarkable effort of community organization and education. To spread their message they published numerous pamphlets on political and economic questions, established more than 1,000 local newspapers, and sent traveling speakers throughout rural America. At great gatherings on the western plains, similar in some ways to religious revival meetings, and in small-town southern country stores, one observer wrote, "people commenced to think who had never thought before, and people talked who had seldom spoken." Here was the last great political expression of the nineteenth-century vision of America as a commonwealth of small producers whose freedom rested on the ownership of productive property and respect for the dignity of labor.

But although the Populists used the familiar language of nineteenth-century radicalism, they were hardly a backward-looking movement. They embraced the modern technologies that made large-scale cooperative enterprise possible—the railroad, the telegraph, and the national market— while looking to the federal government to regulate those technologies in the public interest. They promoted agricultural education and believed farmers should adopt modern scientific methods of cultivation.

The Populist message

A group of Kansas Populists, perhaps on their way to a political gathering, in a photograph from the 1890s.

THE POPULIST CHALLENGE | 515

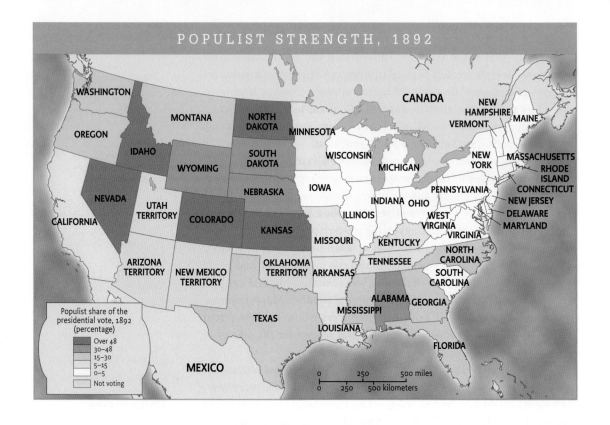

POPULIST STRENGTH, 1892

Populist share of the presidential vote, 1892 (percentage)

- Over 48
- 30–48
- 15–30
- 5–15
- 0–5
- Not voting

0   250   500 miles
0   250   500 kilometers

The Populist Platform

The Populist platform of 1892, adopted at the party's Omaha convention, remains a classic document of American reform. Written by Ignatius Donnelly, a Minnesota editor, it spoke of a nation "brought to the verge of moral, political, and material ruin" by political corruption and economic inequality. The platform put forth a long list of proposals to restore democracy and economic opportunity, many of which would be adopted during the next half-century: the direct election of U.S. senators, government control of the currency, a graduated income tax, a system of low-cost public financing to enable farmers to market their crops, and recognition of the right of workers to form labor unions. In addition, Populists called for public ownership of the railroads to guarantee farmers inexpensive access to markets for their crops. A generation would pass before a major party offered so sweeping a plan for political action to create the social conditions of freedom.

Proposals of reform

The Populist Coalition

In some southern states, the Populists made remarkable efforts to unite black and white small farmers on a common political and economic program. In general, southern white Populists' racial attitudes did not differ significantly from those of their non-Populist neighbors. Nonetheless, recognizing the need for allies to break the Democratic Party's stranglehold on power in the South, some white Populists insisted that black and white farmers shared common grievances and could unite for common goals. Tom Watson, Georgia's leading Populist, worked the hardest to forge a black-white alliance. "You are kept apart," he told interracial audiences, "that you may be separately fleeced of your earnings." While many blacks refused to abandon the party of Lincoln, others were attracted by the Populist appeal. In most of the South, however, Democrats fended off the Populist challenge by resorting to the tactics they had used to retain power since the 1870s—mobilizing whites with warnings about "Negro supremacy," intimidating black voters, and stuffing ballot boxes on election day.

Populism and race

The Populist movement also engaged the energies of thousands of reform-minded women from farm and labor backgrounds. Some, like Mary Elizabeth Lease, a former homesteader and one of the first female lawyers in Kansas, became prominent organizers, campaigners, and strategists. During the 1890s, referendums in Colorado and Idaho approved extending the vote to women, whereas in Kansas and California the proposal went down in defeat. Populists in all these states endorsed woman suffrage.

Populist presidential candidate James Weaver received more than 1 million votes in 1892. The party carried five western states. In his inaugural address in 1893, Lorenzo Lewelling, the new Populist governor of Kansas, anticipated a phrase made famous seventy years later by Martin Luther King Jr.: "I have a dream. . . . A time is foreshadowed when . . . liberty, equality, and justice shall have permanent abiding places in the republic."

The Government and Labor

Were the Populists on the verge of replacing one of the two major parties? The severe depression that began in 1893 led to increased conflict between capital and labor and seemed to create an opportunity for expanding the Populist vote. Time and again, employers brought state or federal authority to bear to protect their own economic power or put down threats to public order. In May 1894, the federal government

Most Populists in the West supported woman suffrage. In this cartoon published in a Colorado Populist newspaper on July 4, 1894, a man and a woman celebrate the passage of a referendum giving women the right to vote in that state.

INDEPENDENCE DAY—COLORADO.

Federal troops pose atop a railroad engine after being sent to Chicago to help suppress the Pullman Strike of 1894.

deployed soldiers to disperse **Coxey's Army**—a band of several hundred unemployed men led by Ohio businessman Jacob Coxey, who marched to Washington demanding economic relief.

The Pullman Strike

Also in 1894, workers in the company-owned town of Pullman, Illinois, where railroad sleeping cars were manufactured, called a strike to protest a reduction in wages. The American Railway Union announced that its members would refuse to handle trains with Pullman cars. When the boycott crippled national rail service, President Grover Cleveland's attorney general, Richard Olney (himself on the board of several railroad companies), obtained a federal court injunction ordering the strikers back to work. Federal troops and U.S. marshals soon occupied railroad centers like Chicago and Sacramento.

Eugene Debs

The strike collapsed when the union's leaders, including its charismatic president, Eugene V. Debs, were jailed for contempt of court for violating the judicial order. In the case of *In re Debs*, the Supreme Court unanimously confirmed the sentences and approved the use of injunctions against striking labor unions. On his release from prison in November 1895, more than 100,000 persons greeted Debs at a Chicago railroad depot.

Populism and Labor

Appealing to industrial workers

In 1894, Populists made determined efforts to appeal to industrial workers. Governor Davis Waite of Colorado, who had edited a labor newspaper before his election, sent the militia to protect striking miners against company police. In the state and congressional elections of that year, as the economic depression deepened, voters by the millions abandoned the Democratic Party of President Cleveland.

In rural areas, the Populist vote increased in 1894. But urban workers did not rally to the Populists, whose core issues—the subtreasury plan and lower mortgage interest rates—had little meaning for them. Urban working-class voters instead shifted en masse to the Republicans, who claimed that raising tariff rates (which Democrats had recently reduced) would restore prosperity by protecting manufacturers and industrial workers from the competition of imported goods and cheap foreign labor. In one of the most decisive shifts in congressional power in American history, the Republicans gained 117 seats in the House of Representatives.

Labor votes

Bryan and Free Silver

In 1896, Democrats and Populists joined to support William Jennings Bryan for the presidency. A thirty-six-year-old congressman from Nebraska, Bryan won the Democratic nomination after delivering to the national convention an electrifying speech that crystallized the farmers' pride and grievances. "Burn down your cities and leave our farms," Bryan proclaimed, "and your cities will spring up again as if by magic; but destroy our farms and grass will grow in the streets of every city in the country." Bryan called for the "free coinage" of silver—the unrestricted minting of silver money. In language ringing with biblical imagery, Bryan condemned the gold standard: "You shall not crucify mankind upon a cross of gold."

Bryan's demand for "free silver" was the latest expression of the view that increasing the amount of currency in circulation would raise the prices farmers received for their crops and make it easier to pay off their debts. His nomination wrested control of the Democratic Party from long-dominant leaders like President Grover Cleveland, who were closely tied to eastern businessmen.

There was more to Bryan's appeal, however, than simply free silver. A devoutly religious man, he was strongly influenced by the Social Gospel movement (discussed in the previous chapter). He championed a vision of the government helping ordinary Americans that anticipated provisions of the New Deal of the 1930s, including a progressive income tax, banking regulation, and the right of workers to form unions. Bryan also broke with tradition and embarked on a nationwide speaking tour, seeking to rally farmers and workers to his cause.

A cartoon from the magazine *Judge*, September 14, 1896, condemns William Jennings Bryan and his "cross of gold" speech for defiling the symbols of Christianity. Bryan tramples on the Bible while holding his golden cross; a vandalized church is visible in the background.

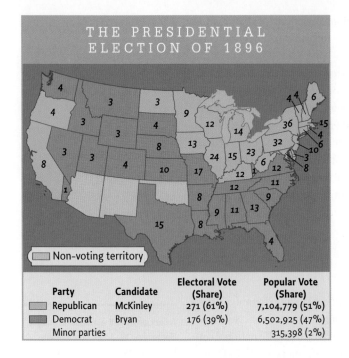

THE PRESIDENTIAL ELECTION OF 1896

Non-voting territory

Party	Candidate	Electoral Vote (Share)	Popular Vote (Share)
Republican	McKinley	271 (61%)	7,104,779 (51%)
Democrat	Bryan	176 (39%)	6,502,925 (47%)
Minor parties			315,398 (2%)

Campaign financing

A Republican majority

The Campaign of 1896

Republicans met the silverite challenge head on, insisting that gold was the only "honest" currency. Abandoning the gold standard, they insisted, would destroy business confidence and prevent recovery from the depression by making creditors unwilling to extend loans, because they could not be certain of the value of the money in which they would be repaid. The party nominated for president Ohio governor William McKinley, who as a congressman in 1890 had shepherded to passage the strongly protectionist McKinley Tariff.

The election of 1896 is sometimes called the first modern presidential campaign because of the amount of money spent by the Republicans and the efficiency of their national organization. Eastern bankers and industrialists, thoroughly alarmed by Bryan's call for monetary inflation and his fiery speeches denouncing corporate arrogance, poured millions of dollars into Republican coffers. (McKinley's campaign raised some $10 million; Bryan's around $300,000.) While McKinley remained at his Ohio home, his political manager Mark Hanna created a powerful national machine that flooded the country with pamphlets, posters, and campaign buttons.

The results revealed a nation as divided along regional lines as in 1860. Bryan carried the South and West and received 6.5 million votes. McKinley swept the more populous industrial states of the Northeast and Midwest, attracting 7.1 million. Industrial America, from financiers and managers to workers, now voted solidly Republican, a loyalty reinforced when prosperity returned after 1897.

McKinley's victory shattered the political stalemate that had persisted since 1876 and created one of the most enduring political majorities in American history. During McKinley's presidency, Republicans placed their stamp on economic policy by passing the Dingley Tariff of 1897, raising rates to the highest level in history, and the Gold Standard Act of 1900. Not until 1932, in the midst of another economic depression, would the Democrats become the nation's majority party.

THE SEGREGATED SOUTH

The Redeemers in Power

The failure of Populism in the South opened the door for the full imposition of a new racial order. The coalition of merchants, planters, and business entrepreneurs who dominated the region's politics after 1877, who called themselves Redeemers, had moved to undo as much as possible of Reconstruction. Hardest hit were the new public school systems. Louisiana spent so little on education that it became the only state in the Union in which the percentage of whites unable to read and write actually increased between 1880 and 1900. Black schools, however, suffered the most, as the gap between expenditures for black and white pupils widened steadily.

Undoing Reconstruction

New laws authorized the arrest of virtually any person without employment and greatly increased the penalties for petty crimes. As the South's prison population rose, the renting out of convicts became a profitable business. Every southern state placed at least a portion of its convicted criminals, the majority of them blacks imprisoned for minor offenses, in the hands of private businessmen. Railroads, mines, and lumber companies competed for this new form of cheap, involuntary labor. Conditions in labor camps were often barbaric, with disease rife and the death rates high. "One dies, get another" was the motto of the system's architects.

Convict labor

The Failure of the New South Dream

During the 1880s, Atlanta editor Henry Grady tirelessly promoted the promise of a **New South**, an era of prosperity based on industrial expansion and agricultural diversification. In fact, while planters, merchants, and industrialists prospered, the region as a whole sank deeper and deeper into poverty. Some industry did develop, such as new upcountry cotton factories that offered jobs to entire families of poor whites from the surrounding countryside. But since the main attractions for investors were the South's low wages and taxes and the availability of convict labor, these enterprises made little contribution to regional economic development. With the exception of Birmingham, Alabama, which by 1900 had developed into an important center for the manufacture of iron and steel, southern cities were mainly export centers for cotton, tobacco, and rice, with little industry or skilled labor. Overall, the region remained dependent on the North for capital and manufactured goods. As late as

A group of Florida convict laborers. Southern states notoriously used convicts for public labor or leased them out to work in dire conditions for private employers.

Coal miners, in a photograph by Lewis Hine. Mining was one occupation in which blacks and whites often worked side by side.

the 1930s, President Franklin D. Roosevelt would declare the South the nation's "number one" economic problem.

Black Life in the South

As the most disadvantaged rural southerners, black farmers suffered the most from the region's condition. In the Upper South, economic development offered some opportunities—mines, iron furnaces, and tobacco factories employed black laborers, and a good number of black farmers managed to acquire land. In the rice kingdom of coastal South Carolina and Georgia, most of the great plantations had fallen to pieces by the turn of the century, and many blacks acquired land and took up self-sufficient farming. In most of the Deep South, however, African-Americans owned a smaller percentage of land in 1900 than they had at the end of Reconstruction.

Growth of a black middle class

In southern cities, the network of institutions created after the Civil War—schools and colleges, churches, businesses, women's clubs, and the like—served as the foundation for increasingly diverse black urban communities. They supported the growth of a black middle class, mostly professionals like teachers and physicians, or businessmen like undertakers and shopkeepers serving the needs of black customers. But the labor market was rigidly divided along racial lines. Black men were excluded from supervisory positions in factories and workshops and white-collar jobs such as clerks in offices. A higher percentage of black women than white worked for wages, but mainly as domestic servants. In most occupations, the few unions that existed in the South excluded blacks, forming yet another barrier to their economic advancement.

The Kansas Exodus

Emigration from the South

Trapped at the bottom of a stagnant economy, some blacks sought a way out through emigration from the South. In 1879 and 1880, an estimated 40,000 to 60,000 African-Americans migrated to Kansas, seeking political equality, freedom from violence, access to education, and eco-

A photograph of townspeople in Nicodemus, a community established by members of the 1879–1880 "Exodus" of southern African-Americans to Kansas.

nomic opportunity. Those promoting the **Kansas Exodus**, including former fugitive slave Benjamin "Pap" Singleton, the organizer of a real estate company, distributed flyers and lithographs picturing Kansas as an idyllic land of rural plenty. Lacking the capital to take up farming, however, most black migrants ended up as unskilled laborers in towns and cities. But few chose to return to the South. In the words of one minister active in the movement, "We had rather suffer and be free."

Despite deteriorating prospects in the South, most African-Americans had little alternative but to stay in the region. The real expansion of job opportunities was taking place in northern cities. But most northern employers refused to offer jobs to blacks in the expanding industrial economy, preferring to hire white migrants from rural areas and immigrants from Europe.

Northern jobs

The Decline of Black Politics

Neither black voting nor black officeholding came to an abrupt end in 1877. A few blacks even served in Congress in the 1880s and 1890s. Nonetheless, political opportunities became more and more restricted. Not until the 1990s would the number of black legislators in the South approach the level seen during Reconstruction.

Fewer black officeholders

With black men of talent and ambition turning away from politics, the banner of political leadership passed to black women activists. The National Association of Colored Women, founded in 1896, brought

Black women reformers

together local and regional women's clubs to press for both women's rights and racial uplift. They aided poor families, offered lessons in home life and childrearing, and battled gambling and drinking in black communities. By insisting on the right of black women to be considered as "respectable" as their white counterparts, the women reformers challenged the racial ideology that consigned all blacks to the status of degraded second-class citizens.

For nearly a generation after the end of Reconstruction, despite fraud and violence, black southerners continued to cast ballots in large numbers. In some states, such as Virginia, Tennessee, Arkansas, and North

Biracial politics

Carolina, the Republican Party remained competitive and formed biracial political coalitions that challenged Democratic Party rule. Despite the limits of these alliances, especially those involving the Populists, the threat of a biracial political insurgency frightened the ruling Democrats and contributed greatly to the disenfranchisement movement.

The Elimination of Black Voting

Between 1890 and 1906, every southern state enacted laws or constitutional provisions meant to eliminate the black vote. Since the Fifteenth Amendment prohibited the use of race as a qualification for the suffrage, how were such measures even possible? Southern legislatures drafted laws that on paper appeared color-blind but that were actually designed

Poll tax

to end black voting. The most popular devices were the poll tax (a fee that each citizen had to pay in order to retain the right to vote), literacy tests, and the requirement that a prospective voter demonstrate to election officials an "understanding" of the state constitution. Six southern states also adopted a **grandfather clause**, exempting from the new requirements descendants of persons eligible to vote before the Civil War (when only whites, of course, could cast ballots in the South). The racial intent of the

Grandfather clause

grandfather clause was so clear that the Supreme Court in 1915 invalidated such laws for violating the Fifteenth Amendment. The other methods of limiting black voting, however, remained on the books.

Although election officials often allowed whites who did not meet the new qualifications to register, numerous poor and illiterate whites also lost the right to vote, a result welcomed by many planters and urban reformers. Louisiana, for example, reduced the number of blacks registered to vote from 130,000 in 1894 to 1,342 a decade later. But 80,000 white voters also lost the right. **Disenfranchisement** led directly to the rise of a generation of southern demagogues, who mobilized white voters by extreme appeals to racism.

Scope of disenfranchisement

As late as 1940, only 3 percent of adult black southerners were registered to vote. The elimination of black and many white voters, which reversed the nineteenth-century trend toward more inclusive suffrage, could not have been accomplished without the acquiescence of the North and the Supreme Court, both of which gave their approval to disenfranchisement laws, in clear violation of the Fourteenth Amendment. As a result, southern congressmen wielded far greater power on the national scene than their tiny electorates warranted.

The Supreme Court's approval of disenfranchisement

The Law of Segregation

Along with disenfranchisement, the 1890s saw the widespread imposition of segregation in the South. Laws and local customs requiring the separation of the races had numerous precedents. They had existed in many parts of the pre–Civil War North. Southern schools and many other institutions had been segregated during Reconstruction. In the 1880s, however, southern race relations remained unsettled. Some railroads, theaters, and hotels admitted blacks and whites on an equal basis while others separated them by race or excluded blacks altogether.

In 1883, in the *Civil Rights Cases*, the Supreme Court invalidated the Civil Rights Act of 1875, which had outlawed racial discrimination by hotels, theaters, railroads, and other public facilities. In 1896, in the landmark decision in **Plessy v. Ferguson**, the Court gave its approval to state laws requiring separate facilities for blacks and whites. The case arose in Louisiana, where the legislature had required railroad companies to maintain a separate car or section for black passengers. In a 7-1 decision, the Court upheld the Louisiana law, arguing that segregated facilities did not discriminate so long as they were "**separate but equal**." The lone dissenter, John Marshall Harlan, reprimanded the majority with an oft-quoted comment: "Our constitution is color-blind." Segregation, he insisted, violated the principle of equal liberty. To Harlan, freedom for the former slaves meant the right to participate fully and equally in American society.

Civil Rights Cases

As Harlan predicted, states reacted to the *Plessy* decision by passing laws mandating racial segregation in every aspect of southern life, from schools to hospitals, waiting rooms, toilets, and cemeteries. Some states

Spread of segregation

In *Plessy v. Ferguson* (1896), the U.S. Supreme Court ruled that laws establishing racial segregation did not violate the equal protection clause of the Fourteenth Amendment so long as facilities were "separate but equal." In fact, this was almost never the case, as illustrated by these photographs of the elementary schools for black and white children in South Boston, Virginia, in the early twentieth century.

forbade taxi drivers to carry members of different races at the same time. Despite the "thin disguise" (Harlan's phrase) of equality required by the Court's "separate but equal" doctrine, facilities for blacks were either non-existent or markedly inferior.

More than a form of racial separation, segregation was one part of an all-encompassing system of white domination, in which each component—disenfranchisement, unequal economic status, inferior education—reinforced the others.

Segregation affected other groups as well as blacks. In some parts of Mississippi where Chinese laborers had been brought in to work the fields after the Civil War, three separate school systems—white, black, and Chinese—were established. In California, black, Hispanic, and American Indian children were frequently educated alongside whites, but state law required separate schools for those of "mongolian or Chinese descent." In Texas and California, although Mexicans were legally considered "white," they found themselves barred from many restaurants, places of entertainment, and other public facilities.

The Rise of Lynching

Those blacks who sought to challenge the system faced not only overwhelming political and legal power but also the threat of violent reprisal. In every year between 1883 and 1905, more than fifty persons, the vast majority of them black men, were lynched in the South—that is, murdered by a mob. **Lynching** continued well into the twentieth century. By

TABLE 17.1 States with Over 200 Lynchings, 1889–1918	
STATE	NUMBER OF LYNCHINGS
Georgia	386
Mississippi	373
Texas	335
Louisiana	313
Alabama	276
Arkansas	214

mid-century, the total number of victims since 1880 had reached nearly 4,000. Some lynchings occurred secretly at night; others were advertised in advance and attracted large crowds of onlookers. Mobs engaged in activities that shocked the civilized world. In 1899, Sam Hose, a plantation laborer who killed his employer in self-defense, was brutally murdered near Newman, Georgia, before 2,000 onlookers, some of whom arrived on a special excursion train from Atlanta. A crowd including young children watched as his executioners cut off Hose's ears, fingers, and genitals, burned him alive, and then fought over pieces of his bones as souvenirs.

Like many victims of lynchings, Hose was accused after his death of having raped a white woman. Yet in nearly all cases, as activist Ida B. Wells argued in a newspaper editorial after a Memphis lynching in 1892, the charge of rape was a "bare lie." Born a slave in Mississippi in 1862, Wells had become a schoolteacher and editor. Her essay condemning the lynching of three black men in Memphis led a mob to destroy her newspaper, the *Memphis Free Press*, while she was out of the city. Wells moved to the North, where she became the nation's leading antilynching crusader. She bluntly insisted that given the conditions of southern blacks, the United States had no right to call itself the "land of the free."

A crowd at the aftermath of the lynching of Laura Nelson and her teenage son L. D. Nelson, African-American residents of Okemah, Oklahoma, in 1911. They were accused of shooting to death a deputy sheriff who had come to the Nelson home to investigate the theft of livestock. A week after being lodged in jail, they were removed by a mob and taken to the bridge. Members of the mob raped Mrs. Nelson before the lynching. The photograph was reproduced as a postcard, sold at local stores. As in most lynchings, no one was prosecuted for the crime.

Politics, Religion, and Memory

As the white North and South moved toward reconciliation in the 1880s and 1890s, one cost was the abandonment of the dream of racial equality written into the laws and Constitution during Reconstruction. In popular literature and memoirs by participants, at veterans' reunions and in public memorials, the Civil War came to be remembered as a tragic family quarrel among white Americans in which blacks had played no significant part. It was a war of "brother against brother" in which both sides fought gallantly for noble causes—local rights on the part of the South, preservation of the Union for the North. Slavery increasingly came to be viewed as a minor issue, not the war's fundamental cause, and Reconstruction as a regrettable period of "Negro rule."

Southern governments erected monuments to **the Lost Cause**, a romanticized version of slavery, the Old South, and the Confederate

Rewriting the Civil War narrative

THE SEGREGATED SOUTH | 527

This carving by an unknown southerner from around 1875 juxtaposes Robert E. Lee and the crucified Christ, illustrating the strong religious overtones in the ideology of the Lost Cause.

experience. Religion was central to the development of Lost Cause mythology—it offered a way for white southerners to come to terms with defeat in the Civil War without abandoning white supremacy. The death of the Confederacy, in many sermons, was equated with the death of Christ, who gave his life for the sins of mankind. Southern churches played a key role in keeping the values of the Old South alive by refusing to reunite with northern counterparts. In the 1840s, the Methodist and Baptist churches had divided into northern and southern branches. Methodists would not reunite until well into the twentieth century; Baptists have yet to do so.

REDRAWING THE BOUNDARIES

As the nineteenth century drew to a close, American society seemed to be fracturing along lines of both class and race. The result, commented economist Simon Patten, was a widespread obsession with redrawing the boundary of freedom by identifying and excluding those unworthy of the blessings of liberty. "The South," he wrote, "has its negro, the city has its slums. . . . The friends of American institutions fear the ignorant immigrant, and the workingman dislikes the Chinese."

The New Immigration and the New Nativism

The 1890s witnessed a major shift in the sources of immigration to the United States. Despite the prolonged depression, 3.5 million newcomers entered the United States during the decade, seeking jobs in the industrial centers of the North and Midwest. Over half arrived not from Ireland, England, Germany, and Scandinavia, the traditional sources of immigration, but from southern and eastern Europe, especially Italy and the Russian and Austro-Hungarian empires. The **new immigrants** were widely described by native-born Americans as members of distinct "races," whose lower level of civilization explained everything from their willingness to work for substandard wages to their supposed inborn tendency toward criminal behavior.

Southern and eastern Europe

Founded in 1894 by a group of Boston professionals, the **Immigration Restriction League** called for reducing immigration by barring the illiterate from entering the United States. Such a measure was adopted by

A cartoon from the magazine *Judge,* entitled *The High Tide,* illustrates anti-immigrant sentiment. A tide of newcomers representing the criminal element of other countries washes up on American shores, to the consternation of Uncle Sam. The words on their hats list undesirable immigrants, including criminals, paupers, and anarchists.

Congress early in 1897 but was vetoed by President Cleveland. Like the South, northern and western states experimented with ways to eliminate undesirable voters. Nearly all the states during the 1890s adopted the secret or "Australian" ballot, meant both to protect voters' privacy and to limit the participation of illiterates (who could no longer receive help from party officials at polling places). Suffrage throughout the country was increasingly becoming a privilege, not a right.

Restricting the vote

Chinese Exclusion and Chinese Rights

The boundaries of nationhood, expanded so dramatically in the aftermath of the Civil War, slowly contracted. Leaders of both parties expressed vicious opinions regarding immigrants from China—they were "odious, abominable, dangerous, revolting," declared Republican leader James G. Blaine.

Beginning in 1882 with the **Chinese Exclusion Act**, Congress temporarily excluded all immigrants from China from entering the country. Although non-whites had long been barred from becoming naturalized citizens, this was the first time that race had been used to exclude an entire group of people. Congress renewed the restriction ten years later and made it

Beginning in 1909, as part of the enforcement of Chinese exclusion, all Chinese in the United States were required to carry a government-issued certificate, the first widespread use of photographs as proof of identity. This certificate, issued in 1924, belonged to Anna May Wong, an American-born movie star.

A Chinese vegetable peddler in Idaho City, Idaho.

Tape v. Hurley

Result of an anti-Chinese riot in Seattle, Washington.

permanent in 1902. Chinese in the United States were required to register with the government and carry identification papers or face deportation. Indeed, the use of photographs for personal identification first came into widespread use as a means of enforcing Chinese exclusion. One Chinese activist complained that the photos, which bore a striking resemblance to "mug shots" of persons under arrest, criminalized people "innocent of any crime" and created a "national rogues' gallery" of Chinese residents. In 2012, Congress passed a Resolution of Regret apologizing for the exclusion laws and acknowledging their role in exacerbating racial discrimination. It was sponsored by Judy Chu, a Chinese-American member of the House of Representatives from California.

By 1930, because of exclusion, the number of Chinese had declined to 75,000. On the West Coast, the Chinese suffered intense discrimination and periodic mob violence. In the late-nineteenth-century West, thousands of Chinese immigrants were expelled from towns and mining camps, and mobs assaulted Chinese residences and businesses. Between 1871 and 1885, San Francisco provided no public education for Chinese children. In 1885, the California Supreme Court, in *Tape v. Hurley*, ordered the city to admit Chinese students to public schools. The state legislature responded by passing a law authorizing segregated education. But Joseph and Mary Tape, who had lived in the United States since the 1860s, insisted that their daughter be allowed to attend her neighborhood school like other children. "Is it a disgrace to be born a Chinese?" Mary Tape wrote. "Didn't God make us all!" But her protest failed. Not until 1947 did California repeal the law authorizing separate schools for the Chinese.

The U.S. Supreme Court also considered the legal status of Chinese-Americans. In *United States v. Wong Kim Ark* (1898), the Court ruled that the Fourteenth Amendment awarded citizenship to children of Chinese immigrants born on American soil. Yet the justices also affirmed the right of Congress to set racial restrictions on immigration. And in its decision in *Fong Yue Ting v. United States* (1893), the Court authorized the federal government to expel Chinese aliens without due process of law. In his dissent, Justice David J. Brewer acknowledged that the power was now directed against a people many Americans found "obnoxious." But "who shall say," he continued, "it will not be exercised tomorrow against other classes and other people?" Brewer proved to be an accurate prophet. In 1904, the Court cited *Fong Yue Ting* in upholding a law barring anarchists from entering the United States, demonstrating how restrictions on the rights of one group can become a precedent for infringing on the rights of others.

The Emergence of Booker T. Washington

The social movements that had helped to expand the nineteenth-century boundaries of freedom now redefined their objectives so that they might be realized within the new economic and intellectual framework. Prominent black leaders, for example, took to emphasizing economic self-help and individual advancement into the middle class as an alternative to political agitation.

Booker T. Washington, advocate of industrial education and economic self-help.

Symbolizing the change was the juxtaposition, in 1895, of the death of Frederick Douglass with Booker T. Washington's widely praised speech, titled the "**Atlanta Compromise**," at the Atlanta Cotton Exposition that urged blacks to adjust to segregation and abandon agitation for civil and political rights. Born a slave in 1856, Washington had studied as a young man at Hampton Institute, Virginia. He adopted the outlook of Hampton's founder, General Samuel Armstrong, who emphasized that obtaining farms or skilled jobs was far more important to African-Americans emerging from slavery than the rights of citizenship. Washington put this view into practice when he became head of Tuskegee Institute in Alabama, a center for vocational education (education focused on training for a job rather than broad learning).

Tuskegee Institute

In his Atlanta speech, Washington repudiated the abolitionist tradition, which stressed ceaseless agitation for full equality. He urged blacks not to try to combat segregation. Washington's ascendancy rested in large part on his success in channeling aid from wealthy northern whites to Tuskegee and to black politicians and newspapers who backed his program. But his support in the black community also arose from a widespread sense that in the world of the late nineteenth century, frontal assaults on white power were impossible and that blacks should concentrate on building up their segregated communities.

Washington's appeal

The Rise of the AFL

Within the labor movement, the demise of the Knights of Labor and the ascendancy of the **American Federation of Labor** (AFL) during the 1890s reflected a similar shift away from a broadly reformist past to more limited goals. As the Homestead and Pullman strikes demonstrated, direct confrontations with the large corporations were likely to prove suicidal.

Limited labor movement

Unions, declared Samuel Gompers, the AFL's founder and longtime president, should not pursue the Knights' utopian dream of creating a "cooperative commonwealth." Rather, the labor movement should devote itself to negotiating with employers for higher wages and better working conditions for its members. Like Washington, Gompers spoke the language of the era's business culture. Indeed, the AFL policies he pioneered were known as "business unionism."

During the 1890s, union membership rebounded from its decline in the late 1880s. But at the same time, the labor movement became less and less inclusive. Abandoning the Knights' ideal of labor solidarity, the AFL

restricted membership to skilled workers—a small minority of the labor force—effectively excluding the vast majority of unskilled workers and, therefore, nearly all blacks, women, and new European immigrants. AFL membership centered on sectors of the economy like printing and building construction that were dominated by small competitive businesses. AFL unions had little presence in basic industries like steel and rubber, or in the large-scale factories that now dominated the economy.

The Women's Era

Changes in the women's movement reflected the same combination of expanding activities and narrowing boundaries. The 1890s launched what would later be called the "women's era"—three decades during which women, although still denied the vote, enjoyed larger opportunities than in the past for economic independence and played a greater and greater

role in public life. Nearly 5 million women worked for wages in 1900. Although most were young, unmarried, and concentrated in traditional jobs such as domestic service and the garment industry, a generation of college-educated women was beginning to take its place in better-paying clerical and professional positions.

Through a network of women's clubs, temperance associations, and social reform organizations, women exerted a growing influence on pub-

lic affairs. Founded in 1874, the Woman's Christian Temperance Union (WCTU) grew to become the era's largest female organization, with a membership by 1890 of 150,000. Under the banner of Home Protection, it moved from demanding the prohibition of alcoholic beverages (blamed for leading men to squander their wages on drink and treat their wives abusively) to a comprehensive program of economic and political reform, including the right to vote. Women, insisted Frances Willard, the group's president, must abandon the idea that "weakness" and dependence were their nature and join assertively in movements to change society.

At the same time, the center of gravity of feminism shifted toward an outlook more in keeping with prevailing racial and ethnic norms. The movement continued to argue for women's equality in employment, education, and politics. But with increasing frequency, the native-born, middle-class women who dominated the suffrage movement claimed the vote as educated members of a "superior race."

Immigrants and former slaves had been enfranchised with "ill-advised haste," declared Carrie Chapman Catt, president of the National American Woman Suffrage Association (created in 1890 to reunite the rival suffrage organizations formed after the Civil War). Indeed, Catt suggested, extending the vote to native-born white women would help to counteract the growing power of the "ignorant foreign vote" in the North and the dangerous potential for a second Reconstruction in the South. In 1895, the same year that Booker T. Washington delivered his Atlanta address, the National American Woman Suffrage Association held its annual convention in that segregated city. Like other American institutions, the organized movement for woman suffrage had made its peace with nativism and racism.

"A Woman's Liquor Raid," an illustration in the *National Police Gazette* in 1879, depicts a group of temperance crusaders destroying liquor containers in a Frederickstown, Ohio, saloon.

BECOMING A WORLD POWER

The New Imperialism

In world history, the last quarter of the nineteenth century is known as the age of imperialism, when rival European empires carved up large parts of the world among themselves. For most of this period, the United States remained a second-rate power.

The "new imperialism" that arose after 1870 was dominated by European powers and Japan. Belgium, Great Britain, and France consolidated their hold on colonies in Africa, and newly unified Germany acquired colonies there as well. By the early twentieth century, most of Asia, Africa, the Middle East, and the Pacific had been divided among these empires.

The global context

American Expansionism

Territorial expansion, of course, had been a feature of American life from well before independence. But the 1890s marked a major turning point in America's relationship with the rest of the world. Americans were increasingly aware of themselves as an emerging world power. "We are a great imperial Republic destined to exercise a controlling influence upon the actions of mankind and to affect the future of the world," proclaimed Henry Watterson, an influential newspaper editor.

"A great imperial Republic"

Until the 1890s, American expansion had taken place on the North American continent. Ever since the Monroe Doctrine (see Chapter 10), to be sure, many Americans had considered the Western Hemisphere an American sphere of influence. The last territorial acquisition before the 1890s had been Alaska, purchased from Russia by Secretary of State William H. Seward in 1867.

Expanding trade

Most Americans who looked overseas were interested in expanded trade, not territorial possessions. The country's agricultural and industrial production could no longer be absorbed entirely at home. By 1890, companies like Singer Sewing Machines and John D. Rockefeller's Standard Oil Company aggressively marketed their products abroad. Especially during economic downturns, business leaders insisted on the necessity of greater access to foreign customers. Middle-class American women, moreover, were becoming more and more desirous of clothing and food from abroad, and their demand for consumer goods such as "Oriental" fashions and exotic spices for cooking spurred the economic penetration of the Far East.

The Lure of Empire

Missionaries

One group of Americans who spread the nation's influence overseas were religious missionaries, thousands of whom ventured abroad in the late nineteenth century to spread Christianity, prepare the world for the second coming of Christ, and uplift the poor. Inspired by Dwight Moody, a Methodist evangelist, the Student Volunteer Movement for Foreign Missions sent more than 8,000 missionaries to "bring light to heathen worlds" across the globe.

Expansionism and international trade

A small group of late-nineteenth-century thinkers actively promoted American expansionism, warning that the country must not allow itself to be shut out of the scramble for empire. Naval officer Alfred T. Mahan, in *The Influence of Sea Power upon History* (1890), argued that no nation could prosper without a large fleet of ships engaged in international trade, protected by a powerful navy operating from overseas bases. His arguments influenced the outlook of James G. Blaine, who served as secretary of state during Benjamin

Harrison's presidency (1889–1893). Blaine urged the president to try to acquire Hawaii, Puerto Rico, and Cuba as strategic naval bases.

Although independent, Hawaii was already closely tied to the United States through treaties that exempted imports of its sugar from tariff duties and provided for the establishment of an American naval base at Pearl Harbor. Hawaii's economy was dominated by American-owned sugar plantations that employed a workforce of native islanders and Chinese, Japanese, and Filipino laborers under long-term contracts. Early in 1893, a group of American planters organized a rebellion that overthrew the Hawaii government of Queen Liliuokalani. On the eve of leaving office, Harrison submitted a treaty of annexation to the Senate. After determining that a majority of Hawaiians did not favor the treaty, Harrison's successor, Grover Cleveland, withdrew it. In July 1898, in the midst of the Spanish-American War, the United States finally annexed the Hawaiian Islands.

The depression that began in 1893 heightened the belief that a more aggressive foreign policy was necessary to stimulate American exports. These were the years when rituals like the Pledge of Allegiance and the practice of standing for the playing of "The Star-Spangled Banner" came into existence. New, mass-circulation newspapers also promoted nationalistic sentiments. By the late 1890s, papers like William Randolph Hearst's *New York Journal* and Joseph Pulitzer's *New York World*—dubbed the **"yellow press"** by their critics after the color in which Hearst printed a popular comic strip—were selling a million copies each day by mixing sensational accounts of crime and political corruption with aggressive appeals to patriotic sentiments.

A cartoon in *Puck*, December 1, 1897, imagines the annexation of Hawaii by the United States as a shotgun wedding. The minister, President McKinley, reads from a book entitled *Annexation Policy*. The Hawaiian bride appears to be looking for a way to escape. Most Hawaiians did not support annexation.

The "Splendid Little War"

All these factors contributed to America's emergence as a world power in the Spanish-American War of 1898. But the immediate origins of the war lay not at home but in the long Cuban struggle for independence from Spain. Ten years of guerrilla war had followed a Cuban revolt in 1868. The movement for independence resumed in 1895. As reports circulated of widespread suffering caused by the Spanish policy of rounding up civilians and moving them into detention camps, the Cuban struggle won growing support in the United States.

Cuban struggle for independence

Demands for intervention escalated after February 15, 1898, when an explosion—probably accidental, a later investigation concluded—destroyed the American battleship **U.S.S. *Maine*** in Havana harbor, with the loss of nearly 270 lives. After Spain rejected an American demand for a cease-fire on the island and eventual Cuban independence, President

BECOMING A WORLD POWER | 535

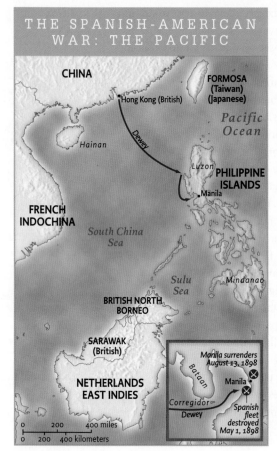

THE SPANISH-AMERICAN WAR: THE PACIFIC

CHINA

FORMOSA (Taiwan) (Japanese)

Hong Kong (British)

Pacific Ocean

Hainan

Dewey

Luzon

PHILIPPINE ISLANDS

Manila

FRENCH INDOCHINA

South China Sea

Sulu Sea

Mindanao

BRITISH NORTH BORNEO

SARAWAK (British)

NETHERLANDS EAST INDIES

0   200   400 miles
0   200   400 kilometers

Bataan

Manila surrenders August 13, 1898

Manila

Corregidor

Dewey

Spanish fleet destroyed May 1, 1898

THE SPANISH-AMERICAN WAR: THE CARIBBEAN

UNITED STATES

Santiago

San Juan Hill July 1, 1898

Spanish fleet destroyed July 3, 1898

Tampa

U.S.S. Maine sunk February 1898

BAHAMAS

Atlantic Ocean

Havana

CUBA

Santiago

HAITI

PUERTO RICO

JAMAICA (British)

DOMINICAN REPUBLIC

Caribbean Sea

Pacific Ocean

0   200   400 miles
0   200   400 kilometers

American victories
American forces
American naval blockade
Spanish forces
Spanish possessions

In both the Caribbean and the Pacific, the United States achieved swift victories over Spain in the Spanish-American War.

The Spanish-American War

McKinley in April asked Congress for a declaration of war. The purpose, declared Senator Henry Teller of Colorado, was to aid Cuban patriots in their struggle for "liberty and freedom." To underscore the government's humanitarian intentions, Congress adopted the Teller Amendment, stating that the United States had no intention of annexing or dominating the island.

Secretary of State John Hay called the Spanish-American conflict a "splendid little war." It lasted only four months and resulted in fewer than 400 American combat deaths. The war's most decisive engagement took place not in Cuba but at Manila Bay, a strategic harbor in the Philippine Islands in the distant Pacific Ocean. Here, on May 1, the American navy under Admiral George Dewey defeated a Spanish fleet. Soon afterward, soldiers went ashore, becoming the first American army units to engage in combat outside the Western Hemisphere. July witnessed another naval victory off Santiago, Cuba, and the landing of American troops on Cuba and Puerto Rico.

Roosevelt at San Juan Hill

The most highly publicized land battle of the war took place in Cuba. This was the charge up San Juan Hill, outside Santiago, by Theodore Roosevelt's Rough Riders. An ardent expansionist, Roosevelt had long believed that a war would reinvigorate the nation's unity and sense of manhood, which had suffered, he felt, during the 1890s. A few months shy of his fortieth birthday when war broke out, Roosevelt resigned his post as assistant secretary of the navy to raise a volunteer cavalry unit, which rushed to Cuba to participate in the fighting. His exploits made Roosevelt a national hero. He was elected governor of New York that fall and in 1900 became McKinley's vice president.

Rough Riders

Theodore Roosevelt

An American Empire

With the backing of the yellow press, the war quickly escalated from a crusade to aid the suffering Cubans to an imperial venture that ended with the United States in possession of a small overseas empire. McKinley became convinced that the United States could neither return the Philippines to Spain nor grant them independence, for which he believed the inhabitants unprepared. In an interview with a group of Methodist ministers, the president spoke of receiving a divine revelation that Americans had a duty to "uplift and civilize" the Filipino people and to train them for self-government. In the treaty with Spain that ended the war, the United States acquired the Philippines, Puerto Rico, and the Pacific island of Guam. As for Cuba, before recognizing its independence, McKinley

Acquiring possessions

Charge of the Rough Riders at San Juan Hill, a painting by Frederic Remington, depicts the celebrated unit, commanded by Theodore Roosevelt, in action in Cuba during the Spanish-American War of 1898. Roosevelt, on horseback, leads the troops. Remington had been sent to the island the previous year by publisher William Randolph Hearst to provide pictures of Spanish atrocities during the Cuban war for independence in the hope of boosting the *New York Journal*'s circulation.

Hacienda La Fortuna, a sugar plantation, as depicted by the Puerto Rican artist Francisco Oller in 1885. From left to right the buildings are a warehouse, plantation home, and modern steam-powered sugar mill. The acquisition of the island by the United States in the Spanish-American War strengthened the hold of "sugar barons" on the Puerto Rican economy.

Platt Amendment

In this cartoon comment on the American effort to suppress the movement for Philippine independence, Uncle Sam tries to subdue a knife-wielding insurgent.

forced the island's new government to approve the **Platt Amendment** to the new Cuban constitution (drafted by Senator Orville H. Platt of Connecticut), which authorized the United States to intervene militarily whenever it saw fit. The United States also acquired a permanent lease on naval stations in Cuba, including what is now the facility at Guantánamo Bay.

America's interest in its new possessions had more to do with trade than with gaining wealth from natural resources or large-scale American settlement. Puerto Rico and Cuba were gateways to Latin America, strategic outposts from which American naval and commercial power could be projected throughout the hemisphere. The Philippines, Guam, and Hawaii lay astride shipping routes to the markets of Japan and China. In 1899, soon after the end of the Spanish-American War, Secretary of State John Hay announced the **Open Door Policy**, demanding that European powers that had recently divided China into commercial spheres of influence grant equal access to American exports. The Open Door referred to the free movement of goods and money, not people. Even as the United States banned the immigration of Chinese into this country, it insisted on access to the markets and investment opportunities of Asia.

The Philippine War

Many Cubans, Filipinos, and Puerto Ricans had welcomed American intervention as a way of breaking Spain's long hold on these colonies. Large planters looked forward to greater access to American markets. Nationalists and labor leaders admired America's democratic ideals and believed that American participation in the destruction of Spanish rule would lead to social reform and political self-government.

American intervention

But the American determination to exercise continued control, direct or indirect, led to a rapid change in local opinion, nowhere more so than in the Philippines. Filipinos had been fighting a war against Spain since 1896. After Dewey's victory at Manila Bay, their leader, Emilio Aguinaldo, established a provisional government with a constitution modeled on that of the United States. But once McKinley decided to retain possession of the islands, the Filipino movement turned against the United States. The result was a second war, far longer (it lasted from 1899 to 1903) and bloodier (it cost the lives of more than 100,000 Filipinos and 4,200 Americans) than the Spanish-American conflict. Today, the **Philippine War** is perhaps the least remembered of all American wars.

Filipino movement

Once in control of the Philippines, the colonial administration took seriously the idea of modernizing the islands. It expanded railroads and harbors, brought in American schoolteachers and public health officials, and sought to modernize agriculture (although efforts to persuade local farmers to substitute corn for rice ran afoul of the Filipino climate and cultural traditions).

The United States, said President McKinley, had an obligation to its "little brown brothers." Yet in all the new possessions, American policies tended to serve the interests of land-based local elites—and bequeathed enduring poverty to the majority of the rural population. Under American rule, Puerto Rico, previously an island of diversified small farmers, became a low-wage plantation economy controlled by absentee American corporations. By the 1920s, its residents were among the poorest in the entire Caribbean.

Simulated drowning or the "water cure," later known as waterboarding, was widely employed by American soldiers to elicit information from captured enemy combatants during the Philippine War. Over a century later, its use during the "war on terror" would arouse worldwide criticism.

Citizens or Subjects?

American rule also brought with it American racial attitudes. In an 1899 poem, the British writer Rudyard Kipling urged the United States to take up the "white man's burden" of imperialism. American proponents of

VOICES OF FREEDOM

From Booker T. Washington, Address at the Atlanta Cotton Exposition (1895)

In 1895, the year of the death of Frederick Douglass, Booker T. Washington delivered a speech at an exposition in Atlanta advocating a new strategy for racial progress. Blacks, he declared, should remain in the South, turn away from agitation for civil and political rights, adjust to segregation, and seek, with white cooperation, to improve their economic condition.

A ship lost at sea for many days suddenly sighted a friendly vessel. From the mast of the unfortunate vessel was seen a signal, "Water, water; we die of thirst!" The answer from the friendly vessel at once came back, "Cast down your bucket where you are." . . . The captain of the distressed vessel, at last heeding the injunction, cast down his bucket, and it came up full of fresh, sparkling water from the mouth of the Amazon River. To those of my race who depend on bettering their condition in a foreign land or who underestimate the importance of cultivating friendly relations with the Southern white man, who is their next door neighbor, I would say: "Cast down your bucket where you are"—cast it down in making friends in every manly way of the people of all races by whom we are surrounded.

Cast it down in agriculture, mechanics, in commerce, in domestic service, and in the professions. . . . Our greatest danger is that in the great leap from slavery to freedom we may overlook the fact that the masses of us are to live by the productions of our hands, and fail to keep in mind that we shall prosper in proportion as we learn to dignify and glorify common labour, and put brains and skill into the common occupations of life. . . . No race can prosper till it learns that there is as much dignity in tilling a field as in writing a poem. . . . Nor should we permit our grievances to overshadow our opportunities.

To those of the white race who look to the incoming of those of foreign birth and strange tongue and habits for the prosperity of the South, were I permitted I would repeat what I say to my own race, "Cast down your bucket where you are." Cast it down among the eight millions of Negroes. . . . In all things that are purely social we can be as separate as the fingers, yet one as the hand in all things essential to mutual progress. . . .

The wisest among my race understand that the agitation of questions of social equality is the extremest folly, and that progress in the enjoyment of all the privileges that will come to us must be the result of severe and constant struggle rather than of artificial forcing. No race that has anything to contribute to the markets of the world is long in any degree ostracized.

From W. E. B. Du Bois, "Of Mr. Booker T. Washington and Others" (1903)

The most powerful critique of Washington's program came from the pen of the black educator and activist W. E. B. Du Bois. In *The Souls of Black Folk*, a collection of essays on the state of American race relations, he sought to revive the tradition of agitation for basic civil, political, and educational rights.

Easily the most striking thing in the history of the American Negro since 1876 is the ascendancy of Mr. Booker T. Washington. . . . The time is come when one may speak in all sincerity and utter courtesy of the mistakes and shortcomings of Mr. Washington's career, as well as of his triumphs. . . .

This is an age of unusual economic development, and Mr. Washington's programme naturally takes an economic cast, becoming a gospel of Work and Money to such an extent as apparently almost completely to overshadow the higher aims of life. . . . The reaction from the sentiment of wartime has given impetus to race prejudice against Negroes, and Mr. Washington withdraws many of the high demands of Negroes as men and American citizens. In other periods of intensified prejudice all the Negro's tendency to self assertion has been called forth; at this period a policy of submission is advocated. In the history of nearly all other races and peoples the doctrine preached at such crises has been that manly self respect is worth more than lands and houses, and that a people who voluntarily surrender such respect, or cease striving for it, are not worth civilizing. Mr. Washington distinctly asks that black people give up, at least for the present, three things,—First, political power, Second, insistence on civil rights, Third, higher education of Negro youth,—and concentrate all their energies on industrial education, the accumulation of wealth, and the conciliation of the South. . . . The question then comes: Is it possible, and probable, that nine millions of men can make effective progress in economic lines if they are deprived of political rights, made a servile caste, and allowed only the most meagre chance for developing their exceptional men? If history and reason give any distinct answer to these questions, it is an emphatic No. . . . [Blacks are] bound to ask of this nation three things. 1. The right to vote. 2. Civic equality 3. The education of youth according to ability. . . . Negroes must insist continually, in season and out of season, that voting is necessary to modern manhood, that color discrimination is barbarism, and that black boys need education as well as white boys. . . . By every civilized and peaceful method we must strive for the rights which the world accords to men.

QUESTIONS

1. *What does Washington believe are the main routes to black advancement?*

2. *Why does Du Bois think that Washington's outlook reflects major elements of social thought in the 1890s?*

3. *How do the two men differ in their understanding of what is required for blacks to enjoy genuine freedom?*

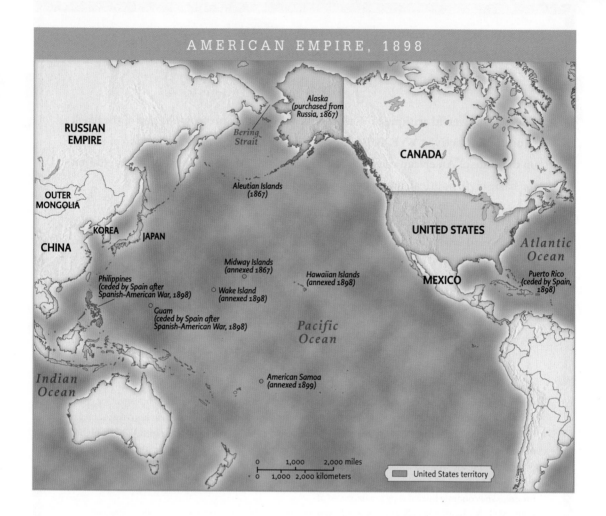

AMERICAN EMPIRE, 1898

RUSSIAN EMPIRE

Alaska (purchased from Russia, 1867)

Bering Strait

CANADA

OUTER MONGOLIA

Aleutian Islands (1867)

KOREA JAPAN

CHINA

UNITED STATES

Atlantic Ocean

Midway Islands (annexed 1867)

Hawaiian Islands (annexed 1898)

MEXICO

Puerto Rico (ceded by Spain, 1898)

Philippines (ceded by Spain after Spanish-American War, 1898)

Wake Island (annexed 1898)

Guam (ceded by Spain after Spanish-American War, 1898)

Pacific Ocean

Indian Ocean

American Samoa (annexed 1899)

0   1,000   2,000 miles
0   1,000 2,000 kilometers

United States territory

As a result of the Spanish-American War, the United States became the ruler of a far-flung overseas empire.

Colonies in the American framework

empire agreed that the domination of non-white peoples by whites formed part of the progress of civilization.

America's triumphant entry into the ranks of imperial powers sparked an intense debate over the relationship among political democracy, race, and American citizenship. The American system of government had no provision for permanent colonies. The right of every people to self-government was one of the main principles of the Declaration of Independence. The idea of an "empire of liberty" assumed that new territories would eventually be admitted as equal states and their residents would be American citizens. In the aftermath of the Spanish-American War, however, nationalism, democracy, and American freedom emerged more closely identified than ever with notions of Anglo-Saxon superiority.

The Foraker Act of 1900 declared Puerto Rico an "insular territory," different from previous territories in the West. Its 1 million inhabitants were defined as citizens of Puerto Rico, not the United States, and denied a future path to statehood. Filipinos occupied a similar status. In a series of cases decided between 1901 and 1904 and known collectively as the **Insular Cases**, the Supreme Court held that the Constitution did not fully apply to the territories recently acquired by the United States—a significant limitation of the scope of American freedom. Thus, two principles central to American freedom since the War of Independence—no taxation without representation and government based on the consent of the governed—were abandoned when it came to the nation's new possessions.

In the twentieth century, the territories acquired in 1898 would follow different paths. Hawaii, which had a sizable population of American missionaries and planters, became a traditional territory. Its population, except for Asian immigrant laborers, became American citizens, and it was admitted as a state in 1959. After nearly a half-century of American rule, the Philippines achieved independence in 1946. Until 1950, the U.S. Navy administered Guam, which remains today an "unincorporated" territory. As for Puerto Rico, it is sometimes called "the world's oldest colony," because ever since the Spanish conquered the island in 1493 it has lacked full self-government. It elects its own government but lacks a voice in Congress (and in the election of the U.S. president).

This propaganda photograph from 1898 depicts the Spanish-American War as a source of national reconciliation in the United States (with Confederate and Union soldiers shaking hands) and of freedom for Cuba (personified by a girl whose arm holds a broken chain).

Drawing the Global Color Line

Just as American ideas about liberty and self-government had circulated around the world in the Age of Revolution, American racial attitudes had a global impact in the age of empire. The turn of the twentieth century was a time of worldwide concern about immigration, race relations, and the "white man's burden," all of which inspired a global sense of fraternity among "Anglo-Saxon" nations. Chinese exclusion in the United States strongly influenced anti-Chinese laws adopted in Canada. The Union of South Africa, inaugurated in 1911, saw its own policy of racial separation—later known as apartheid—as following in the footsteps of segregation in the United States.

"White man's burden"

The first step towards lightening

The White Man's Burden

is through teaching the virtues of cleanliness.

Pears' Soap

is a potent factor in brightening the dark corners of the earth as civilization advances, while amongst the cultured of all nations it holds the highest place—it is the ideal toilet soap.

An advertisement employs the idea of a "white man's burden" (borrowed from a poem by Rudyard Kipling) as a way of promoting the virtues of Pears' Soap. Accompanying text claims that Pears' is "the ideal toilet soap" for "the cultured of all nations," and an agent of civilization in "the dark corners of the earth."

"Republic or Empire?"

The emergence of the United States as an imperial power sparked intense debate. Opponents formed the **Anti-Imperialist League**. It united writers and social reformers who believed American energies should be directed at home, businessmen fearful of the cost of maintaining overseas outposts, and racists who did not wish to bring non-white populations into the United States. America's historic mission, the League declared, was to "help the world by an example of successful self-government," not to conquer other peoples.

In 1900, Democrats again nominated William Jennings Bryan to run against McKinley. The Democratic platform opposed the Philippine War for placing the United States in the "un-American" position of "crushing with military force" another people's desire for "liberty and self-government." George S. Boutwell, president of the Anti-Imperialist League, declared that the most pressing question in the election was the nation's future character—"republic or empire?"

But without any sense of contradiction, proponents of an imperial foreign policy also adopted the language of freedom. America's was a "benevolent" imperialism, they claimed, rooted in a national mission to uplift backward cultures and spread liberty across the globe. Riding the wave of patriotic sentiment inspired by the war, and with the economy having recovered from the depression of 1893–1897, McKinley in 1900 repeated his 1896 triumph.

At the dawn of the twentieth century, the United States seemed poised to take its place among the world's great powers. In 1900, many features that would mark American life for much of the twentieth century were already apparent. The United States led the world in industrial production. The political system had stabilized. The white North and South had achieved reconciliation, while rigid lines of racial exclusion—the segregation of blacks, Chinese exclusion, Indian reservations—limited the boundaries of freedom and citizenship.

Yet the questions central to nineteenth-century debates over freedom—the relationship between political and economic liberty, the role of government in creating the conditions of freedom, and the definition of those entitled to enjoy the rights of citizens—had not been permanently answered. Nor had the dilemma of how to reconcile America's role as an empire with traditional ideas of freedom been resolved. These were the challenges bequeathed by the nineteenth century to the first generation of the twentieth.

CHAPTER REVIEW AND ONLINE RESOURCES

REVIEW QUESTIONS

1. *What economic and political issues gave rise to the Populist Party, and what changes did the party advocate?*

2. *How did employers use state and federal forces to protect their own economic interests, and what were the results?*

3. *Compare and contrast the goals, strategies, and membership of the American Federation of Labor and the Knights of Labor (you may want to refer back to Chapter 16).*

4. *Who were the Redeemers, and how did they change society and politics in the New South?*

5. *Explain how changes in politics, economics, social factors, and violence interacted to affect the situation of African-Americans in the New South.*

6. *How did religion and the idea of the Lost Cause give support to a new understanding of the Civil War?*

7. *What ideas and interests motivated the United States to create an empire in the late nineteenth century?*

8. *Compare the arguments for and against U.S. imperialism. Be sure to consider the views of Alfred T. Mahan and Emilio Aguinaldo.*

9. *What rights did Chinese immigrants and Chinese-Americans gain in these years, and what limitations did they experience? How did their experiences set the stage for other restrictions on immigration?*

KEY TERMS

Populists (p. 515)
Coxey's Army (p. 518)
New South (p. 521)
Kansas Exodus (p. 523)
grandfather clause (p. 524)
disenfranchisement (p. 525)
Plessy v. Ferguson (p. 525)
"separate but equal" (p. 525)
lynching (p. 526)
the Lost Cause (p. 527)
new immigrants (p. 528)
Immigration Restriction League (p. 528)
Chinese Exclusion Act (p. 529)
Atlanta Compromise (p. 531)
American Federation of Labor (p. 531)
yellow press (p. 535)
U.S.S. *Maine* (p. 535)
Platt Amendment (p. 538)
Open Door Policy (p. 538)
Philippine War (p. 539)
Insular Cases (p. 543)
Anti-Imperialist League (p. 544)

Go to INQUIZITIVE

To see what you know—and learn what you've missed—with personalized feedback along the way.

Visit the *Give Me Liberty!* **Student Site** for primary source documents and images, interactive maps, author videos featuring Eric Foner, and more.

1889	Hull House founded
1901	Socialist Party founded in United States
	President McKinley assassinated
1903	Ford Motor Company established
1904	Northern Securities dissolved
1905	Industrial Workers of the World established
1906	Upton Sinclair's *The Jungle*
	Meat Inspection Act
	Pure Food and Drug Act
	Hepburn Act
	John A. Ryan's *A Living Wage*
1908	*Muller v. Oregon*
1911	Triangle Shirtwaist Company fire
	Society of American Indians founded
1912	Theodore Roosevelt organizes the Progressive Party
1913	Sixteenth Amendment
	Seventeenth Amendment
	Federal Reserve established
1914	Federal Trade Commission established
	Clayton Act

CHAPTER 18

THE PROGRESSIVE ERA

★

1900-1916

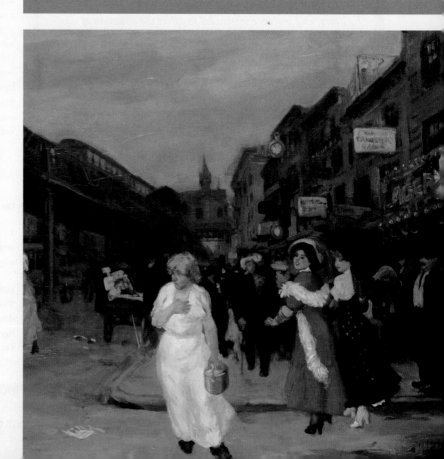

Sixth Avenue and Thirtieth Street, a 1907 painting by John Sloan, depicts a busy street in New York City in an area known as the Tenderloin, with an elevated railroad overhead. Sloan was one of a group of painters called the Ashcan School because of their focus on everyday city life. Here, he emphasizes the vitality of the city and the mingling of people of different social classes on its streets.

It was late afternoon on March 25, 1911, when fire broke out at the Triangle Shirtwaist Company. The factory occupied the top three floors of a ten-story building in the Greenwich Village neighborhood of New York City. Here some 500 workers, mostly young Jewish and Italian immigrant women, toiled at sewing machines producing ladies' blouses, some earning as little as three dollars per week. Those who tried to escape the blaze discovered that the doors to the stairwell had been locked—the owner's way, it was later charged, of discouraging theft and unauthorized bathroom breaks. The fire department rushed to the scene with high-pressure hoses. But their ladders reached only to the sixth floor. Onlookers watched in horror as girls leaped from the upper stories. By the time the blaze had been put out, 46 bodies lay on the street and 100 more were found inside the building.

The Triangle fire was not the worst fire disaster in American history (seven years earlier, over 1,000 people had died in a blaze on the *General Slocum* excursion boat in New York Harbor). But it had an unrivaled impact on public consciousness. In its wake, efforts to organize the city's workers accelerated, and the state legislature passed new factory inspection laws and fire safety codes.

Triangle focused attention on the social divisions that plagued American society during the first two decades of the twentieth century, a period known as the Progressive era. These were years when economic expansion produced millions of new jobs and brought an unprecedented array of goods within reach of American consumers. Cities expanded rapidly—by 1920, for the first time, more Americans lived in towns and cities than in rural areas. Yet severe inequality remained the most visible feature of the urban landscape, and persistent labor strife raised anew the question of government's role in combating it.

The word "Progressive" came into common use around 1910 as a way of describing a broad, loosely defined political movement of individuals and groups who hoped to bring about significant change in American social and political life. Progressives included forward-looking businessmen who realized that workers must be accorded a voice in economic decision making, and labor activists bent on empowering industrial workers. Other major contributors to **Progressivism** were members of female reform organizations who hoped to protect women and children from exploitation, social scientists who believed that academic research would help to solve social problems, and members of an anxious middle class who feared that their status was threatened by the rise of big business.

FOCUS QUESTIONS

- *Why was the city such a central element in Progressive America?*

- *How did the labor and women's movements expand the meanings of American freedom?*

- *In what ways did Progressivism include both democratic and antidemocratic impulses?*

- *How did the Progressive presidents foster the rise of the nation-state?*

As this and the following chapter will discuss, Progressive reformers addressed issues of American freedom in varied, contradictory ways. The era saw the expansion of political and economic freedom through the reinvigoration of the movement for woman suffrage, the use of political power to expand workers' rights, and efforts to improve democratic government by weakening the power of city bosses and giving ordinary citizens more influence on legislation. It witnessed the flowering of understandings of freedom based on individual fulfillment and personal self-determination. At the same time, many Progressives supported efforts to limit the full enjoyment of freedom to those deemed fit to exercise it properly. The new system of white supremacy born in the 1890s became fully consolidated in the South. Growing numbers of native-born Americans demanded that immigrants abandon their traditional cultures and become fully "Americanized." And efforts were made at the local and national levels to place political decision making in the hands of experts who did not have to answer to the electorate. The idea of freedom remained as contested as ever in Progressive America.

AN URBAN AGE AND A CONSUMER SOCIETY

Farms and Cities

Economic growth

The Progressive era was a period of explosive economic growth, fueled by increasing industrial production, a rapid rise in population, and the continued expansion of the consumer marketplace. In the first decade of the twentieth century, the economy's total output rose by about 85 percent. For the last time in American history, farms and cities grew together. Farm families poured into the western Great Plains. More than 1 million claims for free government land were filed under the Homestead Act of 1862—more than in the previous forty years combined. Irrigation transformed the Imperial Valley of California and parts of Arizona into major areas of commercial farming.

Growth of the cities

But it was the city that became the focus of Progressive politics and of a new mass-consumer society. The United States counted twenty-one cities whose population exceeded 100,000 in 1910, the largest of them New York, with 4.7 million residents. The twenty-three square miles of Manhattan Island were home to over 2 million people, more than lived in thirty-three of the states.

The stark urban inequalities of the 1890s continued into the Progressive era. Immigrant families in New York's downtown tenements often had no electricity or indoor toilets. Three miles to the north stood the mansions of Fifth Avenue's Millionaire's Row. According to one estimate, J. P. Morgan's financial firm directly or indirectly controlled 40 percent of all financial and industrial capital in the United States.

TABLE 18.1 Rise of the City, 1880–1920

YEAR	URBAN POPULATION (PERCENTAGE)	NUMBER OF CITIES WITH 100,000+ POPULATION
1880	20%	12
1890	28	15
1900	38	18
1910	50	21
1920	68	26

The Muckrakers

Some observers saw the city as a place where corporate greed undermined traditional American values. At a time when more than 2 million children under the age of fifteen worked for wages, Lewis Hine photographed child laborers to draw attention to persistent social inequality. A new generation of journalists writing for mass-circulation national magazines exposed the ills of industrial and urban life. *The Shame of the Cities* (1904) by Lincoln Steffens showed how party bosses and business leaders profited from political corruption. Theodore Roosevelt disparaged such writing as **muckraking**, the use of journalistic skills to expose the underside of American life.

Major novelists took a similar unsparing approach to social ills. Perhaps the era's most influential novel was Upton Sinclair's *The Jungle* (1906), whose description of unsanitary slaughterhouses and the sale of rotten meat stirred public outrage and led directly to the passage of the Pure Food and Drug Act and the Meat Inspection Act of 1906.

Immigration as a Global Process

If one thing characterized early-twentieth-century cities, it was their immigrant character. The "new immigration" from southern and eastern Europe (discussed in Chapter 17) had begun around 1890 but reached its peak during the Progressive era. Between 1901 and the outbreak of World War I in Europe in 1914, some 13 million immigrants came to the United States, the majority from Italy, Russia, and the Austro-Hungarian empire. In fact, Progressive-era immigration formed part of a larger process

Lewis Hine used his camera to chronicle the plight of child laborers such as this young spinner in a southern cotton factory.

of worldwide migration set in motion by industrial expansion and the decline of traditional agriculture.

During the years from 1840 to 1914 (when immigration to the United States would be virtually cut off, first by the outbreak of World War I and then by legislation), perhaps 40 million persons emigrated to the United States and another 20 million to other parts of the Western Hemisphere, including Canada, Argentina, Brazil, and the Caribbean. Numerous causes inspired this uprooting of population. Rural southern and eastern Europe and large parts of Asia were regions marked by widespread poverty and illiteracy, burdensome taxation, and declining economies. Political turmoil at home, like the revolution that engulfed Mexico after 1911, also inspired emigration.

Causes of emigration

Most European immigrants to the United States entered through **Ellis Island**. Located in New York Harbor, this became in 1892 the nation's main facility for processing immigrants. Millions of Americans today trace their ancestry to immigrants who passed through Ellis Island.

Immigration in the West

At the same time, an influx of Asian and Mexican newcomers was taking place in the West. After the exclusion of immigrants from China in the late nineteenth century, approximately 72,000 Japanese arrived, primarily to work as agricultural laborers in California's fruit and vegetable fields and on Hawaii's sugar plantations. Between 1910 and 1940, Angel Island in San Francisco Bay—the "Ellis Island of the West"—served as the main entry point for immigrants from Asia. Far larger was Mexican immigration. Between 1900 and 1930, some 1 million Mexicans (more than 10 percent of that country's population) entered the United States—a number exceeded by only a few European countries.

By 1910, one-seventh of the American population was foreign-born, the highest percentage in the country's history.

TABLE 18.2 Immigrants and Their Children as Percentage of Population, Ten Major Cities, 1920

CITY	PERCENTAGE
New York City	76%
Cleveland	72
Boston	72
Chicago	71
Detroit	65
San Francisco	64
Minneapolis	63
Pittsburgh	59
Seattle	55
Los Angeles	45

The Immigrant Quest for Freedom

Like their nineteenth-century predecessors, the new immigrants arrived imagining the United States as a land of freedom, where all persons enjoyed equality before the law, could worship as they pleased, enjoyed economic opportunity, and had been emancipated from the oppressive social hierarchies of their homelands. "America is a free country," one Polish immigrant wrote home. "You don't have to be a serf to anyone." Agents sent abroad by the American government to investigate the reasons for large-scale immigration reported that the main impetus was a desire to share in the "freedom and prosperity enjoyed by the people of the United States." Although some of the new immigrants, especially Jews fleeing religious persecution in the Russian empire, thought of themselves as permanent emigrants, the majority initially planned to earn enough money to return home and purchase land. Groups like Mexicans and Italians included many "birds of passage," who remained only temporarily in the United States.

The new immigrants clustered in close-knit "ethnic" neighborhoods with their own shops, theaters, and community organizations, and often continued to speak their native tongues. Although most immigrants earned more than was possible in the impoverished regions from which they came, they endured low wages, long hours, and dangerous working conditions. In the mines and factories of Pennsylvania and the Midwest, eastern European immigrants performed low-wage unskilled labor, whereas native-born workers dominated skilled and supervisory jobs. The vast majority of Mexican immigrants became poorly paid agricultural, mine, and railroad laborers, with little prospect of upward economic mobility. "My people are not in America," remarked one Slavic priest, "they are under it."

A piece of sheet music, published in 1911 and directed at Jewish immigrants, celebrates the United States as the Land of the Free.

Working conditions

Consumer Freedom

Cities, however, were also the birthplace of a mass-consumption society that added new meaning to American freedom. During the Progressive era, large downtown department stores, neighborhood chain stores, and retail mail-order houses made available to consumers throughout the country the vast array of goods now pouring from the nation's factories. By 1910, Americans could purchase, among many other items, electric sewing machines, washing machines, vacuum cleaners, and record players.

The rise of mass consumption

Leisure activities also took on the characteristics of mass consumption. Amusement parks, dance halls, and theaters attracted large crowds of city dwellers. By 1910, 25 million Americans per week, mostly working-class urban residents, were attending "nickelodeons"—motion-picture theaters whose five-cent admission charge was far lower than that of vaudeville shows.

Leisure activities

Women at work in a shoe factory, 1908.

The Working Woman

The new visibility of women in urban public places—at work, as shoppers, and in places of entertainment like cinemas and dance halls—indicated that traditional gender roles were changing dramatically in Progressive America. As the Triangle fire revealed, more and more women were working for wages. Immigrant women were largely confined to low-paying factory employment. But for native-born white women, the kinds of jobs available expanded enormously. By 1920, around 25 percent of employed women were office workers or telephone operators. Female work was no longer confined to young, unmarried white women and adult black women. In 1920, of 8 million women working for wages, one-quarter were married and living with their husbands. The working woman—immigrant and native, working-class and professional—became a symbol of female emancipation. "We enjoy our independence and freedom" was the assertive statement of the Bachelor Girls Social Club, a group of female mail-order clerks in New York.

The desire to participate in the consumer society produced remarkably similar battles within immigrant families of all nationalities between parents and their self-consciously "free" children, especially daughters. Contemporaries, native and immigrant, noted how "the novelties and frivolities of fashion" appealed to young working women, who spent part of their meager wages on clothing and makeup and at places of entertainment. Daughters considered parents who tried to impose curfews or to prevent them from going out alone to dances or movies as old-fashioned and not sufficiently "American."

The Return from Toil, a drawing by John Sloan for the radical magazine *The Masses*, pictures working women not as downtrodden but as independent-minded, stylish, and self-confident.

	TABLE 18.3 Percentage of Women 14 Years and Older in the Labor Force		
YEAR	ALL WOMEN	MARRIED WOMEN	WOMEN AS % OF LABOR FORCE
1900	20.4%	5.6%	18%
1910	25.2	10.7	24
1920	23.3	9.0	24
1930	24.3	11.7	25

The Rise of Fordism

If any individual exemplified the new consumer society, it was Henry Ford. Ford did not invent the automobile, but he developed the techniques of production and marketing that brought it within the reach of ordinary Americans. In 1905, he established the Ford Motor Company, one of dozens of small automobile manufacturing firms that emerged in these years. Three years later, he introduced the Model T, a simple, light vehicle sturdy enough to navigate the country's poorly maintained roads.

In 1913, Ford's factory in Highland Park, Michigan, adopted the method of production known as the moving assembly line, in which car frames were brought to workers on a continuously moving conveyor belt. The process enabled Ford to expand output by greatly reducing the time it took to produce each car. In 1914, he raised wages at his factory to the unheard-of level of five dollars per day (more than double the pay of most industrial workers), enabling him to attract a steady stream of skilled laborers. When other businessmen criticized him for endangering profits by paying high wages, Ford replied that workers must be able to afford the goods being turned out by American factories. Ford's output rose from 34,000 cars, priced at $700 each, in 1910, to 730,000 Model T's that sold at a price of $316 (well within the reach of many workers) in 1916. The economic system based on mass production and mass consumption came to be called **Fordism**.

The Promise of Abundance

As economic production shifted from capital goods (steel, railroad equipment, etc.) to consumer products, the new advertising industry perfected ways of increasing sales, often by linking goods with the idea of freedom. Numerous products took "liberty" as a brand name or used an image of the Statue of Liberty as a sales device. Economic abundance would eventually come to define the "American way of life," in which personal fulfillment was to be found through acquiring material goods.

The maturation of the consumer economy gave rise to concepts—a "living wage" and an **"American standard of living"**—that offered a new

TABLE 18.4 Percentage of Women Workers in Various Occupations

OCCUPATION	1900	1920
Professional, technical	8.2%	11.7%
Clerical	4.0	18.7
Sales workers	4.3	6.2
Unskilled and semiskilled manufacturing	23.7	20.2
Household workers	28.7	15.7

One of the numerous advertisements of the early twentieth century that invoked the Statue of Liberty to market consumer goods, in this case a brand of crackers.

TABLE 18.5 Sales of Passenger Cars	
YEAR	NUMBER OF CARS (IN THOUSANDS)
1900	4.1
1905	24.2
1910	181.0
1915	895.9
1920	1,905.5
1925	3,735.1

language for criticizing the inequalities of wealth and power in Progressive America. Father John A. Ryan's influential book *A Living Wage* (1906) described a decent standard of living (one that enabled a person to participate in the consumer economy) as a "natural and absolute" right of citizenship. His book sought to translate into American terms Pope Leo XIII's powerful statement of 1894, *Rerum Novarum*, which criticized the divorce of economic life from ethical considerations, endorsed the right of workers to organize unions, and repudiated competitive individualism in favor of a more cooperative vision of the good society. For the first time in the nation's history, mass consumption came to occupy a central place in descriptions of American society and its future.

An advertisement for Palmolive soap illustrates how companies marketed goods to consumers by creating anxiety and invoking exotic images. The accompanying text promises "a perfect skin" and includes an imagined image of Cleopatra, claiming that the soap embodies "ancient beauty arts." By 1915, Palmolive was the best-selling soap in the world.

VARIETIES OF PROGRESSIVISM

The immediate task, in the Progressives' view, was to humanize industrial capitalism and find common ground in a society still racked by labor conflict and experiencing massive immigration from abroad. Some Progressives proposed to return to a competitive marketplace populated by small producers. Others accepted the permanence of the large corporation and looked to the government to reverse the growing concentration of wealth and to ensure social justice. Still others would relocate freedom from the economic and political worlds to a private realm of personal fulfillment and unimpeded self-expression. But nearly all Progressives agreed that freedom must be infused with new meaning to deal with the economic and social conditions of the early twentieth century.

Industrial Freedom

In Progressive America, complaints of a loss of freedom came not only from the most poorly paid factory workers but from better-off employees as well. Large firms in the automobile, electrical, steel, and other industries sought to implement greater control over the work process. Efficiency expert Frederick W. Taylor pioneered what he called **scientific management**. Through scientific study, Taylor believed, the "one best way" of producing goods could be determined and implemented. The role of workers was to obey the detailed instructions of supervisors. Not surprisingly, many skilled workers saw the erosion of their traditional influence over the work process as a loss of freedom.

These developments helped to place the ideas of "industrial freedom" and "industrial democracy," which had entered the political vocabulary in the Gilded Age, at the center of political discussion during the Progressive era. Lack of "industrial freedom" was widely believed to lie at the root of the much-discussed "labor problem." Many Progressives believed that the key to increasing industrial freedom lay in empowering workers to participate in economic decision making via strong unions. Louis D. Brandeis, an active ally of the labor movement whom President Woodrow Wilson appointed to the Supreme Court in 1916, maintained that unions embodied an essential principle of freedom—the right of people to govern themselves. The contradiction between "political liberty" and "industrial slavery," Brandeis insisted, was America's foremost social problem.

Roller skaters with socialist leaflets during a New York City strike in 1916. A "scab" is a worker who crosses the picket line during a strike.

The Socialist Presence and Eugene Debs

Economic freedom was also a rallying cry of American socialism, which reached its greatest influence during the Progressive era. Founded in 1901, the **Socialist Party** called for immediate reforms such as free college education, legislation to improve the condition of laborers, and, as an ultimate goal, democratic control over the economy through public ownership of railroads and factories.

Peak of American socialism

By 1912, the Socialist Party claimed 150,000 dues-paying members, published hundreds of newspapers, enjoyed substantial support in the American Federation of Labor (AFL), and had elected scores of local officials. Socialism flourished in diverse communities throughout the country. On the Lower East Side of New York City, it arose from the economic exploitation of immigrant workers and Judaism's tradition of social reform. Here, a vibrant socialist culture developed, complete with Yiddish-language newspapers and theaters, as well as large public meetings and street demonstrations. In 1914, the district elected socialist Meyer London to Congress. Another center of socialist strength was Milwaukee, where Victor Berger, a German-born teacher and newspaper editor, mobilized local AFL unions into a potent political force. Socialism also made inroads among tenant farmers in old Populist areas like Oklahoma, and in the mining regions of Idaho and Montana.

Centers of socialist strength

No one was more important in spreading the socialist gospel or linking it to ideals of equality, self-government, and freedom than Eugene V. Debs,

Eugene V. Debs

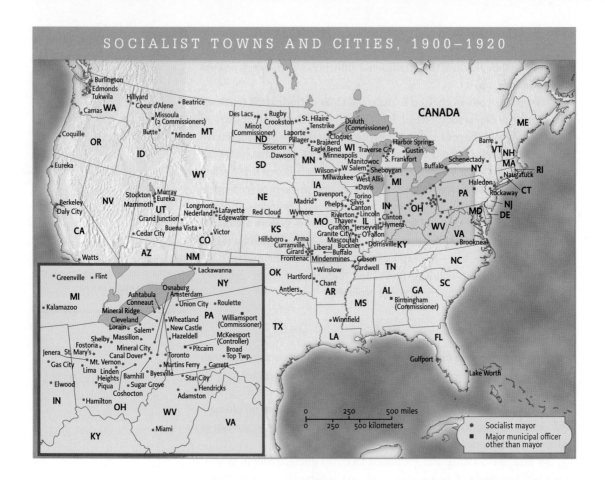

SOCIALIST TOWNS AND CITIES, 1900–1920

Although the Socialist Party never won more than 6 percent of the vote nationally, it gained control of numerous small and medium-sized cities between 1900 and 1920.

the railroad union leader who, as noted in the previous chapter, had been jailed during the Pullman Strike of 1894. For two decades, Debs crisscrossed the country preaching that control of the economy by a democratic government held out the hope of uniting "political equality and economic freedom." "While there is a lower class," proclaimed Debs, "I am in it. . . . While there is a soul in prison, I am not free."

Throughout the Atlantic world of the early twentieth century, socialism was a rising presence. Debs would receive more than 900,000 votes for president (6 percent of the total) in 1912. In that year, the socialist *Appeal to Reason*, published in Girard, Kansas, with a circulation of 700,000, was the largest weekly newspaper in the country.

AFL and IWW

Socialism was only one example of widespread discontent in Progressive America. Having survived the depression of the 1890s, the American

Federation of Labor saw its membership triple to 1.6 million between 1900 and 1904. At the same time, its president, Samuel Gompers, sought to forge closer ties with forward-looking corporate leaders willing to deal with unions as a way to stabilize employee relations. Most employers nonetheless continued to view unions as an intolerable interference with their authority and resisted them stubbornly.

American Federation of Labor (AFL)

The AFL mainly represented the most privileged American workers—skilled industrial and craft laborers, nearly all of them white, male, and native-born. In 1905, a group of unionists who rejected the AFL's exclusionary policies formed the **Industrial Workers of the World** (IWW). Part trade union, part advocate of a workers' revolution that would seize the means of production and abolish the state, the IWW made solidarity its guiding principle. The organization sought to mobilize those excluded from the AFL—the immigrant factory-labor force, migrant timber and agricultural workers, women, blacks, and even the despised Chinese on the West Coast.

Industrial Workers of the World (IWW)

The New Immigrants on Strike

A series of mass strikes among immigrant workers placed labor's demand for the right of **collective bargaining** at the forefront of the reform agenda. These strikes demonstrated that although ethnic divisions among workers impeded labor solidarity, ethnic cohesiveness could also be a basis of unity, so long as strikes were organized on a democratic basis. IWW organizers printed leaflets, posters, and banners in multiple languages and insisted that each nationality enjoy representation on the committee coor-

The right to collective bargaining

Striking New York City garment workers carrying signs in multiple languages, 1913.

dinating a walkout. It drew on the sense of solidarity within immigrant communities to persuade local religious leaders, shopkeepers, and officeholders to support the strikes.

The labor conflict that had the greatest impact on public consciousness took place in Lawrence, Massachusetts. The city's huge woolen mills employed 32,000 men, women, and children representing twenty-five nationalities. When the state legislature in January 1912 enacted a fifty-four-hour limit to the workweek, employers reduced the weekly take-home pay of those who had been laboring longer hours. Workers spontaneously went on strike.

VOICES OF FREEDOM

From Charlotte Perkins Gilman, *Women and Economics* (1898)

Women and Economics, by the prolific feminist social critic and novelist Charlotte Perkins Gilman, influenced the new generation of women aspiring to greater independence. It insisted that how people earned a living shaped their entire lives and that therefore women must free themselves from the home to achieve genuine freedom.

It is not motherhood that keeps the housewife on her feet from dawn till dark; it is house service, not child service. Women work longer and harder than most men. . . . A truer spirit is the increasing desire of young girls to be independent, to have a career of their own, at least for a while, and the growing objection of countless wives to the pitiful asking for money, to the beggary of their position. More and more do fathers give their daughters, and husbands their wives, a definite allowance,—a separate bank account,—something . . . all their own.

The spirit of personal independence in the women of today is sure proof that a change has come. . . . The radical change in the economic position of women is advancing upon us. . . . The growing individualization of democratic life brings inevitable change to our daughters as well as to our sons. . . . One of its most noticeable features is the demand in women not only for their own money, but for their own work for the sake of personal expression. Few girls today fail to manifest some signs of this desire for individual expression. . . .

Economic independence for women necessarily involves a change in the home and family relation. But, if that change is for the advantage of individual and race, we need not fear it. It does not involve a change in the marriage relation except in withdrawing the element of economic dependence, nor in the relation of mother to child save to improve it. But it does involve the exercise of human faculty in women, in social service and exchange rather than in domestic service solely. . . . [Today], when our still developing social needs call for an ever-increasing . . . freedom, the woman in marrying becomes the house-servant, or at least the housekeeper, of the man. . . . When women stand free as economic agents, they will [achieve a] much better fulfilment of their duties as wives and mothers and [contribute] to the vast improvement in health and happiness of the human race.

From John Mitchell, "The Workingman's Conception of Industrial Liberty" (1910)

During the Progressive era, the idea of "industrial liberty" moved to the center of political discussion. Progressive reformers and labor leaders like John Mitchell, head of the United Mine Workers, condemned the prevailing idea of liberty of contract in favor of a broader definition of economic freedom.

While the Declaration of Independence established civil and political liberty, it did not, as you all know, establish industrial liberty.... Liberty means more than the right to choose the field of one's employment. He is not a free man whose family must buy food today with the money that is earned tomorrow. He is not really free who is forced to work unduly long hours and for wages so low that he can not provide the necessities of life for himself and his family; who must live in a crowded tenement and see his children go to work in the mills, the mines, and the factories before their bodies are developed and their minds trained. To have freedom a man must be free from the harrowing fear of hunger and want; he must be in such a position that by the exercise of reasonable frugality he can provide his family with all of the necessities and the reasonable comforts of life. He must be able to educate his children and to provide against sickness, accident, and old age....

A number of years ago the legislatures of several coal producing States enacted laws requiring employers to pay the wages of their workmen in lawful money of the United States and to cease the practice of paying wages in merchandise. From time immemorial it had been the custom of coal companies to conduct general supply stores, and the workingmen were required, as a condition of employment, to accept products in lieu of money in return for services rendered. This system was a great hardship to the workmen.... The question of the constitutionality of this legislation was carried into the courts and by the highest tribunal it was declared to be an invasion of the workman's liberty to deny him the right to accept merchandise in lieu of money as payment of his wages.... [This is] typical of hundreds of instances in which laws that have been enacted for the protection of the workingmen have been declared by the courts to be unconstitutional, on the grounds that they invaded the liberty of the working people.... Is it not natural that the workingmen should feel that they are being guaranteed the liberties they do not want and denied the liberty that is of real value to them? May they not exclaim, with Madame Roland [of the French Revolution], "O Liberty! Liberty! How many crimes are committed in thy name!"

QUESTIONS

1. *What does Gilman see as the main obstacles to freedom for women?*

2. *What does Mitchell believe will be necessary to establish "industrial liberty"?*

3. *How do the authors differ in their view of the relationship of the family to individual freedom?*

A 1900 cartoon from *Puck*, *Divorce the Lesser Evil*. On the left, a quarreling husband and wife are chained to an "unhappy marriage." Justice is about to sever the marriage with her sword, while a minister tries to prevent her. Divorce laws had been liberalized after the Civil War; by the 1890s the United States had the highest divorce rate in the Western world. In the caption, the Church declares divorce an "awful immorality," to which Justice replies, "Divorce is rather an aid to morality."

Forms of political activity

In February, strikers devised the idea of sending strikers' children out of the city for the duration of the walkout. Socialist families in New York City agreed to take them in. The sight of the children, many of whom appeared pale and half-starved, marching up Fifth Avenue from the train station led to a wave of sympathy for the strikers. The governor of Massachusetts soon intervened, and the strike was settled on the workers' terms. A banner carried by the Lawrence strikers gave a new slogan to the labor movement: "We want bread and roses, too"—a declaration that workers sought not only higher wages but the opportunity to enjoy the finer things of life.

Labor and Civil Liberties

The fiery organizer Mary "Mother" Jones, who at the age of eighty-three had been jailed after addressing striking Colorado miners, later told a New York audience that the union "had only the Constitution; the other side had the bayonets." Yet the struggle of workers for the right to strike and of labor radicals against restraints on open-air speaking made free speech a significant public issue in the early twentieth century. By and large, the courts rejected their claims. But these battles laid the foundation for the rise of civil liberties as a central component of freedom in twentieth-century America.

The IWW's battle for freedom of expression is a case in point. Lacking union halls, its organizers relied on songs, street theater, impromptu organizing meetings, and street corner gatherings to spread their message and attract support. In response to IWW activities, officials in Los Angeles, Spokane, Denver, and more than a dozen other cities limited or prohibited outdoor meetings. To arouse popular support, the IWW filled the jails with members who defied local law by speaking in public. In nearly all the free-speech fights, however, the IWW eventually forced local officials to give way. "Whether they agree or disagree with its methods or aims," wrote one journalist, "all lovers of liberty everywhere owe a debt to this organization for . . . [keeping] alight the fires of freedom."

The New Feminism

The word "feminism"

During the Progressive era, the word "feminism" first entered the political vocabulary. In 1914, a mass meeting at New York's Cooper Union debated the question "What is Feminism?" Feminism, said one speaker, meant woman's emancipation "both as a human being and a sex-being."

New feminism's forthright attack on traditional rules of sexual behavior added a new dimension to the idea of personal freedom.

One symbol of the new era was Isadora Duncan, who brought from California a new, expressive dance based on the free movement of a body liberated from the constraints of traditional technique and costume. "I beheld the dance I had always dreamed of," wrote the novelist Edith Wharton on seeing a Duncan performance, "satisfying every sense as a flower does, or a phrase of Mozart's."

During this era, as journalist William M. Reedy jested, it struck "sex o'clock" in America. Issues of intimate personal relations previously confined to private discussion blazed forth in popular magazines and public debates. For the generation of women who adopted the word "feminism" to express their demand for greater liberty, free sexual expression and reproductive choice emerged as critical definitions of women's emancipation.

Isadora Duncan brought a new freedom to an old art form.

The Birth-Control Movement

The growing presence of women in the labor market reinforced demands for access to birth control, an issue that gave political expression to changing sexual behavior. Emma Goldman, who had emigrated to the United States from Lithuania at the age of sixteen, toured the country lecturing on subjects from anarchism to the need for more enlightened attitudes toward homosexuality. She regularly included the right to birth control in her speeches and distributed pamphlets with detailed information about various contraceptive devices.

By forthrightly challenging the laws banning contraceptive information and devices, Margaret Sanger, one of eleven children of an Irish-American working-class family, placed the **birth control movement** at the heart of the new feminism. In 1911, she began a column on sex education, "What Every Girl Should Know," for *The Call*, a New York socialist newspaper. Postal officials barred one issue, containing a column on venereal disease, from the mails. The next issue of *The Call* included a blank page with the headline: "What Every Girl Should Know—Nothing; by order of the U.S. Post Office."

By 1914, the intrepid Sanger was openly advertising birth-control devices in her own journal, *The Woman Rebel*. "No woman can call herself free," she proclaimed, "who does not own and control her own body [and] can choose consciously whether she will or will not be a mother." In 1916, Sanger opened a clinic in a working-class neighborhood of Brooklyn and began distributing contraceptive devices to poor Jewish and Italian women, an action for which she was sentenced to a month in prison.

Emma Goldman

The much-beloved and much-feared Emma Goldman, speaking in favor of birth control to an almost entirely male crowd in New York City in 1916.

Native American Progressivism

Indian intellectuals

Many groups participated in the Progressive impulse. Founded in 1911, the **Society of American Indians** was a reform organization typical of the era. It brought together Indian intellectuals to promote discussion of the plight of Native Americans in the hope that public exposure would be the first step toward remedying injustice. It created a pan-Indian public space independent of white control.

Carlos Montezuma

Many of these Indian intellectuals were not unsympathetic to the basic goals of federal Indian policy, including the transformation of communal landholdings on reservations into family farms. But Carlos Montezuma, a founder of the Society of American Indians, became an outspoken critic. Born in Arizona, he had been captured as a child by members of a neighboring tribe and sold to a traveling photographer, who brought him to Chicago. There Montezuma attended school and eventually obtained a medical degree.

In 1916, Montezuma established a newsletter, *Wassaja* (meaning "signaling"), that called for the abolition of the Bureau of Indian Affairs. Convinced that outsiders exerted too much power over life on the reservations, he insisted that self-determination was the only way for Indians to escape poverty and marginalization. But he also demanded that Indians be granted full citizenship and all the constitutional rights of other Americans. Indian activists would later rediscover him as a forerunner of Indian radicalism.

THE POLITICS OF PROGRESSIVISM

Effective Freedom

Worldwide progressivism

Progressivism was an international movement. In the early twentieth century, cities throughout the world experienced similar social strains arising from rapid industrialization and urban growth. Reformers across the globe exchanged ideas and envisioned new social policies. The Chinese leader Sun Yat-Sen, for example, was influenced by the writings of Henry George and Edward Bellamy.

Social legislation

As governments in Britain, France, and Germany instituted old-age pensions, minimum-wage laws, unemployment insurance, and the regulation of workplace safety, American reformers came to believe they had much to learn from the Old World. The term "social legislation," meaning governmental action to address urban problems and the insecurities of working-class life, originated in Germany but soon entered the political vocabulary of the United States.

Drawing on the reform programs of the Gilded Age and the example of European legislation, Progressives sought to reinvigorate the idea of an activist, socially conscious government. Progressives could reject the traditional assumption that powerful government posed a threat to freedom, because their understanding of freedom was itself in flux. "Effective freedom," wrote the philosopher John Dewey, was a positive, not a negative, concept—the "power to do specific things." It sometimes required the government to act on behalf of those with little wealth or power. Thus, freedom in the Progressive era inevitably became a political question.

A photograph from 1910 depicts needy constituents of New York political boss Timothy "Big Tim" Sullivan receiving free pairs of shoes. Each year, Sullivan distributed two thousand pairs on his mother's birthday. Such largesse endeared political bosses to many voters, to the annoyance of municipal reformers.

State and Local Reforms

In the United States, with a political structure more decentralized than in European countries, state and local governments enacted most of the era's reform measures. In cities, Progressives worked to reform the structure of government to reduce the power of political bosses, establish public control of "natural monopolies" like gas and water works, and improve public transportation. They raised property taxes in order to spend more money on schools, parks, and other public facilities.

Urban Progressivism

Gilded Age mayors and governors pioneered urban Progressivism. A former factory worker who became a successful shoe manufacturer, Hazen Pingree served as mayor of Detroit from 1889 to 1897. He battled the business interests that had dominated city government, forcing gas and telephone companies to lower their rates, and established a municipal power plant.

Progressivism in the West

Although often associated with eastern cities, Progressivism was also a major presence in the West. Former Populists and those who believed in the moral power of the frontier gravitated to Progressive programs to regulate the railroads and other large corporations, and to the idea that direct democracy could revitalize corrupt politics. Important Progressive leaders worked for reform in western states and municipalities, including Hiram Johnson of California and Robert La Follette of Wisconsin.

Progressive reforms

Oregon stood at the forefront of Progressive reform. The leading figure in that state was William U'Ren, a lawyer who had entered politics as a supporter of Henry George's single-tax program. U'Ren was the founder of the Oregon System, which included the initiative and referendum (also known

Children at play at the Hudson-Bank Gymnasium, built in 1898 in a New York immigrant neighborhood by the Outdoor Recreation League, one of many Progressive-era groups that sought to improve life in urban centers.

as direct legislature, which enabled voters to propose and vote on laws), direct primaries to choose candidates for office (an effort to weaken the power of political bosses), and the recall (by which officials could be removed from office by popular vote). Using the initiative, Progressives won the vote for women in the state. The Oregon system, studied and emulated in many other states, came into being via an alliance of the urban middle class with reform-minded farmers and workers. But fault lines appeared when labor-oriented Progressives tried to use the initiative and referendum to increase taxes on the well-to-do and require the state to provide jobs for the unemployed. Both measures failed. Moreover, the initiative system quickly became out of control. In the 1912 election, voters in Portland were asked to evaluate forty measures seeking to become law. Nonetheless, between 1910 and 1912, Oregon's West Coast neighbors, Washington and California, also adopted the initiative and referendum and approved woman suffrage.

In California, where a Republican machine closely tied to the Southern Pacific Railroad had dominated politics for decades, Progressives took power under Governor Hiram Johnson, who held office from 1911 to 1917. As public prosecutor, Johnson had secured the conviction for bribery of a San Francisco political boss. Having promised to "kick the Southern Pacific [Railroad] out of politics," he secured passage of the *Public Utilities Act*

Public Utilities Act, one of the country's strongest railroad-regulation measures, as well as laws banning child labor and limiting the working hours of women.

The most influential Progressive administration at the state level was that of Robert M. La Follette, who made Wisconsin a "laboratory for democracy." After serving as a Republican member of Congress, La Follette became convinced that an alliance of railroad and lumber companies controlled state politics. Elected governor in 1900, he instituted a series of measures known as the Wisconsin Idea, including nominations of candidates for office through primary elections rather than by political bosses, the taxation of corporate wealth, and state regulation of railroads and public utilities. Other measures created a statewide system of insurance against illness, death, and accident, barred the sale to private

Rebert La Follette and the Wisconsin Idea

companies of land, mineral rights, and other natural resources owned by the state, required safety devices on various forms of machinery, and prohibited child labor. To staff his administration, he drew on nonpartisan faculty members from the University of Wisconsin. Wisconsin offered the most striking merger of the social and political impulses that went under the name of Progressivism.

Progressive Democracy

Progressives hoped to reinvigorate democracy by restoring political power to the citizenry and civic harmony to a divided society. Alarmed by the upsurge in violent class conflict and the unrestricted power of corporations, they believed that political reforms could help to create a unified "people" devoted to greater democracy and social reconciliation. Yet increasing the responsibilities of government made it all the more important to identify who was entitled to political participation and who was not.

Civic harmony

The Progressive era saw a host of changes implemented in the political process, many seemingly contradictory in purpose. The electorate was simultaneously expanded and contracted, empowered and removed from direct influence on many functions of government. Democracy was enhanced by the **Seventeenth Amendment** (1913)—which provided that U.S. senators be chosen by popular vote rather than by state legislatures—by widespread adoption of the popular election of judges, and by the use of primary elections among party members to select candidates for office. The era culminated with a constitutional amendment enfranchising women—the largest expansion of democracy in American history.

Constitutional amendments

But the Progressive era also witnessed numerous restrictions on democratic participation, most strikingly the disenfranchisement of blacks in the South, as noted in Chapter 17. To make city government more honest and efficient, many localities replaced elected mayors with appointed nonpartisan commissions or city managers—a change that insulated officials from machine domination but also from popular control. New literacy tests and residency and registration requirements, common in northern as well as southern states, limited the right to vote among the poor. In the eyes of many Progressives, the "fitness" of voters, not their absolute numbers, defined a functioning democracy.

Restricting democratic participation

Most Progressive thinkers were highly uncomfortable with the real world of politics, which seemed to revolve around the pursuit of narrow class, ethnic, and regional interests. Robert M. La Follette's reliance on college professors to staff important posts in his administration reflected a larger Progressive faith in expertise. The government could best exercise intelligent control over society through a democracy run by impartial experts who were in many respects unaccountable to the citizenry. Political freedom was less a matter of direct participation in government than of qualified persons devising the best public policies.

Jane Addams and Hull House

Women reformers and Progressivism

But alongside this elitist politics, Progressivism also included a more democratic vision of the activist state. As much as any other group, organized women reformers spoke for the more democratic side of Progressivism. Still barred from voting and holding office in most states, women nonetheless became central to the political history of the Progressive era. The immediate catalyst was a growing awareness among women reformers of the plight of poor immigrant communities and the emergence of the condition of women and child laborers as a major focus of public concern.

The era's most prominent female reformer was Jane Addams, who had been born in 1860, the daughter of an Illinois businessman. In 1889, she founded Hull House in Chicago, a **settlement house** devoted to improving the lives of the immigrant poor. Unlike previous reformers who had aided the poor from afar, settlement-house workers moved into poor neighborhoods. They built kindergartens and playgrounds for children, established employment bureaus and health clinics, and showed female victims of domestic abuse how to gain legal protection. By 1910, more than 400 settlement houses had been established in cities throughout the country.

Children in the courtyard at Hull House, the settlement house established in Chicago by Jane Addams.

Addams was typical of the Progressive era's "new woman." By 1900, there were more than 80,000 college-educated women in the United States. Many found a calling in providing social services, nursing, and education to poor families in the growing cities. The efforts of middle-class women to uplift the poor, and of laboring women to uplift themselves, helped to shift the center of gravity of politics toward activist government. Women like Addams discovered that even well-organized social work was not enough to alleviate the problems of inadequate housing, income, and health. Government action was essential. Hull House instigated an array of reforms in Chicago, soon adopted elsewhere, including stronger building and sanitation codes, shorter working hours and safer labor conditions, and the right of labor to organize.

The settlement houses have been called "spearheads for reform." Florence Kelley, a veteran of Hull House, went on to mobilize women's power as consumers as a force for social change. Under Kelley's leadership, the National Consumers' League became the nation's leading advocate of laws governing the working conditions of women and children.

Florence Kelley

The Campaign for Woman Suffrage

After 1900, the campaign for woman suffrage moved beyond the elitism of the 1890s to engage a broad coalition ranging from middle-class members of women's clubs to unionists, socialists, and settlement-house workers. For the first time, it became a mass movement. Membership in the National American Woman Suffrage Association grew from 13,000 in 1893 to more than 2 million by 1917. By 1900, more than half the states allowed women to vote in local elections dealing with school issues, and Wyoming, Colorado, Idaho, and Utah had adopted full woman suffrage. Between 1910 and 1914, seven more western states enfranchised women. In 1913, Illinois became the first state east of the Mississippi River to allow women to vote in presidential elections.

A mass movement

These campaigns, which brought women aggressively into the public sphere, were conducted with a new spirit of militancy. They also made effective use of the techniques of advertising, publicity, and mass entertainment characteristic of modern consumer society. California's successful 1911 campaign utilized automobile parades, numerous billboards and electric signs, and countless suffrage buttons and badges. Nonetheless, state campaigns were difficult, expensive, and usually unsuccessful. The movement increasingly focused its attention on securing a national constitutional amendment giving women the right to vote.

Mayor Mary W. Howard (center) and the town council of Kanab, Utah. They served from 1912 to 1914, the first all-female municipal government in American history.

Maternalist Reform

Ironically, the desire to exalt women's role within the home did much to inspire the reinvigoration of the suffrage movement. Female reformers helped to launch a mass movement for direct government action

A woman suffrage parade in Minneapolis/St. Paul, Minnesota, in 1914. The marchers wear traditional costumes of Scandinavian countries and carry the flags of Norway and Sweden.

Government aid to women and children

to improve the living standards of poor mothers and children. Laws providing for mothers' pensions (state aid to mothers of young children who lacked male support) spread rapidly after 1910. These **maternalist reforms** rested on the assumption that the government should encourage women's capacity for bearing and raising children and enable them to be economically independent at the same time. Both feminists and believers in conventional domestic roles supported such measures. The former hoped that these laws would subvert women's dependence on men, the latter that they would strengthen traditional families and the mother-child bond.

Other Progressive legislation recognized that large numbers of women did in fact work outside the home but defined them as a dependent group (like children) in need of state protection in ways male workers were not.

Louis D. Brandeis and Muller v. Oregon

In 1908, in the landmark case of ***Muller v. Oregon***, Louis D. Brandeis filed a brief citing scientific and sociological studies to demonstrate that because they had less strength and endurance than men, long hours of labor were dangerous for women, while their unique ability to bear children gave the government a legitimate interest in their working conditions. Persuaded by Brandeis's argument, the Supreme Court unanimously upheld the constitutionality of an Oregon law setting maximum working hours for women.

Thus, three years after the notorious *Lochner* decision invalidating a New York law limiting the working hours of male bakers (discussed in Chapter 16), the Court created the first large breach in "liberty of contract" doctrine. But the cost was high: at the very time that women in unprecedented numbers were entering the labor market and earning college degrees, Brandeis's brief and the Court's opinion solidified the view of women workers as weak, dependent, and incapable of enjoying the same economic rights as men. By 1917, thirty states had enacted laws limiting the hours of labor of female workers.

The unintended effects of Muller

The maternalist agenda that built gender inequality into the early foundations of the welfare state by extension raised the idea that government should better the living and working conditions of men as well. Indeed, Brandeis envisioned the welfare state as one rooted in the notion of universal economic entitlements, including the right to a decent income and protection against unemployment and work-related accidents.

Right to assistance

This vision, too, enjoyed considerable support in the Progressive era. By 1913, twenty-two states had enacted workmen's compensation laws to benefit workers, male or female, injured on the job. This legislation was the first wedge that opened the way for broader programs of social insurance. But state minimum-wage laws and most laws regulating working hours applied only to women. Women and children may have needed protection, but interference with the freedom of contract of adult male workers was still widely seen as degrading. The establishment of a standard of living and working conditions beneath which no American, male or female, should be allowed to fall would await the coming of the New Deal.

Workmen's compensation laws

Louisine Havemeyer, one of New York City's wealthiest women, was a strong advocate of woman suffrage. Here, in a 1915 photograph, she passes the Torch of Liberty to a group of New Jersey women.

According to this cartoon, giving women the right to vote will clean up political corruption and misgovernment.

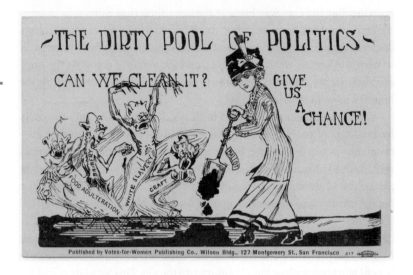

THE PROGRESSIVE PRESIDENTS

Despite creative experiments in social policy at the city and state levels, the tradition of localism seemed to most Progressives an impediment to a renewed sense of national purpose. Poverty, economic insecurity, and lack of industrial democracy were national problems that demanded national solutions. The democratic national state, wrote *New Republic* editor Herbert Croly, offered an alternative to control of Americans' lives by narrow interests that manipulated politics or by the all-powerful corporations. Croly proposed a new synthesis of American political traditions. To achieve the "Jeffersonian ends" of democratic self-determination and individual freedom, he insisted, the country needed to employ the "Hamiltonian means" of government intervention in the economy. Each in his own way, the Progressive presidents—Theodore Roosevelt, William Howard Taft, and Woodrow Wilson—tried to address this challenge.

Herbert Croly

Theodore Roosevelt

In September 1901, the anarchist Leon Czolgosz assassinated William McKinley while the president visited the Pan-American Exposition in Buffalo, New York. At the age of forty-two, Vice President Theodore Roosevelt became the youngest man ever to hold the office of president. In many ways, he became the model for the twentieth-century president, an official actively and continuously engaged in domestic and foreign affairs.

The model for the twentieth-century president

(The foreign policies of the Progressive presidents will be discussed in the next chapter.) He moved aggressively to set the political agenda.

Roosevelt's domestic program, which he called the Square Deal, attempted to confront the problems caused by economic consolidation by distinguishing between "good" and "bad" corporations. The former, among which he included U.S. Steel and Standard Oil, served the public interest. The latter were run by greedy financiers interested only in profit and had no right to exist.

Soon after assuming office, Roosevelt shocked the corporate world by announcing his intention to prosecute under the Sherman Antitrust Act the Northern Securities Company. Created by financier J. P. Morgan, this "holding company" owned the stock and directed the affairs of three major western railroads. It monopolized transportation between the Great Lakes and the Pacific. In 1904, the Supreme Court ordered Northern Securities dissolved, a major victory for the antitrust movement.

Reelected that same year, Roosevelt pushed for more direct federal regulation of the economy. He proposed to strengthen the Interstate Commerce Commission, which the Supreme Court had essentially limited to collecting economic statistics. By this time, journalistic exposés, labor unrest, and the agitation of Progressive reformers had created significant public support for Roosevelt's regulatory program. In 1906, Congress passed the Hepburn Act, giving the ICC the power to examine railroads' business records and to set reasonable rates, a significant step in the development of federal intervention in the corporate economy. That year, as has been noted, also saw passage of the **Pure Food and Drug Act**. Many businessmen supported these measures, recognizing that they would benefit from greater public confidence in the quality and safety of their products. But even they were alarmed by Roosevelt's calls for federal inheritance and income taxes and the regulation of all interstate businesses.

John Muir and the Spirituality of Nature

If the United States lagged behind Europe in many areas of social policy, it led the way in the conservation of natural resources. The first national park, Yellowstone in Wyoming, was created in 1872, partly to preserve an area of remarkable natural beauty and partly at the urging of the Northern Pacific Railroad, which was anxious to promote western tourism. In the 1890s, the Scottish-born naturalist John Muir organized the Sierra Club to help preserve forests from uncontrolled logging by timber companies.

Muir's love of nature stemmed from deep religious feelings. Nearly blinded in an accident in an Indianapolis machine shop where he worked

President Theodore Roosevelt addressing a crowd in 1902.

Public support

Putting the Screws on Him, a 1904 cartoon, depicts President Theodore Roosevelt squeezing ill-gotten gains out of the trusts.

The Old Faithful geyser, the most famous site in Yellowstone, the nation's first national park, in a photograph from the 1880s.

Theodore Roosevelt (center) posing with a group in a grove of giant sequoia trees in California in 1903. He called on Americans to protect these "monuments of beauty."

in his twenties, he found in the restoration of his sight an inspiration to appreciate God's creation. He called forests "God's first temples." In nature, he believed, men could experience directly the presence of God. Muir was inspired by the Transcendentalists of the pre–Civil War era—like Henry David Thoreau, he lamented the intrusions of civilization on the natural environment. But unlike them, Muir developed a broad following. As more and more Americans lived in cities, they came to see nature less as something to conquer and more as a place for recreation and personal growth.

The Conservation Movement

In the 1890s, Congress authorized the president to withdraw "forest reserves" from economic development, a restriction on economic freedom in the name of a greater social good. But it was under Theodore Roosevelt that the **conservation movement** became a concerted federal policy. A dedicated outdoorsman who built a ranch in North Dakota in the 1880s, Roosevelt moved to preserve parts of the natural environment from economic exploitation.

Relying for advice on Gifford Pinchot, the head of the U.S. Forest Service, he ordered that millions of acres be set aside as wildlife preserves and encouraged Congress to create new national parks. In some ways, conservation was a typical Progressive reform. Manned by experts, the government could stand above political and economic battles, serving the public good while preventing "special interests" from causing irreparable damage to the environment. The aim was less to end the economic utilization of natural resources than to develop responsible, scientific plans for their use. Pinchot halted timber companies' reckless assault on the nation's forests. But unlike Muir, he believed that development and conservation could go hand in hand and that logging, mining, and grazing on public lands should be controlled, not eliminated.

Taft in Office

Having served nearly eight years as president, Roosevelt did not run again in 1908. His chosen successor, William Howard Taft, defeated William Jennings Bryan, making his third unsuccessful race for the White House.

Although temperamentally more conservative than Roosevelt, Taft pursued antitrust policy even more aggressively. He persuaded the Supreme Court in 1911 to declare John D. Rockefeller's Standard Oil

Company (one of Roosevelt's "good" trusts) in violation of the Sherman Antitrust Act and to order its breakup into separate marketing, producing, and refining companies. The government also won a case against American Tobacco, which the Court ordered to end pricing policies that were driving smaller firms out of business.

Taft supported the **Sixteenth Amendment** to the Constitution, which authorized Congress to enact a graduated income tax (one whose rate of taxation is higher for wealthier citizens). It was ratified shortly before he left office. A 2 percent tax on incomes over $4,000 had been included in a tariff enacted in 1894 but had been quickly declared unconstitutional by the Supreme Court as a "communistic threat to property." A key step in the modernization of the federal government, the income tax provided a reliable and flexible source of revenue for a national state whose powers, responsibilities, and expenditures were growing rapidly.

The income tax

Despite these accomplishments, Taft seemed to gravitate toward the more conservative wing of the Republican Party. Taft's rift with Progressives grew deeper when Richard A. Ballinger, the secretary of the interior, concluded that Roosevelt had exceeded his authority in placing land in forest reserves. Ballinger decided to return some of this land to the public domain, where mining and lumber companies would have access to it. Gifford Pinchot accused Ballinger of colluding with business interests and repudiating the environmental goals of the Roosevelt administration. When Taft fired Pinchot in 1910, the breach with party Progressives became irreparable. In 1912, Roosevelt challenged Taft for the Republican nomination. Defeated, Roosevelt launched an independent campaign as the head of the new **Progressive Party**.

Ballinger and Pinchot

The Election of 1912

All the crosscurrents of Progressive-era thinking came together in the presidential campaign of 1912. The four-way contest between Taft, Roosevelt, Democrat Woodrow Wilson, and Socialist Eugene V. Debs became a national debate on the relationship between political and economic freedom in the age of big business. At one end of the political spectrum stood Taft, who stressed that economic individualism could remain the foundation of the social order so long as government and private entrepreneurs cooperated in addressing social ills. At the other end was Debs. Relatively few Americans supported the Socialist Party's goal of abolishing the "capitalistic system" altogether, but its immediate demands—including public ownership of the railroads and banking system, government aid to

A key election

Eugene V. Debs, the Socialist Party candidate, speaking in Chicago during the 1912 presidential campaign.

the unemployed, and laws establishing shorter working hours and a minimum wage—summarized forward-looking Progressive thought.

But it was the battle between Wilson and Roosevelt over the role of the federal government in securing economic freedom that galvanized public attention in 1912. The two represented competing strands of Progressivism. Both believed government action necessary to preserve individual freedom, but they differed over the dangers of increasing the government's power and the inevitability of economic concentration.

Competing strands of Progressivism

New Freedom and New Nationalism

Strongly influenced by Louis D. Brandeis, with whom he consulted frequently during the campaign, Wilson insisted that democracy must be reinvigorated by restoring market competition and freeing government from domination by big business. Wilson feared big government as much as he feared the power of the corporations. The **New Freedom**, as he called his program, envisioned the federal government strengthening antitrust laws, protecting the right of workers to unionize, and actively encouraging small businesses—creating, in other words, the conditions for the renewal of economic competition without increasing government regulation of the economy. Wilson warned that corporations were as likely to corrupt government as to be managed by it, a forecast that proved remarkably accurate.

Woodrow Wilson's New Freedom

To Roosevelt's supporters, Wilson seemed a relic of a bygone era; his program, they argued, served the needs of small businessmen but ignored the inevitability of economic concentration and the interests of professionals, consumers, and labor. Espousing the **New Nationalism**, his program of 1912, Roosevelt insisted that only the "controlling and directing power of the government" could restore "the liberty of the oppressed." He called for heavy taxes on personal and corporate fortunes and federal regulation of industries, including railroads, mining, and oil.

Roosevelt's New Nationalism

The Progressive Party platform offered numerous proposals to promote social justice. Drafted by a group of settlement-house activists, labor reformers, and social scientists, the platform laid out a blueprint for a modern, democratic welfare state, complete with woman suffrage, federal supervision of corporate enterprise, national labor and health legislation for women and children, an eight-hour day and "living wage" for all workers, and a national system of social insurance covering unemployment, medical care, and old age. Roosevelt's campaign helped to give freedom a modern social and economic content and established an agenda that would define political liberalism for much of the twentieth century.

The Progressive Party Platform of 1912

Wilson's First Term

The Republican split ensured a sweeping victory for Wilson, who won about 42 percent of the popular vote, although Roosevelt humiliated Taft by winning about 27 percent to the president's 23 percent. In office, Wilson proved himself a strong executive leader. He was the first president to hold regular press conferences, and he delivered messages personally to Congress rather than sending them in written form, as had all his predecessors since John Adams.

Wilson's victory

With Democrats in control of Congress, Wilson moved aggressively to implement his version of Progressivism. The first significant measure of his presidency was the Underwood Tariff, which substantially reduced duties on imports and, to make up for lost revenue, imposed a graduated income tax on the richest 5 percent of Americans. There followed the Clayton Act of 1914, which exempted labor unions from antitrust laws and barred courts from issuing injunctions curtailing the right to strike. In 1916 came the Keating-Owen Act, outlawing child labor in the manufacture of goods sold in interstate commerce; the Adamson Act, establishing an eight-hour workday on the nation's railroads; and the Warehouse Act, reminiscent of the Populist sub-treasury plan, which extended credit to farmers when they stored their crops in federally licensed warehouses.

Wilson's initiatives

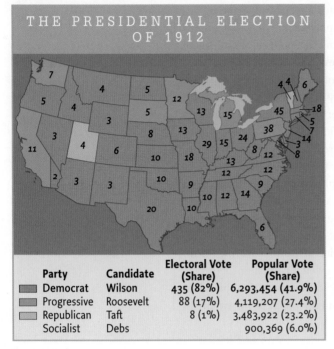

THE PRESIDENTIAL ELECTION OF 1912

Party	Candidate	Electoral Vote (Share)	Popular Vote (Share)
Democrat	Wilson	435 (82%)	6,293,454 (41.9%)
Progressive	Roosevelt	88 (17%)	4,119,207 (27.4%)
Republican	Taft	8 (1%)	3,483,922 (23.2%)
Socialist	Debs		900,369 (6.0%)

The Expanding Role of Government

Some of Wilson's policies seemed more in tune with Roosevelt's New Nationalism than the New Freedom of 1912. Wilson presided over the creation of two powerful new public agencies. In 1913, Congress created the Federal Reserve System, consisting of twelve regional banks. They were overseen by a central board appointed by the president and empowered to handle the issuance of currency, aid banks in danger of failing, and influence interest rates so as to promote economic growth.

A second expansion of national power occurred in 1914, when Congress established the **Federal Trade Commission** (FTC) to investigate and prohibit "unfair" business activities such as price-fixing and monopolistic practices. Both the Federal Reserve and the FTC were welcomed by many business leaders as a means of restoring order to the economic marketplace and warding off more radical measures for curbing corporate power. But they reflected the remarkable expansion of the federal role in the economy during the Progressive era.

A new nation-state

By 1916, the social ferment and political mobilizations of the Progressive era had given birth to a new American state. With new laws, administrative agencies, and independent commissions, government at the local, state, and national levels had assumed the authority to protect and advance "industrial freedom." Government had established rules for labor relations, business behavior, and financial policy, protected citizens from market abuses, and acted as a broker among the groups whose conflicts threatened to destroy social harmony. But a storm was already engulfing Europe that would test the Progressive faith in empowered government as the protector of American freedom.

CHAPTER REVIEW AND ONLINE RESOURCES

REVIEW QUESTIONS

1. Identify the main groups and ideas that drove the Progressive movement.

2. Explain how immigration to the United States in this period was part of a global movement of peoples.

3. Describe how Fordism transformed American industrial and consumer society.

4. Socialism was a rising force across the globe in the early twentieth century. How successful was the movement in the United States?

5. Explain why the Industrial Workers of the World (IWW) grew so rapidly and aroused so much opposition.

6. How did immigrants adjust to life in America? What institutions or activities became important to their adjustment, and why?

7. What did Progressive-era feminists want to change in society, and how did their actions help to spearhead broader reforms?

8. How did ideas of women's roles, shared by maternalist reformers, lead to an expansion of activism by and rights for women?

9. How did each Progressive-era president view the role of the federal government?

10. Pick a Progressive-era reform (a movement, a specific legislation, or an organization) and describe how it shows how Progressives could work for both the expansion of democracy and restrictions on it.

KEY TERMS

Progressivism (p. 547)
muckraking (p. 549)
Ellis Island (p. 550)
Fordism (p. 553)
"American standard of living" (p. 553)
scientific management (p. 554)
Socialist Party (p. 555)
Industrial Workers of the World (p. 557)
collective bargaining (p. 557)
new feminism (p. 561)
birth control movement (p. 561)
Society of American Indians (p. 562)
Seventeenth Amendment (p. 565)
settlement house (p. 566)
maternalist reforms (p. 568)
Muller v. Oregon (p. 568)
Pure Food and Drug Act (p. 571)
conservation movement (p. 572)
Sixteenth Amendment (p. 573)
Progressive Party (p. 573)
New Freedom (p. 574)
New Nationalism (p. 575)
Federal Trade Commission (p. 576)

Go to INQUIZITIVE

To see what you know—and learn what you've missed—with personalized feedback along the way.

Visit the *Give Me Liberty!* **Student Site** for primary source documents and images, interactive maps, author videos featuring Eric Foner, and more.

1903	United States secures the Panama Canal Zone
	W. E. B. Du Bois's *The Souls of Black Folk*
1904	Roosevelt Corollary to the Monroe Doctrine
1905	The Niagara movement established
1907	Gentlemen's Agreement with Japan
1909	National Association for the Advancement of Colored People organized
1910	Mexican Revolution begins
1911	*Bailey v. Alabama*
1914	Assassination of Archduke Ferdinand
1914–1919	World War I
1915	D. W. Griffith's *Birth of a Nation* premieres
	Lusitania sinks
1917	Zimmermann Telegram intercepted
	United States enters the war
	Espionage Act passed
	Russian Revolution
1918	Woodrow Wilson's "Fourteen Points" speech
1918–1920	Worldwide flu epidemic
1919	Eighteenth Amendment
	Treaty of Versailles signed
1919–1920	Red Scare
	Senate rejects the Treaty of Versailles
1920	Nineteenth Amendment ratified
1921	Tulsa Riot

The American painter John Singer Sargent was commissioned by the British government to create a painting depicting World War I and sent to the front lines in France. The result, *Gassed*, completed in 1919 after the war's end, was doubtless not what the authorities had in mind. Revolted by the carnage he had witnessed, Sargent painted a line of soldiers, their eyes bandaged because of exposure to mustard gas, being led off by a medic to receive treatment. More wounded men lie in the foreground. Sargent was one of many artists and intellectuals who concluded that the war had been a ghastly mistake.

CHAPTER 19

SAFE FOR DEMOCRACY: THE UNITED STATES AND WORLD WAR I

1916-1920

In 1902, W. T. Stead published a short volume with the arresting title *The Americanization of the World; or, the Trend of the Twentieth Century,* in which he predicted that the United States would soon emerge as "the greatest of world-powers." But what was most striking about his work was that Stead located the source of American power less in the realm of military might or territorial acquisition than in the country's single-minded commitment to the "pursuit of wealth" and the relentless international spread of American culture—art, music, journalism, even ideas about religion and gender relations. He foresaw a future in which the United States promoted its interests and values through an unending involvement in the affairs of other nations. Stead proved to be an accurate prophet.

The Spanish-American War had established the United States as an international empire. Despite the conquest of the Philippines and Puerto Rico, however, the country's overseas holdings remained tiny compared to those of Britain, France, and Germany. And no more were added, except for a strip of land surrounding the Panama Canal, acquired in 1903, and the Virgin Islands, purchased from Denmark in 1917. In 1900, Great Britain ruled over more than 300 million people in possessions scattered across the globe, and France had nearly 50 million subjects in Asia and Africa. Compared with these, the American presence in the world seemed very small. As Stead suggested, America's empire differed significantly from those of European countries—it was economic, cultural, and intellectual, rather than territorial.

The world economy at the dawn of the twentieth century was already highly globalized. An ever-increasing stream of goods, investments, and people flowed from country to country. Although Britain still dominated world banking and the British pound remained the major currency of international trade, the United States had become the leading industrial power. By 1914, it produced more than one-third of the world's manufactured goods. Spearheads of American culture like movies and popular music were not far behind.

Europeans were fascinated by American ingenuity and mass-production techniques. Many feared American products and culture would overwhelm their own. "What are the chief new features of London life?" one British writer asked in 1901. "They are the telephone, the portable camera, the phonograph, the electric street car, the automobile, the typewriter. . . . In every one of these the American maker is supreme."

America's burgeoning connections with the outside world led to increasing military and political involvement. In the two decades after 1900, many of the basic principles that would guide American foreign

FOCUS QUESTIONS

• *In what ways did the Progressive presidents promote the expansion of American power overseas?*

• *How did the United States get involved in World War I?*

• *How did the United States mobilize resources and public opinion for the war effort?*

• *How did the war affect race relations in the United States?*

• *Why was 1919 such a watershed year for the United States and the world?*

policy for the rest of the century were formulated. The "open door"—the free flow of trade, investment, information, and culture—emerged as a key principle of American foreign relations.

Americans in the twentieth century often discussed foreign policy in the language of freedom. A supreme faith in America's historic destiny and in the righteousness of its ideals enabled the country's leaders to think of the United States simultaneously as an emerging great power and as the worldwide embodiment of freedom.

More than any other individual, Woodrow Wilson articulated this vision of America's relationship to the rest of the world. His foreign policy, called by historians **liberal internationalism**, rested on the conviction that economic and political progress went hand in hand. Thus, greater worldwide freedom would follow inevitably from increased American investment and trade abroad. Frequently during the twentieth century, this conviction would serve as a mask for American power and self-interest. It would also inspire sincere efforts to bring freedom to other peoples. In either case, liberal internationalism represented a shift from the nineteenth-century tradition of promoting freedom primarily by example to active intervention to remake the world in the American image.

AN ERA OF INTERVENTION

Just as they expanded the powers of the federal government in domestic affairs, the Progressive presidents were not reluctant to project American power outside the country's borders. At first, they confined their interventions to the Western Hemisphere, whose affairs the United States had claimed a special right to oversee ever since the Monroe Doctrine of 1823. Between 1901 and 1920, U.S. marines landed in Caribbean countries more than twenty times. Usually, they were dispatched to create a welcoming economic environment for American companies that wanted stable access to raw materials like bananas and sugar, and for bankers nervous that their loans to local governments might not be repaid.

The Caribbean

"I Took the Canal Zone"

Roosevelt's international diplomacy

Theodore Roosevelt became far more active in international diplomacy than most of his predecessors, helping, for example, to negotiate a settlement of the Russo-Japanese War of 1905, a feat for which he was awarded the Nobel Peace Prize. Closer to home, his policies were more aggressive.

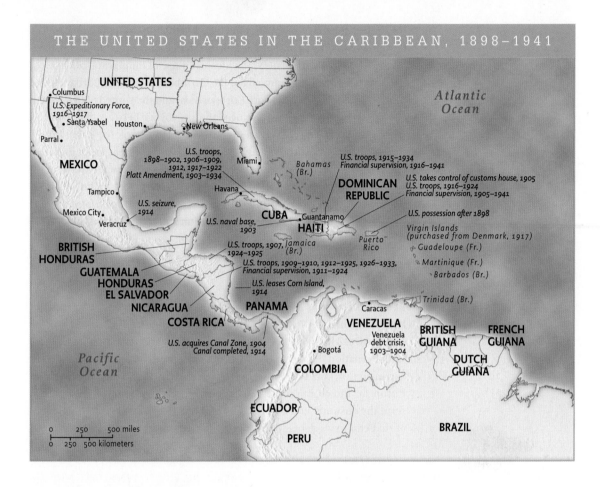

THE UNITED STATES IN THE CARIBBEAN, 1898–1941

UNITED STATES

•Columbus

U.S. Expeditionary Force,
1916–1917
•Santa Ysabel   Houston•   •New Orleans

Parral•

Atlantic
Ocean

MEXICO

Tampico•

Mexico City•
   Veracruz•

U.S. troops,
1898–1902, 1906–1909,
1912, 1917–1922
Platt Amendment, 1903–1934   Miami•   *Bahamas*
(Br.)

Havana•

U.S. seizure,
1914   CUBA   •Guantanamo

U.S. naval base,
1903   HAITI

U.S. troops, 1915–1934
Financial supervision, 1916–1941

DOMINICAN
REPUBLIC

U.S. takes control of customs house, 1905
U.S. troops, 1916–1924
Financial supervision, 1905–1941

U.S. possession after 1898

Puerto
Rico   *Virgin Islands*
(purchased from Denmark, 1917)
🔹*Guadeloupe (Fr.)*

BRITISH
HONDURAS
   GUATEMALA
   HONDURAS
   EL SALVADOR
      NICARAGUA
         COSTA RICA

U.S. troops, 1907, Jamaica
1924–1925   (Br.)

U.S. troops, 1909–1910, 1912–1925, 1926–1933,
Financial supervision, 1911–1924

U.S. leases Corn Island,
1914

PANAMA

U.S. acquires Canal Zone, 1904
Canal completed, 1914

•Bogotá

🔹*Martinique (Fr.)*
🔹*Barbados (Br.)*

Trinidad (Br.)

Caracas•

VENEZUELA
   Venezuela
   debt crisis,
   1903–1904

BRITISH
GUIANA   FRENCH
GUIANA

DUTCH
GUIANA

COLOMBIA

Pacific
Ocean

ECUADOR

PERU

BRAZIL

0   250   500 miles
0   250   500 kilometers

"I have always been fond of the West African proverb," he wrote, "'Speak softly and carry a big stick.'"

The idea of a canal across the fifty-one-mile-wide Isthmus of Panama had a long history. A longtime proponent of American naval development, Roosevelt was convinced that a canal would facilitate the movement of naval and commercial vessels between the two oceans. In 1903, when Colombia, of which Panama was a part, refused to cede land for the project, Roosevelt helped set in motion an uprising by Panamanian conspirators. An American gunboat prevented the Colombian army from suppressing the rebellion.

On establishing its independence, Panama signed a treaty giving the United States both the right to construct and operate a canal and sovereignty over the **Panama Canal Zone**, a ten-mile-wide strip of land through which the route would run. A remarkable feat of engineering, the canal was

Between 1898 and 1941, the United States intervened militarily numerous times in Caribbean countries, generally to protect the economic interests of American banks and investors.

The Panama Canal

the largest construction project in American history to that date. Like the building of the transcontinental railroad in the 1860s and much construction work today, it involved the widespread use of immigrant labor. Most of the 60,000 workers came from the Caribbean islands of Barbados and Jamaica, but others hailed from Europe, Asia, and the United States. When completed in 1914, the canal reduced the sea voyage between the East and West Coasts of the United States by 8,000 miles. "I took the Canal Zone," Roosevelt exulted. But the manner in which the canal had been initiated, and the continued American rule over the Canal Zone, would long remain a source of tension. In 1977, President Jimmy Carter, as a symbol of a new, noninterventionist U.S. attitude toward Latin America, negotiated treaties that led to turning over the canal's operation and control of the Canal Zone to Panama in the year 2000 (see Chapter 26).

Immigrant labor

The Roosevelt Corollary

Roosevelt's actions in Panama anticipated the full-fledged implementation of a principle that came to be called the **Roosevelt Corollary** to the Monroe Doctrine. This held that the United States had the right to exercise "an international police power" in the Western Hemisphere—a significant expansion of James Monroe's pledge to defend the hemisphere against European intervention. In 1904, Roosevelt ordered American forces to seize the customs houses of the Dominican Republic to ensure payment of that country's debts to European and American investors. In 1906, he

An international police power

The World's Constable, a cartoon commenting on Theodore Roosevelt's "new diplomacy," in *Judge*, January 14, 1905, portrays Roosevelt as an impartial policeman, holding in one hand the threat of force and in the other the promise of the peaceful settlement of disputes. Roosevelt stands between the "undisciplined" non-white peoples of the world and the imperialist powers of Europe and Japan.

dispatched troops to Cuba to oversee a disputed election; they remained in the country until 1909.

Roosevelt's successor, William Howard Taft, landed marines in Nicaragua to protect a government friendly to American economic interests. In general, however, Taft emphasized economic investment and loans from American banks, rather than direct military intervention, as the best way to spread American influence. As a result, his foreign policy became known as **Dollar Diplomacy**.

Moral Imperialism

The son of a Presbyterian minister, Woodrow Wilson brought to the presidency a missionary zeal and a sense of his own and the nation's moral righteousness. He appointed as secretary of state William Jennings Bryan, a strong anti-imperialist. Wilson promised a new foreign policy that would respect Latin America's independence and free it from foreign economic domination. But Wilson could not abandon the conviction that the United States had a responsibility to teach other peoples the lessons of democracy.

Woodrow Wilson

Wilson's **moral imperialism** produced more military interventions in Latin America than any president before or since. In 1915, he sent marines to occupy Haiti after the government refused to allow American banks to oversee its financial dealings. In 1916, he established a military government in the Dominican Republic, with the United States controlling the country's customs collections and paying its debts. American soldiers remained in the Dominican Republic until 1924 and in Haiti until 1934. Wilson's foreign policy underscored a paradox of modern American history: the presidents who spoke the most about freedom were likely to intervene most frequently in the affairs of other countries.

Wilson's military interventions in Latin America

Wilson and Mexico

Wilson's major preoccupation in Latin America was Mexico, where in 1911 a revolution led by Francisco Madero overthrew the government of dictator Porfirio Díaz. Two years later, without Wilson's knowledge but with the backing of the U.S. ambassador and of American companies that controlled Mexico's oil and mining industries, military commander Victoriano Huerta assassinated Madero and seized power.

Political turmoil

Wilson was appalled. He would "teach" Latin Americans, he added, "to elect good men." When civil war broke out in Mexico, Wilson ordered American troops to land at Vera Cruz to prevent the arrival of weapons

Vera Cruz

meant for Huerta's forces. But to Wilson's surprise, Mexicans greeted the marines as invaders rather than liberators.

Huerta resigned in 1914 and fled the country. Meanwhile, various Mexican factions turned on one another. A peasant uprising in the southern part of the country, led by Emiliano Zapata, demanded land reform. The Wilson administration offered support to Venustiano Carranza, a leader more devoted to economic modernization. In 1916, several hundred *Pancho Villa* men loyal to Francisco "Pancho" Villa, the leader of another peasant force, raided Columbus, New Mexico, a few miles north of the border, leading to the death of seventeen Americans. With Carranza's approval, Wilson ordered 10,000 troops under the command of General John J. Pershing on an expedition into Mexico that unsuccessfully sought to arrest Villa. Chaos in Mexico continued—within the next few years, Zapata, Carranza, and Villa all fell victim to assassination. Mexico was a warning that it might be difficult to use American might to reorder the internal affairs of other nations.

AMERICA AND THE GREAT WAR

In June 1914, a Serbian nationalist assassinated Archduke Franz Ferdinand, heir to the throne of the Austro-Hungarian empire, in Sarajevo. This deed set in motion a chain of events that plunged Europe into the *Outbreak of war* most devastating war the world had ever seen. In the years before 1914, European nations had engaged in a scramble to obtain colonial possessions overseas and had constructed a shifting series of alliances seeking military domination within Europe. Within a little more than a month, because of the European powers' interlocking military alliances, Britain, France, Russia, and Japan (the Allies) found themselves at war with the Central Powers—Germany, Austria-Hungary, and the Ottoman empire, whose holdings included modern-day Turkey and much of the Middle East.

German forces quickly overran Belgium and part of northern France. The war then settled into a prolonged stalemate, with bloody, indecisive *New technologies* battles succeeding one another. New military technologies—submarines, airplanes, machine guns, tanks, and poison gas—produced unprecedented slaughter. In one five-month battle at Verdun, in 1916, 600,000 French and German soldiers perished—nearly as many deaths as in the entire *Casualties of the Great War* American Civil War. By the time the war ended, an estimated 10 million soldiers, and uncounted millions of civilians, had perished.

In this painting from 1917, the Austrian painter Albin Egger-Lienz portrays World War I soldiers as faceless automatons marching in unison to the slaughter. By this time, the massive loss of life had produced widespread revulsion against the war.

The Great War, or World War I as it came to be called, dealt a severe blow to the optimism and self-confidence of Western civilization. For decades, philosophers, reformers, and politicians had hailed the triumph of reason and human progress, an outlook hard to reconcile with the mass slaughter of World War I. The conflict was also a shock to European socialist and labor movements. Karl Marx had called on the "workers of the world" to unite against their oppressors. Instead, they marched off to kill each other.

Blow to Western optimism

Neutrality and Preparedness

As war engulfed Europe, Americans found themselves sharply divided. British-Americans sided with their nation of origin, as did many other Americans who associated Great Britain with liberty and democracy and Germany with repressive government. On the other hand, German-Americans identified with Germany, and Irish-Americans bitterly opposed any aid to the British. Immigrants from the Russian empire, especially Jews, had no desire to see the United States aid the czar's regime.

Americans divided

When war broke out in 1914, President Wilson proclaimed American neutrality. But naval warfare in Europe reverberated in the United States. Britain declared a naval blockade of Germany and began to stop American merchant vessels. Germany launched submarine warfare against ships entering and leaving British ports. In May 1915, a German submarine sank the British liner **Lusitania** (which was carrying a large cache of arms) off the coast of Ireland, causing the deaths of 1,198 passengers, including 124 Americans. Wilson composed a note of protest so strong that Bryan

American casualties

PEACE·HAS·HER·CONQUESTS·GREATER·FAR·THAN·WAR

R.M.S. LUSITANIA
QUEEN OF THE SEAS

The liner *Lusitania*, pictured on a "peace" postcard. Its sinking by a German submarine in 1915 strengthened the resolve of those who wished to see the United States enter the European war.

Wilson's reelection

A 1916 Wilson campaign truck (a new development in political campaigning), promising peace, prosperity, and preparedness.

resigned as secretary of state, fearing that the president was laying the foundation for military intervention.

The sinking of the *Lusitania* outraged American public opinion and strengthened the hand of those who believed that the United States must prepare for possible entry into the war. Wilson himself had strong pro-British sympathies and viewed Germany as "the natural foe of liberty." By the end of 1915, he had embarked on a policy of "preparedness"—a crash program to expand the American army and navy.

The Road to War

In May 1916, Germany announced the suspension of submarine warfare against noncombatants. Wilson's preparedness program seemed to have succeeded in securing the right of Americans to travel freely on the high seas. "He kept us out of war" became the slogan of his campaign for reelection. With the Republican Party reunited after its split in 1912, the election proved to be one of the closest in American history. Wilson defeated Republican candidate Charles Evans Hughes by only twenty-three electoral votes and about 600,000 popular votes out of more than 18 million cast. Partly because he seemed to promise not to send American soldiers to Europe, Wilson carried ten of the twelve states that had adopted woman suffrage. Without the votes of women, Wilson would not have been reelected.

Almost immediately, however, Germany announced its intention to resume submarine warfare against ships sailing to or from the British Isles, and several American merchant vessels were sunk. In March 1917, British spies intercepted and made public the **Zimmermann Telegram**, a message by German foreign secretary Arthur Zimmermann calling on Mexico to join in a coming war against the United States and promising to help it recover territory lost in the Mexican War of 1846–1848. On April 2, Wilson went before Congress to ask for a declaration of war against Germany. "The world," he proclaimed, "must be made safe for democracy." The war resolution passed the Senate 82–6 and the House 373–50.

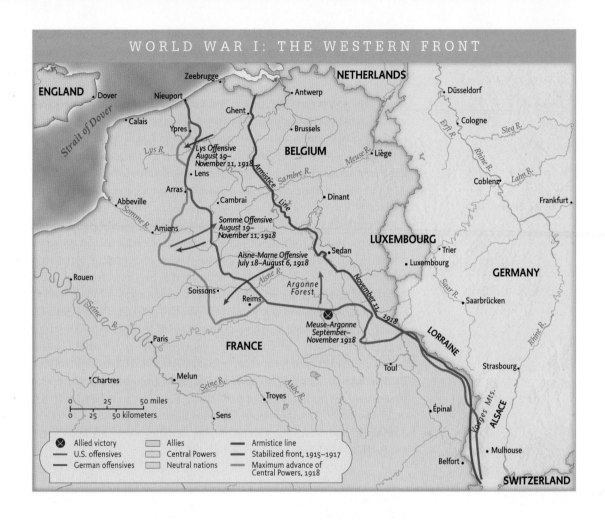

WORLD WAR I: THE WESTERN FRONT

After years of stalemate on the western front in World War I, the arrival of American troops in 1917 and 1918 shifted the balance of power and made possible the Allied victory.

The Fourteen Points

Not until the spring of 1918 did American forces arrive in Europe in large numbers. By then, the world situation had taken a dramatic turn. In November 1917, a communist revolution headed by Vladimir Lenin overthrew the Russian government. Shortly thereafter, Lenin withdrew Russia from the war and published the secret treaties by which the Allies had agreed to divide up conquered territory after the war—an embarrassment for Wilson, who had promised a just peace.

Partly to assure the country that the war was being fought for a moral cause, Wilson in January 1918 issued the **Fourteen Points**, the clearest statement of American war aims and of his vision of a new international order. Among the key principles were self-determination for all nations, freedom of the seas, free trade, open diplomacy (an end to secret treaties), the readjustment of colonial claims with colonized people given "equal weight" in deciding their futures, and the creation of a "general association of nations" to preserve the peace. Wilson envisioned this last provision, which led to the establishment after the war of the League of Nations, as a kind of global counterpart to the regulatory commissions Progressives had created at home to maintain social harmony. The Fourteen Points established the agenda for the peace conference that followed the war.

The United States threw its economic resources and manpower into the war. When American troops finally arrived in Europe, they turned the tide of battle. In the spring of 1918, they helped repulse a German advance near Paris and by July were participating in a major Allied counter-offensive. In September, in the Meuse-Argonne campaign, American soldiers under the command of General John J. Pershing, fresh from his campaign in Mexico, helped push back the German army. With 1.2 million American soldiers taking part and well over 100,000 dead and wounded, Meuse-Argonne, which lasted a month and a half, was the main American engagement of the war and one of the most significant and deadliest battles in American history. It formed part of a massive Allied offensive involving British, French, and Belgian soldiers and those from overseas European possessions. With his forces in full retreat, the German kaiser abdicated on November 9. Two days later, Germany sued for peace. Over 100,000 Americans had died, a substantial number, but they were only 1 percent of the 10 million soldiers killed in the Great War.

THE WAR AT HOME

The Progressives' War

For most Progressives, the war offered the possibility of reforming American society along scientific lines, instilling a sense of national unity and self-sacrifice, and expanding social justice. That American power could now disseminate Progressive values around the globe heightened the war's appeal.

Almost without exception, Progressive intellectuals and reformers, joined by prominent labor leaders and native-born socialists, rallied to Wilson's support. The roster included intellectuals like John Dewey, AFL head Samuel Gompers, socialist writers like Upton Sinclair, and prominent reformers including Florence Kelley and Charlotte Perkins Gilman.

The Wartime State

Like the Civil War, World War I created, albeit temporarily, a national state with unprecedented powers and a sharply increased presence in Americans' everyday lives. Under the **Selective Service Act** of May 1917, 24 million men were required to register with the draft. New federal agencies moved to regulate industry, transportation, labor relations, and agriculture. Headed by Wall Street financier Bernard Baruch, the **War Industries Board** presided over all elements of war production from the distribution of raw materials to the prices of manufactured goods. To spur efficiency, it established standardized specifications for everything from automobile tires to shoe colors (three were permitted—black, brown, and white). The Railroad Administration took control of the nation's transportation system, and the Fuel Agency rationed coal and oil. The Food Administration instructed farmers on modern methods of cultivation and promoted the more efficient preparation of meals.

The War Labor Board, which included representatives of government, industry, and the American Federation of Labor, pressed for the establishment of a minimum wage, an eight-hour workday, and the right to form unions. During the war, wages rose substantially, working conditions in many industries improved, and union membership doubled. To finance the war, corporate and individual income taxes rose enormously. By 1918, the wealthiest Americans were paying 60 percent of their income in taxes. Tens of millions of Americans answered the call to demonstrate their patriotism by purchasing Liberty bonds.

The Propaganda War

During the Civil War, it had been left to private agencies—Union Leagues, the Loyal Publication Society, and others—to mobilize prowar public opinion. But the Wilson administration decided that patriotism was too important to leave to the private sector. Many Americans opposed American participation, notably the Industrial Workers of the World (IWW) and the bulk of the Socialist Party, which in 1917 condemned the declaration of war as "a crime against the people of the United States" and called on "the workers of all countries" to refuse to fight.

In April 1917, the Wilson administration created the Committee on Public Information (CPI) to explain to Americans and the world, as its

All combatants issued propaganda posters. The American poster uses an image of the Statue of Liberty to sell war bonds. The German one, satirically entitled *We Are Barbarians*, refutes the charge of barbarism hurled at Germans by the Allies. It relates that Germany outstrips England and France in Nobel Prizes, provision for the elderly, book publication, education, and literacy.

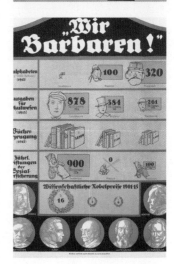

director, George Creel, put it, "the cause that compelled America to take arms in defense of its liberties and free institutions." The CPI flooded the country with prowar propaganda, using every available medium from pamphlets (of which it issued 75 million) to posters, newspaper advertisements, and motion pictures.

The CPI couched its appeal in the Progressive language of social cooperation and expanded democracy. Abroad, this meant a peace based on the principle of national self-determination. At home, it meant improving "industrial democracy." CPI pamphlets foresaw a postwar society complete with a "universal eight-hour day" and a living wage for all.

Although "democracy" served as the key term of wartime mobilization, "freedom" also took on new significance. The war, a CPI advertisement proclaimed, was being fought in "the great cause of freedom." The most common visual image in wartime propaganda was the Statue of Liberty, employed especially to rally support among immigrants. Wilson's speeches cast the United States as a land of liberty fighting alongside a "concert of free people" to secure self-determination for the oppressed peoples of the world. Government propaganda whipped up hatred of the wartime foe by portraying Germany as a nation of barbaric Huns.

The Coming of Woman Suffrage

The enlistment of "democracy" and "freedom" as ideological war weapons inevitably inspired demands for their expansion at home. In 1916, Wilson had cautiously endorsed votes for women. America's entry into the war threatened to tear the suffrage movement apart, because many advocates had been associated with opposition to American involvement. Indeed, among those who voted against the declaration of war was the first woman member of Congress, the staunch pacifist Jeannette Rankin of Montana.

Although defeated in her reelection bid in 1918, Rankin would return to Congress in 1940. She became the only member to oppose the declaration of war against Japan in 1941, which ended her political career. In 1968, at the age of eighty-five, Rankin took part in a giant march on Washington to protest the war in Vietnam.

As during the Civil War, however, most leaders of woman suffrage organizations enthusiastically enlisted in the effort. Women sold war bonds, organized patriotic rallies, and went to work in war production jobs. Some 22,000 served as clerical workers and nurses with American forces in Europe.

At the same time, a new generation of college-educated activists, organized in the National Woman's Party, pressed for the right to vote

THE AWAKENING

A 1915 cartoon showing the western states where women had won the right to vote. Women in the East reach out to a western woman carrying a torch of liberty.

with militant tactics many older suffrage advocates found scandalous. The party's leader, Alice Paul, had studied in England between 1907 and 1910, when the British suffrage movement adopted a strategy that included arrests, imprisonments, and vigorous denunciations of a male-dominated political system. Paul compared Wilson to the kaiser, and a group of her followers chained themselves to the White House fence, resulting in a seven-month prison sentence. When they began a hunger strike, the prisoners were force-fed.

Alice Paul

The combination of women's patriotic service and widespread outrage over the treatment of Paul and her fellow prisoners pushed the administration toward full-fledged support of woman suffrage. In 1920, the long struggle ended with the ratification of the Nineteenth Amendment, which barred states from using sex as a qualification for the suffrage. The United States became the twenty-seventh country to allow women to vote.

The Nineteenth Amendment

Prohibition

The war gave a powerful impulse to other campaigns that had engaged the energies of many women in the Progressive era. Prohibition, a movement inherited from the nineteenth century that had gained new strength and militancy in Progressive America, finally achieved national success during the war. Employers hoped it would create a more disciplined labor force. Urban reformers believed that it would promote a more orderly city environment and undermine urban political machines, which

VOICES OF FREEDOM

From Woodrow Wilson, War Message to Congress (1917)

More than any other individual in the early twentieth century, President Woodrow Wilson articulated a new vision of America's relationship to the rest of the world. In his message to a special session of Congress on April 2, 1917, after Germany launched unrestrained submarine warfare against ships, including American ones, in the Atlantic, Wilson asked for a declaration of war. In his most celebrated sentence, Wilson declared, "The world must be made safe for democracy."

Let us be very clear, and make very clear to all the world what our motives and our objects are. . . . Our object . . . is to vindicate the principles of peace and justice in the life of the world as against selfish and autocratic power and to set up amongst the really free and self-governed peoples of the world such a concert of purpose and of action as will henceforth ensure the observance of those principles. . . . The menace to peace and freedom lies in the existence of autocratic governments backed by organized force which is controlled wholly by their will, not by the will of their people.

A steadfast concert for peace can never be maintained except by a partnership of democratic nations. No autocratic government could be trusted to keep faith within it or observe its covenants. . . . Only free peoples can hold their purpose and their honour steady to a common end and prefer the interests of mankind to any narrow interest of their own. . . .

We are now about to accept gage of battle with this natural foe to liberty and shall, if necessary, spend the whole force of the nation to check and nullify its pretensions and its power. We are glad, now that we see the facts with no veil of false pretense about them, to fight thus for the ultimate peace of the world and for the liberation of its peoples, the German peoples included: for the rights of nations great and small and the privilege of men everywhere to choose their way of life and of obedience. The world must be made safe for democracy. Its peace must be planted upon the tested foundations of political liberty. We have no selfish ends to serve. We desire no conquest, no dominion. . . . If there should be disloyalty, it will be dealt with with a firm hand of stern repression. . . .

It is a fearful thing to lead this great peaceful people into war, into the most terrible and disastrous of all wars, civilization itself seeming to be in the balance. But the right is more precious than peace, and we shall fight for the things which we have always carried nearest our hearts—for democracy, . . . for the rights and liberties of small nations, for a universal dominion of right by such a concert of free peoples as shall bring peace and safety to all nations and make the world itself at last free.

From Eugene V. Debs, Speech to the Jury before Sentencing under the Espionage Act (1918)

Socialist leader Eugene V. Debs was arrested for delivering an antiwar speech and convicted of violating the Espionage Act. In his speech to the jury, he defended the right of dissent in wartime.

Gentlemen, you have heard the report of my speech at Canton [Ohio] on June 16, and I submit that there is not a word in that speech to warrant the charges set out in the indictment. . . . In what I had to say there my purpose was to have the people understand something about the social system in which we live and to prepare them to change this system by perfectly peaceable and orderly means into what I, as a Socialist, conceive to be a real democracy. . . . I have never advocated violence in any form. I have always believed in education, in intelligence, in enlightenment; and I have always made my appeal to the reason and to the conscience of the people.

In every age there have been a few heroic souls who have been in advance of their time, who have been misunderstood, maligned, persecuted, sometimes put to death. . . . Washington, Jefferson, Franklin, Paine, and their compeers were the rebels of their day. . . . But they had the moral courage to be true to their convictions. . . .

William Lloyd Garrison, Wendell Phillips, Elizabeth Cady Stanton . . . and other leaders of the abolition movement who were regarded as public enemies and treated accordingly, were true to their faith and stood their ground. . . . You are now teaching your children to revere their memories, while all of their detractors are in oblivion. . . .

The war of 1812 was opposed and condemned by some of the most influential citizens; the Mexican War was vehemently opposed and bitterly denounced, even after the war had been declared and was in progress, by Abraham Lincoln, Charles Sumner, Daniel Webster. . . . They were not indicted; they were not charged with treason. . . .

Isn't it strange that we Socialists stand almost alone today in upholding and defending the Constitution of the United States? The revolutionary fathers . . . understood that free speech, a free press and the right of free assemblage by the people were fundamental principles in democratic government. . . . I believe in the right of free speech, in war as well as in peace.

QUESTIONS

1. *What does Wilson think is the greatest threat to freedom in the world?*

2. *Why does Debs relate the history of wartime dissent in the United States?*

3. *Does anything in Wilson's speech offer a harbinger of the extreme repression of free speech that occurred during World War I?*

ON TO WASHINGTON!

STORM THE CAPITOL WITH PETITIONS FOR NATIONAL CONSTITUTIONAL
PROHIBITION—NOW IS THE TIME FOR ACTION

A 1916 cartoon from the publication of the Woman's Christian Temperance Union shows petitions for Prohibition flooding into Congress.

Security and freedom

Restrictions on freedom of speech

used saloons as places to organize. Women reformers hoped Prohibition would protect wives and children from husbands who engaged in domestic violence when drunk or who squandered their wages at saloons. Many native-born Protestants saw Prohibition as a way of imposing "American" values on immigrants.

After some success at the state level, Prohibitionists came to see national legislation as their best strategy. The war gave them added ammunition. Many prominent breweries were owned by German-Americans, making beer seem unpatriotic. The Food Administration insisted that grain must be used to produce food, not brewed into beer or distilled into liquor. In December 1917, Congress passed the **Eighteenth Amendment**, prohibiting the manufacture and sale of intoxicating liquor. It was ratified by the states in 1919 and went into effect at the beginning of 1920.

Liberty in Wartime

World War I raised questions already glimpsed during the Civil War that would trouble the nation again during the McCarthy era and in the aftermath of the terrorist attacks of 2001: What is the balance between security and freedom? Does the Constitution protect citizens' rights during wartime? Should dissent be equated with lack of patriotism?

Despite the administration's idealistic language of democracy and freedom, the war inaugurated the most intense repression of civil liberties the nation has ever known.

The Espionage and Sedition Acts

For the first time since the Alien and Sedition Acts of 1798, the federal government enacted laws to restrict freedom of speech. The **Espionage Act** of 1917 prohibited not only spying and interfering with the draft but also "false statements" that might impede military success. The postmaster general barred from the mails numerous newspapers and magazines critical of the administration. In 1918, the **Sedition Act** made it a crime to make spoken or printed statements that intended to cast "contempt, scorn, or disrepute" on the "form of government," or that advocated interference with the war effort. The government charged more than 2,000 persons with violating these laws. Over half were convicted. A court sentenced Ohio farmer John White to twenty-one months in prison for saying that the murder of innocent women and children by German soldiers was no worse than what the United States had done in the Philippines in the war of 1899–1903.

The most prominent victim was Eugene V. Debs, convicted in 1918 under the Espionage Act for delivering an antiwar speech. Germany sent a socialist leader to prison for four years for opposing the war; in the United States, Debs's sentence was ten years. After the war's end, Wilson rejected the advice of his attorney general that he commute Debs's sentence. Debs ran for president while still in prison in 1920 and received 900,000 votes. It was left to Wilson's successor, Warren G. Harding, to release Debs from prison in 1921.

Douglas Fairbanks, one of the era's most celebrated movie stars, addressing a 1918 rally urging people to buy Liberty bonds.

Coercive Patriotism

Even more extreme repression took place at the hands of state governments and private groups. During the war, thirty-three states outlawed the possession or display of red or black flags (symbols, respectively, of communism and anarchism), and twenty-three outlawed a newly created offense, "criminal syndicalism," the advocacy of unlawful acts to accomplish political change or "a change in industrial ownership."

"Criminal syndicalism"

"Who is the real patriot?" Emma Goldman asked when the United States entered the war. She answered, those who "love America with open eyes," who were not blind to "the wrongs committed in the name of patriotism." But from the federal government to local authorities and private groups, patriotism came to be equated with support for the government, the war, and the American economic system. Throughout the country, schools revised their course offerings to ensure their patriotism and required teachers to sign loyalty oaths.

A poster demands that citizens prove they are "100% American" by purchasing war bonds.

The 250,000 members of the newly formed American Protective League (APL) helped the Justice Department identify radicals and critics of the war by spying on their neighbors and carrying out "slacker raids" in which thousands of men were stopped on the streets of major cities and required to produce draft registration cards. Employers cooperated with the government in crushing the Industrial Workers of the World (IWW), a move long demanded by business interests. In September 1917, operating under one of the broadest warrants in American history, federal agents swooped down on IWW offices throughout the country, arresting hundreds of leaders and seizing files and publications.

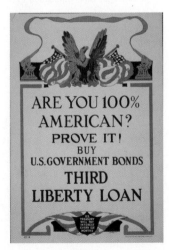

Although some Progressives protested individual excesses, most failed to speak out against the broad suppression of freedom of expression.

Florine Stettheimer's *New York/ Liberty*, painted in 1918, depicts the Statue of Liberty, warships, and airplanes in an exuberant tribute to New York City and to the idea of freedom in the wake of World War I.

Demands for Americanization

Randolph Bourne's "Trans-National America"

Civil liberties, by and large, had never been a major concern of Progressives, who had always viewed the national state as the embodiment of democratic purpose and insisted that freedom flowed from participating in the life of society, not standing in opposition. Strong believers in the use of national power to improve social conditions, Progressives found themselves ill prepared to develop a defense of minority rights against majority or governmental tyranny.

WHO IS AN AMERICAN?

The "Race Problem"

Even before American participation in World War I, what contemporaries called the "race problem"—the tensions that arose from the country's increasing ethnic diversity—had become a major subject of public concern. "Race" referred to far more than black-white relations. The *Dictionary of Races of Peoples*, published in 1911 by the U.S. Immigration Commission, listed no fewer than forty-five immigrant "races," each supposedly with its own inborn characteristics. They ranged from Anglo-Saxons at the top down to Hebrews, Northern Italians, and, lowest of all, Southern Italians—supposedly violent, undisciplined, and incapable of assimilation. The new science of eugenics, which studied the alleged mental characteristics of different races, gave anti-immigrant sentiment an air of professional expertise.

Somehow, the very nationalization of politics and economic life served to heighten awareness of ethnic and racial difference and spurred demands for "Americanization"—the creation of a more homogeneous national culture. A 1908 play by the Jewish immigrant writer Israel Zangwill, *The Melting Pot*, gave a popular name to the process by which newcomers were supposed to merge their identity into existing American nationality. Public and private groups of all kinds—including educators, employers, labor leaders, social reformers, and public officials—took up the task of Americanizing new immigrants. Fearful that adult newcomers remained too stuck in their Old World ways, public schools paid great attention to Americanizing immigrants' children. Moreover, the federal and state governments demanded that immigrants demonstrate their unwavering devotion to the United States.

A minority of Progressives questioned Americanization efforts and insisted on respect for immigrant subcultures. Probably the most penetrating critique issued from the pen of Randolph Bourne, whose 1916 essay "Trans-National America" exposed the fundamental flaw in the

Americanization model. "There is no distinctive American culture," Bourne pointed out. Interaction between individuals and groups had produced the nation's music, poetry, and other cultural expressions. Bourne envisioned a democratic, cosmopolitan society in which immigrants and natives alike submerged their group identities in a new "trans-national" culture.

The Anti-German Crusade

German-Americans bore the brunt of forced Americanization. The first wave of German immigrants had arrived before the Civil War. By 1914, German-Americans numbered nearly 9 million, including immigrants and persons of German parentage. They had created thriving ethnic institutions including clubs, sports associations, schools, and theaters. On the eve of the war, many Americans admired German traditions in literature, music, and philosophy, and one-quarter of all the high school students in the country studied the German language. But after American entry into the war, the use of German and expressions of German culture became a target of prowar organizations.

German culture in America

By 1919, the vast majority of the states had enacted laws restricting the teaching of foreign languages. Popular words of German origin were changed: "hamburger" became "liberty sandwich," and "sauerkraut" "liberty cabbage." The government jailed Karl Muck, the director of the Boston Symphony and a Swiss citizen, as an enemy alien after he insisted on including the works of German composers like Beethoven in his concerts.

Restricting the teaching of foreign languages

Toward Immigration Restriction

Even as Americanization programs sought to assimilate immigrants into American society, the war strengthened the conviction that certain kinds of undesirable persons ought to be excluded altogether. The new immigrants, one advocate of restriction declared, appreciated the values of democracy and freedom far less than "the Anglo-Saxon." Stanford University psychologist Lewis Terman introduced the term "IQ" (intelligence quotient) in 1916, claiming that this single number could measure an individual's mental capacity. Intelligence tests administered to recruits by the army seemed to confirm scientifically that blacks and the new immigrants stood far below native white Protestants on the IQ scale, further spurring demands for immigration restriction.

The war accelerated other efforts to upgrade the American population. Some were inspired by the idea of improving the human race by discouraging reproduction among less "desirable" persons. Indiana in 1907 had passed a law authorizing doctors to sterilize insane and "feeble-minded"

A 1919 cartoon, *Close the Gate*, warns that unrestricted immigration allows dangerous radicals to enter the United States.

inmates in mental institutions so that they would not pass their "defective" genes on to children. Numerous other states now followed suit. In *Buck v. Bell* (1927), the Supreme Court upheld the constitutionality of these laws. Justice Oliver Wendell Holmes's opinion included the famous statement, "Three generations of imbeciles are enough." By the time the practice ended in the 1960s, some 63,000 persons had been involuntarily sterilized.

Groups Apart: Mexicans and Asian-Americans

No matter how coercive, Americanization programs assumed that European immigrants and especially their children could eventually adjust to the conditions of American life, embrace American ideals, and become productive citizens enjoying the full blessings of American freedom. This assumption did not apply to non-white immigrants or to blacks.

Mexicans in the Southwest

The war led to further growth of the Southwest's Mexican population. Wartime demand for labor from the area's mine owners and large farmers led the government to exempt Mexicans temporarily from the literacy test enacted in 1917. Segregation, by law and custom, was common in schools, hospitals, theaters, and other institutions in states with significant Mexican populations. By 1920, nearly all Mexican children in California and the Southwest were educated in their own schools or classrooms. Phoenix, Arizona, established separate public schools for Indians, Mexicans, blacks, and whites. Although in far smaller numbers than blacks, Mexican-Americans also suffered lynchings—over 200 between 1880 and 1930. Discrimination led to the formation of La Grán Liga Mexicanista de Beneficencia y Protección, which aimed to improve the conditions of Mexicans in the United States and "to strike back at the hatred of some bad sons of Uncle Sam who believe themselves better than the Mexicans."

Even more restrictive were policies toward Asian-Americans. In 1906, the San Francisco school board ordered all Asian students confined to a single public school. When the Japanese government protested, President Theodore Roosevelt persuaded the city to rescind the order. *The Gentlemen's Agreement* He then negotiated the Gentlemen's Agreement of 1907, whereby Japan agreed to end migration to the United States except for the wives and children of men already in the country. In 1913, California barred all aliens incapable of becoming naturalized citizens (that is, all Asians) from owning or leasing land.

The Color Line

Exclusion of blacks

By far the largest non-white group, African-Americans were excluded from nearly every Progressive definition of freedom described in Chapter 18. After their disenfranchisement in the South, few could participate in

American democracy. Barred from joining most unions and from skilled employment, black workers had little access to "industrial freedom." Nor could blacks, the majority desperately poor, participate fully in the emerging consumer economy, either as employees in the new department stores (except as janitors and cleaning women) or as purchasers of the consumer goods now flooding the marketplace.

Progressive intellectuals, social scientists, labor reformers, and suffrage advocates displayed a remarkable indifference to the black condition. Most settlement-house reformers accepted segregation as natural and equitable. White leaders of the woman suffrage movement said little about black disenfranchisement. The amendment that achieved woman suffrage left the states free to limit voting by poll taxes and literacy tests. Living in the South, the vast majority of the country's black women still could not vote.

Roosevelt, Wilson, and Race

The Progressive presidents shared prevailing attitudes concerning blacks. Theodore Roosevelt shocked white opinion by inviting Booker T. Washington to dine with him in the White House and by appointing a number of blacks to federal offices. But in 1906, when a small group of black soldiers shot off their guns in Brownsville, Texas, killing one resident, and none of their fellows would name them, Roosevelt ordered the dishonorable discharge of three black companies—156 men in all, including six winners of the Congressional Medal of Honor.

Woodrow Wilson, a native of Virginia, could speak without irony of the South's "genuine representative government" and its exalted "standards of liberty." His administration imposed racial segregation in federal departments in Washington, D.C., and dismissed numerous black federal employees. Wilson allowed D. W. Griffith's film *Birth of a Nation*, which glorified the Ku Klux Klan as the defender of white civilization during Reconstruction, to have its premiere at the White House in 1915.

Blacks subject to disenfranchisement and segregation were understandably skeptical of the nation's claim to embody freedom. In one of hundreds of lynchings during the Progressive era, a white mob in Springfield, Missouri, in 1906 falsely accused three black men of rape, hanged them from an electric light pole, and burned their bodies in a public orgy of violence. Atop the pole stood a replica of the Statue of Liberty.

W. E. B. Du Bois and the Revival of Black Protest

Black leaders struggled to find a strategy to rekindle the national commitment to equality that had flickered brightly, if briefly, during

A poster advertising the 1915 film *The Birth of a Nation*, which had its premiere at Woodrow Wilson's White House. The movie glorified the Ku Klux Klan and depicted blacks during Reconstruction as unworthy of participation in government and a danger to white womanhood.

A cartoon from the *St. Louis Post-Dispatch*, April 17, 1906, commenting on the lynching of three black men in Springfield, Missouri. The shadow cast by the Statue of Liberty forms a gallows on the ground.

Reconstruction. No one thought more deeply, or over so long a period, about the black condition and the challenge it posed to American democracy than the scholar and activist W. E. B. Du Bois. Born in 1868, and educated at Fisk and Harvard universities, Du Bois lived to his ninety-fifth year. The unifying theme of Du Bois's career was his effort to reconcile the contradiction between what he called "American freedom for whites and the continuing subjection of Negroes." His book *The Souls of Black Folk* (1903) issued a clarion call for blacks dissatisfied with the accommodationist policies of Booker T. Washington to press for equal rights. Du Bois believed that educated African-Americans like himself—the "talented tenth" of the black community—must use their education and training to challenge inequality.

In some ways, Du Bois was a typical Progressive who believed that investigation, exposure, and education would lead to solutions for social problems. But he also understood the necessity of political action. In 1905, Du Bois gathered a group of black leaders at Niagara Falls (meeting on the Canadian side because no American hotel would provide accommodations) and organized the Niagara movement, which sought to reinvigorate the abolitionist tradition. "We claim for ourselves," Du Bois wrote in the group's manifesto, "every single right that belongs to a freeborn American." Four years later, Du Bois joined with a group of mostly white reformers, shocked by a lynching in Springfield, Illinois (Lincoln's adult home), to create the **National Association for the Advancement of Colored People**. The NAACP, as it was known, launched a long struggle for the enforcement of the Fourteenth and Fifteenth Amendments.

The NAACP's legal strategy won a few victories. In *Bailey v. Alabama* (1911), the Supreme Court overturned southern "peonage" laws that made it a crime for sharecroppers to break their labor contracts. Six years later, it ruled unconstitutional a Louisville zoning regulation excluding blacks from living in certain parts of the city (primarily because it interfered with whites' right to sell their property as they saw fit). Overall, however, the Progressive era witnessed virtually no progress toward racial justice.

Closing Ranks

Among black Americans, the wartime language of freedom inspired hopes for a radical change in the country's racial system. The black press rallied to the war. Du Bois himself, in a widely reprinted editorial in

The "talented tenth"

The Niagara movement

The NAACP

Bailey v. Alabama

Rallying to the war

the NAACP's monthly magazine, *The Crisis*, called on African-Americans to "close ranks" and enlist in the army, to help "make our own America a real land of the free."

Black participation in the Civil War had helped to secure the destruction of slavery and the achievement of citizenship. But during World War I, closing ranks did not bring significant gains. The navy barred blacks entirely, and the segregated army confined most of the 400,000 blacks who served in the war to supply units rather than combat. Contact with African colonial soldiers fighting alongside the British and French did widen the horizons of black American soldiers. But although colonial troops marched in the victory parade in Paris, the Wilson administration did not allow black Americans to participate.

One of a series of paintings by the black artist Jacob Lawrence called *The Migration Series*, inspired by the massive movement of African-Americans to the North during and after World War I. For each, Lawrence composed a brief title, in this case, "In the North the Negro had better educational facilities."

The Great Migration

Nonetheless, the war unleashed social changes that altered the contours of American race relations. The combination of increased wartime production and a drastic falloff in immigration from Europe once war broke out opened thousands of industrial jobs to black laborers for the first time, inspiring a large-scale migration from South to North. On the eve of World

TABLE 19.1   The Great Migration

CITY	BLACK POPULATION, 1910	BLACK POPULATION, 1920	PERCENT INCREASE
New York	91,709	152,467	66.3%
Philadelphia	84,459	134,229	58.9
Chicago	44,103	109,458	148.2
St. Louis	43,960	69,854	58.9
Detroit	5,741	40,838	611.3
Pittsburgh	25,623	37,725	47.2
Cleveland	8,448	34,451	307.8

War I, 90 percent of the African-American population still lived in the South. But between 1910 and 1920, half a million blacks left the South. The black population of Chicago more than doubled, New York City's rose 66 percent, and smaller industrial cities like Akron, Buffalo, and Trenton showed similar gains. Many motives sustained the **Great Migration**—higher wages in northern factories than were available in the South (even if blacks remained confined to menial and unskilled positions), opportunities for educating their children, escape from the threat of lynching, and the prospect of exercising the right to vote.

Higher wages in northern factories

The black migrants, mostly young men and women, carried with them "a new vision of opportunity, of social and economic freedom," as Alain Locke explained in the preface to his influential book *The New Negro* (1925). Yet the migrants encountered vast disappointments—severely restricted employment opportunities, exclusion from unions, rigid housing segregation, and outbreaks of violence that made it clear that no region of the country was free from racial hostility. The new black presence, coupled with demands for change inspired by the war, created a racial tinderbox that needed only an incident to trigger an explosion.

Racial restrictions in the North

Racial Violence, North and South

Dozens of blacks were killed during a 1917 riot in East St. Louis, Illinois, where employers had recruited black workers in an attempt to weaken unions (most of which excluded blacks from membership). In 1919, more than 250 persons died in riots in the urban North. Most notable was the violence in Chicago, touched off by the drowning by white bathers of a black teenager who accidentally crossed the unofficial dividing line between black and white beaches on Lake Michigan. By the time the National Guard restored order, 38 persons had been killed and more than 500 injured.

Buildings in Tulsa, Oklahoma, burn during the city's riot of June 1921. An estimated 300 people died when white mobs destroyed the city's black neighborhood in the worst outbreak of racial violence in American history.

Violence was not confined to the North. In the year after the war ended, seventy-six persons were lynched in the South, including several returning black veterans wearing their uniforms. The **Tulsa riot**, the worst race riot in American history, occurred in Tulsa, Oklahoma, in 1921 when more than 300 blacks were killed and over 10,000 left homeless after a white mob, including police and National Guardsmen, burned an all-black section of the city to the ground.

The Rise of Garveyism

World War I kindled a new spirit of militancy. The East St. Louis riot of 1917 inspired a widely publicized Silent Protest Parade on New York's Fifth Avenue in which 10,000 blacks silently carried placards reading, "Mr. President, Why Not Make America Safe for Democracy?" In the new densely populated black ghettos of the North, widespread support emerged for the Universal Negro Improvement Association, a movement for African independence and black self-reliance launched by **Marcus Garvey**, a recent immigrant from Jamaica. To Garveyites, freedom meant national self-determination. Blacks, they insisted, should enjoy the same internationally recognized identity enjoyed by other peoples in the aftermath of the war. Du Bois and other established black leaders viewed Garvey as little more than a demagogue. They applauded when the government deported him after a conviction for mail fraud. But the massive following his movement achieved testified to the sense of betrayal that had been kindled in black communities during and after the war.

Marcus Garvey, leader of the largest black movement of the World War I era.

1919

A Worldwide Upsurge

The combination of militant hopes for social change and disappointment with the war's outcome was evident far beyond the black community. In the Union of Soviet Socialist Republics (or Soviet Union), as Russia had been renamed after the revolution, Lenin's government had nationalized landholdings, banks, and factories and proclaimed the socialist dream of a workers' government. The Russian Revolution and the democratic aspirations unleashed by World War I sent tremors of hope and fear throughout the world. General strikes demanding the fulfillment of wartime promises of "industrial democracy" took place in Belfast, Glasgow, and Winnipeg. In Spain, anarchist peasants began seizing land. Crowds in India challenged British rule, and nationalist movements in other colonies demanded independence.

Global uprisings

The worldwide revolutionary upsurge produced a countervailing mobilization by opponents of radical change. Despite Allied attempts to overturn its government, the Soviet regime survived, but in the rest of the world the tide of change receded. By the fall, the mass strikes had been suppressed and conservative governments had been installed in central Europe.

Survival of the Soviet Union

Upheaval in America

The flu epidemic

In the United States, 1919 also brought unprecedented turmoil. It seemed all the more disorienting for occurring in the midst of a worldwide flu epidemic that killed over 20 million persons, including nearly 700,000 Americans. Racial violence, as noted above, was widespread. In June, bombs exploded at the homes of prominent Americans, including the attorney general, A. Mitchell Palmer, who escaped uninjured. Among aggrieved American workers, wartime language linking patriotism with democracy and freedom inspired hopes that an era of social justice and economic empowerment was at hand. In 1917, Wilson had told the AFL, "While we are fighting for freedom, we must see to it among other things that labor is free." Labor took him seriously—more seriously, it seems, than Wilson intended.

In 1919, more than 4 million workers engaged in strikes—the greatest wave of labor unrest in American history. There were walkouts, among many others, by textile workers, telephone operators, and Broadway actors. They were met by an unprecedented mobilization of employers, government, and private patriotic organizations.

The 1919 steel strike

The wartime rhetoric of economic democracy and freedom helped to inspire the era's greatest labor uprising, the 1919 steel strike. Centered in Chicago, it united some 365,000 mostly immigrant workers in demands for union recognition, higher wages, and an eight-hour workday. Before 1917, the steel mills were little autocracies where managers arbitrarily established wages and working conditions and suppressed all efforts at union organizing. During the war, workers won an eight-hour day. "For why this war?" asked one Polish immigrant steelworker at a union meeting. "For why we buy Liberty bonds? For the mills? No, for freedom and America—for everybody."

In response to the strike, steel magnates launched a concerted counterattack. Employers appealed to anti-immigrant sentiment among native-born workers, many of whom returned to work, and conducted a propaganda campaign that associated the strikers with the IWW, communism, and disloyalty. With middle-class opinion having turned against the labor movement and the police in Pittsburgh assaulting workers on the streets, the strike collapsed in early 1920.

Middle-class opinion turns against the labor movement

The Red Scare

Wartime repression of dissent reached its peak with the **Red Scare of 1919–1920**, a short-lived but intense period of political intolerance inspired by the postwar strike wave and the social tensions and fears generated by the Russian Revolution. Convinced that episodes like the steel strike were part of a worldwide communist conspiracy, Attorney General A. Mitchell Palmer in November 1919 and January 1920 dispatched federal agents to raid the offices of radical and labor organizations throughout the country. More than 5,000 persons were arrested, most of them without warrants, and held for months without charge. The government deported hundreds of immigrant radicals, including Emma Goldman.

The abuse of civil liberties in early 1920 was so severe that Palmer came under heavy criticism from Congress and much of the press. Even the explosion of a bomb outside the New York Stock Exchange in September 1920, which killed forty persons, failed to rekindle the repression of the Red Scare. (The perpetrators of this terrorist explosion, the worst on American soil until the Oklahoma City bombing of 1995, were never identified.)

The reaction to the Palmer Raids planted the seeds for a new appreciation of the importance of civil liberties that would begin to flourish during the 1920s. But in their immediate impact, the events of 1919 and 1920 dealt a devastating setback to radical and labor organizations of all kinds and kindled an intense identification of patriotic Americanism with support for the political and economic status quo. The IWW had been effectively destroyed, and many moderate unions lay in disarray. The Socialist Party crumbled under the weight of governmental repression (the New York legislature expelled five Socialist members, and Congress denied Victor Berger the seat to which he had been elected from Wisconsin) and internal differences over the Russian Revolution.

Local police with literature seized from a Communist Party office in Cambridge, Massachusetts, November 1919.

Wilson at Versailles

The beating back of demands for fundamental social change was a severe rebuke to the hopes with which so many Progressives had enlisted in the war effort. Wilson's inability to achieve a just peace based on the Fourteen Points compounded the sense of failure. Late in 1918, the president traveled to France to attend the Versailles peace conference. But he proved a less adept negotiator than his British and French counterparts, David Lloyd George and Georges Clemenceau.

Part of the crowd that greeted President Woodrow Wilson in November 1918 when he traveled to Paris to take part in the peace conference. An electric sign proclaims "Long Live Wilson."

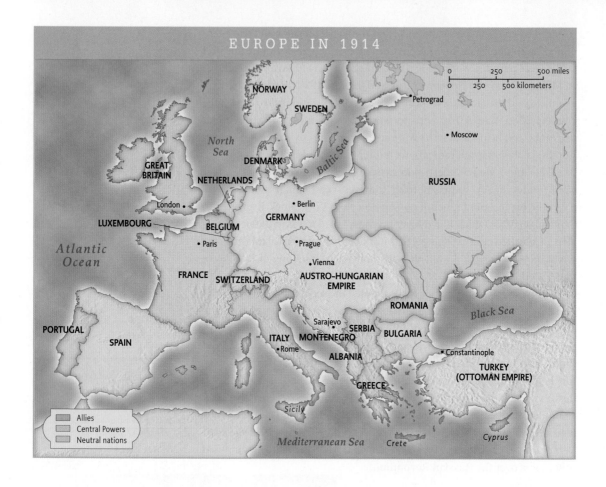

EUROPE IN 1914

World War I and the Versailles Treaty redrew the map of Europe and the Middle East. The Austro-Hungarian and Ottoman empires ceased to exist, and Germany and Russia were reduced in size. A group of new states emerged in eastern Europe, embodying the principle of self-determination, one of Woodrow Wilson's Fourteen Points.

Although the Fourteen Points had called for "open covenants openly arrived at," the negotiations were conducted in secret. The resulting **Versailles Treaty** did accomplish some of Wilson's goals. It established the **League of Nations**, the body central to his vision of a new international order. It applied the principle of self-determination to eastern Europe and redrew the map of that region. From the ruins of the Austro-Hungarian empire and parts of Germany and czarist Russia, new European nations emerged from the war—Finland, Poland, Czechoslovakia, Austria, Hungary, Latvia, Lithuania, Estonia, and Yugoslavia. Some enjoyed ethno-linguistic unity, whereas others comprised unstable combinations of diverse nationalities.

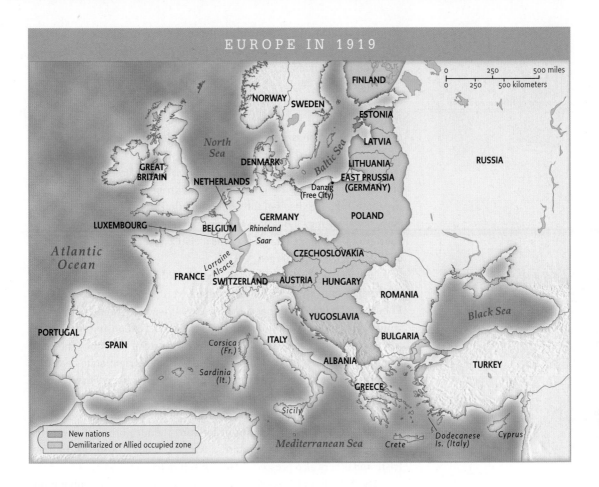

EUROPE IN 1919

> New nations
> Demilitarized or Allied occupied zone

Despite Wilson's pledge of a peace without territorial acquisitions or vengeance, the Versailles Treaty was a harsh document that all but guaranteed future conflict in Europe. Lloyd George persuaded Wilson to agree to a clause declaring Germany morally responsible for the war and setting astronomical reparations payments (they were variously estimated at between $33 billion and $56 billion), which crippled the German economy.

German reparations

The Wilsonian Moment

Like the ideals of the American Revolution, the Wilsonian rhetoric of self-determination reverberated across the globe, especially among colonial peoples seeking independence. In fact, they took Wilson's rhetoric more seriously than he did. Despite his belief in self-determination, he believed that colonial peoples required a long period of tutelage before they were ready for independence.

Spread of Wilsonian ideals

Nonetheless, Wilsonian ideals quickly spread around the globe. In eastern Europe, whose people sought to carve new, independent nations from the ruins of the Austro-Hungarian and Ottoman empires, many considered Wilson a "popular saint." The leading Arabic newspaper, *Al-Ahram*, published in Egypt, then under British rule, gave extensive coverage to Wilson's speech asking Congress to declare war in the name of democracy, and to the Fourteen Points. In Beijing, students demanding that China free itself of foreign domination gathered at the American embassy shouting, "Long live Wilson." Japan proposed to include in the charter of the new League of Nations a clause recognizing the equality of all people, regardless of race.

Self-determination

Outside of Europe, however, the idea of "self-determination" was stillborn. When the Paris peace conference opened, Secretary of State Robert Lansing warned that the phrase was "loaded with dynamite" and would "raise hopes which can never be realized." As Lansing anticipated, advocates of colonial independence descended on Paris to lobby the peace negotiators. Arabs demanded that a unified independent state be carved from the old Ottoman empire in the Middle East. Nguyen That Thanh, a young Vietnamese patriot working in Paris, pressed his people's claim for greater rights within the French empire. W. E. B. Du Bois organized a Pan-African Congress in Paris that put forward the idea of a self-governing nation to be carved out of Germany's African colonies. Koreans, Indians, Irish, and others also pressed claims for self-determination.

Imperial interests

The British and French, however, had no intention of applying this principle to their own empires. During the war, the British had encouraged Arab nationalism as a weapon against the Ottoman empire and had also pledged to create a homeland in Palestine for the persecuted Jews of Europe. In fact, the victors of World War I divided Ottoman territory into a series of new territories, including Syria, Lebanon, Iraq, and Palestine, controlled by the victorious Allies under League of Nations "mandates." South Africa, Australia, and Japan acquired former German colonies in Africa and Asia. Nor did Ireland achieve its independence at Versailles. Only at the end of 1921 did Britain finally agree to the creation of the Irish Free State while continuing to rule the northeastern corner of the island. As for the Japanese proposal to establish the principle of racial equality, Wilson, with the support of Great Britain and Australia, engineered its defeat.

The Seeds of Wars to Come

Disappointment at the failure to apply the Fourteen Points to the non-European world created a pervasive cynicism about Western use of the language of freedom and democracy. Wilson's apparent willingness to accede to the demands of the imperial powers helped to spark a series of popular protest movements across the Middle East and Asia and the rise of a new anti-Western nationalism. Some leaders, like Nguyen That Thanh, who took the name Ho Chi Minh, turned to communism, in whose name he would lead Vietnam's long and bloody struggle for independence. With the collapse of the Wilsonian moment, Lenin's reputation in the colonial world began to eclipse that of the American president. But whether communist or not, these movements announced the emergence of anticolonial nationalism as a major force in world affairs, which it would remain for the rest of the twentieth century.

Interrupting the Ceremony, a 1918 cartoon from the *Chicago Tribune*, depicts Senate opponents of the Versailles Treaty arriving just in time to prevent the United States from becoming permanently ensnared in "foreign entanglements" through the League of Nations.

"Your liberalness," one Egyptian leader remarked, speaking of Britain and America, "is only for yourselves." Yet ironically, when colonial peoples demanded to be recognized as independent members of the international community, they would invoke the heritage of the American Revolution—the first colonial struggle that produced an independent nation.

World War I sowed the seeds not of a lasting peace but of wars to come. German resentment over the peace terms would help to fuel the rise of Adolf Hitler and the coming of World War II. In the breakup of Czechoslovakia and Yugoslavia, violence over the status of Northern Ireland, and seemingly unending conflicts in the Middle East, the world was still haunted by the ghost of Versailles.

Brewing resentment and violence

The Treaty Debate

One final disappointment awaited Wilson on his return from Europe. He viewed the new League of Nations as the war's finest legacy. But many Americans feared that membership in the League would commit

Fear of international involvement

the United States to an open-ended involvement in the affairs of other countries.

A considerable majority of senators would have accepted the treaty with "reservations" ensuring that the obligation to assist League members against attack did not supersede the power of Congress to declare war. Convinced, however, that the treaty reflected "the hand of God," Wilson

refused to negotiate with congressional leaders. In October 1919, in the midst of the League debate, Wilson suffered a serious stroke. Although the extent of his illness was kept secret, he remained incapacitated for the rest of his presidency. In effect, his wife, Edith, headed the government for the next seventeen months. In November 1919 and again in March 1920, the Senate rejected the Versailles Treaty.

American involvement in World War I lasted barely nineteen months, but it cast a long shadow over the following decade—and, indeed, the rest of the century. In its immediate aftermath, the country retreated from international involvements. But in the long run, Wilson's combination

of idealism and power politics had an enduring impact. His appeals to democracy, open markets, and a special American mission to instruct the world in freedom, coupled with a willingness to intervene abroad militarily to promote American interests and values, would create the model for twentieth-century American international relations.

On its own terms, the war to make the world safe for democracy failed. It also led to the eclipse of Progressivism. Republican candidate Warren G. Harding, who had no connection with the party's Progressive wing, swept to victory in the presidential election of 1920. Harding's campaign

centered on a "return to normalcy" and a repudiation of what he called "Wilsonism." He received 60 percent of the popular vote. Begun with idealistic goals and grand hopes for social change, American involvement in the Great War laid the foundation for one of the most conservative decades in the nation's history.

CHAPTER REVIEW AND ONLINE RESOURCES

REVIEW QUESTIONS

1. *Explain the role of the United States in the global economy by 1920.*

2. *What were the assumptions underlying the Roosevelt Corollary? How did the doctrine affect our relations with European nations and those in the Western Hemisphere?*

3. *What did President Wilson mean by "moral imperialism," and what measures were taken to apply this to Latin America?*

4. *How did the ratification of the Eighteenth and Nineteenth Amendments show the restrictive and democratizing nature of Progressivism?*

5. *Why did Progressives see in the expansion of governmental powers in wartime an opportunity to reform American society?*

6. *What were the goals and methods of the Committee on Public Information during World War I?*

7. *What are governmental and private examples of coercive patriotism during the war? What were the effects of those efforts?*

8. *What were the major causes—both real and imaginary—of the Red Scare?*

9. *How did World War I and its aftermath provide African-Americans with opportunities?*

10. *Describe how World War I and the U.S. failure to join the League of Nations sowed the seeds of future twentieth-century wars.*

11. *Identify the goals of those pressing for global change in 1919, and of those who opposed them.*

KEY TERMS

liberal internationalism (p. 580)
Panama Canal Zone (p. 581)
Roosevelt Corollary (p. 582)
Dollar Diplomacy (p. 583)
moral imperialism (p. 583)
Lusitania (p. 585)
Zimmermann Telegram (p. 586)
Fourteen Points (p. 587)
Selective Service Act (p. 589)
War Industries Board (p. 589)
Eighteenth Amendment (p. 594)
Espionage Act (p. 594)
Sedition Act (p. 594)
National Association for the Advancement of Colored People (p. 600)
Great Migration (p. 602)
Tulsa riot (p. 602)
Marcus Garvey (p. 603)
Red Scare of 1919-1920 (p. 604)
Versailles Treaty (p. 606)
League of Nations (p. 606)

Go to 🐰 INQUIZITIVE

To see what you know—and learn what you've missed—with personalized feedback along the way.

Visit the *Give Me Liberty!* **Student Site** for primary source documents and images, interactive maps, author videos featuring Eric Foner, and more.

1915	Reemergence of the Ku Klux Klan
1919	*Schenck v. United States*
	Claude McKay's "If We Must Die"
1920	American Civil Liberties Union established
1921	Trial of Sacco and Vanzetti
1922	Washington Naval Arms Conference
	Hollywood adopts the Hays code
	Herbert Hoover's *American Individualism*
	Meyer v. Nebraska
1924	Immigration Act of 1924
1925	Scopes trial
1927	Charles Lindbergh flies nonstop over the Atlantic
	Sacco and Vanzetti executed
1929	Robert and Helen Lynd's *Middletown*
	Sheppard-Towner Act repealed
	Stock market crashes
1930	Smoot-Hawley Tariff
1932	Reconstruction Finance Corporation established
	Bonus march on Washington

CHAPTER 20

FROM BUSINESS CULTURE TO GREAT DEPRESSION

★

THE TWENTIES, 1920–1932

One of a series of murals painted in 1930 and 1931 by Thomas Hart Benton under the overall title *America Today. Changing West* depicts some of the transformations occurring in that region including oil exploration, factory development, and air travel.

I n May 1920, at the height of the postwar Red Scare, police arrested two Italian immigrants accused of participating in a robbery at a South Braintree, Massachusetts, factory in which a security guard was killed. Nicola Sacco, a shoemaker, and Bartolomeo Vanzetti, an itinerant unskilled laborer, were anarchists who dreamed of a society in which government, churches, and private property would be abolished. They saw violence as an appropriate weapon of class warfare. But very little evidence linked them to this particular crime. In the atmosphere of anti-radical and anti-immigrant fervor, however, their conviction was a certainty.

Although their 1921 trial had aroused little public interest outside the Italian-American community, the case of Sacco and Vanzetti attracted considerable attention during the lengthy appeals that followed. There were mass protests in Europe against their impending execution. On August 23, 1927, Sacco and Vanzetti died in the electric chair.

The **Sacco-Vanzetti case** laid bare some of the fault lines beneath the surface of American society during the 1920s. To many native-born Americans, the two men symbolized an alien threat to their way of life. To Italian-Americans, including respectable middle-class organizations like the Sons of Italy that raised money for the defense, the outcome symbolized the nativist prejudices and stereotypes that haunted immigrant communities.

FOCUS QUESTIONS

- *Who benefited and who suffered in the new consumer society of the 1920s?*

- *In what ways did the government promote business interests in the 1920s?*

- *Why did the protection of civil liberties gain importance in the 1920s?*

- *What were the major flash points between fundamentalism and pluralism in the 1920s?*

- *What were the causes of the Great Depression, and how effective were the government's responses by 1932?*

A 1927 photograph shows Nicola Sacco and Bartolomeo Vanzetti outside the courthouse in Dedham, Massachusetts, surrounded by security agents and onlookers. They are about to enter the courthouse, where the judge will pronounce their death sentences.

In popular memory, the decade that followed World War I is recalled as the Jazz Age or the Roaring Twenties. With its flappers (young, sexually liberated women), speakeasies (nightclubs that sold liquor in violation of Prohibition), and a soaring stock market fueled by easy credit and a get-rich-quick outlook, it was a time of revolt against moral rules inherited from the nineteenth century. Observers from Europe, where class divisions were starkly visible in work, politics, and social relations, marveled at the uniformity of American life. Factories poured out standardized consumer goods, their sale promoted by national advertising campaigns. Conservatism dominated a political system from which radical alternatives seemed to have been purged. Radio and the movies spread mass culture throughout the nation.

Many Americans, however, did not welcome the new secular, commercial culture. They resented and feared the ethnic and racial diversity of America's cities and what they considered the lax moral standards of urban life. The 1920s was a decade of profound social tensions—between rural and urban Americans, traditional and "modern" Christianity, participants in the burgeoning consumer culture and those who did not fully share in the new prosperity.

THE BUSINESS OF AMERICA

A Decade of Prosperity

"The chief business of the American people," said Calvin Coolidge, who became president after Warren G. Harding's sudden death from a heart attack in 1923, "is business." Rarely in American history had economic growth seemed more dramatic, cooperation between business and government so close, and business values so widely shared. Productivity and economic output rose dramatically as new industries—chemicals, aviation, electronics—flourished and older ones like food processing and the manufacture of household appliances adopted Henry Ford's moving assembly line. Annual automobile production tripled during the 1920s, from 1.5 to 4.8 million, stimulating steel, rubber, and oil production, and other sectors of the economy. By 1929, half of all Americans owned a car.

Industrial growth

During the 1920s, American multinational corporations extended their sway throughout the world. With Europe still recovering from the Great War, American investment overseas far exceeded that of other countries. The dollar replaced the British pound as the most important currency

Multinational corporations

of international trade. American companies produced 85 percent of the world's cars and 40 percent of its manufactured goods. General Electric and International Telephone and Telegraph bought up companies in other countries. International Business Machines (IBM) was the world's leader in office supplies. American companies took control of raw materials abroad, from rubber in Liberia to oil in Venezuela.

A New Society

During the 1920s, consumer goods of all kinds proliferated, marketed by salesmen and advertisers who promoted them as ways of satisfying Americans' psychological desires and everyday needs. Frequently purchased on credit through new installment buying plans, they rapidly altered daily life. Telephones made communication easier. Vacuum cleaners, washing machines, and refrigerators transformed work in the home and reduced the demand for domestic servants. Boosted by Prohibition and an aggressive advertising campaign that, according to the company's sales director, made it "impossible for the consumer to *escape*" the product, Coca-Cola became a symbol of American life.

Americans spent more and more of their income on leisure activities like vacations, movies, and sporting events. By 1929, weekly movie attendance had reached 80 million, double the figure of 1922. Hollywood films now dominated the world movie market.

Radios and phonographs brought mass entertainment into American living rooms. The number of radios in American homes rose from 190,000 in 1923 to just under 5 million in 1929. These developments helped create and spread a new celebrity culture, in which recording, film, and sports stars moved to the top of the list of American heroes. During the 1920s, more than 100 million records were sold each year. RCA Victor sold so many recordings of the great opera tenor Enrico Caruso that he is sometimes called the first modern celebrity. He was soon joined by the film actor Charlie Chaplin, baseball player Babe Ruth, and boxer Jack Dempsey. Perhaps the decade's greatest celebrity, in terms of intensive press coverage, was the aviator

Ford's River Rouge auto plant at Dearborn, Michigan, was the world's largest factory complex in the 1920s. It included not only assembly areas but its own steel mill.

Leisure activities

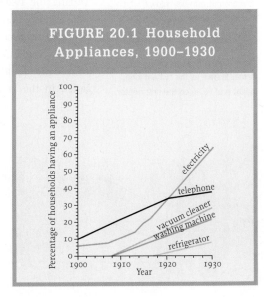

FIGURE 20.1 Household Appliances, 1900–1930

(graph; y-axis: Percentage of households having an appliance, 0–100; x-axis: Year, 1900–1930; lines labeled electricity, telephone, vacuum cleaner, washing machine, refrigerator)

Charles Lindbergh, who in 1927 made the first solo nonstop flight across the Atlantic.

Consumption and entertainment

Widespread acceptance of going into debt to purchase consumer goods replaced the values of thrift and self-denial, central to nineteenth-century notions of upstanding character. Work, once seen as a source of pride in craft skill, now came to be valued as a path to individual fulfillment through consumption and entertainment.

The Limits of Prosperity

But signs of future trouble could be seen beneath the prosperity of the 1920s. The fruits of increased production were very unequally distributed. Real wages for industrial workers (wages adjusted to take account of inflation) rose by one-quarter between 1922 and 1929, but corporate profits rose at more than twice that rate. The process of economic concentration continued unabated. A handful of firms dominated numerous sectors of the economy. In 1929, 1 percent of the nation's banks controlled half of its financial resources. Most of the small auto companies that had existed earlier in the century had fallen by the wayside. General Motors, Ford, and Chrysler now controlled four-fifths of the industry.

Economic concentration and its consequences

At the beginning of 1929, a majority of families had no savings, and an estimated 40 percent of the population remained in poverty, unable to participate in the flourishing consumer economy. Improved productivity meant that goods could be produced with fewer workers. During the 1920s, more Americans worked in the professions, retailing, finance, and education, but the number of manufacturing workers declined by 5 percent, the first such drop in the nation's history. Parts of New England were already experiencing the chronic unemployment caused by deindustrialization. Many of the region's textile companies failed in the face of low-wage competition from southern factories or shifted production to take advantage of the South's cheap labor.

Economic weakness

Kansas agricultural workers breaking new ground with disk plows, which eased the task of readying the sod of the Great Plains for planting and encouraged the emergence of larger farms. Simon Fishman, a Jewish farmer known as the "wheat king," in jacket and tie, is on the first tractor.

The Farmers' Plight

Nor did farmers share in the decade's prosperity. The "golden age" of American farming had reached its peak during World War I, when the need to feed war-torn Europe and government efforts to maintain high farm prices had raised farmers' incomes and promoted the purchase of more land on credit. Thanks to mechanization and the increased use of fertilizer and insecticides, agricultural production continued to rise even when government subsidies ended and world demand stagnated. As a result, farm incomes in the 1920s declined steadily, and banks foreclosed tens of thousands of farms.

Facing dire conditions, some 3 million persons migrated out of rural areas. Many headed for southern California, whose rapidly growing economy needed new labor. The population of Los Angeles, the West's leading industrial center, a producer of oil, automobiles, aircraft, and, of course, Hollywood movies, rose from 575,000 to 2.2 million during the decade, largely because of an influx of displaced farmers from the Midwest. Well before the 1930s, rural America was in an economic depression.

Farmers, such as this family of potato growers in rural Minnesota, did not share in the prosperity of the 1920s.

The 1920s, however, was not simply a period of decline on the farm but of significant technological change. New inventions came into widespread use on the Great Plains, especially the steam tractor and the disk plow, which killed weeds, chopped up the sod, and left the surface layer much easier to plant. Mechanization encouraged an increase in the scale of agriculture. From farms growing wheat to California orange groves, the western states became home to modern "factory farms," employing large numbers of migrant laborers. Massive irrigation projects completed in the previous decades made the Far West much more suitable for farming. Farm output boomed in previously arid parts of California, Arizona, New Mexico, and Texas. With immigration from Asia barred and blacks unwanted, agribusinesses recruited workers from across the southern border, and immigrants from Mexico came to make up the vast majority of the West's low-wage farm migrants.

Factory farms

The Image of Business

Despite America's underlying economic problems, businessmen like Henry Ford and engineers like Herbert Hoover were cultural heroes. Photographers such as Lewis Hine and Margaret Bourke-White and painters like Charles Sheeler celebrated the beauty of machines and factories.

America's image

Numerous firms established public relations departments to justify corporate practices to the public and counteract its long-standing distrust of big business. They even succeeded in changing popular attitudes toward Wall Street.

Rise of the stock market

In the 1920s, as the steadily rising price of stocks made front-page news, the market attracted more investors. Many assumed that stock values would keep rising forever. By 1928, an estimated 1.5 million Americans owned stock—still a small minority of the country's 28 million families, but far more than in the past.

The Decline of Labor

With the defeat of the labor upsurge of 1919 and the dismantling of the wartime regulatory state, business appropriated the rhetoric of Americanism and "industrial freedom" as weapons against labor unions. Some corporations during the 1920s implemented a new style of management. They provided their employees with private pensions and medical insurance plans, job security, and greater workplace safety. They spoke of "welfare capitalism," a more socially conscious kind of business leadership, and trumpeted the fact that they now paid more attention to the "human factor" in employment.

The American Plan

At the same time, however, employers in the 1920s embraced the American Plan, at whose core stood the open shop—a workplace free of both government regulation and unions, except, in some cases, "company unions" created and controlled by management. Even the most forward-looking companies continued to employ strikebreakers, private detectives, and the blacklisting of union organizers to prevent or defeat strikes.

The decline of unions

During the 1920s, organized labor lost more than 2 million members, and unions agreed to demand after demand by employers in an effort to stave off complete elimination. Uprisings by the most downtrodden workers did occur sporadically throughout the decade. Southern textile mills witnessed desperate strikes by workers who charged employers with "making slaves out of the men and women" who labored there. Facing the combined opposition of business, local politicians, and the courts, as well as the threat of violence, such strikes were doomed to defeat.

The Equal Rights Amendment

Like the labor movement, feminists struggled to adapt to the new political situation. The achievement of suffrage in 1920 eliminated the bond of unity among various activists, each "struggling for her own conception of freedom," in the words of labor reformer Juliet Stuart Poyntz. Black feminists insisted that the movement must now demand enforcement of the Fifteenth Amendment in the South, but they won little support from their white counterparts.

The long-standing division between two competing conceptions of woman's freedom—one based on motherhood, the other on individual autonomy and the right to work—now crystallized in the debate over an **Equal Rights Amendment** (ERA) to the Constitution promoted by Alice Paul and the National Woman's Party. This amendment proposed to eliminate all legal distinctions "on account of sex." In Paul's opinion, the ERA followed logically from winning the right to vote. Having gained political equality, she insisted, women no longer required special legal protection—they needed equal access to employment, education, and all the other opportunities of citizens. To supporters of mothers' pensions and laws limiting women's hours of labor, which the ERA would sweep away, the proposal represented a giant step backward. Apart from the National Woman's Party, every major female organization opposed the ERA.

The ERA campaign failed, and only six states ratified a proposed constitutional amendment giving Congress the power to prohibit child labor, which farm groups and business organizations opposed. In 1929, Congress repealed the Sheppard-Towner Act of 1921, a major achievement of the maternalist reformers that had provided federal assistance to programs for infant and child health.

Women's Freedom

If political feminism faded, the prewar feminist demand for personal freedom survived in the vast consumer marketplace and in the actual behavior of the decade's much-publicized liberated young women. No longer one element in a broader program of social reform, sexual freedom now meant individual autonomy or personal rebellion. With her bobbed hair, short skirts, public smoking and drinking, and unapologetic use of birth-control methods such as the diaphragm, the young, single **flapper** epitomized the change in standards of sexual behavior, at least in large cities. She frequented dance halls and attended sexually charged Hollywood films featuring stars like Clara Bow, the provocative "'It' Girl," and Rudolph Valentino, the original on-screen "Latin Lover."

Women's self-conscious pursuit of personal pleasure became a device to market goods from automobiles to cigarettes. In 1904, a woman had been arrested for smoking in public in New York City. Two decades later,

Debate over the ERA

Tipsy, a 1930 painting by the Japanese artist Kobayakawa Kiyoshi, illustrates the global appeal of the "new woman" of the 1920s. The subject, a *moga* ("modern girl" in Japanese), sits alone in a nightclub wearing Western clothing, makeup, and hairstyle and enjoying a cigarette and a martini. The title of the work suggests that Kiyoshi does not entirely approve of her behavior, but he presents her as self-confident and alluring. Japanese police took a dim view of "modern" women, arresting those who applied makeup in public.

(*Left*) Advertisers marketed cigarettes to women as symbols of female independence. The August 27, 1925 cover of *Life* magazine shows a young man and a young woman dressed identically at the beach in revealing bathing suits (by 1920s standards), both enjoying cigarettes. (*Right*) An ad for a washing machine promises to liberate women from the "slavery" of everyday laundering at home.

Edward Bernays, the "father" of modern public relations, masterminded a campaign to persuade women to smoke, dubbing cigarettes women's "torches of freedom." The new freedom, however, was available only during one phase of a woman's life. Marriage, according to one advertisement, remained "the one pursuit that stands foremost in the mind of every girl and woman." Having found husbands, women were expected to seek freedom within the confines of the home.

Marriage and the new freedom

BUSINESS AND GOVERNMENT

Robert and Helen Lynd,
Middletown

In 1929, the sociologists Robert and Helen Lynd published *Middletown*, a classic study of life in Muncie, Indiana, a typical community in the American heartland. The Lynds found that new leisure activities and a new emphasis on consumption had replaced politics as the focus of public concern. Elections were no longer "lively centers" of public attention as in the nineteenth century, and voter participation had fallen dramatically. National statistics bore out their point; the turnout of eligible voters, over 80 percent in 1896, dropped to less than 50 percent in 1924. Many factors helped to explain this decline, including the consolidation of one-party politics in the South, the long period of Republican dominance in national elections, and the enfranchisement of women, who for many years voted in lower numbers than men. But the shift from public to private concerns also played a part. "The American citizen's first importance to his country,"

Decline in voter participation

declared a Muncie newspaper, "is no longer that of a citizen but that of a consumer."

The Republican Era

Government policies reflected the pro-business ethos of the 1920s. Business lobbyists dominated national conventions of the Republican Party. They called on the federal government to lower taxes on personal incomes and business profits, maintain high tariffs, and support employers' continuing campaign against unions. The administrations of Warren G. Harding and Calvin Coolidge obliged. Under William Howard Taft, appointed chief justice in 1921, the Supreme Court remained strongly conservative. A resurgence of laissez-faire jurisprudence eclipsed the Progressive ideal of a socially active national state. The Court struck down a federal law that barred goods produced by child labor from interstate commerce. It even repudiated *Muller v. Oregon* (see Chapter 18) in a 1923 decision (***Adkins v. Children's Hospital***) overturning a minimum wage law for women in Washington, D.C. Now that women enjoyed the vote, the justices declared, they were entitled to the same workplace freedom as men.

The policies of President Calvin Coolidge were music to the ears of big business, according to one 1920s cartoonist, who entitled this image *Yes Sir, He's My Baby*, after a popular song.

Corruption in Government

Warren G. Harding took office as president in 1921 promising a "return to normalcy" after an era of Progressive reform and world war. Reflecting the prevailing get-rich-quick ethos, his administration quickly became one of the most corrupt in American history. Although his cabinet included men

Harding administration

A 1924 cartoon commenting on the scandals of the Harding administration. The White House, Capitol, and Washington Monument have been sold to the highest bidder.

Progressive Optimism, a satirical comment on Robert La Follette's campaign for president in 1924 as the candidate of the Progressive Party, has a disheveled westerner (labeled Wisconsin, La Follette's state) tied to a stake in the desert while a goat dressed as a cowboy and labeled "Third Party" heads off to bring the party's message to the "uneducated East."

of integrity and talent, like Secretary of State Charles Evans Hughes and Secretary of Commerce Herbert Hoover, Harding also surrounded himself with cronies who used their offices for private gain. Attorney General Harry Daugherty accepted payments not to prosecute accused criminals. The most notorious scandal involved Secretary of the Interior Albert Fall, who accepted nearly $500,000 from private businessmen to whom he leased government oil reserves at **Teapot Dome**, Wyoming. Fall became the first cabinet member in history to be convicted of a felony.

The Election of 1924

Harding's successor, Calvin Coolidge, who as governor of Massachusetts had won national fame for using state troops against striking Boston policemen in 1919, was a dour man of few words. But in contrast to his predecessor he seemed to exemplify Yankee honesty. In 1924, Coolidge was elected in a landslide, defeating John W. Davis, a Wall Street lawyer nominated on the 103rd ballot by a badly divided Democratic convention. (This was when the comedian Will Rogers made the quip, often repeated in future years, "I am a member of no organized political party; I am a Democrat.")

One-sixth of the electorate in 1924 voted for Robert La Follette, running as the candidate of a new Progressive Party, which called for greater taxation of wealth, the conservation of natural resources, public ownership of the railroads, farm relief, and the end of child labor. La Follette carried only his native Wisconsin. But his candidacy demonstrated the survival of some currents of dissent in a highly conservative decade.

Economic Diplomacy

Foreign affairs also reflected the close working relationship between business and government. The 1920s marked a retreat from Wilson's goal of internationalism in favor of unilateral American actions mainly designed to increase exports and investment opportunities overseas. Indeed, what is sometimes called the "isolationism" of the 1920s represented a reaction against the disappointing results of Wilson's military and diplomatic pursuit of freedom and democracy abroad. The United States did play host to the Washington Naval Arms Conference of 1922, which negotiated

Isolationism

reductions in the navies of Britain, France, Japan, Italy, and the United States. But the country remained outside the League of Nations. Even as American diplomats continued to press for access to markets overseas, the Fordney-McCumber Tariff of 1922 raised taxes on imported goods to their highest levels in history, a repudiation of Wilson's principle of promoting free trade.

As before World War I, the government dispatched soldiers when a change in government in the Caribbean threatened American economic interests. Having been stationed in Nicaragua since 1912, American marines withdrew in 1925. But the troops soon returned in an effort to suppress a nationalist revolt headed by General Augusto César Sandino. Having created a National Guard headed by General Anastasio Somoza, the marines finally departed in 1933. A year later, Somoza assassinated Sandino and seized power. For the next forty-five years, he and his family ruled and plundered Nicaragua. Somoza's son was overthrown in 1979 by a popular movement calling itself the Sandinistas (see Chapter 26).

Augusto Sandino, who led a rebellion against the U.S. military occupation of Nicaragua in the late 1920s. He was assassinated in 1934 by General Anastasio Somoza, who became dictator and established a family dynasty that ruled Nicaragua until overthrown in 1979 by a popular movement known as the Sandinistas.

THE BIRTH OF CIVIL LIBERTIES

Among the casualties of World War I and the 1920s was Progressivism's faith that an active federal government embodied the national purpose and enhanced the enjoyment of freedom. Wartime and postwar repression, Prohibition, and the pro-business policies of the 1920s all illustrated, in the eyes of many Progressives, how public power could go grievously wrong.

This lesson opened the door to a new appreciation of civil liberties—rights an individual may assert even against democratic majorities—as essential elements of American freedom. In the name of a "new freedom for the individual," the 1920s saw the birth of a coherent concept of civil liberties and the beginnings of significant legal protection for freedom of speech against the government.

Wartime repression continued into the 1920s. Artistic works with sexual themes were subjected to rigorous censorship. The Postal Service removed from the mails books it deemed obscene. The Customs Service barred works by the sixteenth-century French satirist Rabelais, the modern novelist James Joyce, and many others from entering the country. A local crusade against indecency made the phrase "Banned in Boston" a term of ridicule among upholders of artistic freedom. Boston's Watch and Ward Committee excluded sixty-five books from

Censorship

the city's bookstores, including works by the novelists Upton Sinclair, Theodore Dreiser, and Ernest Hemingway. In 1930, the film industry adopted the Hays code, a sporadically enforced set of guidelines that prohibited movies from depicting nudity, long kisses, and adultery, and barred scripts that portrayed clergymen in a negative light or criminals sympathetically.

Disillusionment with the conservatism of American politics and the materialism of the culture inspired some American artists and writers to emigrate to Paris. The Lost Generation of cultural exiles included novelists and poets like Ernest Hemingway, Gertrude Stein, and F. Scott Fitzgerald. Europe, they felt, valued art and culture, and appreciated unrestrained freedom of expression (and, of course, allowed individuals to drink legally).

The Lost Generation

A "Clear and Present Danger"

The arrest of antiwar dissenters under the Espionage and Sedition Acts inspired the formation in 1917 of the Civil Liberties Bureau, which in 1920 became the **American Civil Liberties Union** (ACLU). For the rest of the century, the ACLU would take part in most of the landmark cases that helped to bring about a "rights revolution." Its efforts helped to give meaning to traditional civil liberties like freedom of speech and invented new ones, like the right to privacy. When it began, however, the ACLU was a small, beleaguered organization.

The American Civil Liberties Union

Prior to World War I, the Supreme Court had done almost nothing to protect the rights of unpopular minorities. Now, it was forced to address the question of the permissible limits on political and economic dissent. In 1919, the Court upheld the constitutionality of the Espionage Act and the conviction of Charles T. Schenck, a socialist who had distributed antidraft leaflets through the mails. Speaking for the Court, Justice Oliver Wendell Holmes declared that the First Amendment did not prevent Congress from prohibiting speech that presented a "clear and present danger" of inspiring illegal actions. A week after *Schenck v. United States*, the Court unanimously upheld the conviction of Eugene V. Debs for a speech condemning the war.

Schenck v. United States

The Court and Civil Liberties

Also in 1919, the Court upheld the conviction of Jacob Abrams and five other men for distributing pamphlets critical of American intervention in Russia after the Russian Revolution. This time, however, Holmes and

Louis Brandeis dissented, marking the emergence of a court minority committed to a broader defense of free speech.

The tide of civil-liberties decision making slowly began to turn. By the end of the 1920s, the Supreme Court had voided a Kansas law that made it a crime to advocate unlawful acts to change the political or economic system and one from Minnesota authorizing censorship of the press. The new regard for free speech went beyond political expression. In 1933, a federal court overturned the Customs Service's ban on James Joyce's novel *Ulysses*, a turning point in the battle against the censorship of works of literature.

A judicial defense of civil liberties was slowly being born. As Brandeis insisted, "Those who won our independence believed . . . that freedom to think as you will and to speak as you think are indispensable to the discovery and spread of political truth. . . . The greatest menace to freedom is an inert people."

The defendants in *U.S. v. Abrams*, on the day of their deportation to Russia in 1921. Jacob Abrams is on the right. They were convicted under the Espionage Act of 1918 for impeding the war effort by distributing pamphlets critical of the American intervention in Russia after the Russian Revolution.

THE CULTURE WARS

The Fundamentalist Revolt

Although many Americans embraced modern urban culture with its religious and ethnic pluralism, mass entertainment, and liberated sexual rules, others found it alarming. Many evangelical Protestants felt threatened by the decline of traditional values and the increased visibility of Catholicism and Judaism because of immigration. They also resented the growing presence within mainstream Protestant denominations of "modernists" who sought to integrate science and religion and adapt Christianity to the new secular culture.

Evangelical Protestants

Convinced that the literal truth of the Bible formed the basis of Christian belief, fundamentalists launched a campaign to rid Protestant denominations of modernism and to combat the new individual freedoms that seemed to contradict traditional morality. Their most flamboyant apostle was Billy Sunday, a talented professional baseball player who became a revivalist preacher. Between 1900 and 1930, Sunday drew huge crowds with a highly theatrical preaching style and a message denouncing sins ranging from Darwinism to alcohol. **Fundamentalism** remained an

Billy Sunday

A 1923 lithograph by George Bellows captures the dynamic style of the most prominent evangelical preacher of the 1920s, Billy Sunday.

Selective enforcement of prohibition

Federal agents with confiscated liquor in Colorado in 1920, shortly after the advent of Prohibition.

important strain of 1920s culture and politics. Prohibition, which fundamentalists strongly supported, succeeded in reducing the consumption of alcohol as well as public drunkenness and drink-related diseases. Often portrayed (especially in Hollywood movies) as a glamorous episode of gangland battles and drinkers easily outwitting the police, Prohibition in fact was effectively enforced, albeit selectively. While wealthy Americans continued to enjoy access to liquor, many poor, black, and immigrant communities suffered large-scale arrests and jailings, often accompanied by police violence. Later deemed an unmitigated failure, enforcement of Prohibition in fact led to the building of new federal prisons and laid the foundation for powerful national action against crime and immorality, a precursor to the more recent federal war on drugs.

Prohibition, however, remained a deeply divisive issue. The greatest expansion of national authority since Reconstruction, it raised major questions of local rights, individual freedom, and the wisdom of attempting to impose religious and moral values on the entire society through legislation. It divided the Democratic Party into "wet" and "dry" wings, leading to bitter internal battles at the party's 1924 and 1928 national conventions.

Too many Americans deemed Prohibition a violation of individual freedom for the flow of illegal liquor to stop. In urban areas, Prohibition led to large profits for the owners of illegal speakeasies and the "bootleggers" who supplied them. It produced widespread corruption as police and public officials accepted bribes to turn a blind eye to violations of the law.

The Scopes Trial

In 1925, a trial in Tennessee threw into sharp relief the division between traditional values and modern, secular culture. John Scopes, a teacher in a Tennessee public school, was arrested for violating a state law that prohibited the teaching of Charles Darwin's theory of evolution. His trial became a national sensation.

The **Scopes trial** reflected the enduring tension between two American definitions of freedom. Fundamentalist Christians, strongest in rural areas of the South and West, clung to the traditional idea of "moral" liberty—voluntary adherence to time-honored religious beliefs. The theory that man had evolved over millions of years from ancestors like apes contradicted the biblical account of creation. To Scopes's defenders, including the American Civil Liberties Union, freedom meant above all the right to independent thought and individual self-expression. To them, the Tennessee law offered a lesson in the dangers of religious intolerance and the merger of church and state.

The renowned labor lawyer Clarence Darrow defended Scopes. The trial's highlight came when Darrow called William Jennings Bryan to the stand as an "expert witness" on the Bible. Bryan revealed an almost complete ignorance of modern science and proved unable to respond effectively to Darrow's sarcastic questioning. Asked whether God had actually created the world in six days, Bryan replied that these should be understood as ages, "not six days of twenty-four hours"—thus opening the door to the very nonliteral interpretation of the Bible that the fundamentalists rejected.

The jury found Scopes guilty, although the Tennessee Supreme Court later overturned the decision on a technicality. Fundamentalists retreated for many years from battles over public education, preferring to build their own schools and colleges where teaching could be

A scene on the Canadian side of the border with the state of Washington. One hundred feet into Canada, billboards welcome Americans to a country where it is still legal to consume alcohol.

Because of extreme heat, some sessions of the Scopes trial were held outdoors, in front of the courthouse in Dayton, Tennessee. A photographer snapped this picture of the trial's climactic moment, when Clarence Darrow (standing at the center) questioned William Jennings Bryan (seated) about his interpretation of the Bible.

done as they saw fit. The battle would be rejoined, however, toward the end of the twentieth century. To this day, the teaching of the theory of evolution in public schools arouses intense debate in parts of the United States.

The Second Klan

Few features of urban life seemed more alien to rural and small-town native-born Protestants than their immigrant populations and cultures. The wartime obsession with "100 percent Americanism" continued into the 1920s. In 1922, Oregon became the only state ever to require all students to attend public schools—a measure aimed, said the state's attorney general, at abolishing parochial education and preventing "bolshevists, syndicalists and communists" from organizing their own schools.

"100 percent Americanism"

Perhaps the most menacing expression of the idea that enjoyment of American freedom should be limited on religious and ethnic grounds was the resurgence of the Ku Klux Klan. The Klan had been reborn in Atlanta in 1915 after the lynching of Leo Frank, a Jewish factory manager accused of killing a teenage girl. By the mid-1920s, it claimed more than 3 million members, nearly all white, native-born Protestants, many of whom held respected positions in their communities. Unlike the Klan of Reconstruction, the organization now sank deep roots in parts of the North and West. It became the largest private organization in Indiana and for a time controlled the state Republican Party. American civilization, the new Klan insisted, was endangered not only by blacks but by immigrants (especially Jews and Catholics) and all the forces (feminism, unions, immorality, even, on occasion, the giant corporations) that endangered "individual liberty."

A Ku Klux Klan gathering in Seattle, Washington, in 1923. The unrobed members of the audience are covering their faces to avoid identification. Unlike the Klan of the Reconstruction era, the second Ku Klux Klan was more powerful in the North and West than in the South.

Closing the Golden Door

The Klan's influence faded after 1925, when its leader in Indiana was convicted of assaulting a young woman. But the Klan's attacks on modern secular culture and political radicalism and its demand that control of the nation be returned to "citizens of the old stock" reflected sentiments widely shared in the 1920s.

The 1920s produced a fundamental change in immigration policy. Prior to World War I virtually all the white persons who wished to pass through the "golden door" into the United States and become citizens were able to do so. During the 1920s, however, the pressure for wholesale immigration restriction became irresistible.

In 1921, a temporary measure restricted immigration from Europe to 357,000 per year (one-third of the annual average before the war). Three years later, Congress permanently limited European immigration to 150,000 per year, distributed according to a series of national quotas that severely restricted the numbers from southern and eastern Europe. However, to satisfy the demands of large farmers in California who relied heavily on seasonal Mexican labor, the 1924 law established no limits on immigration from the Western Hemisphere.

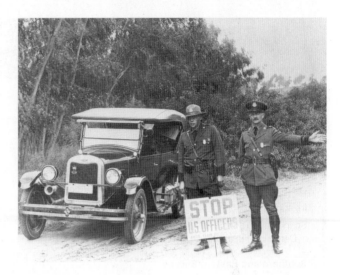

The immigration law of 1924 established the Border Patrol to stop those barred entry from sneaking into the United States from Mexico. At first, the patrol was a modest operation. Here, two officers police the California-Mexico border.

The immigration law also barred the entry of all those ineligible for naturalized citizenship—that is, the entire population of Asia, even though Japan had fought on the American side in World War I.

The law of 1924 established, in effect, for the first time a new category—the **illegal alien**. With it came a new enforcement mechanism, the Border Patrol, charged with policing the land boundaries of the United States and empowered to arrest and deport persons who entered the country in violation of the new nationality quotas or other restrictions. A term later associated almost exclusively with Latinos, "illegal aliens" at first referred mainly to southern and eastern Europeans who tried to sneak across the border from Mexico or Canada.

The "illegal alien"

Race and the Law

The new immigration law reflected the heightened emphasis on "race" as a determinant of public policy. By the early 1920s, political leaders of both North and South agreed on the relegation of blacks to second-class citizenship. But "race policy" meant far more than black-white relations. When President Coolidge signed the new law, his secretary of labor, James J. Davis, commented that immigration policy must now rest on a

"Race policy"

TABLE 20.1 Selected Annual Immigration Quotas under the 1924 Immigration Act

COUNTRY	QUOTA	IMMIGRANTS IN 1914
Northern and Western Europe:		
Great Britain and Northern Ireland	65,721	48,729 (Great Britain only)
Germany	25,957	35,734
Ireland	17,853	24,688 (includes Northern Ireland)
Scandinavia (Sweden, Norway, Denmark, Finland)	7,241	29,391
Southern and Eastern Europe:		
Poland	6,524	(Not an independent state; included in Germany, Russia, and Austria-Hungary)
Italy	5,802	283,738
Russia	2,784	255,660
Other:		
Africa (total of various colonies and countries)	1,000	1,539
Western Hemisphere	No quota limit	122,695
Asia (China, India, Japan, Korea)	0	11,652

A "biologically ideal" population

biological definition of the ideal population. Although enacted by a highly conservative Congress strongly influenced by nativism, the 1924 immigration law also reflected the Progressive desire to improve the "quality" of democratic citizenship and to employ scientific methods to set public policy. It revealed how these aims were overlaid with pseudo-scientific assumptions about the superiority and inferiority of particular "races."

But the entire concept of race as a basis for public policy lacked any rational foundation. The Supreme Court admitted as much in 1923 when it rejected the claim of Bhagat Singh Thind, an Indian-born World War I veteran, who asserted that as a "pure Aryan," he was actually white and could therefore become an American citizen. "White," the Court declared, was not a scientific concept at all, but part of "common speech, to be interpreted with the understanding of the common man" (a forthright statement of what later scholars would call the "social construction" of race).

Promoting Tolerance

In the face of immigration restriction, Prohibition, a revived Ku Klux Klan, and widespread anti-Semitism and anti-Catholicism, immigrant groups asserted the validity of cultural diversity and identified toleration of difference—religious, cultural, and individual—as the essence of American freedom. In effect, they reinvented themselves as "ethnic" Americans, claiming an equal share in the nation's life but, in addition, the right to remain in many respects culturally distinct. The Roman Catholic Church urged immigrants to learn English and embrace "American principles," but it continued to maintain separate schools and other institutions. Throughout the country, organizations like the Anti-Defamation League of B'nai B'rith (founded in 1916 to combat anti-Semitism) and the National Catholic Welfare Council lobbied, in the name of "personal liberty," for laws prohibiting discrimination against immigrants by employers, colleges, and government agencies.

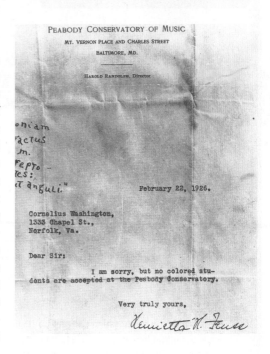

Racism severely limited the opportunities open to black Americans. Here, the internationally renowned Peabody Conservatory of Music informs a black applicant that he cannot pursue his musical education there.

The efforts of immigrant communities to resist coerced Americanization and of the Catholic Church to defend its school system broadened the definition of liberty for all Americans. In landmark decisions, the Supreme Court struck down Oregon's law, mentioned earlier, requiring all students to attend public schools and Nebraska's law prohibiting teaching in a language other than English—one of the anti-German measures of World War I. The *Meyer v. Nebraska* (1923) decision expanded the freedom of all immigrant groups. In its aftermath, federal courts overturned various Hawaii laws imposing special taxes and regulations on private Japanese-language schools. In these cases, the Court also interpreted the Fourteenth Amendment's guarantee of equal liberty to include the right to "marry, establish a home and bring up children" and to practice religion as one chose, "without interference from the state." The decisions gave pluralism a constitutional foundation.

A foundation for pluralism

The Emergence of Harlem

The 1920s also witnessed an upsurge of self-consciousness among black Americans, especially in the North's urban ghettos. With European immigration all but halted, the Great Migration of World War I continued apace as nearly 1 million blacks left the South during the decade. New York's Harlem gained an international reputation as the "capital" of black America, a mecca for migrants from the South and immigrants from

Caribbean immigrants

VOICES OF FREEDOM

From Lucian W. Parrish, Speech in Congress on Immigration (1921)

In the immediate aftermath of World War I, fears of foreign radicalism sparked by labor upheavals, and the increased concern with Americanizing immigrants, greatly strengthened demands to curtail immigration. During a debate in the House of Representatives in April 1921, Lucian W. Parrish, a Democrat from Texas, laid out the case for immigration restriction.

We should stop immigration entirely until such a time as we can amend our immigration laws and so write them that hereafter no one shall be admitted except he be in full sympathy with our Constitution and laws, willing to declare himself obedient to our flag, and willing to release himself from any obligations he may owe to the flag of the country from which he came.

It is time that we act now, because within a few short years the damage will have been done. The endless tide of immigration will have filled our country with a foreign and unsympathetic element. Those who are out of sympathy with our Constitution and the spirit of our Government will be here in large numbers, and the true spirit of Americanism left us by our fathers will gradually become poisoned by this uncertain element.

The time once was when we welcomed to our shores the oppressed and downtrodden people from all the world, but they came to us because of oppression at home and with the sincere purpose of making true and loyal American citizens, and in truth and in fact they did adapt themselves to our ways of thinking and contributed in a substantial sense to the progress and development that our civilization has made. But that time has passed now; new and strange conditions have arisen in the countries over there; new and strange doctrines are being taught. The governments of the Orient are being overturned and destroyed, and anarchy and bolshevism are threatening the very foundation of many of them and no one can foretell what the future will bring to many of those countries of the Old World now struggling with these problems.

Our country is a self-sustaining country. It has taught the principles of real democracy to all the nations of the earth; its flag has been the synonym of progress, prosperity, and the preservation of the rights of the individual, and there can be nothing so dangerous as for us to allow the undesirable foreign element to poison our civilization and thereby threaten the safety of the institutions that our forefathers have established for us. . . .

We must hold this country true to the American thought and the American ideals.

From Majority Opinion, Justice James C. McReynolds, in *Meyer v. Nebraska* (1923)

A landmark in the development of civil liberties, the Supreme Court's decision in *Meyer v. Nebraska* rebuked the coercive Americanization impulse of World War I, overturning a Nebraska law that required all school instruction to take place in English.

The problem for our determination is whether the statute [prohibiting instruction in a language other than English] as construed and applied unreasonably infringes the liberty guaranteed . . . by the Fourteenth Amendment. . . .

The American people have always regarded education and acquisition of knowledge as matters of supreme importance which should be diligently promoted. . . . The calling always has been regarded as useful and honorable, essential, indeed, to the public welfare. Mere knowledge of the German language cannot reasonably be regarded as harmful. Heretofore it has been commonly looked upon as helpful and desirable. [Meyer] taught this language in school as part of his occupation. His right to teach and the right of parents to engage him so to instruct their children, we think, are within the liberty of the Amendment.

It is said the purpose of the legislation was to promote civil development by inhibiting training and education of the immature in foreign tongues and ideals before they could learn English and acquire American ideals. . . . It is also affirmed that the foreign born population is very large, that certain communities commonly use foreign words, follow foreign leaders, move in a foreign atmosphere, and that the children are therefore hindered from becoming citizens of the most useful type and the public safety is impaired.

That the State may do much, go very far, indeed, in order to improve the quality of its citizens, physically, mentally, and morally, is clear; but the individual has certain fundamental rights which must be respected. The protection of the Constitution extends to all, to those who speak other languages as well as to those born with English on the tongue. Perhaps it would be highly advantageous if all had ready understanding of our ordinary speech, but this cannot be coerced by methods which conflict with the Constitution. . . . No emergency has arisen which rendered knowledge by a child of some language other than English so clearly harmful as to justify its inhibition with the consequent infringement of rights long freely enjoyed.

QUESTIONS

1. *Why does Parrish consider continued immigration dangerous?*

2. *How does the decision in* Meyer v. Nebraska *expand the definition of liberty protected by the Fourteenth Amendment?*

3. *How do the two excerpts reflect deep divisions over the nature of American society during the 1920s?*

A black family arriving in Chicago in 1922, as part of the Great Migration from the rural South.

the West Indies, 150,000 of whom entered the United States between 1900 and 1930. Unlike the southern newcomers, most of whom had been agricultural workers, the West Indians included a large number of well-educated professional and white-collar workers. Their encounter with American racism appalled them. "I had heard of prejudice in America," wrote the poet and novelist Claude McKay, who emigrated from Jamaica in 1912, "but never dreamed of it being so intensely bitter."

"Slumming"

The 1920s became famous for "slumming," as groups of whites visited Harlem's dance halls, jazz clubs, and speakeasies in search of exotic adventure. The Harlem of the white imagination was a place of primitive passions, free from the puritanical restraints of mainstream American culture. The real Harlem was a community of widespread poverty, its residents confined to low-wage jobs and, because housing discrimination barred them from other neighborhoods, forced to pay exorbitant rents.

The Harlem Renaissance

Vibrant culture

But Harlem also was home to a vibrant black cultural community that established links with New York's artistic mainstream. Poets and novelists such as Countee Cullen, Langston Hughes, and Claude McKay were befriended and sponsored by white intellectuals and published by white presses. Broadway for the first time presented black actors in serious dramatic roles, as well as shows such as *Dixie to Broadway* and *Blackbirds* that featured great entertainers including the singers Florence Mills and Ethel Waters and the tap dancer Bill Robinson.

The term "**New Negro**," associated in politics with pan-Africanism and the militancy of the Garvey movement, in art meant the rejection of established stereotypes and a search for black values to put in their place. This quest led the writers of what came to be called the **Harlem Renaissance** to the roots of the black experience—Africa, the rural South's folk traditions, and the life of the urban ghetto. Harlem Renaissance writings also contained a strong element of protest. This mood was exemplified by McKay's poem "If We Must Die," a response to the race riots of 1919. The poem affirmed that blacks would no longer allow themselves to be murdered defenselessly by whites:

The "New Negro"

> If we must die, let it not be like hogs
> Hunted and penned in an inglorious spot,
> While round us bark the mad and hungry dogs,
> Making their mock at our accursed lot. . . .
> Like men we'll face the murderous, cowardly pack,
> Pressed to the wall, dying, but fighting back!

Winston Churchill would invoke McKay's words to inspire the British public during World War II.

THE GREAT DEPRESSION

The Election of 1928

Few men elected to the presidency have seemed destined for a more successful term in office than Herbert Hoover. Born in Iowa in 1874, Hoover accumulated a fortune as a mining engineer working for firms in Asia, Africa, and Europe. During and immediately after World War I, he gained international fame by coordinating overseas food relief. In 1922, while serving as secretary of commerce, he published *American Individualism*, which condemned government regulation as an interference with the economic opportunities of ordinary Americans but also insisted that self-interest should be subordinated to public service. Hoover considered himself a Progressive, although he preferred what he called "associational action," in which

A 1928 campaign poster for the Republican ticket of Herbert Hoover and Charles Curtis.

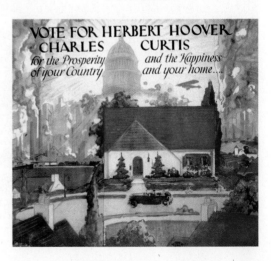

VOTE FOR HERBERT HOOVER *and* CHARLES CURTIS *for the Prosperity of your Country and the Happiness and your home....*

President Herbert Hoover (front row, right), at the opening day baseball game in Washington, D.C., April 17, 1929.

private agencies directed regulatory and welfare policies, to government intervention in the economy.

After "silent Cal" Coolidge in 1927 handed a piece of paper to a group of reporters that stated, "I do not choose to run for president in 1928," Hoover quickly emerged as his successor. Accepting the Republican nomination, Hoover celebrated the decade's prosperity and promised that poverty would "soon be banished from this earth." His Democratic opponent was Alfred E. Smith, the first Catholic to be nominated by a major party. Although he had no family connection with the new immigrants from southern and eastern Europe (his grandparents had emigrated from Ireland), Smith became their symbolic spokesman. He served three terms as governor of New York, securing passage of laws limiting the hours of working women and children and establishing widows' pensions. Smith denounced the Red Scare and called for the repeal of Prohibition.

Smith's Catholicism became the focus of the race. Many Protestant ministers and religious publications denounced him for his faith. For the first time since Reconstruction, Republicans carried several southern states, reflecting the strength of anti-Catholicism and nativism among religious fundamentalists. On the other hand, Smith carried the nation's twelve largest cities and won significant support in economically struggling farm areas. With more than 58 percent of the vote, Hoover was elected by a landslide. But Smith's campaign helped to lay the foundation for the triumphant Democratic coalition of the 1930s, based on urban ethnic voters, farmers, and the South.

The Coming of the Depression

On October 21, 1929, President Hoover traveled to Michigan to take part in the Golden Anniversary of the Festival of Light, organized by Henry Ford to commemorate the invention of the lightbulb by Thomas Edison fifty years earlier. Eight days later, on Black Tuesday, the stock market crashed. As panic selling set in, more than $10 billion in market value (equivalent to more than ten times that amount in today's money) vanished in five hours. Soon, the

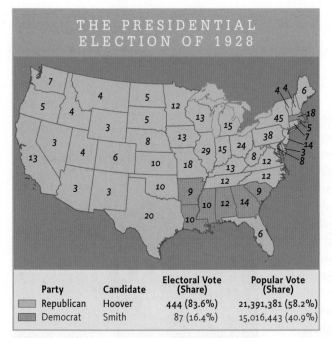

THE PRESIDENTIAL ELECTION OF 1928

Party	Candidate	Electoral Vote (Share)	Popular Vote (Share)
Republican	Hoover	444 (83.6%)	21,391,381 (58.2%)
Democrat	Smith	87 (16.4%)	15,016,443 (40.9%)

United States and, indeed, the entire world found themselves in the grip of the **Great Depression**, the greatest economic disaster in modern history.

The **stock market crash** did not, by itself, cause the Depression. Even before 1929, signs of economic trouble had become evident. Southern California and Florida experienced frenzied real-estate speculation and then spectacular busts, with banks failing, land remaining undeveloped, and mortgages foreclosed. The highly unequal distribution of income and the prolonged depression in farm regions reduced American purchasing power. Sales of new autos and household consumer goods stagnated after 1926. European demand for American goods also declined, partly because industry there had recovered from wartime destruction.

A fall in the bloated stock market, driven ever higher during the 1920s by speculators, was inevitable. But it came with such severity that it destroyed many of the investment companies that had been created to buy and sell stock, wiping out thousands of investors, and it greatly reduced business and consumer confidence.

The global financial system was ill equipped to deal with the downturn. Germany defaulted on reparations payments to France and Britain, leading these governments to stop repaying debts to American banks. Throughout the industrial world, banks failed as depositors withdrew money, fearful that they could no longer count on the promise to redeem paper money in gold. Millions of families lost their life savings.

Global financial system

Although stocks recovered somewhat in 1930, they soon resumed their relentless downward slide. Between 1929 and 1932, the price of a share of U.S. Steel fell from $262 to $22, and General Motors from $73 to $8. Four-fifths of the Rockefeller family fortune disappeared. In 1932, the economy hit rock bottom. Since 1929, the gross national product (the value of all the goods and services in the country) had fallen by one-third, prices by nearly 40 percent, and more than 11 million Americans—25 percent of the labor force—could not find work. U.S. Steel, which had employed 225,000 full-time workers in 1929, had none at the end of 1932. Those who retained their jobs confronted reduced hours and dramatically reduced wages. Every industrial economy suffered, but the United States, which had led the way in prosperity in the 1920s, was hit hardest of all.

Stocks' steady decline

BUY! *REPEATED*
BUY! *PERSISTENT*
BUY! ADVICES

The American Institute of Finance *repeatedly* and *persistently* recommends the purchase of *the same* stock. This persistent repetition on the same stock makes it practically impossible for the advice to escape the attention of clients.

The following nine stocks have been definitely recommended for purchase no less than 113 times in a twenty-month period—an average of over five recommendations a month.

Have *YOU* made *REAL PROFITS* in These Stocks? Did *YOU* BUY

(14 advices in 18 mos.)	Allied Chemical	@	140 up—now 290
(12 advices in 19 mos.)	Air Reduction	@	138 up—now 330
(11 advices in 18 mos.)	American Smelting	@	155 up—now 360
(10 advices in 20 mos.)	Chicago, R. I. & Pacific	@	70 up—now 135
(10 advices in 18 mos.)	Gold Dust Corp.	@	45 up—now 150
(11 advices in 19 mos.)	Inter. Harvester	@	135 up—now 400
(10 advices in 18 mos.)	Jewel Tea	@	58 up—now 170*
(18 advices in 20 mos.)	Mathieson Alkali	@	86 up—now 190
(17 advices in 19 mos.)	Peoples Gas	@	128 up—now 250

* Price includes recent "rights."

Three months before the stock market crash, *The Magazine of Wall Street* was avidly encouraging readers to purchase stocks.

Unemployed men lined up outside a Chicago soup kitchen in 1931. Charitable institutions like this one were overwhelmed by the advent of the Great Depression.

Hoovervilles

Americans and the Depression

The Depression transformed American life. Hundreds of thousands of people took to the road in search of work. Hungry men and women lined the streets of major cities. In Detroit, 4,000 children stood in bread lines each day seeking food. Thousands of families, evicted from their homes, moved into ramshackle shantytowns, dubbed Hoovervilles, that sprang up in parks and on abandoned land. In Chicago, where half the working population was unemployed at the beginning of 1932, Mayor Anton

A Hooverville—a shantytown created by homeless squatters—outside Seattle, Washington, in 1933.

Cermak telephoned people individually, begging them to pay their taxes. When the Soviet Union advertised its need for skilled workers, it received more than 100,000 applications from the United States.

The Depression actually reversed the long-standing movement of population from farms to cities. Many Americans left cities to try to grow food for their families. In 1935, 33 million people lived on farms—more than at any previous point in American history. But rural areas, already poor, saw families reduce the number of meals per day and children go barefoot. With the future shrouded in uncertainty, the American suicide rate rose to the highest level in the nation's history, and the birthrate fell to the lowest.

Deurbanization

The image of big business, carefully cultivated during the 1920s, collapsed as congressional investigations revealed massive irregularities committed by bankers and stockbrokers. Banks had knowingly sold worthless bonds. Prominent Wall Streeters had unloaded their own portfolios while advising small investors to maintain their holdings. Richard Whitney, the president of the New York Stock Exchange, was convicted of stealing from customers, including from a fund to aid widows and orphans. He ended up in jail.

Communist Party headquarters in New York City, 1932. The banners illustrate the variety of activities the party organized in the early 1930s.

Resignation and Protest

Many Americans reacted to the Depression with resignation or blamed themselves for economic misfortune. Others responded with protests that were at first spontaneous and uncoordinated, since unions, socialist organizations, and other groups that might have provided disciplined leadership had been decimated during the 1920s. In the spring of 1932, 20,000 unemployed World War I veterans descended on Washington to demand early payment of a bonus due in 1945, only to be driven away by federal soldiers. That summer, led by the charismatic Milo Reno, a former Iowa Populist, the National Farmers' Holiday Association protested low prices by temporarily blocking roads in the Midwest to prevent farm goods from getting to market.

Only the minuscule Communist Party seemed able to give a political focus to the anger and despair. One labor leader later recalled that the Communists "brought misery out of hiding," forming unemployed

An unemployed man and woman selling apples on a city street during the Great Depression.

councils, sponsoring marches and demonstrations for public assistance, and protesting the eviction of unemployed families from their homes.

Hoover's Response

In the eyes of many Americans, President Hoover's response to the Depression seemed inadequate and uncaring. Leading advisers, including Andrew Mellon, the wealthy secretary of the treasury, told Hoover that economic downturns were a normal part of capitalism, which weeded out unproductive firms and encouraged moral virtue among the less fortunate. Businessmen strongly opposed federal aid to the unemployed, and many publications called for individual "belt-tightening" as the road to recovery.

The federal government had never faced an economic crisis as severe as the Great Depression. Few political leaders understood how important consumer spending had become in the American economy. In 1931, Hoover quoted former president Grover Cleveland from four decades earlier: "The Government should not support the people. . . . Federal aid . . . weakens the sturdiness of our national character."

"Associational action"

Strongly opposed on principle to direct federal intervention in the economy, Hoover remained committed to "associational action." He put his faith in voluntary steps by business to maintain investment and employment—something few found it possible to do—and efforts by local charity organizations to assist needy neighbors. He attempted to restore public confidence, making frequent public statements that "the tide had turned." But these made him increasingly seem out of touch with reality. About the unemployed men who appeared on city streets offering apples at five cents apiece, Hoover would later write, "Many persons left their jobs for the more profitable one of selling apples."

The Worsening Economic Outlook

Some administration remedies, like the **Smoot-Hawley Tariff**, which Hoover signed with some reluctance in 1930, made the economic situation worse. Raising the already high taxes on imported goods, it inspired similar increases abroad, further reducing international trade.

By 1932, Hoover had to admit that voluntary action had failed to stem the Depression. He signed laws creating the **Reconstruction Finance Corporation**, which loaned money to failing banks, railroads, and other businesses, and the Federal Home Loan Bank System, which offered aid to homeowners threatened with foreclosure. Having vetoed previous bills to create employment through public-works projects like road and bridge construction, he now approved a measure appropriating nearly $2 billion for such initiatives and helping to fund local relief efforts. These were dramatic departures from previous federal economic policy. But he adamantly opposed offering direct relief to the unemployed.

Government action

Freedom in the Modern World

In 1927, the New School for Social Research in New York City organized a series of lectures on the theme of freedom in the modern world. The lectures painted a depressing portrait of American freedom on the eve of the Great Depression. The "sacred dogmas of patriotism and Big Business," said the educator Horace Kallen, dominated teaching, the press, and public debate. A definition of freedom reigned supreme that celebrated the unimpeded reign of economic enterprise yet tolerated the surveillance of private life and individual conscience.

Assessing freedom in the 1920s

The prosperity of the 1920s had reinforced this definition of freedom. With the economic crash, compounded by the ineffectiveness of the Hoover administration's response, it would be discredited. By 1932, the seeds had already been planted for a new conception of freedom that combined two different elements in a sometimes uneasy synthesis. One was the Progressive belief in a socially conscious state making constructive changes in economic arrangements. The other, which arose in the 1920s, centered on respect for civil liberties and cultural pluralism and declared that realms of life like group identity, personal behavior, and the free expression of ideas lay outside legitimate state concern. These two principles would become the hallmarks of modern liberalism, which during the 1930s would redefine American freedom.

A new conception of freedom

CHAPTER REVIEW AND ONLINE RESOURCES

REVIEW QUESTIONS

1. *How did consumerism and the idea of the "American way of life" affect people's understanding of American values, including the meaning of freedom, in the 1920s?*

2. *Which groups did not share in the prosperity of the 1920s and why?*

3. *How did business practices and policies lead to a decline in union membership in the 1920s?*

4. *President Calvin Coolidge said, "The chief business of the American people is business." How did the federal government's policies and practices in the 1920s reflect this understanding of the importance of business interests?*

5. *Who supported restricting immigration in the 1920s and why? Why were they more successful in gaining federal legislation to limit immigration in these years?*

6. *Did U.S. society in the 1920s reflect the concept of cultural pluralism as explained by Horace Kallen? Why or why not?*

7. *Identify the causes of the Great Depression.*

8. *What principles guided President Hoover's response to the Great Depression, and how did this restrict his ability to help the American people?*

9. *What issues were of particular concern to fundamentalists in these years and why?*

10. *In what ways did the ideas about (and the reality of) proper roles for women change in these years?*

KEY TERMS

Sacco-Vanzetti case (p. 613)
Equal Rights Amendment (p. 619)
flappers (p. 619)
Adkins v. Children's Hospital (p. 621)
Teapot Dome (p. 622)
American Civil Liberties Union (p. 624)
Schenck v. United States (p. 624)
fundamentalism (p. 625)
Scopes trial (p. 627)
illegal alien (p. 629)
New Negro (p. 635)
Harlem Renaissance (p. 635)
Great Depression (p. 637)
stock market crash (p. 637)
Smoot-Hawley Tariff (p. 640)
Reconstruction Finance Corporation (p. 641)

Go to 🐰 INQUIZITIVE

To see what you know—and learn what you've missed—with personalized feedback along the way.

Visit the *Give Me Liberty!* **Student Site** for primary source documents and images, interactive maps, author videos featuring Eric Foner, and more.

CHAPTER 21

THE NEW DEAL

★

1932-1940

1931   Scottsboro case

1933   FDR inaugurated

        Bank holiday

        The Hundred Days and the
        First New Deal

        Twenty-first Amendment
        ratified

1934   Huey Long launches
        the Share Our Wealth
        movement

1934–   Height of the Dust Bowl
1940

1935   Second New Deal launched

        Social Security Act

        Supreme Court rules
        the National Recovery
        Administration
        unconstitutional

        John L. Lewis organizes
        the Congress of Industrial
        Organizations

1936   Supreme Court rules the
        Agricultural Adjustment Act
        unconstitutional

        New Deal coalition leads to
        Democratic landslide

        John Maynard Keynes's
        *The General Theory of
        Employment, Interest, and
        Money*

1936–   United Auto Workers sit-
1937   down strike

1938   Fair Labor Standards Act
        passed

        House Un-American
        Activities Committee
        established

An unusual piece of folk art, this painting by Frank Teacher Jr., a worker in a coal mine near Pittsburgh, celebrates President Franklin D. Roosevelt and his alliance with organized labor—in this case, the United Mine Workers of America—during the New Deal. Teacher died in a mine accident in 1958.

FOCUS QUESTIONS

- *What were the major policy initiatives of the New Deal in the Hundred Days?*

- *Who were the main proponents of economic justice in the 1930s, and what measures did they advocate?*

- *What were the major initiatives of the Second New Deal?*

- *How did the New Deal recast the meaning of American freedom?*

- *How did New Deal benefits apply to women and minorities?*

- *How did the Popular Front influence American culture in the 1930s?*

The Columbia River winds its way on a 1,200-mile course from Canada through Washington and Oregon to the Pacific Ocean. Because of its steep descent from uplands to sea level, it produces an immense amount of energy. Residents of the economically underdeveloped Pacific Northwest had long dreamed of tapping this unused energy for electricity and irrigation. But not until the 1930s did the federal government launch the program of dam construction that transformed the region. The project created thousands of jobs for the unemployed, and the network of dams produced abundant cheap power.

When the Grand Coulee Dam went into operation in 1941, it was the largest man-made structure in world history. It eventually produced more than 40 percent of the nation's hydroelectric power. The project also had less appealing consequences. From time immemorial, the Columbia River had been filled with salmon. But the Grand Coulee Dam made no provision for the passage of fish, and the salmon all but vanished. This caused little concern during the Depression but became a source of controversy later in the century as Americans became more attuned to preserving the natural environment.

The Columbia River project reflected broader changes in American life and thought during the **New Deal** of the 1930s. Franklin D. Roosevelt believed regional economic development like that in the Northwest would promote economic growth, ease the domestic and working lives of ordinary Americans, and keep control of key natural resources in public rather than private hands. The early Roosevelt administration spent far more money on building roads, dams, airports, bridges, and housing than on any other activity.

Roosevelt also oversaw the transformation of the Democratic Party into a coalition of farmers, industrial workers, the reform-minded urban middle class, liberal intellectuals, northern African-Americans, and, somewhat incongruously, the white supremacist South, united by the belief that the federal government must provide Americans with protection against the dislocations caused by modern capitalism. "Liberalism," traditionally understood as limited government and free-market economics, took on its modern meaning. Thanks to the New Deal, it now referred to active efforts by the national government to uplift less fortunate members of society.

Freedom, too, underwent a transformation during the 1930s. The New Deal elevated a public guarantee of economic security to the forefront of American discussions of freedom. Regional economic planning reflected this understanding of freedom. So did other New Deal measures, including the Social Security Act, which offered aid to the unemployed and aged, and the Fair Labor Standards Act, which established a national minimum wage.

Yet although the New Deal significantly expanded the meaning of freedom, it did not erase freedom's boundaries. Its benefits flowed to industrial workers but not tenant farmers, to men far more fully than women, and to white Americans more than blacks, who, in the South, still were deprived of the basic rights of citizenship.

THE FIRST NEW DEAL

FDR and the Election of 1932

FDR, as he liked to be called, was born in 1882, a fifth cousin of Theodore Roosevelt. After serving as undersecretary of the navy during World War I, he ran for vice president on the ill-fated Democratic ticket of 1920 headed by James M. Cox. In 1921, he contracted polio and lost the use of his legs, a fact carefully concealed from the public in that pre-television era. Very few Americans realized that the president who projected an image of vigorous leadership during the 1930s and World War II was confined to a wheelchair.

Franklin Delano Roosevelt

In his speech accepting the Democratic nomination for president in 1932, Roosevelt promised a "new deal" for the American people. But his campaign offered only vague hints of what this might entail. He advocated a balanced federal budget and criticized his opponent, President Hoover, for excessive government spending. The biggest difference between the parties during the campaign was the Democrats' call for the repeal of Prohibition, although Roosevelt certainly suggested a greater awareness of the plight of ordinary Americans. Battered by the economic crisis, Americans in 1932 were desperate for new leadership, and Roosevelt won a resounding victory. He received 57 percent of the popular vote, and Democrats swept to a commanding majority in Congress.

The Coming of the New Deal

Roosevelt conceived of the New Deal as an alternative to socialism on the left, Nazism on the right, and the inaction of upholders of unregulated capitalism. He hoped to reconcile democracy, individual liberty, and economic recovery and development.

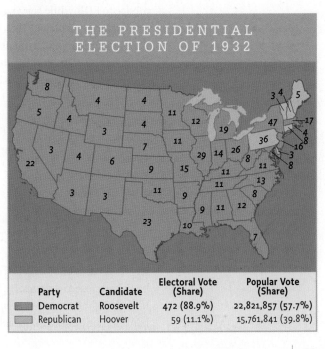

THE PRESIDENTIAL ELECTION OF 1932

Party	Candidate	Electoral Vote (Share)	Popular Vote (Share)
Democrat	Roosevelt	472 (88.9%)	22,821,857 (57.7%)
Republican	Hoover	59 (11.1%)	15,761,841 (39.8%)

This panel depicting the construction of a dam was painted in 1939 by William Gropper as part of a mural for the new Department of the Interior building in Washington, D.C. Like other artists who found it difficult to obtain work during the Depression, Gropper was hired by the Works Projects Administration to paint murals for government buildings. This one was inspired by the construction of the Grand Coulee Dam on the Columbia River, one of the many New Deal projects that expanded the nation's infrastructure and provided employment to victims of the Depression.

FDR's advisers

He did not, however, enter office with a blueprint for dealing with the Depression. At first, he relied heavily for advice on a group of intellectuals and social workers who took up key positions in his administration. They included Secretary of Labor Frances Perkins, a veteran of Hull House and the New York Consumers' League; Harry Hopkins, who had headed emergency relief efforts during Roosevelt's term as governor of New York; Secretary of the Interior Harold Ickes, a veteran of Theodore Roosevelt's Progressive campaign of 1912; and Louis Brandeis, who had advised Woodrow Wilson during the 1912 campaign and now offered political advice to FDR while serving on the Supreme Court.

Brandeis believed that large corporations not only wielded excessive power but had contributed to the Depression by keeping prices artificially high and failing to increase workers' purchasing power. They should be broken up, he insisted, not regulated. But the "brains trust"—a group of academics that included a number of Columbia University professors—saw bigness as inevitable in a modern economy. Large firms needed to be managed and directed by the government, not dismantled. Their view prevailed during what came to be called the First New Deal.

The Banking Crisis

Banking suspended

"This nation asks for action and action now," Roosevelt announced on taking office on March 4, 1933. The new president confronted a banking system on the verge of collapse. As bank funds invested in the stock market lost their value and panicked depositors withdrew their savings, bank after bank had closed its doors. By March 1933, banking had been suspended in a majority of the states—that is, people could not gain access to money in their bank accounts. Roosevelt declared a "bank holiday," temporarily halting all bank operations, and called Congress into special session. On March 9, it rushed to pass the **Emergency Banking Act**, which provided funds to shore up threatened institutions.

Further measures soon followed that transformed the American financial system. The Glass-Steagall Act barred commercial banks from becoming involved in the buying and selling of stocks. Until its repeal in the 1990s, the law prevented many of the irresponsible practices that had contributed to the stock market crash. The same law established the Federal Deposit Insurance Corporation (FDIC), a government system that insured the accounts of individual depositors. Together, these measures rescued the financial system and greatly increased the government's power over it.

The NRA

The Emergency Banking Act was the first of an unprecedented flurry of legislation during the first three months of Roosevelt's administration, a period known as the **Hundred Days**. Seizing on the sense of crisis and the momentum of his electoral victory, Roosevelt won rapid passage of laws he hoped would promote economic recovery. He persuaded Congress to create a host of new agencies, whose initials soon became part of the language of politics—NRA, AAA, CCC.

The centerpiece of Roosevelt's plan for combating the Depression, the **National Industrial Recovery Act**, was to a large extent modeled on the

Presidents Herbert Hoover and Franklin D. Roosevelt on their way to the latter's inauguration on March 4, 1933. The two men strongly disliked one another. They barely spoke during the ride and never saw each other again after that day.

A "run" on a bank: crowds of people wait outside a New York City bank, hoping to withdraw their money.

government–business partnership established by the War Industries Board of World War I. The act established the **National Recovery Administration** (NRA), which would work with groups of business leaders to establish industry codes that set standards for output, prices, and working conditions.

In effect, FDR had repudiated the older idea of liberty based on the idea that the best way to encourage economic activity and ensure a fair distribution of wealth was to allow market competition to operate, unrestrained by the government. And to win support from labor, section 7a of the new law recognized the workers' right to organize unions—a departure from the "open shop" policies of the 1920s and a step toward government support for what workers called "industrial freedom."

Industrial freedom

Headed by Hugh S. Johnson, a retired general and businessman, the NRA quickly established codes that set standards for production, prices, and wages in the textile, steel, mining, and auto industries. But the NRA became mired in controversy. Large companies dominated the code-writing process. They used the NRA to drive up prices, limit production, lay off workers, and divide markets among themselves at the expense of smaller competitors. The NRA produced neither economic recovery nor peace between employers and workers. It did, however, combat the pervasive sense that the government was doing nothing to deal with the economic crisis.

NRA codes

Government Jobs

The Hundred Days also brought the government into providing relief to those in need. Roosevelt and most of his advisers shared the widespread fear that direct government payments to the unemployed would undermine individual self-reliance. But with nearly a quarter of the workforce unemployed, spending on relief was unavoidable. In May 1933, Congress created the Federal Emergency Relief Administration, to make grants to local agencies that aided those impoverished by the Depression. FDR, however, much preferred to create temporary jobs, thereby combating unemployment while improving the nation's infrastructure of roads, bridges, public buildings, and parks.

A Civilian Conservation Corps workforce in Yosemite National Park, 1935.

In March 1933, Congress established the **Civilian Conservation Corps** (CCC), which set unemployed young men to work on projects like forest preservation, flood control, and the improvement of national parks and wildlife preserves. By the time the program ended in 1942, more than 3 million persons had passed through CCC camps, where they received government wages of $30 per month. The CCC made a major contribution to the enhancement of the American environment.

Creating federal jobs

Public-Works Projects

One section of the National Industrial Recovery Act created the **Public Works Administration** (PWA), with an appropriation of $3.3 billion. Directed by Secretary of the Interior Harold Ickes, it built roads, schools, hospitals, and other public facilities, including New York City's Triborough Bridge and the Overseas Highway between Miami and Key West, Florida. In November 1933, yet another agency, the Civil Works Administration (CWA), was launched. By January 1934, it employed more than 4 million persons in the construction of highways, tunnels, courthouses, and airports. But as the cost spiraled upward and complaints multiplied that the New Deal was creating a class of Americans permanently dependent on government jobs, Roosevelt ordered the CWA dissolved.

The **Tennessee Valley Authority** (TVA), another product of the Hundred Days, built a series of dams to prevent floods and deforestation

A map published by the Public Works Administration in 1935 depicts some of the numerous infrastructure projects funded by the New Deal. Among the most famous public-works projects are the Triborough Bridge in New York City, the Overseas Highway in Florida, and the Grand Coulee Dam in Washington. Overall, the New Deal spent $250 billion (in today's money) to construct, among other things, 40,000 public buildings, 72,000 schools, 80,000 bridges, and 8,000 parks.

SERVING THE PEOPLE

A map showing the reach of the Tennessee Valley Authority, covering all or parts of seven southeastern states. Numerous reservoirs and power plants dot the landscape.

along the Tennessee River and to provide cheap electric power for homes and factories in a seven-state region where many families still lived in isolated log cabins. The TVA put the federal government, for the first time, in the business of selling electricity in competition with private companies.

The New Deal and Agriculture

Efforts to raise farm prices

Another policy initiative of the Hundred Days addressed the disastrous plight of American farmers. The **Agricultural Adjustment Act** (AAA) authorized the federal government to set production quotas for major crops and pay farmers to plant less in an attempt to raise farm prices. Many crops already in the field were destroyed. In 1933, the government ordered more than 6 million pigs slaughtered as part of the policy, a step critics found strange at a time of widespread hunger.

The AAA succeeded in significantly raising farm prices and incomes. But not all farmers benefited. Money flowed to property-owning farmers, ignoring the large number who worked on land owned by others. The AAA policy of paying landowning farmers not to grow crops encouraged the eviction of thousands of poor tenants and sharecroppers. Many joined the rural exodus to cities or to the farms of the West Coast.

The onset in 1930 of a period of unusually dry weather in the nation's heartland worsened the Depression's impact on rural America. By mid-decade, the region suffered from the century's most severe drought. Mechanized agriculture in this semi-arid region had pulverized the topsoil and killed native grasses that prevented erosion. Winds now blew much of the soil away, creating the **Dust Bowl**, as the affected areas of Oklahoma, Texas, Kansas, and Colorado were called. The drought and dust storms displaced more than 1 million farmers.

A giant dust storm engulfs a town in western Kansas on April 14, 1935, known as Black Sunday in the American West.

The New Deal and Housing

The Depression devastated the American housing industry. The construction of new residences all but ceased, and banks and savings and loan associations that had financed home ownership collapsed or, to remain afloat, foreclosed on many homes (a quarter of a million in 1932 alone). Millions of Americans lived in overcrowded, unhealthy urban slums or in ramshackle rural dwellings. Private enterprise alone, it seemed clear, was unlikely to solve the nation's housing crisis.

Roosevelt spoke of "the security of the home" as a fundamental right. In 1933 and 1934, his administration moved energetically to protect home owners from foreclosure and to stimulate new construction. The Home Owners Loan Corporation and **Federal Housing Administration** (FHA) insured millions of long-term mortgages issued by private banks. At the same time, the federal government itself built thousands of units of low-rent housing. Thanks to the FHA and, later, the Veterans' Administration, home ownership came within the reach of tens of millions of families. It became cheaper for most Americans to buy single-family homes than to rent apartments.

Other important measures of Roosevelt's first two years in office included the ratification of the Twenty-first Amendment to the Constitution, which repealed Prohibition; the establishment of the Federal Communications Commission to oversee the

As it did in other sectors of the economy, the Great Depression led to a collapse in the construction industry.

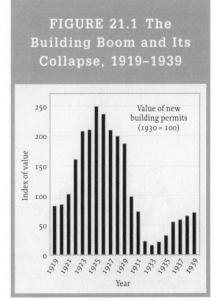

FIGURE 21.1 The Building Boom and Its Collapse, 1919–1939

Value of new building permits (1930 = 100)

Index of value

Year

A MULE AND A PLOW

RESETTLEMENT ADMINISTRATION
Small Loans Give Farmers a New Start

The artist Bernarda Shahn, wife of the more famous painter Ben Shahn, created this lithograph in the mid-1930s for the Resettlement Administration, a New Deal agency that relocated rural and urban families—especially victims of the Dust Bowl—to planned communities.

The Illegal Act, a cartoon critical of the Supreme Court's decision declaring the NRA unconstitutional. FDR tells a drowning Uncle Sam, "I'm sorry, but the Supreme Court says I must chuck you back in."

nation's broadcast airwaves and telephone communications; and the creation of the Securities and Exchange Commission to regulate the stock and bond markets.

Taken together, the First New Deal was a series of experiments, some of which succeeded and some of which did not. They transformed the role of the federal government, constructed numerous public facilities, and provided relief to millions of needy persons. Public employment rescued millions of Americans from the ravages of the Depression. But while the economy improved somewhat, sustained recovery had not been achieved. Some 10 million Americans—more than 20 percent of the workforce—remained unemployed when 1934 came to an end.

The Court and the New Deal

In 1935, the Supreme Court, still controlled by conservative Republican judges who held to the nineteenth-century understanding of freedom as liberty of contract, began to invalidate key New Deal laws. First came the NRA, declared unconstitutional in May in a case brought by the Schechter Poultry Company of Brooklyn, which had been charged with violating the code adopted by the chicken industry. In a unanimous decision, the Court declared the NRA unlawful because in its codes and other regulations it delegated legislative powers to the president and attempted to regulate local businesses that did not engage in interstate commerce. In January 1936, the AAA fell in *United States v. Butler*, which declared it an unconstitutional exercise of congressional power over local economic activities.

Having failed to end the Depression or win judicial approval, the First New Deal ground to a halt. Meanwhile, pressures were mounting outside Washington that propelled the administration toward more radical departures in policy.

THE GRASSROOTS REVOLT

Labor's Great Upheaval

The most striking development of the mid-1930s was the mobilization of millions of workers in mass-production industries that had successfully resisted unionization. "Labor's great upheaval," as this era of unprecedented militancy was called, came as a great surprise. Unlike in the past, however, the federal government now seemed to be on the side of labor.

American-born children of the new immigrants now dominated the industrial labor force, and organizers no longer had to distribute materials in numerous languages as the IWW had done. And a cadre of militant labor leaders, many of them socialists and communists, had survived the repression of the 1920s. They provided leadership to the labor upsurge.

American factories at the outset of the New Deal were miniature dictatorships in which unions were rare, workers could be beaten by supervisors and fired at will, and management determined the length of the workday and speed of the assembly line. Workers' demands during the 1930s went beyond better wages. They included an end to employers' arbitrary power in the workplace, and basic civil liberties for workers, including the right to picket, distribute literature, and meet to discuss their grievances. All these goals required union recognition.

Conditions in American factories

Roosevelt's inauguration unleashed a flood of poignant letters to the federal government describing what a Louisiana sugar laborer called the "terrible and inhuman condition" of many workers. Labor organizers spread the message that the "political liberty for which our forefathers fought" had been "made meaningless by economic inequality" and "industrial despotism."

Labor's great upheaval exploded in 1934, a year that witnessed no fewer than 2,000 strikes. Many produced violent confrontations between workers and the local police. San Francisco experienced the country's first general strike since 1919. It began with a walkout of dockworkers led by the fiery communist Harry Bridges. Workers demanded recognition of the International Longshoremen's Association and an end to the hated "shape up" system in which they had to gather en masse each day to wait for work assignments. The year 1934 also witnessed a strike of 400,000 textile workers in states from New England to the Deep South, demanding recognition of the United Textile Workers. Many of these walkouts won at least some of the workers' demands. But the textile strike failed.

A year of strikes

The Rise of the CIO

The labor upheaval posed a challenge to the American Federation of Labor's traditional policy of organizing workers by craft rather than seeking to mobilize all the workers in a given industry, such as steel manufacturing. In 1934, thirty AFL leaders called for the creation of unions of industrial workers. When the AFL convention of 1935 refused, the head of the United Mine Workers, John L. Lewis, led a walkout that produced a new labor organization, the **Congress of Industrial Organizations** (CIO). It aimed, said Lewis, at nothing less than to secure "economic freedom and

John L. Lewis

industrial democracy" for American workers—a fair share in the wealth produced by their labor, and a voice in determining the conditions under which they worked.

The UAW's sit-down strike

In December 1936, unions, most notably the United Auto Workers (UAW), a fledgling CIO union, unveiled the **sit-down strike**, a remarkably effective tactic that the IWW had pioneered three decades earlier. Rather than walking out of the Fisher Body Plant in Cleveland, thus enabling management to bring in strikebreakers, workers halted production but remained inside. Sit-downs soon spread to General Motors plants in Flint, Michigan, the nerve center of automobile production. Demonstrating a remarkable spirit of unity, the strikers cleaned the plant, oiled the idle machinery, and settled disputes among themselves. Workers' wives shuttled food into the plant. On February 11, General Motors agreed to negotiate with the UAW. By the end of 1937, the UAW claimed 400,000 members.

The victory in the auto industry reverberated throughout industrial America. Steelworkers had suffered memorable defeats in the struggle for unionization, notably at Homestead in 1892 and in the Great Steel Strike of 1919. But in March 1937, fearing a sit-down campaign and aware that it could no longer count on the aid of state and federal authorities, U.S. Steel, the country's single most important business firm, agreed to recognize the Steel Workers Organizing Committee (forerunner of the United Steelworkers of America). Smaller steel firms, however, refused to follow suit.

Growth in union membership

Union membership reached 9 million by 1940, more than double the number in 1930. Workers gained new grievance procedures and seniority systems governing hiring, firing, and promotions. The CIO unions helped to stabilize a chaotic employment situation and offered members a sense of dignity and freedom.

Sit-down strike at a General Motors factory in Flint, Michigan, 1937.

Labor and Politics

Throughout the industrial heartland, the labor upsurge altered the balance of economic power and propelled to the forefront of politics labor's goal of a fairer, freer, more equal America. The CIO put forward an ambitious program for federal action to shield Americans from economic and social insecurity, including public housing, universal health care, and unemployment and old age insurance.

Building on the idea, so prominent in the 1920s, that the key to prosperity lay in an American standard of living based on mass consumption, CIO leaders explained the Depression as the result of an imbalance of wealth and income. The pathbreaking 1937 agreement between the UAW and General Motors spoke of a "rate of pay commensurate with an American standard of living." By mid-decade, many New Dealers accepted the "underconsumptionist" explanation of the Depression, which saw lack of sufficient consumer demand as its underlying cause.

Voices of Protest

Other popular movements of the mid-1930s also placed the question of economic justice on the political agenda. In California, the novelist Upton Sinclair won the Democratic nomination for governor in 1934 as the head of the End Poverty in California movement. Sinclair called for the state to use idle factories and land in cooperative ventures that would provide jobs for the unemployed. He lost the election after being subjected to one of the first modern "negative" media campaigns. Sinclair's opponents circulated false newsreels showing armies of unemployed men marching to California to support his candidacy and a fake endorsement from the Communist Party.

Police break up a gathering along the San Francisco waterfront on the eve of the general strike involving over 200,000 workers in May 1934.

The rise to national prominence of Huey Long offered another sign of popular dissatisfaction with the slow pace of economic recovery. Driven by intense ambition and the desire to help uplift Louisiana's "common people," Long won election as governor in 1928 and in 1930 took a seat in the U.S. Senate. From Washington, he dominated every branch of state government. He used his dictatorial power to build roads, schools, and hospitals and to increase the tax burden on Louisiana's oil companies.

Huey Long, the "Kingfish" of Louisiana politics, in full rhetorical flight. This photo was probably taken in 1934, when Long was in the U.S. Senate but still running the state government.

In 1934, Long launched the **Share Our Wealth movement**, with the slogan "Every Man a King." He called for the confiscation of most of the wealth of the richest Americans in order to finance an immediate grant of $5,000 and a guaranteed job and annual income for all citizens. He was on the verge of announcing a run for president when the son of a defeated political rival assassinated him in 1935.

Dr. Francis Townsend, a California physician, meanwhile won wide support for a plan by which the government would make a monthly payment of $200 to older Americans, with the requirement that they spend it immediately. This, he argued, would boost the economy. Along with the rise of the CIO, these signs of popular discontent helped spark the Second New Deal.

The cover of a songbook to accompany a radio broadcast from the Chicago Gospel Tabernacle. A radio tower dominates the image.

Religion on the Radio

Also in the mid-1930s, the "radio priest," Father Charles E. Coughlin, attracted millions of listeners with weekly broadcasts attacking Wall Street bankers and greedy capitalists, and calling for government ownership of key industries as a way of combating the Depression. Initially a strong supporter of FDR, Coughlin became increasingly critical of the president for what he considered the failure of the New Deal to promote social justice. His crusade would later shift to anti-Semitism and support for European fascism.

Other religious leaders of various denominations took advantage of the mass media to spread their beliefs. Ironically, many fundamentalists used the most modern techniques of communication, including the radio and popular entertainment, to promote their anti-modernist message. They found in the radio a way to bypass established churches and their leaders. Aimee Semple McPherson, a Los Angeles revivalist, had her own radio station, which broadcast sermons from the International Church of the Foursquare Gospel she had founded. By the 1940s, national religious broadcast networks emerged, with a reliable and dedicated listening audience.

THE SECOND NEW DEAL

Economic security

Buoyed by Democratic gains in the midterm elections of 1934, Roosevelt in 1935 launched the Second New Deal. The First had focused on economic recovery. The emphasis of the Second was economic security—a guarantee that Americans would be protected against unemployment and poverty.

The idea that lack of consumer demand caused the Depression had been popularized by Huey Long, Francis Townsend, and the CIO. More and more New Dealers concluded that the government should no longer try to plan business recovery but should try to redistribute the national income so as to sustain mass purchasing power in the consumer economy. A series of measures in 1935 attacked head-on the problem of weak demand and economic inequality. Congress levied a highly publicized tax on large fortunes and corporate profits—a direct response to the popularity of Huey Long's Share Our Wealth campaign. It created the Rural Electrification Agency (REA) to bring electric power to homes that lacked it—80 percent of farms were still without electricity in 1934—in part to enable more Americans to purchase household appliances.

The Rural Electrification Agency

By 1950, 90 percent of the nation's farms had been wired for electricity, and almost all now possessed radios, electric stoves, refrigerators, and mechanical equipment to milk cows. In addition, the federal government under the Second New Deal tried to promote soil conservation and family farming. This effort resulted from the belief that the country would never achieve prosperity so long as farmers' standard of living lagged well behind that of city dwellers, and that rural poverty resulted mainly from the poor use of natural resources. Thus, farmers received federal assistance in reducing soil loss in their fields. These measures (like those of the AAA) mainly benefited landowners, not sharecroppers, tenants, or migrant workers. In the long run, the Second New Deal failed to arrest the trend toward larger farms and fewer farmers.

The WPA and the Wagner Act

In 1934, Roosevelt had severely curtailed federal employment for those in need. Now, he approved the establishment of the **Works Progress Administration** (WPA), which hired some 3 million Americans, in virtually every walk of life, each year until it ended in 1943. It constructed thousands of public buildings and bridges, more than 500,000 miles of roads, and 600 airports. It built stadiums, swimming pools, and sewage treatment plants. Unlike previous work relief programs, the WPA employed many out-of-work white-collar workers and professionals, even doctors and dentists.

A poster by the artist Vera Bock for the Federal Art Project of the Works Progress Administration depicts farmers and laborers joining hands to produce prosperity.

Employing white-collar workers

An art exhibit in a New York City alley in 1938. The Works Progress Administration tried to broaden the audience for art by displaying it in unusual venues.

Funding the arts

Perhaps the most famous WPA projects were in the arts. The WPA set hundreds of artists to work decorating public buildings with murals. It hired writers to produce local histories and guidebooks to the forty-eight states and to record the recollections of ordinary Americans, including hundreds of former slaves. Thanks to the WPA, audiences across the country enjoyed their first glimpse of live musical and theatrical performances and their first opportunity to view exhibitions of American art.

The Wagner Act

Another major initiative of the Second New Deal, the **Wagner Act**, brought democracy into the American workplace by empowering the National Labor Relations Board to supervise elections in which employees voted on union representation. It also outlawed "unfair labor practices," including the firing and blacklisting of union organizers.

The American Welfare State: Social Security

The centerpiece of the Second New Deal was the **Social Security Act** of 1935. It embodied Roosevelt's conviction that the national government had a responsibility to ensure the material well-being of ordinary Americans. It created a system of unemployment insurance, old age pensions, and aid to the disabled, the elderly poor, and families with dependent children.

Progressive legacy

None of these were original ideas. The Progressive platform of 1912 had called for old age pensions. Assistance to poor families with dependent children descended from the mothers' pensions promoted by maternalist reformers. Many European countries had already adopted national unemployment insurance plans. What was new, however, was that in the name of economic security, the American government would now supervise not simply temporary relief but a permanent system of social insurance.

A 1935 poster promoting the new Social Security system.

The Social Security Act launched the American version of the **welfare state**—a term that originated in Britain during World War II to refer to a system of income assistance, health coverage, and social services for all citizens. Compared with similar programs in Europe, the American welfare state has always been far more decentralized, involved lower levels of public spending, and covered fewer citizens. The original Social Security bill, for example, envisioned a national system of health insurance. But Congress dropped this after ferocious opposition from the American Medical Association, which feared government regulation of doctors' activities and incomes. And the fact that domestic and agricultural workers were not covered by unemployment and old age benefits meant that Social Security at first excluded large numbers of Americans, especially unmarried women and non-whites.

Nonetheless, Social Security represented a dramatic departure from the traditional functions of government. The Second New Deal transformed the relationship between the federal government and American citizens. Before the 1930s, national political debate often revolved around the question of *whether* the federal government should intervene in the economy. After the New Deal, debate rested on *how* it should intervene. In addition, the government assumed a responsibility, which it has never wholly relinquished, for guaranteeing Americans a living wage and protecting them against economic and personal misfortune.

A RECKONING WITH LIBERTY

The Depression made inevitable, in the words of one writer, a "reckoning with liberty." For too many Americans, Roosevelt proclaimed, "life was no longer free, liberty no longer real, men could no longer follow the pursuit of happiness."

FDR delivering one of his "fireside chats" in 1938. Roosevelt was the first president to make effective use of the radio to promote his policies.

Along with being a superb politician, Roosevelt was a master of political communication. At a time when his political opponents controlled most newspapers, he harnessed radio's power to bring his message directly into American homes. By the mid-1930s, more than two-thirds of American families owned radios. They listened avidly to Roosevelt's radio addresses, known as "fireside chats."

FDR's "fireside chats"

Roosevelt adeptly appealed to traditional values in support of new policies. He gave the term "liberalism" its modern meaning. As we have seen, in the nineteenth century, liberalism had been a shorthand for limited government and free-market economics. Roosevelt consciously chose to employ it to describe a large, active, socially conscious state. He reclaimed the word "freedom" from conservatives and made it a rallying cry for the New Deal. In his second fireside chat, Roosevelt juxtaposed his own definition of liberty as "greater security for the average man" to the older notion of liberty of contract, which served the interests of "the privileged few." Henceforth, he would consistently link freedom with economic security and identify entrenched economic inequality as its greatest enemy. "The liberty of a democracy," he declared in 1938, was not safe if citizens could not "sustain an acceptable standard of living."

Freedom and economic security

Even as Roosevelt invoked the word to uphold the New Deal, "liberty"—in the sense of freedom from powerful government—became the fighting slogan of his opponents. When conservative businessmen and politicians in 1934 formed an organization to mobilize opposition to Roosevelt's policies, they called it the American Liberty League.

Opposition to the New Deal

VOICES OF FREEDOM

From Franklin D. Roosevelt, "Fireside Chat" (1934)

President Roosevelt pioneered the use of the new mass medium of radio to speak directly to Americans in their homes. He used his "fireside chats" to mobilize support for New Deal programs, link them with American traditions, and outline his definition of freedom.

To those who say that our expenditures for public works and other means for recovery are a waste that we cannot afford, I answer that no country, however rich, can afford the waste of its human resources. Demoralization caused by vast unemployment is our greatest extravagance. Morally, it is the greatest menace to our social order. Some people try to tell me that we must make up our minds that in the future we shall permanently have millions of unemployed just as other countries have had them for over a decade. What may be necessary for those countries is not my responsibility to determine. But as for this country, I stand or fall by my refusal to accept as a necessary condition of our future a permanent army of unemployed. . . .

In our efforts for recovery we have avoided, on the one hand, the theory that business should and must be taken over into an all-embracing Government. We have avoided, on the other hand, the equally untenable theory that it is an interference with liberty to offer reasonable help when private enterprise is in need of help. The course we have followed fits the American practice of Government, a practice of taking action step by step, of regulating only to meet concrete needs, a practice of courageous recognition of change. I believe with Abraham Lincoln, that "the legitimate object of Government is to do for a community of people whatever they need to have done but cannot do at all or cannot do so well for themselves in their separate and individual capacities."

I am not for a return to that definition of liberty under which for many years a free people were being gradually regimented into the service of the privileged few. I prefer and I am sure you prefer that broader definition of liberty under which we are moving forward to greater freedom, to greater security for the average man than he has ever known before in the history of America.

From John Steinbeck, *The Harvest Gypsies: On the Road to the Grapes of Wrath* (1938)

John Steinbeck's popular novel *The Grapes of Wrath* (1939), and the film version that followed shortly thereafter, focused national attention on the plight of homeless migrants displaced from their farms as a result of the Great Depression. Before that book appeared, Steinbeck had published a series of newspaper articles based on eyewitness accounts of the migrants, which became the basis for his novel.

In California, we find a curious attitude toward a group that makes our agriculture successful. The migrants are needed, and they are hated. . . . The migrants are hated for the following reasons, that they are ignorant and dirty people, that they are carriers of disease, that they increase the necessity for police and the tax bill for schooling in a community, and that if they are allowed to organize they can, simply by refusing to work, wipe out the season's crops. . . .

Let us see what kind of people they are, where they come from, and the routes of their wanderings. In the past they have been of several races, encouraged to come and often imported as cheap labor. Chinese in the early period, then Filipinos, Japanese and Mexicans. These were foreigners, and as such they were ostracized and segregated and herded about. . . . But in recent years the foreign migrants have begun to organize, and at this danger they have been deported in great numbers, for there was a new reservoir from which a great quantity of cheap labor could be obtained.

The drought in the middle west has driven the agricultural populations of Oklahoma, Nebraska and parts of Kansas and Texas westward. . . . Thousands of them are crossing the borders in ancient rattling automobiles, destitute and hungry and homeless, ready to accept any pay so that they may eat and feed their children. . . .

The earlier foreign migrants have invariably been drawn from a peon class. This is not the case with the new migrants. They are small farmers who have lost their farms, or farm hands who have lived with the family in the old American way. . . . They have come from the little farm districts where democracy was not only possible but inevitable, where popular government, whether practiced in the Grange, in church organization or in local government, was the responsibility of every man. And they have come into the country where, because of the movement necessary to make a living, they are not allowed any vote whatever, but are rather considered a properly unprivileged class. . . .

As one little boy in a squatter's camp said, "When they need us they call us migrants, and when we've picked their crop, we're bums and we got to get out."

QUESTIONS

1. *What does Roosevelt mean by the difference between the definition of liberty that has existed in the past and his own "broader definition of liberty"?*

2. *According to Steinbeck, how do Depression-era migrant workers differ from those in earlier periods?*

3. *Do the migrant workers described by Steinbeck enjoy liberty as Roosevelt understands it?*

The Election of 1936

Politics and class divisions

By 1936, with working-class voters providing massive majorities for the Democratic Party and businesses large and small bitterly estranged from the New Deal, politics reflected class divisions more completely than at any other time in American history. Conceptions of freedom divided sharply as well.

A fight for the possession of "the ideal of freedom," reported the *New York Times*, emerged as the central issue of the presidential campaign of 1936. In his speech accepting renomination, Roosevelt launched a blistering attack against "economic royalists" who, he charged, sought to establish a new tyranny over the "average man." Economic rights, he went on, were the precondition of liberty—poor men "are not free men." Throughout the campaign, FDR would insist that the threat posed to economic freedom by the "new despotism" of large corporations was the main issue of the election.

Economic freedom

As Roosevelt's opponent, Republicans chose Kansas governor Alfred Landon, a former Theodore Roosevelt Progressive. Landon denounced Social Security and other measures as threats to individual liberty. Opposition to the New Deal planted the seeds for the later flowering of an antigovernment conservatism bent on upholding the free market and dismantling the welfare state. But in 1936 Roosevelt won a landslide reelection, with more than 60 percent of the popular vote. His success stemmed from strong backing from organized labor and his ability to unite southern white and northern black voters, Protestant farmers and urban Catholic and Jewish ethnics, industrial workers and middle-class home owners. These groups made up the so-called New Deal coalition, which would dominate American politics for nearly half a century.

The New Deal coalition

Fall In!, a cartoon commenting on Roosevelt's proposal to "pack" the Supreme Court, from the *Richmond Times-Dispatch*, January 8, 1937.

The Court Fight

Roosevelt's second inaugural address was the first to be delivered on January 20. In order to shorten a newly elected president's wait before taking office, the recently ratified Twentieth Amendment had moved inauguration day from March 4. The Depression, he admitted, had not been conquered: "I see one-third of a nation ill-housed, ill-clad, and ill-nourished." Emboldened by his electoral triumph, Roosevelt now made what many considered a serious political miscalculation. On the pretext that several members of the Supreme Court were too old to perform their functions, he proposed that the president be allowed to appoint a new justice for each one who remained on the Court past age seventy (an age that six of the nine had already passed). FDR's aim, of course, was to change the balance of power on a Court that, he feared, might well invalidate Social Security, the Wagner Act, and other measures of the Second New Deal.

Congress rejected the **Court packing plan**. But Roosevelt accomplished his underlying purpose. Coming soon after Roosevelt's landslide victory of 1936, the threat of "Court packing" inspired an astonishing about-face by key justices. Beginning in March 1937, the Court suddenly revealed a new willingness to support economic regulation by both the federal government and the states. It turned aside challenges to Social Security and the Wagner Act. In subsequent cases, the Court affirmed federal power to regulate wages, hours, child labor, agricultural production, and numerous other aspects of economic life.

The about-face for the Court

The Court's new attitude marked a permanent change in judicial policy. Having declared dozens of economic laws unconstitutional in the decades leading up to 1937, the justices have rarely done so since.

The End of the Second New Deal

Even as the Court made its peace with Roosevelt's policies, the momentum of the Second New Deal slowed. The landmark United States Housing Act did pass in 1937, initiating the first major national effort to build homes for the poorest Americans. But the Fair Labor Standards bill failed to reach the floor for over a year. When it finally passed in 1938, it banned goods produced by child labor from interstate commerce, set forty cents as the hourly minimum wage, and required overtime pay for hours of work exceeding forty per week. This last major piece of New Deal legislation established the practice of federal regulation of wages and working conditions, another radical departure from pre-Depression policies.

The New Deal did not really solve the problem of unemployment, which fell below 10 percent only in 1941, as the United States prepared to enter World War II.

The year 1937 also witnessed a sharp downturn of the economy. With economic conditions improving in 1936, Roosevelt had reduced federal funding for farm subsidies and WPA work relief. The result was disastrous. Unemployment, still 14 percent at the beginning of 1937, rose to nearly 20 percent by year's end.

In 1936, in *The General Theory of Employment, Interest, and Money*, John Maynard Keynes had challenged economists' traditional belief in the sanctity of balanced budgets. Large-scale government spending, he insisted, was necessary to sustain purchasing power and stimulate economic activity during downturns. Such spending should be enacted even at the cost of a budget deficit (a situation in which the government spends more money than it takes in). By 1938, Roosevelt was ready to follow

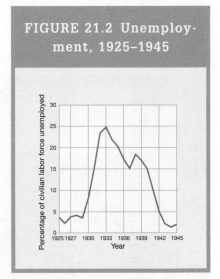

FIGURE 21.2 Unemployment, 1925–1945

Keynesian economics

this prescription, which would later be known as Keynesian economics. In April, he asked Congress for billions more for work relief and farm aid. The events of 1937–1938 marked a major shift in New Deal philosophy. Public spending would now be the government's major tool for combating unemployment and stimulating economic growth. The Second New Deal had come to an end.

THE LIMITS OF CHANGE

Roosevelt conceived of the Second New Deal, and especially Social Security, as expanding the meaning of freedom by extending assistance to broad groups of needy Americans—the unemployed, elderly, and dependent—as a right of citizenship, not charity or special privilege. But political realities, especially the power of inherited ideas about gender and black disenfranchisement in the South, powerfully affected the drafting of legislation. Different groups of Americans experienced the New Deal in radically different ways.

The New Deal and American Women

Eleanor Roosevelt

Eleanor Roosevelt transformed the role of First Lady by taking an active and visible part in public life. Here she visits a West Virginia coal mine in 1933.

The New Deal brought more women into government than ever before in American history. A number of talented women, including Secretary of Labor Frances Perkins, advised the president and shaped public policy. Most prominent of all was Eleanor Roosevelt, FDR's distant cousin, whom he had married in 1905. She transformed the role of First Lady, turning a position with no formal responsibilities into a base for political action. She traveled widely, spoke out on public issues, wrote a regular newspaper column, and worked to enlarge the scope of the New Deal in areas like civil rights, labor legislation, and work relief.

But even as the New Deal increased women's visibility in national politics, organized feminism, already in disarray during the 1920s, disappeared as a political force. Indeed, the Depression inspired widespread demands for women to remove themselves from the labor market to make room for unemployed men. Because the Depression hit industrial employment harder than low-wage clerical and service jobs where women predominated, the proportion of the workforce made up of women rose. The government tried to reverse this trend.

This photograph from 1933 depicts a march in New York City organized by the Association of Unemployed Single Women. Many men believed that public-works jobs and governmental relief should not go to women, who could be supported by their husbands or fathers.

The Economy Act of 1933 prohibited both members of a married couple from holding federal jobs. Until its repeal in 1937, it led to the dismissal of numerous female civil service employees whose husbands worked for the government. Employers from banks to public school systems barred married women from jobs.

Women and the labor market

Most New Deal programs did not exclude women from benefits (although the CCC restricted its camps to men). But the ideal of the male-headed household powerfully shaped social policy. Since paying taxes on one's wages made one eligible for the most generous Social Security programs—old age pensions and unemployment insurance—they left most women uncovered, because they did not work outside the home. The program excluded the 3 million mostly female domestic workers altogether.

A 1936 photograph shows a black farmer, with his son, repaying a loan from the Farm Security Administration, which sought to improve the conditions of poor land-owning farmers and sharecroppers. The client wears what is probably his nicest attire to meet with the government official.

The Southern Veto

Roosevelt made the federal government the symbolic representative of all the people, including racial and ethnic groups generally ignored by previous administrations. Yet the power of the Solid South helped to mold the New Deal welfare state into an entitlement of white Americans. After the South's blacks lost the right to vote around the turn of the century, Democrats enjoyed a political monopoly in the region. Democratic members of Congress were elected again and again. Committee chairmanships in Congress rest on seniority—how many years a member has served in office. Thus, beginning in 1933, when Democrats took control of Congress, southerners assumed the key leadership positions. At their insistence, the Social Security law excluded agricultural and domestic workers, the largest categories of black employment.

Blacks and Social Security

Black organizations like the Urban League and the NAACP lobbied strenuously for a system that enabled agricultural and domestic workers to receive unemployment and old age benefits and that established national relief standards. The Social Security Act, however, complained the *Pittsburgh Courier*, a black newspaper, reflected the power of "reactionary elements in the South who cannot bear the thought of Negroes getting pensions and compensations" and who feared that the inclusion of black workers would disrupt the region's low-wage, racially divided labor system.

The Stigma of Welfare

Public assistance

Because of the "southern veto," the majority of black workers found themselves confined to the least generous and most vulnerable wing of the new welfare state. The public assistance programs established by Social Security, notably aid to dependent children and to the poor elderly, were open to all Americans who could demonstrate financial need. But they set benefits at extremely low levels and authorized the states to determine eligibility standards, including "moral" behavior as defined by local authorities. As a result, public assistance programs allowed for widespread discrimination in the distribution of benefits. Recipients came to bear the humiliating stigma of dependency on government handouts, which would soon come to be known as "welfare."

Welfare discrimination

The situation seemed certain to identify blacks as recipients of unearned government assistance, and welfare as a program for minorities, thus dooming it forever to inadequate "standards of aid." Over time, this is precisely what happened, until the federal government abolished its responsibility for welfare entirely in 1996, during the presidency of Bill Clinton.

The Indian New Deal

Changes in Indian policy

Overall, the Depression and New Deal had a contradictory impact on America's racial minorities. Under Commissioner of Indian Affairs John Collier, the administration launched an **Indian New Deal**. Collier ended the policy of forced assimilation and allowed Indians unprecedented cultural autonomy. He replaced boarding schools meant to eradicate the tribal heritage of Indian children with schools on reservations, and dramatically increased spending on Indian health. He secured passage of the Indian Reorganization Act of 1934, ending the policy, dating back to the Dawes

Act of 1887, of dividing Indian lands into small plots for individual families and selling off the rest. Federal authorities once again recognized Indians' right to govern their own affairs.

The New Deal marked the most radical shift in Indian policy in the nation's history. But living conditions on the desperately poor reservations did not significantly improve.

The New Deal and Mexican-Americans

For Mexican-Americans, the Depression was a wrenching experience. With demand for their labor plummeting, more than 400,000 (one-fifth of the population of Mexican origin) returned to Mexico, some voluntarily, others at the strong urging of local authorities in the Southwest. A majority of those "encouraged" to leave the country were recent immigrants, but they included perhaps 200,000 Mexican-American children who had been born in the United States and were therefore citizens. Those who remained mostly worked in grim conditions in California's vegetable and fruit fields, whose corporate farms benefited enormously from New Deal dam construction that provided them with cheap electricity and water for irrigation. The Wagner and Social Security acts did not apply to agricultural laborers.

Mexican-American leaders struggled to develop a consistent strategy for their people. They sought greater rights by claiming to be white Americans—in order not to suffer the same discrimination as African-Americans—but also sought the backing of the Mexican government and promoted a mystical sense of pride and identification with Mexican heritage later given the name *la raza*.

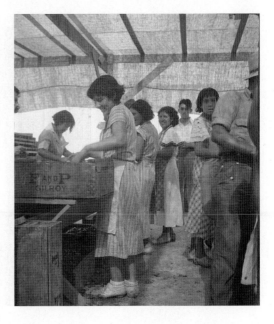

The Farm Security Administration hired noted photographers to document American life. This image by Dorothea Lange, from 1938, shows Hispanic women packing apricots in Brentwood, California.

Conflicting strategies

Last Hired, First Fired

As the "last hired and first fired," African-Americans were hit hardest by the Depression. Even those who retained their jobs now faced competition from unemployed whites who had previously considered positions like waiter and porter beneath them. With an unemployment rate double that of whites, blacks benefited disproportionately from direct government relief and, especially in northern cities, jobs on New Deal public-works projects. Half of the families in Harlem received public assistance during the 1930s.

Unemployment for blacks

Future congressman Adam Clayton Powell Jr. (at center with billboard), taking part in a "Don't Buy Where You Can't Work" demonstration in Harlem during the Depression. The campaign targeted stores that served black customers but refused to hire black employees.

Race in federal government

Shift in the black vote

Demonstrations in Harlem demanded jobs in the neighborhood's white-owned stores, with the slogan "Don't Buy Where You Can't Work."

Although Roosevelt seems to have had little personal interest in race relations or civil rights, he appointed Mary McLeod Bethune, a prominent black educator, as a special adviser on minority affairs and a number of other blacks to important federal positions. Key members of his administration, including his wife, Eleanor, and Secretary of the Interior Harold Ickes, a former president of the Chicago chapter of the NAACP, directed national attention to the injustices of segregation, disenfranchisement, and lynching. In 1939, Eleanor Roosevelt resigned from the Daughters of the American Revolution when the organization refused to allow the black singer Marian Anderson to present a concert at Constitution Hall in Washington. The president's wife arranged for Anderson to sing on the steps of the Lincoln Memorial and for the concert to be broadcast nationally on the radio.

The decade witnessed a historic shift in black voting patterns. In the North and West, where they enjoyed the right to vote, blacks in 1934 and 1936 abandoned their allegiance to the party of Lincoln and emancipation in favor of Democrats and the New Deal. But despite a massive lobbying campaign, southern congressmen prevented passage of a federal antilynching law. FDR offered little support. Because of the exclusion of agricultural and domestic workers, Social Security's old age pensions and unemployment benefits and the minimum wages established by the Fair

Labor Standards Act left uncovered 60 percent of all employed blacks and 85 percent of black women.

Federal Discrimination

Federal housing policy, which powerfully reinforced residential segregation, revealed the limits of New Deal freedom. As in the case of Social Security, local officials put national housing policy into practice in a way that reinforced existing racial boundaries. Nearly all municipalities, North as well as South, insisted that housing built or financially aided by the federal government be racially segregated. The Federal Housing Administration, moreover, had no hesitation about insuring mortgages that contained clauses barring future sales to non-white buyers, and it refused to channel money into integrated neighborhoods. Along with discriminatory practices by private banks and real estate companies, federal policy became a major factor in further entrenching housing segregation in the United States.

Federal employment practices also discriminated on the basis of race. As late as 1940, of the 150,000 blacks holding federal jobs, only 2 percent occupied positions other than clerk or custodian. In the South, many New Deal construction projects refused to hire blacks at all. The New Deal began the process of modernizing southern agriculture, but tenants, black and white, footed much of the bill. Tens of thousands of sharecroppers, as noted earlier, were driven off the land as a result of the AAA policy of raising crop prices by paying landowners to reduce cotton acreage.

Not until the Great Society of the 1960s would those left out of Social Security and other New Deal programs—racial minorities, many women, migrants and other less privileged workers—win inclusion in the American welfare state.

A NEW CONCEPTION OF AMERICA

But if the New Deal failed to dismantle the barriers that barred non-whites from full participation in American life, the 1930s witnessed the absorption of other groups into the social mainstream. With Catholics and Jews occupying prominent posts in the Roosevelt administration and new immigrant voters forming an important part of its electoral support,

A map of Philadelphia prepared by the Home Owners' Loan Corporation illustrates how federal agencies engaged in "redlining" of neighborhoods containing blue-collar and black residents. The colors correspond to the agency's perception of an area's real-estate prospects. Wealthy neighborhoods, colored green and given the best credit ratings, were expected to be racially and ethnically homogeneous. White-collar districts, in blue, were second best. Red districts, the worst, had an "undesirable population." The Corporation prepared maps like this for many cities and shared them with private lenders and the Federal Housing Administration, resulting in massive disinvestment in "red" neighborhoods, whose residents found it almost impossible to obtain housing loans.

the New Deal made ethnic pluralism a living reality in American politics.

Thanks to the virtual cutoff of southern and eastern European immigration in 1924; the increasing penetration of movies, chain stores, and mass advertising into ethnic communities; and the common experience of economic crisis, the 1930s witnessed an acceleration of cultural assimilation. For the children of the new immigrants, labor and political activism became agents of a new kind of Americanization. "Unionism is Americanism" became a CIO rallying cry.

During the 1930s, the South remained rigidly segregated. This 1939 photograph by Dorothea Lange depicts a "colored" movie theater in the Mississippi Delta.

The Heyday of American Communism

In the mid-1930s, for the first time in American history, the left—an umbrella term for socialists, communists, labor radicals, and many New Deal liberals—enjoyed a shaping influence on the nation's politics and culture. The CIO and Communist Party became focal points for a broad social and intellectual impulse that helped to redraw the boundaries of American freedom. An obscure, faction-ridden organization when the Depression began, the Communist Party experienced remarkable growth during the 1930s. The party's membership never exceeded 100,000, but several times that number passed through its ranks.

Growth of Communist Party

It was not so much the party's ideology as its vitality—its involvement in a mind-boggling array of activities, including demonstrations by the unemployed, struggles for industrial unionism, and a renewed movement for black civil rights—that for a time made it the center of gravity for a broad democratic upsurge. At the height of the **Popular Front**—a period during the mid-1930s when the Communist Party sought to ally itself with socialists and New Dealers in movements for social change, urging reform of the capitalist system rather than revolution—Communists gained an unprecedented respectability.

Respectability for Communists

Redefining the People

In theater, film, and dance, the Popular Front vision of American society sank deep roots and survived much longer than the political moment from which it sprang. In this broad left-wing culture, social and economic radicalism, not support for the status quo, defined true Americanism. Ethnic and racial diversity was the glory of American society, and the "American way of life" meant unionism and social citizenship, not the unbridled pursuit of wealth.

During the 1930s, artists and writers who strove to create socially meaningful works eagerly took up the task of depicting the daily lives of ordinary farmers and city dwellers. Art about the people—such as Dorothea Lange's photographs of migrant workers and sharecroppers—and art created by the people—such as black spirituals—came to be seen as expressions of genuine Americanism. Films celebrated populist figures who challenged and defeated corrupt businessmen and politicians, as in *Mr. Deeds Goes to Town* (1936) and *Mr. Smith Goes to Washington* (1939). Earl Robinson's song "Ballad for Americans," a typical expression of Popular Front culture that celebrated the religious, racial, and ethnic diversity of American society, became a national hit and was performed in 1940 at the Republican national convention.

History of Southern Illinois, a mural sponsored by the Illinois Federal Art Project, illustrates the widespread fascination during the 1930s with American traditions and the lives of ordinary Americans. On the left, a man strums a guitar, while workers labor on the waterfront.

Challenging the Color Line

It was fitting that "Ballad for Americans" reached the top of the charts in a version performed by the magnificent black singer Paul Robeson. Popular Front culture moved well beyond New Deal liberalism in condemning racism as incompatible with true Americanism. In the 1930s, groups like the American Jewish Committee and the National Conference of Christians and Jews actively promoted ethnic and religious tolerance, defining pluralism as "the American way." But whether in Harlem or East Los Angeles, the Communist Party was the era's only predominantly white organization to make fighting racism a top priority. Communist influence spread even to the South. The Communist-dominated International Labor Defense mobilized popular support for black defendants victimized by a racist criminal justice system. It helped to make the **Scottsboro case** an international

Promoting racial tolerance

A NEW CONCEPTION OF AMERICA | 671

A Dorothea Lange photograph of a sharecropper and his family outside their modest home.

The "Scottsboro boys," flanked by two prison guards, with their lawyer, Samuel Liebowitz.

cause célèbre. The case revolved around nine young black men arrested for the rape of two white women in Alabama in 1931. Despite the weakness of the evidence against the "Scottsboro boys" and the fact that one of the two accusers recanted, Alabama authorities three times put them on trial and three times won convictions. Landmark Supreme Court decisions overturned the first two verdicts and established legal principles that greatly expanded the definition of civil liberties—that defendants have a constitutional right to effective legal representation and that states cannot systematically exclude blacks from juries. But the Court allowed the third set of convictions to stand, which led to prison sentences for five of the defendants.

The CIO brought large numbers of black industrial workers into the labor movement for the first time and ran extensive educational campaigns to persuade white workers to recognize the interests they shared with their black counterparts. Black workers, many of them traditionally hostile to unions because of their long experience of exclusion, responded with enthusiasm to CIO organizing efforts.

Labor and Civil Liberties

Another central element of Popular Front public culture was its mobilization for civil liberties, especially the right of labor to organize. The struggle to launch industrial unions encountered sweeping local restrictions on freedom of speech as well as repression by private and public police forces.

Labor militancy helped to produce an important shift in the understanding of civil liberties. Previously conceived of as individual rights that must be protected against infringement by the government, the concept now expanded to include violations of free speech and assembly by powerful private groups. As a result, just as the federal government emerged as a guarantor of economic security, it also became a protector of freedom of expression.

By the eve of World War II, civil liberties had assumed a central place in the New Deal understanding of freedom. In 1939, Attorney General Frank Murphy established a Civil Liberties Unit in the Department of Justice. Meanwhile, the same Supreme Court that in 1937 relinquished its role as a judge of economic legislation moved to expand its authority over civil liberties. The justices insisted that constitutional guarantees of free thought and expression were essential to "nearly every other form of free-

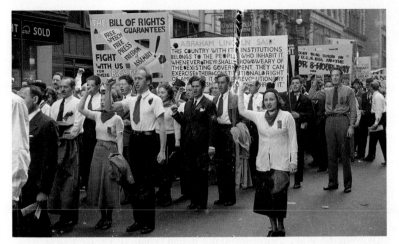

A May Day parade in New York City in 1935 includes a placard celebrating the Bill of Rights.

dom" and therefore deserved special protection by the courts. Since 1937, the large majority of state and national laws overturned by the courts have been those that infringe on civil liberties, not the property rights of business.

Pushback against free expression

The new appreciation of free expression was hardly universal. In 1938, the House of Representatives established the **House Un-American Activities Committee** to investigate disloyalty. Its expansive definition of "un-American" included communists, labor radicals, and the left of the Democratic Party, and its hearings led to the dismissal of dozens of federal employees on charges of subversion. Two years later, Congress enacted the Smith Act, which made it a federal crime to "teach, advocate, or encourage" the overthrow of the government.

The End of the New Deal

By then the New Deal, as an era of far-reaching social reform, had already begun to recede. One reason was that more and more southern Democrats were finding themselves at odds with Roosevelt's policies. In 1938, the administration released a "Report on Economic Conditions in the South," along with a letter by the president referring to the region as "the nation's No. 1 economic problem." The document revealed that the South lagged far behind other parts of the country in industrialization and invest-ment in education and public health. Also in 1938, a new generation of home-grown radicals—southern New Dealers, black activists, labor leaders, communists, even a few elected officials—founded the Southern Conference for Human Welfare to work for unionization, unemployment relief, and racial justice.

Southern leaders and the New Deal

Southern business and political leaders feared that continuing federal intervention in their region would encourage unionization and upset race relations. Roosevelt concluded that the enactment of future New Deal measures required a liberalization of the southern Democratic Party. In 1938, he tried to persuade the region's voters to replace conservative congressmen with ones who would support his policies. The South's small electorate dealt him a stinging rebuke.

A period of political stalemate followed the congressional election of 1938. For many years, a conservative coalition of southern Democrats and northern Republicans dominated Congress. Further reform initiatives became almost impossible, and Congress moved to abolish existing ones. It repealed an earlier tax on corporate profits and rejected a proposed program of national medical insurance. The administration, moreover, increasingly focused its attention on the storm gathering in Europe. Even before December 1941, when the United States entered World War II, "Dr. Win the War," as Roosevelt put it, had replaced "Dr. New Deal."

"Dr. Win the War"

The New Deal in American History

Given the scope of the economic calamity it tried to counter, the New Deal seems in many ways limited. Compared with later European welfare states, Social Security remained restricted in scope and modest in cost. The New Deal failed to address the problem of racial inequality, which in some ways it actually worsened.

Failures and accomplishments of the New Deal

Yet even as the New Deal receded, its substantial accomplishments remained. It greatly expanded the federal government's role in the American economy and made it an independent force in relations between industry and labor. The government influenced what farmers could and could not plant, required employers to deal with unions, insured bank deposits, regulated the stock market, loaned money to home owners, and provided payments to a majority of the elderly and unemployed. It transformed the physical environment through hydroelectric dams, reforestation projects, rural electrification, and the construction of innumerable public facilities. It restored faith in democracy and made the government an institution directly experienced in Americans' daily lives and directly concerned with their welfare. It redrew the map of American politics. It helped to inspire, and was powerfully influenced by, a popular upsurge that recast the idea of freedom to include a public guarantee of economic security for ordinary citizens and that identified economic inequality as the greatest threat to American freedom.

Legacy of the New Deal

The New Deal certainly improved economic conditions in the United States. But more than 15 percent of the workforce remained unemployed in 1940. Only the mobilization of the nation's resources to fight World War II would finally end the Great Depression.

CHAPTER REVIEW AND ONLINE RESOURCES

REVIEW QUESTIONS

1. Discuss how regional development such as the Tennessee Valley Authority and the Columbia River project reflected broader changes in American life during the New Deal.

2. What actions did President Roosevelt and Congress take to help the banking system recover as well as to reform how it operated in the long run?

3. How did the actions of the AAA benefit many farmers, injure others, and provoke attacks by conservatives?

4. Explain what labor did in the 1930s to secure "economic freedom and industrial democracy" for American workers.

5. How did the emphasis of the Second New Deal differ from that of the First New Deal?

6. How did the entrenched power of southern white conservatives limit African-Americans' ability to enjoy the full benefits of the New Deal and eliminate racial violence and discrimination? Why did African-Americans still support the Democratic Party?

7. Analyze the effects of the Indian Reorganization Act of 1934 on Native Americans.

8. Explain how New Deal programs contributed to the stigma of blacks as welfare-dependent.

9. How did the New Deal build on traditional ideas about the importance of home ownership to Americans, and how did it change Americans' ability to own their own homes?

10. What were the major characteristics of liberalism by 1939?

KEY TERMS

New Deal (p. 644)
Emergency Banking Act (p. 647)
Hundred Days (p. 647)
National Industrial Recovery Act (p. 647)
National Recovery Administration (p. 648)
Civilian Conservation Corps (p. 648)
Public Works Administration (p. 649)
Tennessee Valley Authority (p. 649)
Agricultural Adjustment Act (p. 650)
Dust Bowl (p. 651)
Federal Housing Administration (p. 651)
Congress of Industrial Organizations (p. 653)
sit-down strike (p. 654)
Share Our Wealth movement (p. 655)
Works Progress Administration (p. 657)
Wagner Act (p. 658)
Social Security Act (p. 658)
welfare state (p. 658)
Court packing plan (p. 663)
Indian New Deal (p. 666)
Popular Front (p. 670)
Scottsboro case (p. 671)
House Un-American Activities Committee (p. 673)

Go to 🐇 INQUIZITIVE

To see what you know—and learn what you've missed—with personalized feedback along the way.

Visit the *Give Me Liberty!* **Student Site** for primary source documents and images, interactive maps, author videos featuring Eric Foner, and more.

1931   Japan invades Manchuria

1933   U.S. recognizes Soviet
        Union

1935–   Congress passes
1939   Neutrality Acts

1937   Sino-Japanese War begins

1938   Munich agreement

1939   Germany invades Poland

1940   Draft established

1941   Four Freedoms speech

        Henry Luce's *The American
        Century*

        Executive Order 8802

        Lend-Lease Act

        Pearl Harbor attacked

1942   Executive Order 9066

        Battle of Midway Island

        Congress of Racial Equality
        (CORE) formed

1943   Zoot suit riots

        Detroit race riot

        Congress lifts Chinese
        Exclusion Act

1944   *Smith v. Allwright*

        D-Day

        GI Bill of Rights

        Bretton Woods conference

        Korematsu v. United States

        Battle of the Bulge

1945   Yalta conference

        Roosevelt dies; Harry
        Truman becomes president

        V-E Day (May)

        Atomic bombs dropped on
        Japan

        End of war in Pacific

CHAPTER 22

FIGHTING FOR THE FOUR FREEDOMS: WORLD WAR II

★

1941-1945

Members of the U.S. Marine Corps, Navy, and Coast Guard taking part in an amphibious assault during the "island hopping" campaign in the Pacific theater of World War II.

By far the most popular works of art produced during World War II were paintings of the **Four Freedoms** by the magazine illustrator Norman Rockwell. In his State of the Union Address, delivered before Congress on January 6, 1941, President Roosevelt spoke eloquently of a future world order founded on the "essential human freedoms": freedom of speech, freedom of worship, freedom from want, and freedom from fear. The Four Freedoms became Roosevelt's favorite statement of Allied aims. They embodied, Roosevelt declared in a 1942 radio address, the "rights of men of every creed and every race, wherever they live," and made clear "the crucial difference between ourselves and the enemies we face today."

Rockwell's paintings succeeded in linking the Four Freedoms with the defense of traditional American values. Drawing on the lives of his Vermont neighbors, Rockwell translated the Four Freedoms into images of real people situated in small-town America. Each of the paintings focuses on an instantly recognizable situation. An ordinary citizen rises to speak at a town meeting; members of different religious groups are seen at prayer; a family enjoys a Thanksgiving dinner; a mother and father stand over their sleeping children.

Even as Rockwell invoked images of small-town life to rally Americans to the war effort, however, the country experienced changes as deep as at any time in its history. As during World War I, but on a far larger scale, wartime mobilization expanded the size and scope of government and energized the economy. The gross national product more than doubled and unemployment disappeared as war production finally conquered the Depression. The demand for labor drew millions of women into the workforce and sent a tide of migrants from rural America to the industrial cities of the North and West, permanently altering the nation's social geography.

World War II gave the country a new and lasting international role and greatly strengthened the idea that American security was global in scope and could be protected only by the worldwide triumph of core American values. Government military spending sparked the economic development of the South and West, laying the foundation for the rise of the modern Sunbelt. The war created a close link between big business and a militarized federal government—a "military-industrial complex," as President Dwight D. Eisenhower would later call it—that long survived the end of fighting.

FOCUS QUESTIONS

- *What steps led to American participation in World War II?*

- *How did the United States mobilize economic resources and promote popular support for the war effort?*

- *What visions of America's postwar role began to emerge during the war?*

- *How did American minorities face threats to their freedom at home and abroad during World War II?*

- *How did the end of the war begin to shape the postwar world?*

Part of a sheet of fifty miniature reproductions of World War II posters. The themes include invocations of freedom, depictions of the enemy, calls for disciplined labor, and warnings against inadvertently revealing military secrets. Artists for Victory, an organization founded in 1942, sponsored a national poster competition to encourage artists to use their talents to promote the Allied war effort.

The immensely popular Office of War Information poster reproducing Norman Rockwell's paintings of the Four Freedoms, President Franklin D. Roosevelt's shorthand for American purposes in World War II.

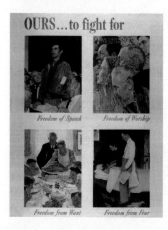

OURS...to fight for

Freedom of Speech   Freedom of Worship

Freedom from Want   Freedom from Fear

World War II also redrew the boundaries of American nationality. In contrast to World War I, the government recognized the "new immigrants" of the early twentieth century and their children as loyal Americans. Black Americans' second-class status assumed, for the first time since Reconstruction, a prominent place on the nation's political agenda. But toleration had its limits. With the United States at war with Japan, the federal government removed more than 110,000 Japanese-Americans, the majority of them American citizens, from their homes and confined them to internment camps.

As a means of generating support for the struggle, the Four Freedoms provided a crucial language of national unity. But this unity obscured underlying divisions concerning freedom. Although some Americans looked forward to a worldwide New Deal, others envisioned "free enterprise" replacing government intervention in the economy. The movement of women into the labor force challenged traditional gender relations, but most men and not a few women longed for the restoration of family life with a male breadwinner and a wife responsible for the home.

FIGHTING WORLD WAR II

Good Neighbors

During the 1930s, with Americans preoccupied by the economic crisis, international relations played only a minor role in public affairs. From the outset of his administration, nonetheless, FDR embarked on a number of departures in foreign policy. In 1933, hoping to stimulate American trade, he exchanged ambassadors with the Soviet Union, whose government his Republican predecessors had stubbornly refused to recognize.

Roosevelt also formalized a policy initiated by Herbert Hoover by which the United States repudiated the right to intervene militarily in the internal affairs of Latin American countries. This **Good Neighbor Policy**, as it was called, offered a belated recognition of the sovereignty of America's neighbors. But the United States lent its support to dictators like Anastasio Somoza in Nicaragua, Rafael Trujillo Molina in the Dominican Republic, and Fulgencio Batista in Cuba. "He may be a son of a bitch, but he's *our* son of a bitch," FDR said of Somoza.

The Road to War

Ominous developments in Asia and Europe quickly overshadowed events in Latin America. By the mid-1930s, it seemed clear that the rule of law was disintegrating in international relations and that war was on the horizon. In 1931, seeking to expand its military and economic power in Asia, Japan invaded Manchuria, a province of northern China. Six years later, its troops moved farther into China. When the Japanese overran the city of Nanjing, they massacred an estimated 300,000 Chinese prisoners of war and civilians.

Aggression in Europe and Asia

An aggressive power threatened Europe as well. After brutally consolidating his rule in Germany, Adolf Hitler embarked on a campaign to control the entire continent. In 1936, he sent troops to occupy the Rhineland, a demilitarized zone between France and Germany established after World War I. The failure of Britain, France, and the United States to oppose this action convinced Hitler that the democracies could not muster the will to halt his aggressive plans. The Italian leader Benito Mussolini, the founder of fascism, a movement similar to Hitler's Nazism, invaded and conquered Ethiopia. As part of a campaign to unite all Europeans of German origin in a single empire, Hitler in 1938 annexed Austria and the Sudetenland, an ethnically German part of Czechoslovakia. Shortly thereafter, he gobbled up all of that country.

Adolf Hitler

As the 1930s progressed, Roosevelt became more and more alarmed at Hitler's aggression as well as his accelerating campaign against Germany's Jews, whom the Nazis stripped of citizenship and property and began to deport to concentration camps. But Roosevelt had little choice but to follow the policy of "appeasement" adopted by Britain and France, which hoped that agreeing to Hitler's demands would prevent war.

Isolationism

To most Americans, the threat arising from Japanese and German aggression seemed very distant. Moreover, Hitler had more than a few admirers in the United States. Obsessed with the threat of communism, some Americans approved of his expansion of German power as a counterweight to the Soviet Union. Businessmen did not wish to

In a 1940 cartoon, war clouds engulf Europe, while Uncle Sam observes that the Atlantic Ocean no longer seems to shield the United States from involvement.

give up profitable overseas markets. Henry Ford did business with Nazi Germany throughout the 1930s. Trade with Japan also continued, including shipments of American trucks and aircraft and considerable amounts of oil.

Many Americans remained convinced that involvement in World War I had been a mistake. Ethnic allegiances reinforced Americans' traditional reluctance to enter foreign conflicts. Many Americans of German and Italian descent celebrated the expansion of national power in their countries of origin, even as they disdained their dictatorial governments. Irish-Americans remained strongly anti-British.

Isolationism—the 1930s version of Americans' long-standing desire to avoid foreign entanglements—dominated Congress. Beginning in 1935, lawmakers passed a series of **Neutrality Acts** that banned travel on belligerents' ships and the sale of arms to countries at war. These policies, Congress hoped, would allow the United States to avoid the conflicts over freedom of the seas that had contributed to involvement in World War I.

War in Europe

In the Munich agreement of 1938, Britain and France had caved in to Hitler's aggression. In 1939, the Soviet Union proposed an international agreement to oppose further German demands for territory. Britain and France, who distrusted Stalin and saw Germany as a bulwark against the spread of communist influence in Europe, refused. Stalin then astonished the world by signing a nonaggression pact with Hitler, his former sworn enemy. On September 1, immediately after the signing of the Nazi–Soviet pact, Germany invaded Poland. This time, Britain and France, which had pledged to protect Poland against aggression, declared war. But Germany appeared unstoppable. Within a year, the Nazi *blitzkrieg* (lightning war) had overrun Poland and much of Scandinavia, Belgium, and the Netherlands. On June 14, 1940, German troops occupied Paris. Hitler now dominated nearly all of Europe, as well as North Africa. In September 1940, Germany, Italy, and Japan created a military alliance known as the Axis.

For one critical year, Britain stood virtually alone in fighting Germany. In the Battle of Britain of 1940–1941, German planes launched devastating attacks on London and other cities. The Royal Air Force eventually turned back the air assault.

A newsreel theater in New York's Times Square announces Hitler's *blitzkrieg* in Europe in the spring of 1940.

Toward Intervention

Roosevelt viewed Hitler as a mad gangster whose victories posed a direct threat to the United States. But most Americans remained desperate to stay out of the conflict. After a tumultuous debate, Congress in 1940 agreed to allow the sale of arms to Britain on a "cash and carry" basis—that is, they had to be paid for in cash and transported in British ships. It also approved plans for military rearmament. But with a presidential election looming, Roosevelt was reluctant to go further. Opponents of involvement in Europe organized the America First Committee, with hundreds of thousands of members and a leadership that included such well-known figures as Henry Ford, Father Coughlin, and Charles A. Lindbergh.

"Cash and carry"

In 1940, breaking with a tradition that dated back to George Washington, Roosevelt announced his candidacy for a third term as president. The international situation was too dangerous and domestic recovery too fragile, he insisted, for him to leave office. Republicans chose as his opponent a political amateur, Wall Street businessman and lawyer Wendell Willkie. Willkie, who endorsed New Deal social legislation, captured more votes than Roosevelt's previous opponents. But FDR still emerged with a decisive victory. Soon after his victory, in a fireside chat in December 1940, Roosevelt announced that the United States would become the "arsenal of democracy," providing Britain and China with military supplies in their fight against Germany and Japan.

A third term

During 1941, the United States became more and more closely allied with those fighting Germany and Japan. At Roosevelt's urging, Congress passed the **Lend-Lease Act**, which authorized military aid so long as countries promised somehow to return it all after the war. Under the law's provisions, the United States funneled billions of dollars' worth of arms to Britain and China, as well as the Soviet Union, after Hitler renounced his nonaggression pact and invaded that country in June 1941. FDR also froze Japanese assets in the United States, halting virtually all trade between the countries, including the sale of oil vital to Japan.

Financial support

Pearl Harbor

Until November 1941, the administration's attention focused on Europe. But at the end of that month, intercepted Japanese messages revealed that an assault in the Pacific was imminent. No one, however, knew where it would come. On December 7, 1941, Japanese planes, launched from aircraft carriers, bombed the naval base at Pearl Harbor in Hawaii, the first attack

Pearl Harbor attack

by a foreign power on American soil since the War of 1812. Japan launched the attack in the hope of crippling American naval power in the Pacific. With a free hand in its campaign of conquest in East Asia, Japan would gain access to supplies of oil and other resources it could no longer obtain from the United States. It hoped that destroying the American fleet would establish Japan for years to come as the dominant power in the region.

Pearl Harbor was a complete and devastating surprise. In a few hours, more than 2,000 American servicemen were killed, and 187 aircraft and 18 naval vessels, including 8 battleships, had been destroyed or damaged.

Secretary of Labor Frances Perkins, who saw the president after the attack, remarked that he seemed calm—"his terrible moral problem had been resolved." Terming December 7 "a date which will live in infamy," Roosevelt asked Congress for a declaration of war against Japan. The combined vote in Congress was 477 in favor and 1 against—pacifist Jeanette Rankin of Montana, who had also voted against American entry into World War I. The next day, Germany declared war on the United States. America had finally joined the largest war in human history.

Declaration of war

The War in the Pacific

World War II has been called a "gross national product war," meaning that its outcome turned on which coalition of combatants could outproduce the other. In retrospect, it appears inevitable that the entry of the United States, with its superior industrial might, would ensure the defeat of the **Axis powers**. But the first few months of American involvement witnessed an unbroken string of military disasters. Japan in early 1942 conquered Burma (Myanmar) and Siam (Thailand). Japan also took control of the Dutch East Indies (Indonesia), whose extensive oil fields could replace supplies from the United States. And it occupied Guam, the Philippines, and other Pacific islands. At Bataan, in the Philippines, the Japanese forced 78,000 American and Filipino troops to lay down their arms—the largest surrender in American military history. Thousands perished on the ensuing "death march" to a prisoner-of-war camp. At the same time, German submarines sank hundreds of Allied merchant and naval vessels during the Battle of the Atlantic.

Military disasters

Soon, however, the tide of battle began to turn. In May 1942, in the Battle of the Coral Sea, the American navy turned back a Japanese fleet intent on attacking Australia. The following month, it inflicted devastating losses on the Japanese navy in the Battle of Midway Island. American code-breakers had managed to decipher the Japanese communications code, so the navy was forewarned about the timing of the assault at Midway and

Battle of Midway Island

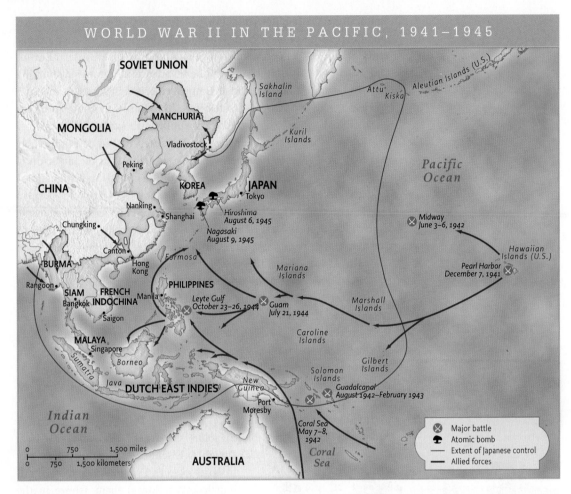

WORLD WAR II IN THE PACIFIC, 1941–1945

prepared an ambush for the attacking fleet. In the battle, four Japanese aircraft carriers, along with other vessels, were destroyed. Midway was the turning point of the Pacific naval war. The victories there and in the Coral Sea allowed American forces to launch the bloody campaigns that one by one drove the Japanese from fortified islands like Guadalcanal and the Solomons in the western Pacific and brought American troops ever closer to Japan.

Although the Japanese navy never fully recovered from its defeats at the Coral Sea and Midway in 1942, it took three more years for American forces to near the Japanese homeland.

The War in Europe

The "Grand Alliance" of World War II in Europe brought together the United States, Great Britain, and the Soviet Union, each led by an iron-willed, larger-than-life figure: Roosevelt, Winston Churchill, and Joseph

Stalin. United in their determination to defeat Nazi Germany, they differed not only in terms of the societies they represented but in their long-range goals. Stalin was set on establishing enough control over eastern Europe that his country would never again be invaded from the west. Churchill hoped to ensure that the British Empire emerged intact from the war. Roosevelt, like Woodrow Wilson before him, hoped to establish a new international order so that world wars would never again take place.

Facing wars in two hemispheres, Roosevelt had to determine how best to deploy American manpower and resources. Bearing the brunt of the fighting after Hitler invaded the Soviet Union in 1941, Stalin demanded an early Allied attack across the English Channel to confront German forces in occupied France and relieve pressure on his beleaguered army. Churchill's strategy was to attack the "soft underbelly" of Axis power through Allied operations in the Mediterranean, starting with an invasion of North Africa. Churchill's approach prevailed, and the cross-Channel invasion did not come until 1944.

By the spring of 1943, the Allies also gained the upper hand in the Atlantic, as British and American destroyers and planes devastated the German submarine fleet. In July 1943, American and British forces invaded Sicily, beginning the liberation of Italy. A popular uprising in Rome overthrew the Mussolini government, whereupon Germany occupied most of the country. Fighting there raged throughout 1944.

The major involvement of American troops in Europe did not begin until June 6, 1944. On that date, known as **D-Day**, nearly 200,000 American, British, and Canadian soldiers under the command of General Dwight D. Eisenhower landed in Normandy in northwestern France. More than a million troops followed them ashore in the next few weeks, in the most massive sea-land operation in history. After fierce fighting, German armies retreated eastward. By August, Paris had been liberated.

The crucial fighting in Europe, however, took place on the eastern front, the scene of an epic struggle between Germany and the Soviet Union. More than 3 million German soldiers took part in the 1941 invasion. After sweeping through western Russia, German armies in August 1942 launched a siege of Stalingrad, a city located deep inside Russia on the Volga River. This

German prisoners of war guarded by an American soldier shortly after D-Day in June 1944. By this time, the Germans were drafting very young men into their armies.

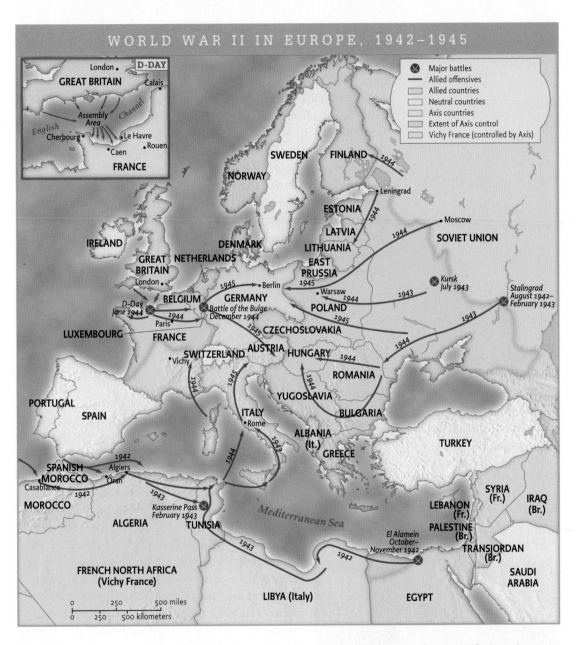

WORLD WAR II IN EUROPE, 1942–1945

D-DAY

GREAT BRITAIN

London
Calais
Le Havre
Rouen
Cherbourg
Caen
Assembly Area
English Channel
FRANCE

Major battles
Allied offensives
Allied countries
Neutral countries
Axis countries
Extent of Axis control
Vichy France (controlled by Axis)

SWEDEN
FINLAND
1944
NORWAY
Leningrad
ESTONIA
1944
LATVIA
Moscow
LITHUANIA
1944
SOVIET UNION
IRELAND
DENMARK
EAST PRUSSIA
Kursk July 1943
GREAT BRITAIN
NETHERLANDS
1945
Berlin
London
1945
Warsaw
Stalingrad August 1942– February 1943
BELGIUM
GERMANY
1944
POLAND
1943
D-Day June 1944
Battle of the Bulge December 1944
1944
1945
1943
LUXEMBOURG
Paris
1945
CZECHOSLOVAKIA
1945
1944
FRANCE
AUSTRIA
HUNGARY
1944
SWITZERLAND
Vichy
1944
ROMANIA
PORTUGAL
1945
YUGOSLAVIA
BULGARIA
SPAIN
ITALY
Rome
1943
TURKEY
ALBANIA (It.)
GREECE
1942
SPANISH MOROCCO
Algiers
Oran
Mediterranean Sea
SYRIA (Fr.)
IRAQ (Br.)
Casablanca
1942
LEBANON (Fr.)
MOROCCO
1943
Kasserine Pass February 1943
PALESTINE (Br.)
ALGERIA
TUNISIA
El Alamein October– November 1942
TRANSJORDAN (Br.)
1943
SAUDI ARABIA
FRENCH NORTH AFRICA (Vichy France)
1942
LIBYA (Italy)
EGYPT

0   250   500 miles
0   250   500 kilometers

Most of the land fighting in Europe during World War II took place on the eastern front between the German and Soviet armies.

proved to be a catastrophic mistake. Bolstered by an influx of military supplies from the United States, the Russians surrounded the German troops and forced them to surrender in January 1943. Stalingrad marked the turning point of the European war.

Stalingrad

Of 13.6 million German casualties in World War II, 10 million came on the Russian front. They were only part of the war's vast toll in human lives. Millions of Poles and at least 20 million Russians, probably many more, perished—not only soldiers but civilian victims of starvation, disease, and massacres by German soldiers. After his armies had penetrated eastern Europe in 1941, moreover, Hitler embarked on the "final solution"—the mass extermination of "undesirable" peoples—Slavs, gypsies, homosexuals, and, above all, Jews. By 1945, 6 million Jewish men, women, and children had died in Nazi death camps. What came to be called the **Holocaust** was the horrifying culmination of the Nazi belief that Germans constituted a "master race" destined to rule the world.

Hitler's "final solution"

THE HOME FRONT

Mobilizing for War

By the end of World War II, some 50 million men had registered for the draft and 10 million had been inducted into the military. The army exemplified how the war united American society in new ways. Military service threw together Americans from every region and walk of life, and almost every racial and ethnic background (African-Americans continued to serve in segregated units). It brought into contact young men who would never have encountered each other in peacetime. Many were the children of immigrants who now emerged from urban ethnic communities to fight alongside Americans from rural regions with very different cultures and outlooks. The federal government ended voluntary enlistment in 1942, relying entirely on the draft for manpower. This ensured that wartime sacrifice was widely shared throughout American society. By contrast, in the decades following the Vietnam War, the armed forces have been composed entirely of volunteers and the military includes very few men and women from middle- and upper-class backgrounds.

War-related production essentially ended the Great Depression. In this photograph from 1942, workers wait to be paid at a Maryland shipyard.

World War II also transformed the role of the national government. FDR created federal agencies like the War Production Board, the War Manpower Commission, and the Office of Price Administration to regulate the allocation of labor, control the shipping industry, establish manufacturing quotas, and fix wages, prices, and rents. The number of federal workers rose from 1 million to 4 million, helping to push the unemployment rate down from 14 percent in 1940 to 2 percent three years later.

The government built housing for war workers and forced civilian industries to retool for war production. Michigan's auto factories now turned out trucks, tanks, and jeeps for the army. The gross national product rose from $91 billion to $214 billion during the war, and the federal government's expenditures amounted to twice the combined total of the previous 150 years. The government marketed billions of dollars' worth of war bonds, increased taxes, and began the practice of withholding income tax directly from weekly paychecks.

Bombers being manufactured at Ford's Willow Run factory, "the greatest single manufacturing plant the world has ever seen," according to the *Washington Post*. During the war, Ford, General Motors, and other automakers produced tanks, armored vehicles, and airplanes for the armed forces rather than cars for consumers.

Business and the War

Americans marveled at the achievements of wartime manufacturing. Thousands of aircraft, 100,000 armored vehicles, and 2.5 million trucks rolled off American assembly lines, and entirely new products like synthetic rubber replaced natural resources now controlled by Japan. Government-sponsored scientific research perfected inventions like radar, jet engines, and early computers that helped to win the war and would have a large impact on postwar life. These accomplishments not only made it possible to win a two-front war but also helped to restore the reputation of business and businessmen, which had reached a low point during the Depression.

Innovation in manufacturing

Federal funds reinvigorated established manufacturing areas and created entirely new industrial centers. World War II saw the West Coast emerge as a focus of military-industrial production. The government invested billions of dollars in the shipyards of Seattle, Portland, and San Francisco and in the steel plants and aircraft factories of southern California. By the war's end, California had received one-tenth of all federal spending. Nearly 2 million Americans moved to California for jobs in defense-related industries, and millions more passed through for military training and embarkation to the Pacific war.

Industrial centers on the West Coast

TABLE 22.1 Labor Union Membership

YEAR	NUMBER OF MEMBERS
1933	2,857,000
1934	3,728,000
1935	3,753,000
1936	4,107,000
1937	5,780,000
1938	8,265,000
1939	8,980,000
1940	8,944,000
1941	10,489,000
1942	10,762,000
1943	13,642,000
1944	14,621,000
1945	14,796,000

In the South, the combination of rural out-migration and government investment in military-related factories and shipyards hastened a shift from agricultural to industrial employment. The South remained very poor when the war ended. Much of its rural population still lived in small wooden shacks with no indoor plumbing.

Labor in Wartime

During the war, labor entered a three-sided arrangement with government and business that allowed union membership to soar to unprecedented levels. In order to secure industrial peace and stabilize war production, the federal government forced reluctant employers to recognize unions. In 1944, when Montgomery Ward, the large mail-order company, defied a pro-union order, the army seized its headquarters and physically evicted its president. For their part, union leaders agreed not to strike.

By 1945, union membership stood at nearly 15 million, one-third of the non-farm labor force and the highest proportion in American history. But if labor became a partner in government, it was very much a junior partner. Congress continued to be dominated by a conservative alliance of Republicans and southern Democrats. Despite the "no-strike" pledge, 1943 and 1944 witnessed numerous brief walkouts in which workers protested the increasing speed of assembly-line production and the disparity between wages frozen by government order and expanding corporate profits.

Fighting for the Four Freedoms

The Good War

Previous conflicts, including the Mexican War and World War I, had deeply divided American society. In contrast, World War II came to be remembered as the Good War, a time of national unity in pursuit of indisputably noble goals. But all wars require the mobilization of patriotic public opinion. By 1940, "To sell *goods*, we must sell *words*" had become a motto of advertisers. Foremost among the words that helped to "sell" World War II was "freedom."

Talk of freedom pervaded wartime America. In 1941, the administration celebrated with considerable fanfare the 150th anniversary of the Bill of Rights (the first ten amendments to the Constitution). FDR described their protections against tyrannical government as defining characteristics of American life, central to the rights of "free men and free women."

The "most ambiguous" of the Four Freedoms, *Fortune* magazine remarked, was freedom from want. Yet this "great inspiring phrase," as a Pennsylvania steelworker put it in a letter to the president, seemed to strike the deepest chord in a nation just emerging from the Depression. Roosevelt initially meant it to refer to the elimination of barriers to international trade. But he quickly came to link freedom from want to an economic goal more relevant to the average citizen—protecting the future "standard of living of the American worker and farmer" by guaranteeing that the Depression would not resume after the war. This, he declared, would bring "real freedom for the common man."

The Fifth Freedom

Under the watchful eye of the War Advertising Council, private companies joined in the campaign to promote wartime patriotism, while positioning themselves and their brand names for the postwar world. Alongside advertisements urging Americans to purchase war bonds, guard against revealing military secrets, and grow "victory gardens" to allow food to be sent to the army, the war witnessed a burst of messages marketing

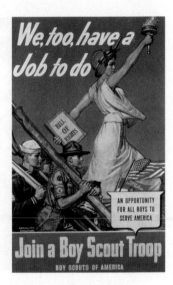

In this recruitment poster for the Boy Scouts, a svelte Miss Liberty prominently displays the Bill of Rights, widely celebrated during World War II as the centerpiece of American freedom.

In this advertisement by the Liberty Motors and Engineering Corporation, published in the February 1944 issue of *Fortune*, Uncle Sam offers the Fifth Freedom—"free enterprise"—to war-devastated Europe. To spread its message, the company offered free enlargements of its ad.

A female lathe operator in a Texas plant that produced transport planes.

This photograph captures the enthusiasm of three "fly girls"—female pilots employed by the air force to deliver cargo and passengers and test military aircraft. Known as WASPs (Women Airforce Service Pilots), they eventually numbered over 1,000 aviators, who trained at an all-female base at Avenger Field in Sweetwater, Texas. They did not take part in combat, but thirty-eight died in service.

advertisers' definition of freedom. Without directly criticizing Roosevelt, they repeatedly suggested that he had overlooked a fifth freedom. The National Association of Manufacturers and individual companies bombarded Americans with press releases, radio programs, and advertisements attributing the amazing feats of wartime production to "free enterprise."

With the memory of the Depression still very much alive, businessmen predicted a postwar world filled with consumer goods, with "freedom of choice" among abundant possibilities assured if only private enterprise were liberated from government controls.

Women at Work

During the war, the nation engaged in an unprecedented mobilization of "womanpower" to fill industrial jobs vacated by men. Hollywood films glorified the independent woman, and private advertising celebrated the achievements of Rosie the Riveter, the female industrial laborer depicted as muscular and self-reliant in Norman Rockwell's famous magazine cover. With 15 million men in the armed forces, women in 1944 made up more than one-third of the civilian labor force, and 350,000 served in auxiliary military units.

Even though most women workers still labored in clerical and service jobs, new opportunities suddenly opened in industrial, professional, and government positions previously restricted to men. On the West Coast, one-third of the workers in aircraft manufacturing and shipbuilding were women. For the first time in history, married women in their thirties outnumbered the young and single among female workers. Women forced unions like the United Auto Workers to confront issues like equal pay for equal work, maternity leave, and child-care facilities for working mothers. Having enjoyed what one wartime worker called "a taste of freedom"—doing "men's" jobs for men's wages and, sometimes, engaging in sexual activity while unmarried—many women hoped to remain in the labor force once peace returned.

"We as a nation," proclaimed one magazine article, "must change our basic attitude toward the work of women." But change proved difficult.

The government, employers, and unions depicted work as a temporary necessity, not an expansion of women's freedom. When the war ended, most female war workers, especially those in better-paying industrial employment, did indeed lose their jobs.

Despite the upsurge in the number of working women, the advertisers' "world of tomorrow" rested on a vision of family-centered prosperity. Advertisements portrayed working women dreaming of their boyfriends in the army and emphasized that with the proper makeup, women could labor in a factory and remain attractive to men. Men in the army seem to have assumed that they would return home to resume traditional family life.

...where the family is a sacred institution. Where children love, honor and respect their parents ...where a man's home is his castle * This is *your* America

... *Keep it Free!*

VISIONS OF POSTWAR FREEDOM

Toward an American Century

The prospect of an affluent future provided a point of unity between New Dealers and conservatives, business and labor. And the promise of prosperity to some extent united two of the most celebrated blueprints for the postwar world. One was *The American Century*, the publisher Henry Luce's 1941 effort to mobilize the American people both for the coming war and for an era of postwar world leadership. Americans, Luce's book insisted, must embrace the role history had thrust on them as the "dominant power in the world." After the war, American power and American values would underpin a previously unimaginable prosperity—"the abundant life," Luce called it—produced by "free economic enterprise."

Luce's essay anticipated important aspects of the postwar world. But its bombastic rhetoric and a title easily interpreted as a call for an American imperialism aroused immediate opposition among liberals and the left. Henry Wallace offered their response in "The Price of Free World Victory," an address delivered in May 1942 to the Free World Association. Wallace, secretary of agriculture during the 1930s, had replaced Vice President John Nance Garner as Roosevelt's running mate in 1940. In contrast to Luce's American Century, a world of business dominance no less than of American power, Wallace predicted that the war would usher in a "century of the common man." Governments acting to "humanize" capitalism and redistribute economic resources would eliminate hunger, illiteracy, and poverty.

Despite the new independence enjoyed by millions of women, propaganda posters during World War II emphasized the male-dominated family as an essential element of American freedom.

Luce's The American Century

Henry Wallace

Luce and Wallace had one thing in common—a new conception of America's role in the world, tied to continued international involvement, the promise of economic abundance, and the idea that the American experience should serve as a model for all other nations.

"The Way of Life of Free Men"

NRPB

Even as Congress moved to dismantle parts of the New Deal, liberal Democrats and their left-wing allies unveiled plans for a postwar economic policy that would allow all Americans to enjoy freedom from want. In 1942 and 1943, the reports of the National Resources Planning Board (NRPB) offered a blueprint for a peacetime economy based on full employment, an expanded welfare state, and a widely shared American standard of living. The board called for a "new bill of rights" that would include all Americans in an expanded Social Security system and guarantee access to education, health care, adequate housing, and jobs for able-bodied adults. The NRPB's plan for a "full-employment economy" with a "fair distribution of income," said *The Nation*, embodied "the way of life of free men."

An Economic Bill of Rights

Mindful that public-opinion polls showed a large majority of Americans favoring a guarantee of employment for those who could not find work, the president in 1944 called for an "Economic Bill of Rights." The original Bill of Rights restricted the power of government in the name of liberty. FDR proposed to expand its power in order to secure full employment, an adequate income, medical care, education, and a decent home for all Americans.

GI Bill

Already ill and preoccupied with the war, Roosevelt spoke only occasionally of the Economic Bill of Rights during the 1944 presidential campaign. The replacement of Vice President Henry Wallace by Harry S. Truman, then a little-known senator from Missouri, suggested that the president did not intend to do battle with Congress over social policy. Congress did not enact the Economic Bill of Rights. But in 1944, it extended to the millions of returning veterans an array of benefits, including unemployment pay, scholarships for further education, low-cost mortgage loans, pensions, and job training. The Servicemen's Readjustment Act, or **GI Bill of Rights**, was one of the farthest-reaching pieces of social legislation in American history. Aimed at rewarding members of the armed forces for their service and preventing the widespread unemployment and economic disruption that had followed World War I, it profoundly shaped postwar society. By 1946, more than 1 million veterans were attending college under its provisions, making up half of total college enrollment. Almost 4 million would receive home mortgages, spurring the postwar suburban housing boom.

The Road to Serfdom

The Road to Serfdom (1944), a surprise best-seller by Friedrich A. Hayek, a previously obscure Austrian-born economist, claimed that even the best-intentioned government efforts to direct the economy posed a threat to individual liberty. Coming at a time when the miracles of war production had reinvigorated belief in the virtues of capitalism, and with the confrontation with Nazism highlighting the danger of merging economic and political power, Hayek offered a new intellectual justification for opponents of active government. In a complex economy, he insisted, no single person or group of experts could possibly possess enough knowledge to direct economic activity intelligently. A free market, he wrote, mobilizes the fragmented and partial knowledge scattered throughout society far more effectively than a planned economy.

Friedrich A. Hayek and laissez-faire economics

By equating fascism, socialism, and the New Deal and by identifying economic planning with a loss of freedom, he helped lay the foundation for the rise of modern conservatism and a revival of laissez-faire economic thought. As the war drew to a close, the stage was set for a renewed battle over the government's proper role in society and the economy, and the social conditions of American freedom.

THE AMERICAN DILEMMA

The unprecedented attention to freedom as the defining characteristic of American life had implications that went far beyond wartime mobilization. The struggle against Nazi tyranny and its theory of a master race discredited ethnic and racial inequality. A pluralist vision of American society now became part of official rhetoric. What set the United States apart from its wartime foes, the government insisted, was not only dedication to the ideals of the Four Freedoms but also the principle that Americans of all races, religions, and national origins could enjoy those freedoms equally. Racism was the enemy's philosophy; Americanism rested on toleration of diversity and equality for all. By the end of the war, the new immigrant groups had been fully accepted as loyal ethnic Americans, rather than members of distinct and inferior "races." And the contradiction between the principle of equal freedom and the actual status of blacks had come to the forefront of national life.

In this patriotic war poster the words of Abraham Lincoln are linked to the struggle against Nazi tyranny.

"THIS WORLD CANNOT EXIST HALF SLAVE AND HALF FREE"

FIGHT FOR FREEDOM!

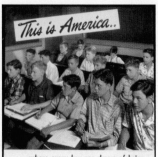

This is America..

... where every boy can dream of being President. Where free schools, free opportunity, free enterprise, have built the most decent nation on earth. A nation built upon the rights of all men • This is your America

... Keep it Free!

Another *This Is America* propaganda poster emphasizes the American dream of equal opportunity for all. All the children in the classroom, however, are white.

Patriotic Assimilation

Among other things, World War II created a vast melting pot, especially for European immigrants and their children. Millions of Americans moved out of urban ethnic neighborhoods and isolated rural enclaves into the army and industrial plants, where they came into contact with people of very different backgrounds. What one historian has called their "patriotic assimilation" differed sharply from the forced Americanization of World War I.

Horrified by the uses to which the Nazis put the idea of inborn racial difference, biological and social scientists abandoned belief in a link among race, culture, and intelligence, an idea only recently central to their disciplines. Ruth Benedict's *Races and Racism* (1942) described racism as "a travesty of scientific knowledge." By the war's end, racism and nativism had been stripped of intellectual respectability, at least outside the South, and were viewed as psychological disorders.

The persistence of prejudice

Intolerance, of course, hardly disappeared from American life. Many business and government circles still excluded Jews. Along with the fact that early reports of the Holocaust were too terrible to be believed, anti-Semitism contributed to the government's unwillingness to allow more than a handful of European Jews (21,000 during the course of the war) to find refuge in the United States. Roosevelt himself learned during the war of the extent of Hitler's "final solution" to the Jewish presence in Europe. But he failed to authorize air strikes that might have destroyed German death camps.

The *Bracero* Program

Racial barriers

The war had a far more ambiguous meaning for non-white groups than for whites. On the eve of Pearl Harbor, racial barriers remained deeply entrenched in American life. Southern blacks were still trapped in a rigid system of segregation. Asians could not emigrate to the United States or become naturalized citizens. Most American Indians still lived on reservations in dismal poverty.

The war set in motion changes that would reverberate in the postwar years. Under the ***bracero* program** agreed to by the Mexican and American governments in 1942 (the name derives from *brazo*, the Spanish word for arm), tens of thousands of contract laborers crossed into the United States to take up jobs as domestic and agricultural workers. Initially designed as a temporary response to the wartime labor shortage, the program lasted until 1964. During that period, more than 4.5 million Mexicans entered the

Mexican contract workers

United States under labor contracts (while a slightly larger number were arrested for illegal entry by the Border Patrol).

Although the *bracero* program reinforced the status of immigrants from Mexico as an unskilled labor force, wartime employment opened new opportunities for second-generation Mexican-Americans. Hundreds of thousands of men and women emerged from ethnic neighborhoods, or *barrios*, to work in defense industries and serve in the army (where, unlike blacks, they fought alongside whites). For Mexican-American women in particular, the war afforded new opportunities for public participation and higher incomes. "Rosita the Riveter" took her place alongside "Rosie" in the West Coast's multiethnic war production factories. Government publications and newspaper accounts celebrated their role as patriotic mothers who encouraged their sons to enlist in the army and offered moral support while they were away at war. Contact with other groups led many to learn English and sparked a rise in interethnic marriages.

The **zoot suit riots** of 1943, in which club-wielding sailors and policemen attacked Mexican-American youths wearing flamboyant clothing on the streets of Los Angeles, illustrated the limits of wartime tolerance. But the contrast between the war's rhetoric of freedom and pluralism and the reality of continued discrimination inspired a heightened consciousness of civil rights. Mexican-Americans brought complaints of discrimination before the Fair Employment Practices Commission (FEPC) to fight the practice in the Southwest of confining them to the lowest-paid work or paying them lower wages than white workers doing the same jobs. Perhaps half a million Mexican-American men and women served in the armed forces.

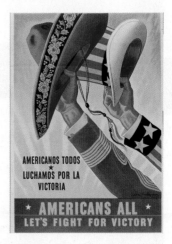

AMERICANOS TODOS ★ LUCHAMOS POR LA VICTORIA

★ AMERICANS ALL ★ LET'S FIGHT FOR VICTORY

One series of posters issued by the Office of War Information to mobilize support for the war effort emphasized respect for the country's racial and ethnic diversity. This one, directed at Hispanics, suggests that there is no contradiction between pride in ethnic heritage and loyalty to the United States.

Indians during the War

The war also brought many American Indians closer to the mainstream of American life. Some 25,000 served in the army (including the famous Navajo "code-talkers," who transmitted messages in their complex native language, which the Japanese could not decipher). Insisting that the United States lacked the authority to draft Indian men into the army, the Iroquois issued their own declaration of war against the Axis powers. Tens of thousands of Indians left reservations for jobs in war industries. Exposed for the first time to urban life and industrial society, many chose not to return to the reservations after the war ended. (Indeed, the reservations did not share in wartime prosperity.) Some Indian veterans took advantage of the GI Bill to attend college after the war, an opportunity that had been available to very few Indians previously.

The Navajo "code-talkers"

VOICES OF FREEDOM

From League of United Latin American Citizens, "World War II and Mexican Americans" (1945)

Founded in 1929, the League of United Latin American Citizens (LULAC) campaigned for equal treatment for Americans of Latino descent and their full integration into American life. Soon after the war ended, an editorial in its publication *LULAC News* condemned continuing discrimination, reflecting how the war sparked a rising demand for equal rights among many minority groups.

"We do not serve Mexicans here." "You will have to get out as no Mexicans are allowed." "Your uniform and service ribbons mean nothing here. We still do not allow Mexicans."

These, and many other stronger-worded ones, are the embarrassing and humiliating retorts given our returning veterans of Latin American descent and their families. They may all be worded differently, and whereas some are toned with hate and loathness while others are toned with sympathy and remorse, still the implication remains that these so-called "Mexicans" are considered unworthy of equality, regardless of birthright or service. . . .

Why this hate, this prejudice, this tendency to discriminate against a people whose only fault seems to be that they are heirs of a culture older than any known "American Culture," to find themselves a part of a land and people they have helped to build and to defend, to find themselves a part of a minority group whose acquired passive nature keeps them from boldly demanding those rights and privileges which are rightfully theirs? Can it be the result of difference in race, nationality, language, loyalty, or ability?

There is no difference in race. Latin Americans, or so-called "Mexicans," are Caucasian or white. . . . There is no difference in nationality. These "Mexicans" were born and bred in this country and are just as American as Jones or Smith. . . . Difference in language? No, these "Mexicans" speak English. Accented, perhaps, in some cases, but English all over the United States seems to be accented. . . . Difference in loyalty? How can that be when all revere the same stars and stripes, when they don the same service uniforms for the same principles? Difference in intelligence and ability? Impossible. . . .

This condition is not a case of difference; it is a case of ignorance. . . . An ignorance of the cultural contributions of Americans of Latin American descent to the still young American Culture; . . . an ignorance of a sense of appreciation for a long, profitable, and loyal association with a group of Americans whose voice cries out in desperate supplication: "We have proved ourselves true and loyal Americans . . . now give us social, political, and economic equality."

From Charles H. Wesley, "The Negro Has Always Wanted the Four Freedoms," in *What the Negro Wants* (1944)

In 1944, the University of North Carolina Press published *What the Negro Wants*, a book of essays by fourteen prominent black leaders. Virtually every contributor called for the right to vote in the South, the dismantling of segregation, and access to the "American standard of living." Several essays also linked the black struggle for racial justice with movements against European imperialism in Africa and Asia. When he read the manuscript, W. T. Couch, the director of the press, was stunned. "If this is what the Negro wants," he told the book's editor, "nothing could be clearer than what he needs, and needs most urgently, is to revise his wants." In this excerpt, the historian Charles H. Wesley explains that blacks are denied each of the Four Freedoms and also illustrates how the war strengthened black internationalism.

[Negroes] have wanted what other citizens of the United States have wanted. They have wanted freedom and opportunity. They have wanted the pursuit of the life vouchsafed to all citizens of the United States by our own liberty documents. They have wanted freedom of speech, [but] they were supposed to be silently acquiescent in all aspects of their life. . . . They have wanted freedom of religion, for they had been compelled to "steal away to Jesus" . . . in order to worship God as they desired. . . . They have wanted freedom from want. . . . However, the Negro has remained a marginal worker and the competition with white workers has left him in want in many localities of an economically sufficient nation. They have wanted freedom from fear. They have been cowed, browbeaten or beaten, as they have marched through the years of American life. . . .

The Negro wants democracy to begin at home. . . . The future of our democratic life is insecure so long as the hatred, disdain and disparagement of Americans of African ancestry exist. . . .

The Negro wants not only to win the war but also to win the peace. . . . He wants the peace to be free of race and color restrictions, of imperialism and exploitation, and inclusive of the participation of minorities all over the world in their own governments. When it is said that we are fighting for freedom, the Negro asks, "Whose freedom?" Is it the freedom of a peace to exploit, suppress, exclude, debase and restrict colored peoples in India, China, Africa, Malaya in the usual ways? . . . Will Great Britain and the United States specifically omit from the Four Freedoms their minorities and subject peoples? The Negro does not want such a peace.

QUESTIONS

1. *What evidence does the editorial offer that Latinos are deserving of equality?*

2. *Why does Wesley believe that black Americans are denied the Four Freedoms?*

3. *What differences and what commonalities exist between these two claims for greater rights in American society?*

Asian-Americans in Wartime

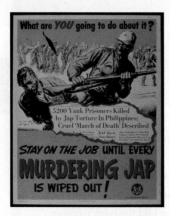

Wartime propaganda in the United States sought to inspire hatred against the Pacific foe. This poster, issued by the U.S. Army, recalls the Bataan death march in the Philippines.

Asian-Americans' war experience was paradoxical. More than 50,000—the children and grandchildren of immigrants from China, Japan, Korea, and the Philippines—fought in the army, mostly in all-Asian units. With China an ally in the Pacific war, Congress in 1943 ended decades of complete exclusion by establishing a nationality quota for Chinese immigrants. The annual limit of 105 hardly suggested a desire for a large-scale influx. But the image of the Chinese as gallant fighters defending their country against Japanese aggression called into question long-standing racial stereotypes.

The experience of Japanese-Americans was far different. Both sides saw the Pacific war as a race war. Japanese propaganda depicted Americans as a self-indulgent people contaminated by ethnic and racial diversity as opposed to the racially "pure" Japanese. In the United States, long-standing prejudices and the shocking attack on Pearl Harbor combined to produce an unprecedented hatred of Japan. Government propaganda and war films portrayed the Japanese foe as rats, dogs, gorillas, and snakes—bestial and subhuman. They blamed Japanese aggression on a violent racial or national character, not, as in the case of Germany and Italy, on tyrannical rulers.

Prejudice against Japanese-Americans

About 70 percent of Japanese-Americans in the continental United States lived in California, where they dominated vegetable farming in the Los Angeles area. One-third were first-generation immigrants, or *issei*, but a substantial majority were *nisei*—American-born, and therefore citizens. Many of the latter spoke only English, had never been to Japan, and had tried to assimilate despite prevailing prejudice. The government bent over backward to include German-Americans and Italian-Americans in the war effort. It ordered the arrest of only a handful of the more than 800,000 German and Italian nationals in the United States when the war began. But it viewed every person of Japanese ethnicity as a potential spy.

Japanese-American Internment

Inspired by exaggerated fears of a Japanese invasion of the West Coast and pressured by whites who saw an opportunity to gain possession of Japanese-American property, the military persuaded FDR to issue Executive Order 9066. Promulgated in February 1942, this ordered the relocation of all persons of Japanese descent from the West Coast. That spring and summer, authorities removed more than 110,000 men, women, and children—nearly two-thirds of them American citizens—to camps far from their homes. The order did not apply to persons of Japanese

Internment camps

JAPANESE-AMERICAN INTERNMENT, 1942–1945

Legend:
- ■ Internment camps
- Figures show highest number interned at each camp.
- — Demarcates area from which Japanese-Americans were excluded

descent living in Hawaii, where they made up nearly 40 percent of the population. Despite Hawaii's vulnerability, its economy could not function without Japanese-American labor.

The internees were subjected to a quasi-military discipline in the camps. Living in former horse stables, makeshift shacks, or barracks behind barbed-wire fences, they were awakened for roll call at 6:45 each morning and ate their meals (which rarely involved the Japanese cooking to which they were accustomed) in giant mess halls. Nonetheless, the internees did their best to create an atmosphere of home, decorating their accommodations with pictures, flowers, and curtains, planting vegetable gardens, and setting up activities like sports clubs and art classes for themselves.

Japanese-American internment revealed how easily war can undermine basic freedoms. There were no court hearings, no due process, and no writs of habeas corpus. One searches the wartime record in vain for public

More than 100,000 Japanese-Americans—the majority American citizens—were forcibly moved from their homes to internment camps during World War II.

Life in internment camps

Fumiko Hayashida holds her thirteen-month-old daughter, while waiting for relocation to an internment camp. Both wear baggage tags, as if they were pieces of luggage. This photo, taken by a journalist for the *Seattle Post-Intelligencer*, came to symbolize the entire internment experience. Ms. Hayashida celebrated her 100th birthday in 2011.

protests among non-Japanese against the gravest violation of civil liberties since the end of slavery.

The courts refused to intervene. In 1944, in ***Korematsu v. United States***, the Supreme Court denied the appeal of Fred Korematsu, a Japanese-American citizen who had been arrested for refusing to present himself for internment. Speaking for a 6-3 majority, Justice Hugo Black, usually an avid defender of civil liberties, upheld the legality of the internment policy, insisting that an order applying only to persons of Japanese descent was not based on race. The Court has never overturned the *Korematsu* decision. As Justice Robert H. Jackson warned in his dissent, it "lies about like a loaded weapon ready for the hand of any authority that can bring forward a plausible claim" of national security.

The government established a loyalty oath program, expecting Japanese-Americans to swear allegiance to the government that had imprisoned them and to enlist in the army. Some young men refused, and about 200 were sent to prison for resisting the draft. But 20,000 Japanese-Americans joined the armed forces from the camps, along with another 13,000 from Hawaii.

Contradictions abounded in the wartime experiences of Japanese-Americans. In 1944, Sono Isato danced the role of an American beauty queen in the musical *On the Town* on Broadway, and her brother fought for the U.S. Army in the Pacific theater, while the government interned their father because he had been born in Japan. A long campaign for acknowledgment of the injustice done to Japanese-Americans followed the end

Apology and restitution

of the war. In 1988, Congress apologized for internment and provided $20,000 in compensation to each surviving victim.

Blacks and the War

Although the treatment of Japanese-Americans revealed the stubborn hold of racism in American life, the wartime message of freedom portended a major transformation in the status of blacks. Nazi Germany cited American

Segregation during wartime

practices as proof of its own race policies. Washington remained a rigidly segregated city, and the Red Cross refused to mix blood from blacks and whites in its blood banks (thereby, critics charged, in effect accepting Nazi race theories). Charles Drew, the black scientist who pioneered the techniques of storing and shipping blood plasma—a development of immense importance to the treatment of wounded soldiers—protested bitterly against this policy, pointing out that it had no scientific basis.

Second Great Migration

The war spurred a movement of black population from the rural South to the cities of the North and West that dwarfed the Great Migration of World War I and the 1920s. In the **second Great Migration**, about 700,000 black migrants poured out of the South on what they called "liberty trains," seeking jobs in the industrial heartland. They encountered sometimes violent hostility. In 1943, a fight at a Detroit city park spiraled into a race riot that left thirty-four persons dead, and a "hate strike" of 20,000 workers protested the upgrading of black employees in a plant manufacturing aircraft engines.

Blacks and Military Service

When World War II began, the air force and marines had no black members. The army restricted the number of black enlistees and contained only five black officers, three of them chaplains. The navy accepted blacks only as waiters and cooks.

During the war, more than 1 million blacks served in the armed forces. They did so in segregated units, largely confined to construction, transport, and other noncombat tasks. Black soldiers sometimes had to give up their seats on railroad cars to accommodate Nazi prisoners of war.

Segregation in the armed forces

When southern black veterans returned home and sought benefits through the GI Bill, they encountered even more evidence of racial discrimination. On the surface, the GI Bill contained no racial differentiation in offering benefits like health care, college tuition assistance, job training, and loans to start a business or purchase a farm. But local authorities who administered its provisions allowed southern black veterans to use its education benefits only at segregated colleges, limited their job training to unskilled work and low-wage service jobs, and restricted loans for farm purchase to white veterans.

Postwar segregation

Birth of the Civil Rights Movement

The war years witnessed the birth of the modern civil rights movement. Angered by the almost complete exclusion of African-Americans from jobs in the rapidly expanding war industries (of 100,000 aircraft workers in 1940, fewer than 300 were blacks), the black labor leader A. Philip Randolph in July 1941 called for a March on Washington. His demands included access to defense employment, an end to segregation, and a national antilynching law.

Randolph's March on Washington

The prospect of thousands of angry blacks descending on Washington, remarked one official, "scared the government half to death." To persuade Randolph to call off the march, Roosevelt issued Executive Order 8802, which banned discrimination in defense jobs and established a Fair Employment Practices Commission (FEPC) to monitor compliance. The

FEPC

first federal agency since Reconstruction to campaign for equal opportunity for black Americans, the FEPC played an important role in obtaining jobs for black workers in industrial plants and shipyards. By 1944, more than 1 million blacks, 300,000 of them women, held manufacturing jobs. ("My sister always said that Hitler was the one that got us out of the white folks' kitchen," recalled one black woman.)

The Double-V

CORE

During the war, NAACP membership grew from 50,000 to nearly 500,000. The Congress of Racial Equality (CORE), founded by an interracial group of pacifists in 1942, held sit-ins in northern cities to integrate restaurants and theaters. In February of that year, the *Pittsburgh Courier* coined the phrase that came to symbolize black attitudes during the war—the **double-V**. Victory over Germany and Japan, it insisted, must be accompanied by victory over segregation at home. Whereas the Roosevelt administration and the white press saw the war as an expression of American ideals, black newspapers pointed to the gap between those ideals and reality.

Surveying wartime public opinion, a political scientist concluded that "symbols of national solidarity" had very different meanings to white and black Americans. To blacks, freedom from fear meant, among other things, an end to lynching, and freedom from want included doing away with "discrimination in getting jobs." If, in whites' eyes, freedom was a "possession to be defended," he observed, to blacks and other racial minorities it remained a "goal to be achieved."

The War and Race

During the war, a broad political coalition centered on the left but reaching well beyond it called for an end to racial inequality in America. The NAACP and American Jewish Congress cooperated closely in advocating laws to ban discrimination in employment and housing. Despite considerable resistance from rank-and-file white workers, CIO unions, especially those with strong left-liberal and communist influence, made significant efforts to organize black workers and win them access to skilled positions.

The new black militancy alarmed southern politicians. The "war emergency," insisted Governor Frank Dixon of Alabama, "should not be used as a pretext to bring about the abolition of the color line." Even as the war gave birth to the modern civil rights movement, it also planted the seeds for the South's "massive resistance" to desegregation during the 1950s.

This is the Enemy, a 1942 poster by Victor Ancona and Karl Koehler, suggests a connection between Nazism abroad and lynching at home.

This is the Enemy

WINNER R. HOE & CO., INC. AWARD – NATIONAL WAR POSTER COMPETITION

Although progress was slow, it was measurable. The National War Labor Board banned racial wage differentials. In *Smith v. Allwright* (1944), the Supreme Court outlawed all-white primaries, one of the mechanisms by which southern states deprived blacks of political rights. In the same year, the navy began assigning small numbers of black sailors to previously all-white ships. In the final months of the war, it ended segregation altogether, and the army established a few combat units that included black and white soldiers.

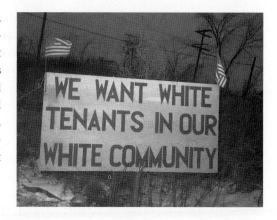

A sign displayed opposite a Detroit housing project in 1942 symbolizes one aspect of what Gunnar Myrdal called "the American Dilemma"—the persistence of racism in the midst of a worldwide struggle for freedom.

An American Dilemma

No event reflected the new concern with the status of black Americans more than the publication in 1944 of *An American Dilemma*, a sprawling account of the country's racial past, present, and future written by the Swedish social scientist Gunnar Myrdal. The book offered an uncompromising portrait of how deeply racism was entrenched in law, politics, economics, and social behavior. But Myrdal combined this sobering analysis with admiration for what he called the American Creed—belief in equality, justice, equal opportunity, and freedom. He concluded that "there is bound to be a redefinition of the Negro's status as a result of this War."

Myrdal's notion of a conflict between American values and American racial policies was hardly new—Frederick Douglass and W. E. B. Du Bois

The American Creed

Paul Robeson, the black actor, singer, and battler for civil rights, leading Oakland dockworkers in singing the national anthem in 1942. World War II gave a significant boost to the vision, shared by Robeson and others on the left, of an America based on genuine equality.

had said much the same thing. But in the context of a worldwide struggle against Nazism and rising black demands for equality at home, his book struck a chord. It identified a serious national problem and seemed to offer an almost painless path to peaceful change, in which the federal government would take the lead in outlawing discrimination.

Black Internationalism

Black international consciousness

In the nineteenth century, black radicals like David Walker and Martin Delany had sought to link the fate of African-Americans with that of peoples of African descent in other parts of the world, especially the Caribbean and Africa. In the first decades of the twentieth century, this kind of international consciousness was reinvigorated. At the home of George Padmore, a West Indian labor organizer and editor living in London, black American leaders like W. E. B. Du Bois and Paul Robeson came into contact with future leaders of African independence movements such as Jomo Kenyatta (Kenya), Kwame Nkrumah (Ghana), and Nnamdi Azikiwe (Nigeria).

A global cause

Through these gatherings, Du Bois, Robeson, and others developed an outlook that linked the plight of black Americans with that of people of color worldwide. Freeing Africa from colonial rule, they came to believe, would encourage greater equality at home. World War II stimulated among African-Americans an even greater awareness of the links between racism in the United States and colonialism abroad.

THE END OF THE WAR

As 1945 opened, Allied victory was assured. In December 1944, in a desperate gamble, Hitler launched a surprise counterattack in France that pushed Allied forces back fifty miles, creating a large bulge in their lines. The largest single battle ever fought by the U.S. Army, the Battle of the Bulge produced more than 70,000 American casualties. But by early 1945 the assault had failed.

V-E Day

In March, American troops crossed the Rhine River and entered the industrial heartland of Germany. Hitler took his own life, and shortly afterward Soviet forces occupied Berlin. On May 8, known as **V-E Day** (for victory in Europe), came the formal end to the war against Germany. In the Pacific, American forces moved ever closer to Japan.

"The Most Terrible Weapon"

Franklin D. Roosevelt defeated Republican nominee Thomas E. Dewey, the governor of New York, to win an unprecedented fourth term in 1944. But FDR did not live to see the Allied victory. He succumbed to a stroke on April 12, 1945. To his successor, Harry S. Truman, fell one of the most momentous decisions ever confronted by an American president— whether to use the atomic bomb against Japan. Truman did not know about the bomb until after he became president. Then, Secretary of War Henry L. Stimson informed him that the United States had secretly developed "the most terrible weapon ever known in human history."

Truman and the atomic bomb

The bomb was a practical realization of the theory of relativity, a rethinking of the laws of physics developed early in the twentieth century by the German scientist Albert Einstein. Energy and matter, Einstein showed, were two forms of the same phenomenon. By using certain forms of uranium, or the man-made element plutonium, scientists could create an atomic reaction that transformed part of the mass into energy. This energy could be harnessed to provide a form of controlled power—or it could be unleashed in a tremendous explosion.

Albert Einstein

In 1940, FDR authorized what came to be known as the **Manhattan Project**, a top-secret program in which American scientists developed an atomic bomb during World War II. The weapon was tested successfully in the New Mexico desert in July 1945.

The Dawn of the Atomic Age

On August 6, 1945, an American plane dropped an atomic bomb that detonated over Hiroshima, Japan—a target chosen because almost alone among major Japanese cities, it had not yet suffered damage. In an instant, nearly every building in the city was destroyed. Of the city's population of 280,000 civilians and 40,000 soldiers, approximately 70,000 died immediately. Because atomic bombs release deadly radiation, the death toll kept rising in the months that followed. By the end of the year, it reached at least 140,000. On August 9, the United States exploded a second bomb over Nagasaki, killing 70,000 persons. On the same day, the Soviet Union declared war on Japan and invaded Manchuria. Within a week, Japan surrendered.

"Fat Man," the atomic bomb dropped on Nagasaki, Japan, on August 9, 1945.

Because of the enormous cost in civilian lives—more than twice America's military fatalities in the entire

After the dropping of the atomic bomb on Hiroshima, Japan, the federal government restricted the circulation of images of destruction. But soon after the end of the war, it dispatched photographers to compile a Strategic Bombing Survey to assess the bomb's impact. This photograph, which long remained classified, shows the remains of an elementary school.

A controversial choice

Pacific war—the use of the bomb remains controversial. An American invasion of Japan, some advisers warned Truman, might cost as many as 250,000 American lives. No such invasion was planned to begin, however, until the following year, and considerable evidence had accumulated that Japan was nearing surrender. Japan's economy had been crippled and its fleet destroyed, and it would now have to fight the Soviet Union as well as the United States. Some of the scientists who had worked on the bomb urged Truman to demonstrate its power to international observers. But Truman did not hesitate. The bomb was a weapon, he reasoned, and weapons are created to be used.

The Nature of the War

The dropping of the atomic bombs was the logical culmination of the way World War II had been fought. All wars inflict suffering on non-combatants. But never before had civilian populations been so ruthlessly targeted. Of the estimated 50 million persons who perished during World War II (including 400,000 American soldiers), perhaps 20 million were civilians. Germany had killed millions of members of "inferior races." The Allies carried out deadly air assaults on civilian populations. Early in 1945, the firebombing of Dresden killed some 100,000 people, mostly women,

The war and civilian populations

children, and elderly men. On March 9, nearly the same number died in an inferno caused by the bombing of Tokyo.

Four years of war propaganda had dehumanized the Japanese in Americans' eyes, and few persons criticized Truman's decision in 1945. But public doubts began to surface, especially after John Hersey published *Hiroshima* (1946), a graphic account of the horrors suffered by the civilian population. General Dwight D. Eisenhower, who thought the use of the bomb unnecessary, later wrote, "I hated to see our country be the first to use such a weapon."

Hersey's Hiroshima

Planning the Postwar World

Even as the war raged, a series of meetings between Allied leaders formulated plans for the postwar world. Churchill, Roosevelt, and Soviet chief Joseph Stalin met at Tehran, Iran, in 1943, and at Yalta, in the southern Soviet Union, early in 1945, to hammer out agreements. The final "Big Three" conference took place at Potsdam, near Berlin, in July 1945. It involved Stalin, Truman, and Churchill (replaced midway in the talks by Clement Attlee, who became prime minister when his Labour Party swept the British elections). At the **Potsdam conference**, the Allied leaders established a military administration for Germany and agreed to place top Nazi leaders on trial for war crimes.

The "Big Three" conferences

Relations among the three Allies were often uneasy, as each maneuvered to maximize its postwar power. Neither Britain nor the United States trusted Stalin. But since Stalin's troops had won the war on the eastern front, it was difficult to resist his demand that eastern Europe become a Soviet sphere of influence (a region whose governments can be counted on to do a great power's bidding).

The Big Three—Stalin, Roosevelt, and Churchill—at their first meeting, in Tehran, Iran, in 1943, where they discussed the opening of a second front against Germany in western Europe.

Yalta and Bretton Woods

At the **Yalta conference**, Roosevelt and Churchill entered only a mild protest against Soviet plans to retain control of the Baltic states (Estonia, Latvia, and Lithuania) and a large part of eastern Poland, in effect restoring Russia's pre–World War I western borders. Stalin agreed to enter the war against Japan later in 1945 and to allow "free and unfettered elections" in Poland, but he was intent on establishing communism in eastern

Europe. Yalta saw the high-water mark of wartime American–Soviet cooperation. But it planted seeds of conflict, since the participants soon disagreed over the fate of eastern Europe.

Tension also existed between Britain and the United States. Churchill rejected American pressure to place India and other British colonies on the road to independence. He concluded private deals with Stalin to divide southern and eastern Europe into British and Soviet spheres of influence.

Shaping the postwar economic order

Britain also resisted, unsuccessfully, American efforts to reshape and dominate the postwar economic order. A meeting of representatives of forty-five nations at Bretton Woods, New Hampshire, in July 1944 replaced the British pound with the dollar as the main currency for international transactions. The **Bretton Woods conference** also created two American-dominated financial institutions. The World Bank would provide money to developing countries and to help rebuild Europe. The International Monetary Fund would work to prevent governments from devaluing their currencies to gain an advantage in international trade, as many had done during the Depression. Both of these institutions, American leaders believed, would encourage free trade and the growth of the world economy, an emphasis that remains central to American foreign policy to this day.

The United Nations

Early in the war, the Allies also agreed to establish a successor to the League of Nations. In a 1944 conference at Dumbarton Oaks, near Washington, D.C., they developed the structure of the **United Nations** (UN). There would be a General Assembly—essentially a forum for discussion where each member enjoyed an equal voice—and a Security Council responsible for maintaining world peace. Along with six rotating members, the Council would have five permanent ones—Britain, China, France, the Soviet Union, and the United States—each with the power to veto resolutions. In June 1945, representatives of fifty-one countries met in San Francisco to adopt the UN Charter, which outlawed force or the threat of force as a means of settling international disputes. In July, the U.S. Senate endorsed the charter. In contrast to the bitter dispute over membership in the League of Nations after World War I, only two members of the U.S. Senate voted against joining the UN.

Structure of the UN

Peace, but Not Harmony

World power redistributed

World War II produced a radical redistribution of world power. Japan and Germany, the two dominant military powers in their regions before the war, were utterly defeated. Britain and France, though victorious, were substantially weakened. Only the United States and the Soviet Union were able to project significant influence beyond their national borders.

Overall, however, the United States was clearly the dominant world power. But peace did not usher in an era of international harmony. The Soviet occupation of eastern Europe created a division soon to be solidified in the Cold War. The dropping of the atomic bombs left a worldwide legacy of fear.

The dominant world power

The Four Freedoms speech had been intended primarily to highlight the differences between Anglo-American ideals and Nazism. Nonetheless, it had unanticipated consequences. As one of Roosevelt's speechwriters remarked, "when you state a moral principle, you are stuck with it, no matter how many fingers you have kept crossed at the moment." The language with which World War II was fought helped to lay the foundation for postwar ideals of human rights that extend to all mankind.

Human rights

During the war, Mahatma Gandhi, the Indian nationalist leader, wrote to Roosevelt that the idea "that the Allies are fighting to make the world safe for freedom of the individual and for democracy seems hollow, so long as India, and for that matter, Africa, are exploited by Great Britain, and America has the Negro problem in her own home." Allied victory saved mankind from a living nightmare—a worldwide system of dictatorial rule and slave labor in which peoples deemed inferior suffered the fate of European Jews and the victims of Japanese outrages in Asia. But disputes over the freedom of colonial peoples overseas and non-whites in the United States foretold wars and social upheavals to come.

Unresolved disputes

CHAPTER REVIEW AND ONLINE RESOURCES

REVIEW QUESTIONS

1. Why did most Americans support isolationism in the 1930s?

2. What factors after 1939 led to U.S. involvement in World War II?

3. How did government, business, and labor work together to promote wartime production? How did the war affect each group?

4. How did different groups understand or experience the Four Freedoms differently?

5. Explain how conservatives in Congress and business used the war effort to attack the goals and legacy of the New Deal.

6. How did the war alter the lives of women on the home front, and what did different groups think would happen after the war?

7. How did a war fought to bring "essential human freedoms" to the world fail to protect the home front liberties of blacks, Indians, Japanese-Americans, and Mexican-Americans?

8. Explain how World War II promoted an awareness of the links between racism in the United States and colonialism around the world.

9. What was the impact of the GI Bill of Rights on American society, including minorities?

10. Describe how the decisions made at the Bretton Woods conference in 1944 created the framework for postwar U.S. economic and foreign policy.

KEY TERMS

Four Freedoms (p. 677)
Good Neighbor Policy (p. 678)
isolationism (p. 680)
Neutrality Acts (p. 680)
Lend-Lease Act (p. 681)
Axis powers (p. 682)
D-Day (p. 684)
Holocaust (p. 686)
GI Bill of Rights (p. 692)
bracero program (p. 694)
zoot suit riots (p. 695)
Japanese-American internment (p. 699)
Korematsu v. United States (p. 700)
second Great Migration (p. 701)
double-V (p. 702)
V-E Day (p. 704)
Manhattan Project (p. 705)
Potsdam conference (p. 707)
Yalta conference (p. 707)
Bretton Woods conference (p. 708)
United Nations (p. 708)

Go to 🐰 **INQUIZITIVE**

To see what you know—and learn what you've missed—with personalized feedback along the way.

Visit the *Give Me Liberty!* **Student Site** for primary source documents and images, interactive maps, author videos featuring Eric Foner, and more.

CHAPTER 23

THE UNITED STATES AND THE COLD WAR

★

1945-1953

TREASURE CHEST

...IS IS THE VOICE OF YOUR COMMUNIST ...VERNMENT SPEAKING. TODAY, COMMUNIST ...RCES HAVE COMPLETED THE OCCUPATION ...F YOUR COUNTRY. THE UNITED STATES ...O LONGER EXISTS. IT IS NOW THE UNION ...E SOVIET STATES OF AMERICA! LONG LIVE THE U.S.S.A.!!

1947	Truman Doctrine
	Federal Employee Loyalty program
	Jackie Robinson integrates major league baseball
	Marshall Plan
	Taft-Hartley Act
	Freedom Train exhibition
	House Un-American Activities Committee investigates Hollywood
1948	UN adopts Universal Declaration of Human Rights
	Truman desegregates military
1948–1949	Berlin blockade and airlift
1949	North Atlantic Treaty Organization established
	Soviet Union tests atomic bomb
	People's Republic of China established
1950	McCarthy's Wheeling, W.V., speech
	NSC-68 issued
	McCarran Internal Security Act
1950–1953	Korean War
1953	Julius and Ethel Rosenberg executed for spying
1954	Army-McCarthy hearings
1955	Warsaw Pact organized

The Cold War led to widespread fears of a communist takeover in the United States (a task far beyond the capacity of the minuscule American Communist Party or the Soviet Union). This image is from the first page of *This Godless Communism*, an issue of a comic book series called *Treasure Chest* published from 1946 to 1972. The issue warned of the danger that communists might overthrow the government, and detailed the horrors of life in a communist America, including the arrest and jailing of priests and ministers. It was circulated to parochial schools by the Roman Catholic Church and contained an introduction by J. Edgar Hoover, head of the Federal Bureau of Investigation.

FOCUS
QUESTIONS

• *What series of events
and ideological conflicts
prompted the Cold War?*

• *How did the Cold War
reshape ideas of American
freedom?*

• *What major domestic
policy initiatives did
Truman undertake?*

• *What effects did the
anticommunism of the Cold
War have on American
politics and culture?*

On September 16, 1947, the 160th anniversary of the signing of the Constitution, the Freedom Train opened to the public in Philadelphia. A traveling exhibition of 133 historical documents, the train, bedecked in red, white, and blue, soon embarked on a sixteen-month tour that took it to more than 300 American cities. Never before or since have so many cherished pieces of Americana—among them the Mayflower Compact, the Declaration of Independence, and the Gettysburg Address—been assembled in one place.

The idea for the Freedom Train originated in 1946 with the Department of Justice. President Harry S. Truman endorsed it as a way of contrasting American freedom with "the destruction of liberty by the Hitler tyranny." Since direct government funding raised fears of propaganda, however, the administration turned the project over to a nonprofit group, the American Heritage Foundation.

By any measure, the Freedom Train was an enormous success. Behind the scenes, however, the Freedom Train demonstrated that the meaning of freedom remained as controversial as ever.

The liberal staff members at the National Archives who proposed the initial list of documents had included the Wagner Act of 1935, which guaranteed workers the right to form unions, as well as President Roosevelt's Four Freedoms speech of 1941, with its promise to fight "freedom from want." The more conservative American Heritage Foundation removed these documents. They also deleted from the original list the Fourteenth and Fifteenth Amendments, which had established the principle of equal civil and political rights regardless of race after the Civil War. In the end, nothing on the train referred to organized labor or any twentieth-century social legislation. The only documents relating to African-Americans were the Emancipation Proclamation, the Thirteenth Amendment, and a 1776 letter by South Carolina patriot Henry Laurens criticizing slavery.

On the eve of the train's unveiling, the poet Langston Hughes wondered whether there would be "Jim Crow on the Freedom Train." "When it stops in Mississippi," Hughes asked, "will it be made plain / Everybody's got a right to board the Freedom Train?" In fact, with the Truman administration about to make civil rights a major priority, the train's organizers announced that they would not permit segregated viewing. In an unprecedented move, the American Heritage Foundation canceled visits to Memphis, Tennessee, and Birmingham, Alabama, when local authorities insisted on separating visitors by race. The Freedom Train visited forty-seven other southern cities without incident.

Even as the Freedom Train reflected a new sense of national unease about expressions of racial inequality, its journey also revealed the growing impact of the **Cold War**. In the spring of 1947, a few months before the train was dedicated, President Truman committed the United States to the worldwide **containment** of Soviet power and inaugurated a program to root out "disloyal" persons from government employment. The Federal Bureau of Investigation began compiling reports on those who found the train objectionable. The Freedom Train revealed how the Cold War helped to reshape freedom's meaning, identifying it ever more closely with anticommunism, "free enterprise," and the defense of the social and economic status quo.

ORIGINS OF THE COLD WAR

The Two Powers

The United States emerged from World War II as by far the world's greatest power. The United States accounted for half the world's manufacturing capacity. It alone possessed the atomic bomb. American leaders believed that the nation's security depended on the security of Europe and Asia, and that American prosperity required global economic reconstruction.

The only power that in any way could rival the United States was the Soviet Union, whose armies now occupied most of eastern Europe, including the eastern part of Germany. Its crucial role in defeating Hitler and its claim that communism had wrested a vast backward nation into modernity gave the Soviet Union considerable prestige in Europe and among colonial peoples struggling for independence. Having lost more than 20 million dead and suffered immense devastation during the war, however, Stalin's government was in no position to embark on new military adventures. But the Soviet government remained determined to establish a sphere of influence in eastern Europe, through which Germany had twice invaded Russia in the past thirty years.

The Roots of Containment

In retrospect, it seems all but inevitable that the two major powers to emerge from the war would come into conflict. Born of a common foe rather than common long-term interests, values, or history, the wartime alliance between the United States and the Soviet Union began to unravel almost from the day that peace was declared.

The cover of a comic book promoting the Freedom Train in 1948. The image links the train to Paul Revere's ride and, more broadly, the Revolutionary era.

Soviet power

Alliance unraveled

The first confrontation of the Cold War took place in the Middle East. At the end of World War II, Soviet troops had occupied parts of northern Iran, hoping to pressure that country to grant it access to its rich oil fields. Under British and American pressure, Stalin quickly withdrew Soviet forces. At the same time, however, the Soviets installed procommunist governments in Poland, Romania, and Bulgaria, a step they claimed was no different from American domination of Latin America or Britain's determination to maintain its own empire.

Early in 1946, in his famous **Long Telegram** from Moscow, American diplomat George Kennan advised the Truman administration that the Soviets could not be dealt with as a normal government. Communist ideology drove them to try to expand their power throughout the world, he claimed, and only the United States had the ability to stop them. His telegram laid the foundation for what became known as the policy of "containment," according to which the United States committed itself to preventing any further expansion of Soviet power.

Shortly afterward, in a speech at Fulton, Missouri, Britain's former wartime prime minister Winston Churchill declared that an **iron curtain** had descended across Europe, partitioning the free West from the communist East. But not until March 1947, in a speech announcing what came to be known as the **Truman Doctrine**, did the president officially embrace the Cold War as the foundation of American foreign policy and describe it as a worldwide struggle over the future of freedom.

The Truman Doctrine

Harry S. Truman never expected to become president. When he assumed the presidency after Roosevelt's death in April 1945, Truman found himself forced to decide foreign policy debates in which he had previously played virtually no role.

Convinced that Stalin could not be trusted and that the United States had a responsibility to provide leadership to a world that he tended to view in stark, black-and-white terms, Truman soon determined to put the policy of containment into effect. The immediate occasion for this epochal decision came early in 1947 when Britain informed the United States that because its economy had been shattered by the war, it had no choice but to end military and financial aid to two crucial governments—Greece, a monarchy threatened by a communist-led rebellion, and Turkey, from which the Soviets were demanding joint control of the straits linking the Black Sea and the Mediterranean. Britain asked the United States to fill the vacuum.

The Soviet Union had little to do with the internal problems of Greece and Turkey, where opposition to corrupt, undemocratic regimes was largely homegrown. But the two countries occupied strategically important sites at the gateway to southeastern Europe and the oil-rich Middle East. Truman had been told by Senate leader Arthur Vandenberg that the only way a reluctant public and Congress would support aid to these governments was for the president to "scare hell" out of the American people. Truman rolled out the heaviest weapon in his rhetorical arsenal—the defense of freedom. As the leader of the "free world," the United States must now shoulder the responsibility of supporting "freedom-loving peoples" wherever communism threatened them. Twenty-four times in the eighteen-minute speech, Truman used the words "free" and "freedom."

President Harry S. Truman delivering his Truman Doctrine speech before Congress on March 12, 1947.

Truman succeeded in persuading both Republicans and Democrats in Congress to support his policy, beginning a long period of bipartisan support for the containment of communism. As Truman's speech to Congress suggested, the Cold War was, in part, an ideological conflict. Both sides claimed to be promoting freedom and social justice while defending their own security, and each offered its social system as a model the rest of the world should follow.

Truman's rhetoric suggested that the United States had assumed a permanent global responsibility. The speech set a precedent for American assistance to anticommunist regimes throughout the world, no matter how undemocratic, and for the creation of a set of global military alliances directed against the Soviet Union. There soon followed the creation of new national security bodies immune from democratic oversight, such as the Atomic Energy Commission, National Security Council, and Central Intelligence Agency (CIA), the last established in 1947 to gather intelligence and conduct secret military operations abroad.

Consequences of the Truman Doctrine

The Marshall Plan

The threat of American military action overseas formed only one pillar of containment. Secretary of State George C. Marshall spelled out the other in a speech at Harvard University in June 1947. Marshall pledged the United States to contribute billions of dollars to finance the economic recovery of Europe. Two years after the end of the war, much of the continent still lay

Postwar foreign aid to Europe

Bales of American cotton in a warehouse at the French port of Le Havre, 1949. Part of the Marshall Plan aid program, the shipment helped to revive the French cotton industry.

in ruins with widespread food shortages and rampant inflation. The economic chaos had strengthened the communist parties of France and Italy. American policymakers feared that these countries might fall into the Soviet orbit.

The **Marshall Plan** offered a positive vision to go along with containment. Avoiding Truman's language of a world divided between free and unfree blocs, Marshall insisted, "Our policy is directed not against any country or doctrine, but against hunger, poverty, desperation, and chaos."

The Marshall Plan proved to be one of the most successful foreign aid programs in history. By 1950, western European production exceeded prewar levels and the region was poised to follow the United States down the road to a mass-consumption society. Because the Soviet Union refused to participate, fearing American control over the economies of eastern Europe, the Marshall Plan further solidified the division of the continent. At the same time, the United States worked out with twenty-three other Western nations the General Agreement on Tariffs and Trade (GATT), which proposed to stimulate freer trade among the participants, creating an enormous market for American goods and investment.

The Reconstruction of Japan

A democratic constitution

Under the guidance of General Douglas MacArthur, the "supreme commander" in Japan until 1948, that country adopted a new, democratic constitution. Thanks to American insistence, and against the wishes of most Japanese leaders, the new constitution gave women the right to vote for the first time in Japan's history. Furthermore, Article 9 of the new constitution stated that Japan would renounce forever the policy of war and armed aggression, and would maintain only a modest self-defense force.

Japan's recovery

The United States also oversaw the economic reconstruction of Japan. Initially, the United States proposed to dissolve Japan's giant industrial corporations, which had contributed so much to the nation's war effort. But this plan was abandoned in 1948 in favor of an effort to rebuild Japan's industrial base as a bastion of anticommunist strength in Asia. By the 1950s, thanks to American economic assistance, the adoption of new technologies, and low spending on the military, Japan's economic recovery was in full swing.

The Berlin Blockade and NATO

Meanwhile, the Cold War intensified and, despite the Marshall Plan, increasingly took a militaristic turn. At the end of World War II, each of the four victorious powers assumed control of a section of occupied Germany, and of Berlin, located deep in the Soviet zone. In June 1948, the United States, Britain, and France introduced a separate currency in their zones, a prelude to the creation of a new West German government that would be aligned with them in the Cold War. In response, the Soviets cut off road and rail traffic from the American, British, and French zones of occupied Germany to Berlin.

Occupation of Germany

An eleven-month airlift followed, with Western planes supplying fuel and food to their zones of the city. When Stalin lifted the blockade in May 1949, the Truman administration had won a major victory. Soon, two new nations emerged, East and West Germany, each allied with a side in the Cold War. Berlin itself remained divided. Not until 1991 would Germany be reunified.

The Berlin airlift

Also in 1949, the Soviet Union tested its first atomic bomb, ending the American monopoly of that weapon. In the same year, the United States, Canada, and ten western European nations established the **North Atlantic Treaty Organization** (NATO), pledging mutual defense against any future Soviet attack. Soon, West Germany became a crucial part of NATO. The North Atlantic Treaty was the first long-term military alliance between the United States and Europe since the Treaty of Amity and Commerce with France during the American Revolution. The Soviets formalized their own eastern European alliance, the Warsaw Pact, in 1955.

A poster issued by the Defense Department's Office of Public Information in 1950 seeks to drum up popular support for the Korean War. An armed, determined Uncle Sam stands before an idealized rural landscape, an embodiment of "all the things we have" that needed to be defended by war, even though by this time most Americans lived in cities or suburbs.

The Growing Communist Challenge

In 1949, communists led by Mao Zedong emerged victorious in the long Chinese civil war—a serious setback for the policy of containment. Assailed by Republicans for having "lost" China (which, of course, the United States never "had" in the first place), the Truman administration refused to recognize the new government—the People's Republic of China—and blocked it from occupying China's seat at the United Nations. Until the 1970s, the United States insisted that the ousted regime, which had been forced into

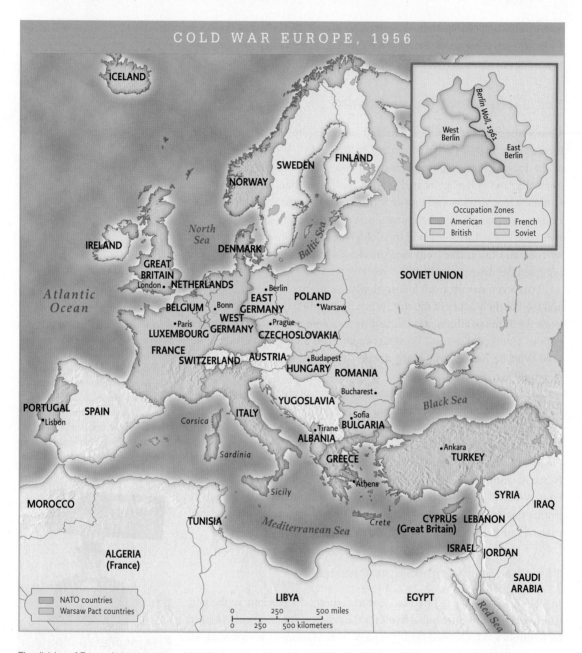

COLD WAR EUROPE, 1956

ICELAND

SWEDEN   FINLAND

NORWAY

North Sea

IRELAND

DENMARK

Occupation Zones
American   French
British   Soviet

West Berlin

Berlin Wall, 1961

East Berlin

SOVIET UNION

GREAT BRITAIN
London•   NETHERLANDS   •Berlin   POLAND
BELGIUM   •Bonn   EAST GERMANY   •Warsaw
•Paris   WEST GERMANY   •Prague
LUXEMBOURG   CZECHOSLOVAKIA
FRANCE
SWITZERLAND   AUSTRIA   •Budapest
HUNGARY   ROMANIA

Atlantic Ocean

PORTUGAL   SPAIN   *Corsica*   ITALY   YUGOSLAVIA   Bucharest•
•Lisbon   •Sofia   *Black Sea*
•Tirane   BULGARIA
Sardinia   ALBANIA
GREECE   Ankara•
TURKEY

Sicily   •Athens   SYRIA
MOROCCO   *Crete*   CYPRUS   LEBANON   IRAQ
TUNISIA   *Mediterranean Sea*   (Great Britain)
ISRAEL   JORDAN
ALGERIA
(France)   SAUDI ARABIA

NATO countries   LIBYA   EGYPT
Warsaw Pact countries   *Red Sea*

0   250   500 miles
0   250   500 kilometers

The division of Europe between communist and noncommunist nations, solidified by the early 1950s, would last for nearly forty years.

exile on the island of Taiwan, remained the legitimate government of China.

In the wake of Soviet-American confrontations in Europe, the communist victory in China, and Soviet success in developing an atomic bomb, the National Security Council approved a call for a permanent military build-up to enable the United States to pursue a global crusade against communism. Known as **NSC-68**, this 1950 manifesto described the Cold War as an epic struggle between "the idea of freedom" and the "idea of slavery under the grim oligarchy of the Kremlin."

In the shadow of the Eiffel Tower in Paris in 1955, NATO delegates vote to admit West Germany to membership, symbolizing the political and military integration of western Europe.

The Korean War

Initially, American postwar policy focused on Europe. But it was in Asia that the Cold War suddenly turned hot. Occupied by Japan during World War II, Korea had been divided in 1945 into Soviet and American zones. These zones soon evolved into two governments: communist North Korea and anticommunist South Korea, undemocratic but aligned with the United States. In June 1950, the North Korean army invaded the south, hoping to reunify the country under communist control. North Korean soldiers soon occupied most of the peninsula. The Truman administration persuaded the United Nations Security Council to authorize the use of force to repel the invasion. (The Soviets, who could have vetoed the resolution, were boycotting Security Council meetings to protest the refusal to seat communist China.)

American troops did the bulk of the fighting on this first battlefield of the Cold War. In September 1950, General Douglas MacArthur launched a daring counterattack at Inchon, behind North Korean lines. MacArthur's army soon occupied most of North Korea. Truman now hoped to unite Korea under a pro-American government. But in October 1950, when UN forces neared the Chinese border, hundreds of thousands of Chinese troops intervened, driving them back in bloody fighting. MacArthur demanded the right to push north again and possibly even invade China and use nuclear weapons against it. But Truman, fearing an all-out war on the Asian mainland, refused. MacArthur did not fully accept the principle of civilian control of the military. When he went public with criticism of the president, Truman removed him from command. The war then settled into a stalemate around the thirty-eighth parallel, the original boundary

A divided Korea

MacArthur in Korea

The Chinese in Korea

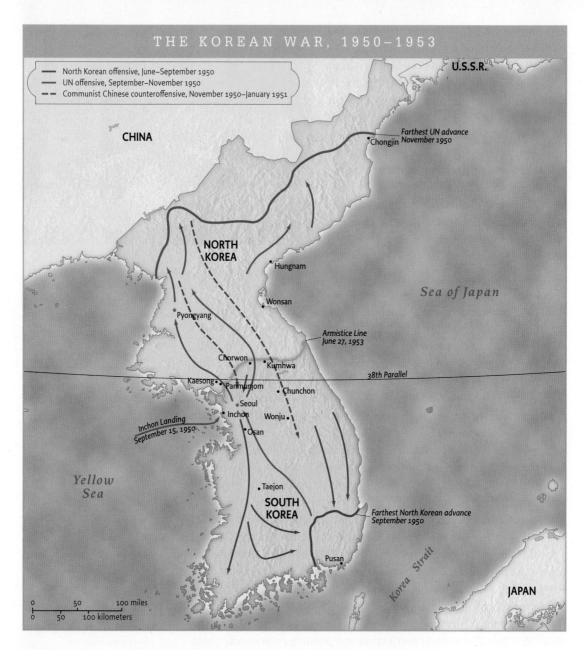

THE KOREAN WAR, 1950–1953

— North Korean offensive, June–September 1950
— UN offensive, September–November 1950
-- Communist Chinese counteroffensive, November 1950–January 1951

U.S.S.R.

CHINA

Chongjin • — Farthest UN advance November 1950

NORTH KOREA

Hungnam •

Sea of Japan

Wonsan •

Pyongyang ◦

— Armistice Line June 27, 1953

Chorwon •

Kumhwa •

Kaesong •

Panmunjom • Chunchon •

38th Parallel

◦ Seoul
Inchon •

Wonju •

Inchon Landing
September 15, 1950

Osan •

Yellow Sea

Taejon •

SOUTH KOREA

— Farthest North Korean advance
September 1950

Pusan •

Korea Strait

JAPAN

0   50   100 miles
0   50   100 kilometers

As this map indicates, when General Douglas MacArthur launched his surprise landing at Inchon, North Korean forces controlled nearly the entire Korean peninsula.

between the two Koreas. Not until 1953 was an armistice agreed to, essentially restoring the prewar status quo. There has never been a formal peace treaty ending the **Korean War**.

More than 33,000 Americans died in Korea. The Asian death toll reached an estimated 1 million Korean soldiers and 2 million civilians, along with hundreds of thousands of Chinese troops. Korea made it clear that the Cold War, which began in Europe, had become a global conflict.

A photograph of a street battle in Seoul, South Korea, during the Korean War illustrates the ferocity of the fighting.

Cold War Critics

In the Soviet Union, Stalin had consolidated a brutal dictatorship that jailed or murdered millions of Soviet citizens. With its one-party rule, stringent state control of the arts and intellectual life, and government-controlled economy, the Soviet Union presented a stark opposite of democracy and "free enterprise." As a number of contemporary critics, few of them sympathetic to Soviet communism, pointed out, however, casting the Cold War in terms of a worldwide battle between freedom and slavery had unfortunate consequences.

In a penetrating critique of Truman's policies, Walter Lippmann, one of the nation's most prominent journalists, objected to turning foreign policy into an "ideological crusade." To view every challenge to the status quo as part of a contest with the Soviet Union, Lippmann correctly predicted, would require the United States to recruit and subsidize an "array of satellites, clients, dependents and puppets." It would have to intervene continuously in the affairs of nations whose political problems did not arise from Moscow and could not be easily understood in terms of the battle between freedom and slavery. World War II, he went on, had shaken the foundations of European empires. In the tide of revolutionary nationalism now sweeping the world, communists were certain to play an important role.

Walter Lippmann

Imperialism and Decolonization

World War II had increased American awareness of the problem of imperialism. Many movements for colonial independence borrowed the language of the American Declaration of Independence in demanding the right to

Imperialism

self-government. Liberal Democrats and black leaders urged the Truman administration to take the lead in promoting worldwide **decolonization**, insisting that a Free World worthy of the name should not include colonies and empires. But as the Cold War developed, the United States backed away from pressuring its European allies to grant self-government to colonies like French Indochina, the Dutch East Indies, and British possessions like the Gold Coast and Nigeria in Africa and Malaya in Asia.

The Free World

No matter how repressive to its own people, if a nation joined the worldwide anticommunist alliance led by the United States, it was counted as a member of the Free World. The Republic of South Africa, for example, was considered a part of the Free World even though its white minority had deprived the black population of nearly all their rights.

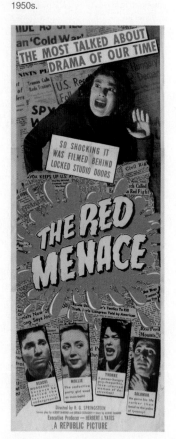

A poster for *The Red Menace*, one of numerous anticommunist films produced by Hollywood during the 1950s.

THE COLD WAR AND THE IDEA OF FREEDOM

Among other things, the Cold War was an ideological struggle, a battle, in a popular phrase of the 1950s, for the "hearts and minds" of people throughout the world. During the 1950s, freedom became an inescapable theme of academic research, popular journalism, mass culture, and official pronouncements.

One of the more unusual Cold War battlefields involved American history and culture. National security agencies encouraged Hollywood to produce anticommunist movies, such as *The Red Menace* (1949) and *I Married a Communist* (1950), and urged that film scripts be changed to remove references to less-than-praiseworthy aspects of American history, such as Indian removal and racial discrimination.

To counteract the widespread European view of the United States as a cultural backwater, the CIA secretly funded an array of overseas publications, conferences, publishing houses, concerts, and art exhibits. And to try to improve the international image of American race relations, the government sent jazz musicians and other black performers abroad, especially to Africa and Asia.

Freedom and Totalitarianism

Along with freedom, the Cold War's other great mobilizing concept was **totalitarianism**. The term originated in Europe between the world wars to describe fascist Italy and Nazi Germany—aggressive, ideologically driven states that sought to subdue all of civil society, including churches, unions, and other voluntary associations, to their control. By the 1950s, the term had become shorthand for describing those on the Soviet side in the Cold War. As the eventual collapse of communist governments in eastern Europe and the Soviet Union would demonstrate, the idea of totalitarianism greatly exaggerated the totality of government control of private life and thought in these countries.

Just as the conflict over slavery redefined American freedom in the nineteenth century and the confrontation with the Nazis shaped understandings of freedom during World War II, the Cold War reshaped them once again. Whatever Moscow stood for was by definition the opposite of freedom, including anything to which the word "socialized" could be attached. In the largest public relations campaign in American history, the American Medical Association raised the specter of "socialized medicine" to defeat Truman's proposal for national health insurance.

Mark Rothko was a painter whose works seemed to exemplify American artists' freedom from the constraints of European traditions. The painting has no subject other than color itself, with the different shades of red meant to evoke what Rothko called "the basic human emotions—tragedy, ecstasy, and doom."

The Rise of Human Rights

The Cold War also affected the emerging concept of human rights. The atrocities committed during World War II, as well as the global language of the Four Freedoms, forcefully raised the issue of human rights in the postwar world. After the war, the victorious Allies put numerous German officials on trial before special courts at Nuremberg for crimes against humanity. For the first time, individuals were held directly accountable to the international community for violations of human rights. The trials resulted in prison terms for many Nazi officials and the execution of ten leaders.

In 1948, the UN General Assembly approved the Universal Declaration of Human Rights, drafted by a committee chaired by Eleanor Roosevelt. It identified a broad range of rights to be enjoyed by people everywhere, including freedom of speech, religious toleration, and protection against arbitrary government, as well as social and economic entitlements like the right to an adequate standard of living and access to housing, education, and medical care. The document had no enforcement mechanism. Some considered it an exercise in empty rhetoric. But the core principle—that a nation's treatment of its own citizens should be subject

The Universal Declaration of Human Rights

to outside evaluation—slowly became part of the language in which freedom was discussed.

Ambiguities of Human Rights

Human rights in world affairs

One reason for the lack of an enforcement mechanism in the Universal Declaration of Human Rights was that both the United States and the Soviet Union refused to accept outside interference in their internal affairs. In 1947, the NAACP did file a petition with the United Nations asking it to investigate racism in the United States as a violation of human rights. But the UN decided that it lacked jurisdiction. Nonetheless, since the end of World War II, the enjoyment of human rights has increasingly taken its place in definitions of freedom across the globe, especially where such rights are flagrantly violated.

Partial acceptance of human rights

After the Cold War ended, the idea of human rights would play an increasingly prominent role in world affairs. But during the 1950s, Cold War imperatives shaped the concept. Neither the United States nor the Soviet Union could resist emphasizing certain provisions of the Universal Declaration while ignoring others. The Soviets claimed to provide all citizens with social and economic rights, but violated democratic rights and civil liberties. Many Americans condemned these nonpolitical rights as a path to socialism.

THE TRUMAN PRESIDENCY

The Fair Deal

Economic transition

With the end of World War II, President Truman's first domestic task was to preside over the transition from a wartime to a peacetime economy. More than 12 million men remained in uniform in August 1945. Most wanted nothing more than to return home to their families. Some returning soldiers found the adjustment to civilian life difficult. The divorce rate in 1945 rose to double its prewar level. Others took advantage of the GI Bill of Rights (discussed in the previous chapter) to obtain home mortgages, set up small businesses, and embark on college educations. The majority of returning soldiers entered the labor force—one reason why more than 2 million women workers lost their jobs. The government abolished wartime agencies that regulated industrial production and labor relations, and it dismantled wartime price controls, leading to a sharp rise in prices.

In the immediate aftermath of World War II, President Truman, backed by party liberals and organized labor, moved to revive the stalled momentum of the New Deal. Truman's program, which he announced in September 1945 and would later call the **Fair Deal**, focused on improving the social safety net and raising the standard of living of ordinary Americans. He called on Congress to increase the minimum wage, enact a program of national health insurance, and expand public housing, Social Security, and aid to education.

The Postwar Strike Wave

In 1946, a new wave of labor militancy swept the country. The AFL and CIO launched **Operation Dixie**, a campaign to bring unionization to the South and, by so doing, shatter the hold of anti-labor conservatives on the region's politics. More than 200 labor organizers entered the region, seeking support especially in the southern textile industry, the steel industry in the Birmingham region, and agriculture. As inflation soared following the removal of price controls, the resulting drop in workers' real income sparked the largest strike wave in American history. Nearly 5 million workers—including those in the steel, auto, coal, and other key industries—walked off their jobs, demanding wage increases. The strike of 750,000 steelworkers represented the largest single walkout in American history to that date.

A few of the numerous World War II veterans who attended college after the war, thanks to the GI Bill.

National strikes

The Republican Resurgence

In the congressional elections of 1946, large numbers of middle-class voters, alarmed by the labor turmoil, voted Republican. For the first time since the 1920s, Republicans swept to control of both houses of Congress. Meanwhile, in the face of vigorous opposition from southern employers and public officials and the reluctance of many white workers to join interracial labor unions, Operation Dixie failed to unionize the South or dent the political control of conservative Democrats in the region. The election of 1946 ensured that a conservative coalition of Republicans and southern Democrats would continue to dominate Congress.

A conservative coalition

Congress turned aside Truman's Fair Deal program. It enacted tax cuts for wealthy Americans and, over the president's veto, in 1947 passed the

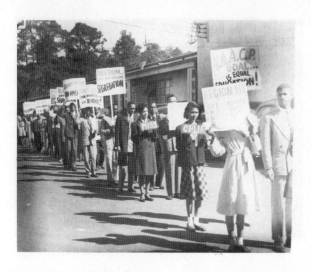

An NAACP youth march against racial segregation in Houston, Texas, in 1947 illustrates the civil rights upsurge of the years immediately following the end of World War II.

Jackie Robinson sliding into third base, 1949.

Taft-Hartley Act, which sought to reverse some of the gains made by organized labor in the past decade. The measure authorized the president to suspend strikes by ordering an eighty-day "cooling-off period," and it banned sympathy strikes and secondary boycotts (labor actions directed not at an employer but at those who did business with him). It outlawed the closed shop, which required a worker to be a union member when taking up a job, and authorized states to pass "right-to-work" laws, prohibiting other forms of compulsory union membership. It also forced union officials to swear that they were not communists. Over time, as population and capital investment shifted to states with "right-to-work" laws like Texas, Florida, and North Carolina, Taft-Hartley contributed to the decline of organized labor's share of the nation's workforce.

Postwar Civil Rights

During his first term, Truman reached out in unprecedented ways to the nation's black community. In the years immediately following World War II, the status of black Americans enjoyed a prominence in national affairs unmatched since Reconstruction.

Between 1945 and 1951, eleven states from New York to New Mexico established fair employment practices commissions, and numerous cities passed laws against discrimination in access to jobs and public accommodations. A broad civil rights coalition involving labor, religious groups, and black organizations supported these measures. By 1952, 20 percent of black southerners were registered to vote, nearly a seven-fold increase since 1940. (Most of the gains took place in the Upper South—in Alabama and Mississippi, the heartland of white supremacy, the numbers barely budged.) Also in 1952, for the first time since record keeping began seventy years earlier, no lynchings took place in the United States. In 1946, the Superman radio show devoted several episodes to the man of steel fighting the Ku Klux Klan, a sign of changing race relations in the wake of World War II.

In another indication that race relations were in flux, the Brooklyn Dodgers in 1947 challenged the long-standing exclusion of black players from major league baseball by adding Jackie Robinson to their team. Robinson, who possessed both remarkable athletic ability and a passion for equality, had been tried and acquitted for insubordination in 1944 when he refused to move to the back of a bus at Fort Hood, Texas, while serving in the army. But he promised Dodger owner Branch Rickey that he would not retaliate when subjected to racist taunts by opposing fans and players. His dignity in the face of constant verbal abuse won Robinson nationwide respect, and his baseball prowess earned him the Rookie of the Year award. His success opened the door to the integration of baseball and led to the demise of the Negro Leagues, to which black players had previously been confined.

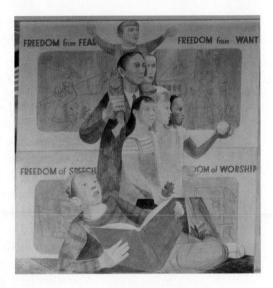

Part of a series of giant murals painted for the lobby of the Rincon Center (formerly a post office, now a shopping mall in San Francisco), this work by the artist Anton Refregier links the Four Freedoms of World War II to a multicultural vision of American society. (In Norman Rockwell's celebrated paintings, shown in Chapter 22, nearly all the figures depicted are white.)

To Secure These Rights

In October 1947, a Commission on Civil Rights appointed by the president issued *To Secure These Rights*, one of the most devastating indictments ever published of racial inequality in America. It called on the federal government to assume the responsibility for abolishing segregation and ensuring equal treatment in housing, employment, education, and the criminal justice system.

In February 1948, Truman presented an ambitious civil rights program to Congress, calling for a permanent federal civil rights commission, national laws against lynching and the poll tax, and action to ensure equal access to jobs and education. Congress, as Truman anticipated, approved none of his proposals. But in July 1948, just as the presidential campaign was getting under way, Truman issued an executive order desegregating the armed forces. The armed services became the first large institution in American life to promote racial integration actively and to attempt to root out long-standing racist practices. The Korean War would be the first American conflict fought by an integrated army since the War of Independence.

Desegregating the armed forces

The Democratic platform of 1948 was the most progressive in the party's history. Led by Hubert Humphrey, the young mayor of

Minneapolis, party liberals overcame southern resistance and added a strong civil rights plank to the platform.

The Dixiecrat and Wallace Revolts

The 1948 Democratic national convention

"I say the time has come," Humphrey told the Democratic national convention, "to walk out of the shadow of states' rights and into the sunlight of human rights." Whereupon numerous southern delegates—dubbed **Dixiecrats** by the press—walked out of the gathering. They soon formed the States' Rights Democratic Party and nominated for president Governor Strom Thurmond of South Carolina. His platform called for the "complete segregation of the races" and his campaign drew most of its support from those alarmed by Truman's civil rights initiatives.

Also in 1948, a group of left-wing critics of Truman's foreign policy formed the Progressive Party and nominated former vice president Henry A. Wallace for president. Wallace advocated an expansion of social welfare programs at home and denounced racial segregation even more vigorously than Truman. When he campaigned in the South, angry white crowds attacked him. But his real difference with the president concerned the Cold War. Wallace called for international control of nuclear weapons and a renewed effort to develop a relationship with the Soviet Union based on economic co-operation rather than military confrontation. The influence of the now much-reduced Communist Party in Wallace's campaign led to an exodus of New Deal liberals and severe attacks on his candidacy. A vote for Wallace, Truman declared, was in effect a vote for Stalin.

Wallace threatened to draw votes from Truman on the left, and Thurmond to undermine the president's support in the South, where whites had voted solidly for the Democrats throughout the twentieth century. But Truman's main opponent, fortunately for the president, was the colorless Republican Thomas A. Dewey. Certain of victory and an ineffective speaker and campaigner, Dewey seemed unwilling to commit himself on controversial issues. Truman, by contrast, ran an aggressive campaign. He criss-

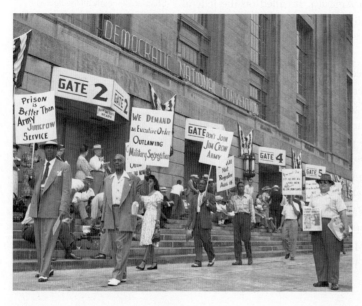

Blacks, led by A. Philip Randolph (*left*), picketing at the 1948 Democratic national convention. The delegates' adoption of a strong civil rights plank led representatives of several southern states to withdraw and nominate their own candidate for president, Strom Thurmond.

crossed the country by train, delivering fiery attacks on the Republican-controlled "do-nothing Congress."

Virtually every public-opinion poll and newspaper report predicted a Dewey victory. Truman's success—by 303 to 189 electoral votes—represented one of the greatest upsets in American political history. For the first time since 1868, blacks (in the North, where they enjoyed the right to vote) played a decisive role in the outcome. Thurmond carried four Deep South states, demonstrating that the race issue, couched in terms of individual freedom, had the potential to lead traditionally Democratic white voters to desert their party. In retrospect, the States' Rights campaign offered a preview of the political transformation that by the end of the twentieth century would leave every southern state in the Republican column. As for Wallace, he suffered the humiliation of polling fewer popular votes than Thurmond.

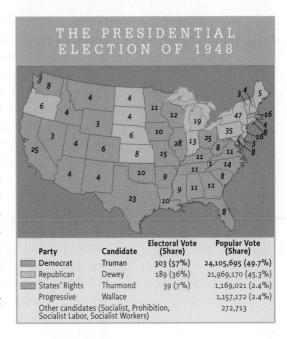

THE PRESIDENTIAL ELECTION OF 1948

Party	Candidate	Electoral Vote (Share)	Popular Vote (Share)
Democrat	Truman	303 (57%)	24,105,695 (49.7%)
Republican	Dewey	189 (36%)	21,969,170 (45.3%)
States' Rights	Thurmond	39 (7%)	1,169,021 (2.4%)
Progressive	Wallace		1,157,172 (2.4%)
Other candidates (Socialist, Prohibition, Socialist Labor, Socialist Workers)			272,713

THE ANTICOMMUNIST CRUSADE

For nearly half a century, the Cold War profoundly affected American life. There would be no return to "normalcy" as after World War I. The military-industrial establishment created during World War II would

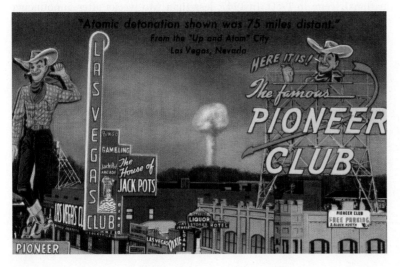

A postcard promoting tourism to Las Vegas highlights as one attraction the city's proximity to a nuclear test site. Witnessing nearby atomic explosions became a popular pastime in the city. The government failed to issue warnings of the dangers of nuclear fallout, and only years later did it admit that many onlookers had contracted diseases from radiation.

become permanent, not temporary. National security became the stated reason for a host of government projects, including aid to higher education and the building of a new national highway system (justified by the need to speed the evacuation of major cities in the event of nuclear war). The Cold War encouraged a culture of secrecy and dishonesty. American nuclear tests, conducted on Pacific islands and in Nevada, exposed thousands of civilians to radiation that caused cancer and birth defects.

Cold War military spending helped to fuel economic growth and support scientific research that not only perfected weaponry but also led to improved aircraft, computers, medicines, and other products with a large impact on civilian life. The Cold War reshaped immigration policy, with refugees from communism being allowed to enter the United States regardless of national-origin quotas. The international embarrassment caused by American racial policies contributed to the dismantling of segregation. And like other wars, the Cold War encouraged the drawing of a sharp line between patriotic Americans and those accused of being disloyal. At precisely the moment when the United States celebrated freedom as the foundation of American life, the right to dissent came under attack.

*Scientific innovation and
social changes*

Loyalty and Disloyalty

Dividing the world between liberty and slavery automatically made those who could be linked to communism enemies of freedom. Although the assault on civil liberties came to be known as **McCarthyism**, it began before Senator Joseph R. McCarthy of Wisconsin burst onto the national scene in 1950. In 1947, less than two weeks after announcing the Truman Doctrine, the president established a loyalty review system that required government employees to demonstrate their patriotism without being allowed to confront accusers or, in some cases, knowing the charges against them. Along with persons suspected of disloyalty, the new national security system also targeted homosexuals who worked for the government. They were deemed particularly susceptible to blackmail by Soviet agents as well as supposedly lacking the manly qualities needed to maintain the country's resolve in the fight against communism. Ironically, the government conducted an anti-gay campaign at the very time that gay men enjoyed a powerful presence in realms of culture and commercial life being promoted as expressions of American freedom—modern art and ballet, fashion, and advertising. The loyalty program failed to uncover any cases of espionage. But the federal government dismissed several hundred persons from their jobs.

*Gays and the loyalty review
system*

Also in 1947, the House Un-American Activities Committee (HUAC) launched a series of hearings about communist influence in Hollywood. Calling well-known screenwriters, directors, and actors to appear before the committee ensured itself a wave of national publicity, which its members relished. Celebrities like producer Walt Disney and actors Gary Cooper and Ronald Reagan testified that the movie industry harbored numerous communists. But ten "unfriendly witnesses" refused to answer the committee's questions about their political beliefs or to "name names" (identify individual communists) on the grounds that the hearings violated the First Amendment's guarantees of freedom of speech and political association. The committee charged the **Hollywood Ten**, who included the prominent screenwriters Ring Lardner Jr. and Dalton Trumbo, with contempt of Congress, and they served jail terms of six months to a year. Hollywood studios blacklisted them (denied them employment), along with more than 200 others who were accused of communist sympathies or who refused to name names.

Movie stars, led by actors Humphrey Bogart and Lauren Bacall, on their way to attend the 1947 hearings of the House Un-American Activities Committee, in a demonstration of support for those called to testify about alleged communist influence in Hollywood.

The Spy Trials

A series of highly publicized legal cases followed, which fueled the growing anticommunist hysteria. Whittaker Chambers, an editor at *Time* magazine, testified before HUAC that during the 1930s, Alger Hiss, a high-ranking State Department official, had given him secret government documents to pass to agents of the Soviet Union. Hiss vehemently denied the charge, but a jury convicted him of perjury and he served five years in prison. A young congressman from California and a member of HUAC, Richard Nixon, achieved national prominence because of his dogged pursuit of Hiss.

The most sensational trial involved Julius and Ethel Rosenberg, a working-class Jewish communist couple from New York City (quite different from Hiss, a member of the eastern Protestant "establishment"). In 1951, a jury convicted the Rosenbergs of conspiracy to pass secrets concerning the atomic bomb to Soviet agents during World War II (when the Soviets were American allies). Their chief accuser was David Greenglass,

The trial of Julius and Ethel Rosenberg

Ethel Rosenberg's brother, who had worked at the Los Alamos nuclear research center.

The case against Julius Rosenberg rested on highly secret documents that could not be revealed in court. (When they were released many years later, the scientific information they contained seemed too crude to justify the government's charge that Julius had passed along the "secret of the atomic bomb," although he may have helped the Soviets speed up their atomic program.) The government had almost no evidence against Ethel Rosenberg, and Greenglass later admitted that he had lied in some of his testimony about her. Indeed, prosecutors seem to have indicted her in the hope of pressuring Julius to confess and implicate others. But in the atmosphere of hysteria, their conviction was certain. Even though they had been convicted of conspiracy, a far weaker charge than spying or treason, Judge Irving Kaufman called their crime "worse than murder." They had helped, he declared, to "cause" the Korean War. Despite an international outcry, their death sentences were carried out in 1953.

Anticommunist hysteria

McCarthy and McCarthyism

In this atmosphere, a little-known senator from Wisconsin suddenly emerged as the chief national pursuer of subversives and gave a new name to the anticommunist crusade. Joseph R. McCarthy had won election to the Senate in 1946, partly on the basis of a fictional war record (he falsely claimed to have flown combat missions in the Pacific). In a speech at Wheeling, West Virginia, in February 1950, McCarthy announced that he had a list of 205 communists working for the State Department. The charge was preposterous, the numbers constantly changed, and McCarthy never identified a single person guilty of genuine disloyalty. But with a genius for self-promotion, McCarthy used the Senate subcommittee he chaired to hold hearings and level wild charges against numerous individuals as well as the Defense Department, the Voice of America, and other government agencies.

Few political figures had the courage to speak up against McCarthy's crusade. One who did was Margaret Chase Smith of Maine,

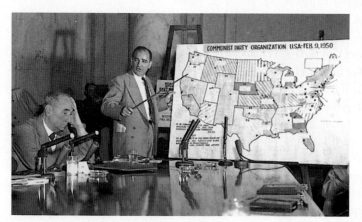

Senator Joseph R. McCarthy at the Army-McCarthy hearings of 1954. McCarthy points to a map detailing charges about the alleged extent of the communist menace, while the army's lawyer, Joseph Welch, listens in disgust.

the Senate's only woman member. On June 1, 1950, soon after McCarthy's Wheeling speech, Smith addressed the Senate with what she called a "declaration of conscience." She did not name McCarthy, but few could mistake the target of her condemnation of a "campaign of hate and character assassination." Most of her colleagues, however, remained silent.

McCarthy's downfall came in 1954, when a Senate committee investigated his charges that the army had harbored and "coddled" communists. The nationally televised **Army-McCarthy hearings** revealed McCarthy as a bully who browbeat witnesses and made sweeping accusations with no basis in fact. The dramatic high point came when McCarthy attacked the loyalty of a young attorney in the firm of Joseph Welch, the army's chief lawyer. "Let us not assassinate this lad further," Welch pleaded. "You have done enough. Have you no sense of decency, sir?" After the hearings ended, the Republican-controlled Senate voted to "condemn" McCarthy for his behavior. But the word "McCarthyism" had entered the political vocabulary, a shorthand for character assassination, guilt by association, and abuse of power in the name of anticommunism.

"Fire!" The cartoonist Herbert Block, known as "Herblock," offered this comment in 1949 on the danger to American freedom posed by the anticommunist crusade.

An Atmosphere of Fear

States created their own committees, modeled on HUAC, that investigated suspected communists and other dissenters. States and localities required loyalty oaths of teachers, pharmacists, and members of other professions, and they banned communists from fishing, holding a driver's license, and, in Indiana, working as professional wrestlers. Throughout the country in the late 1940s and 1950s, those who failed to testify about their past and present political beliefs and to inform on possible communists frequently lost their jobs.

State and local actions

Local anticommunist groups forced public libraries to remove from their shelves "un-American" books like the tales of Robin Hood, who took from the rich to give to the poor. Universities refused to allow left-wing speakers to appear on campus and fired teachers who refused to sign loyalty oaths or to testify against others.

Library and university measures

The Uses of Anticommunism

There undoubtedly were Soviet spies in the United States. Yet the tiny U.S. Communist Party hardly posed a threat to American security. And the vast majority of those jailed or deprived of their livelihoods during the

VOICES OF FREEDOM

From Joseph R. McCarthy, Speech at Wheeling (1950)

During the 1950s, the demagogic pursuit of supposed communists in government and other places of influence became known as McCarthyism, after Senator Joseph R. McCarthy, Republican of Wisconsin. In a speech in West Virginia in February 1950, McCarthy claimed to have a list of 205 communists working for the State Department. When he entered the speech into the Congressional Record a few days later, he reduced the number to fifty-seven. He never named any of them.

Today we are engaged in a final, all-out battle between communistic atheism and Christianity. The modern champions of communism have selected this as the time. And, ladies and gentlemen, the chips are down—they are truly down.

Six years ago, at the time of the first conference to map out peace . . . there was within the Soviet orbit 180 million people. Lined up on the antitotalitarian side there were in the world at that time roughly 1.625 billion people. Today, only six years later, there are 800 million people under the absolute domination of Soviet Russia—an increase of over 400 percent. On our side, the figure has shrunk to around 500 million. . . .

The reason why we find ourselves in a position of impotency is not because our only powerful, potential enemy has sent men to invade our shores, but rather because of the traitorous actions of those who have been treated so well by this nation. It has not been the less fortunate or members of minority groups who have been selling this nation out, but rather those who have had all the benefits that the wealthiest nation on earth has had to offer—the finest homes, the finest college education, and the finest jobs in government we can give.

This is glaringly true in the State Department. There the bright young men who are born with silver spoons in their mouths are the ones who have been worst. . . . In my opinion the State Department, which is one of the most important government departments, is thoroughly infested with communists.

I have in my hand 57 cases of individuals who would appear to be either card carrying members or certainly loyal to the Communist Party, but who nevertheless are still helping to shape our foreign policy. . . . One thing to remember in discussing the communists in our government is that we are not dealing with spies who get 30 pieces of silver to steal the blueprints of new weapons. We are dealing with a far more sinister type of activity because it permits the enemy to guide and shape our policy.

From Margaret Chase Smith, Speech in the Senate (1950)

Most of McCarthy's colleagues were cowed by his tactics. One who was not was Margaret Chase Smith of Maine, the Senate's only female member. On June 1, she delivered a brief speech, along with a Declaration of Conscience, signed by six other Republican senators.

The United States Senate has long enjoyed worldwide respect as the greatest deliberative body in the world. But recently that deliberative character has too often been debased to the level of a forum of hate and character assassination sheltered by the shield of congressional immunity. . . .

I think that it is high time for the United States Senate and its members to do some soul searching—for us to weigh our consciences—on the manner in which we are performing our duty to the people of America—on the manner in which we are using or abusing our individual powers and privileges. . . . I think that it is high time that we remembered; that the Constitution, as amended, speaks not only of the freedom of speech but also of trial by jury instead of trial by accusation.

Those of us who shout the loudest about Americanism in making character assassinations are all too frequently those who, by our own words and acts, ignore some of the basic principles of Americanism—

The right to criticize; The right to hold unpopular beliefs; The right to protest; The right of independent thought.

The exercise of these rights should not cost one single American citizen his reputation or his right to a livelihood nor should he be in danger of losing his reputation or livelihood merely because he happens to know some one who holds unpopular beliefs. Who of us doesn't? Otherwise none of us could call our souls our own. Otherwise thought control would have set in.

The American people are sick and tired of being afraid to speak their minds lest they be politically smeared as "Communists" or "Fascists" by their opponents. Freedom of speech is not what it used to be in America. It has been so abused by some that it is not exercised by others. The American people are sick and tired of seeing innocent people smeared and guilty people whitewashed.

The nation sorely needs a Republican victory. But I don't want to see the Republican Party ride to political victory on the Four Horsemen of Calumny—Fear, Ignorance, Bigotry and Smear. . . .

As a United States Senator, I am not proud of the way in which the Senate has been made a publicity platform for irresponsible sensationalism.

QUESTIONS

1. *What kind of social resentments are evident in McCarthy's speech?*

2. *What does Smith believe is the essence of freedom of speech?*

3. *What do these documents suggest about how the Cold War affected discussions of freedom in the early 1950s?*

McCarthy era were guilty of nothing more than holding unpopular beliefs and engaging in lawful political activities.

Anticommunism had many faces and purposes. A popular mass movement, it grew especially strong among ethnic groups like Polish-Americans, with roots in eastern European countries now dominated by the Soviet Union, and among American Catholics in general, who resented and feared communists' hostility to religion. Government agencies like the Federal Bureau of Investigation (FBI) used anticommunism to expand their power. Under director J. Edgar Hoover, the FBI developed files on thousands of American citizens, including political dissenters, homosexuals, and others, most of whom had no connection to communism. For business, anticommunism became part of a campaign to identify labor unions and government intervention in the economy with socialism. White supremacists employed anticommunism as a weapon against black civil rights. Upholders of sexual morality and traditional gender roles raised the cry of subversion against feminism and homosexuality, both supposedly responsible for eroding the country's fighting spirit.

Anticommunist groups and goals

Anticommunist Politics

At its height, from the late 1940s to around 1960, the anticommunist crusade powerfully structured American politics and culture. After launching the government's loyalty program in 1947, Truman had become increasingly alarmed at the excesses of the anticommunist crusade. He vetoed the McCarran Internal Security Bill of 1950, which required "subversive" groups to register with the government, allowed the denial of passports to their members, and authorized their deportation or detention on presidential order. But Congress quickly gave the measure the two-thirds majority necessary for it to become law.

McCarran Internal Security Bill of 1950

The **McCarran-Walter Act** of 1952, the first major piece of immigration legislation since 1924, also passed over the president's veto. Truman had called for replacing the quotas based on national origins with a more flexible system taking into account family reunion, labor needs, and political asylum. But the McCarran-Walter Act kept the quotas in place. It also authorized the deportation of immigrants identified as communists, even if they had become citizens. But the renewed fear of aliens sparked by the anticommunist crusade went far beyond communists. In 1954, the federal government launched Operation "Wetback," which employed the military to invade Mexican-American neighborhoods and round up and deport noncitizens. Within a year, some 1 million Mexicans had been deported. ("Wetback" is an insulting term sometimes directed at Mexican immigrants.)

Immigration quotas retained

Truman did secure passage of a 1950 law that added previously excluded self-employed and domestic workers to Social Security. Otherwise, however, the idea of expanding the New Deal welfare state faded. In its place, private welfare arrangements proliferated. The labor contracts of unionized workers established health insurance plans, automatic cost-of-living wage increases, paid vacations, and pension plans that supplemented Social Security. Western European governments provided these benefits to all citizens. In the United States, union members in major industries enjoyed them, but not the nonunionized majority of the population, a situation that created increasing inequality among laboring Americans.

The privatization of social benefits

Organized labor emerged as a major supporter of the foreign policy of the Cold War. Internal battles over the role of communists and their allies led to the purging of some of the most militant union leaders, often the ones most committed to advancing equal rights to women and racial minorities in the workplace.

Purging militant union leaders

Cold War Civil Rights

The civil rights movement also underwent a transformation. Although a few prominent black leaders, notably the singer and actor Paul Robeson and the veteran crusader for equality W. E. B. Du Bois, became outspoken critics of the Cold War, most felt they had no choice but to go along. The NAACP purged communists from local branches. When the government deprived Robeson of his passport and indicted Du Bois for failing to register as an agent of the Soviet Union, few prominent Americans, white or black, protested. (The charge against Du Bois was so absurd that even at the height of McCarthyism, the judge dismissed it.)

Black organizations and the Cold War

Black organizations embraced the language of the Cold War and used it for their own purposes. They insisted that by damaging the American image abroad, racial inequality played into the Russians' hands. Thus, they helped to cement Cold War ideology as the foundation of the political culture, while complicating the idea of American freedom.

American image abroad

President Truman, as noted above, had called for greater attention to civil rights in part to improve the American image abroad. All in all, however, the height of the Cold War was an unfavorable time to raise questions about the imperfections of American society. In 1947, two months after the Truman Doctrine speech, Undersecretary of State Dean Acheson delivered a major address defending the president's pledge to aid "free peoples" seeking to preserve their "democratic institutions." Acheson chose as his audience the Delta Council, an organization of Mississippi planters, bankers, and merchants. He seemed unaware that to make the case for the Cold War, he had ventured into what one historian has called the "American Siberia," a place of grinding poverty whose black population (70 percent of the total) enjoyed neither genuine freedom nor democracy. Most of the Delta's citizens were denied the very liberties supposedly endangered by communism.

The waning civil rights impulse

By 1948, the Truman administration's civil rights flurry had subsided. State and local laws banning discrimination in employment and housing remained largely unenforced. In 1952, the Democrats showed how quickly the issue had faded by nominating for president Adlai Stevenson of Illinois, a candidate with little interest in civil rights, with southern segregationist John Sparkman as his running mate.

Rising affluence

Time would reveal that the waning of the civil rights impulse was only temporary. Yet it came at a crucial moment—the late 1940s and early 1950s, when the United States experienced the greatest economic boom in its history. The rise of an "affluent society" transformed American life, opening new opportunities for tens of millions of white Americans in rapidly expanding suburbs. But it left blacks trapped in the declining rural areas of the South and urban ghettos of the North. The contrast between new opportunities and widespread prosperity for whites and continued discrimination for blacks would soon inspire a civil rights revolution and, with it, yet another redefinition of American freedom.

CHAPTER REVIEW AND ONLINE RESOURCES

REVIEW QUESTIONS

1. *What major ideological conflicts, security interests, and events brought about the Cold War?*

2. *President Truman referred to the Truman Doctrine and the Marshall Plan as "two halves of the same walnut." Explain the similarities and differences between these two aspects of containment.*

3. *How did the tendency of both the United States and the Soviet Union to see all international events through the lens of the Cold War lessen each country's ability to understand what was happening in various countries around the world?*

4. *Why did the United States not support movements for colonial independence around the world?*

5. *How did the government attempt to shape public opinion during the Cold War?*

6. *Explain the differences between the United States' and the Soviet Union's application of the UN Universal Declaration of Human Rights.*

7. *How did the anticommunist crusade affect organized labor in the postwar period?*

8. *What accounts for the Republican resurgence in these years?*

9. *What were the major components of Truman's Fair Deal? Which ones were implemented, and which ones were not?*

10. *How did the Cold War affect civil liberties in the United States?*

KEY TERMS

Cold War (p. 713)

containment (p. 713)

Long Telegram (p. 714)

iron curtain (p. 714)

Truman Doctrine (p. 714)

Marshall Plan (p. 716)

North Atlantic Treaty Organization (p. 717)

NSC-68 (p. 719)

Korean War (p. 721)

decolonization (p. 722)

totalitarianism (p. 722)

Fair Deal (p. 725)

Operation Dixie (p. 725)

Taft-Hartley Act (p. 726)

Dixiecrats (p. 728)

McCarthyism (p. 730)

Hollywood Ten (p. 731)

Army-McCarthy hearings (p. 733)

McCarran-Walter Act (p. 736)

Go to 🐰 INQUIZITIVE

To see what you know—and learn what you've missed—with person-alized feedback along the way.

Visit the *Give Me Liberty!* **Student Site** for primary source documents and images, interactive maps, author videos featuring Eric Foner, and more.

1946   *Mendez v. Westminster*

1947   Levittown development starts

1950   David Riesman's *The Lonely Crowd*

1952   United States detonates first hydrogen bomb

1953   Soviet Union detonates hydrogen bomb

1954   *Brown v. Board of Education*

       CIA-led Guatemalan coup

       Geneva Accords for Vietnam

1955   AFL and CIO merge

       Allen Ginsberg's *Howl*

1955–   Montgomery bus boycott
1956

1956   "Southern Manifesto"

       Start of interstate highway system

1957   Southern Christian Leadership Conference organized

       Integration of Little Rock's Central High School

       Sputnik launched

1958   National Defense Education Act

1959   Nixon-Khrushchev "kitchen debate"

1960   John F. Kennedy elected president

CHAPTER 24

AN AFFLUENT SOCIETY

★

1953 – 1960

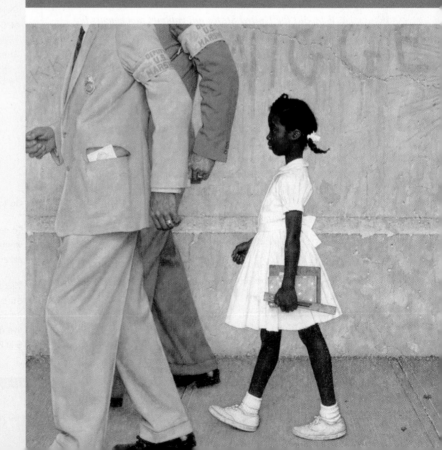

The Problem We All Live With. This 1964 painting by Norman Rockwell depicts federal marshals escorting six-year-old Ruby Bridges to kindergarten in New Orleans in 1960 in accordance with a court order to integrate the city's schools. Rockwell, intent on focusing on the child, presents the mob of angry onlookers only through their graffiti and tomatoes thrown against the wall, and does not show the faces of the marshals. Because of the decision to send her to the formerly white school, Bridges's father lost his job, and her grandparents, sharecroppers in Mississippi, were evicted from their land. In 2001, President Bill Clinton presented her with the Presidential Citizens Medal.

I n 1958, during a "thaw" in the Cold War, the United States and the Soviet Union agreed to exchange national exhibitions in order to allow citizens of each "superpower" to become acquainted with life in the other. The Soviet Exhibition, unveiled in New York City in June 1959, featured factory machinery, scientific advances, and other illustrations of how communism had modernized a backward country. The following month, the American National Exhibition opened in Moscow. A showcase of consumer goods and leisure equipment, complete with stereo sets, a movie theater, home appliances, and twenty-two different cars, the exhibit, *Newsweek* observed, hoped to demonstrate the superiority of "modern capitalism with its ideology of political and economic freedom." Yet the exhibit's real message was not freedom but consumption—or, to be more precise, the equating of the two. Vice President Richard Nixon opened the exhibit with an address entitled "What Freedom Means to Us." He spoke of the "extraordinarily high standard of living" in the United States, with its 56 million cars and 50 million television sets.

The Moscow exhibition became the site of a classic Cold War confrontation over the meaning of freedom—the "kitchen debate" between Nixon and Soviet premier Nikita Khrushchev. Nixon and Khrushchev engaged in unscripted debate, first in the kitchen of a model suburban ranch house, then in a futuristic "miracle kitchen" complete with a mobile robot that swept the floors. Supposedly the home of an average steelworker, the ranch house represented, Nixon declared, the mass enjoyment of American freedom within a suburban setting—freedom

FOCUS QUESTIONS

- *What were the main characteristics of the affluent society of the 1950s?*

- *How were the 1950s a period of consensus in both domestic policies and foreign affairs?*

- *What were the major thrusts of the civil rights movement in this period?*

- *What was the significance of the presidential election of 1960?*

Vice President Richard Nixon, with hands folded, and Soviet premier Nikita Khrushchev during the "kitchen debate," a discussion, among other things, of the meaning of freedom, which took place in 1959 at the American National Exposition in Moscow. Khrushchev makes a point while a woman demonstrates a washing machine.

AN AFFLUENT SOCIETY | **741**

of choice among products, colors, styles, and prices. It also implied a particular role for women. Throughout his exchanges with Khrushchev, Nixon used the words "women" and "housewives" interchangeably. His stance reflected the triumph during the 1950s of a conception of freedom centered on economic abundance and consumer choice within the context of traditional family life—a vision that seemed to offer far more opportunities for the "pursuit of happiness" to men than women.

THE GOLDEN AGE

The end of World War II was followed by what one scholar has called the "golden age" of capitalism, a period of economic expansion, stable prices, low unemployment, and rising standards of living that continued until 1973. Between 1946 and 1960, the American gross national product more than doubled. Much of the benefit flowed to ordinary citizens in rising wages. In every measurable way—diet, housing, income, education, recreation—most Americans lived better than their parents and grandparents had. The official poverty rate, 30 percent of all families in 1950, had declined to 22 percent a decade later (still, to be sure, representing more than one in five Americans).

Economic growth

Numerous innovations came into widespread use in these years, transforming Americans' daily lives. They included television, home air-conditioning, automatic dishwashers, inexpensive long-distance telephone calls, and jet air travel.

Between 1950 and 1973, the average real wages of manufacturing workers doubled. Wages rose faster for low-income than high-income Americans, lessening economic inequality. Significant numbers of blue-collar men were able to earn enough at an early age to marry and support a family. At the time, widespread affluence and the narrowing gap between rich and poor seemed to have become a permanent feature of American society, a model for other

FIGURE 24.1   Real Gross Domestic Product per Capita, 1790–2014

countries to follow. History would show that this was, in fact, an exceptional moment, made possible by government policies, a strong union movement, and the country's global economic dominance in the wake of World War II. When the long postwar boom ended in 1973, it would be succeeded by an even longer period of stagnant incomes for most Americans and increasing inequality.

A Changing Economy

Like other wars, the Cold War fueled U.S. industrial production and promoted a redistribution of the nation's population and economic resources. The West, especially the Seattle area, southern California, and the Rocky Mountain states, benefited enormously from government contracts for aircraft, guided missiles, and radar systems. The South became the home of numerous military bases and government-funded shipyards.

In retrospect, the 1950s appear as the last decade of the industrial age in the United States. Since then, the American economy has shifted rapidly toward services, education, information, finance, and entertainment, while employment in manufacturing has declined. Unions' very success in raising wages inspired employers to mechanize more and more elements of manufacturing in order to reduce labor costs. In 1956, for the first time in American history, white-collar workers outnumbered blue-collar factory and manual laborers.

Industrial strength

The decade witnessed an acceleration of the transformation of southern life that had begun during World War II. New tractors and harvesting machinery and a continuing shift from cotton production to less labor-intensive soybean and poultry raising reduced the need for farm workers. More than 3 million black and white hired hands and sharecroppers migrated out of the region. The large corporate farms of California, worked by Latino and Filipino migrant laborers, poured forth an endless supply of fruits and vegetables for the domestic and world markets. Items like oranges and orange juice, once luxuries, became an essential part of the American diet.

Regional changes

A Suburban Nation

The main engines of economic growth during the 1950s, however, were residential construction and spending on consumer goods. The postwar baby boom (discussed later) and the shift of population from cities to suburbs created an enormous demand for housing, television sets, home appliances, and cars.

Consumer demand

THE INTERSTATE HIGHWAY SYSTEM

Begun in 1956 and completed in 1993, the interstate highway system dramatically altered the American landscape and Americans' daily lives. It made possible more rapid travel by car and stimulated the growth of suburbs along its many routes.

Suburbs and the automobile

During the 1950s, the number of houses in the United States doubled, nearly all of them built in the suburbs that sprang up across the landscape. William and Alfred Levitt, who shortly after the war built the first **Levittown** on 1,200 acres of potato fields on Long Island near New York City, became the most famous suburban developers. Levittown's more than 10,000 houses were assembled quickly from prefabricated parts and priced well within the reach of most Americans. Levittown was soon home to 40,000 people. At the same time, suburbs required a new form of shopping center—the mall—to which people drove in their cars.

The automobile, the pivot on which suburban life turned, transformed the nation's daily life, just as the interstate highway system (discussed later) transformed Americans' travel habits, making possible long-distance vacationing by car and commuting to work from ever-increasing distances. The result was an altered American landscape, leading to the construction of motels, drive-in movie theaters, and roadside eating establishments.

A portrait of affluence: In this photograph by Alex Henderson, Steve Czekalinski, an employee of the DuPont Corporation, poses with his family and the food they consumed in a single year, 1951. The family spent $1,300 (around $12,000 in today's money) on food, including 699 bottles of milk, 578 pounds of meat, and 131 dozen eggs. Nowhere else in the world was food so available and inexpensive.

The first McDonald's fast food restaurant opened in Illinois in 1954. Within ten years, having been franchised by the California business-man Ray Kroc, approximately 700 McDonald's stands had been built, which had sold over 400 million hamburgers. The car symbolized the identification of freedom with individual mobility and private choice. Americans could imagine themselves as modern versions of western pioneers, able to leave behind urban crowds and workplace pressures for the "open road."

McDonald's

The Growth of the West

The modern West emerged in the postwar years. Unlike the 1930s, when most migrants to the West came from the South and the Dust Bowl states, all parts of the country now contributed to the region's growth. Federal spending on dams, highways, and military installations helped to fuel the flow of people. So did the pleasant climate of many parts of the region, and the diffusion of air-conditioning in warmer places such as Arizona and southern California. The rapid expansion of oil production (a result of the tremendous increase in automobile ownership) led to the explosive growth of urban centers connected to the oil industry such as Denver, Dallas, and Houston.

Ernst Haas's 1969 photograph of Albuquerque, New Mexico, could have been taken in any one of scores of American communities. As cities spread out, "strips," consisting of motels, gas stations, and nationally franchised businesses, became common. Meanwhile, older downtown business sections stagnated.

Indeed, it was California that became the most prominent symbol of the postwar suburban boom. Between World War II and 1975, more than 30 million Americans moved west of the Mississippi River. In 1963, California surpassed New York to become the nation's most populous state.

"Centerless" western cities like Houston, Phoenix, and Los Angeles differed greatly from traditional urban centers in the East. Rather than consisting of downtown business districts linked to residential neighborhoods by public transportation, western cities were decentralized clusters of single-family homes and businesses united by a web of highway. Life centered around the car; people drove to and from work and did their shopping at malls reachable only by driving. In other sections of the country as well, shopping shifted to suburban centers, and old downtown business districts stagnated. The spread of suburban homes created millions of new lawns. Today, more land is cultivated in grass than any agricultural crop in the United States.

Decentralized cities

The TV World

Thanks to television, images of middle-class life and advertisements for consumer goods blanketed the country. By the end of the 1950s, nearly nine of ten American families owned a TV set. Television replaced newspapers as the most common source of information about public events, and TV watching became the nation's leading leisure activity. Television changed Americans' eating habits (the frozen TV dinner, heated and eaten while diners watched a program, went on sale in 1954).

TV journalism and entertainment

With a few exceptions, like the Army-McCarthy hearings mentioned in the previous chapter, TV avoided controversy and projected a bland image of middle-class life. The dominant programs were quiz shows, westerns, and comedies set in suburban homes, like *Leave It to Beaver* and *The Adventures of Ozzie and Harriet*. Television also became the most effective advertising medium ever invented.

TV advertising

Women at Work and at Home

The emergence of suburbia placed pressure on the family—and especially on women—to live up to freedom's promise. After a sharp postwar drop in female employment, the number of women at work soon began to rise. By 1955, it exceeded the level during World War II. But the nature and aims of women's work had changed. The modern woman worked part-time to help support the family's middle-class lifestyle, not to help pull it out of poverty or to pursue personal fulfillment or an independent career.

**FIGURE 24.2
Average Daily
Television Viewing,
1950–1970**

1950
4 hrs. 36 mins.

1960
5 hrs. 6 mins.

1970
5 hrs. 54 mins.

Working women in 1960 earned, on average, only 60 percent of the income of men.

Despite the increasing numbers of wage-earning women, the suburban family's breadwinner was assumed to be male, while the wife remained at home. Films, TV shows, and advertisements portrayed marriage as the most important goal of American women. And during the 1950s, men and women married younger (at an average age of twenty-two for men and twenty for women), divorced less frequently than in the past, and had more children (3.2 per family). A **baby boom** that lasted into the mid-1960s followed the end of the war. At a time of low immigration, the American population rose by nearly 30 million (almost 20 percent) during the 1950s.

Like other forms of dissent, feminism seemed to have disappeared from American life or was widely dismissed as evidence of mental disorder. Prominent psychologists insisted that the unhappiness of individual women or even the desire to work for wages stemmed from a failure to accept the "maternal instinct."

Advertisers during the 1950s sought to convey the idea that women would enjoy their roles as suburban homemakers, as in this ad for a vacuum cleaner, which equates housework with a game of golf.

A Segregated Landscape

For millions of city dwellers, the suburban utopia fulfilled the dream, postponed by depression and war, of home ownership and middle-class incomes. The move to the suburbs also promoted Americanization, cutting residents off from urban ethnic communities and bringing them fully into the world of mass consumption. But if the suburbs offered a new site for the enjoyment of American freedom, they retained at least one familiar characteristic—rigid racial boundaries.

Suburbia has never been as uniform as either its celebrants or its critics claimed. There are upper-class suburbs, working-class suburbs, industrial suburbs, and "suburban" neighborhoods within city limits. But suburbia's racial uniformity was all too real. As late as the 1990s, nearly 90 percent of suburban whites lived in communities with non-white populations of less than 1 percent—the legacy of decisions by government, real-estate developers, banks, and residents.

During the postwar suburban boom, federal agencies continued to insure mortgages that barred resale of houses to non-whites, thereby financing housing segregation. Even after the Supreme Court in 1948 declared such provisions legally unenforceable, banks and private

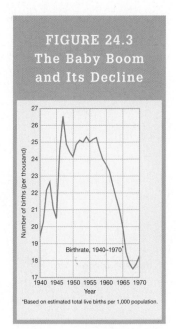

FIGURE 24.3
The Baby Boom and Its Decline

Birthrate, 1940–1970[*]

*Based on estimated total live births per 1,000 population.

Students at an East Harlem elementary school in 1947. Most have recently migrated from Puerto Rico to the mainland with their families, although some are probably children of the area's older Italian-American community.

developers barred non-whites from the suburbs. The government refused to subsidize their mortgages, except in segregated enclaves. The vast new communities built by the Levitts refused to allow blacks, including army veterans, to rent or purchase homes. A lawsuit forced Levitt to begin selling to non-whites in the 1960s, but by 1990, his Long Island community, with a population of 53,000, included only 127 black residents.

At the same time, under programs of **urban renewal**, cities demolished poor neighborhoods in city centers that occupied potentially valuable real estate. In their place, developers constructed retail centers and all-white middle-income housing complexes, and states built urban public universities like Wayne State in Detroit and the University of Illinois at Chicago. White residents displaced by urban renewal often moved to the suburbs. Non-whites, unable to do so, found housing in run-down city neighborhoods.

The Divided Society

Suburbanization hardened the racial lines of division in American life. Between 1950 and 1970, about 7 million white Americans left cities for the suburbs. Meanwhile, nearly 3 million blacks moved from the South to the North, greatly increasing the size of existing urban ghettos and creating entirely new ones. And half a million Puerto Ricans, mostly small coffee and tobacco farmers and agricultural laborers forced off the land when American sugar companies expanded their landholdings on the island, moved to the mainland.

Self-reinforced racial exclusion

The process of racial exclusion became self-reinforcing. Non-whites remained concentrated in manual and unskilled jobs, the result of employment discrimination and their virtual exclusion from educational opportunities at public and private universities, including those outside the South. As the white population and industrial jobs fled the old city centers for the suburbs, poorer blacks and Latinos remained trapped in urban ghettos, seen by many whites as places of crime, poverty, and welfare.

Religion and Anticommunism

Both Protestant and Roman Catholic religious leaders played crucial roles in the spread of anticommunism and Cold War culture. Official American values celebrated the nation's religiosity as opposed to "godless" communism. During the 1950s, a majority of Americans—the highest percentage in the nation's history—were affiliated with a church or synagogue. In 1954, to "strengthen our national resistance to communism," Congress added the words "under God" to the Pledge of Allegiance. In

Height of American religiosity

1957, **"In God We Trust"** was included on paper money. Big-budget Hollywood films like *The Ten Commandments* and *Ben Hur* celebrated early Judaism and Christianity. Leading clerics like Bishop Fulton J. Sheen of the Catholic Church and Protestant evangelist Billy Graham used radio and television to spread to millions a religious message heavily imbued with anticommunism. Communism, Graham declared, was not only an economic and political outlook but a religion—one "inspired, directed and motivated by the Devil himself."

Selling Free Enterprise

The economic content of Cold War freedom increasingly came to focus on consumer capitalism, or, as it was now universally known, "free enterprise." More than political democracy or freedom of speech, which many allies of the United States outside western Europe lacked, an economic system resting on private ownership united the nations of the Free World.

Free enterprise seemed an odd way of describing an economy in which a few large corporations dominated key sectors. Until well into the twentieth century, most ordinary Americans had been deeply suspicious of big business, associating it with images of robber barons who manipulated politics, suppressed economic competition, and treated their workers unfairly.

In 1953, 4.5 million Americans—only slightly more than in 1928—owned shares of stock. By the mid-1960s, the number had grown to 25 million. In the face of widespread abundance, who could deny that the capitalist marketplace embodied individual freedom or that poverty would soon be a thing of the past? "It was American Freedom," proclaimed *Life* magazine, "by which and through which this amazing achievement of wealth and power was fashioned."

The Libertarian Conservatives and the New Conservatives

During the 1950s, a group of thinkers began the task of reviving conservatism and reclaiming the idea of freedom from liberals. Although largely ignored outside their own immediate circle, they developed ideas that would define conservative thought for the next half-century. One was opposition to a strong national government, an outlook that had been given new political life in conservatives' bitter reaction against the New Deal. To these "libertarian" conservatives, freedom meant individual autonomy, limited government, and unregulated capitalism. These ideas had great appeal to conservative entrepreneurs, especially in the rapidly

An image from a booklet issued by the American Economic Foundation illustrates the linkage of anticommunism and religious faith during the Cold War. The hairy hand in the bottom half of the drawing represents the communist threat, which endangers religious freedom in the United States. Most of the booklet, however, dealt with the superiority of free enterprise to communism.

Opposition to strong national government

growing South and West, who desired to pursue their economic fortunes free of government regulation, high taxes, and labor unions.

A second strand of thought became increasingly prominent in the 1950s. Convinced that the Free World needed to arm itself morally and intellectually, not just militarily, for the battle against communism, "new conservatives" insisted that toleration of difference—a central belief of modern liberalism—offered no substitute for the search for absolute truth. The West, they warned, was suffering from moral decay, and they called for a return to a civilization based on values grounded in the Christian tradition and in timeless notions of good and evil. The "new conservatives" understood freedom as first and foremost a moral condition. It required a decision by independent men and women to lead virtuous lives or governmental action to force them to do so.

Freedom and morality

Here lay the origins of a division in conservative ranks that would persist into the twenty-first century. Unrestrained individual choice and moral virtue are radically different starting points from which to discuss freedom. Was the purpose of conservatism, one writer wondered, to create the "free man" or the "good man"? Libertarian conservatives spoke the language of progress and personal autonomy; the "new conservatives" emphasized tradition, community, and moral commitment. The former believed that too many barriers existed to the pursuit of individual liberty. The latter condemned an excess of individualism and a breakdown of common values.

Division in conservatism

Fortunately for conservatives, political unity often depends less on intellectual coherence than on the existence of a common foe. And two powerful enemies became focal points for the conservative revival—the Soviet Union abroad and the federal government at home. Republican control of the presidency did not lessen conservatives' hostility to the federal government, partly because they did not consider President Eisenhower one of their own.

THE EISENHOWER ERA

Ike and Nixon

Dwight D. Eisenhower

Dwight D. Eisenhower, or "Ike," as he was affectionately called, emerged from World War II as the military leader with the greatest political appeal, partly because his public image of fatherly warmth set him apart from other successful generals like the arrogant Douglas MacArthur. Eisenhower became convinced that Senator Robert A. Taft of Ohio, a leading contender for the Republican nomination, would lead the United States back toward isolationism. Eisenhower entered the contest and won the Republican nomination.

For his running mate, Eisenhower chose Richard Nixon of California, a World War II veteran who had made a name for himself with his vigorous anticommunism. Nixon won election to the U.S. Senate in 1950 in a campaign in which he suggested that the Democratic candidate, Congresswoman Helen Gahagan Douglas, had communist sympathies.

These tactics gave Nixon a lifelong reputation for opportunism and dishonesty. But Nixon was also a shrewd politician who pioneered efforts to transform the Republican Party's image from defender of business to champion of the "forgotten man"—the hardworking citizen burdened by heavy taxation and unresponsive government bureaucracies. In using populist language to promote free market economics, Nixon helped to lay the foundation for the triumph of conservatism a generation later.

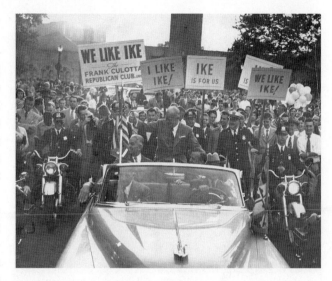

Dwight D. Eisenhower's popularity was evident at this appearance in Baltimore during the 1952 presidential campaign.

The 1952 Campaign

Television was beginning to transform politics by allowing candidates to bring carefully crafted images directly into Americans' living rooms. The 1952 campaign became the first to make extensive use of TV ads. Parties, one observer complained, were "selling the president like toothpaste."

More important to the election's outcome, however, was Eisenhower's popularity (invoked in the Republican campaign slogan "I Like Ike") and the public's weariness with the Korean War. Ike's pledge to "go to Korea" in search of peace signaled his intention to bring the conflict to an end. He won a resounding victory over the Democratic candidate, Adlai Stevenson. Four years later, Eisenhower again defeated Stevenson by an even wider margin. His popularity, however, did not extend to his party. Republicans won a razor-thin majority in Congress in 1952, but Democrats regained control in 1954 and retained it for the rest of the decade. In 1956, Eisenhower became the first president to be elected without his party controlling either house of Congress.

During the 1950s, voters at home and abroad seemed to find reassurance in selecting familiar, elderly leaders to govern them. At age sixty-two, Eisenhower was one of the oldest men ever elected president. But he seemed positively youthful compared with Winston Churchill,

A poster for Adlai Stevenson, Democratic candidate for president in 1952. The party's main argument, it seems, was that Republican victory would usher in a return of the Great Depression. Stevenson was soundly defeated by Dwight D. Eisenhower.

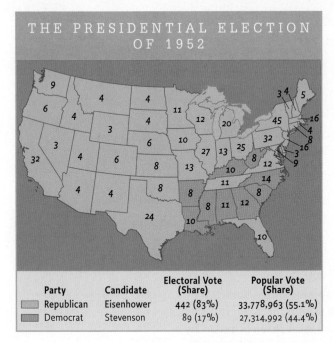

THE PRESIDENTIAL ELECTION OF 1952

Party	Candidate	Electoral Vote (Share)	Popular Vote (Share)
Republican	Eisenhower	442 (83%)	33,778,963 (55.1%)
Democrat	Stevenson	89 (17%)	27,314,992 (44.4%)

who returned to office as prime minister of Great Britain at age seventy-seven; Charles De Gaulle, who assumed the presidency of France at sixty-eight; and Konrad Adenauer, who served as chancellor of West Germany from age seventy-three until well into his eighties. In retrospect, Eisenhower's presidency seems almost uneventful, at least in domestic affairs—an interlude between the bitter party battles of the Truman administration and the social upheavals of the 1960s.

Modern Republicanism

With a Republican serving as president for the first time in twenty years, the tone in Washington changed. Wealthy businessmen dominated Eisenhower's cabinet. Defense Secretary Charles Wilson, the former president of General Motors, made the widely publicized statement: "What is good for the country is good for General Motors, and vice versa." A champion of the business community and a fiscal conservative, Ike worked to scale back government spending, including the military budget. But although right-wing Republicans saw his victory as an invitation to roll back the New Deal, Eisenhower realized that such a course would be disastrous. "Should any political party attempt to abolish Social Security, unemployment insurance, and eliminate labor laws and farm programs," he declared, "you would not hear of that party again in our political history."

Scaling back government spending

Eisenhower called his domestic agenda Modern Republicanism. It aimed to sever his party's identification in the minds of many Americans with the Great Depression. The core New Deal programs not only remained in place but expanded.

Accepting the New Deal

Eisenhower presided over the largest public-works enterprise in American history, the building of the 41,000-mile **interstate highway system**. As noted in the previous chapter, Cold War arguments—especially the need to provide rapid exit routes from cities in the event of nuclear war—justified this multibillion-dollar project. But automobile manufacturers, oil companies, suburban builders, and construction unions had very practical reasons for supporting highway construction regardless of any Soviet threat. When the Soviets launched *Sputnik*, the first artificial

Public works

earth satellite, in 1957, the administration responded with the **National Defense Education Act**, which for the first time offered direct federal funding to higher education.

All in all, rather than dismantling the New Deal, Eisenhower's Modern Republicanism consolidated and legitimized it. By accepting its basic premises, he ensured that its continuation no longer depended on Democratic control of the presidency.

Legitimizing the New Deal

The Social Contract

The 1950s also witnessed an easing of the labor conflict of the two previous decades. The passage of the Taft-Hartley Act in 1947 (discussed in the previous chapter) had reduced labor militancy. In 1955, the AFL and CIO merged to form a single organization representing 35 percent of all nonagricultural workers. In leading industries, labor and management hammered out what has been called a new **social contract**. Unions signed long-term agreements that left decisions regarding capital investment, plant location, and output in management's hands. Employers stopped trying to eliminate existing unions and granted wage increases and fringe benefits such as private pension plans, health insurance, and automatic cost-of-living adjustments to pay.

Labor and management cooperation

Unionized workers shared fully in 1950s prosperity. Although the social contract did not apply to the majority of workers, who did not belong to unions, it did bring benefits to those who labored in nonunion jobs. For example, trade unions in the 1950s and 1960s were able to use their political power to win a steady increase in the minimum wage, which was earned mostly by nonunion workers at the bottom of the employment pyramid. But the majority of workers did not enjoy anything close to the wages, benefits, and job security of unionized workers in such industries as automobiles and steel.

Nonunion workers

By the end of the 1950s, the social contract was weakening. In 1959, the steel industry sought to tighten work rules and limit wage increases in an attempt to boost profits battered by a recession that hit two years earlier. The plan sparked a strike of 500,000 steelworkers, which successfully beat back the proposed changes.

Massive Retaliation

Soon after he entered office, Eisenhower approved an armistice that ended fighting in Korea. But this failed to ease international tensions. Ike took office at a time when the Cold War had entered an extremely dangerous phase. In 1952, the United States exploded the first hydrogen bomb—a

The hydrogen bomb

weapon far more powerful than those that had devastated Hiroshima and Nagasaki. The following year, the Soviets matched this achievement. Both sides feverishly developed long-range bombers capable of delivering weapons of mass destruction around the world.

John Foster Dulles

A professional soldier, Ike hated war, which he viewed as a tragic waste. "Every gun that is made," he said in 1953, "every warship launched . . . signifies a theft from those who hunger and are not fed." But his secretary of state, John Foster Dulles, was a grim Cold Warrior. In 1954, Dulles announced an updated version of the doctrine of containment. **Massive retaliation**, as it was called, declared that any Soviet attack on an American ally would be countered by a nuclear assault on the Soviet Union itself.

Fear of MAD

Massive retaliation ran the risk that any small conflict, or even a miscalculation, could escalate into a war that would destroy both the United States and the Soviet Union. The reality that all-out war would result in "mutual assured destruction" (or MAD, in military shorthand) did succeed in making both great powers cautious in their direct dealings with one another. But it also inspired widespread fear of impending nuclear war. Government programs encouraging Americans to build bomb shelters in their backyards and school drills that trained children to hide under their desks in the event of an atomic attack aimed to convince Americans that nuclear war was survivable.

Ike and the Russians

A man helps his daughter into a backyard bomb shelter in Garden City, Long Island, New York, in a photograph from 1955. Manufacturers of such shelters assured purchasers that occupants could survive for five days after a nuclear attack.

The end of the Korean War and the death of Stalin, both of which occurred in 1953, convinced Eisenhower that rather than being blind zealots, the Soviets were reasonable and could be dealt with in conventional diplomatic terms. In 1955, Ike met in Geneva, Switzerland, with Nikita Khrushchev, the new Soviet leader, at the first "summit" conference since Potsdam a decade earlier. The following year, Khrushchev delivered a speech to the Communist Party Congress in Moscow that detailed Stalin's crimes, including purges of political opponents numbering in the millions.

Khrushchev's call in the same 1956 speech for "peaceful coexistence" with the United States raised the possibility of an easing of the Cold War. The "thaw" was abruptly shaken that fall, however, when Soviet troops put down an anticommunist uprising in Hungary. Eisenhower refused to extend aid to the Hungarian rebels, an indication that he believed it impossible to "roll back" Soviet domination of eastern Europe.

In 1958, the two superpowers agreed to a voluntary halt to the testing of nuclear weapons. The pause lasted until 1961. It had been demanded by the National Committee for a Sane Nuclear Policy, which publicized the danger to public health posed by radioactive fallout from nuclear tests.

But the spirit of cooperation ended abruptly in 1960, when the Soviets shot down an American U-2 spy plane over their territory. Eisenhower first denied that the plane had been involved in espionage and refused to apologize even after the Russians produced the captured pilot. The incident torpedoed another planned summit meeting.

The Emergence of the Third World

Even as Europe, where the Cold War began, settled into what appeared to be a permanent division between a communist East and a capitalist West, an intense rivalry, which sometimes took a military form, persisted in what came to be called the Third World. The term was invented to describe developing countries aligned with neither of the two Cold War powers and desirous of finding their own model of development between Soviet centralized economic planning and free market capitalism. But none of these countries could avoid being strongly affected by the political, military, and economic contest of the Cold War.

Nonaligned developing countries

The post–World War II era witnessed the crumbling of European empires. Decolonization began when India and Pakistan (the latter carved out of India to give Muslims their own nation) achieved independence in 1947. Ten years later, Britain's Gold Coast colony in West Africa emerged as the independent nation of Ghana. Other new nations—including Indonesia, Malaysia, Nigeria, Kenya, and Tanzania—soon followed.

Decolonization begins

The Soviet Union strongly supported the dissolution of Europe's overseas empires, and communists participated in movements for colonial independence. Most of the new Third World nations resisted alignment with either major power bloc, hoping to remain neutral in the Cold War.

By the end of the 1950s, much of the focus of the Cold War shifted to the Third World. The policy of containment easily slid over into opposition to any government, whether communist or not, that seemed to threaten American strategic or economic interests. Jacobo Arbenz Guzmán in Guatemala and Mohammed Mossadegh in Iran were elected, homegrown nationalists, not agents of Moscow. But they were determined to reduce foreign corporations' control over their countries' economies. Arbenz embarked on a sweeping land-reform policy that threatened the domination of Guatemala's economy by the American-owned United Fruit Company. Mossadegh nationalized the Anglo-Iranian Oil Company, whose refinery in Iran was Britain's largest remaining overseas asset. In 1953 and 1954, the Central Intelligence Agency organized the ouster of both governments—a clear violation of the UN Charter, which barred a member state from taking military action against another except in self-defense.

Containment

In 1956, Israel, France, and Britain—without prior consultation with the United States—invaded Egypt after the country's nationalist leader, Gamal Abdel Nasser, nationalized the Suez Canal, jointly owned by Britain and France. A furious Eisenhower forced them to abandon the invasion. After the Suez fiasco, the United States moved to replace Britain as the major Western power in the Middle East.

Origins of the Vietnam War

In Vietnam, the expulsion of the Japanese in 1945 led not to independence but to a French military effort to preserve France's Asian empire against Ho Chi Minh's nationalist forces. Anticommunism led the United States into deeper and deeper involvement. Following a policy initiated by Truman, the Eisenhower administration funneled billions of dollars in aid to bolster French efforts. By the early 1950s, the United States was paying four-fifths of the cost of the war. Wary of becoming bogged down in another land war in Asia immediately after Korea, however, Ike declined to send in American troops when France requested them to avert defeat in 1954, leaving France no alternative but to agree to Vietnamese independence.

The military junta installed in Guatemala by the CIA in 1954 enters Guatemala City in a Jeep driven by CIA agent Carlos Castillo Armas. Although hailed by the Eisenhower administration as a triumph for freedom, the new government suppressed democracy in Guatemala and embarked on a murderous campaign to stamp out opposition.

Geneva agreements

Issued from a peace conference in 1954, the **Geneva Accords** divided Vietnam temporarily into northern and southern districts, with elections scheduled for 1956 to unify the country. But the staunchly anticommunist southern leader Ngo Dinh Diem, urged on by the United States, refused to hold elections, which would almost certainly have resulted in a victory for Ho Chi Minh's communists. American aid poured into South Vietnam in order to bolster the Diem regime. By the time Eisenhower left office in 1961, Diem nevertheless faced a full-scale guerrilla revolt by the communist-led National Liberation Front.

U.S. interventions

Little by little, the United States was becoming accustomed to intervention, both open and secret, in far-flung corners of the world. Despite the Cold War rhetoric of freedom, American leaders seemed more comfortable dealing with reliable military regimes than democratic governments. A series of military governments succeeded Arbenz in Guatemala. The shah of Iran replaced Mossadegh and remained in office until 1979 as one of the world's most tyrannical rulers, until his overthrow in a revolution led by the fiercely anti-American radical Islamist Ayatollah Khomeini. In Vietnam, the American decision to prop up Diem's regime laid the groundwork for what would soon become the most disastrous military involvement in American history.

Mass Society and Its Critics

The fatherly Eisenhower seemed the perfect leader for the placid society of the 1950s. Consensus was the dominant ideal in an era in which McCarthyism had defined criticism of the social and economic order as disloyalty and most Americans located the enjoyment of freedom in private pleasures rather than the public sphere. Even *Life* magazine commented that American freedom might be in greater danger from "disuse" than from communist subversion.

Dissenting voices could be heard. The sociologist C. Wright Mills challenged the self-satisfied vision of democratic pluralism that dominated mainstream social science in the 1950s. Mills wrote of a "power elite"—an interlocking directorate of corporate leaders, politicians, and military men whose domination of government and society had made political democracy obsolete. Freedom, Mills insisted, rested on the ability "to formulate the available choices," and this most Americans were effectively denied.

Other writers worried that modern mass society inevitably produced loneliness and anxiety, causing mankind to yearn for stability and authority, not freedom. In *The Lonely Crowd* (1950), the decade's most influential work of social analysis, the sociologist David Riesman described Americans as "other-directed" conformists who lacked the inner resources to lead

Commuters returning from work in downtown Chicago, leaving the railroad station at suburban Park Forest, Illinois, in 1953. Social critics of the 1950s claimed that Americans had become "organization men," too conformist to lead independent lives.

The Lonely Crowd

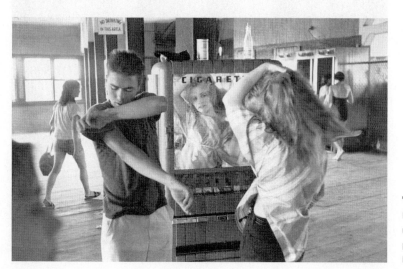

Rebels without a cause. Teenage members of a youth gang, photographed at Coney Island, Brooklyn, in the late 1950s.

Elvis Presley's gyrating hips appealed to teenagers but alarmed many adults during the 1950s.

Rock and roll

A poetry meeting at a Beat coffeehouse in New York City, photographed in 1959, where poets, artists, and others who rejected 1950s mainstream culture gathered.

truly independent lives. Other social critics charged that corporate bureaucracies had transformed employees into "organization men" incapable of independent thought.

William Whyte's *The Organization Man* (1956) and Vance Packard's *The Hidden Persuaders* (1957), which criticized the monotony of modern work, the emptiness of suburban life, and the pervasive influence of advertising, created the vocabulary for an assault on the nation's social values that lay just over the horizon.

Rebels without a Cause

The social critics did not offer a political alternative or have any real impact on the parties or government. Nor did other stirrings of dissent. With teenagers a growing part of the population thanks to the baby boom, the rise of a popular culture geared to the emerging youth market suggested that significant generational tensions lay beneath the bland surface of 1950s life. The 1955 films *Blackboard Jungle* and *Rebel without a Cause* (the latter starring James Dean as an aimlessly rebellious youth) highlighted the alienation of at least some young people from the world of adult respectability. These works helped to spur a mid-1950s panic about juvenile delinquency.

Cultural life during the 1950s seemed far more daring than politics. Teenagers wore leather jackets and danced to rock-and-roll music that brought the hard-driving rhythms and sexually provocative movements of black musicians and dancers to enthusiastic young white audiences.

They made Elvis Presley, a rock-and-roll singer with an openly sexual performance style, an immensely popular entertainment celebrity.

In New York City and San Francisco, as well as college towns like Madison, Wisconsin, and Ann Arbor, Michigan, **the Beats**, a small group of poets and writers, railed against mainstream culture. "I saw the best minds of my generation destroyed by madness, starving hysterical naked," wrote the Beat poet Allen Ginsberg in *Howl* (1955), a brilliant protest against materialism and conformism written while the author was under the influence of hallucinogenic drugs. Ginsberg became nationally known when San Francisco police in 1956 confiscated his book and arrested bookstore owners for selling an obscene work. (A judge later overturned the ban on the grounds that *Howl* possessed redeeming social value.) Rejecting the work ethic, the "desperate materialism" of the suburban middle class, and the militarization of American life by the Cold War, the Beats celebrated impulsive action, immediate pleasure (often enhanced by drugs), and sexual experimentation. Despite Cold War slogans, they insisted, personal and political repression, not freedom, were the hallmarks of American society.

Allen Ginsberg

Rejecting repressive society

THE FREEDOM MOVEMENT

Not until the 1960s would young white rebels find their cause, as the seeds of dissent planted by the social critics and Beats flowered in an outpouring of political activism, new attitudes toward sexuality, and a full-fledged generational rebellion. A more immediate challenge to the complacency of the 1950s arose from the twentieth century's greatest citizens' movement—the black struggle for equality.

Origins of the Movement

Today, with the birthday of Martin Luther King Jr. a national holiday and the struggles of Montgomery, Little Rock, Birmingham, and Selma celebrated as heroic episodes in the history of freedom, it is easy to forget that at the time, the civil rights revolution came as a great surprise. Few predicted the emergence of the southern mass movement for civil rights.

With blacks' traditional allies on the left decimated by McCarthyism, most union leaders unwilling to challenge racial inequalities within their own ranks, and the NAACP concentrating on court battles, new constituencies and new tactics were sorely needed. The movement found in the southern black church the organizing power for a militant, nonviolent assault on segregation.

The southern black church

The United States in the 1950s was still a segregated, unequal society. Half of the nation's black families lived in poverty. In the South, evidence of Jim Crow abounded—in separate public institutions and the signs "white" and "colored" at entrances to buildings, train carriages, drinking fountains, restrooms, and the like. In the North and West, the law did not require segregation, but custom barred blacks from many colleges, hotels, and restaurants, and from most suburban housing. Las Vegas, Nevada, for example, was as strictly segregated as any southern city. Hotels and casinos did not admit blacks except in the most menial jobs. Lena Horne, Sammy Davis Jr., Louis Armstrong, and other black entertainers played the hotel-casinos on the "strip" but could not stay as guests where they performed.

The persistence of Jim Crow

In 1950, seventeen southern and border states and Washington, D.C., had laws requiring the racial segregation of public schools, and several others permitted local districts to impose it. In northern communities housing patterns and school district lines created de facto segregation—separation in fact if not in law. Few white Americans felt any urgency about confronting racial inequality.

Legal or de facto segregation

The Legal Assault on Segregation

With the Eisenhower administration reluctant to address the issue, it fell to the courts to confront the problem of racial segregation. In the Southwest, the **League of United Latin American Citizens** (LULAC), the equivalent of the NAACP, challenged restrictive housing, employment discrimination, and the segregation of Latino students. It won an impor-

LULAC and Mendez v. Westminster

A segregated school in West Memphis, Arkansas, photographed for *Life* magazine in 1949. Education in the South was separate but hardly equal.

tant victory in 1946 in the case of *Mendez v. Westminster*, when a federal court ordered the schools of Orange County, California, desegregated. In response, the state legislature repealed all school laws requiring racial segregation. The governor who signed the measure, Earl Warren, had presided over the internment of Japanese-Americans during World War II as the state's attorney general. After the war, he became convinced that racial inequality had no place in American life. When Chief Justice Fred Vinson died in 1953, Eisenhower appointed Earl Warren to replace him on the U.S. Supreme Court.

Desegregation in California

For years, the NAACP, under the leadership of attorneys Charles Hamilton Houston and Thurgood Marshall, had pressed legal challenges to the "separate but equal" doctrine laid down by the Court in 1896 in *Plessy v. Ferguson* (see Chapter 17). At first, the NAACP sought to gain admission to white institutions of higher learning for which no black equivalent existed. In 1938, the Supreme Court ordered the University of Missouri Law School to admit Lloyd Gaines, a black student, because the state had no such school for blacks. Missouri responded by setting up a segregated law school, satisfying the courts. But in 1950, the Supreme Court unanimously ordered Heman Sweatt admitted to the University of Texas Law School even though the state had established a "school" for him in a basement containing three classrooms and no library.

Thurgood Marshall and the NAACP

The *Brown* Case

Marshall now launched a frontal assault on segregation itself. He brought the NAACP's support to local cases that had arisen when black parents challenged unfair school policies. For parents to do so required remarkable courage. In Clarendon County, South Carolina, Levi Pearson, a black farmer who brought a lawsuit on behalf of his children, saw his house burned to the ground. The Clarendon case attacked not segregation itself but the unequal funding of schools. Black children attended class in buildings with no running water or indoor toilets and were not provided with buses to transport them to classes. Five such cases from four states and the District of Columbia were combined in a single appeal that reached the Supreme Court late in 1952.

When cases are united, they are listed alphabetically and the first case gives the entire decision its name. In this instance, the first case arose from a state outside the old Confederacy. Oliver Brown went to court because his daughter, a third grader, was forced to walk across dangerous railroad tracks each morning rather than being allowed to attend a nearby school restricted to whites. His lawsuit became ***Brown v. Board of Education*** of *Topeka, Kansas.*

Linda Brown's parents sued the school board of Topeka, Kansas, demanding that it admit their daughter to a school near her home restricted to whites, rather than requiring her to walk across dangerous railroad tracks each day, as in this photograph, to attend a black school. The result was the Supreme Court's landmark *Brown* decision outlawing school segregation.

Thurgood Marshall decided that the time had come to attack the "separate but equal" doctrine itself. Even with the same funding and facilities, he insisted, segregation was inherently unequal because it stigmatized one group of citizens as unfit to associate with others. In its legal brief, the Eisenhower administration did not directly support Marshall's position, but it urged the justices to consider "the problem of racial discrimination . . . in the context of the present world struggle between freedom and tyranny." Other peoples, it noted, "cannot understand how such a practice can exist in a country which professes to be a staunch supporter of freedom, justice, and democracy."

The Warren Court

The new chief justice, Earl Warren, managed to create unanimity on a divided Court, some of whose members disliked segregation but feared that a decision to outlaw it would spark widespread violence. On May 17, 1954, Warren himself read aloud the decision, only eleven pages long. Segregation in public education, he concluded, violated the equal protection of the laws guaranteed by the Fourteenth Amendment. "In the field of education, the doctrine of 'separate but equal' has no place. Separate educational facilities are inherently unequal."

The decision did not order immediate implementation but instead called for hearings as to how segregated schooling should be dismantled. But *Brown* marked the emergence of the Warren Court as an active agent of social change. And it inspired a wave of optimism that discrimination would soon disappear.

The Montgomery Bus Boycott

Brown did not cause the modern civil rights movement, which, as noted in the previous two chapters, began during World War II and continued in cities like New York after the war. But the decision did ensure that when the movement resumed after waning in the early 1950s, it would have the backing of the federal courts. Mass action against Jim Crow soon reappeared. On December 1, 1955, Rosa Parks, a black tailor's assistant who had just completed her day's work in a Montgomery, Alabama, department store, refused to surrender her seat on a city bus to a white rider, as required by local law. Parks's arrest sparked a yearlong **Montgomery bus boycott**, the beginning of the mass phase of the civil rights movement in the South. In 2000, *Time* magazine named Rosa Parks one of the 100 most significant persons of the twentieth century.

Parks is widely remembered today as a "seamstress with tired feet," a symbol of ordinary blacks' determination to resist the daily injustices and indignities of the Jim Crow South. In fact, her life makes clear that the civil

The mug shot of Rosa Parks taken in December 1955 at a Montgomery, Alabama, police station after she was arrested for refusing to give up her seat on a city bus to a white passenger.

rights revolution built on earlier struggles. Parks was a veteran of black politics. During the 1930s, she took part in meetings protesting the conviction of the Scottsboro Boys. She served for many years as secretary to E. D. Nixon, the local leader of the NAACP. In 1943, she tried to register to vote, only to be turned away because she supposedly failed a literacy test. After two more attempts, Parks succeeded in becoming one of the few blacks in Montgomery able to cast a ballot.

Rosa Parks

When news of Parks's arrest spread, hundreds of blacks gathered in a local church and vowed to refuse to ride the buses until accorded equal treatment. For 381 days, despite legal harassment and occasional violence, black maids, janitors, teachers, and students walked to their destinations or rode an informal network of taxis. Finally, in November 1956, the Supreme Court ruled segregation in public transportation unconstitutional. The boycott ended in triumph.

Successful boycott

The Daybreak of Freedom

The Montgomery bus boycott marked a turning point in postwar American history. It launched the movement for racial justice as a nonviolent crusade based in the black churches of the South. It gained the support of northern liberals and focused unprecedented and unwelcome international attention on the country's racial policies. And it marked the emergence of the twenty-six-year-old Martin Luther King Jr., who had recently arrived in Montgomery to become pastor of a Baptist church, as the movement's national symbol. On the night of the first protest meeting, King's call to action electrified the audience: "We, the disinherited of this land, we who have been oppressed so long, are tired of going through the long night of captivity. And now we are reaching out for the daybreak of freedom and justice and equality."

The rise of Martin Luther King Jr.

From the beginning, the language of freedom pervaded the black movement. It resonated in the speeches of civil rights leaders and in the hand-lettered placards of the struggle's foot soldiers. During the summer of 1964, when civil rights activists established "freedom schools" for black children across Mississippi, lessons began with students being asked to define the word. Some gave specific answers ("going to public libraries"), some more abstract ("standing up for your rights"). Some insisted that freedom meant legal equality, others saw it as liberation from years of deference to and fear of whites. "Freedom of the mind," wrote one, was the greatest freedom of all.

For adults as well, freedom had many meanings. It meant enjoying the political rights and economic opportunities taken for granted by whites.

The movement and freedom

It required eradicating historic wrongs such as segregation, disenfranchisement, confinement to low-wage jobs, and the ever-present threat of violence. It meant the right to be served at lunch counters and downtown department stores, central locations in the consumer culture, and to be addressed as "Mr.," "Miss," and "Mrs.," rather than "boy" and "auntie."

The Leadership of King

"I Have a Dream"

In King's soaring oratory, the protesters' understandings of freedom fused into a coherent whole. His most celebrated oration, the "I Have a Dream" speech of 1963, began by invoking the unfulfilled promise of emancipation ("one hundred years later, the Negro still is not free") and closed with a cry borrowed from a black spiritual: "Free at last! Free at last! Thank God Almighty, we are free at last!"

Peaceful civil disobedience

King presented the case for black rights in a vocabulary that merged the black experience with that of the nation. Having studied the writings of Henry David Thoreau and Mahatma Gandhi on peaceful civil disobedience, King outlined a philosophy of struggle in which evil must be met with good, hate with Christian love, and violence with peaceful demands for change.

Echoing Christian themes derived from his training in the black church, King's speeches resonated deeply in both black communities and the broader culture. He repeatedly invoked the Bible to preach justice and forgiveness. Like Frederick Douglass before him, King appealed to white America by stressing the protesters' love of country and devotion to national values. If Africa was gaining its freedom, he asked, why must black America lag behind?

Massive Resistance

Southern Christian Leadership Conference

Buoyed by success in Montgomery, King in 1956 took the lead in forming the **Southern Christian Leadership Conference**, a coalition of black ministers and civil rights activists, to press for desegregation. But despite the movement's success in popular mobilization, the fact that Montgomery's city fathers agreed to the boycott's demands only after a Supreme Court ruling indicated that without national backing, local action might not be enough to overturn Jim Crow. The white South's refusal to accept the *Brown* decision reinforced the conviction that black citizens could not gain their constitutional rights without Washington's intervention. This was not immediately forthcoming. When the Supreme Court finally issued its implementation ruling in 1955, the justices declared that desegregation should proceed "with all deliberate speed." This vague formulation unintentionally encouraged a campaign of "massive resistance" that paralyzed civil rights progress in much of the South.

In 1956, 96 of 106 southern congressmen—and every southern senator except Lyndon B. Johnson of Texas and Albert Gore and Estes Kefauver of Tennessee—signed a **Southern Manifesto**, denouncing the *Brown* decision as a "clear abuse of judicial power," and calling for resistance to "forced integration" by "any lawful means." State after state passed laws to block desegregation. Virginia pioneered the strategy of closing any public schools ordered to desegregate and offering funds to enable white pupils, but not black, to attend private institutions. Prince Edward County, Virginia, shut its schools entirely in 1959; not until 1964 did the Supreme Court order them reopened.

A women's demonstration against racial integration in Poolesville, Maryland, 1956.

Eisenhower and Civil Rights

The federal government tried to remain aloof from the black struggle. Thanks to the efforts of Senate majority leader Lyndon B. Johnson, who hoped to win liberal support for a run for president in 1960, Congress in 1957 passed the first national civil rights law since Reconstruction. It targeted the denial of black voting rights in the South, but with weak

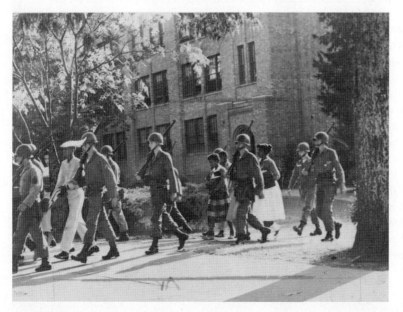

Federal troops escort black children to Little Rock Central High School, enforcing a court order for integration in 1957.

VOICES OF FREEDOM

From Martin Luther King Jr., Speech at Montgomery, Alabama (December 5, 1955)

On the evening of Rosa Parks's arrest for refusing to give up her seat on a Montgomery bus to a white passenger, a mass rally of local African-Americans decided to boycott city buses in protest. In his speech to the gathering, the young Baptist minister Martin Luther King Jr. invoked Christian and American ideals of justice and democracy—themes he would strike again and again during his career as the leading national symbol of the civil rights struggle.

We are here this evening . . . because first and foremost we are American citizens, and we are determined to apply our citizenship to the fullness of its means. We are here also because of our love for democracy. . . . Just the other day . . . one of the finest citizens in Montgomery—not one of the finest Negro citizens but one of the finest citizens in Montgomery—was taken from a bus and carried to jail and arrested because she refused to give her seat to a white person. . . .

Mrs. Rosa Parks is a fine person. And since it had to happen I'm happy that it happened to a person like Mrs. Parks, for nobody can doubt the boundless outreach of her integrity! Nobody can doubt the height of her character, nobody can doubt that depth of her Christian commitment and devotion to the teachings of Jesus. And I'm happy since it had to happen, it happened to a person that nobody can call a disturbing factor in the community. Mrs. Parks is a fine Christian person, unassuming, and yet there is integrity and character there. And just because she refused to get up, she was arrested.

I want to say, that we are not here advocating violence. We have never done that. . . . We believe in the teachings of Jesus. The only weapon that we have in our hands this evening is the weapon of protest. . . . There will be no white persons pulled out of their homes and taken out to some distant road and lynched. . . .

We are not wrong in what we are doing. If we are wrong, then the Supreme Court of this nation is wrong. If we are wrong, the Constitution of the United States is wrong. If we are wrong, God Almighty is wrong. . . . If we are wrong, justice is a lie. . . .

We, the disinherited of this land, we who have been oppressed so long, are tired of going through the long night of captivity. And now we are reaching out for the daybreak of freedom and justice and equality. . . . Right here in Montgomery when the history books are written in the future, somebody will have to say, "There lived a race of people, a black people, . . . a people who had the moral courage to stand up for their rights. And thereby they injected a new meaning into the veins of history and of civilization."

From The Southern Manifesto (1956)

Drawn up early in 1956 and signed by ninety-six southern members of the Senate and House of Representatives, the Southern Manifesto repudiated the Supreme Court decision in *Brown v. Board of Education* and offered support to the campaign of resistance in the South.

The unwarranted decision of the Supreme Court in the public school cases is now bearing the fruit always produced when men substitute naked power for established law. . . .

We regard the decisions of the Supreme Court in the school cases as a clear abuse of judicial power. It climaxes a trend in the Federal Judiciary undertaking to legislate, in derogation [violation] of the authority of Congress, and to encroach upon the reserved rights of the States and the people.

The original Constitution does not mention education. Neither does the 14th Amendment nor any other amendment. The debates preceding the submission of the 14th Amendment clearly show that there was no intent that it should affect the system of education maintained by the States.

In the case of *Plessy v. Ferguson* in 1896 the Supreme Court expressly declared that under the 14th Amendment no person was denied any of his rights if the States provided separate but equal facilities. This decision . . . restated time and again, became a part of the life of the people of many of the States and confirmed their habits, traditions, and way of life. It is founded on elemental humanity and commonsense, for parents should not be deprived by Government of the right to direct the lives and education of their own children.

Though there has been no constitutional amendment or act of Congress changing this established legal principle almost a century old, the Supreme Court of the United States, with no legal basis for such action, undertook to exercise their naked judicial power and substituted their personal political and social ideas for the established law of the land.

This unwarranted exercise of power by the Court, contrary to the Constitution, is creating chaos and confusion in the States principally affected. It is destroying the amicable relations between the white and Negro races that have been created through 90 years of patient effort by the good people of both races. It has planted hatred and suspicion where there has been heretofore friendship and understanding.

With the gravest concern for the explosive and dangerous condition created by this decision and inflamed by outside meddlers: . . . we commend the motives of those States which have declared the intention to resist forced integration by any lawful means. . . .

QUESTIONS

1. *How do religious convictions shape King's definition of freedom?*

2. *Why does the Southern Manifesto claim that the Supreme Court decision is a threat to constitutional government?*

3. *How do these documents illustrate contrasting understandings of freedom at the dawn of the civil rights movement?*

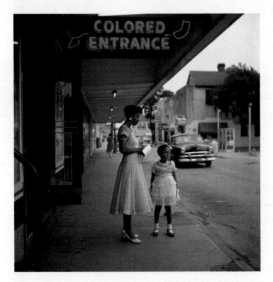

A photograph by Gordon Parks shows a well-dressed black woman and her daughter at the "colored" entrance to a Mobile, Alabama, department store in 1956.

International criticism

enforcement provisions it added few voters to the rolls. President Eisenhower failed to provide moral leadership. He called for Americans to abide by the law, but he made it clear that he found the whole civil rights issue distasteful.

In 1957, however, after Governor Orval Faubus of Arkansas used the National Guard to prevent the court-ordered integration of Little Rock's Central High School, Eisenhower dispatched federal troops to the city. In the face of a howling mob, soldiers of the 101st Airborne Division escorted nine black children into the school. Events in Little Rock showed that in the last instance, the federal government would not allow the flagrant violation of court orders. But because of massive resistance, the pace of the movement slowed in the final years of the 1950s. When Eisenhower left office, fewer than 2 percent of black students attended desegregated schools in the states of the old Confederacy.

Ever since the beginning of the Cold War, American leaders had worried about the impact of segregation on the country's international reputation. Foreign nations and colonies paid close attention to the unfolding of the American civil rights movement. The global reaction to the *Brown* decision was overwhelmingly positive. But the slow pace of change led to criticism that embarrassed American diplomats seeking to win the loyalty of people in the non-white world. Of course, the Soviet Union played up American race relations as part of the global "battle for hearts and minds of men" that was a key part of the Cold War.

THE ELECTION OF 1960

Kennedy and Nixon

JFK

The presidential campaign of 1960 turned out to be one of the closest in American history. Republicans chose Vice President Richard Nixon as their candidate to succeed Eisenhower. Democrats nominated John F. Kennedy, a senator from Massachusetts and a Roman Catholic, whose father, a millionaire Irish-American businessman, had served as ambassador to Great Britain during the 1930s. Kennedy's chief rivals for the nomination were Hubert Humphrey, leader of the party's liberal wing, and Lyndon B. Johnson of Texas, the Senate majority leader, who accepted Kennedy's offer to run for vice president.

The 1960 presidential campaign produced a flood of anti-Catholic propaganda. Kennedy's victory, the first for an American Catholic, was a major step in the decline of this long-standing prejudice.

Kennedy's Catholicism

The atmosphere of tolerance promoted by World War II had weakened traditional anti-Catholicism. But many Protestants remained reluctant to vote for a Catholic, fearing that Kennedy would be required to support church doctrine on controversial public issues or, in a more extreme version, take orders from the pope. Kennedy addressed the question directly. "I do not speak for my church on public matters," he insisted, and "the church does not speak for me." At age forty-three, Kennedy became the youngest major-party nominee for president in the nation's history.

Both Kennedy and Nixon were ardent Cold Warriors. But Kennedy pointed to Soviet success in putting *Sputnik*, the first earth satellite, into orbit and subsequently testing the first intercontinental ballistic missile (ICBM) as evidence that the United States had lost the sense of national purpose necessary to fight the Cold War. He warned that Republicans had allowed a **missile gap** to develop in which the Soviets had achieved technological and military superiority over the United States. In fact, as both Kennedy and Nixon well knew, American economic and military capacity far exceeded that of the Soviets. But the charge persuaded many Americans that the time had come for new

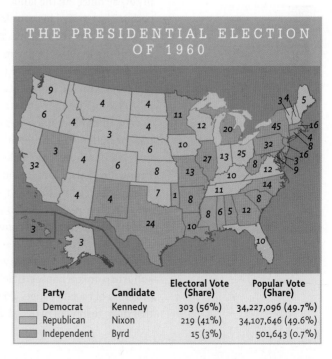

THE PRESIDENTIAL ELECTION OF 1960

Party	Candidate	Electoral Vote (Share)	Popular Vote (Share)
Democrat	Kennedy	303 (56%)	34,227,096 (49.7%)
Republican	Nixon	219 (41%)	34,107,646 (49.6%)
Independent	Byrd	15 (3%)	501,643 (0.7%)

A photograph of John F. Kennedy and his wife, Jacqueline, strolling along the pier at Hyannis Port, Massachusetts, illustrates their youthful appeal.

Eisenhower's Farewell Address

Pollution

leadership. The stylishness of Kennedy's wife, Jacqueline, reinforced the impression that Kennedy would conduct a more youthful, vigorous presidency.

In the first televised debate between presidential candidates, judging by viewer response, the handsome Kennedy bested Nixon, who was suffering from a cold and appeared tired and nervous. Those who heard the encounter on the radio thought Nixon had won, but, on TV, image counted for more than substance. In November, Kennedy eked out a narrow victory, winning the popular vote by only 120,000 out of 69 million votes cast (and, Republicans charged, benefiting from a fraudulent vote count by the notoriously corrupt Chicago Democratic machine).

The End of the 1950s

In January 1961, shortly before leaving office, Eisenhower delivered a televised Farewell Address, modeled to some extent on George Washington's address of 1796. Knowing that the missile gap was a myth, Ike warned against the drumbeat of calls for a new military buildup. He urged Americans to think about the dangerous power of what he called the **military-industrial complex**—the conjunction of "an immense military establishment" with a "permanent arms industry"—with an influence felt in "every office" in the land. "We must never let the weight of this combination," he advised his countrymen, "endanger our liberties or democratic processes." Few Americans shared Ike's concern—far more saw the alliance of the Defense Department and private industry as a source of jobs and national security rather than a threat to democracy. A few years later, however, with the United States locked in an increasingly unpopular war in Vietnam, Eisenhower's warning would come to seem prophetic.

By then, other underpinnings of 1950s life were also in disarray. The tens of millions of cars that made suburban life possible were spewing toxic lead, an additive to make gasoline more efficient, into the atmosphere. Penned in to the east by mountains that kept automobile emissions from being dispersed by the wind, Los Angeles had become synonymous with smog, a type of air pollution produced by cars. The chemical insecticides that enabled agricultural conglomerates to produce the country's remarkable abundance of food were poisoning farm workers, consumers, and the water supply. Housewives were rebelling against a life centered in suburban dream houses. Blacks were increasingly impatient with the slow progress of racial change. The United States, in other words, had entered that most turbulent of decades, the 1960s.

CHAPTER REVIEW AND ONLINE RESOURCES

REVIEW QUESTIONS

1. Explain the meaning of the "American standard of living" during the 1950s.

2. Describe how the automobile transformed American communities and culture in the 1950s.

3. Identify the prescribed roles and aspirations for women during the social conformity of the 1950s.

4. How did governmental policies, business practices, and individual choices contribute to racially segregated suburbs?

5. Explain the ideological rifts among conservatives in the 1950s. Why did many view President Eisenhower as "not one of them"?

6. What was the new "social contract" between labor and management, and how did it benefit both sides as well as the nation as a whole?

7. How did the United States and Soviet Union shift the focus of the Cold War to the Third World?

8. What were the most significant factors that contributed to the growing momentum of the civil rights movement in the 1950s?

9. How did many southern whites, led by their elected officials, resist desegregation and civil rights in the name of "freedom"?

10. How and why did the federal government's concern with U.S. relations overseas shape its involvement with the Brown v. Board of Education case?

KEY TERMS

Levittown (p. 744)

baby boom (p. 747)

urban renewal (p. 748)

"In God We Trust" (p. 749)

interstate highway system (p. 752)

Sputnik (p. 752)

National Defense Education Act (p. 753)

social contract (p. 753)

massive retaliation (p. 754)

Geneva Accords (p. 756)

the Beats (p. 759)

League of United Latin American Citizens (p. 760)

Brown v. Board of Education (p. 761)

Montgomery bus boycott (p. 762)

Southern Christian Leadership Conference (p. 764)

Southern Manifesto (p. 765)

missile gap (p. 769)

military-industrial complex (p. 770)

Go to 🐰 INQUIZITIVE

To see what you know—and learn what you've missed—with personalized feedback along the way.

Visit the *Give Me Liberty!* **Student Site** for primary source documents and images, interactive maps, author videos featuring Eric Foner, and more.

1960   Greensboro, NC, sit-in

        Young Americans for
        Freedom founded

1961   Bay of Pigs

        Freedom Rides

        Berlin Wall constructed

1962   Port Huron Statement

        University of Mississippi
        desegregated

        Rachel Carson's *Silent
        Spring*

        Cuban missile crisis

1963   Betty Friedan's *The
        Feminine Mystique*

        King's "Letter from
        Birmingham Jail"

        March on Washington

        Kennedy assassinated

1964   Freedom Summer

        Civil Rights Act passed

        Gulf of Tonkin resolution

1965–   Great Society
1967

1965   Voting Rights Act

        Watts riots

        Hart-Celler Act

1966   National Organization for
        Women organized

1968   Tet offensive

        Martin Luther King Jr.
        assassinated

        American Indian movement
        founded

        Richard Nixon elected

1969   Police raid on Stonewall Inn

        Woodstock festival

1973   *Roe v. Wade*

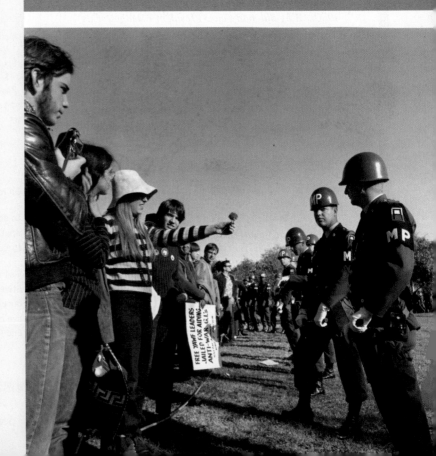

CHAPTER 25

THE SIXTIES

★

1960-1968

An antiwar demonstrator offers a flower
to military police stationed outside the
Pentagon at a 1967 rally against the
Vietnam War. Some 100,000 protesters
took part in this demonstration.

On the afternoon of February 1, 1960, four students from North Carolina Agricultural and Technical State University, a black college in Greensboro, North Carolina, entered the local Woolworth's department store. After making a few purchases, they sat down at the lunch counter, an area reserved for whites. Told that they could not be served, they remained in their seats until the store closed. They returned the next morning and the next. After resisting for five months, Woolworth's in July agreed to serve black customers at its lunch counters.

More than any other event, the Greensboro **sit-in** launched the 1960s: a decade of political activism and social change. Similar demonstrations soon took place throughout the South as activists demanded the integration not only of lunch counters but of parks, pools, restaurants, bowling alleys, libraries, and other facilities as well. By the end of 1960, some 70,000 demonstrators had taken part in sit-ins. Angry whites often assaulted them. But having been trained in nonviolent resistance, the protesters did not strike back.

Even more than elevating blacks to full citizenship, declared the writer James Baldwin, the civil rights movement challenged the United States to rethink "what it really means by freedom"—including whether freedom applied to all Americans or only to part of the population. With

FOCUS QUESTIONS

- *What were the major events in the civil rights movement of the early 1960s?*

- *What were the major crises and policy initiatives of the Kennedy presidency?*

- *What were the purposes and strategies of Johnson's Great Society programs?*

- *How did the civil rights movement change in the mid-1960s?*

- *How did the Vietnam War transform American politics and culture?*

- *What were the sources and significance of the rights revolution of the late 1960s?*

- *In what ways was 1968 a climactic year for the Sixties?*

Participants in a sit-in in Raleigh, North Carolina, in 1960. The protesters, probably students from a local college, brought books and newspapers to emphasize the seriousness of their intentions and their commitment to nonviolence.

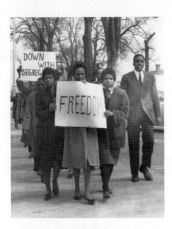

Civil rights demonstrators in Orangeburg, South Carolina, in 1960.

their freedom rides, freedom schools, freedom marches, and the insistent cry "Freedom now," black Americans and their white allies risked physical and economic retribution to lay claim to freedom. Their courage inspired a host of other challenges to the status quo, including a student movement known as the New Left, the "second wave" of feminism, and activism among other minorities.

By the time the decade ended, these movements had challenged the 1950s' understanding of freedom linked to the Cold War abroad and consumer choice at home. They made American society confront the fact that certain groups, including students, women, members of racial minorities, and homosexuals, felt themselves excluded from full enjoyment of American freedom.

Reflecting back years later on the struggles of the 1960s, one black organizer in Memphis remarked, "All I wanted to do was to live in a free country." Of the movement's accomplishments, he added, "You had to fight for every inch of it. Nobody gave you anything. Nothing."

THE CIVIL RIGHTS REVOLUTION

The Rising Tide of Protest

Ella Baker and SNCC

With the sit-ins, college students for the first time stepped onto the stage of American history as the leading force for social change. In April 1960, Ella Baker, a longtime civil rights organizer, called a meeting of young activists in Raleigh, North Carolina. Out of the gathering came the **Student Nonviolent Coordinating Committee** (SNCC), dedicated to replacing the culture of segregation with a "beloved community" of racial justice and to empowering ordinary blacks to take control of the decisions that affected their lives.

In 1961, the Congress of Racial Equality (CORE) launched the **Freedom Rides**. Integrated groups traveled by bus into the Deep South to test compliance with court orders banning segregation on interstate buses and trains and in terminal facilities. Violent mobs assaulted them. Near Anniston, Alabama, a firebomb was thrown into the vehicle and the passengers beaten as they escaped. In Birmingham, Klansmen attacked riders with bats and chains while police refused to intervene. But the Interstate Commerce Commission ordered buses and terminals desegregated.

James Meredith

As protests escalated, so did the resistance of local authorities. In September 1962, a court ordered the University of Mississippi to admit James Meredith, a black student. The state police stood aside as a mob, encouraged by Governor Ross Barnett, rampaged through the streets of Oxford, where the university is located. Two bystanders lost their lives in the riot. President Kennedy was forced to dispatch the army to restore order.

Birmingham

The high point of protest came in the spring of 1963, when demonstrations took place in towns and cities across the South. In one week in June, there were more than 15,000 arrests in 186 cities. The dramatic culmination came in Birmingham, Alabama, a citadel of segregation. Even for the Deep South, Birmingham was a violent city—there had been over fifty bombings of black homes and institutions since World War II.

Violence in Birmingham

With the movement flagging, some of its leaders invited Martin Luther King Jr. to come to Birmingham. While serving a nine-day prison term in April 1963 for violating a ban on demonstrations, King composed one of his most eloquent pleas for racial justice, the "Letter from Birmingham Jail." Responding to local clergymen who counseled patience, King related the litany of abuses faced by black southerners, from police brutality to the daily humiliation of having to explain to their children why they could not enter amusement parks or public swimming pools. The "white moderate," King declared, must put aside fear of disorder and commit himself to racial justice.

In May, King made the bold decision to send black schoolchildren into the streets of Birmingham. Police chief Eugene "Bull" Connor unleashed his forces against the thousands of young marchers. The images, broadcast on television, of children being assaulted with nightsticks, high-pressure fire hoses, and attack dogs produced a wave of revulsion throughout the world. It led President Kennedy, as will be related later, to endorse the movement's goals. Leading businessmen, fearing that the city was becoming an international symbol of brutality, brokered an end to the demonstrations that desegregated downtown stores and restaurants and promised that black salespeople would be hired.

A fireman assaulting young African-American demonstrators with a high-pressure hose during the climactic demonstrations in Birmingham. Broadcast on television, such pictures proved a serious problem for the United States in its battle for the "hearts and minds" of people around the world and forced the Kennedy administration to confront the contradiction between the rhetoric of freedom and the reality of racism.

In June 1963, a sniper killed Medgar Evers, field secretary of the NAACP in Mississippi. In September, a bomb exploded at a black Baptist church in Birmingham, killing four young girls. (Not until 2002

Three participants in the 1963 March on Washington stand in front of the White House with signs invoking freedom and the memory of slavery.

Tensions within civil rights movement

Placing hope in the federal government

was the last of those who committed this act of domestic terrorism tried and convicted.)

The March on Washington

On August 28, 1963, two weeks before the Birmingham church bombing, 250,000 black and white Americans converged on the nation's capital for the **March on Washington**, often considered the high point of the nonviolent civil rights movement. Calls for the passage of a civil rights bill pending before Congress took center stage. But the march's goals also included a public-works program to reduce unemployment, an increase in the minimum wage, and a law barring discrimination in employment. These demands, and the marchers' slogan, "Jobs and Freedom," revealed how the black movement had, for the moment, forged an alliance with white liberal groups. On the steps of the Lincoln Memorial, King delivered his most famous speech, including the words, "I have a dream that one day this nation will rise up and live out the true meaning of its creed: 'We hold these truths to be self-evident, that all men are created equal.' "

The movement was not without internal tensions. March organizers ordered SNCC leader John Lewis (later a congressman from Georgia) to tone down his speech, the original text of which called on blacks to "free ourselves of the chains of political and economic slavery" and march "through the heart of Dixie the way Sherman did . . . and burn Jim Crow to the ground." Lewis's rhetoric forecast the more militant turn many in the movement would soon be taking.

Civil rights activists also resurrected the Civil War–era vision of national authority as the custodian of American freedom. Despite the fact that the federal government had for many decades promoted segregation, blacks' historical experience suggested that they had more hope for justice from national power than from local governments or civic institutions—home owners' associations, businesses, private clubs—still riddled with racism. It remained unclear whether the federal government would take up this responsibility.

THE KENNEDY YEARS

John F. Kennedy served as president for less than three years and, in domestic affairs, had few tangible accomplishments. But his administration is widely viewed today as a moment of youthful glamour, soaring hopes, and dynamic leadership at home and abroad.

Kennedy's inaugural address of January 1961 announced a watershed in American politics: "The torch has been passed," he declared, "to a new generation of Americans" who would "pay any price, bear any burden," to "assure the survival and success of liberty." But although the sit-ins were by now a year old, the speech said nothing about segregation or race. At the outset of his presidency, Kennedy regarded civil rights as a distraction from his main concern—vigorous conduct of the Cold War.

"The torch has been passed"

Kennedy and the World

Kennedy's agenda envisioned new initiatives aimed at countering communist influence in the world. One of his first acts was to establish the Peace Corps, which sent young Americans abroad to aid in the economic and educational progress of developing countries and to improve the image of the United States there. When the Soviets in April 1961 launched a satellite carrying the first man into orbit around the earth, Kennedy announced that the United States would mobilize its resources to land a man on the moon by the end of the decade. The goal seemed almost impossible when announced, but it was stunningly accomplished in 1969.

The Peace Corps

Like his predecessors, Kennedy viewed the entire world through the lens of the Cold War. This outlook shaped his dealings with Fidel Castro, who had led a revolution that in 1959 ousted Cuban dictator Fulgencio Batista. Until Castro took power, Cuba was an economic dependency of the United States. When his government began nationalizing American landholdings and other investments and signed an agreement to sell sugar to the Soviet Union, the Eisenhower administration suspended trade and diplomatic relations with the island. The CIA began training anti-Castro exiles for an invasion of Cuba.

Kennedy as Cold Warrior

In April 1961, Kennedy allowed the CIA to launch its invasion at a site known as the Bay of Pigs. But the **Bay of Pigs invasion** proved to be a total failure and only strengthened Cuba's ties to the Soviet Union. The Kennedy administration tried other methods, including assassination attempts, to get rid of Castro's government.

Bay of Pigs

The Missile Crisis

Meanwhile, relations between the two "superpowers" deteriorated. In August 1961, in order to stem a growing tide of emigrants fleeing from East to West Berlin, the Soviets constructed a wall separating the two parts of the city. Until its demolition in 1989, the Berlin Wall would stand as a tangible symbol of the Cold War and the division of Europe.

The most dangerous crisis of the Kennedy administration, and in many ways of the entire Cold War, came in October 1962, when American spy planes discovered that the Soviet Union was installing missiles in Cuba capable of reaching the United States with nuclear weapons. Rejecting advice from military leaders that he authorize an attack on Cuba, which would almost certainly have triggered a Soviet response in Berlin and perhaps a nuclear war, Kennedy imposed a blockade, or "quarantine," of the island and demanded the missiles' removal. After tense behind-the-scenes negotiations, Soviet premier Nikita Khrushchev agreed to withdraw the missiles; Kennedy pledged that the United States would not invade Cuba and secretly agreed to remove American Jupiter missiles from Turkey, from which they could reach the Soviet Union.

The **Cuban missile crisis** seems to have lessened Kennedy's passion for the Cold War. Indeed, he appears to have been shocked by the casual way military leaders spoke of "winning" a nuclear exchange in which tens of millions of Americans and Russians were certain to die. In 1963, he called for greater cooperation with the Soviets. That summer, the two countries agreed to a treaty banning the testing of nuclear weapons in the atmosphere and in space. In announcing the agreement, Kennedy paid tribute to the small movement against nuclear weapons that had been urging such a ban for several years.

Kennedy and Civil Rights

In his first two years in office, Kennedy was preoccupied with foreign policy. But in 1963, the crisis over civil rights eclipsed other concerns. Until then, Kennedy had been reluctant to take a forceful stand on black demands. He used federal force when obstruction of civil rights law became acute, as at the University of Mississippi. But he failed to protect activists from violence, insisting that law enforcement was a local matter.

Events in Birmingham in May 1963 forced Kennedy's hand. In June, he went on national television to call for the passage of a law banning discrimination in all places of public accommodation, a major goal of the civil rights movement. The nation, he asserted, faced a moral crisis: "We preach freedom around the world, . . . but are we to say to the world, and much more importantly, to each other, that this is a land of the free except for Negroes?"

Kennedy did not live to see his civil rights bill enacted. On November 22, 1963, while riding in a motorcade through Dallas, Texas, he was shot and killed. Most likely, the assassin was Lee Harvey Oswald, a

James Meredith, the first black student to attend the University of Mississippi, in a classroom where white classmates refused to sit near him.

troubled former marine. Partly because Oswald was murdered two days later by a local nightclub owner while in police custody, speculation about a possible conspiracy continues to this day. In any event, Kennedy's death brought an abrupt and utterly unexpected end to his presidency. It fell to his successor, Lyndon B. Johnson, to secure passage of the civil rights bill and to launch a program of domestic liberalism far more ambitious than anything Kennedy had envisioned.

LYNDON JOHNSON'S PRESIDENCY

Unlike John F. Kennedy, raised in a wealthy and powerful family, Lyndon Johnson grew up in one of the poorest parts of the United States, the central Texas hill country. Johnson never forgot the poor Mexican and white children he had taught in a Texas school in the early 1930s. Far more interested than Kennedy in domestic reform, he continued to hold the New Deal view that government had an obligation to assist less-fortunate members of society.

New York City train passengers reading the news of President Kennedy's assassination, November 22, 1963.

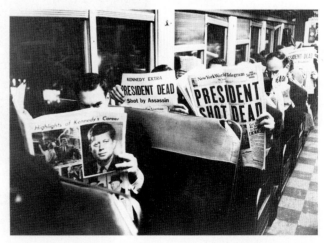

The Civil Rights Act of 1964

Just five days after Kennedy's assassination, Johnson called on Congress to enact the civil rights bill as the most fitting memorial to his slain predecessor.

In 1964, Congress passed the **Civil Rights Act**, which prohibited racial discrimination in employment, institutions like hospitals and schools, and privately owned public accommodations such as restaurants, hotels, and theaters. It also banned discrimination on the grounds of sex—a provision added by opponents of civil rights in an effort to derail the entire bill and embraced by liberal and female members of Congress as a way to broaden its scope. Johnson knew that many whites opposed the new law. After signing it, he turned to an aide and remarked, "I think we delivered the South to the Republican Party."

Landmark legislation

Freedom Summer

The 1964 voter registration drive

The 1964 law did not address a major concern of the civil rights movement—the right to vote in the South. That summer, a coalition of civil rights groups launched a voter registration drive in Mississippi. Hundreds of white college students from the North traveled to the state to take part in Freedom Summer. An outpouring of violence greeted the campaign, including thirty-five bombings and numerous beatings of civil rights workers. In June, three young activists—Michael Schwerner and

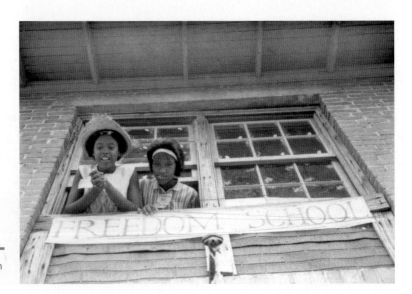

Two students at a Freedom School in Mississippi, photographed in 1964.

Andrew Goodman, white students from the North, and James Chaney, a local black youth—were kidnapped by a group headed by a deputy sheriff and murdered near Philadelphia, Mississippi. Although many black lives had been lost in the movement, the deaths of the two white students now focused unprecedented attention on Mississippi and on the apparent inability of the federal government to protect citizens seeking to exercise their constitutional rights.

Mississippi

Freedom Summer led directly to one of the most dramatic confrontations of the civil rights era—the campaign by the Mississippi Freedom Democratic Party (MFDP) to take the seats of the state's all-white official party at the 1964 Democratic national convention in Atlantic City, New Jersey. The civil rights movement in Mississippi had created the MFDP, open to all residents of the state. At televised hearings before the credentials committee, Fannie Lou Hamer of the MFDP held a national audience spellbound with her account of growing up in poverty in the Yazoo-Mississippi Delta and of the savage beatings she had endured at the hands of police. Party liberals, including Johnson's running mate, Hubert Humphrey, pressed for a compromise in which two black delegates would be granted seats. But the MFDP rejected the proposal.

The MFDP

Fannie Lou Hamer

The 1964 Election

The events at Atlantic City severely weakened black activists' faith in the responsiveness of the political system and forecast the impending breakup of the coalition between the civil rights movement and the liberal wing of the Democratic Party. For the moment, however, the movement rallied behind Johnson's campaign for reelection. Johnson's opponent, Senator Barry Goldwater of Arizona, demanded a more aggressive conduct of the Cold War. But Goldwater directed most of his critique against "internal" dangers to freedom, especially the New Deal welfare state, which he believed stifled individual initiative and independence. He voted against the Civil Rights Act of 1964. His acceptance speech at the Republican national convention contained the explosive statement, "Extremism in the defense of liberty is no vice."

Barry Goldwater's platform

Stigmatized by the Democrats as an extremist who would repeal Social Security and risk nuclear war, Goldwater went down to a disastrous defeat. Johnson received almost 43 million votes to Goldwater's 27 million. Democrats swept to two-to-one majorities in both houses of Congress. But Goldwater's message enabled him to carry five Deep South states, and segregationist governor George Wallace of Alabama showed in several Democratic primaries that politicians could strike electoral gold

Social conservatism in the South

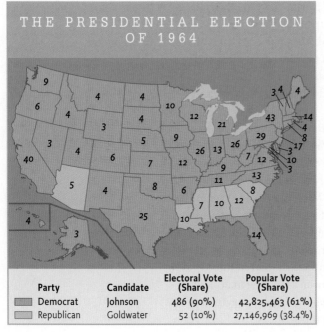

THE PRESIDENTIAL ELECTION OF 1964

Party	Candidate	Electoral Vote (Share)	Popular Vote (Share)
Democrat	Johnson	486 (90%)	42,825,463 (61%)
Republican	Goldwater	52 (10%)	27,146,969 (38.4%)

by appealing to white opposition to the civil rights movement. Although few realized it, the 1964 campaign marked a milestone in the resurgence of American conservatism.

The Conservative Sixties

The 1960s, today recalled as a decade of radicalism, clearly had a conservative side as well. With the founding in 1960 of Young Americans for Freedom (YAF), conservative students emerged as a force in politics. There were striking parallels between the Sharon Statement, issued by ninety young people who gathered at the estate of conservative intellectual William F. Buckley in Sharon, Connecticut, to establish YAF, and the Port Huron Statement of SDS of 1962 (discussed later in this chapter). Both manifestos portrayed youth as the cutting edge of a new radicalism, and both claimed to offer a route to greater freedom. The Sharon Statement summarized beliefs that had circulated among conservatives during the past decade—the free market underpinned "personal freedom," government must be strictly limited, and "international communism," the gravest threat to liberty, must be destroyed.

Conservative strength

Goldwater also brought new constituencies to the conservative cause. His campaign aroused enthusiasm in the rapidly expanding suburbs of southern California and the Southwest. Orange County, California, many of whose residents had recently arrived from the East and Midwest and worked in defense-related industries, became a nationally known center of grassroots conservative activism. And by carrying five states of the Deep South, Goldwater showed that the civil rights revolution had redrawn the nation's political map, opening the door to a "southern strategy" that would eventually lead the entire region into the Republican Party.

Well before the rise of Black Power, a reaction against civil rights gains offered conservatives new opportunities and threatened the stability of the Democratic coalition. In 1962, YAF bestowed its Freedom Award

Strom Thurmond

on Senator Strom Thurmond of South Carolina, one of the country's most prominent segregationists. During the 1960s, most conservatives abandoned talk of racial superiority and inferiority. But conservative appeals to

Ronald Reagan and his wife Nancy, at the center, along with popular singer Pat Boone, next to a replica of the Statue of Liberty, at an anticommunist "youth night" in Los Angeles in 1961. At this event, Boone made the widely circulated remark that he would rather have his four daughters shot than see them live under communism.

law and order, "freedom of association," and the evils of welfare often had strong racial overtones. Racial divisions would prove to be a political gold mine for conservatives.

The Voting Rights Act

One last legislative triumph, however, lay ahead for the civil rights movement. In January 1965, King launched a voting rights campaign in Selma, Alabama, a city where only 355 of 15,000 black residents had been allowed to register to vote. In March, defying a ban by Governor Wallace, King attempted to lead a march from Selma to the state capital, Montgomery. When the marchers reached the bridge leading out of the city, state police assaulted them with cattle prods, whips, and tear gas.

Selma, Alabama

Once again, violence against nonviolent demonstrators flashed across television screens throughout the world. Calling Selma a milestone in "man's unending search for freedom," Johnson asked Congress to enact a law securing the right to vote. He closed his speech by quoting the demonstrators' song, "We Shall Overcome." Never before had the movement received so powerful an endorsement from the federal government. Congress quickly passed the **Voting Rights Act** of 1965, which allowed federal officials to register voters. In addition, the Twenty-fourth

LBJ's support

A sharecropper's shack alongside Jefferson Davis Highway, the route followed from Selma to Montgomery, Alabama, in 1965, by marchers demanding voting rights. The photograph, by James "Spider" Martin, who chronicled the march, suggests the deep-seated inequalities that persisted a century after the end of the Civil War.

New wave of immigration

American pluralism

Expanding social programs

Amendment to the Constitution outlawed the poll tax, which had long prevented poor blacks (and some whites) from voting in the South.

Immigration Reform

By 1965, the civil rights movement had succeeded in eradicating the legal bases of second-class citizenship. The belief that racism should no longer serve as a foundation of public policy spilled over into other realms. In 1965, the **Hart-Celler Act** abandoned the national-origins quota system of immigration, which had excluded Asians and severely restricted southern and eastern Europeans. The law established new, racially neutral criteria for immigration, notably family reunification and possession of skills in demand in the United States. On the other hand, because of growing hostility in the Southwest to Mexican immigration, the law established the first limit, 120,000, on newcomers from the Western Hemisphere.

The new law had many unexpected results. At the time, immigrants represented only 5 percent of the American population—the lowest proportion since the 1830s. No one anticipated that the new quotas not only would lead to an explosive rise in immigration but also would spark a dramatic shift in which newcomers from Latin America, the Caribbean, and Asia came to outnumber those from Europe. Taken together, the civil rights revolution and immigration reform marked the triumph of a pluralist conception of Americanism. By 1976, 85 percent of respondents to a public-opinion survey agreed with the statement, "The United States was meant to be . . . a country made up of many races, religions, and nationalities."

The Great Society

After his landslide victory of 1964, Johnson outlined the most sweeping proposal for governmental action to promote the general welfare since the New Deal. Johnson's initiatives of 1965–1967, known collectively as the **Great Society**, provided health services to the poor and elderly in the new Medicaid and Medicare programs and poured federal funds into education and urban development. New agencies, such as the Equal Employment Opportunity Commission, the National Endowments for the Humanities and for the Arts, and a national public broadcasting network, were created. These measures greatly expanded the powers of the federal government, and they completed and extended the social agenda (with the exception of national health insurance) that had been stalled in Congress since 1938.

Expansion of federal government

Unlike the New Deal, the Great Society was a response to prosperity, not depression. The mid-1960s was a time of rapid economic expansion, fueled by increased government spending and a tax cut on individuals and businesses initially proposed by Kennedy and enacted in 1964. Johnson and Democratic liberals believed that economic growth made it possible to fund ambitious new government programs and to improve the quality of life.

The War on Poverty

The centerpiece of the Great Society, however, was the crusade to eradicate poverty, launched by Johnson early in 1964. Michael Harrington's 1962 book *The Other America* revealed that 40 to 50 million Americans lived in poverty.

During the 1930s, Democrats had attributed poverty to an imbalance of economic power and flawed economic institutions. In the 1960s, the administration attributed it to an absence of skills and a lack of proper attitudes and work habits. Thus, the **War on Poverty** did not address the economic changes that were reducing the number of well-paid manufacturing jobs and leaving poor families in rural areas like Appalachia and decaying urban ghettos with little hope of economic advancement.

Causes of poverty

As part of his War on Poverty, President Lyndon Johnson visited Appalachia, one of the poorest places in the United States.

One of the Great Society's most popular and successful components, food stamps, offered direct aid to the poor. But, in general, the War on Poverty concentrated on equipping the poor with skills and rebuilding their spirit and motivation. It provided Head Start (an early childhood education program), job training, legal services, and scholarships for poor college students. It also created VISTA, a domestic version of the Peace Corps for the inner cities. The War on Poverty required that poor people play a leading part in the design and implementation of local policies, a recipe for continuing conflict with local political leaders accustomed to controlling the flow of federal dollars.

Freedom and Equality

Recognizing that black poverty was fundamentally different from white, because its roots lay in "past injustice and present prejudice," Johnson sought to redefine the relationship between freedom and equality.

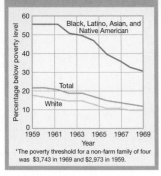

During the 1960s, an expanding economy and government programs assisting the poor produced a steady decrease in the percentage of Americans living in poverty.

Economic liberty, he insisted, meant more than equal opportunity: "You do not wipe away the scars of centuries by saying: Now you are free to go where you want, do as you desire, and choose the leaders you please. . . . We seek . . . not just equality as a right and a theory, but equality as a fact and as a result."

Johnson's Great Society may not have achieved equality "as a fact." But it represented the most expansive effort in the nation's history to mobilize the powers of the national government to address the needs of the least-advantaged Americans.

Coupled with the decade's high rate of economic growth, the War on Poverty succeeded in reducing the incidence of poverty from 22 percent to 13 percent of American families during the 1960s. It has fluctuated around the latter figure ever since. By the 1990s, thanks to the civil rights movement and the Great Society, the historic gap between whites and blacks in education, income, and access to skilled employment narrowed considerably. But nearly a quarter of all black children still lived in poverty.

THE CHANGING BLACK MOVEMENT

In the mid-1960s, economic issues rose to the forefront of the civil rights agenda. Violent outbreaks in black ghettos outside the South drew attention to the national scope of racial injustice and to inequalities in jobs, education, and housing that the dismantling of legal segregation left intact.

The Ghetto Uprisings

Riots

The first riots—really, battles between angry blacks and the predominantly white police (widely seen by many ghetto residents as an occupying army)—erupted in Harlem in 1964. Far larger was the Watts uprising of 1965, which took place in the black ghetto of Los Angeles only days after Johnson signed the Voting Rights Act. An estimated 50,000 persons took part in this "rebellion," attacking police and firemen, looting white-owned businesses, and burning buildings. It required 15,000 police and National Guardsmen to restore order, by which time thirty-five people lay dead, 900 were injured, and $30 million worth of property had been destroyed.

A semblance of normal life resumes amid the rubble of the Watts uprising of August 1965.

By the summer of 1967, urban uprisings left twenty-three dead in Newark and forty-three in Detroit, where entire blocks went up in flames and property damage ran into the hundreds of millions of dollars. The violence led Johnson to appoint a commission headed by Illinois governor Otto Kerner to study the causes of urban rioting. Released in 1968, the Kerner Report blamed the violence on "segregation and poverty" and offered a powerful indictment of "white racism." But the report failed to offer any clear proposals for change.

Detroit and Newark

With black unemployment twice that of whites and the average black family income little more than half the white norm, the movement looked for ways to "make freedom real" for black Americans. In 1964, King called for a "Bill of Rights for the Disadvantaged" to mobilize the nation's resources to abolish economic deprivation. His proposal was directed against poverty in general, but King also insisted that after "doing something special *against* the Negro for hundreds of years," the United States had an obligation to "do something special *for* him now"—an early call for what would come to be known as "affirmative action."

Early affirmative action

In 1966, King launched the Chicago Freedom Movement, with demands quite different from its predecessors in the South—an end to discrimination by employers and unions, equal access to mortgages, the integration of public housing, and the construction of low-income housing scattered throughout the region. Confronting the entrenched power of Mayor Richard J.

Chicago Freedom Movement

Malcolm X in Harlem in 1962 distributing a newspaper publicizing charges of police brutality toward blacks.

Daley's political machine and the ferocious opposition of white home owners, the movement failed.

Malcolm X

The civil rights movement's first phase had produced a clear set of objectives, far-reaching accomplishments, and a series of coherent if sometimes competitive organizations. The second witnessed political fragmentation and few significant victories. Even during the heyday of the integration struggle, the fiery orator Malcolm X had insisted that blacks must control the political and economic resources of their communities and rely on their own efforts rather than working with whites. Malcolm Little dropped his "slave surname" in favor of "X," symbolizing blacks' separation from their African ancestry. He became a spokesman for the Nation of Islam, or Black Muslims, and a sharp critic of the ideas of integration and nonviolence.

On a 1964 trip to Mecca, Saudi Arabia, Islam's spiritual home, Malcolm X witnessed harmony among Muslims of all races. He now began to speak of the possibility of interracial cooperation for radical change in the United States. But when members of the Nation of Islam assassinated *Legacy of Malcolm X* him in February 1965 after he had formed his own Organization of Afro-American Unity, Malcolm X left neither a consistent ideology nor a coherent movement. However, his call for blacks to rely on their own resources struck a chord among the urban poor and younger civil rights activists.

The Rise of Black Power

Malcolm X was the intellectual father of **Black Power**, a slogan that came to national attention in 1966 when SNCC leader Stokely Carmichael used it during a civil rights march in Mississippi.

A highly imprecise idea, Black Power suggested everything from the election of more black officials (hardly a radical notion) to the belief that black Americans were a colonized people whose freedom could be won only through a revolutionary struggle for self-determination. In many communities where black parents felt that the local public education system failed to educate their children adequately, it inspired the establishment of black-operated local schools that combined traditional learning *African-American pride* with an emphasis on pride in African-American history and identity. But however employed, the idea reflected the radicalization of young civil rights activists and sparked an explosion of racial self-assertion, reflected in the slogan "Black Is Beautiful." The abandonment of the word "Negro" in favor of "Afro-American," as well as the popularity of African styles of dress and the "natural," or "Afro," hairdo among both men and women reflected a new sense of racial pride and a rejection of white norms.

Inspired by the idea of black self-determination, SNCC and CORE repudiated their previous interracialism, and new militant groups sprang into existence. Most prominent of the new groups, in terms of public-ity, if not numbers, was the Black Panther Party. Founded in Oakland, California, in 1966, it became notorious for advocating armed self-defense in response to police brutality. The party's youthful members alarmed whites by wearing military garb, although they also ran health clinics, schools, and children's breakfast programs. But internal disputes and a campaign against the Black Panthers by police and the FBI, which left sev-eral leaders dead in shootouts, destroyed the organization.

By 1967, with the escalation of U.S. military involvement in Vietnam, the War on Poverty ground to a halt. By then, with ghetto uprisings punctuating the urban landscape, the antiwar movement assuming mas-sive proportions, and millions of young people ostentatiously rejecting mainstream values, American society faced its greatest crisis since the Depression.

Female students on the campus of Howard University in Washington, D.C., sport the Afro, a hairstyle representative of the "Black Is Beautiful" campaign of the 1960s.

Social crisis

VIETNAM AND THE NEW LEFT

Old and New Lefts

To most Americans, the rise of a protest movement among white youth came as a complete surprise. If blacks' grievances appeared self-evident, those of white college students were difficult to understand. What per-suaded large numbers of children of affluence to reject the values and institutions of their society? In part, the answer lay in a redefinition of the meaning of freedom by what came to be called the **New Left**.

The New Left

The New Left challenged not only mainstream America but also what it dismissively called the Old Left. Unlike the Communist Party, it did not take the Soviet Union as a model or see the working class as the main agent of social change. Instead of economic equality, the language of New Deal liberals, the New Left spoke of loneliness, isolation, and alienation, of pow-erlessness in the face of bureaucratic institutions and a hunger for authen-ticity that affluence could not provide. By 1968, thanks to the coming of age of the baby-boom generation and the growing number of jobs that required post–high school skills, more than 7 million students attended college, more than the number of farmers or steelworkers.

The New Left's greatest inspiration was the black freedom movement. More than any other event, the sit-ins catalyzed white student activism. Here was the unlikely combination that created the upheaval known as the Sixties—the convergence of society's most excluded members demanding full access to all its benefits, with the children of the middle class rejecting the social mainstream.

The Fading Consensus

Pivotal books of social criticism

The years 1962 and 1963 witnessed the appearance of several pathbreaking books that challenged one or another aspect of the 1950s consensus. James Baldwin's *The Fire Next Time* gave angry voice to the black revolution. Rachel Carson's *Silent Spring* exposed the environmental costs of economic growth. Michael Harrington's *The Other America* revealed the persistence of poverty amid plenty. *The Death and Life of Great American Cities*, by Jane Jacobs, criticized urban renewal, the removal of the poor from city centers, and the destruction of neighborhoods to build highways.

Yet in some ways the most influential critique of all arose in 1962 from **Students for a Democratic Society** (SDS), an offshoot of the socialist League for Industrial Democracy. Meeting at Port Huron, Michigan, some sixty college students adopted a document that captured the mood and summarized the beliefs of this generation of student protesters.

The **Port Huron Statement** offered a new vision of social change. "We seek the establishment," it proclaimed, of "a democracy of individual participation, [in which] the individual shares in those social decisions determining the quality and direction of his life." Freedom, for the New Left, meant "participatory democracy." Although rarely defined with precision, this became a standard by which students judged existing social arrangements—workplaces, schools, government—and found them wanting.

In 1964, events at the University of California, Berkeley, revealed the possibility for a mobilization of students in the name of participatory democracy. Berkeley was an immense, impersonal institution where enrollments in many classes approached 1,000 students. The spark that

Members of Students for a Democratic Society (SDS) at the University of Delaware in their yearbook photo. Despite their raised fists, they appear eminently respectable compared to radicals who emerged later in the decade. The group is entirely white.

set student protests alight was a new rule prohibiting political groups from using a central area of the campus to spread their ideas. Students responded by creating the Free Speech movement.

Thousands of Berkeley students became involved in the protests in the months that followed. Their program moved from demanding a repeal of the new rule to a critique of the entire structure of the university and of an education geared toward preparing graduates for corporate jobs. The university gave in on the speech ban early in 1965.

Mario Savio, a leader of the 1964 Free Speech movement at the University of California, Berkeley, addressing a crowd on campus from the roof of a police car.

America and Vietnam

By 1965 the black movement and the emergence of the New Left had shattered the climate of consensus of the 1950s. But what transformed protest into a full-fledged generational rebellion was the war in Vietnam. The war tragically revealed the danger that Walter Lippmann had warned of at the outset of the Cold War—viewing the entire world and every local situation within it through the either-or lens of an anticommunist crusade. A Vietnam specialist in the State Department who attended a policy meeting in August 1963 later recalled "the abysmal ignorance around the table of the particular facts of Vietnam. . . . They [believed] that we could manipulate other states and build nations; that we knew all the answers."

Vietnam and anticommunism

As noted in the previous chapter, the Truman and Eisenhower administrations cast their lot with French colonialism in the region. After the French defeat, they financed the creation of a pro-American South Vietnamese government. By the 1960s, the United States was committed to the survival of this corrupt regime.

Commitment to South Vietnam

Fear that voters would not forgive them for "losing" Vietnam made it impossible for presidents Kennedy and Johnson to remove the United States from an increasingly untenable situation. Kennedy's foreign policy advisers saw Vietnam as a test of whether the United States could, through "counterinsurgency"—intervention to counter internal uprisings in non-communist countries—halt the spread of Third World revolutions. South Vietnamese leader Ngo Dinh Diem resisted American advice to broaden his government's base of support. In October 1963, after large Buddhist demonstrations against his regime, the United States approved a military coup

VOICES OF FREEDOM

From Barry Goldwater, Speech at Republican National Convention (1964)

In his speech accepting the Republican nomination for president in 1964, Senator Barry Goldwater of Arizona outlined a political vision rooted in the conservatism of the Southwest and California. Charged with being an extremist, Goldwater responded, "Extremism in the defense of liberty is no vice," an explosive statement that enabled President Lyndon Johnson to portray him as a dangerous radical.

My fellow Americans, the tide has been running against freedom. Our people have followed false prophets. We must, and we shall, return to proven ways—not because they are old, but because they are true. We must, and we shall, set the tide running again in the cause of freedom. And this party, with its every action, every word, every breath, and every heartbeat, has but a single resolve, and that is freedom—freedom made orderly for this Nation by our constitutional government; freedom under a government limited by laws of nature and of nature's God; freedom—balanced so that liberty lacking order will not become the slavery of the prison cell; balanced so that liberty lacking order will not become the license of the mob and of the jungle.

Now, we Americans understand freedom. We have earned it, we have lived for it, and we have died for it. This Nation and its people are freedom's model in a searching world. We can be freedom's missionaries in a doubting world. But, ladies and gentlemen, first we must renew freedom's mission in our own hearts and in our own homes. . . .

Tonight there is violence in our streets, corruption in our highest offices, aimlessness among our youth, anxiety among our elders and there is a virtual despair among the many who look beyond material success for the inner meaning of their lives. . . .

We Republicans seek a government that attends to its inherent responsibilities of maintaining a stable monetary and fiscal climate, encouraging a free and a competitive economy and enforcing law and order. . . .

Our towns and our cities, then our counties, then our states, then our regional contacts and only then, the national government. That, let me remind you, is the ladder of liberty, built by decentralized power. On it also we must have balance between the branches of government at every level. . . .

I would remind you that extremism in the defense of liberty is no vice. And let me remind you also that moderation in the pursuit of justice is no virtue.

From Statement of Purpose, National Organization for Women (1966)

Founded in 1966, the National Organization for Women gave voice to the movement for equality for women known as the "second wave" of feminism. Written by Betty Friedan, and adopted at the group's organizing meeting in Washington, D.C., the statement of purpose outlined a wide range of areas, public and private, where women continued to be denied full freedom.

The time has come for a new movement toward true equality for all women in America, and toward a fully equal partnership of the sexes, as part of the world-wide revolution of human rights now taking place within and beyond our national borders.

The purpose of NOW is to take action to bring women into full participation in the mainstream of American society now, exercising all the privileges and responsibilities thereof in truly equal partnership with men. . . .

The actual position of women in the United States has declined, and is declining, to an alarming degree throughout the 1950's and '60s. . . . Working women are becoming increasingly—not less—concentrated on the bottom of the job ladder. . . . Today, women earn only one in three of the B.A.'s and M.A.'s granted, and one in ten of the Ph.D.'s. In all the professions considered of importance to society, and in the executive ranks of industry and government, women are losing ground. Where they are present it is only a token handful. Women comprise less than 1% of federal judges; less than 4% of all lawyers; 7% of doctors. . . .

We do not accept the traditional assumption that a woman has to choose between marriage and motherhood, on the one hand, and serious participation in industry or the professions on the other. . . . True equality of opportunity and freedom of choice for women requires such practical, and possible innovations as a nationwide network of child-care centers, which will make it unnecessary for women to retire completely from society until their children are grown. . . .

We believe that a true partnership between the sexes demands a different concept of marriage, and equitable sharing of the responsibilities of home and children and of the economic burdens of their support. We believe that proper recognition should be given to the economic and social value of homemaking and child-care.

QUESTIONS

1. *Why does Goldwater stress the interconnection of order and liberty?*

2. *What social changes does NOW believe necessary to enable women to enjoy equality and freedom?*

3. *How do the two documents differ in assessing the dangers to American freedom?*

that led to Diem's death. When Kennedy was assassinated the following month, there were 17,000 American military advisers in South Vietnam.

Lyndon Johnson's War

Lyndon B. Johnson came to the presidency with little experience in foreign relations. But he was an adept politician and knew that Republicans had used the "loss" of China as a weapon against Truman.

In August 1964, North Vietnamese vessels encountered an American ship on a spy mission off its coast. When North Vietnamese patrol boats fired on the American vessel, Johnson proclaimed that the United States was a victim of "aggression." In response, Congress passed the **Gulf of Tonkin resolution**, authorizing the president to take "all necessary measures to repel armed attack" in Vietnam. Only two members—senators Ernest Gruening of Alaska and Wayne Morse of Oregon—voted against giving Johnson this blank check.

Authorizing military action

Immediately after Johnson's 1964 election, the National Security Council recommended that the United States begin air strikes against North Vietnam and introduce American ground troops in the south. Johnson put the plan into effect. At almost the same time, he intervened in the Dominican Republic. Here, military leaders in 1963 had overthrown the left-wing but noncommunist Juan Bosch, the country's first elected president since 1924. In April 1965, another group of military men attempted to restore Bosch to power but were defeated by the ruling junta. Fearing the unrest would lead to "another Cuba," Johnson dispatched 22,000 American troops. The operation's success seemed to bolster Johnson's determination in Vietnam.

Secretary of Defense Robert McNamara, on the left, and his deputy, Cyrus Vance, at a May 1965 meeting at the White House where the war in Vietnam was discussed. A bust of President Kennedy stands in the background. McNamara later wrote in his memoirs that his misgivings only grew as the war progressed.

By 1968, the number of American troops in Vietnam exceeded half a million, and the conduct of the war had become more and more brutal. The North Vietnamese mistreated American prisoners of war held in a camp known sardonically by the inmates as the Hanoi Hilton. American planes dropped more tons of bombs on the small countries of North and South Vietnam than both sides had used in all of World War II. They spread chemicals that destroyed forests to deprive the Viet Cong of hiding places and dropped incendiary bombs filled with napalm, a gelatinous form of gasoline that clings to the skin of anyone exposed to it as it burns.

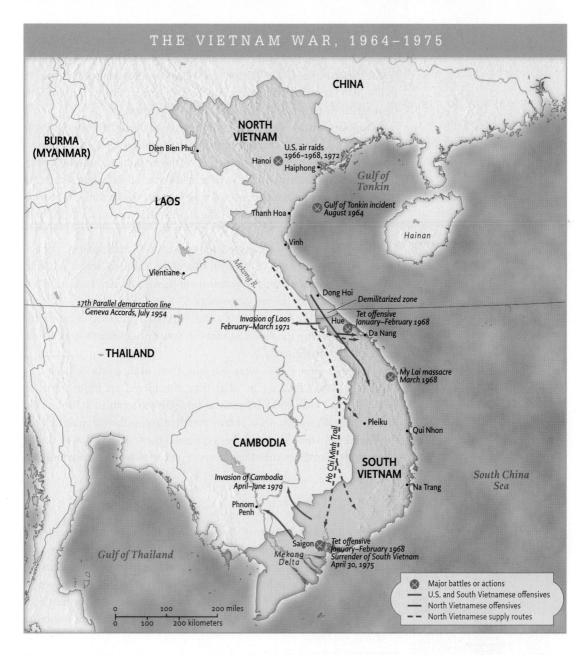

THE VIETNAM WAR, 1964–1975

A war of aerial bombing and small guerrilla skirmishes rather than fixed land battles, Vietnam was among the longest wars in American history and the only one the United States has lost.

The Antiwar Movement

As casualties mounted and American bombs poured down on North and South Vietnam, the Cold War foreign policy consensus began to unravel. By 1968, the war had sidetracked much of the Great Society and had torn families, universities, and the Democratic Party apart.

Opposition to the war became the organizing theme that united people with all kinds of doubts and discontents. With college students exempted from the draft, the burden of fighting fell on the working class and the poor. In 1967, Martin Luther King Jr. condemned the administration's Vietnam policy as an unconscionable use of violence and for draining resources from needs at home. At this point, King was the most prominent American to speak out against the war.

As for SDS, the war seemed the opposite of participatory democracy, since American involvement had come through secret commitments and decisions made by political elites, with no real public debate. In April 1965, SDS invited opponents of American policy in Vietnam to assemble in Washington, D.C. The turnout of 25,000 amazed the organizers, offering the first hint that the antiwar movement would soon enjoy a mass constituency.

By 1967, young men were burning their draft cards or fleeing to Canada to avoid fighting in what they considered an unjust war. In October of that year, 100,000 antiwar protesters assembled at the Lincoln Memorial in Washington, D.C. Many marched across the Potomac River to the Pentagon, where photographers captured them placing flowers in the rifle barrels of soldiers guarding the nerve center of the American military.

The Counterculture

The New Left's definition of freedom initially centered on participatory democracy, a political concept. But as the 1960s progressed, young Americans' understanding of freedom increasingly expanded to include cultural freedom as well. By the late 1960s, millions of young people openly rejected the values and behavior of their elders. For the first time in American history, the flamboyant rejection of respectable norms in clothing, language, sexual behavior, and drug use, previously confined to artists and bohemians, became the basis of a mass movement. Its rallying cry was "liberation."

"Your sons and your daughters are beyond your command," Bob Dylan's song "The Times They Are A-Changin' " bluntly informed mainstream America. To be sure, the **counterculture** in some ways represented

Opposition to the Vietnam War

A poster listing some of the performers who took part in the Woodstock festival in 1969. A dove of peace sits on the guitar, symbolizing the overlap between the antiwar movement and counterculture.

not rebellion but the fulfillment of the consumer marketplace. It extended into every realm of life the definition of freedom as the right to individual choice. Self-indulgence and self-destructive behavior were built into the counterculture.

Personal Liberation and the Free Individual

But there was far more to the counterculture than new consumer styles or the famed trio of sex, drugs, and rock and roll. To young dissenters, personal liberation meant a search for a way of life in which friendship and pleasure eclipsed the single-minded pursuit of wealth. It also encouraged new forms of radical action. "Underground" newspapers pioneered a personal and politically committed style of journalism. The Youth International Party, or "yippies," introduced humor and theatricality as elements of protest. From the visitors' gallery of the New York Stock Exchange, yippie founder Abbie Hoffman showered dollar bills onto the floor, bringing trading to a halt as brokers scrambled to retrieve the money.

New forms of radical action

Rock festivals, like Woodstock in upstate New York in 1969, brought together hundreds of thousands of young people to celebrate their alternative lifestyle and independence from adult authority. The opening song at Woodstock, performed by Richie Havens, began with eight repetitions of the single word "freedom."

Woodstock

Faith and the Counterculture

Religious conviction, as has been noted, helped to inspire the civil rights movement. A different religious development, the sweeping reforms

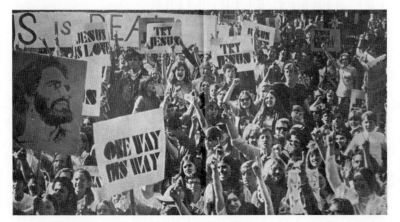

A gathering of "Jesus People," one of the religious groups that sprang up in the 1960s.

Among the religious developments of the 1960s was the spread of interest in eastern religions and religious practices. The cover of Yoga Journal illustrates how one practice entered the mainstream of American life.

initiated in Roman Catholic practice (such as the delivery of the Mass in local languages, not Latin) by the Second Vatican Council of 1962–1965, led many priests, nuns, and lay Catholics to become involved in social justice movements, producing a growing split in the Church between liberals and conservatives. Many members of the New Left were motivated by a quest for a new sense of brotherhood and social responsibility, which often sprang from Christian roots. Many young people came to believe that a commitment to social change was a fulfillment of Christian values.

The quest for personal authenticity, a feature of the counterculture, led to a flowering of religious and spiritual creativity and experimentation. The Jesus People (called by their detractors Jesus Freaks) saw the hippy lifestyle, with its long hair, unconventional attire, and quest for universal love, as an authentic expression of the outlook of the early church. The Sixties also witnessed a burgeoning interest in eastern religions. The Beats of the 1950s had been attracted to Buddhism as a religion that rejected violence and materialism, which they saw as key features of American society. Now, Buddhist practices like yoga and meditation became popular with members of the counterculture and even in the suburban mainstream as a way of promoting spiritual and physical well-being. Some Americans traveled to Tibet and India to seek spiritual guidance from "gurus" (religious leaders) there.

THE NEW MOVEMENTS AND THE RIGHTS REVOLUTION

The civil rights revolution, soon followed by the rise of the New Left, inspired other Americans to voice their grievances and claim their rights. By the late 1960s, new social movements dotted the political landscape.

The counterculture's notion of liberation centered on the free individual. Starting in 1960, the mass marketing of birth-control pills made possible what "free lovers" had long demanded—the separation of sex from procreation. By the late 1960s, sexual freedom had become as much an element of the youth rebellion as long hair and drugs. The sexual revolution was central to another mass movement that emerged in the 1960s—the "second wave" of feminism.

"Second wave" feminism

The Feminine Mystique

During the 1950s, some commentators had worried that the country was wasting its "woman power," a potential weapon in the Cold War. But the public reawakening of feminist consciousness did not get its start until the publication in 1963 of Betty Friedan's **The Feminine Mystique**. Friedan had written pioneering articles during the 1940s on pay discrimination against women workers and racism in the workplace for the newspaper of the United Electrical Workers' union. But, like other social critics, she now took as her themes the emptiness of consumer culture and the discontents of the middle class. Her opening chapter, "The Problem That Has No Name," painted a devastating picture of talented, educated women trapped in a world that viewed marriage and motherhood as their primary goals.

Betty Friedan

Few books have had the impact of *The Feminine Mystique*. Friedan was deluged by desperate letters from female readers relating how the suburban dream had become a nightmare.

The law slowly began to address feminist concerns. In 1963, Congress passed the Equal Pay Act, barring sex discrimination among holders of the same jobs. The Civil Rights Act of 1964, as noted earlier, prohibited inequalities based on sex as well as race. Deluged with complaints of discrimination by working women, the Equal Employment Opportunity Commission established by the law became a major force in breaking down barriers to female employment. In 1966 the **National Organization for Women** (NOW) was formed, with Friedan as president. Modeled on civil rights organizations, it demanded equal opportunity in jobs, education, and political participation and attacked the "false image of women" spread by the mass media.

Sex discrimination and the law

Women's Liberation

A different female revolt was brewing within the civil rights and student movements. Young women who had embraced an ideology of social equality and personal freedom and learned methods of political organizing encountered inequality and sexual exploitation in organizations like SNCC and SDS. Many women in the movement found themselves relegated to typing, cooking, and cleaning for male coworkers.

By 1967, women throughout the country were establishing "consciousness-raising" groups to discuss the sources of their discontent. The new feminism burst onto the national scene at the Miss America beauty pageant of 1968, when protesters filled a "freedom trash can" with

Raising consciousness

In 1967, in a celebrated incident arising from the new feminism, a race official tried to eject Kathrine Switzer from the Boston Marathon, only to be pushed aside by other runners. Considered too fragile for the marathon (whose course covers more than twenty-six miles), women were prohibited from running. Switzer completed the race, and today hundreds of thousands of women around the world compete in marathons each year.

objects of "oppression"—girdles, brassieres, high-heeled shoes, and copies of *Playboy* and *Cosmopolitan*. (Contrary to legend, they did not set the contents on fire, but the media invented a new label for radical women—"bra burners.") Inside the hall, demonstrators unfurled banners carrying the slogans "Freedom for Women" and "Women's Liberation."

Personal Freedom

The women's liberation movement inspired a major expansion of the idea of freedom by insisting that it should be applied to the most intimate realms of life. It contended that sexual relations, conditions of marriage, and standards of beauty were as much "political" questions as the war, civil rights, and the class tensions that had traditionally inspired the Left to action. The idea that family life is not off limits to considerations of power and justice repudiated the family-oriented public culture of the 1950s, and it permanently changed Americans' definition of freedom.

Radical feminists' first public campaign demanded the repeal of state laws that underscored women's lack of self-determination by banning abortions or leaving it up to physicians to decide whether a pregnancy could be terminated. In 1969, a group of feminists disrupted legislative hearings on New York's law banning abortions, where the experts scheduled to testify consisted of fourteen men and a Roman Catholic nun.

By this time, feminist ideas had entered the mainstream. In 1962, a poll showed that two-thirds of American women did not feel themselves to be victims of discrimination. By 1974, two-thirds did.

Gay Liberation

In a decade full of surprises, perhaps the greatest of all was the emergence of the movement for gay liberation. Gay men and lesbians had long been stigmatized as sinful or mentally disordered. Most states made homosexual acts illegal, and police regularly harassed the gay subcultures that existed in major cities like San Francisco and New York. Although homosexuals had achieved considerable success in the arts and fashion, most kept their sexual orientation secret, or "in the closet."

If one moment marked the advent of "gay liberation," it was a 1969 police raid on the **Stonewall Inn** in New York's Greenwich Village, a gathering place for homosexuals. Rather than bowing to police harassment, as in the past, gays fought back. Five days of rioting followed, and

Social and legal homophobia

Stonewall Inn

a militant movement was born. Gay men and lesbians stepped out of the "closet" to insist that sexual orientation is a matter of rights, power, and identity. Prejudice against homosexuals persisted. But within a few years, "gay pride" marches were being held in numerous cities.

Latino Activism

As in the case of blacks, a movement for legal rights had long flourished among Mexican-Americans. But the mid-1960s saw the flowering of a new militancy challenging the group's second-class economic status. Like Black Power advocates, the movement emphasized pride in both the Mexican past and the new Chicano culture that had arisen in the United States. Unlike the Black Power movement and SDS, it was closely linked to labor struggles. Beginning in 1965, César Chavez, the son of migrant farm workers and a disciple of King, led a series of nonviolent protests, including marches, fasts, and a national boycott of California grapes, to pressure growers to agree to labor contracts with the United Farm Workers union (UFW). The UFW was as much a mass movement for civil rights as a campaign for economic betterment. The boycott mobilized Latino communities throughout the Southwest and drew national attention to the pitifully low wages and oppressive working conditions of migrant laborers. In 1970, the major growers agreed to contracts with the UFW.

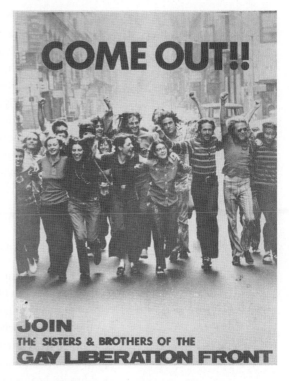

A 1970 poster urging male and female homosexuals to join the Gay Liberation Front, one of the numerous movements that sprang to life in the late 1960s.

Red Power

The 1960s also witnessed an upsurge of Native American militancy. The Truman and Eisenhower administrations had sought to dismantle the reservation system and integrate Indians into the American mainstream—a policy known as "termination," since it meant ending recognition of the remaining elements of Indian sovereignty. Many Indian leaders protested vigorously against this policy, and it was abandoned by President Kennedy. Johnson's War on Poverty channeled increased federal funds to reservations. But like other minority groups, Indian activists demanded not simply economic aid but self-determination.

Indian activism

The occupation of Alcatraz Island in San Francisco Bay in 1969 by "Indians of All Tribes" symbolized the emergence of a new militancy among Native Americans.

Founded in 1968, the **American Indian movement** staged protests demanding greater tribal self-government and the restoration of economic resources guaranteed in treaties. In 1969, a group calling itself "Indians of All Tribes" occupied (or, from their point of view, re-occupied) Alcatraz Island in San Francisco Bay, claiming that it had been illegally seized from its original inhabitants. In the years that followed, many Indian tribes would win greater control over education and economic development on the reservations. Indian activists would bring land claims suits, demanding and receiving monetary settlements for past dispossession. In an atmosphere of rising Native American pride, the number of Americans identifying themselves as Indians doubled between 1970 and 1990.

Environmentalism and the Consumer Movement

Another movement, environmentalism, called into question different pillars of American life—the equation of progress with endless increases in consumption and the faith that science, technology, and economic growth would advance social welfare. In keeping with the spirit of the Sixties, the new environmentalism reflected the very affluence celebrated by proponents of the American Way. As the "quality of life"—including physical fitness, health, and opportunities to enjoy leisure activities—occupied a greater role in the lives of middle-class Americans, the environmental consequences of economic growth received increased attention.

Environmentalism advanced through affluence

The publication in 1962 of **_Silent Spring_** by the marine biologist Rachel Carson brought home to millions of readers the effects of DDT, an insecticide widely used by home owners and farmers against mosquitoes, gypsy moths, and other insects. In chilling detail, Carson related how DDT killed birds and animals and caused sickness among humans.

Rachel Carson

Carson's work launched the modern environmental movement. The Sierra Club, founded in the 1890s to preserve forests, saw its membership more than triple, and other groups sprang into existence to alert the country to the dangers of water contamination, air pollution, lead in paint, and the extinction of animal species. Nearly every state quickly banned the use of DDT.

Despite vigorous opposition from business groups that considered its proposals a violation of property rights, environmentalism attracted the broadest bipartisan support of any of the new social movements. Under Republican president Richard Nixon, Congress during the late 1960s and early 1970s passed a series of measures to protect the environ-

Bipartisan support

ment, including the Clean Air and Clean Water Acts and the Endangered Species Act. On April 22, 1970, the first Earth Day, some 20 million people, most of them under the age of thirty, participated in rallies, concerts, and teach-ins.

Closely related to environmentalism was the consumer movement, spearheaded by the lawyer Ralph Nader. His book *Unsafe at Any Speed* (1965) exposed how auto manufacturers produced highly dangerous vehicles. General Motors, whose Chevrolet Corvair Nader singled out for its tendency to roll over in certain driving situations, hired private investigators to discredit him.

Consumer activism

Nader's campaigns laid the groundwork for the numerous new consumer protection laws and regulations of the 1970s. Unlike 1960s movements that emphasized personal liberation, environmentalism and the consumer movement called for limiting some kinds of freedom—especially the right to use private property in any way the owner desired—in the name of a greater common good.

Consumer protection laws

The Rights Revolution

It is one of the more striking ironies of the 1960s that although the "rights revolution" began in the streets, it achieved constitutional legitimacy through the Supreme Court, historically the most conservative branch of government. Under the guidance of Chief Justice Earl Warren, the Court vastly expanded the rights enjoyed by all Americans and placed them beyond the reach of legislative and local majorities.

The Court moved to rein in the anticommunist crusade. The justices overturned convictions of individuals for advocating the overthrow of the government, failing to answer questions before the House Un-American Activities Committee, and refusing to disclose their political beliefs to state officials. By the time Warren retired in 1969, the Court had reaffirmed the right of even the most unpopular viewpoints to First Amendment protection.

The landmark ruling in *New York Times v. Sullivan* (1964) overturned a libel judgment by an Alabama jury against the nation's leading newspaper for carrying an advertisement critical of how local officials treated civil rights demonstrators. Before the 1960s, few Supreme Court cases had dealt with newspaper publishing. *Sullivan* created the modern constitutional law of freedom of the press.

The Court in the 1960s continued the push toward racial equality, overturning numerous local Jim Crow laws. In *Loving v. Virginia* (1967),

Karl Hubenthal's December 8, 1976, cartoon for the *Los Angeles Herald-Examiner* celebrates the rights revolution as an expansion of American liberty.

Richard and Mildred Loving with their children in a 1965 photograph by Grey Villet. Their desire to live in Virginia as husband and wife led to a Supreme Court decision declaring unconstitutional state laws that barred interracial marriages.

"One man, one vote"

Religion in schools

it declared unconstitutional the laws still on the books in sixteen states that prohibited interracial marriage. This aptly named case arose from the interracial marriage of Richard and Mildred Loving. Barred by Virginia law from marrying, they did so in Washington, D.C., and later returned to their home state. Two weeks after their arrival, the local sheriff entered their home in the middle of the night, roused the couple from bed, and arrested them.

The Court simultaneously pushed forward the process of imposing on the states the obligation to respect the liberties outlined in the Bill of Rights. Among the most important of these decisions was the 5-4 ruling in *Miranda v. Arizona* (1966). This held that an individual in police custody must be informed of the rights to remain silent and to confer with a lawyer before answering questions and must be told that any statements might be used in court. The decision made "Miranda warnings" standard police practice.

The Court also assumed the power to oversee the fairness of democratic procedures at the state and local levels. *Baker v. Carr* (1962) established the principle that districts electing members of state legislatures must be equal in population. This "one man, one vote" principle overturned apportionment systems in numerous states that had allowed individuals in sparsely inhabited rural areas to enjoy the same representation as residents of populous city districts.

The justices also moved to reinforce the "wall of separation" between church and state. In *Engel v. Vitale*, they decreed that prayers and Bible readings in public schools violated the First Amendment. These rulings proved to be the most unpopular of all the Warren Court's decisions.

The Right to Privacy

The Warren Court not only expanded existing liberties but also outlined entirely new rights in response to the rapidly changing contours of American society. Most dramatic was its assertion of a constitutional right to privacy in **Griswold v. Connecticut** (1965), which overturned a state law prohibiting the use of contraceptives. Justice William O. Douglas, who wrote the decision, had once declared, "The right to be let alone is the beginning of all freedom."

Griswold linked privacy to the sanctity of marriage. But the Court soon transformed it into a right of individuals. It extended access to birth control to unmarried adults and ultimately to minors—an admission by the Court that law could not reverse the sexual revolution. These decisions led directly to the most controversial decision that built on the rulings of the Warren Court (even though it occurred in 1973, four years after Warren's retirement). This was ***Roe v. Wade***, which created a constitutional right to terminate a pregnancy. *Roe* provoked vigorous opposition that has continued to this day.

The rights revolution completed the transformation of American freedom from a set of entitlements enjoyed mainly by white men into an open-ended claim to equality, recognition, and self-determination.

The cartoonist Herbert Block's comment on critics of the Supreme Court's decision barring prayer in public schools.

1968

A Year of Turmoil

The Sixties reached their climax in 1968, a year when momentous events succeeded each other so rapidly that the foundations of society seemed to be dissolving. Late January 1968 saw the **Tet offensive**, in which Viet Cong and North Vietnamese troops launched well-organized uprisings in cities throughout South Vietnam, completely surprising American military leaders. The intensity of the fighting, brought into America's homes on television, shattered public confidence in the Johnson administration, which had repeatedly proclaimed victory to be "just around the corner." Eugene McCarthy, an antiwar senator from Minnesota, announced that he would seek the Democratic nomination for president. Aided by a small army of student volunteers, McCarthy received more than 40 percent of the vote in the New Hampshire primary. Johnson then stunned the nation by announcing that he had decided not to seek reelection.

Meanwhile, Martin Luther King Jr. was organizing a Poor People's March, hoping to bring thousands of demonstrators to Washington to demand increased anti-poverty efforts. On April 4, having traveled to Memphis to support a strike of the city's grossly underpaid black garbage collectors, King was killed by a white assassin. The greatest outbreak of urban violence in the nation's history followed in black neighborhoods

Setbacks in the war

Eugene McCarthy's challenge

Martin Luther King Jr.'s assassination

Striking sanitation workers in Memphis, Tennessee. As their signs suggest, they demanded respect as well as higher wages. Having traveled to Memphis to support the strikers, Martin Luther King Jr. was assassinated on April 4, 1968.

across the country. Washington, D.C., had to be occupied by soldiers before order was restored.

In June, a young Palestinian nationalist assassinated Robert F. Kennedy, who was seeking the Democratic nomination as an opponent of the war. In August, tens of thousands of antiwar activists descended on Chicago for protests at the Democratic national convention, where the delegates nominated Vice President Hubert Humphrey as their presidential candidate. The city's police, never known for restraint, assaulted the marchers with nightsticks, producing hundreds of injuries outside the convention hall and pandemonium inside it.

The Global 1968

International antiwar movements

Like 1848 and 1919, 1968 was a year of worldwide upheaval. In many countries, young radicals challenged existing power structures, often borrowing language and strategies from the decade's social movements in the United States and adapting them to their own circumstances.

Massive antiwar demonstrations took place in London, Rome, Paris, Munich, and Tokyo, leading to clashes with police and scores of injuries. In Paris, a nationwide student uprising began in May 1968 that echoed American demands for educational reform and personal liberation. Unlike in the United States, millions of French workers soon joined the protest, adding their own demands for higher wages and greater democracy in the workplace. The result was a general strike that paralyzed the country. In communist Czechoslovakia, leaders bent on reform came to power by promising to institute "socialism with a human face," only to be ousted by a Soviet invasion. Soldiers fired on students demonstrating for greater democracy on the eve of the opening of the Olympic Games in Mexico City, leading to more than 500 deaths. In Northern Ireland, which remained part of Great Britain after the rest of Ireland achieved independence, the police attacked a peaceful march of Catholics demanding an end to religious discrimination who were inspired by the American civil rights movement. This event marked the beginning of the Troubles, a period of both peaceful protest and violent conflict in the region that did not end until the turn of the twenty-first century.

Nixon's Comeback

In the United States, instead of radical change, the year's events opened the door for a conservative reaction. Turmoil in the streets produced a demand for public order. Black militancy produced white "backlash."

In August, Richard Nixon capped a remarkable political comeback by winning the Republican nomination. He called for a renewed commitment to "law and order." With 43 percent of the vote, Nixon had only a razor-thin margin over his Democratic rival. But George Wallace, running as an independent and appealing to resentments against blacks' gains, Great Society programs, and the Warren Court, received an additional 13 percent. Taken together, the Nixon and Wallace totals indicated that four years after Johnson's landslide election ushered in the Great Society, liberalism was on the defensive.

The Legacy of the Sixties

The 1960s transformed American life in ways unimaginable when the decade began. It produced new rights and new understandings of freedom. It made possible the entrance of numerous members of racial minorities into the mainstream of American life, while leaving unsolved the problem of urban poverty. It set in motion a transformation of the status of women.

As the country became more conservative, the Sixties would be blamed for every imaginable social ill, from crime and drug abuse to a decline of respect for authority. Yet during the 1960s, the United States became a more open, more tolerant—in a word, a freer—country.

A mural in Belfast, Northern Ireland, depicts the black American abolitionist Frederick Douglass, illustrating how the movement for Catholic civil rights associated itself with the struggle for racial justice in the United States. The text points out that Douglass lectured in Ireland in the 1840s on abolitionism, women's rights, and Irish independence.

CHAPTER REVIEW AND ONLINE RESOURCES

REVIEW QUESTIONS

1. How did the idea of a "zone of privacy" build on or change earlier notions of rights and freedom?

2. In what ways were President Kennedy's foreign policy decisions shaped by Cold War ideology?

3. How did immigration policies change in these years, and what were the consequences for the makeup of the population in the United States?

4. Explain why many blacks, especially in the North, did not believe that civil rights legislation went far enough in promoting black freedom.

5. What were the effects of President Johnson's Great Society and War on Poverty programs?

6. In what ways was the New Left not as new as it claimed?

7. How did the goals and actions of the United States in Vietnam cause controversy at home and abroad?

8. Discuss the impact of the civil rights movement on at least two other movements for social change in the 1960s.

9. Identify the origins, goals, and composition of the feminist, or women's liberation, movement.

10. Describe how the social movements of the 1960s in the United States became part of global movements for change by 1968. How did those connections affect the United States' position in the world?

11. How did the counterculture expand the meaning of freedom in these years?

KEY TERMS

sit-in (p. 773)
Student Nonviolent Coordinating Committee (p. 774)
Freedom Rides (p. 774)
March on Washington (p. 776)
Bay of Pigs invasion (p. 777)
Cuban missile crisis (p. 778)
Civil Rights Act (p. 780)
Voting Rights Act (p. 783)
Hart-Celler Act (p. 784)
Great Society (p. 784)
War on Poverty (p. 785)
Black Power (p. 788)
New Left (p. 789)
Students for a Democratic Society (p. 790)
Port Huron Statement (p. 790)
Gulf of Tonkin resolution (p. 794)
counterculture (p. 796)
The Feminine Mystique (p. 799)
National Organization for Women (p. 799)
Stonewall Inn (p. 800)
American Indian movement (p. 802)
Silent Spring (p. 802)
Griswold v. Connecticut (p. 804)
Roe v. Wade (p. 805)
Tet offensive (p. 805)

Go to 🐰 INQUIZITIVE

To see what you know—and learn what you've missed—with personalized feedback along the way.

Visit the *Give Me Liberty!* **Student Site** for primary source documents and images, interactive maps, author videos featuring Eric Foner, and more.

CHAPTER 26

THE TRIUMPH OF CONSERVATISM

1969-1988

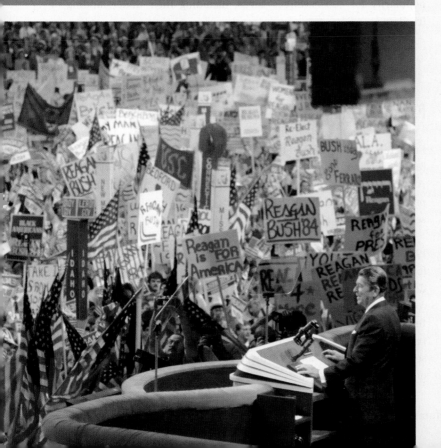

1968	My Lai massacre
1970	United States invades Cambodia
1971	Pentagon Papers published
	United States goes off the gold standard
1972	Nixon travels to the People's Republic of China
	Congress passes the Equal Rights Amendment for ratification
	SALT is signed
	Congress approves Title IX
1973	War Powers Act
	CIA-aided Chilean coup
	Paris Peace Accords end U.S. involvement in Vietnam War
1974	Nixon resigns in Watergate scandal
1975	Collapse of South Vietnamese government
1976	Jimmy Carter elected
1978	*Regents of the University of California v. Bakke*
	Camp David Accords signed between Israel and Egypt
1979	Three Mile Island accident
	Sagebrush Rebellion
	Fifty-three Americans taken hostage in Iran
1980	Ronald Reagan elected
1981	Air traffic controllers strike
1983	Strategic Defense Initiative
1985– 1987	Iran-Contra affair
1986	*Bowers v. Hardwick*

Ronald Reagan addressing the Republican national convention of 1980, which nominated him for president. His election that fall brought modern conservatism to the White House and launched the Reagan Revolution.

FOCUS QUESTIONS

- *What were the major policies of the Nixon administration on social and economic issues?*

- *How did Vietnam and the Watergate scandal affect popular trust in the government?*

- *In what ways did the opportunities of most Americans diminish in the 1970s?*

- *What were the roots of the rise of conservatism in the 1970s?*

- *How did the Reagan presidency affect American aims at home and abroad?*

Beginning with the dramatic 1960 contest between John F. Kennedy and Richard M. Nixon, the journalist Theodore White published best-selling accounts of four successive races for the presidency. Covering the 1964 election, White attended civil rights demonstrations and rallies for Barry Goldwater, the Republican nominee. White noticed something that struck him as odd: "The dominant word of these two groups, which loathe each other, is 'freedom.'"

White had observed firsthand the struggle over the meaning of freedom that emerged in the 1960s, as well as the revival of conservatism in the midst of an era known for radicalism.

The second half of the 1960s and the 1970s witnessed pivotal developments that reshaped American politics—the breakup of the political coalition forged by Franklin D. Roosevelt; an economic crisis that traditional liberal remedies seemed unable to solve; a shift of population and economic resources to conservative strongholds in the Sunbelt of the South and West; the growth of an activist, conservative Christianity increasingly aligned with the Republican Party; and a series of setbacks for the United States overseas. Together, they led to growing popularity for conservatives' ideas, including their understanding of freedom.

PRESIDENT NIXON

From the vantage point of the early twenty-first century, it is difficult to recall how marginal conservatism seemed at the end of World War II. Associated in many minds with conspiracy theories, anti-Semitism, and preference for social hierarchy over democracy and equality, conservatism seemed a relic of a discredited past.

Nonetheless, as noted in the previous two chapters, the 1950s and 1960s witnessed a conservative rebirth. And in 1968, a "backlash" among formerly Democratic voters against both black assertiveness and antiwar demonstrations helped to propel Richard Nixon into the White House. But conservatives found Nixon no more to their liking than his predecessors. In office, he expanded the welfare state and moved to improve American relations with the Soviet Union and China. During his presidency, the social changes set in motion by the 1960s—seen by conservatives as forces of moral decay—continued apace.

Nixon's Domestic Policies

Having won the presidency by a very narrow margin, Nixon moved toward the political center on many issues. A shrewd politician, he worked to solidify his support among Republicans while reaching out to disaffected elements of the Democratic coalition. Mostly interested in foreign policy, he had no desire to battle Congress, still under Democratic control, on domestic issues. Just as Eisenhower had helped to institutionalize the New Deal, Nixon accepted and even expanded many elements of the Great Society.

Conservatives applauded Nixon's New Federalism, which offered federal "block grants" to the states to spend as they saw fit, rather than for specific purposes dictated by Washington. On the other hand, the Nixon administration created a host of new federal agencies. The Environmental Protection Agency oversaw programs to combat water and air pollution, cleaned up hazardous wastes, and required "environmental impact" statements from any project that received federal funding. The Occupational Safety and Health Administration sent inspectors into the nation's workplaces. The National Transportation Safety Board instructed automobile makers on how to make their cars safer.

Nixon's New Federalism

Environmental Protection Agency

Nixon also signed measures that expanded the food stamp program and made Social Security benefits adjust automatically to the rising cost of living. His environmental initiatives included the Endangered Species Act and the Clean Air Act, which set air quality standards for carbon monoxide and other chemicals released by cars and factories.

Nixon and Welfare

Perhaps Nixon's most startling initiative was his proposal for a Family Assistance Plan, or "negative income tax," that would replace Aid to Families with Dependent Children (AFDC) by having the federal government guarantee a minimum income for all Americans. Originally a New Deal program that mainly served the white poor, welfare had come to be associated with blacks, who by 1970 accounted for nearly half the recipients. The AFDC rolls expanded rapidly during the 1960s. This arose from an increase in births to unmarried women, which produced a sharp rise in the number of poor female-headed households, and from an aggressive campaign by welfare rights groups to encourage people to apply for benefits. Conservative politicians now attacked recipients of welfare as people who preferred to live at the expense of honest taxpayers rather than by working. A striking example of

Richard Nixon (on the right) and former Alabama governor George Wallace at an "Honor America" celebration in February 1974. Nixon's "southern strategy" sought to woo Wallace's supporters into the Republican Party.

Nixon's willingness to break the political mold, his plan to replace welfare with a guaranteed annual income failed to win approval by Congress.

Nixon and Race

Nixon's racial policies offer a similarly mixed picture. To consolidate support in the white South, he nominated to the Supreme Court Clement Haynsworth and G. Harrold Carswell, conservative southern jurists with records of support for segregation. Both were rejected by the Senate. On the other hand, in Nixon's first three years in office, the proportion of southern black students attending integrated schools rose from 32 percent to 77 percent.

For a time, the Nixon administration also pursued **affirmative action** programs to upgrade minority employment. The Philadelphia Plan required that construction contractors on federal projects hire specific numbers of minority workers. Secretary of Labor George Shultz, who initiated the idea, sincerely hoped to open more jobs for black workers. Nixon seems to have viewed the plan mainly as a way of fighting inflation by weakening the power of the building trades unions. Their control over the labor market, he believed, pushed wages to unreasonably high levels, raising the cost of construction.

Trade unions of skilled workers like plumbers and electricians, which had virtually no black members, strongly opposed the Philadelphia Plan. After a widely publicized incident in May 1970, when a group of construction workers assaulted antiwar demonstrators in New York City, Nixon suddenly decided that he might be able to woo blue-collar workers in preparation for his 1972 reelection campaign. He abandoned the Philadelphia Plan in favor of an ineffective one that stressed voluntary local efforts toward minority hiring instead of federal requirements.

Rise in southern school integration

The battle over busing students to achieve racial integration in Boston public schools produced a series of violent incidents, this one in April 1976. The photographer, Stanley Forman, won a Pulitzer Prize for this image, to which he gave the title *The Soiling of Old Glory*.

The Burger Court

When Earl Warren retired as chief justice in 1969, Nixon appointed Warren Burger, a federal court-of-appeals judge, to succeed him.

In 1971, in *Swann v. Charlotte-Mecklenburg Board of Education*, which arose from North Carolina, the justices unanimously approved a lower court's plan that required the extensive transportation of students to achieve school integration. The decision led to hundreds of cases in which judges throughout the country ordered the use of **busing** as a tool to achieve integration. With many white parents determined to keep their children in neighborhood schools and others willing to move to the suburbs or enroll them in private academies to avoid integration, busing became a lightning rod for protests. One of the most bitter fights took place in Boston in the mid-1970s. Residents of the tightly knit Irish-American community of South Boston demonstrated vociferously and sometimes violently against a busing plan decreed by a local judge.

The Supreme Court soon abandoned the idea of overturning local control of schools or moving students great distances to achieve integration. In *Milliken v. Bradley* (1974), the justices overturned a lower court order that required Detroit's predominantly white suburbs to enter into a regional desegregation plan with the city's heavily minority school system. By absolving suburban districts of responsibility for assisting in integrating urban schools, the decision guaranteed that housing segregation would be mirrored in public education. Indeed, by the 1990s, public schools in the North were considerably more segregated than those in the South.

Milliken v. Bradley

Many whites came to view affirmative action programs as a form of **reverse discrimination**. Even as such programs quickly spread from blacks to encompass women, Latinos, Asian-Americans, and Native Americans, conservatives demanded that the Supreme Court invalidate them all.

Opposition to affirmative action

The justices proved increasingly hostile to governmental affirmative action policies. In *Regents of the University of California v. Bakke* (1978), the Court overturned an admissions program of the University of California at Davis, a public university, which set aside 16 of 100 places in the entering medical school class for minority students. Justice Lewis F. Powell, a Nixon appointee who cast the deciding vote in the 5-4 decision, rejected the idea of fixed affirmative action quotas. He added, however, that race could be used as one factor among many in admissions decisions, so affirmative action continued at most colleges and universities. *Bakke* continues to be the standard by which affirmative action programs are judged today.

The Continuing Sexual Revolution

As noted in the previous chapter, the social activism associated with the 1960s continued in the following decade. Both right and left took part in grassroots movements, ranging from campaigns against nuclear weapons and nuclear power plants and struggles to aid migrant workers to battles to stop the court-ordered busing of public school children and movements against abortion rights. But the most profound changes in American life arose from the continuing sexual revolution.

To the alarm of conservatives, during the 1970s the sexual revolution passed from the counterculture into the social mainstream. The number of

Mainstream sexual revolution

**FIGURE 26.1
Median Age at
First Marriage,
1947–1981**

divorces soared, reaching more than 1 million in 1975, double the number ten years earlier. The age at which both men and women married rose dramatically. As a result of women's changing aspirations and the availability of birth control and legal abortions, the American birthrate declined dramatically. By 1976, the average woman was bearing 1.7 children during her lifetime, less than half the figure of 1957 and below the level at which a population reproduces itself. A 1971 survey of the last five graduating classes at Bryn Mawr, an elite women's college, reported the birth of more than seventy children. A similar survey covering the classes of 1971 through 1975 found that only three had been born. (Of course, many of these women eventually did marry and have children. But unlike their mothers of the "baby-boom" generation, they postponed these decisions to pursue careers.)

During the Nixon years, women made inroads into areas from which they had long been excluded. In 1972, Congress approved **Title IX**, which banned gender discrimination in higher education. The giant corporation American Telephone and Telegraph (AT&T) entered into a landmark agreement in which it paid millions of dollars to workers who had suffered gender discrimination and to upgrade employment opportunities for women. The number of women at work continued its upward climb. Working women were motivated by varied aims. Some sought careers in professions and skilled jobs previously open only to men. Others, spurred by the need to bolster family income as the economy faltered, flooded into the traditional, low-wage, "pink-collar" sector, working as cashiers, secretaries, and telephone operators.

Expansion of gay and lesbian movement

In addition, the gay and lesbian movement, born at the end of the 1960s, expanded greatly during the 1970s and became a major concern of the right. In 1969, there had been about fifty local gay rights groups in the United States; ten years later, their numbers reached into the thousands. They began to elect local officials, persuaded many states to decriminalize homosexual relations, and succeeded in convincing cities with large gay populations to pass antidiscrimination laws. They actively encouraged gay men and lesbians to "come out of the closet"—that is, to reveal their sexual orientation.

Nixon and Détente

"Soft" approach to communism

Just as domestic policies and social trends under Nixon disappointed conservatives, they viewed his foreign policy as dangerously "soft" on communism. To be sure, Nixon and Henry Kissinger, his national security adviser and secretary of state, continued their predecessors' policy of attempting to undermine Third World governments deemed dangerous to American strategic or economic interests. Nixon funneled arms to dictatorial pro-American regimes in Iran, the Philippines, and South Africa. After Chile in 1970 elected socialist Salvador Allende as president, the CIA worked with his domestic opponents to destabilize the regime. On September 11, 1973, Allende was overthrown and killed in a military coup, which installed a bloody dictatorship under General Augusto Pinochet. Thousands of Allende backers, including a few Americans then in Chile, were tortured and murdered, and many others fled the country. The Nixon administration continued to back Pinochet despite his brutal policies. Democracy did not return to Chile until the end of the 1980s.

The Allende affair

In his relations with the major communist powers, however, Nixon fundamentally altered Cold War policies. In the language of foreign relations, he and Kissinger were "realists." They had more interest in power than ideology and preferred international stability to relentless conflict. Nixon also hoped that if relations with the Soviet Union improved, the Russians would influence North Vietnam to agree to an end to the Vietnam War on terms acceptable to the United States.

Nixon and Kissinger's "realist" foreign policy

Nixon realized that far from being part of a unified communist bloc, China had its own interests, different from those of the Soviet Union, and was destined to play a major role on the world stage. The policy of refusing to recognize China's communist government had reached a dead end. In 1971, Kissinger flew secretly to China, paving the way for Nixon's own astonishing public visit of February 1972. The trip led to the Beijing government's taking up China's seat at the United Nations, previously occupied by the exiled regime on Taiwan.

Nixon in China

Three months after his trip to Beijing, Nixon became the first Cold War American president to visit the Soviet Union, where he engaged in intense negotiations with his Soviet counterpart, Leonid Brezhnev. Out of this summit meeting came agreements for increased trade and two landmark arms-control treaties. SALT (named for the **Strategic Arms Limitation Talks** under way since 1969) froze each country's arsenal of intercontinental missiles capable of carrying nuclear warheads. The Anti–Ballistic Missile Treaty banned the development of systems designed to intercept incoming missiles, so that neither side would be tempted to attack the other without fearing devastating retaliation. Nixon and Brezhnev proclaimed a new era of "peaceful coexistence," in which **détente** (cooperation) would replace the hostility of the Cold War.

Richard Nixon at a banquet celebrating his visit to China in February 1972. To his right is Premier Zhou Enlai.

VIETNAM AND WATERGATE

Nixon and Vietnam

Despite Nixon's foreign policy triumphs, one issue would not go away—Vietnam. On taking office, he announced a new policy, Vietnamization. Under this plan, American troops would gradually be withdrawn while South Vietnamese soldiers, backed by continued American bombing, did more and more of the fighting. But Vietnamization neither limited the war nor ended the antiwar movement. Hoping to cut North Vietnamese supply lines, Nixon in 1970 ordered American troops into neutral Cambodia. The invasion did not achieve its military goals, but it destabilized the Cambodian government and set in motion a chain of events that eventually brought to power the Khmer Rouge. Before being ousted by a Vietnamese invasion in 1979, this local communist movement attempted to force virtually all Cambodians into rural communes and committed widespread massacres in that unfortunate country.

The invasion of Cambodia and its consequences

As the war escalated, protests again spread on college campuses, partly because the policy of exempting students from the draft had ended. In the wake of the killing of four antiwar protesters at Kent State University by the Ohio National Guard and two by police at Jackson State University in Mississippi, the student movement reached its high-water mark. In the spring of 1970, more than 350 colleges and universities experienced strikes, and troops occupied 21 campuses. The protests at Kent State, a public university with a largely working-class student body, and Jackson State, a black institution, demonstrated how antiwar sentiment had spread far beyond elite campuses.

The same social changes sweeping the home front were evident among troops in Vietnam. Soldiers experimented with drugs, openly wore peace and Black-Power symbols, refused orders, and even assaulted unpopular officers. In 1971, thousands deserted the army, while at home Vietnam veterans held antiwar demonstrations. The decline of discipline within the army convinced increasing numbers of high-ranking officers that the United States must extricate itself from Vietnam.

Public support for the war was rapidly waning. In 1969, the *New York Times* published details of the **My Lai massacre** of 1968, in which a company of American troops killed some 350 South Vietnamese civilians. After a military

Tear gas envelops the campus as members of the Ohio National Guard prepare to fire on student demonstrators at Kent State University. Shortly after this photo was taken, four students lay dead.

investigation, one soldier, Lieutenant William Calley, was found guilty of directing the atrocity. (The courts released him from prison in 1974.) While hardly typical of the behavior of most servicemen, My Lai further undermined public support for the war. In 1971, the *Times* began publishing the **Pentagon Papers**, a classified report prepared by the Defense Department that traced American involvement in Vietnam back to World War II and revealed how successive presidents had misled the American people about it. In a landmark freedom-of-the-press decision, the Supreme Court rejected Nixon's request for an injunction to halt publication. In 1973, Congress passed the **War Powers Act**. The most vigorous assertion of congressional control over foreign policy in the nation's history, it required the president to seek congressional approval for the commitment of American troops overseas.

The Pentagon Papers

The End of the Vietnam War

Early in 1973, Nixon achieved what had eluded his predecessors—a negotiated settlement in Vietnam. The Paris peace agreement, the result of five years of talks, made possible the final withdrawal of American troops. The compromise left in place the government of South Vietnam, but it also left North Vietnamese and Viet Cong soldiers in control of parts of the South. The U.S. military draft came to an end. Henceforth, volunteers would make up the armed forces. But in the spring of 1975, the North Vietnamese launched a final military offensive. The government of South Vietnam collapsed. The United States did not intervene except to evacuate the American embassy, and Vietnam was reunified under communist rule.

The only war the United States has ever lost, Vietnam was a military, political, and social disaster. By the time it ended, 58,000 Americans had been killed, along with 3 million to 4 million Vietnamese. Vietnam undermined Americans' confidence in their own institutions and challenged long-standing beliefs about the country and its purposes.

Two decades after the war ended, former secretary of defense Robert McNamara published a memoir in which he admitted that the policy he had helped to shape had been "terribly wrong." Ignorance of the history and culture of Vietnam and a misguided belief that every communist movement in the world was a puppet of Moscow, he wrote, had led the country into a war that he now profoundly regretted. The political establishment had supported the war for most of its duration. For far too long, they had accepted its basic premise—that the United States had the right to decide the fate of a faraway people about whom it knew almost nothing.

A campaign poster from the 1972 election does not even name Richard Nixon, referring to him only as "the president." It includes images of some of his accomplishments, including pursuing détente with China (bottom) and the Soviet Union (above and to the left).

Watergate

By the time the war ended, Richard Nixon was no longer president. His domestic policies and foreign policy successes had contributed greatly to his reelection in 1972. He won a landslide victory over liberal Democrat George McGovern, receiving 60 percent of the popular vote. Nixon made deep inroads into former Democratic strongholds in the South and among working-class white northerners. He carried every state but Massachusetts. But his triumph soon turned into disaster.

Nixon's reelection

Nixon was obsessed with secrecy. He viewed every critic as a threat to national security and developed an "enemies list" that included reporters, politicians, and celebrities unfriendly to the administration. In June 1972, five former employees of Nixon's reelection committee took part in a break-in at Democratic Party headquarters in the **Watergate** apartment complex in Washington, D.C. A security guard called police, who arrested the intruders.

The break-in

No one knows precisely what the Watergate burglars were looking for (perhaps they intended to install listening devices), and the botched robbery played little role in the 1972 presidential campaign. But in 1973, Judge John J. Sirica, before whom the burglars were tried, determined to find out who had sponsored the break-in. A pair of *Washington Post* journalists began publishing investigative stories that made it clear that persons close to the president had ordered the burglary and then tried to "cover up" White House involvement. Congressional hearings followed that revealed a wider pattern of wiretapping, break-ins, and attempts to sabotage political opposition. When it became known that Nixon had made tape recordings of conversations in his office, Archibald Cox, a special prosecutor the president had reluctantly appointed to investigate the Watergate affair, demanded the tapes. In October 1973, Nixon proposed to allow Senator John C. Stennis of Mississippi to review the tapes, rather than release them. When Cox refused, Nixon fired him, whereupon Attorney General Elliot Richardson and his deputy resigned in protest. These events, known as the Saturday Night Massacre, further undermined Nixon's standing. The Supreme Court unanimously ordered Nixon to provide the tapes—a decision that reaffirmed the principle that the president is not above the law.

The Watergate hearings

Nixon's Fall

Week after week, revelations about the scandal unfolded. By mid-1974, it had become clear that whether or not Nixon knew in advance of the Watergate break-in, he had become involved immediately afterward in authorizing payments to the burglars to remain silent or commit perjury, and he had ordered the FBI to halt its investigation of the crime. In August 1974, the House Judiciary Committee voted to recommend that Nixon be impeached for conspiracy to obstruct justice. His political support having evaporated, Nixon became the only president in history to resign.

Nixon's resignation

Nixon's presidency remains a classic example of the abuse of political power. In 1973, his vice president, Spiro T. Agnew, resigned after revelations that he had accepted bribes from construction firms while serving as governor of Maryland. Nixon's attorney general, John Mitchell, and White House aides H. R. Haldeman and John Ehrlichman, were convicted of obstruction of justice in the Watergate affair and went to jail. As for the president, he insisted that he had done nothing wrong.

The aftermath of Watergate

His departure from office was followed by Senate hearings headed by Frank Church of Idaho that laid bare a history of abusive actions involving every administration since the beginning of the Cold War. In violation of the law, the FBI had spied on millions of Americans and had tried to disrupt the civil rights movement. The CIA had conducted secret operations to overthrow foreign governments and had tried to assassinate foreign leaders. Abuses of power, in other words, went far beyond the misdeeds of a single president.

The Church Committee revelations led Congress to enact new restrictions on the power of the FBI and CIA to spy on American citizens or conduct operations abroad without the knowledge of lawmakers. Congress also strengthened the Freedom of Information Act (FOIA), initially enacted in 1966. Since 1974, the FOIA has allowed scholars, journalists, and ordinary citizens to gain access to millions of pages of records of federal agencies.

Freedom of Information Act

Liberals, who had despised Nixon throughout his career, celebrated his downfall. Nixon's fall and the revelations of years of governmental misconduct helped to convince many Americans that conservatives were correct when they argued that to protect liberty it was necessary to limit Washington's power over Americans' lives.

THE END OF THE GOLDEN AGE

The Decline of Manufacturing

During the 1970s, the long period of postwar economic expansion and consumer prosperity came to an end, succeeded by slow growth and high inflation. For the only time in the twentieth century, other than the 1930s,

TABLE 26.1 The Misery Index, 1970–1980

YEAR	RATE OF INFLATION (%)	RATE OF UNEMPLOYMENT (%)	MISERY INDEX (%)
1970	5.9	4.9	10.8
1971	4.3	5.9	10.2
1972	3.3	5.6	8.9
1973	6.2	4.9	11.1
1974	11.0	5.6	16.6
1975	9.1	8.5	17.6
1976	5.8	7.7	13.5
1977	6.5	7.1	13.6
1978	7.7	6.1	13.8
1979	11.3	5.8	17.1
1980	13.5	7.1	20.6

the average American ended the 1970s poorer than when the decade began. There were many reasons for the end of capitalism's "golden age." With American prosperity seemingly unassailable and the military-industrial complex thriving, successive administrations had devoted little attention to the less positive economic consequences of the Cold War. To strengthen its anticommunist allies, the United States promoted the industrial reconstruction of Japan and Germany and the emergence of new centers of manufacturing in places like South Korea and Taiwan. It encouraged American companies to invest in overseas plants. The strong dollar, linked to gold by the Bretton Woods agreement of 1944, made it harder to sell American goods overseas (discussed in Chapter 22).

Economic weakness

In 1971, for the first time in the twentieth century, the United States experienced a merchandise trade deficit—that is, it imported more goods than it exported. By 1980, nearly three-quarters of goods produced in the United States were competing with foreign-made products, and the number of manufacturing workers, 38 percent of the American workforce in 1960, had fallen to 28 percent.

Trade deficit

In 1971, Nixon announced the most radical change in economic policy since the Great Depression. He took the United States off the gold standard, ending the Bretton Woods agreement that fixed the value of the dollar and other currencies in terms of gold. Henceforth, the world's currencies would "float" in relation to one another, their worth determined not by treaty but by

Currency values and trade

international currency markets. Nixon hoped that lowering the dollar's value in terms of the German mark and Japanese yen would promote exports by making American goods cheaper overseas and reduce imports, because foreign products would be more expensive in the United States. But the end of fixed currency rates injected a new element of instability into the world economy. Nixon also ordered wages and prices frozen for ninety days.

Stagflation

Nixon's policies temporarily curtailed inflation and reduced imports. But in 1973, a brief war broke out between Israel and its neighbors Egypt and Syria. Middle Eastern Arab states retaliated against Western support of Israel by quadrupling the price of oil and suspending the export of oil to the United States for several months. During the **oil embargo**, long lines of cars appeared at American gas stations, which either ran out of fuel or limited how much a customer could buy. A second "oil shock" occurred in 1979 as a result of the revolution that overthrew the shah of Iran, discussed later.

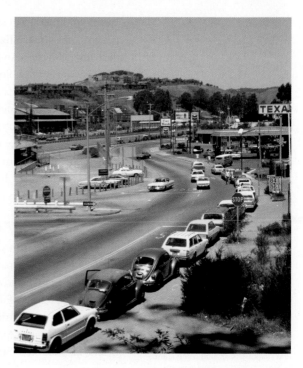

Drivers lining up to purchase gas during the oil crisis of 1973–1974.

Rising oil prices rippled through the world economy, contributing to the combination of stagnant economic growth and high inflation known as **stagflation**. Between 1973 and 1981, the rate of inflation in developed countries was 10 percent per year and the rate of economic growth only 2.4 percent, a sharp deterioration from the economic conditions of the 1960s. The so-called misery index—the sum of the unemployment and inflation rates—stood at 10.8 percent when the decade began. By 1980, it had almost doubled. As oil prices rose, many Americans shifted from large, domestically produced cars, known for high gasoline consumption, to smaller, more fuel-efficient imports. By the end of the decade, Japan had become the world's leading automobile producer, and imports accounted for nearly 25 percent of car sales in the United States.

The World Trade Center under construction in New York City in the 1970s.

The Beleaguered Social Compact

The economic crisis contributed to a breakdown of the postwar social compact. Faced with declining profits and rising overseas competition, corporations stepped up the trend, already under way before 1970, toward eliminating well-paid manufacturing jobs through automation and

FIGURE 26.2
Real Average
Weekly Wages,
1955–1990

Because of economic dislocations and deindustrialization, Americans' real wages (wages adjusted to take account of inflation) peaked in the early 1970s and then began a sharp, prolonged decline.

President Gerald Ford tried to enlist Americans in his "Whip Inflation Now" program. It did not succeed.

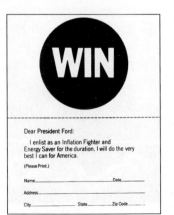

shifting production to low-wage areas of the United States and overseas. By 1980, **deindustrialization** in Detroit and Chicago included the loss of more than half the manufacturing jobs in existence three decades earlier.

The accelerating flow of jobs, investment, and population to the non-union, low-wage states of the **Sunbelt** increased the political influence of this conservative region.

In some manufacturing centers, political and economic leaders welcomed the opportunity to remake their cities as finance, information, and entertainment hubs. In New York, the construction of the World Trade Center, completed in 1977, symbolized this shift in the economy. Until destroyed by terrorists twenty-four years later, the 110-story "twin towers" stood as a symbol of New York's grandeur. But to make way for the World Trade Center, the city displaced hundreds of small electronics, printing, and other firms, causing the loss of thousands of manufacturing jobs.

Always a junior partner in the Democratic coalition, the labor movement found itself forced onto the defensive. It has remained there ever since.

The weakening of unions and the continuation of the economy's long-term shift from manufacturing to service employment had an adverse impact on ordinary Americans. Between 1953 and 1973, median family income had doubled. But in 1973, real wages began to fall.

Ford as President

Economic problems dogged the presidencies of Nixon's successors. Gerald Ford, who had been appointed to replace Vice President Agnew, succeeded to the White House when Nixon resigned. Ford named Nelson Rockefeller of New York as his own vice president. Thus, for the only time in American history, both offices were occupied by persons for whom no one had actually voted. Among his first acts as president, Ford pardoned Nixon, shielding him from prosecution for obstruction of justice. Ford claimed that he wanted the country to put the Watergate scandal behind it. But the pardon proved to be widely unpopular.

In domestic policy, Ford's presidency lacked significant accomplishment. To combat inflation, Ford urged Americans to shop wisely, reduce expenditures, and wear WIN buttons (for "Whip Inflation Now"). Although inflation fell, joblessness continued to rise. During the steep recession of 1974–1975 unemployment exceeded 9 percent, the highest level since the Depression.

In the international arena, 1975 witnessed the major achievement of Ford's presidency. In a continuation of Nixon's policy of détente, the United States and Soviet Union signed an agreement at Helsinki, Finland, that recognized the permanence of Europe's post–World War II boundaries (including the division of Germany). In addition, both superpowers agreed to respect the basic liberties of their citizens. Secretary of State Henry Kissinger and his Soviet counterpart, Andrey Gromyko, assumed that this latter pledge would have little practical effect. But over time, the **Helsinki Accords** inspired movements for greater freedom within the communist countries of eastern Europe.

The Helsinki Accords

The Carter Administration

In the presidential election of 1976, Jimmy Carter, a former governor of Georgia, narrowly defeated Ford. A graduate of the U.S. Naval Academy who later became a peanut farmer, Carter was virtually unknown outside his state when he launched his campaign for the Democratic nomination. But realizing that Watergate and Vietnam had produced a crisis in confidence in the federal government, he turned his obscurity into an advantage. Carter ran for president as an "outsider," making a virtue of the fact that he had never held federal office. A devout "born-again" Baptist, he spoke openly of his religious convictions. His promise, "I'll never lie to you," resonated with an electorate tired of official dishonesty.

Jimmy Carter's background

Carter had much in common with Progressives of the early twentieth century. His passions were making government more efficient, protecting the environment, and raising the moral tone of politics. Unlike the Progressives, however, he embraced the aspirations of black Americans. As president, Carter appointed an unprecedented number of blacks to important positions, including Andrew Young, a former lieutenant of Martin Luther King Jr., as ambassador to the United Nations.

Carter and race

Carter and the Economic Crisis

The Democratic Party found itself ill-equipped to deal with the economic crisis. The social upheavals of the 1960s had led to the emergence of politicians known collectively as the New Democrats. Representing affluent urban and suburban districts, they viewed issues like race relations, gender equality, the environment, and improving the political process as more central than traditional economic matters. Although his party controlled both houses, Carter often found himself at odds with Congress. He viewed inflation, not unemployment, as the country's main economic problem, and to combat it he promoted cuts in spending on domestic programs. In the hope that increased competition would reduce prices, his administration enacted **deregulation** in the trucking and airline industries. In 1980, with Carter's approval, Congress repealed usury laws—laws that limit how

The New Democrats

Carter's economic plan

The deregulation of the airline industry brought lower fares but also a drastic decline in service. Before deregulation, with prices fixed, airlines sought to attract customers by providing good service. Today, fares may be lower, but passengers are jammed in like sardines and have to pay for checked baggage, onboard meals, and other amenities.

much interest lenders can charge—allowing credit card companies to push their interest rates up to 20 percent or even higher.

Carter also believed that expanded use of nuclear energy could help reduce dependence on imported oil. For years, proponents of nuclear power had hailed it as an inexpensive way of meeting the country's energy needs. By the time Carter took office, more than 200 nuclear plants were operating or on order. But in 1979 the industry suffered a near-fatal blow when an accident at the **Three Mile Island** plant in Pennsylvania released a large amount of radioactive steam into the atmosphere. The Three Mile Island mishap reinforced fears about the environmental hazards associated with nuclear energy and put a halt to the industry's expansion.

Since the New Deal, Democrats had presented themselves as the party of affluence and economic growth. But Carter seemed to be presiding over a period of national decline. It did not help his popularity when, in a speech in 1979, he spoke of a national "crisis of confidence" and seemed to blame it on the American people themselves and their "mistaken idea of freedom" as "self-indulgence and consumption."

The Emergence of Human Rights Politics

Carter's human rights foreign policy

Under Carter, a commitment to promoting human rights became a centerpiece of American foreign policy for the first time. He was influenced by the proliferation of information about global denials of human rights spread by nongovernmental agencies like Amnesty International and the International League for Human Rights. Their reports marked a significant break with dominant ideas about international affairs since World War II, which had viewed the basic division in the world as between communist and noncommunist countries. Such reports, along with congressional hearings, exposed misdeeds not only by communist countries but also by American allies, especially the death squads of Latin American dictatorships.

Argentina

In 1978, Carter cut off aid to the brutal military dictatorship governing Argentina, which in the name of anticommunism had launched a "dirty war" against its own citizens, kidnapping off the streets and secretly murdering an estimated 10,000 to 30,000 persons. Carter's action was a dramatic gesture, as Argentina was one of the most important powers in Latin America, and previous American administrations had turned a blind eye to human rights abuses by Cold War allies. By the end of his presidency, the phrase "human rights" had acquired political potency.

Carter believed that in the post-Vietnam era, American foreign policy should de-emphasize Cold War thinking. Combating poverty in the Third World, preventing the spread of nuclear weapons, and promoting human rights should take priority over what he called "the inordinate fear of communism that once led us to embrace any dictator who joined us in that fear." In one of his first acts as president, he offered an unconditional pardon to Vietnam-era draft resisters.

President Jimmy Carter (*center*), Egyptian president Anwar Sadat (*left*), and Israeli prime minister Menachem Begin (*right*) celebrating the signing of the 1979 peace treaty between Israel and Egypt.

Carter's emphasis on pursuing peaceful solutions to international problems and his willingness to think outside the Cold War framework yielded important results. In 1979, he brought the leaders of Egypt and Israel to the presidential retreat at Camp David and brokered a historic peace agreement, the **Camp David Accords**, between the two countries. He improved American relations with Latin America by agreeing to a treaty, ratified by the Senate in 1978, that provided for the transfer of the Panama Canal to local control by the year 2000. Carter attempted to curb the murderous violence of death squads allied to the right-wing government of El Salvador, and in 1980 he suspended military aid after the murder of four American nuns by members of the country's army.

Both conservative Cold Warriors and foreign policy "realists" severely criticized Carter's emphasis on human rights. He himself found it impossible to translate rhetoric into action. He criticized American arms sales to the rest of the world. But with thousands of jobs and billions of dollars in corporate profits at stake, he did nothing to curtail them. The United States continued its support of allies with records of serious human rights violations such as the governments of Guatemala, the Philippines, South Korea, and Iran. Indeed, the American connection with the shah of Iran, whose secret police regularly jailed and tortured political opponents, proved to be Carter's undoing.

Carter's effectiveness

The Iran Crisis and Afghanistan

Occupying a strategic location on the southern border of the Soviet Union, Iran was a major supplier of oil and an importer of American military equipment. At the end of 1977, Carter traveled there to help celebrate the shah's rule, causing the internal opposition to become more and more

American hostages being paraded by their Iranian captors on the first day of the occupation of the American embassy in Tehran in 1979. Television gave extensive coverage to the plight of the hostages, leading many Americans to view the Carter administration as weak and inept.

anti-American. Early in 1979, a popular revolution inspired by the exiled Muslim cleric Ayatollah Khomeini overthrew the shah and declared Iran an Islamic republic.

When Carter in November 1979 allowed the deposed shah to seek medical treatment in the United States, Khomeini's followers invaded the American embassy in Tehran and seized sixty-six hostages. They did not regain their freedom until January 1981, on the day Carter's term as president ended. Events in Iran made Carter seem helpless and inept and led to a rapid fall in his popularity.

Another crisis that began in 1979 undermined American relations with Moscow. At the end of that year, the Soviet Union sent thousands of troops into Afghanistan to support a friendly government threatened by an Islamic rebellion. In the long run, Afghanistan became the Soviet Vietnam, an unwinnable conflict whose mounting casualties seriously weakened the government at home. Initially, however, it seemed another example of declining American power.

Actions in Afghanistan

Declaring the invasion the greatest crisis since World War II (a considerable exaggeration), the president announced the Carter Doctrine, declaring that the United States would use military force, if necessary, to protect its interests in the Persian Gulf. He organized a Western boycott of the 1980 Olympics, which took place in Moscow, and dramatically increased American military spending. In a reversion to the Cold War principle that any opponent of the Soviet Union deserved American support, the United States funneled aid to fundamentalist Muslims in Afghanistan who fought a decade-long guerrilla war against the Soviets. The alliance had unforeseen consequences. A faction of Islamic fundamentalists known as the Taliban eventually came to power in Afghanistan. Tragically, they would prove as hostile to the United States as to Moscow.

THE RISING TIDE OF CONSERVATISM

Issues for conservatives

The combination of domestic and international dislocations during the 1970s created a widespread sense of anxiety among Americans and offered conservatives new political opportunities. Economic problems heightened the appeal of lower taxes, reduced government regulation, and cuts in social spending to spur business investment. Fears about a decline of American power in the world led to calls for a renewal of the Cold War. The civil rights and sexual revolutions produced resentments that undermined the Democratic coalition. Rising urban crime rates reinforced demands for law and order and attacks on courts considered too lenient toward criminals. These issues brought new converts to the conservative cause.

As the 1970s went on, conservatives abandoned overt opposition to the black struggle for racial justice. The fiery rhetoric and direct confrontation tactics of Bull Connor, George Wallace, and other proponents of massive resistance were succeeded by appeals to freedom of association, local control, and resistance to the power of the federal government. This language of individual freedom resonated throughout the country, appealing especially to the growing, predominantly white, suburban population that was fleeing the cities and their urban problems. The suburbs would become one of the bastions of modern conservatism.

Conservatives and freedom

One set of recruits was the **neoconservatives**, a group of intellectuals who charged that the 1960s had produced a decline in moral standards and respect for authority. Once supporters of liberalism, they had come to believe that even well-intentioned government social programs did more harm than good. Neoconservatives repudiated the attempts by Nixon, Ford, and Carter to reorient foreign policy away from the Cold War. Conservative "think tanks" created during the 1970s, like the Heritage Foundation and the American Enterprise Institute, refined and spread these ideas.

Neoconservatives

The Religious Right

The rise of religious fundamentalism during the 1970s expanded conservatism's popular base. Even as membership in mainstream denominations like Episcopalianism and Presbyterianism declined, evangelical Protestantism flourished. Some observers spoke of a Third Great Awakening (like those of the 1740s and early nineteenth century). The election of Carter, the first "born-again" Christian to become president, highlighted the growing influence of evangelical religion. But unlike Carter, most fundamentalists who entered politics did so as conservatives.

Evangelical religion

Evangelical Christians had become more and more alienated from a culture that seemed to them to trivialize religion and promote immorality. Although it spoke of restoring traditional values, the Religious Right proved remarkably adept at using modern technology, including mass mailings and televised religious programming, to raise funds for its crusade and spread its message. In 1979, Jerry Falwell, a Virginia minister,

Conservatism and the evangelicals

VOICES OF FREEDOM

From Barry Commoner, *The Closing Circle* (1971)

Environmentalism, a movement born in the 1960s, expanded rapidly in the following decade. In *The Closing Circle*, Barry Commoner, a biologist later called the Paul Revere of the movement, warned that technological development and the pursuit of economic growth regardless of consequences were creating an environmental crisis. He called on Americans to alter their lifestyles to bring them into harmony with the "ecosphere"—the natural environment within which people live.

The environment has just been rediscovered by the people who live in it. In the United States the event was celebrated in April 1970, during Earth Week. It was a sudden, noisy awakening. School children cleaned up rubbish; college students organized new demonstrations; determined citizens recaptured the streets from the automobile, at least for a day. Everyone seemed to be aroused to the environmental danger and eager to do something about it.

They were offered lots of advice. Almost every writer, almost every speaker, on the college campuses, in the streets and on television and radio broadcasts, was ready to fix the blame and pronounce a cure for the environmental crisis.

Some blamed pollution on the rising population. . . . Some blamed man's innate aggressiveness. . . . Having spent some years in the effort simply to detect and describe the growing list of environmental problems—radioactive fallout, air and water pollution, the deterioration of the soil—and in tracing some of their links to social and political processes, the identification of a single cause and cure seemed a rather bold step. . . .

Any living thing that hopes to live on the earth must fit into the ecosphere or perish. The environmental crisis is a sign that the finely sculpted fit between life and its surroundings has begun to corrode. As the links between one living thing and another, and between all of them and their surroundings, begin to break down, the dynamic interactions that sustain the whole have begun to falter and, in some places, stop. . . .

We have broken out of the circle of life, converting its endless cycles into man-made, linear events; oil is taken from the ground, distilled into fuel, burned in an engine, converted thereby into noxious fumes, which are emitted into the air. At the end of the line is smog. Other man-made breaks in the ecosphere's cycle spew out toxic chemicals, sewage, heaps of rubbish—the testimony to our power to tear the ecological fabric that has, for millions of years, sustained the planet's life.

From Richard E. Blakemore, Report on the Sagebrush Rebellion (1979)

The rapid growth of the environmentalist movement sparked a conservative reaction, especially in the western states. What came to be called the Sagebrush Rebellion denounced federal control of large areas of western land as well as new environmental regulations that, the "rebels" claimed, threatened energy production and long-standing grazing rights. Richard E. Blakemore, a member of the Nevada state senate, offered this explanation of the outlook of many westerners.

The "sagebrush rebellion" is a catchy but somewhat misleading term used to describe the western states' demands for a greater role in determining the future of the west. Unlike the dictionary definition, in this rebellion there is no armed or unlawful resistance to government. Neither is western land desolate or worthless as the term "sagebrush" connoted. Moreover, if much of the land in the west ever was considered of little worth, the need for energy has changed that.

Statistics show that much of the west is controlled by the federal government. . . . On average, the federal government controls 52.6 percent of the land in the 12 western states. . . . For many years, the public domain was open to ranching, mining, and outdoor recreation. But a number of federal acts, passed to protect and conserve the environment, have closed great parts of the public domain to traditional uses. . . .

The west today is at the confluence of two major movements—that for protection of the environment and that for production of energy. To a great extent, the success of the attempt for U.S. energy independence depends on resources of the west. In addition, the west is looked to for increased agricultural production and for its reserves of minerals necessary to modern industry. The environmental movement prompted the passage of federal legislation aimed at protecting the environment and maintaining great portions of the country in a natural state. Among the major environmental acts of the past 15 years are the Wilderness Act, the National Environmental Protection Act, the Federal Land Policy Management Act, the Wild and Scenic Rivers Act, and the National Forest Management Act.

The genesis of the sagebrush rebellion can be found in the conflict between the desires to protect and preserve the environment and the demands for food, minerals, and energy from the west. . . .

QUESTIONS

1. *How and why does Commoner ask Americans to rethink their definition of freedom?*

2. *What elements of environmental policy does Blakemore see as a threat to "our freedoms"?*

3. *How do the two writers differ in their visions of the future of American society?*

founded the self-styled Moral Majority, devoted to waging a "war against sin" and electing "pro-life, pro-family, pro-America" candidates to office.

Christian conservatives seemed most agitated by the ongoing sexual revolution, which they saw as undermining the traditional family and promoting immorality. As a result of the 1960s, they believed, American freedom was out of control.

The Battle over the Equal Rights Amendment

During the 1970s, "family values" moved to the center of conservative politics, nowhere more so than in the battle over the Equal Rights Amendment (ERA). Originally proposed during the 1920s by Alice Paul and the Women's Party, the ERA had been revived by second-wave feminists. In the wake of the rights revolution, the amendment's affirmation that "equality of rights under the law" could not be abridged "on account of sex" hardly seemed controversial. In 1972, with little opposition, Congress approved the ERA and sent it to the states for ratification. Designed to eliminate obstacles to the full participation of women in public life, it aroused unexpected protest from those who claimed it would discredit the role of wife and homemaker.

The ERA

The ERA debate reflected a division among women as much as a battle of the sexes. To its supporters, the amendment offered a guarantee of women's freedom in the public sphere. To its foes, freedom for women still resided in the divinely appointed roles of wife and mother. They claimed that the ERA would let men "off the hook" by denying their responsibility

Women divided

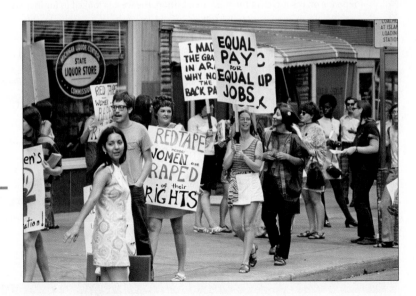

A women's liberation march in Detroit in 1970 highlights the issue of equal pay for equal work. At the time, women earned less than men in virtually every category of employment.

to provide for their wives and children. Polls consistently showed that a majority of Americans, male and female, favored the ERA. But thanks to the mobilization of conservative women, the amendment failed to achieve ratification by the required thirty-eight states.

The Abortion Controversy

An even more acrimonious battle emerged in the 1970s over abortion rights, another example, to conservatives, of how liberals in office promoted sexual immorality at the expense of moral values. The movement to reverse the 1973 *Roe v. Wade* decision began among Roman Catholics, whose church condemned abortion under any circumstances. But it soon enlisted evangelical Protestants and social conservatives more generally. Life, the movement insisted, begins at conception, and abortion is nothing less than murder. Between this position and the feminist insistence that a woman's right to control her body includes the right to a safe, legal abortion, compromise was impossible.

The abortion issue drew a bitter, sometimes violent line through American politics. It affected battles over nominees to judicial positions and led to demonstrations at family-planning and abortion clinics. The anti-abortion movement won its first victory in 1976 when Congress, over President Ford's veto, ended federal funding for abortions for poor women through the Medicaid program. By the 1990s, a few fringe anti-abortion activists were placing bombs at medical clinics and murdering doctors who terminated pregnancies.

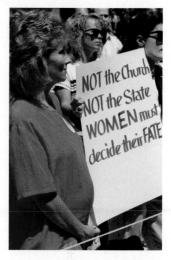

Demonstrators at a rally supporting abortion rights.

Violent anti-abortion activism

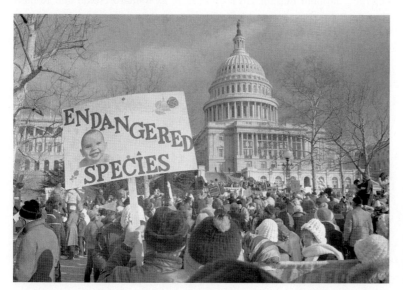

A 1979 anti-abortion rally in Washington, D.C., on the sixth anniversary of the Supreme Court's decision in *Roe v. Wade*, which barred states from limiting a woman's right to terminate a pregnancy.

The Tax Revolt

Conservative economics

With liberals unable to devise an effective policy to counteract deindustrialization and declining real wages, economic anxieties also created a growing constituency for conservative economics. Unlike during the Great Depression, economic distress inspired a critique of government rather than of business. New environmental regulations led to calls for less government intervention in the economy. The descent from affluence to "stagflation" increased the appeal of the conservative argument that government regulation raised business costs and eliminated jobs.

Demands for lower taxes

Economic decline also broadened the constituency receptive to demands for lower taxes. To conservatives, tax reductions served the dual purposes of enhancing business profits and reducing the resources available to government, thus making new social programs financially impossible.

Conservatism in the West

The West has always both reflected and contributed to national political trends. In the 1970s and 1980s it offered fertile soil for various strands of conservatism. The population movements of previous decades stimulated this development. Many southerners had left their homes for southern California, bringing with them their distinctive form of evangelical Christianity. Increasingly alienated from a Democratic Party that embraced the rights revolution and with it, evangelicals felt, the decline of traditional values, they gravitated to the California Republican Party, from which emerged national Republican leaders such as Richard Nixon and Ronald Reagan. California conservatives also embraced the new anti-tax mood.

California conservatives

California's Proposition 13

In 1978, conservatives sponsored and California voters approved Proposition 13, a ban on further increases in property taxes. The vote demonstrated that the level of taxation could be a powerful political issue. Proposition 13 proved to be a windfall for businesses and home owners while reducing funds available for schools, libraries, and other public services. Many voters, however, proved willing to accept this result of lower taxes. As anti-tax sentiment flourished throughout the country, many states followed California's lead.

There have always been voices in the West insisting that the region has a colonial relationship with the rest of the country. They point to federal ownership of large swaths of western land, and the dependence of western development on investment from the East. In the late nineteenth century, this view helped give rise to western Populism, when the targets of protest were eastern banks and railroad companies, as well as a national economic policy that favored these corporations. Nearly a century later it became associated with a conservative upsurge known as the Sagebrush Rebellion (the name given to a bill passed by the Nevada legislature in 1979) directed at the federal government. The roots of this "rebellion" lie as far back as the 1920s, when the U.S. Forest Service announced plans to increase grazing fees and mineral rights in national forests and other public lands. Nevada's ranchers went to court to block these fees but were rebuffed by the Supreme Court. In the 1970s, new environmental regulations won fresh recruits to the movement. The Clean Air Act alarmed western coal operators. Westerners who believed the environmental policies of the Carter administration were closing the public domain to exploitation eagerly supported Ronald Reagan's presidential candidacy.

Sagebrush Rebellion

The Election of 1980

By 1980, Carter's approval rating had fallen to 21 percent—lower than Nixon's at the time of his resignation. Ronald Reagan's 1980 campaign for the presidency brought together the many strands of 1970s conservatism. He pledged to end stagflation and restore the country's dominant role in the world and its confidence in itself. "Let's make America great again," he proclaimed. "The era of self-doubt is over."

Reagan's appeal

Reagan also appealed skillfully to "white backlash." He kicked off his campaign in Philadelphia, Mississippi, where three civil rights workers had been murdered in 1964, with a speech emphasizing his belief in states' rights. Many white southerners understood this doctrine as including opposition to federal intervention on behalf of civil rights. During the campaign, Reagan repeatedly condemned welfare "cheats," school busing, and affirmative action. The Republican platform reversed the party's long-standing support for the Equal Rights Amendment and condemned moral permissiveness. Although not personally religious and the first divorced man to run for president, Reagan won the support of the Religious Right and conservative upholders of "family values."

Riding a wave of dissatisfaction with the country's condition, Reagan swept into

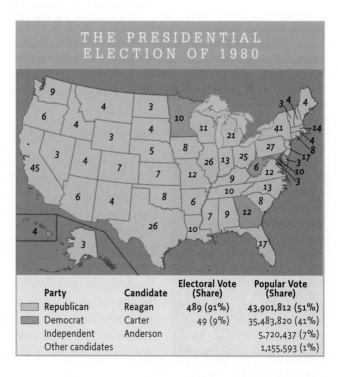

THE PRESIDENTIAL ELECTION OF 1980

Party	Candidate	Electoral Vote (Share)	Popular Vote (Share)
Republican	Reagan	489 (91%)	43,901,812 (51%)
Democrat	Carter	49 (9%)	35,483,820 (41%)
Independent	Anderson		5,720,437 (7%)
Other candidates			1,155,593 (1%)

Before entering politics, Ronald Reagan was a prominent actor and a spokesperson for General Electric. In this 1958 photograph, he demonstrates the use of a GE oven.

A delegate to the Republican national convention of 1980 wears a hat festooned with the flags of the United States and Texas and a button with a picture of her hero, Ronald Reagan.

the White House. Because moderate Republican John Anderson, running for president as an independent, received about 7 percent of the popular vote, Reagan won only a bare majority, although he commanded an overwhelming margin in the electoral college. Carter received 41 percent, a humiliating defeat for a sitting president.

The election of 1980 launched the **Reagan Revolution**, which completed the transformation of freedom from the rallying cry of the left to a possession of the right.

THE REAGAN REVOLUTION

Ronald Reagan followed a most unusual path to the presidency. Originally a New Deal Democrat and head of the Screen Actors Guild (he was the only union leader ever to reach the White House), he emerged in the 1950s as a spokesman for the General Electric Corporation, preaching the virtues of unregulated capitalism. His nominating speech for Barry Goldwater at the 1964 Republican convention brought Reagan to national attention. Two years later, California voters elected Reagan as governor. His victory in 1980 brought to power a diverse coalition of old and new conservatives: Sunbelt suburbanites and urban working-class ethnics, antigovernment crusaders and advocates of a more aggressive foreign policy, libertarians who believed in freeing the individual from restraint, and the Christian Right, which sought to restore what they considered traditional moral values to American life.

Reagan and American Freedom

Reagan's opponents often underestimated him. By the time he left office at the age of seventy-seven, he had become the oldest man ever to serve as president. Unlike most modern presidents, he was content to outline broad policy themes and leave their implementation to others.

Reagan, however, was hardly a political novice. He was an excellent public speaker, and his optimism and affability appealed to large numbers of Americans. Reagan made conservatism seem progressive, rather than an attempt to turn back the tide of progress. Reagan repeatedly invoked the idea that America has a divinely appointed mission as a "beacon of liberty and freedom." Freedom, indeed, became the watchword of the Reagan Revolution. In his public appearances and state papers, Reagan used the word more often than any president before him.

Reagan reshaped the nation's agenda and political language more effectively than any president since Franklin D. Roosevelt. On issues ranging from taxes to government spending, national security, crime, welfare, and "traditional values," he put Democrats on the defensive. But he also proved to be a pragmatist, recognizing when to compromise so as not to fragment his diverse coalition of supporters.

Reagan as leader

Reagan's Economic Policies

In 1981, Reagan persuaded Congress to reduce the top tax rate from 70 percent to 50 percent and to index tax brackets to take inflation into account. Five years later, the Tax Reform Act reduced the rate on the wealthiest Americans to 28 percent. These measures marked a sharp retreat from the principle of progressivity (the idea that the wealthy should pay a higher percentage of their income in taxes than other citizens), one of the ways twentieth-century societies tried to address the unequal distribution of wealth. Reagan also appointed conservative heads of regulatory agencies, who cut back on environmental protection and workplace safety rules, about which business had complained for years.

Tax reform

Since the New Deal, liberals had tried to promote economic growth by using the power of the government to bolster ordinary Americans' purchasing power. Reagan's economic program, known as "supply-side economics" by proponents and "trickle-down economics" by critics, relied on high interest rates to curb inflation and lower tax rates, especially for businesses and high-income Americans, to stimulate private investment. The policy assumed that cutting taxes would inspire Americans at all income levels to work harder, because they would keep more of the money they earned.

Supply-side economics

Reagan and Labor

Reagan inaugurated an era of hostility between the federal government and organized labor. In August 1981, when 13,000 members of PATCO, the union of air traffic controllers, began a strike in violation of federal law, Reagan fired them all. He used the military to oversee the nation's air traffic system until new controllers could be trained. Reagan's action inspired many private employers to launch anti-union offensives. The hiring of workers to replace permanently those who had gone on strike, a rare occurrence before 1980, became widespread. Manufacturing employment, where union membership was concentrated, meanwhile continued its long-term decline. By the mid-1990s, the steel industry employed only 170,000 persons—down from 600,000 in 1973.

The air traffic controllers' strike

Reaganomics, as critics dubbed the administration's policies, initially produced the most severe recession since the 1930s. A long period of economic expansion, however, followed the downturn of 1981–1982. As companies "downsized" their workforces, shifted production overseas, and took advantage of new technologies such as satellite communications, they became more profitable. At the same time, the rate of inflation, 13.5 percent at the beginning of 1981, declined to 3.5 percent in 1988, partly because a period of expanded oil production that drove down prices succeeded the shortages of the 1970s. By the end of Reagan's presidency in 1989, the real gross domestic product had risen by 25 percent and unemployment was down to 5.5 percent. These were significant accomplishments.

Downsizing

The Problem of Inequality

Together, Reagan's policies, rising stock prices, and deindustrialization resulted in a considerable rise in economic inequality. By the mid-1990s, the richest 1 percent of Americans owned 40 percent of the nation's wealth, twice their share twenty years earlier. Most spent their income not on productive investments and charity as supply-side economists had promised, but on luxury goods, real-estate speculation, and corporate buyouts that often led to plant closings as operations were consolidated. The income of middle-class families, especially those with a wife who did not work outside the home, stagnated while that of the poorest one-fifth of the population declined.

During the 1970s, Jim Crow had finally ended in many workplaces and unions. But just as decades of painful efforts to obtain better jobs bore fruit, hundreds of thousands of black workers lost their jobs when factories closed their doors. In South Gate, a working-class suburb of Los Angeles, for example, the giant Firestone tire factory shut down in 1980, only a few years after black and Latino workers made their first breakthroughs in employment. When the national unemployment rate reached 8.9 percent at the end of 1981, the figure for blacks exceeded 20 percent.

The wealthiest American families benefited the most from economic expansion during the 1980s, whereas the poorest 40 percent of the population saw their real incomes decline. (Real income indicates income adjusted to take account of inflation.)

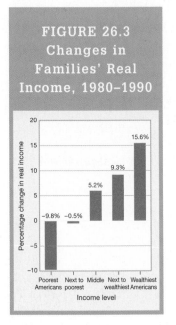

FIGURE 26.3
Changes in Families' Real Income, 1980–1990

The Second Gilded Age

In retrospect, the 1980s, like the 1890s, would be widely remembered as a decade of misplaced values. Buying out companies generated more profits than running them; making deals, not making products, became the way to get rich. The merger of Nabisco and R. J. Reynolds Tobacco Company in 1988 produced close to $1 billion in fees for lawyers, economic advisers, and stockbrokers. "Greed is healthy," declared Wall Street financier Ivan

This photograph of the remains of the Bethlehem Steel plant in Lackawanna, New York, which closed in 1982, depicts the aftermath of deindustrialization. Today, the site is a wind farm, with eight windmills helping to provide electricity for the city.

Boesky (who ended up in prison for insider stock trading). "Yuppie"—the young urban professional who earned a high income working in a bank or stock-brokerage firm and spent lavishly on designer clothing and other trappings of the good life—became a household word.

Yuppies

Taxpayers footed the bill for some of the consequences. The deregulation of savings and loan associations—banks that had generally confined themselves to financing home mortgages—allowed those institutions to invest in unsound real-estate ventures and corporate mergers. Losses piled up, and the Federal Savings and Loan Insurance Corporation, which insured depositors' accounts, faced bankruptcy. After Reagan left office, the federal government bailed out the savings and loan institutions at a cost to taxpayers estimated at $250 billion.

Federal bailout

Supply-side advocates insisted that lowering taxes would enlarge government revenue by stimulating economic activity. But spurred by large increases in funds for the military, federal spending far outstripped income, producing large budget deficits, despite assurances by supply-siders that this would not happen. During Reagan's presidency, the national debt tripled to $2.7 trillion.

A homeless St. Louis mother and her children, forced to live in their car, photographed in 1987.

Nonetheless, Reagan remained immensely popular. He won a triumphant reelection in 1984. His opponent, Walter Mondale (best remembered for choosing Congresswoman Geraldine Ferraro of New York as his running mate, the first woman candidate on a major-party presidential ticket), carried only his home state of Minnesota and the District of Columbia.

First lady Nancy Reagan promoting her "Just Say No" campaign against the use of drugs, in a photo from 1986.

Conservatives and Reagan

Although he implemented their economic policies, Reagan in some ways disappointed ardent conservatives. The administration left intact core elements of the welfare state, such as Social Security, Medicare, and Medicaid, which many conservatives wished to curtail significantly or repeal. The Reagan era did little to advance the social agenda of the Christian Right. Abortion remained legal, women continued to enter the labor force in unprecedented numbers, and Reagan even appointed the first female member of the Supreme Court, Sandra Day O'Connor. In 1986, in *Bowers v. Hardwick*, in a rare victory for cultural conservatives, the Supreme Court did uphold the constitutionality of state laws outlawing homosexual acts. (In 2003, the justices would reverse the *Bowers* decision, declaring unconstitutional laws that criminalized homosexuality.)

Reagan and the Cold War

In foreign policy, Reagan resumed vigorous denunciation of the Soviet Union—calling it an "evil empire"—and sponsored the largest military buildup in American history, including new long-range bombers and missiles. In 1983, he proposed an entirely new strategy, the Strategic Defense Initiative, which would develop a space-based system to intercept and destroy enemy missiles. The idea was not remotely feasible technologically, and, if deployed, it would violate the Anti-Ballistic Missile Treaty of 1972. But it appealed to Reagan's desire to reassert America's worldwide power.

Hollywood joined enthusiastically in the revived Cold War. The 1984 film *Red Dawn* depicted a Soviet invasion of the United States.

Reagan came into office determined to overturn the **"Vietnam Syndrome"**—as widespread public reluctance to commit American forces overseas was called. He sent American troops to the Caribbean island of Grenada to oust a pro-Cuban government. In 1982, Reagan dispatched marines as a peacekeeping force to Lebanon, where a civil war raged between the Christian government, supported by Israeli forces, and Muslim insurgents. But he quickly withdrew them after

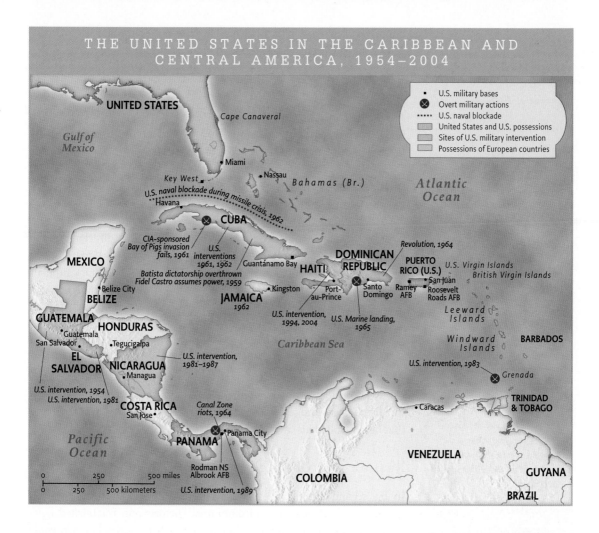

THE UNITED STATES IN THE CARIBBEAN AND CENTRAL AMERICA, 1954–2004

Legend:
- U.S. military bases
- Overt military actions
- U.S. naval blockade
- United States and U.S. possessions
- Sites of U.S. military intervention
- Possessions of European countries

UNITED STATES
Cape Canaveral
Gulf of Mexico
Miami
Key West
Nassau
Bahamas (Br.)
Atlantic Ocean
U.S. naval blockade during missile crisis, 1962
Havana
CUBA
CIA-sponsored Bay of Pigs invasion fails, 1961
U.S. interventions 1961, 1962
Guantánamo Bay
Batista dictatorship overthrown Fidel Castro assumes power, 1959
MEXICO
Belize City
BELIZE
GUATEMALA
Guatemala
San Salvador
HONDURAS
Tegucigalpa
EL SALVADOR
NICARAGUA
Managua
U.S. intervention, 1954
U.S. intervention, 1981
COSTA RICA
San José
Canal Zone riots, 1964
PANAMA
Panama City
Rodman NS
Albrook AFB
U.S. intervention, 1989
Pacific Ocean
JAMAICA
1962
Kingston
HAITI
Port-au-Prince
U.S. intervention, 1994, 2004
DOMINICAN REPUBLIC
Santo Domingo
U.S. Marine landing, 1965
Revolution, 1964
PUERTO RICO (U.S.)
San Juan
Ramey AFB
Roosevelt Roads AFB
U.S. Virgin Islands
British Virgin Islands
Leeward Islands
Caribbean Sea
Windward Islands
U.S. intervention, 1983
Grenada
BARBADOS
TRINIDAD & TOBAGO
Caracas
U.S. intervention, 1981–1987
VENEZUELA
GUYANA
COLOMBIA
BRAZIL

0   250   500 miles
0   250   500 kilometers

a bomb exploded at their barracks, killing 241 Americans. The public, Reagan realized, would support minor operations like Grenada but remained unwilling to sustain heavy casualties abroad.

Abandoning the Carter administration's emphasis on human rights, Reagan embraced the idea, advanced in 1979 by neoconservative writer Jeane Kirkpatrick, that the United States should oppose "totalitarian" communists but assist "authoritarian" noncommunist regimes. The United States stepped up its alliances with Third World anticommunist dictatorships like the governments of Chile and South Africa. The administration poured in funds to combat insurgencies against the governments of El Salvador and Guatemala, whose armies and associated death squads committed flagrant abuses against their own citizens. When El Salvador's army massacred

As in the first part of the twentieth century, the United States intervened frequently in Caribbean and Central American countries during and immediately after the Cold War.

Latin America

hundreds of civilians in the town of El Mozote in 1981, the State Department denied that the event, widely reported in the press, had taken place.

The Iran-Contra Affair

American involvement in Central America produced the greatest scandal of Reagan's presidency, the **Iran-Contra affair**. In 1984, Congress banned military aid to the Contras (derived from the Spanish word for "against") fighting the Sandinista government of Nicaragua, which had ousted the American-backed dictator Anastasio Somoza in 1979. In 1985, Reagan secretly authorized the sale of arms to Iran—now involved in a war with its neighbor, Iraq—in order to secure the release of a number of American hostages held by Islamic groups in the Middle East. CIA director William Casey and Lieutenant Colonel Oliver North of the National Security Council set up a system that diverted some of the proceeds to buy military supplies for the Contras in defiance of the congressional ban. The scheme continued for nearly two years.

Arms for hostages

In 1987, after a Middle Eastern newspaper leaked the story, Congress held televised hearings that revealed a pattern of official duplicity and violation of the law reminiscent of the Nixon era. Eleven members of the administration eventually were convicted of perjury or destroying documents, or pleaded guilty before being tried. Reagan denied knowledge of the illegal proceedings, but the Iran-Contra affair undermined confidence that he controlled his own administration.

President Reagan visited Moscow in 1988, cementing his close relationship with Soviet leader Mikhail Gorbachev. They were photographed in Red Square.

Reagan and Gorbachev

In his second term, to the surprise of both his foes and his supporters, Reagan softened his anticommunist rhetoric and established good relations with Soviet premier Mikhail Gorbachev. Gorbachev had come to power in 1985, bent on reforming the Soviet Union's repressive political system and reinvigorating its economy. Gorbachev inaugurated policies known as *glasnost* (political openness) and *perestroika* (economic reform).

Gorbachev realized that significant change would be impossible without reducing his country's military budget. Reagan was ready to negotiate. A series of talks between 1985 and 1987 yielded more progress on arms control than in the entire postwar period to that point, including an agreement to eliminate intermediate- and short-range nuclear missiles in Europe. In 1988, Gorbachev began pulling Soviet troops out of Afghanistan. Having entered office as an ardent Cold Warrior, Reagan left with hostilities between the superpowers much diminished. He even repudiated his earlier comment that the Soviet Union was an "evil empire," saying that it referred to "another era."

Reagan's Legacy

Reagan's presidency revealed the contradictions at the heart of modern conservatism. In some ways, the Reagan Revolution undermined the very values and institutions conservatives held dear. Intended to discourage reliance on government handouts by rewarding honest work and business initiative, Reagan's policies inspired a speculative frenzy that enriched architects of corporate takeovers and investors in the stock market while leaving in their wake plant closings, job losses, and devastated communities. Nothing proved more threatening to local traditions or family stability than deindustrialization, insecurity about employment, and the relentless downward pressure on wages.

Social and economic repurcussions

Nonetheless, few figures have so successfully changed the landscape and language of politics. Reagan's vice president, George H. W. Bush, defeated Michael Dukakis, the governor of Massachusetts, in the 1988 election partly because Dukakis could not respond effectively to the charge that he was a "liberal"—now a term of political abuse. Conservative assumptions about the virtues of the free market and the evils of "big government" dominated the mass media and political debates. During the 1990s, these and other conservative ideas would be embraced almost as fully by President Bill Clinton, a Democrat, as by Reagan and the Republicans.

Reagan's impact

The Election of 1988

The 1988 election seemed to show politics sinking to new lows. Television advertisements and media exposés now dominated political campaigns. The race for the Democratic nomination had hardly begun before the front-runner, Senator Gary Hart of Colorado, withdrew after a newspaper reported that he had spent the night at his Washington town house with a woman other than his wife. Democrats ridiculed the Republican vice presidential nominee, Senator Dan Quayle of Indiana, for factual and linguistic mistakes. Republicans spread unfounded rumors that Michael Dukakis's wife had burned an American flag during the 1960s. The low point of the campaign came in a Republican television ad depicting the threatening image of Willie Horton, a black murderer and rapist who had been furloughed from prison during Dukakis's term as governor of Massachusetts. Rarely in the modern era had a major party appealed so blatantly to racial fears.

A dismal campaign

Bush achieved a substantial majority, winning 54 percent of the popular vote. Democratic success in retaining control of Congress suggested that an electoral base existed for a comeback. But this would only occur if the party fashioned a new appeal to replace traditional liberalism, which had been eclipsed by the triumph of conservatism.

CHAPTER REVIEW AND ONLINE RESOURCES

REVIEW QUESTIONS

1. Why were social issues associated with the sexual revolution so contested by all sides?

2. What were continuing challenges to the cohesiveness of the Democratic (New Deal) coalition? What were the consequences of those divisions?

3. What were the main features of Nixon's policy of "realism" in dealing with China and the Soviet Union?

4. Describe the basic events and the larger significance of the Watergate scandal.

5. What were the major causes for the decline of the U.S. economy during the 1970s?

6. What were the causes and consequences of the public's disillusionment with the federal government in the 1970s and 1980s?

7. Identify the groups and their agendas that combined to create the new conservative base in the 1970s and 1980s.

8. What impact did Ronald Reagan have on the American political scene?

9. Why was there growth in economic inequality in the 1980s?

10. How did various groups see the relationship between women's rights and freedom differently?

KEY TERMS

affirmative action (p. 812)
busing (p. 812)
reverse discrimination (p. 813)
Title IX (p. 814)
Strategic Arms Limitation Talks (p. 815)
détente (p. 815)
My Lai massacre (p. 816)
Pentagon Papers (p. 817)
War Powers Act (p. 817)
Watergate (p. 818)
oil embargo (p. 821)
stagflation (p. 821)
deindustrialization (p. 822)
Sunbelt (p. 822)
Helsinki Accords (p. 823)
deregulation (p. 823)
Three Mile Island (p. 824)
Camp David Accords (p. 825)
neoconservatives (p. 827)
Reagan Revolution (p. 834)
Reaganomics (p. 836)
Vietnam Syndrome (p. 838)
Iran-Contra affair (p. 840)

Go to 🐇 INQUIZITIVE

To see what you know—and learn what you've missed—with personalized feedback along the way.

Visit the *Give Me Liberty!* **Student Site** for primary source documents and images, interactive maps, author videos featuring Eric Foner, and more.

CHAPTER 27

FROM TRIUMPH TO TRAGEDY

★

1989-2001

1989   Communism falls in eastern Europe

U.S.-led Panamanian coup

1990   Americans with Disabilities Act

Germany reunifies

1991   Gulf War

Dissolution of the Soviet Union

1992   Los Angeles riots

Casey v. Planned Parenthood of Pennsylvania

William Jefferson Clinton elected president

1993   North American Free Trade Agreement approved

1994   Republicans win in Congress; Contract with America

Rwandan genocide

1995   Oklahoma City federal building bombed

1996   Clinton eliminates Aid to Families with Dependent Children

1998–   Clinton impeachment
1999   proceedings

Kosovo War

1999   Protests in Seattle against the World Trade Organization

Glass-Steagall Act repealed

2000   *Bush v. Gore*

2001   9/11 attacks

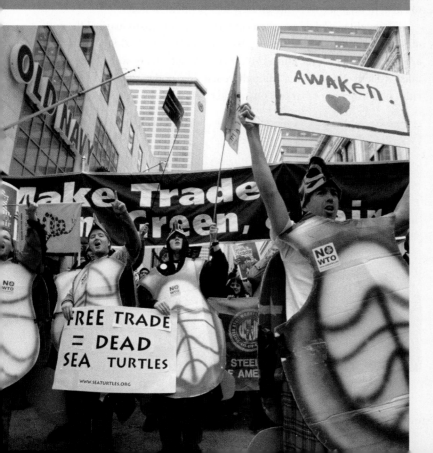

Protesters dressed as sea turtles, an endangered species, at the demonstrations against the World Trade Organization in Seattle, December 1999.

The year 1989 was one of the most momentous of the twentieth century. In April, tens of thousands of student demonstrators occupied Tiananmen Square in the heart of Beijing, demanding greater democracy in China. The students erected a figure reminiscent of the Statue of Liberty, calling it "The Goddess of Democracy and Freedom." In June, Chinese troops crushed the protest, killing an unknown number of people, possibly thousands.

In the fall of 1989, pro-democracy demonstrations spread across eastern Europe. Mikhail Gorbachev made it clear that unlike in the past, the Soviet Union would not intervene. The climactic event took place on November 9 when crowds breached the Berlin Wall, which since 1961 had stood as the Cold War's most prominent symbol. One by one, the region's communist governments agreed to give up power. In 1990, a reunified German nation absorbed East Germany. The remarkably swift and almost entirely peaceful collapse of communism in eastern Europe became known as the "velvet revolution."

Meanwhile, the Soviet Union itself slipped deeper and deeper into crisis. One after another, the republics of the Soviet Union declared themselves sovereign states. By the end of 1991, the Soviet Union ceased to exist; in its place were fifteen new independent nations.

The sudden and unexpected collapse of communism marked the end of the Cold War and a stunning triumph for the United States and its allies. For the first time since 1917, there existed a truly worldwide capitalist system. Even China, though remaining under Communist Party rule, had already embarked on market reforms and rushed to attract

Demonstrators dancing atop the Berlin Wall on November 10, 1989. The next day, crowds began dismantling it, in the most dramatic moment of the collapse of communist rule in eastern Europe.

EASTERN EUROPE AFTER THE COLD WAR

foreign investment. Other events suggested that the 1990s would also be a "decade of democracy." In 1990, South Africa released Nelson Mandela, head of the African National Congress, from prison. Four years later, as a result of the first democratic elections in the country's history, Mandela became president, ending the system of state-sponsored racial inequality, known as "apartheid," and white minority government. Throughout Latin America and Africa, civilian governments replaced military rule.

The end of the Cold War and breakup of the Soviet Union, Czechoslovakia, and Yugoslavia redrew the map of eastern Europe (compare this map with the map of Cold War Europe in Chapter 23). Two additional nations that emerged from the Soviet Union lie to the east and are not indicated here: Kyrgyzstan and Tajikistan.

THE POST–COLD WAR WORLD

The sudden shift from a bipolar world to one of unquestioned American predominance promised to redefine the country's global role. President George H. W. Bush spoke of the coming of a **new world order**. But no

The Goddess of Democracy and Freedom, a statue reminiscent of the Statue of Liberty, was displayed by pro-democracy advocates during the 1989 demonstrations in Beijing's Tiananmen Square. After allowing it to continue for two months, the Chinese government sent troops to crush the peaceful occupation of the square.

one knew what its characteristics would be and what new challenges to American power might arise.

A New World Order?

Bush's first major foreign policy action was a throwback to the days of American interventionism in the Western Hemisphere. At the end of 1989, he dispatched troops to Panama to overthrow the government of General Manuel Antonio Noriega, a former ally of the United States who had become involved in the international drug trade.

The Gulf War

A far more serious crisis arose in 1990 when Iraq invaded and annexed Kuwait, an oil-rich sheikdom on the Persian Gulf. Fearing that Iraqi dictator Saddam Hussein might next attack Saudi Arabia, a longtime ally that supplied more oil to the United States than any other country, Bush rushed troops to defend Kuwait and warned Iraq to withdraw from the country or face war.

In February 1991, the United States launched Operation Desert Storm, which quickly drove the Iraqi army from Kuwait. The United Nations ordered Iraq to disarm and imposed economic sanctions that produced widespread civilian suffering for the rest of the decade. But Hussein remained in place. So did a large American military establishment in Saudi Arabia, to the outrage of Islamic fundamentalists who deemed its presence an affront to their faith. In the **Gulf War's** immediate aftermath, Bush's public approval rating rose to an unprecedented 89 percent.

Public approval

Visions of America's Role

In a speech to Congress, President Bush identified the Gulf War as the first step in the struggle to create a world rooted in democracy and global free trade. But it remained unclear how this broad vision would be translated into policy. Soon after the end of the war, General Colin Powell, chairman of the Joint Chiefs of Staff, and Dick Cheney, the secretary of defense, outlined different visions of the future. Powell predicted that the post–Cold War world would be a dangerous environment with conflicts popping

Conflicting visions

up in unexpected places. To avoid being drawn into an unending role as global policeman, he insisted, the United States should not commit its troops abroad without clear objectives and a timetable for withdrawal. Cheney argued that with the demise of the Soviet Union, the United States possessed the power to reshape the world and prevent hostile states from achieving regional power. For the rest of the 1990s, it was not certain which definition of the American role in the post–Cold War world would predominate.

The Election of Clinton

Had a presidential election been held early in 1991, Bush would undoubtedly have been victorious. But later that year, the economy slipped into recession. Despite victory in the Cold War and the Gulf, more and more Americans believed the country was on the wrong track. No one seized more effectively on this widespread sense of unease than Bill Clinton, a former governor of Arkansas. In 1992, Clinton won the Democratic nomination by combining social liberalism (he supported abortion rights, gay rights, and affirmative action for racial minorities) with elements of conservatism (he pledged to reduce government bureaucracy and, borrowing a page from Republicans, promised to "end welfare as we know it").

Bill Clinton's appeal

A charismatic campaigner, Clinton conveyed sincere concern for voters' economic anxieties. Bush, by contrast, seemed out of touch with the day-to-day lives of ordinary Americans. On the wall of Democratic headquarters, Clinton's campaign director posted the slogan, "It's the Economy, Stupid"—a reminder that the economic downturn was the Democrats' strongest card. Bush was further weakened when conservative leader Pat Buchanan delivered a fiery televised speech at the Republican national convention that declared cultural war against gays, feminists, and supporters of abortion rights. This rhetoric seemed to confirm the Democratic portrait of Republicans as intolerant and divisive.

Economic and social issues

A third candidate, the eccentric Texas billionaire Ross Perot, also entered the fray. He attacked Bush and Clinton as lacking the economic know-how to deal with the recession and the ever-increasing national debt. That millions of Americans considered Perot a credible candidate—at one point, polls showed him leading both Clinton and Bush—testified to widespread dissatisfaction with the major parties. Perot's support faded, but he still received 19 percent of the popular vote, the best result for a third-party candidate since Theodore Roosevelt in 1912. Clinton won by

Bush's weakness

a substantial margin, a humiliating outcome for Bush, given his earlier popularity.

Clinton in Office

Clinton's domestic policy

In his first two years in office, Clinton turned away from some of the social and economic policies of the Reagan and Bush years. He appointed several blacks and women to his cabinet, including Janet Reno, the first female attorney general, and named two supporters of abortion rights, Ruth Bader Ginsburg and Stephen Breyer, to the Supreme Court. He modified the military's strict ban on gay soldiers, instituting a "**Don't ask, don't tell**" policy by which officers would not seek out gays for dismissal from the armed forces. His first budget raised taxes on the wealthy and significantly expanded the Earned Income Tax Credit (EITC)—a cash payment for low-income workers

Earned Income Tax Credit

begun during the Ford administration. The most effective antipoverty policy since the Great Society, the EITC raised more than 4 million Americans, half of them children, above the poverty line during Clinton's presidency.

Clinton shared his predecessor's passion for free trade. Despite strong opposition from unions and environmentalists, he obtained congressional approval in 1993 of the **North American Free Trade Agreement** (NAFTA), a treaty negotiated by Bush that created a free-trade zone consisting of Canada, Mexico, and the United States.

The major policy initiative of Clinton's first term was a plan devised

Clinton's universal health plan

by a panel headed by his wife, Hillary, to address the rising cost of health care and the increasing number of Americans who lacked health insurance. In Canada and western Europe, governments provided universal medical coverage. The United States had the world's most advanced medical technology but a woefully incomplete system of health insurance. Tens of millions of Americans lacked any coverage at all.

Announced with great fanfare by Hillary Rodham Clinton at congressional hearings in 1993, Clinton's plan would have provided universal coverage through large groupings of medical care businesses. Doctors and health insurance and drug companies attacked it vehemently, fearing government regulations that would limit reimbursement for medical procedures and the cost of drugs. Too complex to be easily understood by most voters, and vulnerable to criticism for further expanding the unpopular federal bureaucracy, the plan died in 1994.

The "Freedom Revolution"

With the economy recovering slowly from the recession and Clinton's first two years in office seemingly lacking in significant accomplishments, voters in 1994 turned against the administration. For the first time since the 1950s, Republicans won control of both houses of Congress. They proclaimed their triumph the "Freedom Revolution." Newt Gingrich, a conservative congressman from Georgia who became the new Speaker of the House, masterminded their campaign. Gingrich had devised a platform called the **Contract with America**, which promised to curtail the scope of government, cut back on taxes and economic and environmental regulations, overhaul the welfare system, and end affirmative action.

A twenty-acre tire pile in Smithfield, Rhode Island, shown here in 1999, exemplifies the threat posed by industrial waste to the natural environment. It sits less than ten miles from the state's main water supply.

Republicans moved swiftly to implement its provisions. The House approved deep cuts in social, educational, and environmental programs, including the popular Medicare system. With the president and Congress unable to reach agreement on a budget, the government in December 1995 shut down all nonessential operations, including Washington, D.C., museums and national parks. Most Americans blamed Congress for the impasse, however, and Congress soon retreated.

Clinton's Political Strategy

Like Truman after the Republican sweep of 1946, Clinton rebuilt his popularity by campaigning against a radical Congress. He opposed the most extreme parts of his opponents' program, while adopting others. In his state of the union address of January 1996, he announced that "the era of big government is over," in effect turning his back on the tradition of Democratic Party liberalism and embracing the antigovernment outlook associated with Republicans.

Ending AFDC

Also in 1996, ignoring the protests of most Democrats, Clinton signed into law a Republican bill that abolished the program of Aid to Families with Dependent Children (AFDC), commonly known as "welfare." Grants of money to the states, with strict limits on how long recipients could receive payments, replaced it. At the time of its abolition, AFDC assisted 14 million individuals, 9 million of them children. Thanks to stringent new

VOICES OF FREEDOM

From Bill Clinton,
Speech on Signing of NAFTA (1993)

The North American Free Trade Agreement was signed by President Bill Clinton early in his first term. It created a free-trade zone (an area where goods can travel freely without import duties) composed of Canada, the United States, and Mexico. Clinton asked Americans to accept economic globalization as an inevitable form of progress and the path to future prosperity. "There will be no job loss," he promised. Things did not entirely work out that way.

As President, it is my duty to speak frankly to the American people about the world in which we now live. Fifty years ago, at the end of World War II, an unchallenged America was protected by the oceans and by our technological superiority and, very frankly, by the economic devastation of the people who could otherwise have been our competitors. We chose then to try to help rebuild our former enemies and to create a world of free trade supported by institutions which would facilitate it. . . . As a result, jobs were created, and opportunity thrived all across the world. . . .

For the last 20 years, in all the wealthy countries of the world—because of changes in the global environment, because of the growth of technology, because of increasing competition—the middle class that was created and enlarged by the wise policies of expanding trade at the end of World War II has been under severe stress. Most Americans are working harder for less. They are vulnerable to the fear tactics and the averseness to change that are behind much of the opposition to NAFTA. But I want to say to my fellow Americans: When you live in a time of change, the only way to recover your security and to broaden your horizons is to adapt to the change—to embrace, to move forward. . . . The only way we can recover the fortunes of the middle class in this country so that people who work harder and smarter can, at least, prosper more, the only way we can pass on the American dream of the last 40 years to our children and their children for the next 40, is to adapt to the changes which are occurring.

In a fundamental sense, this debate about NAFTA is a debate about whether we will embrace these changes and create the jobs of tomorrow or try to resist these changes, hoping we can preserve the economic structures of yesterday. . . . I believe that NAFTA will create 1 million jobs in the first 5 years of its impact. . . . NAFTA will generate these jobs by fostering an export boom to Mexico by tearing down tariff walls. . . . There will be no job loss.

From Global Exchange, Seattle, Declaration for Global Democracy (December 1999)

The demonstrations that disrupted the December 1999 meeting of the World Trade Organization in Seattle brought to public attention a widespread dissatisfaction with the effects of economic globalization. In this declaration, organizers of the protest offered their critique.

As citizens of global society, recognizing that the World Trade Organization is unjustly dominated by corporate interests and run for the enrichment of the few at the expense of all others, we demand:

Representatives from all sectors of society must be included in all levels of trade policy formulations. All global citizens must be democratically represented in the formulation, implementation, and evaluation of all global social and economic policies.

Global trade and investment must not be ends in themselves, but rather the instruments for achieving equitable and sustainable development including protection for workers and the environment.

Global trade agreements must not undermine the ability of each nation-state or local community to meet its citizens' social, environmental, cultural or economic needs.

The World Trade Organization must be replaced by a democratic and transparent body accountable to citizens—not to corporations.

No globalization without representation!

QUESTIONS

1. *Why does Clinton feel that free trade is necessary to American prosperity?*

2. *Why do the Seattle protesters feel that the World Trade Organization is a threat to democracy?*

3. *How do these documents reflect contradictory arguments about the impact of globalization in the United States?*

eligibility requirements imposed by the states and the economic boom of the late 1990s, welfare rolls plummeted. But the number of children living in poverty remained essentially unchanged.

Clinton's strategy enabled him to neutralize Republican claims that Democrats were the party of high taxes and lavish spending on persons who preferred dependency to honest labor. Clinton's passion for free trade alienated many working-class Democrats but convinced much of the middle class that the party was not beholden to the unions.

The presidential election of 1996

Clinton easily defeated Republican Bob Dole in the presidential contest of 1996, becoming the first Democrat elected to two terms since FDR. Clinton had accomplished for Reaganism what Eisenhower had done for the New Deal and Nixon for the Great Society—consolidating a basic shift in American politics by accepting many of the premises of his opponents.

Clinton and World Affairs

Like Jimmy Carter before him, Clinton took steps to encourage the settlement of long-standing international conflicts and tried to elevate support for human rights to a central place in international relations. He achieved only mixed success.

Massacres in Rwanda

Like Carter, Clinton found it difficult to balance concern for human rights with strategic and economic interests and to formulate clear guidelines for humanitarian interventions overseas. For example, the United States did nothing in 1994 when tribal massacres racked Rwanda, in central Africa. More than 800,000 people were slaughtered in the **Rwandan genocide**, and 2 million refugees fled the country.

The most complex foreign policy crisis of the Clinton years arose from the disintegration of Yugoslavia, a multi-ethnic state in southeastern Europe that had been carved from the old Austro-Hungarian empire after World War I. As in the rest of eastern Europe, the communist government that had ruled Yugoslavia since the 1940s collapsed in 1989. Within a few years, the country's six provinces dissolved into five new states. During the ensuing **Balkan crisis**, ethnic conflict plagued several of these new nations. **Ethnic cleansing**—a terrible new term meaning the forcible

The Balkan crisis

expulsion from an area of a particular ethnic group—now entered the international vocabulary.

With the Cold War over, protection of human rights in the Balkans gave NATO a new purpose. In 1998, Yugoslavian troops and local Serbs conducted ethnic cleansing against the Albanian population of Kosovo,

Serbian refugees fleeing a Croat offensive during the 1990s. By the fall of 1995, the wars that followed the breakup of Yugoslavia and accompanying "ethnic cleansing" had displaced over 3 million people.

a province of Serbia. More than 800,000 Albanians fled the region. To halt the bloodshed, NATO launched a two-month war in 1999 against Yugoslavia that led to the deployment of American and UN forces in Kosovo.

Human Rights

During Clinton's presidency, human rights played an increasingly important role in international affairs. Hundreds of nongovernmental agencies throughout the world defined themselves as protectors of human rights. During the 1990s, the agenda of international human rights organizations expanded to include access to health care, women's rights, and the rights of indigenous peoples like the Aborigines of Australia and the descendants of the original inhabitants of the Americas. The United States dispatched the military to distant parts of the world to assist in international missions to protect civilians.

An expanding agenda

New institutions emerged that sought to punish violations of human rights. The Rwandan genocide produced a UN-sponsored war crimes court that sentenced the country's former prime minister to life in prison. An international tribunal put Yugoslav president Slobodan Milošević on trial for sponsoring the massacre of civilians. It remained to be seen whether these initiatives would grow into an effective international system of protecting human rights across national boundaries.

Punishing human rights violations

GLOBALIZATION AND ITS DISCONTENTS

In December 1999, delegates from around the world gathered in Seattle for a meeting of the World Trade Organization (WTO), a 135-nation group created five years earlier to reduce barriers to international commerce and settle trade disputes. To the astonishment of residents of the city, more than 30,000 persons gathered to protest the meeting. Their marches and rallies brought together factory workers, who claimed that global free trade encouraged corporations to shift production to low-wage centers overseas, and "tree-huggers," as some reporters called environmentalists, who complained about the impact on the earth's ecology of unregulated economic development.

Protests in Seattle

Once a center of labor radicalism, the Seattle area in 1999 was best known as the home of Microsoft, developer of the Windows operating system used in most of the world's computers. The company's worldwide reach symbolized **globalization**, the process by which people, investment, goods, information, and culture increasingly flowed across national boundaries. Globalization has been called "*the* concept of the 1990s."

Globalization

Globalization, of course, was hardly a new phenomenon. The internationalization of commerce and culture and the reshuffling of the world's peoples had been going on since the explorations of the fifteenth century. But the scale and scope of late-twentieth-century globalization was unprecedented. Thanks to satellites and the Internet, information and popular culture flowed instantaneously to every corner of the world. Manufacturers and financial institutions scoured the world for profitable investment opportunities.

Perhaps most important, the collapse of communism between 1989 and 1991 opened almost the entire world to the spread of market capitalism and to the idea that government should interfere as little as possible with economic activity. American politicians and social commentators increasingly criticized the regulation of wages and working conditions, assistance to the less fortunate, and environmental protections as burdens on international competitiveness. During the 1990s, presidents Bush, a Republican, and Clinton, a Democrat, both spoke of an American mission to create a single global free market as the path to rising living standards, the spread of democracy, and greater worldwide freedom.

Spread of market capitalism

The media called the loose coalition of groups who organized the Seattle protests and others like it the "antiglobalization" movement. In fact, they challenged not globalization itself but its social consequences. Globalization, the demonstrators claimed, accelerated the worldwide creation of wealth but widened gaps between rich and poor countries and between haves and have-nots within societies. Decisions affecting the day-to-day lives of millions of people were made by institutions—the World Trade Organization, International Monetary Fund, World Bank, and multinational corporations—that operated without any democratic input. Demonstrators demanded not an end to global trade and capital flows but the establishment of international standards for wages, labor conditions, and the environment, and greater investment in health and education in poor countries.

Gap between haves and have-nots

The Battle of Seattle placed on the national and international agendas a question that promises to be among the most pressing concerns of the twenty-first century—the relationship between globalization, economic justice, and freedom.

The economy's performance in the 1990s at first seemed to justify the claims of globalization's advocates. Clinton's popularity rested in part on the American economy's remarkable performance in the mid- and late 1990s. After recovery from the recession of 1990–1991, economic expansion continued for the rest of the decade. By 2000, unemployment stood below 4 percent, a figure not seen since the 1960s. Because Reagan and Bush had left behind massive budget deficits, Clinton worked hard to balance the federal budget—a goal traditionally associated with fiscal conservatives. Because economic growth produced rising tax revenues, Clinton during his second term not only balanced the budget but actually produced budget surpluses.

Economic growth

The Computer Revolution

Many commentators spoke of the 1990s as the dawn of a "new economy," in which computers and the Internet would produce vast new efficiencies and the production and sale of information would occupy the central place once held by the manufacture of goods. Computers had first been developed during and after World War II to solve scientific problems and do calculations involving enormous amounts of data. The early ones were extremely large, expensive, and, by modern standards, slow. Research for the space program of the 1960s spurred the development of the microchip, on which circuits could be imprinted.

Origins of computers

Microchips made possible the development of entirely new consumer products. Video cassette recorders, handheld video games, cellular phones, and digital cameras were mass produced at affordable prices during the 1990s, mostly in Asia and Latin America rather than the

Two architects of the computer revolution, Steve Jobs (on the left), the head of Apple Computer, and Bill Gates, founder of Microsoft, which makes the operating system used in most of the world's computers.

United States. But it was the computer that transformed American life. As computers became smaller, faster, and less expensive, they found a place in businesses of every kind. They also changed private life. By the year 2000, nearly half of all American households owned a personal computer, used for entertainment, shopping, and sending and receiving electronic mail. Centers of computer technology, such as Silicon Valley south of San Francisco, the Seattle and Austin metropolitan areas, and lower Manhattan, boomed during the 1990s.

The Internet, first developed as a high-speed military communications network, was simplified and opened to commercial and individual use through personal computers. The Internet expanded the flow of information and communications more radically than any invention since the printing press. The fact that anyone with a computer could post his or her ideas for worldwide circulation led "netizens" ("citizens" of the Internet) to hail the advent of a new, democratic public sphere in cyberspace.

The Stock Market Boom and Bust

Economic growth and talk of a new economy sparked a frenzied boom in the stock market that was reminiscent of the 1920s. Investors, large and small, poured funds into stocks, spurred by the rise of discount and online firms that advertised aggressively and charged lower fees than traditional brokers. By 2000, a majority of American households owned stocks outright or through investment in mutual funds and pension and retirement accounts.

Dot-com bubble

Investors were especially attracted to the new "dot coms"—companies that conducted business via the Internet and seemed to symbolize the promise of the new economy. The NASDAQ, a stock exchange dominated by new technology companies, rose more than 500 percent from 1998 to 1999. Many of these "high-tech" companies never turned a profit. But economic journalists and stockbrokers explained that the new economy had so revolutionized business that traditional methods of assessing a company's value no longer applied.

Inevitably, the bubble burst. On April 14, 2000, stocks suffered their largest one-day point drop in history. For the first time since the

Depression, stock prices declined for three successive years (2000–2002), wiping out billions of dollars in Americans' net worth and pension funds. The value of NASDAQ stocks fell by nearly 80 percent between 2000 and 2002. By 2001, the American economy had fallen into a recession. Talk of a new economy, it appeared, had been premature.

The Enron Syndrome

Only after the market dropped did it become apparent that the stock boom of the 1990s had been fueled in part by fraud. During the late 1990s, accounting firms like Arthur Andersen, giant banks like JPMorgan, Chase, and Citigroup, and corporate lawyers pocketed extravagant fees for devising complex schemes to help push up companies' stock prices by hiding their true financial condition. Enron, a Houston-based energy company that epitomized the new economy—it bought and sold electricity rather than actually producing it—reported as profits billions of dollars in operating losses.

Corporate fraud

In the early twenty-first century, the bill came due for many corporate criminals. Kenneth Lay and Jeffrey Skilling, chief officers of Enron, were convicted by a Texas jury of multiple counts of fraud.

Fruits of Deregulation

At the height of the 1990s boom, with globalization in full swing, stocks rising, and the economy expanding, the economic model of free trade and deregulation appeared unassailable. But the retreat from government economic regulation, a policy embraced by both the Republican Congress and President Clinton, left no one to represent the public interest. The sectors of the economy most affected by the scandals—energy, telecommunications, and stock trading—had all been subjects of deregulation.

Many stock frauds stemmed from the repeal in 1999 of the Glass-Steagall Act, a New Deal measure that separated commercial banks, which accept deposits and make loans, from investment banks, which invest in stocks and real estate and take larger risks.

Cartoonist David Jacobson's comment on the Enron scandal.

"Let's say I was Enron, how would you do my taxes?"

Banks took their new freedom as an invitation to engage in all sorts of misdeeds, knowing that they had become so big that if disaster struck, the federal government would have no choice but to rescue them. They poured money into risky mortgages. When the housing bubble collapsed in 2007–2008, the banks suffered losses that threatened to bring down the entire financial system. The George W. Bush and Obama administrations felt they had no choice but to expend hundreds of billions of dollars of taxpayer money to save the banks from their own misconduct.

Rising Inequality

The boom that began in 1995 benefited nearly all Americans. For the first time since the early 1970s, average real wages and family incomes began to grow significantly. Economic expansion at a time of low unemployment brought rapid increases in wages for families at all income levels.

Yet, despite these gains, in the last two decades of the twentieth century, the poor and the middle class became worse off while the rich became significantly richer. The wealth of the richest Americans exploded during the 1990s. Sales of luxury goods like yachts and mansions boomed. Bill Gates, head of Microsoft and the country's richest person, owned as much wealth as the bottom 40 percent of the American population put together.

Barbie's Liberty, a satirical work by the artist Hans Haacke, recasts the Barbie doll, one of America's most successful toys, in the image of the Statue of Liberty to comment on the loss of manufacturing jobs to low-wage areas overseas.

Companies continued to shift manufacturing jobs overseas. Thanks to NAFTA, which eliminated barriers to imports from Mexico, a thriving industrial zone emerged just across the southern border of the United States, where American manufacturers built plants to take advantage of cheap labor and weak environmental and safety regulations. Despite low unemployment, companies' threats to shut down and move exerted downward pressure on American wages. Business, moreover, increasingly relied on financial operations for profits rather than making things. The financial sector of the economy accounted for around 10 percent of total profits in 1950; by 2000 the figure was up to 40 percent. Companies like Ford and General Electric made more money from interest on loans to customers and other financial operations than from selling their products.

The outsourcing of jobs soon moved from manufacturing to other areas, including accounting, legal services, banking, and other skilled positions where companies could employ workers overseas for a fraction of their cost in the United States. All this lowered prices for consumers but also threw millions of American workers into competition with those around the globe, producing a relentless downward pressure on American wages.

In 1970, General Motors had been the country's largest corporate employer. In the early twenty-first century, it had been replaced by Wal-Mart, a giant discount retail chain that paid most of its 1.6 million workers slightly more than the minimum wage. Wal-Mart aggressively opposed efforts at collective bargaining. Not a single one of its employees belonged to a union. Thanks to NAFTA, which enabled American companies to expand their business in Mexico, by 2010 Wal-Mart was also the largest employer in that country. Overall, between 1990 and 2008, companies that did business in global markets contributed almost nothing to job growth in the United States.

Huge companies and little job growth

CULTURE WARS

The end of the Cold War ushered in hopes for a new era of global harmony. Instead, what one observer called a "rebellion of particularisms"—renewed emphasis on group identity and insistent demands for group recognition and power—has racked the international arena. The declining power of nation-states arising from globalization seemed to unleash long-simmering ethnic and religious antagonisms. Partly in reaction to the global spread of a secular culture based on consumption and mass entertainment, intense religious movements attracted increasing numbers of followers—Hindu nationalism in India, orthodox Judaism in Israel, Islamic fundamentalism in much of the Muslim world, and evangelical Christianity in the United States. Like other nations, although in a far less extreme way and with little accompanying violence, the United States has experienced divisions arising from the intensification of ethnic and racial identities and religious fundamentalism.

A "rebellion of particularisms"

The Newest Immigrants

Because of shifts in immigration, cultural and racial diversity have become increasingly visible in the United States. Until the immigration law of 1965, the vast majority of twentieth-century newcomers hailed from Europe. Between 1965 and 2010, nearly 38 million immigrants entered the United States, substantially more than the 27 million during the peak period of immigration between 1880 and 1924. About 50 percent came from Latin America and the Caribbean, 35 percent from Asia, and smaller numbers from the Middle East and Africa. Only 10 percent arrived from Europe, mostly from the war-torn Balkans and the former Soviet Union.

Erected on U.S. 5, an interstate highway running from the Mexican to Canadian borders along the Pacific Coast, this sign warns motorists to be on the lookout for people (i.e., undocumented immigrant families) crossing the road on foot. The sign's placement north of San Diego, about thirty miles north of Mexico, illustrates how the "border" had become an entire region, not simply a geographical boundary.

TABLE 27.1 Immigration to the United States, 1961–2010

DECADE	TOTAL	EUROPE	ASIA	WESTERN HEMISPHERE	OTHER AREAS
1961–1970	3,321,584	1,123,492	427,642	1,716,374	54,076
1971–1980	4,493,302	800,368	1,588,178	1,982,735	122,021
1981–1990	7,336,940	761,550	2,738,157	3,615,225	222,008
1991–2000	9,042,999	1,359,737	2,795,672	4,486,806	400,784
2001–2010	14,974,975	1,165,176	4,088,455	8,582,601	1,138,743

Shifts in immigration

The immigrant influx changed the country's religious and racial map. By 2010, more than 4 million Muslims resided in the United States, and the combined population of Buddhists and Hindus exceeded 1 million.

Unlike in the past, rather than being concentrated in one or two parts of city centers, immigrants quickly moved into outlying neighborhoods and older suburbs. By the turn of the century, more than half of all Latinos lived in suburbs. Orange County, California, which had been a stronghold of suburban conservatism between 1960 and 1990, elected a Latina Democrat to Congress in the late 1990s. Immigrants brought cultural and racial diversity to once-homogeneous communities in the American heartland.

Recent immigrants at a naturalization ceremony held at Fenway Park, Boston, in 2008. Over 3,000 people became U.S. citizens at this event.

Post-1965 immigration formed part of the worldwide uprooting of labor arising from globalization. Those who migrated to the United States included poor, illiterate refugees from places of economic and political crisis—Central Americans escaping the region's civil wars and poverty, Haitians and Cambodians fleeing repressive governments. But many immigrants were well-educated professionals from countries like India and South Korea, where the availability of skilled jobs had not kept pace with the spread of higher education. In the year 2000, more than 40 percent of all immigrants to the United States had a college education.

For the first time in American history, women made up the majority of newcomers, reflecting the decline of manufacturing jobs that had previously absorbed immigrant men, as well as the spread of employment opportunities in traditionally female

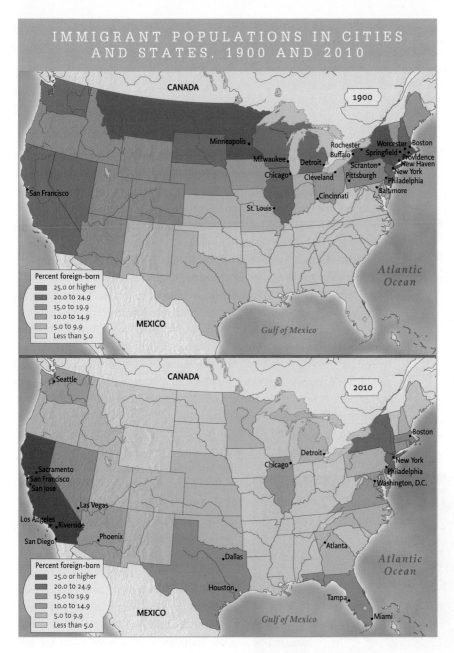

IMMIGRANT POPULATIONS IN CITIES
AND STATES, 1900 AND 2010

Maps illustrating states foreign-born populations and the twenty metropolitan areas with the most immigrants in 1900 and 2010. In 1900 nearly all went to the Northeast and Upper Midwest, the heartland of the industrial economy. In 2010 the largest number headed for cities in the South and West, especially California, although major cities of the Northeast also attracted many newcomers.

fields like care of children and the elderly and retail sales. Thanks to cheap global communications and jet travel, modern-day immigrants retain strong ties with their countries of origin, frequently phoning and visiting home.

The New Diversity

Latino immigrants

Latinos formed the largest single immigrant group. This term was invented in the United States and includes people of quite different origins— Mexicans, Central and South Americans, and migrants from Spanish-speaking Caribbean island nations such as Cuba, the Dominican Republic, and Puerto Rico (although the last group, of course, are American citizens, not immigrants). With 95 million people, Mexico in 2000 had become the world's largest Spanish-speaking nation. Its poverty, high birthrate, and proximity to the United States made it a source of massive legal and illegal immigration. In 2000, Mexican-Americans made up a majority of the Hispanic population of the United States and nearly half the residents of Los Angeles. But almost every state witnessed an influx of Mexican immigrants. In 1930, 90 percent of the Mexican population of the United States lived in states that had once been part of Mexico. Today, there is a significant Mexican-American presence in almost every state, including such places as Kansas, Minnesota, and Georgia, with very little experience, until recently, with ethnic diversity.

Latina nannies pushing baby carriages in Beverly Hills, California, in the 1990s. For the first time in American history, female immigrants outnumbered male immigrants.

Numbering around 50 million in 2010, Latinos had become the largest minority group in the United States. Between 1990 and 2010, 30 million Hispanics were added to the American population, representing half the nation's total growth. Latinos were highly visible in entertainment, sports, and politics. Indeed, the Hispanic presence transformed American life. José was now the most common name for baby boys in Texas and the third most popular in California. Smith remained the most common American surname, but Garcia, Rodriguez, Gonzales, and other Hispanic names were all in the top fifty.

Latino communities remained far poorer than the rest of the country. The influx of legal and undocumented immi-

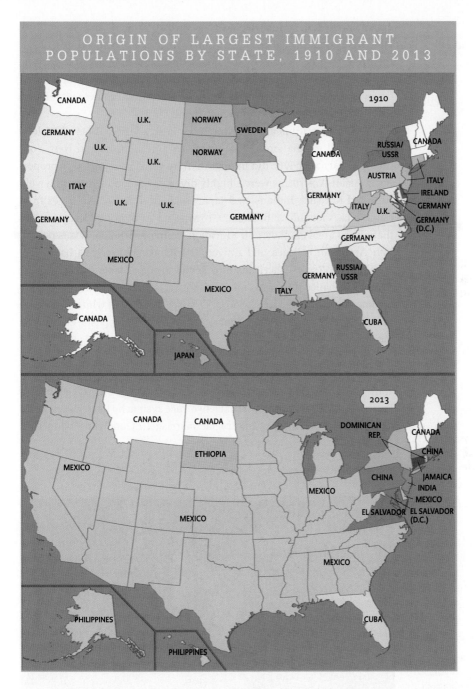

ORIGIN OF LARGEST IMMIGRANT
POPULATIONS BY STATE, 1910 AND 2013

Maps depicting the birthplace of each state's largest immigrant population in 1910 and 2013. A century ago, most immigrants hailed from Europe, and the leading country of origin varied among the states. Today, in almost every state outside the Northeast, those born in Mexico constitute the largest number of immigrants.

grants swelled the ranks of low-wage urban workers and agricultural laborers. Latinos lagged far behind other Americans in education. In 2010, their poverty rate stood at nearly double the national figure of 15 percent. Living and working conditions among predominantly Latino farm workers in the West fell back to levels as dire as when César Chavez established the United Farm Workers union in the 1960s.

Asian-Americans also became increasingly visible. There had long been a small population of Asian ancestry in California and New York City, but only after 1965 did immigration from Asia assume large proportions. Asian-Americans were a highly diverse population, including well-educated Koreans, Indians, and Japanese, as well as poor refugees from Cambodia, Vietnam, and China. Growing up in tight-knit communities that placed great emphasis on education, young Asian-Americans poured into American colleges and universities. Once subjected to harsh discrimination, Asian-Americans now achieved remarkable success. White Americans hailed them as a "model minority." By 2007, the median family income of Asian-Americans, $66,000, surpassed that of whites. But more than any other group, Asian-Americans clustered at opposite ends of the income spectrum.

The United States, of course, had long been a multiracial society. But for centuries race relations had been shaped by the black-white divide and the experience of slavery and segregation. The growing visibility of Latinos and Asians suggested that a two-race system no longer adequately described American life. Interracial marriage, at one time banned in

Young Korean girls rehearsing a dance at the Veterans Administration Medical Center in Columbia, South Carolina, an illustration of the growing diversity of American society.

forty-two states, became more common and acceptable. Among Asian-Americans, half of all marriages involved a non-Asian partner. The figure for Latinos was 30 percent.

One thing seemed clear at the dawn of the twenty-first century: diversity was here to stay. Because the birthrate of racial minorities is higher than that of whites, the Census Bureau projected that by 2050, less than 50 percent of the American population would be white.

The Changing Face of Black America

Compared with the situation in 1900 or 1950, the most dramatic change in American life at the turn of the century was the absence of legal segregation and the presence of blacks in areas of American life from which they had once been almost entirely excluded. Thanks to the decline in overt discrimination and the effectiveness of many affirmative action programs, blacks now worked in unprecedented numbers alongside whites in corporate board rooms, offices, and factories.

One major change in black life was the growing visibility of Africans among the nation's immigrants. Between 1970 and 2010, more than twice as many Africans immigrated to the United States as had entered during the entire period of the Atlantic slave trade. For the first time, all the elements of the African diaspora—natives of Africa, Caribbean, Central and South Americans of African descent, Europeans with African roots—could be found in the United States alongside the descendants of American slaves.

More than half the African newcomers had college educations, the highest percentage for any immigrant group. Indeed, some African countries complained of a "brain drain" as physicians, teachers, and other highly skilled persons sought opportunities in the United States that did not exist in their own underdeveloped countries.

Most African-Americans, nonetheless, remained in a more precarious situation than whites or many recent immigrants. In the early twenty-first century, half of all black children lived in poverty, two-thirds were born out of wedlock, and in every index of social well-being from health to quality of housing, blacks continued to lag. Housing segregation remained pervasive.

FIGURE 27.1 The Projected Non-White Majority: Racial and Ethnic Breakdown

2008: Non-Hispanic white 66%, Black 15%, Hispanic 13%, Asian 4%, Other 3%

2050: Non-Hispanic white 46%, Hispanic 30%, Black 13%, Asian 8%, Other 5%

Legend: Non-Hispanic white | Black | Hispanic | Asian | Other

	1970	1980	1990	2000
Whites	65.0%	67.8%	68.2%	73.8%
Blacks	41.6	44.4	43.4	47.2
Latinos	43.7	43.4	42.4	46.3
All families	62.9	64.4	64.2	67.4

TABLE 27.2 Home Ownership Rates by Group, 1970–2000

Despite the nation's growing racial diversity, school segregation—now resulting from housing patterns and the divide between urban and suburban school districts rather than laws requiring racial separation—was on the rise. Most city public school systems consisted overwhelmingly of minority students, large numbers of whom failed to receive an adequate education. By 2000, the nation's black and Latino students were more isolated from white pupils than in 1970. Since school funding rested on property taxes, poor communities continued to have less to spend on education than wealthy ones.

The Spread of Imprisonment

During the 1960s, the nation's prison population declined. But in the 1970s, with urban crime rates rising, politicians of both parties sought to convey the image of being "tough on crime." They insisted that the judicial system should focus on locking up criminals for long periods rather than rehabilitating them. They treated drug addiction as a violation of

the law rather than as a disease. As a result, the number of Americans in prison rose dramatically, most of them incarcerated for nonviolent drug offenses.

During the 1990s, thanks to the waning of the crack epidemic and more effective urban police tactics, crime rates dropped dramatically across the country. But this did nothing to stem the increase of the prison population. In 2011, it reached 2.3 million. Ten times the figure of 1970, this number represented one-quarter of the entire world's inmates and far exceeded the number in any other country. Several million more

A private, for-profit, maximum-security prison under construction in 1999 in California City, in the Mohave Desert, illustrates the expansion of the "prison-industrial complex."

Americans were on parole, on probation, or under some other kind of criminal supervision.

Members of racial minorities experienced most strongly the paradox of growing islands of unfreedom in a nation that prided itself on liberty. In 1950, whites accounted for 70 percent of the nation's prison population and non-whites 30 percent. By 2010, these figures had been reversed. One reason was that severe penalties faced those convicted of using or selling crack, a particularly potent form of cocaine concentrated among the urban poor, whereas the use of powder cocaine, the drug of choice in suburban America, led to far lighter sentences.

The percentage of the black population in prison stood five times higher than the proportion of white Americans. More than one-quarter of all black men could expect to serve time in prison at some time during their lives. Partly because so many young men were in prison, blacks had a significantly lower rate of marriage than other Americans.

The continuing frustration of urban blacks exploded in 1992 when an all-white suburban jury found four Los Angeles police officers not guilty in the beating of black motorist Rodney King, even though an onlooker had captured their assault on videotape. The deadliest urban uprising since the New York draft riots of 1863 followed. Some fifty-two people died, and property damage approached $1 billion. Many Latino youths, who shared blacks' resentment over mistreatment by the police, joined in the violence. The uprising suggested that despite the civil rights revolution, the nation had failed to address the plight of the urban poor.

The AIDS quilt, each square of which represents a person who died of AIDS, on display in Washington, D.C. The quilt was exhibited throughout the country, heightening public awareness of the AIDS epidemic.

The Continuing Rights Revolution

Reflecting the continued power of the rights revolution, in 1990, newly organized disabled Americans won passage of the **Americans with Disabilities Act**. This far-reaching measure prohibited discrimination in hiring and promotion against persons with disabilities and required that entrances to public buildings be redesigned so as to ensure access for the disabled.

Some movements that were descended from the late 1960s achieved great visibility in the 1990s. Prominent among these was the campaign for gay rights, which turned its attention to combating acquired immunodeficiency syndrome (AIDS), a fatal disease spread by sexual contact, drug use, and transfusions of contaminated blood. AIDS first emerged in the early 1980s. It quickly became epidemic among homosexual men. The gay movement mobilized to promote "safe sex" and press the federal government to devote greater resources to fighting the disease. The Gay Men's Health Crisis organized educational programs and assistance to those affected by the disease, and demanded that drug companies put AZT, a drug with some success in treating AIDS, on the market. A more radical group, ACT UP, disrupted a mass at New York's St. Patrick's Cathedral to protest what it called the Catholic Church's prejudices against gays. By 2000, even though more than 400,000 Americans had died of AIDS, its spread among gays had been sharply curtailed.

Gay groups also played an increasing role in politics. In cities with large gay populations, such as New York and San Francisco, politicians vied to attract their votes. Overall, the growth of public tolerance of homosexuality was among the most striking changes in American social attitudes in the last two decades of the century. In the second decade of the twenty-first century, this would lead to the remarkably rapid acceptance of the right of gay Americans to form legal marriages.

This work by the contemporary Eastern Band Cherokee artist Shan Goshorn, entitled *Unintended Legacy*, reproduces historical documents that are woven into a basket (a traditional Native American craft) such as the names and images of Indian children and adults at a typical boarding school. That history, she suggests, still affects Indian life today.

Native Americans in the New Century

Another social movement spawned by the 1960s that continued to flourish was the American Indian movement. The Indian population reached over

5 million (including people choosing more than one race) in the 2010 census—a sign not only of population growth but also of a renewed sense of pride that led many Indians for the first time to identify themselves as such to census enumerators.

The legal position of Indians as American citizens who enjoy a kind of quasi-sovereignty still survives in some cases. Notable examples are the lucrative Indian casinos now operating in states that otherwise prohibit gambling. In 2011, Indian casinos took in over $27 billion, making some tribes very rich. One such group is the Pequot tribe of Connecticut. In 1637, as the result of a brief, bloody war, Puritan New Englanders exterminated or sold into slavery most of the tribe's members. The treaty that restored peace decreed that the tribe's name should be wiped from the historical record. Today, the few hundred members of the Pequot tribe operate Foxwoods, reputedly the world's largest casino. However, because of the recession that began in 2007, Foxwoods' receipts plummeted and its survival remains uncertain.

Although some tribes have reinvested casino profits in improved housing and health care and college scholarships for Native American students, most Indian casinos are marginal operations whose low-wage jobs as cashiers, waitresses, and the like have done little to relieve Indian poverty. Native Americans continue to occupy the lowest rung on the economic ladder.

Continued economic hardship

Multiculturalism

Among some Americans, the heightened visibility of immigrants, racial minorities, and inheritors of the sexual revolution inspired not celebration of pluralism and **multiculturalism** but alarm over perceived cultural fragmentation.

Increased cultural diversity and changes in educational policy inspired harsh debates over whether immigrant children should be required to learn English and whether further immigration should be discouraged. These issues entered politics most dramatically in California, whose voters in 1994 approved Proposition 187, which denied undocumented immigrants and their children access to welfare, education, and most health services. A federal judge soon barred implementation of the measure on the grounds that control over immigration policy rests with the federal government. By 2000, twenty-three states had passed laws establishing English as their official language.

But efforts to appeal to prejudice for political gain often backfired. In California, Republicans' anti-immigrant campaigns inspired minorities to mobilize politically and offended many white Americans. In 2000, Republican presidential candidate George W. Bush emphasized that his brand of conservatism was multicultural, not exclusionary.

Immigration occupied only one front in what came to be called the **Culture Wars**—battles over moral values that raged throughout the 1990s. The Christian Coalition, founded by evangelical minister Pat Robertson, launched crusades against gay rights, abortion, secularism in public schools, and government aid to the arts.

It sometimes appeared during the 1990s that the country was refighting old battles between traditional religion and modern secular culture. In an echo of the 1920s, a number of localities required the teaching of creationism, a religious alternative to Darwin's theory of evolution.

At the beginning of the twenty-first century, less than one-quarter of American households consisted of a "traditional" family—a married couple living with their children.

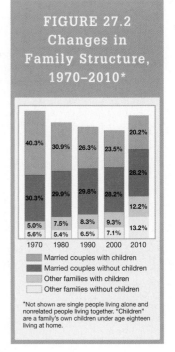

FIGURE 27.2
Changes in Family Structure, 1970–2010*

Married couples with children
Married couples without children
Other families with children
Other families without children

*Not shown are single people living alone and nonrelated people living together. "Children" are a family's own children under age eighteen living at home.

Figure 27.3 Median Ages of First Marriages, 1970–2010

MEN
Age at first marriage

NEW MOTHERS
Age at first birth

WOMEN
Age at first marriage

Median age in years

Year

Both men and women are getting married later, shifting marriage to an act of later adulthood and increasing the number of births to unmarried parents.

Casey v. Planned Parenthood of Pennsylvania

Private militias

Many conservatives railed against the erosion of the nuclear family, the changing racial landscape produced by immigration, and what they considered a general decline of traditional values.

Family Values in Retreat

The censuses of 2000 and 2010 showed **family values** increasingly in disarray. Half of all marriages ended in divorce (70 percent on the West Coast). In 2010, over 40 percent of births were to unmarried women, not only sexually active teenagers but growing numbers of professional women in their thirties and forties as well. For the first time, less than half of all households consisted of married couples, and only one-fifth were "traditional" families—a wife, husband, and their children. Two-thirds of married women worked outside the home. The pay gap between men and women, although narrowing, persisted. In 2010, the weekly earnings of women with full-time jobs stood at 82 percent of those of men—up from 63 percent in 1980. In only two occupational categories did women earn more than men: postal service clerks and special education teachers.

Although dominated by conservatives, the Supreme Court, in *Casey v. Planned Parenthood of Pennsylvania* (1992), reaffirmed a woman's right to terminate a pregnancy. The decision allowed states to enact mandatory waiting periods and anti-abortion counseling, but it overturned a requirement that the husband be given notification before the procedure was undertaken. "At the heart of liberty," said the Court, "is the right to . . . make the most intimate and personal choices" without outside interference.

The Antigovernment Extreme

At the radical fringe of conservatism, the belief that the federal government posed a threat to American freedom led to the creation of private militias who armed themselves to fend off oppressive authority. Groups like Aryan Nation, Posse Comitatus, and other self-proclaimed "Christian patriots" spread a mixture of racist, anti-Semitic, and antigovernment ideas.

Rescue workers sifting the wreckage of a federal office building in Oklahoma City after it was heavily damaged by a bomb in 1995, the worst act of terrorism in the United States during the twentieth century.

By 2000, women made up nearly half of the American workforce. Unlike in the nineteenth century, a majority of women working outside the home were married.

Although such organizations had been growing for years, they burst into the national spotlight in 1995 when Timothy McVeigh, a member of the militant antigovernment movement, exploded a bomb at a federal office building in Oklahoma City. The blast killed 168 persons, including numerous children at a day-care center. McVeigh was captured, convicted, and executed. The bombing alerted the nation to the danger of violent antigovernment right-wing groups.

IMPEACHMENT AND THE ELECTION OF 2000

The unusually intense partisanship of the 1990s seemed ironic, given Clinton's move toward the political center. Republicans' intense dislike of Clinton could be explained only by the fact that he seemed to symbolize everything conservatives hated about the 1960s. As a college student, the president had smoked marijuana and participated in antiwar demonstrations. He had married a feminist, made a point of leading a multicul-

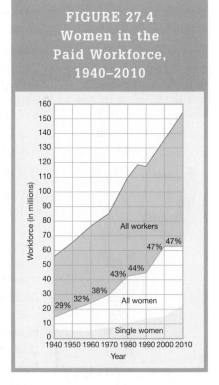

FIGURE 27.4 Women in the Paid Workforce, 1940–2010

tural administration, and supported gay rights. Clinton's popularity puzzled and frustrated conservatives, reinforcing their conviction that something was deeply amiss in American life. From the very outset of his administration, Clinton's political opponents and a scandal-hungry media stood ready to pounce. Clinton himself provided the ammunition.

The Impeachment of Clinton

Monica Lewinsky

From the day Clinton took office, charges of misconduct bedeviled him. In 1998, it became known that he had carried on an affair with Monica Lewinsky, a White House intern. Kenneth Starr, the special counsel who had been appointed to investigate a previous scandal, shifted his focus to Lewinsky. He issued a lengthy report containing details of Clinton's sexual acts with the young woman. In December 1998, the Republican-controlled House of Representatives voted to impeach Clinton for perjury and obstruction of justice. He became the second president to be tried before the Senate. Early in 1999, the vote took place. Neither charge mustered a simple majority, much less than the two-thirds required to remove Clinton from office.

Polls suggested that the obsession of Kenneth Starr and members of Congress with Clinton's sexual acts appalled Americans far more than the president's irresponsible behavior. Clinton's continuing popularity throughout the impeachment controversy demonstrated how profoundly traditional attitudes toward sexual morality had changed.

Herbert Block's 1998 cartoon comments humorously on Clinton's talent for political survival.

The Disputed Election

Had Clinton been eligible to run for reelection in 2000, he would probably have won. But after the death of FDR, the Constitution had been amended to limit presidents to two terms in office. Democrats nominated Vice President Al Gore to succeed Clinton (pairing him with Senator Joseph Lieberman of Connecticut, the first Jewish vice presidential nominee). Republicans chose George W. Bush, the governor of Texas and son of Clinton's predecessor, as their candidate, with former secretary of defense Dick Cheney as his running mate.

The election proved to be one of the closest in the nation's history. The outcome remained uncertain until a month after the ballots had been cast. Gore won the popular vote by a tiny margin—540,000 votes of 100 million cast, or one-half of 1 percent. Victory in the electoral college hinged on which candidate had carried Florida. There, amid widespread confusion at the polls and claims of irregularities in counting the ballots, Bush claimed a margin of a few hundred votes. In the days after the election, Democrats demanded a hand recount of the Florida ballots for which machines could not determine a voter's intent.

It fell to Supreme Court justices to decide the outcome. On December 12, 2000, by a 5-4 vote, the Court ordered a halt to the recounting of Florida ballots, allowing the state's governor Jeb Bush (George W. Bush's brother) to certify that the Republican candidate had carried the state and had therefore won the presidency.

The decision in ***Bush v. Gore*** was one of the oddest in Supreme Court history. The majority justified their decision by insisting that the "equal protection" clause of the Fourteenth Amendment required that all ballots within a state be counted in accordance with a single standard, something impossible given the wide variety of machines and paper ballots used in Florida. Perhaps recognizing that this new constitutional principle threatened to throw into question results throughout the country—since many states had voting systems as complex as Florida's—the Court added that it applied only in this single case.

The most remarkable thing about the election of 2000 was not so much its controversial ending as the even division of the country it revealed. Bush and Gore each received essentially half of the popular vote. The final count in the electoral college stood at 271–266, the narrowest margin since 1876. The Senate ended up divided 50–50 between the two parties.

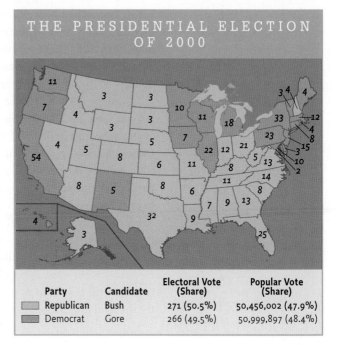

THE PRESIDENTIAL ELECTION OF 2000

Party	Candidate	Electoral Vote (Share)	Popular Vote (Share)
Republican	Bush	271 (50.5%)	50,456,002 (47.9%)
Democrat	Gore	266 (49.5%)	50,999,897 (48.4%)

A member of a Florida election board trying to determine a voter's intent during the recount of presidential ballots in November 2000. The U.S. Supreme Court eventually ordered the recount halted.

A Challenged Democracy

Coming at the end of the "decade of democracy," the 2000 election revealed troubling features of the American political system. The electoral college, devised by the founders to enable the country's prominent men rather than ordinary voters to choose the president, gave the White House to a candidate who did not receive the most votes, an odd result in a political democracy. A country that prided itself on modern technology had a voting system in which citizens' choices could not be reliably determined. Counting both congressional and presidential races, the campaign cost more than $1.5 billion, mostly raised from wealthy individuals and corporate donors. This amount reinforced the widespread belief that money dominated the political system.

Evidence abounded of a broad disengagement from public life. As governments at all levels competed to turn their activities over to private contractors, and millions of Americans walled themselves off from their fellow citizens by taking up residence in socially homogeneous gated communities, the very idea of a shared public sphere seemed to dissolve. Nearly half the eligible voters did not bother to go to the polls. In state and local elections, turnouts typically ranged between only 20 and 30 percent. More people watched the televised Nixon-Kennedy debates of 1960 than the Bush-Gore debates of 2000, even though the population had risen by 100 million. Major issues like health care, race relations, and economic inequality went virtually unmentioned during the campaign. And no one discussed the issue that would soon come to dominate Bush's presidency—the threat of international terrorism.

A shrinking public sphere

The twin towers of the World Trade Center after being struck by hijacked airplanes on September 11, 2001. Shortly after this photograph was taken, the towers collapsed.

THE ATTACKS OF SEPTEMBER 11

September 11, 2001, a beautiful late-summer morning, began with the sun rising over the East Coast of the United States in a crystal-clear sky. But September 11 soon became one of the most tragic dates in American history.

Around 8 AM, hijackers seized control of four jet airliners filled with passengers. They crashed two into the World Trade Center in New York City, igniting infernos that soon caused these buildings, which dominated the lower Manhattan skyline, to collapse. A third plane hit a wing of the Pentagon, the country's military headquarters, in Washington, D.C. On the fourth aircraft, passengers who had learned of these events via their cell phones overpowered the hijackers. The plane crashed in a field near Pittsburgh, killing all aboard. Counting the nineteen hijackers, the more than 200 passengers, pilots, and flight attendants, and the victims on the ground, around 3,000 people died on September 11. The victims included nearly 400 police and firefighters who had rushed to the World Trade Center in a rescue effort.

The administration of George W. Bush quickly blamed Al Qaeda, a shadowy terrorist organization headed by Osama bin Laden, for the attacks. A wealthy Islamic fundamentalist from Saudi Arabia, bin Laden had joined the fight against the Soviet occupation of Afghanistan in the 1980s. He had developed a relationship with the Central Intelligence Agency and received American funds to help build his mountain bases. But after the Gulf War of 1991, his anger increasingly turned against the United States. Bin Laden was especially outraged by the presence of American military bases in Saudi Arabia and by American support for Israel in its ongoing conflict with the Palestinians.

A bystander gazes at some of the missing-persons posters with photographs of those who died on September 11.

Terrorists associated with Al Qaeda exploded a truck bomb at the World Trade Center in 1993, killing six persons, and set off blasts in 1998 at two American embassies in Africa, killing over 200 persons. Nonetheless, the attack of September 11 came as a complete surprise. With the end of the Cold War in 1991, most Americans felt more secure, especially within their own borders, than they had for decades.

The attacks and events that followed lent new urgency to questions that had recurred many times in American history: Should the United States act in the world as a republic or an empire? What is the proper balance between liberty and security? Who deserves the full enjoyment of American freedom? None had an easy answer.

CHAPTER REVIEW AND ONLINE RESOURCES

REVIEW QUESTIONS

1. Why was the year 1989 one of the most momentous in the twentieth century?

2. Describe the different visions of the U.S. role in the post–Cold War world as identified by President George H. W. Bush and President Clinton.

3. Explain Clinton's political strategy of combining social liberalism with conservative economic ideas.

4. Identify the factors that, in the midst of 1990s prosperity, increased the levels of inequality in the United States.

5. What are the similarities and differences between immigration patterns of the 1990s and earlier?

6. What main issues gave rise to the Culture Wars of the 1990s?

7. Assess the role of the Supreme Court in the presidential election of 2000.

8. What is globalization, and how did it affect the United States in the 1990s?

KEY TERMS

new world order (p. 845)

Gulf War (p. 846)

"Don't ask, don't tell" (p. 848)

North American Free Trade Agreement (p. 848)

Contract with America (p. 849)

Rwandan genocide (p. 852)

Balkan crisis (p. 852)

ethnic cleansing (p. 852)

globalization (p. 854)

Americans with Disabilities Act (p. 867)

multiculturalism (p. 869)

Culture Wars (p. 869)

family values (p. 870)

Bush v. Gore (p. 873)

Go to INQUIZITIVE

To see what you know—and learn what you've missed—with personalized feedback along the way.

Visit the *Give Me Liberty!* **Student Site** for primary source documents and images, interactive maps, author videos featuring Eric Foner, and more.

CHAPTER 28

A NEW CENTURY AND NEW CRISES

★

2001	United States launches air strikes in Afghanistan
	United States enters war in Afghanistan
	USA Patriot Act
2002	Bush identifies "axis of evil"
	Department of Homeland Security established
2003	Iraq War begins
2005	Hurricane Katrina hits the Gulf Coast
2007	Great Recession begins
2008	Federal bailout of banks and companies
	Barack Obama elected
2009	Sonia Sotomayor named to Supreme Court
	Federal stimulus package
	Tea Party movement develops
2010	Affordable Care Act
2011	Arab Spring
	Osama bin Laden killed
	Occupy Wall Street movement
2012	Obama reelected
2013	Edward Snowden revelations
2015	Supreme Court declares constitutional right to gay marriage
	U.S. reestablishes relations with Cuba

Barack Obama and his family greet enthusiastic supporters at an outdoor celebration in Chicago on the night of his election as president on November 4, 2008.

- *What were the major policy elements of the war on terror in the wake of September 11, 2001?*

- *How did the war in Iraq unfold in the wake of 9/11?*

- *How did the war on terror affect the economy and American liberties?*

- *What events eroded support for President Bush's policies during his second term?*

- *What kinds of change did voters hope for when they elected Barack Obama?*

- *What were the major challenges of Obama's first term?*

- *What were the prevailing ideas of American freedom at the beginning of the 21st century?*

The presidential election of 2008 produced not only a great political surprise but a historic moment in American history. Whatever one's opinion of Barack Obama's policies, there is no question that in view of the nation's racial history, the election of the first African-American president was an enormously important symbolic turning point.

A little-known forty-seven-year-old senator from Illinois when the campaign began in 2007, Obama owed his success both to his own exceptional skills as a speaker and campaigner and to the evolution of American politics.

Obama's life story exemplified the enormous changes American society had undergone since 1960. Without the civil rights movement, his election would have been inconceivable. He was the product of an interracial marriage, which ended in divorce when he was two years old, between a Kenyan immigrant and a white American woman. When Obama was born in 1961, his parents' marriage was still illegal in many states. He attended Columbia College and Harvard Law School, and worked in Chicago as a community organizer before going into politics. Obama was elected to the U.S. Senate in 2004 and first gained national attention with an eloquent speech at the Democratic national convention that year.

Hillary Rodham Clinton sought the Democratic nomination by emphasizing her political experience, both as First Lady and as a senator from New York. Obama realized that in 2008 people were hungry for change, not experience. Indeed, although Clinton's nomination would also have been pathbreaking—no woman has ever been the presidential candidate of a major party—Obama succeeded in making her seem a representative of the status quo. His early opposition to the Iraq War (discussed below), for which Clinton had voted in the Senate, won the support of the party's large antiwar element; his race galvanized the support of black voters; and his youth and promise of change appealed to the young.

Obama recognized how the Internet had changed politics. He established an e-mail list containing the names of millions of voters with whom he could communicate instantaneously, and his campaign used web-based networks to raise enormous sums of money in small donations. With its widespread use of modern technology and massive mobilization of new voters, Obama's was the first political campaign of the twenty-first century. But his election also rested on the deep unpopularity of his predecessor, George W. Bush, because of the seemingly endless war he launched in Iraq and the collapse of the American economy in 2008.

THE WAR ON TERROR

Bush before September 11

From the outset, Bush pursued a strongly conservative agenda. In 2001, he persuaded Congress to enact the largest tax cut in American history. With the economy slowing, he promoted the plan as a way of stimulating renewed growth. In keeping with the "supply-side" economic outlook embraced twenty years earlier by Ronald Reagan, most of the tax cuts were directed toward the wealthiest Americans, on the assumption that they would invest the money they saved in taxes in economically productive activities.

Tax cuts

In foreign policy, Bush emphasized American freedom of action, unrestrained by international treaties and institutions. To great controversy, the Bush administration announced that it would not abide by the **Kyoto Protocol** of 1997, which sought to combat global warming—a slow rise in the earth's temperature that scientists warned could have disastrous effects on the world's climate. Global warming is caused when gases released by burning fossil fuels such as coal and oil remain in the upper atmosphere, trapping heat reflected from the earth. Most scientists consider global warming a serious situation. Climate change threatens to disrupt long-established patterns of agriculture, and the melting of glaciers and the polar ice caps because of rising temperatures may raise ocean levels and flood coastal cities. Since, at the time, the United States burned far more fossil fuel than any other nation, Bush's repudiation of the treaty, on the grounds that it would weaken the American economy, infuriated much of the world, as well as environmentalists at home.

Global warming

Is This the End? by the artist Owen Freeman offers a warning about global warming, one of whose consequences in coming decades will be a rise in sea levels, flooding many low-lying coastal communities.

"They Hate Freedom"

September 11, 2001, transformed the international situation, the domestic political environment, and the Bush presidency. An outpouring of popular patriotism followed the terrorist attacks, all the more impressive because it was spontaneous, not orchestrated by the government or private organizations. Throughout the country, people demonstrated their sense of resolve and their sympathy for the victims by displaying the American flag.

Patriotism

The Bush administration benefited from this patriotism and identification with government. The president's popularity soared. Bush seized the opportunity to give his administration a new direction and purpose. Like presidents before him, he made freedom the rallying cry for a nation at war.

On September 20 Bush addressed a joint session of Congress and a national television audience. His speech echoed the words of FDR, Truman, and Reagan: "Freedom and fear are at war. The advance of human freedom . . . now depends on us." The country's antagonists, Bush went on, "hate our freedoms, our freedom of religion, our freedom of speech, our freedom to assemble and disagree with each other." In later speeches, he repeated this theme. Why did terrorists attack the United States? the president repeatedly asked. His answer: "Because we love freedom, that's why. And they hate freedom."

The Bush Doctrine

A war on terrorism

Bush's speech announced a new foreign policy principle, which quickly became known as **the Bush Doctrine**. The United States would launch a **war on terrorism**. Unlike previous wars, this one had a vaguely defined enemy—terrorist groups around the world that might threaten the United States or its allies—and no predictable timetable for victory. The new war would recognize no middle ground: "Either you are with us, or you are with the terrorists." Bush demanded that Afghanistan, ruled by a group of Islamic fundamentalists called the Taliban, surrender Osama bin Laden, the architect of 9/11 attacks who had established a base in the country. When the Taliban refused, the United States on October 7, 2001, launched air strikes against its strongholds.

Supporters of the Bush administration who turned out in Washington, D.C., late in 2001 to confront demonstrators opposed to the war in Afghanistan.

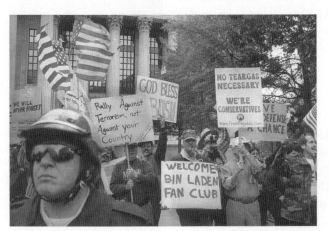

By the end of the year, the Taliban had been driven from power. A new government, friendly to and dependent on the United States, took its place. It repealed Taliban laws denying women the right to attend school and banning movies, music, and other expressions of Western culture but found it difficult to establish full control over the country. U.S. forces would remain in the country at least into 2017, making the **war in Afghanistan** the longest in American history.

The "Axis of Evil"

In his State of the Union address of January 2002, President Bush accused Iraq, Iran, and North Korea of harboring terrorists and developing "weapons of mass destruction"—nuclear, chemical, and biological—that posed a potential threat to the United States. He called the three countries an "axis of evil," even though no evidence connected them with the attacks of September 11 and they had never cooperated with one another.

"Axis of evil"

AN AMERICAN EMPIRE?

The "axis of evil" speech sent shock waves around the world. In the immediate aftermath of September 11, a wave of sympathy for the United States had swept across the globe. Most of the world supported the war in Afghanistan as a legitimate response to the terrorist attacks. By late 2002, however, many persons overseas feared that the United States was claiming the right to act as a world policeman in violation of international law.

Critics, including leaders of close American allies, wondered whether dividing the world into friends and enemies of freedom ran the danger of repeating some of the mistakes of the Cold War. Charges quickly arose that the United States was bent on establishing itself as a new global empire. Indeed, September 11 and its aftermath highlighted not only the vulnerability of the United States but also its overwhelming strength. In every index of power—military, economic, cultural—the United States far outpaced the rest of the world. It was not surprising that in such circumstances many American policymakers felt that the country had a responsibility to impose order in a dangerous world, even if this meant establishing its own rules of international conduct.

The global response

Steve Benson's 2003 cartoon, which alters a renowned World War II photograph of soldiers raising an American flag, illustrates widespread skepticism about American motivations in the Iraq War.

Confronting Iraq

These tensions became starkly evident in the Bush administration's next initiative. The Iraqi dictatorship of Saddam Hussein had survived its defeat in the Gulf War of 1991. Hussein's opponents charged that he had flouted United Nations resolutions barring his regime from developing new weapons.

From the outset of the Bush administration, a group of conservative policymakers including Vice President Dick Cheney, Secretary of Defense Donald Rumsfeld, and Deputy Defense Secretary Paul D. Wolfowitz were determined to oust Hussein from power. They insisted that the oppressed Iraqi people would welcome an American army as liberators and quickly establish a democratic government, allowing for the early departure of American soldiers. Secretary of State Colin Powell, who believed the conquest and stabilization of Iraq would require hundreds of thousands of American soldiers and should not be undertaken without the support of America's allies, found himself marginalized in the administration.

Regime change in Iraq

Even though Hussein was not an Islamic fundamentalist and no known evidence linked him to the terrorist attacks of September 11, the Bush administration in 2002 announced a goal of "regime change" in Iraq. Hussein, administration spokesmen insisted, must be ousted from power because he had developed an arsenal of chemical and bacterial "weapons of mass destruction" and was seeking to acquire nuclear arms. American newspaper and television journalists repeated these claims with almost no independent investigation. Early in 2003, despite his original misgivings, Secretary of State Powell delivered a speech before the UN outlining the administration's case. He claimed that Hussein possessed a mobile chemical weapons laboratory, had hidden weapons of mass destruction in his many palaces, and was seeking to acquire uranium in Africa to build nuclear weapons. (Every one of these assertions later turned out to be false.)

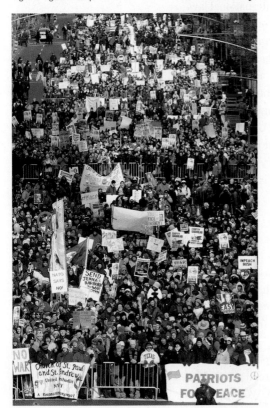

Part of the massive crowd that gathered in New York City on February 15, 2003, a day of worldwide demonstrations against the impending war against Iraq.

The Iraq War

Foreign policy "realists," including members of previous Republican administrations like Brent Scowcroft, the national security adviser under the first President Bush, warned that the administration's preoccupation with Iraq deflected attention from its real foe, Al Qaeda, which remained capable of launching terrorist attacks. They insisted that the United States could not unilaterally transform the Middle East into a bastion of democracy, as the administration claimed was its long-term aim.

The decision to begin the **Iraq War** split the Western alliance and inspired a massive antiwar movement throughout the world. In February 2003, between 10 million and 15 million people across the globe demonstrated against the impending war.

Both traditional foes of the United States like Russia and China and traditional allies like Germany and France refused to support a "preemptive" strike against Iraq. Unable to obtain approval from the United Nations for attacking Iraq, the United States went to war anyway in March 2003, with Great Britain as its sole significant ally. President Bush called the war "Operation Iraqi Freedom." Within a month, American troops occupied Baghdad. After hiding out for several months, Hussein was captured by American forces and subsequently put on trial before an Iraqi court. Late in 2006, he was found guilty of ordering the killing of many Iraqis during his reign, and was sentenced to death and executed.

President Bush standing on the deck of the aircraft carrier *Abraham Lincoln* on May 10, 2003, announcing the end of combat operations in Iraq. A banner proclaims, "Mission Accomplished." Unfortunately, the war was not in fact over.

Soon after the fall of Baghdad, a triumphant President Bush appeared on the deck of an aircraft carrier beneath a banner reading "Mission Accomplished." But after the fall of Hussein, everything seemed to go wrong. Rather than parades welcoming American liberators, looting and chaos followed the fall of the Iraqi regime. An insurgency quickly developed that targeted American soldiers and Iraqis cooperating with them. Sectarian violence soon swept throughout Iraq, with militias of Shiite and Sunni Muslims fighting each other. (Under Hussein, Sunnis, a minority of Iraq's population, had dominated the government and army; now, the Shiite majority sought to exercise power and exact revenge.)

With no end in sight to the conflict, comparisons with the American experience in Vietnam became commonplace. In both wars, American policy was made by officials who had little or no knowledge of the countries to which they were sending troops and distrusted State Department experts on these regions, who tended to be skeptical about the possibility of achieving quick military and long-term political success.

In 2008, a church in Miami displayed nearly 4,500 small American flags in honor of each of the American soldiers who to that date had died in Afghanistan and Iraq.

The World and the War

The war marked a departure in American foreign policy. The United States had frequently intervened unilaterally in the affairs of Latin American countries. But outside the Western Hemisphere it had

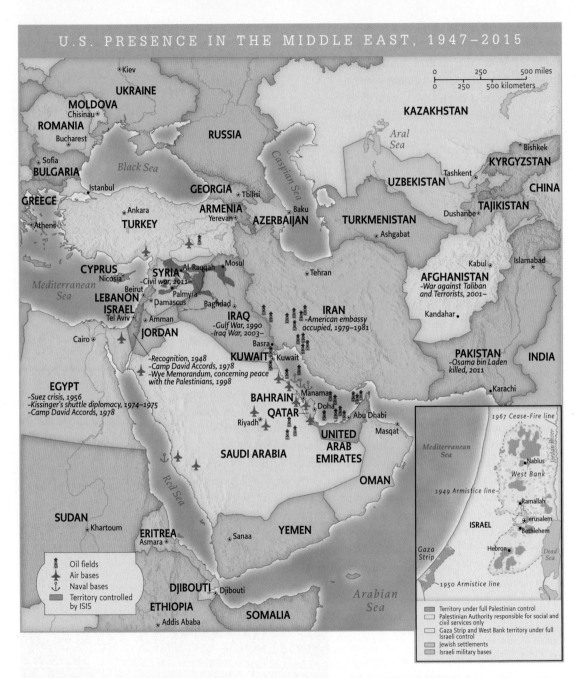

U.S. PRESENCE IN THE MIDDLE EAST, 1947–2015

0   250   500 miles

0   250   500 kilometers

Kiev

UKRAINE

MOLDOVA
Chisinau

ROMANIA
Bucharest

Sofia

BULGARIA

Black Sea

Istanbul

GREECE

Athens

Mediterranean
Sea

CYPRUS
Nicosia

SYRIA
-Civil war, 2011–

Al-Raqqah   Mosul

Palmyra

LEBANON
Beirut   Damascus

ISRAEL
Tel Aviv

Baghdad

IRAQ
-Gulf War, 1990
-Iraq War, 2003–

Amman

JORDAN

Cairo

-Recognition, 1948
-Camp David Accords, 1978
-Wye Memorandum, concerning peace
with the Palestinians, 1998

Basra

KUWAIT   Kuwait

EGYPT
-Suez crisis, 1956
-Kissinger's shuttle diplomacy, 1974–1975
-Camp David Accords, 1978

BAHRAIN   Manama

QATAR   Doha

Riyadh

SAUDI ARABIA

UNITED
ARAB
EMIRATES

Abu Dhabi

Masqat

OMAN

RUSSIA

Caspian Sea

GEORGIA   Tbilisi

ANKARA
Ankara

TURKEY

ARMENIA
Yerevan   Baku

AZERBAIJAN

Tehran

IRAN
-American embassy
occupied, 1979–1981

Aral
Sea

KAZAKHSTAN

Bishkek

KYRGYZSTAN

Tashkent

UZBEKISTAN

CHINA

TAJIKISTAN
Dushanbe

TURKMENISTAN

Ashgabat

Kabul   Islamabad

AFGHANISTAN
-War against Taliban
and Terrorists, 2001–

Kandahar

PAKISTAN
-Osama bin Laden
killed, 2011

INDIA

Karachi

SUDAN

Khartoum

DJIBOUTI   Djibouti

ETHIOPIA

Addis Ababa

ERITREA
Asmara

Sanaa

YEMEN

SOMALIA

Red Sea

Arabian
Sea

Oil fields
Air bases
Naval bases
Territory controlled
by ISIS

Inset map

1967 Cease-Fire line

Mediterranean
Sea

Nablus

West Bank

1949 Armistice line

Ramallah

Jerusalem
Bethlehem

ISRAEL

Gaza
Strip

Hebron

Dead
Sea

1950 Armistice line

Jordan River

Territory under full Palestinian control
Palestinian Authority responsible for social and
civil services only
Gaza Strip and West Bank territory under full
Israeli control
Jewish settlements
Israeli military bases

Since World War II, the United States has become more and more deeply involved in the affairs of the Middle East, whose countries are together the world's largest exporters of oil. Note that the ISIS-controlled territory shown here is as of the end of 2015.

previously been reluctant to use force except as part of an international coalition. Never before had it occupied a nation in the center of the world's most volatile region.

Rarely in its history had the United States found itself so isolated from world public opinion. Initially, the war in Iraq proved to be popular in the United States. Many Americans believed the administration's claims that Saddam Hussein had something to do with September 11 and had stockpiled weapons of mass destruction. The realization that in fact Hussein had no such weapons discredited the administration's rationale for the war. By early 2007, polls showed that a large majority of Americans considered the invasion of Iraq a mistake and the war a lost cause. The fact that Iraq possessed the world's second-largest reserves of oil reinforced suspicions that American motives had less to do with freedom than self-interest.

An isolated position

THE AFTERMATH OF SEPTEMBER 11 AT HOME

Security and Liberty

Like earlier wars, the war on terrorism raised anew the problem of balancing security and liberty. In the immediate aftermath of the attacks, Congress rushed to pass the **USA Patriot Act**, a mammoth bill (it ran to more than 300 pages) that few members of the House or Senate had actually read. It conferred unprecedented powers on law enforcement agencies charged with preventing the new, vaguely defined crime of "domestic terrorism," including the authority to wiretap, spy on citizens, open letters, read e-mail, and obtain personal records from third parties like universities and libraries without the knowledge of a suspect. At least 5,000 foreigners with Middle Eastern connections were rounded up and more than 1,200 arrested. Many with no link to terrorism were held for months, without either a formal charge or a public notice of their fate. The administration also set up a detention camp at the U.S. naval

Before the Cuban Revolution of 1959, Guantánamo Bay was mostly known as an American naval base where the families of servicemen enjoyed a slice of suburban life, as in this photograph from the 1950s. Today, Guantánamo is famous as the site of the world's most notorious prison.

base at **Guantánamo Bay**, Cuba, for persons captured in Afghanistan or otherwise accused of terrorism. More than 700 persons, nationals of many foreign countries, were detained there.

In November 2001, the Bush administration issued an executive order authorizing the holding of secret military tribunals for noncitizens deemed to have assisted terrorism. In such trials, traditional constitutional protections, such as the right of the accused to choose a lawyer and see all the evidence, would not apply.

Suspension of due process

The Power of the President

In the new atmosphere of heightened security, numerous court orders and regulations of the 1970s, inspired by abuses of the CIA, FBI, and local police forces, were rescinded, allowing these agencies to resume surveillance of Americans without evidence that a crime had been committed. Some of these measures were authorized by Congress, but the president implemented many of them unilaterally, claiming the authority to ignore laws that restricted his power as commander-in-chief in wartime.

Privacy violations

The debate over liberty and security seemed certain to last as long as the war on terrorism itself.

The Torture Controversy

Officials of the Bush administration also insisted in the aftermath of September 11 that the United States need not be bound by international law in pursuing the war on terrorism. They were especially eager to sidestep the Geneva Conventions and the International Convention Against Torture, which regulate the treatment of prisoners of war and prohibit torture and other forms of physical and mental coercion. In January 2002, the Justice Department produced a memorandum stating that these rules did not apply to captured members of Al Qaeda as they were "unlawful combatants," not members of regularly constituted armies. The Defense Department approved methods of interrogation that most observers considered torture.

The United States and international law

In this atmosphere and lacking clear rules of behavior, some military personnel—in Afghanistan, at Abu Ghraib prison in Iraq, and at Guantánamo—beat prisoners who were being held for interrogation, subjected them to electric shocks and simulated drowning (so-called water-boarding), let them be attacked by dogs, and forced them to strip naked and lie atop other prisoners. Photographs of the abuse of prisoners eventually became public. Their publication around the world in newspapers, on television, and on the Internet undermined the reputation of the United States as a country that adheres to standards of civilized behavior and the rule of law.

The full extent of the torture policy did not become known until 2014, when a Senate committee released a scathing report stemming from a long investigation. It revealed a pattern of brutality and deception, while concluding that no useful information had been obtained from tortured prisoners. Torture, it concluded, did not arise from the actions of a few "bad apples" but was systematically employed at secret U.S. prisons around the world.

Based on an infamous photograph circulated around the world of an Iraqi prisoner abused while in American custody, this 2004 cartoon suggests how such mistreatment damaged the image of the United States.

The Economy under Bush

Continuing chaos in Iraq began to undermine support for Bush's foreign policy. But the main threat to the president's reelection appeared to be the condition of the American economy. During 2001, the economy slipped into a recession—that is, it contracted rather than grew. Growth resumed at the end of the year, but, with businesses reluctant to make new investments after the overexpansion of the 1990s, it failed to generate new jobs.

Recession

Ninety percent of the jobs lost during the recession of 2001–2002 were in manufacturing. Despite the renewed spirit of patriotism, deindustrialization continued. Textile firms closed southern plants and shifted production to cheap-labor factories in China and India. Maytag, a manufacturer of washing machines, refrigerators, and other home appliances, announced plans to close its factory in Galesburg, Illinois, where wages averaged fifteen dollars per hour, to open a new one in Mexico, where workers earned less than one-seventh that amount.

Job loss

THE WINDS OF CHANGE

The 2004 Election

With Bush's popularity sliding because of the war in Iraq and a widespread sense that many Americans were not benefiting from economic growth, Democrats in 2004 sensed a golden opportunity to retake the

White House. They nominated as their candidate John Kerry, a senator from Massachusetts and the first Catholic to run for president since John F. Kennedy in 1960. A decorated combat veteran in Vietnam, Kerry had joined the antiwar movement after leaving the army.

Kerry proved a surprisingly ineffective candidate. An aloof man who lacked the common touch, he failed to generate the same degree of enthusiasm among his supporters as Bush did among his. The Bush campaign consistently and successfully appealed to fear, with continuous reminders of September 11 and warnings of future attacks.

Bush won a narrow victory, with a margin of 2 percent of the popular vote and thirty-four electoral votes. The results revealed a remarkable electoral stability. Both sides spent tens of millions of dollars in advertising and mobilized new voters—nearly 20 million since 2000. But in the end, only three states voted differently from four years earlier—New Hampshire, which Kerry carried, and Iowa and New Mexico, which swung to Bush.

Bush's Second Term

In his second inaugural address, in January 2005, Bush outlined a new American goal—"ending tyranny in the world." Striking a more conciliatory tone than during his first administration, he promised that the United States would not try to impose "our style of government" on others and that it would in the future seek the advice of allies. He said nothing specific about Iraq but tried to shore up falling support for the war by invoking the ideal of freedom. In his first inaugural, in January 2001, Bush had used the words "freedom," "free," or "liberty" seven times. In his second, they appeared forty-nine times. But the ongoing chaos in Iraq, coupled with a

spate of corruption scandals surrounding Republicans in Congress and the White House, eroded Bush's standing.

Hurricane Katrina

A further blow to the Bush administration's standing came in August 2005, when **Hurricane Katrina** slammed ashore near New Orleans. Situated below sea level between the Mississippi River and Lake Pontchartrain and protected by levees, New Orleans has always been vulnerable to flooding. For years, scientists had predicted a catastrophe if a hurricane hit the city. When the storm hit on August 29 the levees broke. Nearly the entire city, with a population of half a million, was inundated. Nearby areas of the Louisiana and Mississippi Gulf Coast were also hard hit.

The natural disaster quickly became a man-made one, with ineptitude evident from local government to the White House. The mayor of New Orleans had been slow to order an evacuation, fearing it would damage the city's tourist trade. The Federal Emergency Management Agency (FEMA) had made almost no preparations. If the Bush administration had prided itself on anything, it was competence in dealing with disaster. Katrina shattered that image.

For days, vast numbers of people, most of them poor African-Americans, remained abandoned amid the floodwaters. Bodies floated in the streets, and people died in city hospitals and nursing homes. By the time aid began to arrive, damage stood at $80 billion, the death toll was around 1,500, and two-thirds of the city's population had been displaced. The televised images of misery in the streets of New Orleans shocked the world and shamed the country.

Hurricane Katrina also shone a bright light on the heroic side of American life. Where government failed, individual citizens stepped into the breach. People with boats rescued countless survivors from rooftops and attics, private donations flowed in to aid the victims, and neighboring states like Texas opened their doors to thousands of refugees.

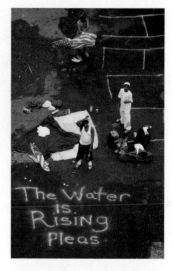

Residents of New Orleans, stranded on a rooftop days after flood waters engulfed the city, frantically attempt to attract the attention of rescue helicopters.

Battle over the Border

The attacks of September 11 and subsequent war on terror threw into sharp relief the status of American borders and borderlands, especially in the Southwest. The existence of the borderland embracing parts of the United States and Mexico, with people enjoying well-developed connections with communities in both countries, has always been a source of tension and insecurity in the eyes of many Americans. Fears of terrorists crossing the border merged with older worries about undocumented immigration and the growth of Hispanic culture in the Southwest. When the Swedish vodka-maker Absolut posted an advertisement in Mexico showing the pre-1848 map of Mexico and the United States, the ad angered enough Americans (who saw it on the Internet) that the company withdrew it.

In 2015, the artist JR took photographs of immigrants and affixed them to the walls of New York City buildings and to other public places. This image is of Kamola Akilova, from Uzbekistan. The purpose, according to the artist, is to take immigrants out of the shadows and make people aware of their presence in the city.

The Bush and Obama administrations greatly accelerated efforts to police the border. By 2013, the number of U.S. Border Patrol officers stood at 20,000, making it the nation's second-largest police force after the New York City Police Department, and 400,000 undocumented immigrants were being deported annually, far more than in the past. Latino communities

Members of the Texas Minutemen patrolling the U.S.-Mexico border. Claiming that the federal government was failing to prevent undocumented immigrants from entering the United States, vigilantes tried to do so on their own.

The U.S.-Canada boundary, which stretches for over 3,000 miles, has long been called the world's "longest undefended border." With borders becoming more contested lately, however, it has seen increased restrictions on crossing (but, as yet, no armed patrols, unlike the Mexican border).

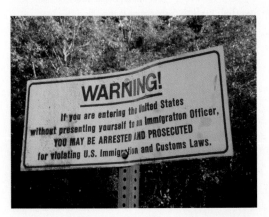

WARNING!
If you are entering the United States without presenting yourself to an Immigration Officer, YOU MAY BE ARRESTED AND PROSECUTED for violating U.S. Immigration and Customs Laws.

experienced the southwestern borderlands as increasingly militarized, since the "border" stretched far inland and persons accused of having entered the country illegally—almost all of them from Mexico, Guatemala, Honduras, and El Salvador—could be apprehended many miles north of Mexico. Nonetheless, some Americans in the region, claiming that the federal government was not doing enough to enforce the border's status as a dividing line, set up unofficial militias to police the area.

In the spring of 2006, the immigration issue suddenly burst again onto the center stage of politics. Alongside legal immigrants, millions of undocumented newcomers had made their way to the United States, mostly from Mexico. Economists disagree about their impact. It seems clear that the presence of large numbers of uneducated, low-skilled workers pushes down wages at the bottom of the economic ladder, especially affecting African-Americans. On the other hand, immigrants both legal and undocumented receive regular paychecks, spend money, and pay taxes. They fill jobs for which American workers seem to be unavailable because the wages are so low. It is estimated that more than one-fifth of construction workers, domestic workers, and agricultural workers are in the United States illegally.

In 2006, with many Americans convinced that the United States had lost control of its borders and that immigration was in part responsible for the stagnation of real wages, the House of Representatives approved a bill making it a felony to be in the country illegally and a crime to offer aid to undocumented immigrants. The response was utterly unexpected: a series of massive demonstrations in the spring of 2006 by immigrants—legal and undocumented—and their supporters, demanding the right to remain in the country as citizens. In cities from New York to Chicago, Los Angeles, Phoenix, and Dallas, hundreds of thousands of protesters took to the streets. All Congress could agree on, however, was a measure to build a 700-mile wall along part of the U.S.-Mexico border. The immigration issue was at a stalemate.

Islam, America, and the "Clash of Civilizations"

The events of September 11, 2001, placed new pressures on religious liberty. Even before the terrorist attacks, the political scientist Samuel P. Huntington had published a widely noted book, *The Clash of Civilizations and the Remaking of the World Order* (1996), which argued that with the Cold War over, a new global conflict impended between Western and Islamic "civilizations."

Many readers, including politicians, interpreted Huntington, not entirely correctly, as reducing politics and culture to a single characteristic—in this case, religion—that remains forever static, divorced from historical development. "Islam," in fact, consists of well over a billion people, in very different countries ranging from South Asia to the Middle East, Africa, Europe, and the Americas. Nonetheless, in the aftermath of 9/11, the formula that pitted a freedom-loving United States against militant, authoritarian Muslims became popular as a way of making sense of the terrorist attacks.

What did this mean for the nearly 5 million Americans who practiced the Muslim religion? President Bush insisted that the war on terror was not a war against Islam. But many Americans found it difficult to separate the two, even though most American Muslims were as appalled by the terrorist attacks as their fellow countrymen. Some critics claimed that Islam was fundamentally incompatible with American life—a position reminiscent of prejudice in the nineteenth century against Catholics and Mormons. In a number of states, politicians appealed for votes by opposing the construction of new mosques and raising the nonexistent threat that courts would impose "sharia law"—the religious rules laid down in the Koran—on all Americans.

In April 2006, millions of people demonstrated for immigrant rights. This photograph shows part of the immense crowd in Chicago, bearing the flags of many nations.

Islam and terrorism

The Constitution and Liberty

Two significant Supreme Court decisions in June 2003 revealed how the largely conservative justices had come to accept that the social revolution that began during the 1960s could not be undone.

In two cases arising from challenges to the admissions policies of the University of Michigan, the Supreme Court issued its most important rulings on affirmative action since the *Bakke* case twenty-five years earlier. A 5-4 majority upheld the right of colleges and universities to take race into account in admissions decisions. Writing for the majority, Justice Sandra Day O'Connor argued that such institutions have a legitimate interest in creating a "diverse" student body to enhance education.

Revisiting the Bakke *case*

In the second decision, in *Lawrence v. Texas*, a 6-3 majority declared unconstitutional a Texas law making homosexual acts a crime. The majority opinion overturned the Court's 1986 ruling in *Bowers v. Hardwick*, which had upheld a similar Georgia law. The *Lawrence* decision paved the way for an even more momentous Supreme Court ruling in 2015, in **Obergefell v. Hodges**, which overturned state laws barring marriages for same-sex couples. Public opinion on this question had evolved with remarkable rapidity, especially among younger Americans. In 2003, two-thirds of Americans opposed legalizing such marriages; by the time of the 2015 ruling, over 60 percent were in favor.

Both decisions relating to gay Americans, written by Justice Anthony Kennedy, repudiated the conservative view that constitutional interpretation must rest either on the "original intent" of the founders and authors of constitutional amendments or on a narrow reading of the document's text. Instead, Kennedy, generally a conservative, reaffirmed the liberal view of the Constitution as a living document whose protections expand as society changes. "The nature of injustice is such," he wrote in *Obergefell*, "that we may not always see it in our own times. The generations that wrote and ratified the Bill of Rights and the Fourteenth Amendment did not presume to know the extent of freedom in all of its dimensions, and so they entrusted to future generations a charter protecting the right of all persons to enjoy liberty as we learn its meaning."

The Court and the President

Nor did the Supreme Court prove receptive to President Bush's claim of authority to disregard laws and treaties and to suspend constitutional protections of individual liberties. In a series of decisions, the Court reaffirmed the rule of law both for American citizens and for foreigners held prisoner by the United States. It ruled that an American citizen who had moved to Saudi Arabia and been captured in Afghanistan had a right to a judicial hearing. The justices offered a stinging rebuke to the key presumptions of the Bush administration—that the Geneva Conventions do not apply to prisoners captured in the war on terrorism, that the president can unilaterally set up secret military tribunals in which defendants have very few if any rights, and that the Constitution does not apply at Guantánamo.

In June 2008, the Supreme Court rebuffed the Bush administration's strategy of denying detainees at Guantánamo Bay the normal protections guaranteed by the Constitution. Written by Justice Anthony Kennedy, the 5-4 decision in *Boumediene v. Bush* affirmed the detainees' right to challenge their detention in U.S. courts. "The laws and Constitution are designed,"

Kennedy wrote, "to survive, and remain in force, in extraordinary times." Security, he added, consists not simply in military might, but "in fidelity to freedom's first principles," including freedom from arbitrary arrest and the right of a person to go to court to challenge his or her imprisonment.

The Midterm Elections of 2006

With President Bush's popularity having plummeted because of the war in Iraq and the Hurricane Katrina disaster, Congress beset by scandal after scandal, and public-opinion polls revealing that a majority of Americans believed the country to be "on the wrong track," Democrats expected to reap major gains in the congressional elections of 2006. They were not disappointed. In a sweeping repudiation of the administration, voters gave Democrats control of both houses of Congress for the first time since 1994. In January 2007, Democrat Nancy Pelosi of California became the first female Speaker of the House in American history.

Democratic majorities in Congress

In January 2009, as Bush's presidency came to an end, only 22 percent of Americans approved of his performance in office—the lowest figure since such polls began in the mid-twentieth century. Indeed, it was difficult to think of many substantive achievements during Bush's eight years in office. His foreign policy alienated most of the world, leaving the United States militarily weakened and diplomatically isolated. Because of the tax cuts for the wealthy that he pushed through Congress during his first term, as well as the cost of the wars in Iraq and Afghanistan, the large budget surplus he had inherited was transformed into an immense deficit.

George W. Bush's legacy

The Housing Bubble

At one point in his administration, Bush might have pointed to the economic recovery that began in 2001 as a major success. But late in 2007, the economy entered a recession. And in 2008, the American banking system suddenly found itself on the brink of collapse, threatening to drag the national and world economies into a repeat of the Great Depression.

The economy in crisis

The roots of the crisis of 2008 lay in a combination of public and private policies that favored economic speculation, free-wheeling spending, and get-rich-quick schemes over more traditional avenues to economic growth and personal advancement. For years, the Federal Reserve Bank kept interest rates at unprecedented low levels, first to help the economy recover from the bursting of the technology bubble in 2000 and then to enable more Americans to borrow money to purchase homes. Housing prices rose rapidly. Consumer indebtedness also rose dramatically as people who owned houses took out second mortgages or simply spent

An Arizona house left unfinished when the housing bubble collapsed. When prices were at their peak, housing developers rushed to build new residences; many were abandoned when prices plunged.

Selling debut

Causes of the recession

to the limits on their credit cards. In mid-2008, when the median family income was around $50,000, the average American family owed an $84,000 home mortgage, $14,000 in auto and student loans, $8,500 to credit card companies, and $10,000 in home equity loans.

All this borrowing fueled increased spending. An immense influx of cheap goods from China accelerated the loss of manufacturing jobs in the United States but also enabled Americans to keep buying, even though for most, household income stagnated during the Bush years. Indeed, China helped to finance the American spending spree by buying up hundreds of billions of dollars' worth of federal bonds—in effect loaning money to the United States so that it could purchase Chinese-made goods. Banks and other lending institutions issued more and more "subprime" mortgages—risky loans to people who lacked the income to meet their monthly payments.

Wall Street bankers developed complex new ways of repackaging and selling these mortgages to investors. Insurance companies, including the world's largest, American International Group (AIG), insured these new financial products against future default. Credit-rating agencies gave these securities their highest ratings, even though they were based on loans that clearly would never be repaid. Believing that the market must be left to regulate itself, the Federal Reserve Bank and other regulatory agencies did nothing to slow the speculative frenzy. Banks and investment firms reported billions of dollars in profits and rewarded their executives with unheard-of bonuses.

The Great Recession

In 2006 and 2007, overbuilding had reached the point where home prices began to fall. More and more home owners found themselves owing more money than their homes were worth. As mortgage rates reset, increasing numbers of borrowers defaulted—that is, they could no longer meet their monthly mortgage payments. Banks suddenly found themselves with billions of dollars of worthless investments on their books. In 2008, the situation became a full-fledged crisis, as banks stopped making loans, business dried up, and the stock market collapsed. Once above 14,000, the Dow Jones Industrial Average plunged to around 8,000—the worst percentage decline since 1931. Lehman Brothers, a venerable investment house, recorded a $2.3 billion loss and went out of existence in history's biggest bankruptcy. Leading banks seemed to be on the verge of failure.

With the value of their homes and stock market accounts in free fall, Americans cut back on spending, leading to business failures and a rapid rise in unemployment. By the end of 2008, 2.5 million jobs had been lost—the most in any year since the end of World War II. Unemployment was concentrated in manufacturing and construction, sectors dominated by men. As a result, by mid-2009, for the first time in history, more women than men in the United States held paying jobs.

Even worse than the economic meltdown was the meltdown of confidence as millions of Americans lost their jobs and/or their homes and saw their retirement savings and pensions, if invested in the stock market, disappear. In April 2009, the recession that began in December 2007 known as the **Great Recession** became the longest since the Great Depression.

FIGURE 28.1
Portrait of a Recession

These graphs offer a vivid visual illustration of the steep decline in the American economy in 2008 and the first part of 2009, and the slow recovery to 2012.

"A Conspiracy against the Public"

In *The Wealth of Nations* (1776), Adam Smith wrote: "People of the same trade seldom meet together, even for merriment and diversion, but the conversation ends in a conspiracy against the public." This certainly seemed an apt description of the behavior of leading bankers and investment houses whose greed helped bring down the American economy.

Amid mounting revelations of corporate misdeeds, the reputation of stockbrokers and bankers fell to lows last seen during the Great Depression. One poll showed that of various social groups, bankers ranked third from the bottom in public esteem—just above prostitutes and convicted felons. Resentment was fueled by the fact that Wall Street had long since abandoned the idea that pay should be linked to results. By the end of 2008, the worst year for the stock market since the Depression, Wall Street firms had

*Resentment toward
Wall Street*

This cartoon suggests that the near-collapse of the financial system in 2008 indicates the need for "a little more regulation."

fired 240,000 employees. But they also paid out $20 billion in bonuses to top executives.

In 2010, Goldman Sachs, the Wall Street banking and investment firm, paid a fine of half a billion dollars to settle charges that it had knowingly marketed to clients mortgage-based securities it knew were bound to fail and then in effect bet on their failure. (This was like a real-estate agency selling an unsuspecting customer a house with faulty wiring and then taking out insurance so that the agency would be paid when the house burned down.)

Overall, during the next few years, an incredible litany of malfeasance by the world's largest banks became public. Between 2009 and 2015, major banks, American and foreign, were forced by their respective governments to pay fines totaling in excess of $100 billion for such actions as facilitating tax evasion by wealthy clients, fixing foreign currency exchange rates and international interest rates to boost their own profits, often at the expense of their customers, and misleading regulators about their activities. Yet bank profits are so large that the institutions accepted these fines as simply a minor cost of doing business. Even when J. P. Morgan Chase and Citibank pleaded guilty to felony conspiracy charges, no meaningful punishment followed. No individual executive was charged with a crime, and the Securities and Exchange Commission granted waivers from penalties that are supposed to punish criminal behavior, such as being barred from certain kinds of financial transactions.

Waived penalties for banks

It was also revealed in 2010 that Bernard Madoff, a Wall Street investor who claimed to have made enormous profits for his clients, had in fact run a Ponzi scheme in which investors who wanted to retrieve their money were paid with funds from new participants. Madoff sent fictitious monthly financial statements to his clients, but he never actually made stock purchases for them. When the scheme collapsed, Madoff's investors suffered losses amounting to around $50 billion. The crisis exposed the dark side of market fundamentalism—the ethos of deregulation that had dominated world affairs for the preceding thirty years.

The Bernard Madoff scandal

Every president from Ronald Reagan onward had lectured the rest of the world on the need to adopt the American model of unregulated economic competition and berated countries like Japan and Germany for assisting failing businesses. Now, the American model lay in ruins and a new role for government in regulating economic activity seemed inevitable.

Bush and the Crisis

In the fall of 2008, with the presidential election campaign in full swing, the Bush administration seemed unable to come up with a response to the crisis. In keeping with the free market ethos, it allowed Lehman Brothers to fail. But this immediately created a domino effect, with the stock prices of other banks and investment houses collapsing, and the administration quickly reversed course. It persuaded a reluctant Congress to appropriate $700 billion dollars to bail out other floundering firms. Insurance companies like AIG, banks like Citigroup and Bank of America, and giant financial companies like the Federal Home Loan Mortgage Corporation (popularly known as Freddie Mac) and the Federal National Mortgage Association (Fannie Mae), which insured most mortgages in the country, were deemed "too big to fail"—that is, they were so interconnected with other institutions that their collapse would drive the economy into a full-fledged depression. Through the federal bailout, taxpayers in effect took temporary ownership of these companies, absorbing the massive losses created by the companies' previous malfeasance. Giant banks and investment houses that received public money redirected some of it to enormous bonuses to top employees. But despite the bailout, the health of the banking system remained fragile.

The bailout

"Too big to fail"

The crisis also revealed the limits of the American social "safety net" compared with those of other industrialized countries. In western Europe, workers who lose their jobs typically receive many months of unemployment insurance amounting to a significant percentage of their lost wages. In the United States, only one-third of out-of-work persons even qualify for unemployment insurance, and it runs out after a few months. The abolition of "welfare" (the national obligation to assist the neediest Americans) during the Clinton administration left the American safety net a patchwork of a few national programs such as food stamps, supplemented by locally administered aid. The poor were dependent on aid from the states, which found their budgets collapsing as revenues from property and sales taxes dried up.

The limits of the American social safety net

A cartoon in the *Boston Globe* suggests the progress that has been made since Rosa Parks refused to give up her seat on a bus to a white passenger.

The 2008 Campaign

In 2008, Obama faced Senator John McCain, the Republican nominee, in the general election. At age seventy-two, McCain was the oldest man ever to run for president. He sur prised virtually everyone by choosing as his running mate Sarah Palin, the little-known governor of Alaska, in part as an attempt to woo Democratic women disappointed at their party's rejection of Hillary Clinton, who had sought the Democratic nomination. Palin proved extremely popular with the Republican Party's conservative base. But her performances in speeches and interviews soon made it clear that she lacked familiarity with many of the domestic and foreign issues a new administration would confront.

But the main obstacles for the McCain campaign were President Bush's low popularity and the financial crisis that reached bottom in September and October. Obama's promise of change seemed more appealing than ever.

On election day, he swept to victory with 53 percent of the popular vote and a large majority in the electoral college. His election redrew the nation's political map. Obama carried not only Democratic strongholds in New England, the mid-Atlantic states, the industrial Midwest, and the West Coast but also states that had been reliably Republican for years. He cracked the solid South, winning Virginia, North Carolina, and Florida. He did extremely well in suburbs throughout the country. He even carried Indiana, where Bush had garnered 60 percent of the vote in 2004 but which now was hard hit by unemployment. He did exceptionally well among young voters. Obama carried every age group except persons over sixty-five. Thus, he was elected even though he received only 43 percent of the nation's white vote.

The Age of Obama?

Obama's victory seemed to mark the end of a political era that began with Richard Nixon and his "southern strategy." In the wake of the Iraq War, the economic meltdown, and the enthusiasm aroused by Obama's candidacy, Republican appeals to patriotism, low taxes, and resentment against the social changes sparked by the 1960s seemed oddly out of date. Democrats not only regained the presidency but ended up with 60 of the 100 seats in the Senate and a large majority in the House.

Obama's First Inauguration

Few presidents have come into office facing as serious a set of problems as did Barack Obama. The economy was in crisis and the country involved in two wars. But Americans, including many who had not voted for him, viewed Obama's election as

On inauguration day, January 20, 2009, a photograph of the outgoing president, George W. Bush, is replaced by one of Barack Obama at the headquarters of the U.S. naval station at Guantánamo, Cuba.

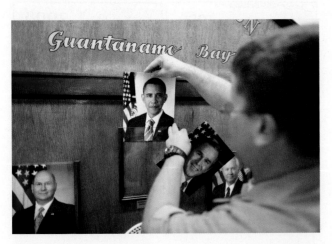

a cause for optimism. On January 20, 2009, a day after the Martin Luther King Jr. holiday and more than forty-five years after King's "I Have a Dream" speech, Obama was inaugurated as president. More than 1 million people traveled to Washington to view the historic event. In his inaugural address Obama offered a stark rebuke to eight years of Bush policies and, more broadly, to the premises that had shaped government policy since the election of Reagan. He promised a foreign policy based on diplomacy rather than unilateral force, pledged to protect the environment, spoke of the need to combat income inequality and lack of access to health care, and blamed a culture of "greed and irresponsibility" for helping to bring on the economic crisis. He promised to renew respect for the Constitution. Instead of freedom, he spoke of community and responsibility. His address harked back to the revolutionary-era ideal of putting the common good before individual self-interest.

Obama's first inaugural address

OBAMA IN OFFICE

In many ways, Obama's first policy initiatives lived up to the promise of change. In his first three months, he barred the use of torture, launched a diplomatic initiative to repair relations with the Muslim world, reversed the previous administration's executive orders limiting women's reproductive rights, and abandoned Bush's rhetoric about a God-given American mission to spread freedom throughout the world. When Supreme Court justice David Souter announced his retirement, Obama named **Sonia Sotomayor**, the first Hispanic and third woman in the Court's history, to replace him. In 2010, Obama appointed a second woman, Elena Kagan, to the Court.

Obama's first budget recalled the New Deal and Great Society. Breaking with the Reagan-era motto, "Government is the problem, not the solution," it anticipated active government support for health-care reform, clean energy, and public education, paid for in part by allowing Bush's tax cuts for the wealthy to expire in 2010. He pushed through Congress a "stimulus" package amounting to nearly $800 billion in new government spending—for construction projects, the extension of unemployment benefits, and aid to the states to enable them to balance their budgets. The largest single spending appropriation in American

In the spring of 2009, Republicans and independents opposed to President Obama's "stimulus" plan held "tea parties" around the country, seeking to invoke the tradition of the Boston Tea Party and its opposition to taxation. In this demonstration in Austin, Texas, some participants wore hats reminiscent of the revolutionary era. One participant carries a sign urging the state to secede from the Union.

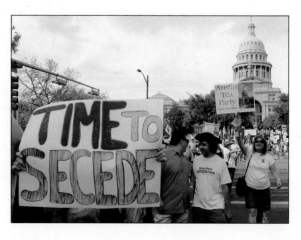

history, the bill was meant to pump money into the economy in order to save and create jobs and to ignite a resumption of economic activity.

The Health-Care Debate

For most of Obama's first year in office, congressional debate revolved around a plan to restructure the nation's health-care system so as to provide insurance coverage to the millions of Americans who lacked it, and to end abusive practices by insurance companies, such as their refusal to cover patients with existing illnesses. After months of increasingly bitter debate, in March 2010, Congress passed a sweeping health-care

Health-care reform

bill that required all Americans to purchase health insurance and most businesses to provide it to their employees. It also offered subsidies to persons of modest incomes so they could afford insurance and required insurance companies to accept all applicants. The legislation aroused strong partisan opposition. Claiming that it amounted to a "government takeover" of the health-care industry, every Republican in Congress voted against the bill.

Republican opposition

Throughout Obama's presidency, Republicans remained bitterly opposed to the new law, and vowed to repeal it when they could. Indeed, in October 2013, in an effort to get the president to abandon the health-care law, the Republican-dominated Congress shut down the federal government—a tactic that, as during the Clinton administration, backfired. By 2015, what came to be known as Obamacare proved to be a remarkably successful policy. Sixteen million uninsured Americans had obtained medical coverage under its provisions, most of them less affluent Americans who received some sort of government subsidy. Moreover, despite a general conservative majority on the Supreme Court, the justices twice rejected challenges to the constitutionality of Obamacare.

Financial Reform

Another far-reaching piece of legislation followed in July 2010. This was a law to overhaul regulation of the financial industry so as to prevent a repetition of the abuses that had led to the economic crash. It subjected to

Regulatory reform

public oversight the huge market in derivatives—exotic financial instruments that were basically bets that some element of the economy would fail; limited banks' speculative investments; and established a Consumer Protection Agency to stop predatory lending and fees by banks, credit card companies, and mortgage companies. The law marked an end to several decades when banks had been given a free hand to engage in any practice, honest or dishonest, they deemed profitable.

Obama had come into office promising an era of cooperation between the parties. But with Republicans overwhelmingly opposing every one of his policy initiatives, the atmosphere in Washington became more and more partisan. One of his key proposals, a plan to combat global warming by limiting factory emissions, had to be abandoned because it could not muster the 60 votes needed to end debate in the Senate. Immigration reform remained stalled, as the recession inflamed hostility to undocumented immigrants and to any proposal that offered them a path to legalized status.

Increased partisanship in Washington

Taken together, the measures of Obama's first year and a half in office saw the most dramatic domestic reform legislation since the Great Society of the 1960s. "Change"—the slogan of his election campaign—was significant but did not go far enough for many of his supporters. The health-care bill failed to include a "public option," in which the government itself would offer medical insurance to those who desired it (much like Medicare for elderly Americans). Obama chose his economic advisers from Wall Street, who underestimated the depth of the crisis, and continued the Bush administration policy of pouring taxpayer money into the banks. Little was done to help home owners facing foreclosure.

Not enough change for supporters

The Problem of Inequality

In 2014 and 2015, the economic recovery finally gathered momentum, although growth remained weak by historic standards. Nonetheless, consumer spending and confidence were on the rise, unemployment was falling, home sales were rising, and the stock market reached record highs. The one exception to these favorable trends, however, was a significant one—Americans' wages remained stagnant. In fact, because of the growing number of low-paid jobs, the continuing decline in the power of unions, and the rising value of stocks, owned primarily by upper-income Americans, virtually the entire benefit of the recovery that began in 2009 went to the top 1 percent of earners, while the real incomes of most families declined, deepening the long-term trend toward greater and greater economic inequality. In 2013, the top 10 percent of Americans received nearly half the total income. Meanwhile, the percentage of families in the middle class continued to shrink while that of those living in poverty continued to grow.

Economic recovery for the wealthy

At the bottom of the social scale, Americans employed by some of the country's largest corporations, including McDonald's and Wal-Mart,

VOICES OF FREEDOM

From Opinion of the Court in
Obergefell v. Hodges (2015)

In 2015, in a 5-4 decision, the Supreme Court ruled that the Constitution's Fourteenth Amendment establishes a constitutional right to marriage for gay Americans. The ruling reflected a remarkably rapid shift in public opinion regarding gay marriage in the previous few years. Written by Justice Anthony Kennedy, the majority opinion included a powerful exposition of the meaning of freedom in the early twenty-first century.

The history of marriage is one of both continuity and change. That institution—even as confined to opposite-sex relations—has evolved over time. For example, marriage was once viewed as an arrangement by the couple's parents based on political, religious, and financial concerns; but by the time of the Nation's founding it was understood to be a voluntary contract between a man and a woman.... As the role and status of women changed, the institution further evolved. Under the centuries-old doctrine of coverture, a married man and woman were treated by the State as a single, male-dominated legal entity. As women gained legal, political, and property rights, and as society began to understand that women have their own equal dignity, the law of coverture was abandoned....

New dimensions of freedom become apparent to new generations, often through perspectives that begin in pleas or protests....

The identification and protection of fundamental rights is an enduring part of the judicial duty to interpret the Constitution.... The nature of injustice is such that we may not always see it in our own times. The generations that wrote and ratified the Bill of Rights and the Fourteenth Amendment did not presume to know the extent of freedom in all of its dimensions, and so they entrusted to future generations a charter protecting the right of all persons to enjoy liberty as we learn its meaning. When new insight reveals discord between the Constitution's central protections and a received legal structure, a claim to liberty must be addressed....

The right to marry is a fundamental right inherent in the liberty of the person, and . . . couples of the same sex may not be deprived of that right and that liberty.

From Barack Obama, Eulogy at Emanuel African Methodist Episcopal Church (2015)

In the summer of 2015, the nation was shocked by the murder of nine black parishioners in a black church in Charleston by a white supremacist gunman. President Obama traveled to the city to deliver a eulogy for one of the victims, Clementa Pinckney, the church's pastor and a member of the South Carolina Senate. His speech reflected on the history of race relations and the condition of black America fifty years after the height of the civil rights revolution.

The church is and always has been the center of African American life . . . a place to call our own in a too-often hostile world, a sanctuary from so many hardships. . . .

There's no better example of this tradition than Mother Emanuel, . . . a church built by blacks seeking liberty, burned to the ground because its founders sought to end slavery only to rise up again, a phoenix from these ashes. . . .

We do not know whether the killer of Reverend Pinckney and eight others knew all of this history, but he surely sensed the meaning of his violent act. It was an act that drew on a long history of bombs and arson and shots fired at churches, not random but as a means of control, a way to terrorize and oppress. . . .

For too long, we've been blind to the way past injustices continue to shape the present. Perhaps we see that now. Perhaps this tragedy causes us to ask some tough questions about how we can permit so many of our children to languish in poverty . . . or attend dilapidated schools or grow up without prospects for a job or for a career. Perhaps it causes us to examine what we're doing to cause some of our children to hate. Perhaps it softens hearts towards those lost young men, tens and tens of thousands caught up in the criminal-justice system and leads us to make sure that that system's not infected with bias. . . .

None of us can or should expect a transformation in race relations overnight. . . . Whatever solutions we find will necessarily be incomplete. But it would be a betrayal of everything Reverend Pinckney stood for, I believe, if we allow ourselves to slip into a comfortable silence again. . . .

QUESTIONS

1. *How does Justice Kennedy believe we should understand the meaning of freedom?*

2. *Why does President Obama believe that the freedom of some Americans is interconnected with the freedom of others?*

3. *What do these documents suggest about how much has changed in American life in the past half-century and how much has not changed?*

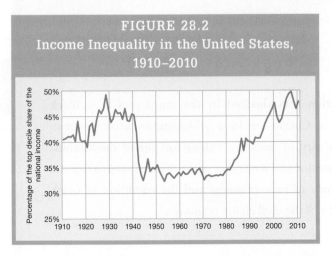

FIGURE 28.2
Income Inequality in the United States, 1910–2010

(y-axis: Percentage of the top decile share of the national income, 25%–50%; x-axis: 1910–2010)

A chart showing how much of the nation's total income has been enjoyed by the top 10 percent of families from 1910 to 2010. This is an index of income inequality. There was a sharp drop during World War II, which persisted until 1980, when the share began to rise. Today, income inequality is near historic highs.

An Occupy Wall Street demonstrator expresses her concern about rising economic inequality.

received pitiably low wages, at or just slightly above the federal minimum wage of $7.25 per hour (a figure lower, in income adjusted for inflation, than fifty years before). Nearly three-quarters of people helped by programs designed for the poor, such as food stamps and Medicaid, include a working member, so in effect taxpayers are subsidizing the low-wage policies of highly profitable corporations by enabling their employees to survive. McDonald's had a helpful website to assist its workers in making ends meet. It urged them to try to have two full-time jobs, spend no more than twenty dollars per month on health insurance, and break food into small pieces so that it would seem to go further.

The Occupy Movement

The problem of inequality burst into public discussion in 2011. On September 17, a few dozen young protesters unrolled sleeping bags in Zuccotti Park, in the heart of New York City's financial district. They vowed to remain—to **Occupy Wall Street** as they put it—as a protest against growing economic inequality, declining opportunity, and the banks' malfeasance.

Over the next few weeks, hundreds of people camped out in the park, and thousands took part in rallies organized by the Occupy movement. Similar encampments sprang up in cities across the country. Using social media and the Internet, the Occupy movement spread its message far and wide. In the spring of 2012, public authorities began to evict the protesters. But its language, especially the charge that "the 1 percent" (the very richest Americans) dominated political and economic life, had entered the political vocabulary. And it spurred a movement among low-paid workers, especially in fast-food establishments, demanding a rise in the hourly minimum wage. States and cities are allowed to establish higher minimum-wage rates than the federal government and many do so, although some large states, including Texas, Florida, and Pennsylvania, make no such provision. In 2014, Seattle and Los Angeles raised their minimums to $15 per hour. New York State followed in 2015 by announcing a $15 minimum for workers in fast-food restaurants. What began as a quixotic movement of the least empowered workers against some of the

PERCENTAGE OF POPULATION BELOW
THE POVERTY LINE, 2014

Percent of population below
the poverty line, 2014

40%
30%
20%
10%

A map showing the distribution of poverty in the United States. The darker the color, the higher the percentage of families living below the poverty line. Areas with concentrations of African-Americans, Latinos, and Native Americans, along with portions of Appalachia inhabited by whites, have the highest poverty rates.

country's most prominent corporations had achieved some remarkable successes.

The United States was by far the world's most unequal developed economy. In a variety of social statistics, it was falling further and further behind other advanced countries. More than one-fifth of American children lived in poverty in 2015, the highest figure in the industrialized world. In 1980, the United States ranked thirteenth among advanced countries in life expectancy at birth; in 2015 it ranked twenty-ninth. In a reversal of the historic pattern, the size of the American middle class continued to shrink, average family income and the number of low-income students graduating from college trailed that of several other countries, and social mobility—the opportunity for people to move up the economic ladder—stood at a lower level in the United States than in western Europe.

Shrinking middle class

THE OBAMA PRESIDENCY

Postracial America?

African-Americans and the recession

Ironically, under the nation's first black president, African-Americans suffered most severely from the recession. A far higher proportion of blacks' family wealth was in their homes compared with whites, so the collapse of the housing bubble devastated their economic status. In 2012, the median family wealth of white families was $110,000, that of blacks only $6,300.

Despite this grim reality, Obama's election spurred discussions among political commentators and ordinary Americans that the nation had finally put the legacy of racial inequality behind it. Talk proliferated of a new, "postracial" America, in which racial differences no longer affected public policy or private attitudes. In 2013, the Supreme Court employed this very logic in a 5-4 decision that invalidated the heart of the Voting Rights Act of 1965, a milestone of the civil rights era. Since states identified in the law, most of them in the Old South, no longer discriminated on the basis of race, the majority declared, they should no longer be required to gain permission from the Justice Department before changing their election laws. The decision unleashed a flood of laws, such as limits on early voting and requiring voters to possess state-issued identification. These measures were intended to limit the right to vote for poor people of all races, many of whom do not possess driver's licenses or other official IDs.

Voting limitations

Police killings of unarmed African-Americans

A series of events involving the deaths of unarmed black men at the hands of police or other authorities also suggested that any self-congratulation about the end of racial inequality was premature. In 2012, Trayvon Martin, a black teenager walking through a Florida neighborhood to visit his father, was accosted by George Zimmerman, a white member of the "neighborhood watch." An altercation followed in which Zimmerman shot and killed Martin. Subsequently, a jury acquitted Zimmerman of all charges related to the incident. In 2014, Eric Garner, a forty-four-year-old black man selling cigarettes on the street in Staten Island, a borough of New York City, died after being wrestled to the ground and choked by police. Although "choke holds" were illegal, a grand jury declined to bring charges. In ensuing months other such incidents followed including the death of a twenty-five-year-old black man in Baltimore while in a police van after being arrested for carrying a small knife (legal in Maryland). In Ferguson, Missouri, a suburb of St. Louis, Michael Brown, an unarmed black eighteen-year-old, was shot in disputed circumstances by a white police officer, whom a grand jury subsequently cleared of potential charges. In Baltimore, by contrast, the local district attorney moved to indict the police implicated in these cities' deaths.

Michael Brown

This cascade of events spurred the emergence of a national movement, **Black Lives Matter**, which demanded that police practices be changed and officers who used excessive force be held accountable. It gave public voice to the countless African-Americans who had experienced disrespect, harassment, or violence at the hands of police. The movement used social media and current technology to organize protests and disseminate videos of encounters between black persons and the police. The Black Lives Matter movement was less an articulation of specific policy demands than a broad claim to black humanity. In this sense, it had historical precedents in abolitionism, with its slogan "Am I Not a Man and a Brother?," and in "I Am a Man," the defiant claim of Memphis sanitation workers during their 1968 strike, where Martin-Luther King Jr. was assassinated.

Black Lives Matter movement

In Ferguson, Missouri, Brown's death inspired weeks of sometimes violent street demonstrations. These led to the deployment of state police and National Guardsmen dressed in battle gear and armed with assault rifles and armored personnel carriers, as if equipped for a war zone overseas—a sign of how policing had become increasingly militarized since the 1960s. In Ferguson, investigations after the death of Michael Brown revealed that the almost entirely white police, city government, and local judiciary regularly preyed on black residents, seeing them not as citizens to be served and protected but as a source of revenue to balance the local budget. Blacks were hauled into court to pay fines for nonexistent driving violations, jaywalking, even walking on the sidewalks too close to the street. Nationally, public reaction to the Black Lives Matter movement revealed a sharp divide between white and black Americans. In public opinion polls, over 80 percent of blacks but just 30 percent of whites agreed with the statement that blacks are victims of discriminatory treatment by the police.

Mass demonstrations

Heavily armed police confront a resident of Ferguson, Missouri, during demonstrations there.

Obama and the World

The most dramatic achievement of Obama's presidency in foreign affairs was fulfillment of his campaign promise to end American involvement in the Iraq War. At the end of 2011, the last American soldiers came home. Nearly 5,000 Americans and, according to the estimates of U.S. and Iraqi analysts, hundreds of thousands of Iraqis, most of them civilians, had died during this eight-year conflict. The war had cost the United States nearly $2 trillion, an almost unimaginable sum. Whether it would produce a stable, democratic Iraq remained to be seen.

End of Iraq War

At the same time, Obama continued many of the policies of the Bush administration. He dramatically increased the American troop presence in Afghanistan, while pledging to withdraw American forces by the end of 2014, although he failed to meet this deadline. By 2012, polls showed that a large majority of Americans felt the war was a mistake and wanted it to end.

Like many of his predecessors, Obama found that criticizing presidential power from outside is one thing, dismantling it another. He reversed his previous promise to abolish the military tribunals Bush had established and to close the military prison at Guantánamo, Cuba. And in 2011 he signed a four-year extension of key provisions of the USA Patriot Act originally passed under Bush. In May 2011, to wide acclaim in the United States, Obama authorized an armed raid into Pakistan that resulted in the death of Osama bin Laden, who had been hiding there for years. More controversially, Obama claimed the right to order the assassination of American citizens in foreign countries if evidence indicated their connection with terrorism. And in 2011 he sent the air force to participate in a NATO campaign that assisted rebels who overthrew Libyan dictator Muammar Gadhafi. But a seemingly endless civil war followed, not the restoration of democracy. Obama did not seek congressional approval of the action.

Fighting terrorism

International diplomacy

In 2014, Obama abandoned the half-century-old policy of isolating Cuba and moved to resume diplomatic relations with the island nation. The policy of isolation had long outlived its Cold War origins and had made the United States seem petty and vindictive in the eyes of Latin Americans. In the following year, the administration, in conjunction with the European Union, Russia, and China, worked out an arrangement with Iran to ensure that that nation's nuclear energy program was confined to peaceful purposes and did not lead to the manufacture of nuclear weapons. This was a remarkable achievement in view of the decades of hostility between the United States and Iran dating back to the hostage crisis of 1979–1981. Also in 2015, the United States played a major role in the forging of an agreement committing every country in the world to reduce emissions (notably from the burning of coal and oil) that contributed to global warming.

Events overseas presented new challenges and opportunities for the Obama administration. To the surprise of almost everyone, beginning in 2011 popular revolts swept the Middle East. Uprisings brought millions of people into the streets, toppling long-serving dictators in Tunisia, Egypt, and Libya. Freedom emerged as the rallying cry of those challenging autocratic governments. "I'm in Tahrir Square," one demonstrator yelled into his cell phone while standing at the epicenter of the Egyptian revolution. "In freedom, in freedom, in freedom." Once again, the tension between the ideals of freedom and democracy and American strategic interests posed a difficult challenge for policymakers. After some hesitation, the United States sided with those seeking the ouster of Egyptian dictator Hosni Mubarak, a staunch American ally. It then stood on the sidelines throughout 2011 and 2012 as Egypt lurched from popular uprising to military rule to electoral victory by the Muslim Brotherhood, a previously illegal Islamic group, to a military coup in 2013, with the final outcome of the revolution always in doubt. When a military coup in 2013 ousted the elected president and instituted a regime even more repressive than Mubarak's, the Obama administration suspended shipments of military equipment to Egypt, but soon resumed them. In general, like his predecessors during the Cold War, Obama used "human rights" as a political weapon, condemning abuses by adversaries like China while remaining largely silent in the face of serious abuses by allies in the war on terror such as Pakistan, Ethiopia, and Saudi Arabia. In Bahrain, an oil-rich principality in the Persian Gulf and home base of the American Fifth Fleet, the Obama administration looked the other way when the autocratic government suppressed popular discontent with force.

In his second term, Obama faced a new crisis when the self-proclaimed Islamic State took control of parts of Iraq, Syria, and Libya. **ISIS**, as it was called, conducted campaigns of exceptional brutality, beheading prisoners of war and driving religious minorities out of territory it conquered. The videos of these acts posted by ISIS on social media horrified most of the world but also attracted recruits to the organization. ISIS also sponsored terror attacks outside the Middle East. In 2015 over 100 persons were killed in a series of coordinated attacks in Paris. A few weeks later, two followers of ISIS in the United States killed fourteen people in San

President Barack Obama, Vice President Joe Biden, Secretary of State Hillary Clinton, and other members of Obama's national security team receiving an update on the mission against Osama bin Laden at the White House on May 1, 2011.

Revolts in the Middle East

Acts of Terrorism

"Get me everything on everybody."

A cartoon in the magazine the *New Yorker* inspired by revelations that the National Security Agency has been spying on the phone conversations and e-mails of millions of Americans.

Privacy versus national security

Bernardino, California. It remained to be seen whether the rampages of ISIS would draw the United States into further combat in the Middle East.

Another area in which Obama continued the policies initiated during the Bush administration's war on terror was governmental surveillance, both domestic and overseas. The extent of such activity became known in 2013 when **Edward Snowden**, a former employee of the National Security Agency, released documents online that detailed NSA programs that monitored virtually all telephone, instant messaging, and e-mail traffic in the United States, tracked the location of numerous American cell phones, and spied on the private communications of world leaders, including close allies of the United States such as Chancellor Angela Merkel of Germany and French president François Hollande. The government also secretly worked with major Internet and communications companies like AT&T and Verizon to gain access to the private data of their users. Of course, the overwhelming majority of the people subject to government surveillance had no connection to terrorism or to any crime at all. To avoid prosecution, Snowden took up residence in Russia. But his revelations rekindled the age-old debate over the balance between national security and Americans' civil liberties and offered another example of how, whichever party is in power, the balance always seems to shift in favor of the former. In 2015, Congress approved a measure curtailing the government's sweeping surveillance of phone records. But much of the government's prying into Americans' communications continued.

The Republican Resurgence

In nearly all midterm elections in American history the party in power has lost seats in Congress. But Democrats faced more serious difficulties than usual in the midterm elections of 2010. Grassroots Republicans were energized by hostility to Obama's sweeping legislative enactments. The **Tea Party**, named for the Boston Tea Party of the 1770s and inspired by its opposition to taxation by a faraway government, mobilized grassroots opposition to the administration. For a time, some activists denied that Obama was legally president at all, claiming that he had been born in Africa, not in the United States. (In fact, he was born in Hawaii.)

With their opponents energized and their own supporters demoralized by the slow pace of economic recovery, Democrats suffered a severe

Grassroots support

reversal. Republicans swept to control of the House of Representatives and substantially reduced the Democratic majority in the Senate. The result was political gridlock that lasted for the remainder of Obama's presidency.

Tea Party–inspired conservative gains at the state level in 2010 unleashed a rash of new legislation. Several states moved to curtail abortion rights. New conservative legislatures also took aim at undocumented immigrants. Alabama, which has no land border with a foreign country and a small population of immigrants, enacted the harshest measure, making it a crime for undocumented immigrants to apply for a job and for anyone to transport them, even to a church or hospital. During the contest for the Republican presidential nomination in early 2012, candidates vied with each other to demonstrate their determination to drive undocumented immigrants from the country. Oddly, all this took place at a time when illegal immigration from Mexico, the largest source of undocumented workers, had ceased almost completely because of stricter controls at the border and the drying up of available jobs because of the recession. These measures associated the Republican Party with intense nativism in the minds of many Hispanic voters.

The immigration issue

The 2012 Campaign

Despite the continuing economic crisis, sociocultural issues played a major role in the campaign for the Republican presidential nomination in 2012, as candidates vied to win the support of the evangelical Christians who formed a major part of the party's base. The front-runner was Mitt Romney, the former governor of Massachusetts. Romney had made a fortune directing Bain Capital, a firm that specialized in buying up other companies and then reselling them at a profit after restructuring them, which often involved firing large numbers of employees. But the party's powerful conservative wing disliked Romney because of his moderate record (as governor he had instituted a state health-care plan remarkably similar to Obama's 2010 legislation) and a distrust of his Mormon faith among many evangelical Christians.

Mitt Romney

Eventually, using his personal fortune to outspend his rivals by an enormous amount, Romney emerged as the Republican candidate, the first Mormon to win a major party's nomination—a significant moment in the history of religious toleration in the United States. He chose as his running mate Congressman Paul D. Ryan of Wisconsin, a favorite of the Tea Party and a Roman Catholic. For the first time in its history, the Republican Party's ticket did not contain a traditional Protestant.

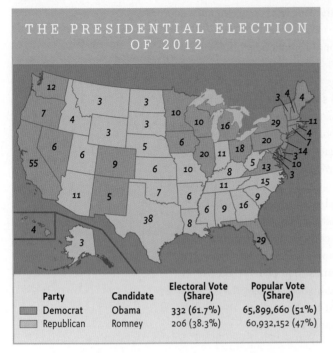

THE PRESIDENTIAL ELECTION OF 2012

Party	Candidate	Electoral Vote (Share)	Popular Vote (Share)
Democrat	Obama	332 (61.7%)	65,899,660 (51%)
Republican	Romney	206 (38.3%)	60,932,152 (47%)

President Obama began the 2012 campaign with numerous liabilities. The enthusiasm that greeted his election had long since faded as the worst economic slump since the Great Depression dragged on, and voters became fed up with both the president and Congress because of the intensity of partisanship and legislative gridlock. The war in Afghanistan was increasingly unpopular and his signature health-care law under ferocious assault by Republicans.

Nonetheless, after a heated campaign, Obama emerged victorious, winning 332 electoral votes to Romney's 206, and 51 percent of the popular vote to his opponent's 47 percent. At the same time, while Democrats gained a few seats in the House and Senate, the balance of power in Washington remained unchanged. This set the stage for continued partisan infighting and political gridlock during Obama's second term.

Obama's victory stemmed from many causes, including an extremely efficient get-out-the-vote organization on election day and Romney's weaknesses as a campaigner. Romney never managed to shed the image of a millionaire who used loopholes to avoid paying taxes (his federal tax rate of 14 percent was lower than that of most working-class Americans). Many people believed he held ordinary people in contempt, particularly after he was videotaped making an off-the-cuff remark that 47 percent of the people would not vote for him because they were "victims" dependent on government payments like Medicare and Social Security. But more important, as in 2008, the result reflected the new diversity of the American population in the twenty-first century. Romney won 60 percent of the white vote, which in previous elections would have guaranteed victory. But Obama carried over 90 percent of the black vote and over 70 percent of Asians and Hispanics. With the minority population on the increase, these figures heralded future difficulties for the Republican Party unless it modified its strong anti-immigration rhetoric. Nonetheless, as frequently happens in midterm elections, the party that did not hold the White House, in this case the Republicans, made significant gains, strengthening its hold on the House in 2014 and taking control of the Senate.

A rising Hispanic population

The 2012 election reflected the new diversity in other ways as well. Hawaii elected Tulsi Gabbard, the first Hindu to serve in the House of Representatives, and the first Buddhist, Mazie K. Hirono, to the Senate. But perhaps the most striking feature of the election was the unprecedented amount of money spent on the campaign. In 2010, in *Citizens United v. Federal Elections Commission,* the conservative majority on the Supreme Court had overturned federal restrictions on political contributions by corporations. At the same time, political action committees were allowed to spend as much money as they wished supporting or denigrating candidates for office so long as they did not coordinate their activities with the candidates' campaigns. Meanwhile, the Romney and Obama campaigns themselves raised and spent hundreds of millions of dollars from individual donors. All this resulted in an election that cost, for presidential and congressional races combined, some $6 billion.

Campaign funding

FREEDOM IN THE TWENTY-FIRST CENTURY

The century that ended in 2000 witnessed vast human progress and unimaginable human tragedy. It saw the decolonization of Asia and Africa, the emergence of women into full citizenship in most parts of the world, and amazing advances in science, medicine, and technology. Thanks to the spread of new products, available at ever-cheaper prices, it brought more improvement in the daily conditions of life to more human beings than any other century in history. But the twentieth century also witnessed the death of uncounted millions in wars and genocides and the widespread degradation of the natural environment, the underside of progress.

International development and tragedy

Exceptional America

In the early twenty-first century, people in the United States lived longer and healthier lives compared with previous generations, and they enjoyed a level of material comfort unimagined a century before. In 1900, the typical American had no indoor plumbing, no telephone or car, and had not graduated from high school. As late as 1940, one-third of American households did not have running water. In 2013, health conditions had improved so much that the average life expectancy for men had risen to seventy-six and for women to eighty-one (from forty-six and forty-eight in

America from 1900 to 2013

1900). On the other hand, poverty, income inequality, and infant mortality in the United States considerably exceeded that of other economically advanced countries, and fewer than 10 percent of workers in private firms belonged to unions, a figure not seen since the nineteenth century.

Many of the changes affecting American life have taken place in all economically advanced societies. In other ways, however, the United States at the dawn of the twenty-first century differed sharply from other developed countries. Prevailing ideas of freedom in the United States seemed more attuned to individual advancement than to broad social welfare. The United States was a far more religious country. Sixty percent of Americans agreed with the statement, "Religion plays a very important part in my life," whereas the comparable figure was 32 percent in Britain, 26 percent in Italy, and only 11 percent in France.

Other forms of **American exceptionalism** had a darker side. Among advanced countries, the United States has by far the highest rate of murder using guns. In 2012, there were 9,146 murders with guns in the United States as opposed to 158 in Germany, 173 in Canada, and 11 in Japan.

Indeed, in the last years of the twentieth century and the beginning of the twenty-first, the United States was the scene of a horrifying number of mass murders, often committed at schools. In 1999, two students killed twelve students and a teacher at Columbine High School in Colorado. In 2007, a student at Virginia Tech University shot and killed thirty-two people. Five years later, a lone gunman killed twenty children aged five and six and seven adults at Sandy Hook Elementary School in Newtown, Connecticut. In the 1950s, schools across the country had conducted drills to enable students to survive a nuclear attack. Now they trained pupils in seeking shelter if a gunman entered the building. There were also mass killings at a movie theater in Aurora, Colorado, and at the Washington Navy Yard. In 2015, a gunman influenced by racist Internet sites murdered nine black participants in a Bible study group, including the minister, at Emanuel African Methodist Episcopal Church in Charleston, South Carolina. Other countries also experienced instances of mass violence, but not with the frequency of the United States. While each of these events led to calls for stricter regulations on the purchase of firearms, the strong commitment of many Americans to the Second Amendment's guarantee of the right to bear arms, coupled with the remarkable power of the National Rifle Association, one of the country's most influential lobbies, ensured that no new regulations were enacted.

A lock-down drill in Belle Plaine, Minnesota, trains an eighth-grade class how to respond in the event of a school shooting.

The United States continued to lag behind other countries in providing social rights to its citizens. In Europe, workers are guaranteed by law a paid vacation each year and a number of paid sick days. American employers are not required to offer either to their workers. Only four countries in the world have no national provision for paid maternity leave after a woman gives birth to a child: Liberia, Papua New Guinea, Suriname, and the United States. And as noted in the previous chapter, the United States has by far the world's highest rate of imprisonment.

It was an irony of early-twenty-first-century life that Americans enjoyed more personal freedom than ever before but less of what earlier generations called "industrial freedom." The sustained recovery from the recession of the early 1990s did not entirely relieve a widespread sense of economic insecurity. Globalization—which treated workers at home and abroad as interchangeable factors of production, capable of being uprooted or dismissed without warning—seemed to render individual and even national sovereignty all but meaningless. Because economic liberty has long been associated with economic security, and rights have historically been linked to democratic participation and membership in a nation-state, these processes had ominous implications for traditional understandings of freedom. It remained to be seen whether a conception of freedom grounded in access to the consumer marketplace and the glorification of individual self-fulfillment unrestrained by government, social citizenship, or a common public culture could provide an adequate way to comprehend the world of the twenty-first century.

American writers and artists continue to reflect on the history and symbolism of freedom. In a work entitled *Chillin' with Liberty*, the artist Renée Cox poses herself atop the Statue of Liberty, audaciously staking her own claim to American freedom.

Learning from History

"The owl of Minerva takes flight at dusk." Minerva was the Roman goddess of wisdom, and this saying suggests that the meaning of events only becomes clear once they are over. It is still far too soon to assess the full impact of September 11 on American life and the long-term consequences of the changes at home and abroad it inspired.

As of the end of 2015, the world seemed far more unstable than anyone could have predicted when the Cold War ended. An end to the war on terror seemed as remote as ever. The future of Iraq, Afghanistan, and indeed the entire Middle East remained uncertain. No settlement of the long-standing conflict between Israel and its Arab neighbors seemed in sight.

An unstable world

Other regions of the world also presented daunting problems for American policymakers, most notably China's rapidly growing economic power, which challenged American predominance. Relations with Russia,

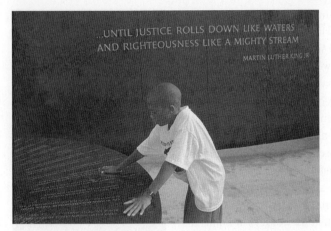

Seeking the lessons of history: a young visitor at the Civil Rights Memorial in Montgomery, Alabama.

which was supporting a separatist movement in eastern Ukraine, were at their lowest point since the end of the Cold War.

No one could predict how any of these crises, or others yet unimagined, would be resolved.

What *is* clear is that as in the past, freedom is central to Americans' sense of themselves as individuals and as a nation. Americans continue to debate contemporary issues in a political landscape shaped by ideas of freedom. Indeed, freedom remains, as it has always been, an evolving concept, its definition open to disagreement, its boundaries never fixed or final. Freedom is neither self-enforcing nor self-correcting. It cannot be taken for granted, and its preservation requires eternal vigilance, especially in times of crisis.

More than half a century ago, the African-American poet Langston Hughes urged Americans both to celebrate the freedoms they enjoy and to remember that freedom has always been incomplete:

> There are words like *Freedom*
> Sweet and wonderful to say.
> On my heartstrings freedom sings
> All day everyday.
>
> There are words like *Liberty*
> That almost make me cry.
> If you had known what I know
> You would know why.

CHAPTER REVIEW AND ONLINE RESOURCES

REVIEW QUESTIONS

1. How did the foreign policy initiatives of the George W. Bush administration depart from the policies of other presidents since World War II?

2. How did the September 11 attacks transform Americans' understanding of their security? How did the response compare with that after Pearl Harbor?

3. What are the similarities of and differences between America's involvement in Afghanistan and Iraq since 2001?

4. In what ways did Americans—leaders and citizens— draw lessons from Vietnam when considering U.S. involvement in Iraq?

5. What does the war on terrorism suggest about the tension between freedom and security as priorities of the United States?

6. What were the goals and impact of the Bush administration's economic policies?

7. How did Supreme Court decisions since 2001 indicate that the rights revolution was here to stay?

8. What were the political and social effects of Hurricane Katrina? Which were lasting?

9. In what ways did the Obama administration diverge from the policies of other recent administrations? In what ways was it similar?

10. How did the 2012 election reveal changes in American political and social practices? How did it represent continuities?

11. What is meant by American exceptionalism? In what ways is the United States different from the rest of the world, and how is it similar?

KEY TERMS

Kyoto Protocol (p. 879)
the Bush Doctrine (p. 880)
war on terrorism (p. 880)
war in Afghanistan (p. 880)
Iraq War (p. 882)
USA Patriot Act (p. 885)
Guantánamo Bay (p. 886)
Hurricane Katrina (p. 888)
Obergefell v. Hodges (p. 892)
Great Recession (p. 895)
Sonia Sotomayor (p. 899)
Occupy Wall Street (p. 904)
Black Lives Matter (p. 907)
ISIS (p. 909)
Edward Snowden (p. 910)
Tea Party (p. 910)
American exceptionalism (p. 914)

Go to 🐰 IN**QUIZITIVE**

To see what you know—and learn what you've missed—with personalized feedback along the way.

Visit the *Give Me Liberty!* **Student Site** for primary source documents and images, interactive maps, author videos featuring Eric Foner, and more.

★

APPENDIX

★

DOCUMENTS

The Declaration of Independence (1776)   A-2

The Constitution of the United States (1787)   A-5

From George Washington's Farewell Address (1796)   A-17

The Seneca Falls Declaration of Sentiments and
    Resolutions (1848)   A-22

From Frederick Douglass's "What, to the Slave, Is the Fourth of
    July?" Speech (1852)   A-25

The Gettysburg Address (1863)   A-29

Abraham Lincoln's Second Inaugural Address (1865)   A-30

The Populist Platform of 1892   A-31

Franklin D. Roosevelt's First Inaugural Address (1933)   A-34

From The Program for the March on Washington for Jobs and
    Freedom (1963)   A-37

Ronald Reagan's First Inaugural Address (1981)   A-38

Barack Obama's First Inaugural Address (2009)   A-42

TABLES AND FIGURES

Presidential Elections   A-46

Admission of States   A-54

Population of the United States   A-55

Historical Statistics of the United States:
    Labor Force—Selected Characteristics Expressed as a
        Percentage of the Labor Force, 1800–2010   A-56
    Immigration, by Origin   A-56
    Unemployment Rate, 1890–2015   A-57
    Union Membership as a Percentage of Nonagricultural
        Employment, 1880–2015   A-57
    Voter Participation in Presidential Elections, 1824–2016   A-57
    Birthrate, 1820–2015   A-57

SUGGESTED READING ... A-59

GLOSSARY... A-73

CREDITS... A-105

INDEX... A-109

THE DECLARATION OF INDEPENDENCE (1776)

When in the course of human events, it becomes necessary for one people to dissolve the political bands which have connected them with another, and to assume among the Powers of the earth, the separate and equal station to which the Laws of Nature and of Nature's God entitle them, a decent respect to the opinions of mankind requires that they should declare the causes which impel them to the separation.

We hold these truths to be self-evident, that all men are created equal, that they are endowed by their Creator with certain unalienable rights, that among these are Life, Liberty, and the pursuit of Happiness. That to secure these rights, Governments are instituted among Men, deriving their just powers from the consent of the governed. That whenever any Form of Government becomes destructive of these ends, it is the Right of the People to alter or to abolish it, and to institute new Government, laying its foundation on such principles and organizing its powers in such form, as to them shall seem most likely to effect their Safety and Happiness. Prudence, indeed, will dictate that Governments long established should not be changed for light and transient causes; and accordingly all experience hath shown, that mankind are more disposed to suffer, while evils are sufferable, than to right themselves by abolishing the forms to which they are accustomed. But when a long train of abuses and usurpations, pursuing invariably the same Object evinces a design to reduce them under absolute Despotism, it is their right, it is their duty, to throw off such Government, and to provide new Guards for their future security.—Such has been the patient sufferance of these Colonies; and such is now the necessity which constrains them to alter their former Systems of Government. The history of the present King of Great Britain is a history of repeated injuries and usurpations, all having in direct object the establishment of an absolute Tyranny over these States. To prove this, let Facts be submitted to a candid world.

He has refused his Assent to Laws, the most wholesome and necessary for the public good.

He has forbidden his Governors to pass Laws of immediate and pressing importance, unless suspended in their operation till his Assent should be obtained; and when so suspended, he has utterly neglected to attend to them.

He has refused to pass other Laws for the accommodation of large districts of people, unless those people would relinquish the right of Representation in the Legislature, a right inestimable to them and formidable to tyrants only.

He has called together legislative bodies at places unusual, uncomfortable, and distant from the depository of their public Records, for the sole purpose of fatiguing them into compliance with his measures.

He has dissolved Representative Houses repeatedly, for opposing with manly firmness his invasions on the rights of the people.

He has refused for a long time, after such dissolutions, to cause others to be elected; whereby the Legislative powers, incapable of Annihilation, have returned to the People at large for their exercise; the State remaining in the mean time exposed to all dangers of invasion from without, and convulsions within.

He has endeavoured to prevent the population of these States; for that purpose obstructing the Laws of Naturalization of Foreigners; refusing to pass others to encourage their migrations hither, and raising the conditions of new Appropriations of Lands.

He has obstructed the Administration of Justice, by refusing his Assent to Laws for establishing Judiciary powers.

He has made Judges dependent on his Will alone, for the tenure of their offices, and the amount and payment of their salaries.

He has erected a multitude of New Offices, and sent hither swarms of Officers to harass our People, and eat out their substance.

He has kept among us, in times of peace, Standing Armies without the Consent of our legislatures.

He has affected to render the Military independent of and superior to the Civil Power.

He has combined with others to subject us to a jurisdiction foreign to our constitution, and unacknowledged by our laws; giving his Assent to their Acts of pretended Legislation:

For quartering large bodies of armed troops among us:

For protecting them, by a mock Trial, from Punishment for any Murders which they should commit on the Inhabitants of these States:

For cutting off our Trade with all parts of the world:

For imposing taxes on us without our Consent:

For depriving us of many cases, of the benefits of Trial by jury:

For transporting us beyond Seas to be tried for pretended offences:

For abolishing the free System of English Laws in a neighbouring Province, establishing therein an Arbitrary government, and enlarging its Boundaries so as to render it at once an example and fit instrument for introducing the same absolute rule into these Colonies:

For taking away our Charters, abolishing our most valuable Laws, and altering fundamentally the Forms of our Governments:

For suspending our own Legislatures, and declaring themselves invested with Power to legislate for us in all cases whatsoever.

He has abdicated Government here, by declaring us out of his Protection and waging War against us.

He has plundered our seas, ravaged our Coasts, burnt our towns, and destroyed the lives of our people.

He is at this time transporting large armies of foreign mercenaries to compleat the works of death, desolation, and tyranny, already begun with circumstances of Cruelty & perfidy scarcely paralleled in the most barbarous ages, and totally unworthy the Head of a civilized nation.

He has constrained our fellow Citizens taken Captive on the high Seas to bear Arms against their Country, to become the executioners of their friends and Brethren, or to fall themselves by their Hands.

He has excited domestic insurrections amongst us, and has endeavoured to bring on the inhabitants of our frontiers, the merciless Indian Savages, whose known rule of warfare, is an undistinguished destruction of all ages, sexes, and conditions.

In every stage of these Oppressions We have Petitioned for Redress in the most humble terms: Our repeated Petitions have been answered only by repeated injury. A Prince, whose character is thus marked by every act which may define a Tyrant, is unfit to be the ruler of a free people.

Nor have We been wanting in attention to our British brethren. We have warned them from time to time of attempts by their legislature to extend an unwarrantable jurisdiction over us. We have reminded them of the circumstances of our emigration and settlement here. We have appealed to their native justice and magnanimity, and we have conjured them by the ties of our common kindred to disavow these usurpations, which, would inevitably interrupt our connections and correspondence. They too must have been deaf to the voice of justice and of consanguinity. We must, therefore, acquiesce in the necessity, which denounces our Separation, and hold them, as we hold the rest of mankind, Enemies in War, in Peace Friends.

WE, THEREFORE, the Representatives of the UNITED STATES OF AMERICA, in General Congress, Assembled, appealing to the Supreme Judge of the world for the rectitude of our intentions, do, in the Name, and by Authority of the good People of these Colonies, solemnly publish and declare, That these United Colonies are, and of Right ought to be FREE AND INDEPENDENT STATES; that they are Absolved from all Allegiance to the British Crown, and that all political connection between them and the State of Great Britain, is and ought to be totally dissolved; and that as Free and Independent States, they have full Power to levy War, conclude Peace, contract Alliances, establish Commerce, and to do all other Acts and Things which Independent States may of right do. And for the support of this Declaration, with a firm reliance on the Protection of Divine Providence, we mutually pledge to each other our Lives, our Fortunes, and our sacred Honor.

The foregoing Declaration was, by order of Congress, engrossed, and signed by the following members:

John Hancock

NEW HAMPSHIRE
Josiah Bartlett
William Whipple
Matthew Thornton

MASSACHUSETTS BAY
Samuel Adams
John Adams
Robert Treat Paine
Elbridge Gerry

RHODE ISLAND
Stephen Hopkins
William Ellery

CONNECTICUT
Roger Sherman
Samuel Huntington
William Williams
Oliver Wolcott

NEW YORK
William Floyd
Philip Livingston
Francis Lewis
Lewis Morris

NEW JERSEY
Richard Stockton
John Witherspoon
Francis Hopkinson
John Hart
Abraham Clark

PENNSYLVANIA
Robert Morris
Benjamin Rush
Benjamin Franklin
John Morton
George Clymer
James Smith
George Taylor
James Wilson
George Ross

DELAWARE
Caesar Rodney
George Read
Thomas M'Kean

MARYLAND
Samuel Chase
William Paca
Thomas Stone
Charles Carroll, of Carrollton

VIRGINIA
George Wythe
Richard Henry Lee
Thomas Jefferson
Benjamin Harrison
Thomas Nelson, Jr.
Francis Lightfoot Lee
Carter Braxton

NORTH CAROLINA
William Hooper
Joseph Hewes
John Penn

SOUTH CAROLINA
Edward Rutledge
Thomas Heyward, Jr.
Thomas Lynch, Jr.
Arthur Middleton

GEORGIA
Button Gwinnett
Lyman Hall
George Walton

Resolved, That copies of the Declaration be sent to the several assemblies, conventions, and committees, or councils of safety, and to the several commanding officers of the continental troops; that it be proclaimed in each of the United States, at the head of the army.

THE CONSTITUTION OF THE UNITED STATES (1787)

We the People of the United States, in order to form a more perfect Union, establish Justice, insure domestic Tranquility, provide for the common defence, promote the general Welfare, and secure the Blessings of Liberty to ourselves and our Posterity, do ordain and establish this Constitution for the United States of America.

ARTICLE. I.

Section. 1. All legislative Powers herein granted shall be vested in a Congress of the United States, which shall consist of a Senate and House of Representatives.

Section. 2. The House of Representatives shall be composed of Members chosen every second Year by the People of the several States, and the Electors in each State shall have the Qualifications requisite for Electors of the most numerous Branch of the State Legislature.

No Person shall be a Representative who shall not have attained to the Age of twenty five Years, and been seven Years a Citizen of the United States, and who shall not, when elected, be an Inhabitant of that State in which he shall be chosen.

Representatives and direct Taxes shall be apportioned among the several States which may be included within this Union, according to their respective Numbers, which shall be determined by adding to the whole Number of free Persons, including those bound to Service for a Term of Years, and excluding Indians not taxed, three fifths of all other Persons. The actual Enumeration shall be made within three Years after the first Meeting of the Congress of the United States, and within every subsequent Term of ten Years, in such Manner as they shall by Law direct. The Number of Representatives shall not exceed one for every thirty Thousand, but each State shall have at Least one Representative; and until such enumeration shall be made, the State of New Hampshire shall be entitled to chuse three, Massachusetts eight, Rhode-Island and Providence Plantations one, Connecticut five, New York six, New Jersey four, Pennsylvania eight, Delaware one, Maryland six, Virginia ten, North Carolina five, South Carolina five, and Georgia three.

When vacancies happen in the Representation from any state, the Executive Authority thereof shall issue Writs of Election to fill such Vacancies.

The House of Representatives shall chuse their Speaker and other Officers; and shall have the sole Power of Impeachment.

Section. 3. The Senate of the United States shall be composed of two Senators from each State, chosen by the legislature thereof, for six Years; and each Senator shall have one Vote.

Immediately after they shall be assembled in Consequence of the first Election, they shall be divided as equally as may be into three Classes. The Seats of the Senators of the first Class shall be vacated at the Expiration of the second Year, of the second Class at the Expiration of the fourth Year, and of the third Class at the Expiration of the sixth Year, so that one third may be chosen every second Year; and if Vacancies happen by Resignation, or otherwise, during the Recess of the Legislature of any State, the Executive thereof may make temporary Appointments until the next Meeting of the Legislature, which shall then fill such Vacancies.

No Person shall be a Senator who shall not have attained to the Age of thirty Years, and been nine Years a Citizen of the United States, and who shall not, when elected, be an Inhabitant of that State for which he shall be chosen.

The Vice President of the United States shall be President of the Senate, but shall have no Vote, unless they be equally divided.

The Senate shall chuse their other Officers, and also a President pro tempore, in the Absence of the

Vice President, or when he shall exercise the Office of President of the United States.

The Senate shall have the sole Power to try all Impeachments. When sitting for that Purpose, they shall be on Oath or Affirmation. When the President of the United States is tried, the Chief Justice shall preside: And no Person shall be convicted without the Concurrence of two thirds of the Members present.

Judgment in Cases of Impeachment shall not extend further than to removal from Office, and disqualification to hold and enjoy any Office of honor, Trust or Profit under the United States: but the Party convicted shall nevertheless be liable and subject to Indictment, Trial, Judgment and Punishment, according to Law.

Section. 4. The Times, Places and Manner of holding Elections for Senators and Representatives, shall be prescribed in each State by the Legislature thereof; but the Congress may at any time by Law make or alter such Regulations, except as to the Places of chusing Senators.

The Congress shall assemble at least once in every Year, and such Meeting shall be on the first Monday in December, unless they shall by Law appoint a different Day.

Section. 5. Each House shall be the Judge of the Elections, Returns and Qualifications of its own Members, and a Majority of each shall constitute a Quorum to do Business; but a smaller Number may adjourn from day to day, and may be authorized to compel the Attendance of absent Members, in such Manner, and under such Penalties as each House may provide.

Each House may determine the Rules of its Proceedings, punish its Members for disorderly Behaviour, and, with the Concurrence of two thirds, expel a Member.

Each House shall keep a Journal of its Proceedings, and from time to time publish the same, excepting such Parts as may in their Judgment require Secrecy; and the Yeas and Nays of the Members of either House on any question shall, at the Desire of one fifth of those Present, be entered on the Journal.

Neither House, during the Session of Congress, shall, without the Consent of the other, adjourn for more than three days, not to any other Place than that in which the two Houses shall be sitting.

Section. 6. The Senators and Representatives shall receive a Compensation for their Services, to be ascertained by Law, and paid out of the Treasury of the United States. They shall in all Cases, except Treason, Felony and Breach of the Peace, be privileged from Arrest during their Attendance at the Session of their respective Houses, and in going to and returning from the same; and for any Speech or Debate in either House, they shall not be questioned in any other Place.

No Senator or Representative shall, during the Time for which he was elected, be appointed to any civil Office under the Authority of the United States, which shall have been created, or the Emoluments whereof shall have been encreased during such time; and no Person holding any Office under the United States, shall be a Member of either House during his Continuance in Office.

Section. 7. All Bills for raising Revenue shall originate in the House of Representatives; but the Senate may propose or concur with Amendments as on other Bills.

Every Bill which shall have passed the House of Representatives and the Senate shall, before it become a Law, be presented to the President of the United States; If he approve he shall sign it, but if not he shall return it, with his Objections to that House in which it shall have originated, who shall enter the Objections at large on their Journal, and proceed to reconsider it. If after such Reconsideration two thirds of that House shall agree to pass the Bill, it shall be sent, together with the Objections, to the other House, by which it shall likewise be reconsidered, and if approved by two thirds of that House, it shall become a Law. But in all such Cases the Votes of both Houses shall be determined by Yeas and Nays, and the Names of the Persons voting for and against the Bill shall be entered on the Journal of each House respectively. If any Bill shall not be returned by the President within ten Days (Sundays excepted) after it shall have been presented to him, the Same shall be a Law, in like Manner as if he had signed it, unless the Congress by their Adjournment prevent its Return, in which Case it shall not be a Law.

Every Order, Resolution, or Vote to which the Concurrence of the Senate and House of Representatives may be necessary (except on a question of Adjournment) shall be presented to the President of the United States; and before the Same shall take Effect, shall be approved by him, or being disapproved by him, shall be repassed by two thirds of the Senate and House of Representatives, according to the Rules and Limitations prescribed in the Case of a Bill.

Section. 8. The Congress shall have Power To lay and collect Taxes, Duties, Imposts and Excises, to pay the Debts and provide for the common Defence and general Welfare of the United States; but all Duties, Imposts and Excises shall be uniform throughout the United States;

To borrow Money on the credit of the United States;

To regulate Commerce with foreign Nations, and among the several States, and with the Indian Tribes;

To establish an uniform Rule of Naturalization, and uniform Laws on the subject of Bankruptcies throughout the United States;

To coin Money, regulate the Value thereof, and of foreign Coin, and fix the Standard of Weights and Measures;

To provide for the Punishment of counterfeiting the Securities and current Coin of the United States;

To establish Post Offices and Post Roads;

To promote the Progress of Science and useful Arts, by securing for limited Times to Authors and Inventors the exclusive Right to their respective Writings and Discoveries;

To constitute Tribunals inferior to the supreme Court;

To define and punish Piracies and Felonies committed on the high Seas, and Offences against the Law of Nations;

To declare War, grant Letters of Marque and Reprisal, and make Rules concerning Captures on Land and Water;

To raise and support Armies, but no Appropriation of Money to that Use shall be for a longer Term than two Years;

To provide and maintain a Navy;

To make Rules for the Government and Regulation of the land and naval Forces;

To provide for calling forth the Militia to execute the Laws of the Union, suppress Insurrections and repel Invasions;

To provide for organizing, arming, and disciplining, the Militia, and for governing such Part of them as may be employed in the Service of the United States, reserving to the States respectively, the Appointment of the Officers, and the Authority of training the Militia according to the discipline prescribed by Congress;

To exercise exclusive Legislation in all Cases whatsoever, over such District (not exceeding ten Miles square) as may, by Cession of Particular States, and the Acceptance of Congress, become the Seat of the Government of the United States, and to exercise like Authority over all Places purchased by the Consent of the Legislature of the State in which the Same shall be, for the Erection of Forts, Magazines, Arsenals, dock-Yards, and other needful Buildings;—And

To make all Laws which shall be necessary and proper for carrying into Execution the foregoing Powers, and all other Powers vested by this Constitution in the Government of the United States, or in any Department or Officer thereof.

Section. 9. The Migration or Importation of such Persons as any of the States now existing shall think proper to admit, shall not be prohibited by the Congress prior to the Year one thousand eight hundred and eight, but a Tax or duty may be imposed on such Importation, not exceeding ten dollars for each Person.

The Privilege of the Writ of Habeas Corpus shall not be suspended, unless when in Cases of Rebellion or Invasion the public Safety may require it.

No Bill of Attainder or ex post facto Law shall be passed.

No Capitation, or other direct, Tax shall be laid, unless in Proportion to the Census or Enumeration herein before directed to be taken.

No Tax or Duty shall be laid on Articles exported from any State.

No Preference shall be given by any Regulation of Commerce or Revenue to the Ports of one State over those of another: nor shall Vessels bound to, or from, one State, be obliged to enter, clear, or pay Duties in another.

No Money shall be drawn from the Treasury, but in Consequence of Appropriations made by Law; and a regular Statement and Account of the Receipts and Expenditures of all public Money shall be published from time to time.

No Title of Nobility shall be granted by the United States: And no Person holding any Office of Profit or Trust under them, shall, without the Consent of the Congress, accept of any present, Emolument, Office, or Title, of any kind whatever, from any King, Prince, or foreign State.

Section. 10. No State shall enter into any Treaty, Alliance, or Confederation; grant Letters of Marque and Reprisal; coin Money; emit Bills of Credit; make any Thing but gold and silver Coin a Tender in Payment of Debts; pass any Bill of Attainder, ex post facto Law, or Law impairing the Obligation of Contracts, or grant any Title of Nobility.

No State shall, without the Consent of the Congress, lay any Imposts or Duties on Imports or Exports, except what may be absolutely necessary for executing its inspection Laws: and the net Produce of all Duties and Imposts, laid by any State on Imports or Exports, shall be for the Use of the Treasury of the United States; and all such Laws shall be subject to the Revision and Controul of the Congress.

No State shall, without the Consent of Congress, lay any Duty of Tonnage, keep Troops, or Ships of War in time of Peace, enter into any Agreement or Compact with another State, or with a foreign Power, or engage in War, unless actually invaded, or in such imminent Danger as will not admit of delay.

ARTICLE. II.

Section. 1. The executive Power shall be vested in a President of the United States of America. He shall hold his Office during the term of four Years, and,

together with the Vice President, chosen for the same Term, be elected, as follows:

Each State shall appoint, in such Manner as the Legislature thereof may direct, a Number of Electors, equal to the whole Number of Senators and Representatives to which the State may be entitled in the Congress: but no Senator or Representative, or Person holding an Office of Trust or Profit under the United States, shall be appointed an Elector.

The Electors shall meet in their respective States, and vote by Ballot for two Persons, of whom one at least shall not be an Inhabitant of the same State with themselves. And they shall make a List of all the Persons voted for, and of the Number of Votes for each; which List they shall sign and certify, and transmit sealed to the Seat of the Government of the United States, directed to the President of the Senate. The President of the Senate shall, in the Presence of the Senate and House of Representatives, open all the Certificates, and the Votes shall then be counted. The Person having the greatest Number of Votes shall be the President, if such Number be a Majority of the whole Number of Electors appointed; and if there be more than one who have such Majority, and have an equal Number of Votes, then the House of Representatives shall immediately chuse by Ballot one of them for President; and if no Person have a Majority, then from the five highest on the List the said House shall in like Manner chuse the President. But in chusing the President, the Votes shall be taken by States, the Representation from each State having one Vote; A quorum for this Purpose shall consist of a Member or Members from two thirds of the States, and a Majority of all the States shall be necessary to a Choice. In every Case, after the Choice of the President, the Person having the greatest Number of Votes of the Electors shall be the Vice President. But if there should remain two or more who have equal Votes, the Senate shall chuse from them by Ballot the Vice President.

The Congress may determine the Time of chusing the Electors, and the Day on which they shall give their Votes; which Day shall be the same throughout the United States.

No Person except a natural born Citizen, or a Citizen of the United States, at the time of the Adoption of this Constitution, shall be eligible to the Office of

President; neither shall any Person be eligible to that Office who shall not have attained to the Age of thirty five Years, and been fourteen Years a Resident within the United States.

In Case of the Removal of the President from Office, or of his Death, Resignation, or Inability to discharge the Powers and Duties of the said Office, the Same shall devolve on the Vice President, and the Congress may by Law provide for the Case of Removal, Death, Resignation or Inability, both of the President and Vice President, declaring what Officer shall then act as President, and such Officer shall act accordingly, until the Disability be removed, or a President shall be elected.

The President shall, at stated Times, receive for his Services, a Compensation, which shall neither be encreased or diminished during the Period for which he shall have been elected, and he shall not receive within that Period any other Emolument from the United States, or any of them.

Before he enters on the Execution of his Office, he shall take the following Oath or Affirmation:—"I do solemnly swear (or affirm) that I will faithfully execute the Office of President of the United States, and will to the best of my Ability, preserve, protect and defend the Constitution of the United States."

Section. 2. The President shall be Commander in Chief of the Army and Navy of the United States, and of the Militia of the several States, when called into the actual Service of the United States; he may require the Opinion, in writing, of the principal Officer in each of the executive Departments, upon any Subject relating to the Duties of their respective Offices, and he shall have Power to grant Reprieves and Pardons for Offences against the United States, except in Cases of Impeachment.

He shall have Power, by and with the Advice and Consent of the Senate, to make Treaties, provided two thirds of the Senators present concur; and he shall nominate, and by and with the Advice and Consent of the Senate, shall appoint Ambassadors, other public Ministers and Consuls, Judges of the supreme Court, and all other Officers of the United States, whose Appointments are not herein otherwise

provided for, and which shall be established by Law; but the Congress may by Law vest the Appointment of such inferior Officers, as they think proper, in the President alone, in the Courts of Law, or in the Heads of Departments.

The President shall have Power to fill up all Vacancies that may happen during the Recess of the Senate, by granting Commissions which shall expire at the End of their next Session.

Section. 3. He shall from time to time give to the Congress Information of the State of the Union, and recommend to their Consideration such Measures as he shall judge necessary and expedient; he may, on extraordinary Occasions, convene both Houses, or either of them, and in Case of Disagreement between them, with Respect to the Time of Adjournment, he may adjourn them to such Time as he shall think proper; he shall receive Ambassadors and other public Ministers; he shall take Care that the Laws be faithfully executed, and shall Commission all the Officers of the United States.

Section. 4. The President, Vice President and all civil Officers of the United States, shall be removed from Office on Impeachment for, and Conviction of, Treason, Bribery, or other high Crimes and Misdemeanors.

ARTICLE. III.

Section. 1. The judicial Power of the United States, shall be vested in one supreme Court, and in such inferior Courts as the Congress may from time to time ordain and establish. The Judges, both of the supreme and inferior Courts, shall hold their Offices during good Behavior, and shall, at stated Times, receive for their Services, a Compensation, which shall not be diminished during their Continuance in Office.

Section. 2. The judicial Power shall extend to all Cases, in Law and Equity, arising under this Constitution, the Laws of the United States, and Treaties made, or which shall be made, under their Authority;—to all Cases affecting Ambassadors, other public Ministers and Consuls;—to all Cases of admiralty and maritime Jurisdiction;—the Controversies to which the United States shall be a Party;—to Controversies between two or more States;—between a State and Citizens of another State;—between Citizens of different States;—between Citizens of the same State claiming Lands under Grants of different States, and between a State, or the Citizens thereof, and foreign States, Citizens or Subjects.

In all cases affecting Ambassadors, other public Ministers and Consuls, and those in which a State shall be Party, the supreme Court shall have original Jurisdiction. In all the other Cases before mentioned, the supreme Court shall have appellate Jurisdiction, both as to Law and Fact, with such Exceptions, and under such Regulations as the Congress shall make.

The Trial of all Crimes, except in Cases of Impeachment, shall be by Jury; and such Trial shall be held in the State where the said Crimes shall have been committed; but when not committed within any State, the Trial shall be at such Place or Places as the Congress may by Law have directed.

Section. 3. Treason against the United States, shall consist only in levying War against them, or in adhering to their Enemies, giving them Aid and Comfort. No Person shall be convicted of Treason unless on the Testimony of two Witnesses to the same overt Act, or on Confession in open Court.

The Congress shall have Power to declare the Punishment of Treason, but no Attainder of Treason shall work Corruption of Blood, or Forfeiture except during the Life of the Person attainted.

ARTICLE. IV.

Section. 1. Full Faith and Credit shall be given in each State to the public Acts, Records, and judicial Proceedings of every other State. And the Congress may by general Laws prescribe the Manner in which such Acts, Records and Proceedings shall be proved, and the Effect thereof.

Section. 2. The Citizens of each State shall be entitled to all Privileges and Immunities of Citizens in the several States.

A Person charged in any State with Treason, Felony, or other Crime, who shall flee from Justice, and be found in another State, shall on Demand of the executive Authority of the State from which he fled, be delivered up, to be removed to the State having Jurisdiction of the Crime.

No Person held to Service or Labour in one State, under the Laws thereof, escaping into another, shall, in Consequence of any Law or Regulation therein, be discharged from such Service or Labour, but shall be delivered up on Claim of the Party to whom such Service or Labour may be due.

Section. 3. New States may be admitted by the Congress into this Union; but no new State shall be formed or erected within the Jurisdiction of any other State; nor any State be formed by the Junction of two or more States, or Parts of States, without the consent of the Legislatures of the States concerned as well as of the Congress.

The Congress shall have Power to dispose of and make all needful Rules and Regulations respecting the Territory or other Property belonging to the United States; and nothing in this Constitution shall be so construed as to Prejudice any Claims of the United States, or of any particular States.

Section. 4. The United States shall guarantee to every State in this Union a Republican Form of Government, and shall protect each of them against Invasion; and on Application of the Legislature, or of the Executive (when the Legislature cannot be convened) against domestic Violence.

ARTICLE. V.

The Congress, whenever two thirds of both Houses shall deem it necessary, shall propose Amendments to this Constitution, or, on the Application of the Legislatures of two thirds of the several States, shall call a Convention for proposing Amendments, which, in either Case, shall be valid to all Intents and Purposes, as Part of this Constitution, when ratified by the Legislatures of three fourths of the several States, or by Conventions in three fourths thereof, as the one or the other Mode of Ratification may be proposed by the Congress; Provided that no Amendment which may be made prior to the Year One thousand eight hundred and eight shall in any Manner affect the first and fourth Clauses in the Ninth Section of the first Article; and that no State, without its Consent, shall be deprived of its equal Suffrage in the Senate.

ARTICLE. VI.

All Debts contracted and Engagements entered into, before the Adoption of this Constitution, shall be as valid against the United States under this Constitution, as under the Confederation.

This Constitution, and the Laws of the United States which shall be made in Pursuance thereof; and all Treaties made, or which shall be made, under the Authority of the United States, shall be the supreme Law of the Land; and the Judges in every State shall be bound thereby, any Thing in the Constitution or Laws of any State to the Contrary notwithstanding.

The Senators and Representatives before mentioned, and the Members of the several State Legislatures, and all executive and judicial Officers, both of the United States and of the several States, shall be bound by Oath or Affirmation, to support this Constitution; but no religious Test shall ever be required as a Qualification to any Office or public Trust under the United States.

ARTICLE. VII.

The Ratification of the Conventions of nine States, shall be sufficient for the Establishment of this Constitution between the States so ratifying the Same.

Done in Convention by the Unanimous Consent of the States present the Seventeenth Day of September in the Year of our Lord one thousand seven hundred and Eighty seven and of the Independence of the United States of America the Twelfth. In witness thereof We have hereunto subscribed our Names,

G⁰. WASHINGTON—Presdᵗ.
and deputy from Virginia

NEW HAMPSHIRE
John Langdon
Nicholas Gilman

MASSACHUSETTS
Nathaniel Gorham
Rufus King

CONNECTICUT
Wᵐ Samˡ Johnson
Roger Sherman

NEW YORK
Alexander Hamilton

NEW JERSEY
Wil: Livingston
David A. Brearley
Wᵐ Paterson
Jona: Dayton

PENNSYLVANIA
B Franklin
Thomas Mifflin
Robᵗ Morris
Geo. Clymer
Thoˢ FitzSimons
Jared Ingersoll
James Wilson
Gouv Morris

DELAWARE
Geo: Read
Gunning Bedford jun
John Dickinson
Richard Bassett
Jaco: Broom

MARYLAND
James MᶜHenry
Dan of Sᵗ Thoˢ Jenifer
Danˡ Carroll

VIRGINIA
John Blair—
James Madison Jr.

NORTH CAROLINA
Wᵐ Blount
Richᵈ Dobbs Spaight
Hu Williamson

SOUTH CAROLINA
J. Rutledge
Charles Cotesworth
Pinckney
Charles Pinckney
Pierce Butler

GEORGIA
William Few
Abr Baldwin

AMENDMENTS TO THE CONSTITUTION

Articles in addition to, and Amendment of the Constitution of the United States of America, proposed by Congress, and ratified by the Legislatures of the several States, pursuant to the fifth Article of the original Constitution.

AMENDMENT I.

Congress shall make no law respecting an establishment of religion, or prohibiting the free exercise thereof; or abridging the freedom of speech, or of the press; or the right of the people peaceably to assemble, and to petition the Government for a redress of grievances.

AMENDMENT II.

A well regulated Militia, being necessary to the security of a free State, the right of the people to keep and bear Arms, shall not be infringed.

AMENDMENT III.

No Soldier shall, in time of peace be quartered in any house, without the consent of the Owner, nor in time of war, but in a manner to be prescribed by law.

AMENDMENT IV.

The right of the people to be secure in their persons, houses, papers, and effects, against unreasonable searches and seizures, shall not be violated, and no Warrants shall issue, but upon probable cause, supported by Oath or affirmation, and particularly describing the place to be searched, and the persons or things to be seized.

AMENDMENT V.

No person shall be held to answer for a capital, or otherwise infamous crime, unless on a presentment or indictment of a Grand Jury, except in cases arising in the land or naval forces, or in the Militia, when in actual service in time of War or public danger; nor shall any person be subject for the same offence to be twice put in jeopardy of life or limb; nor shall be compelled in any criminal case to be a witness against himself, nor be deprived of life, liberty, or property, without due process of law; nor shall private property be taken for public use, without just compensation.

AMENDMENT VI.

In all criminal prosecutions, the accused shall enjoy the right to a speedy and public trial, by an impartial jury of the State and district wherein the crime shall have been committed, which district shall have been previously ascertained by law, and to be informed of the nature and cause of the accusation; to be confronted with the witnesses against him; to have compulsory process for obtaining witnesses in his favor, and to have the Assistance of Counsel for his defence.

AMENDMENT VII.

In Suits at common law, where the value in controversy shall exceed twenty dollars, the right of trial by jury shall be preserved, and no fact tried by a jury, shall be otherwise re-examined in any Court of the United States, than according to the rules of the common law.

AMENDMENT VIII.

Excessive bail shall not be required, nor excessive fines imposed, nor cruel and unusual punishments inflicted.

AMENDMENT IX.

The enumeration in the Constitution, of certain rights, shall not be construed to deny or disparage others retained by the people.

AMENDMENT X.

The powers not delegated to the United States by the Constitution, nor prohibited by it to the States, are reserved to the States respectively, or to the people.

AMENDMENT XI.

The Judicial power of the United States shall not be construed to extend to any suit in law or equity, commenced or prosecuted against one of the United States by Citizens of another State, or by Citizens or Subjects of any Foreign State. [January 8, 1798]

AMENDMENT XII.

The Electors shall meet in their respective states, and vote by ballot for President and Vice-President, one of whom, at least, shall not be an inhabitant of the same state with themselves; they shall name in their ballots the person voted for as President, and in distinct ballots the person voted for as Vice-President, and they shall make distinct lists of all persons voted for as President, and of all persons voted for as Vice President, and of the number of votes for each, which lists they shall sign and certify, and transmit sealed to the seat of the government of the United States, directed to the President of the Senate;—The President of the Senate shall, in the presence of the Senate and House of Representatives, open all the certificates and the votes shall then be counted;—The person having the greatest number of votes for President, shall be the President, if such number be a majority of the whole number of Electors appointed; and if no person have such majority, then from the persons having the highest numbers not exceeding three on the list of those voted for as President, the House of Representatives shall choose immediately, by ballot, the President. But in choosing the President, the votes shall be taken by states, the representation from each state having one vote; a quorum for this purpose shall consist of a member or members from two-thirds of the states, and a majority of all the states shall be necessary to a choice. And if the House of Representatives shall not choose a President whenever the right of choice shall devolve upon them, before the fourth day of March next following, then the Vice-President shall act as President, as in the case of the death or other constitutional disability of the President.—The person having the greatest number of votes as Vice-President, shall be the Vice-President, if such number be a majority of the whole number of Electors appointed, and if no person have a majority, then from the two highest numbers on the list, the Senate shall choose the Vice-President; a quorum for the purpose shall consist of two-thirds of the whole number of Senators, and a majority of the whole number shall be necessary to a choice. But no person constitutionally ineligible to the office of President shall be eligible to that of Vice-President of the United States. [September 25, 1804]

AMENDMENT XIII.

Section 1. Neither slavery nor involuntary servitude, except as a punishment for crime whereof the party shall have been duly convicted, shall exist within the United States, or any place subject to their jurisdiction.

Section 2. Congress shall have power to enforce this article by appropriate legislation. [December 18, 1865]

AMENDMENT XIV.

Section 1. All persons born or naturalized in the United States, and subject to the jurisdiction thereof, are citizens of the United States and of the State wherein they reside. No State shall make or enforce any law which shall abridge the privileges or immunities of citizens of the United States; nor shall any State deprive any person of life, liberty, or property, without due process of law; nor deny to any person within its jurisdiction the equal protection of the laws.

Section 2. Representatives shall be apportioned among the several States according to their respective numbers, counting the whole number of persons in each State, excluding Indians not taxed. But when the right to vote at any election for the choice of electors for President and Vice President of the United States, Representatives in Congress, the Executive and Judicial officers of a State, or the members of the Legislature thereof, is denied to any of the male inhabitants of such State, being twenty-one years of age, and citizens of the United States, or in any way abridged, except for participation in rebellion, or other crime, the basis of representation therein shall be reduced in the proportion which the number of such male citizens shall bear to the whole number of male citizens twenty-one years of age in such State.

Section 3. No person shall be a Senator or Representative in Congress, or elector of President and Vice President, or hold any office, civil or military, under the United States, or under any State, who, having previously taken an oath, as a member of Congress, or as an officer of the United States, or as a member of any State legislature, or as an executive or judicial officer of any State, to support the Constitution of the United States, shall have engaged in insurrection or rebellion against the same, or given aid or comfort to the enemies thereof. But Congress may by a vote of two-thirds of each House, remove such disability.

Section 4. The validity of the public debt of the United States, authorized by law, including debts incurred for payment of pensions and bounties for services in suppressing insurrection or rebellion, shall not be questioned. But neither the United States nor any State shall assume or pay any debt or obligation incurred in aid of insurrection or rebellion against the United States, or any claim for the loss or emancipation of any slave; but all such debts, obligations and claims shall be held illegal and void.

Section 5. The Congress shall have power to enforce, by appropriate legislation, the provisions of this article. [July 28, 1868]

AMENDMENT XV.

Section 1. The right of citizens of the United States to vote shall not be denied or abridged by the United States or by any State on account of race, color, or previous condition of servitude—

Section 2. The Congress shall have power to enforce this article by appropriate legislation. [March 30, 1870]

AMENDMENT XVI.

The Congress shall have power to lay and collect taxes on incomes, from whatever source derived, without apportionment among the several States, and without regard to any census or enumeration. [February 25, 1913]

AMENDMENT XVII.

The Senate of the United States shall be composed of two senators from each State, elected by the people thereof, for six years; and each Senator shall have one vote. The electors in each State shall have the qualifications requisite for electors of the most numerous branch of the State legislatures.

When vacancies happen in the representation of any State in the Senate, the executive authority of such State shall issue writs of election to fill such vacancies: *Provided*, That the legislature of any State may empower the executive thereof to make temporary appointments until the people fill the vacancies by election as the legislature may direct.

This amendment shall not be so construed as to affect the election or term of any senator chosen before it becomes valid as part of the Constitution. [May 31, 1913]

AMENDMENT XVIII.

After one year from the ratification of this article, the manufacture, sale, or transportation of intoxicating liquors within, the importation thereof into, or the exportation thereof from the United States and all territory subject to the jurisdiction thereof for beverage purposes is hereby prohibited.

The Congress and the several States shall have concurrent power to enforce this article by appropriate legislation.

This article shall be inoperative unless it shall have been ratified as an amendment to the Constitution by the legislatures of the several States, as provided in the Constitution, within seven years from the date of the submission thereof to the States by Congress. [January 29, 1919]

AMENDMENT XIX.

The right of citizens of the United States to vote shall not be denied or abridged by the United States or by any State on account of sex.

The Congress shall have power by appropriate legislation to enforce the provisions of this article. [August 26, 1920]

AMENDMENT XX.

Section 1. The terms of the President and Vice-President shall end at noon on the twentieth day of January, and the terms of Senators and Representatives at noon on the third day of January, of the years in which such terms would have ended if this article had not been ratified; and the terms of their successors shall then begin.

Section 2. The Congress shall assemble at least once in every year, and such meeting shall begin at noon on the third day of January, unless they shall by law appoint a different day.

Section 3. If, at the time fixed for the beginning of the term of the President, the President-elect shall have died, the Vice-President-elect shall become President. If a President shall not have been chosen before the time fixed for the beginning of his term, or if the President-elect shall have failed to qualify, then the Vice-President-elect shall act as President until a President shall have qualified; and the Congress may by law provide for the case wherein neither a President-elect nor a Vice-President-elect shall have qualified, declaring who shall then act as President, or the manner in which one who is to act shall be selected, and such person shall act accordingly until a President or Vice-President shall have qualified.

Section 4. The Congress may by law provide for the case of the death of any of the persons from whom the House of Representatives may choose a President whenever the right of choice shall have devolved upon them, and for the case of the death of any of the persons from whom the Senate may choose a Vice-President whenever the right of choice shall have devolved upon them.

Section 5. Sections 1 and 2 shall take effect on the 15th day of October following the ratification of this article.

Section 6. This article shall be inoperative unless it shall have been ratified as an amendment to the Constitution by the legislatures of three-fourths of the several States within seven years from the date of its submission. [February 6, 1933]

AMENDMENT XXI.

Section 1. The eighteenth article of amendment to the Constitution of the United States is hereby repealed.

Section 2. The transportation or importation into any State, Territory or possession of the United States for delivery or use therein of intoxicating liquors, in violation of the laws thereof, is hereby prohibited.

Section 3. This article shall be inoperative unless it shall have been ratified as an amendment to the Constitution by convention in the several States, as provided in the Constitution, within seven years from the date of the submission thereof to the States by the Congress. [December 5, 1933]

AMENDMENT XXII.

Section 1. No person shall be elected to the office of the President more than twice, and no person who has held the office of President, or acted as President, for more than two years of a term to which some other person was elected President shall be elected to the office of the President more than once. But this Article shall not apply to any person holding the office of President when this Article was proposed by the Congress, and shall not prevent any person who may be holding the office of President, or acting as President, during the term within which this Article becomes operative from holding the office of President or acting as President during the remainder of such term.

Section 2. This article shall be inoperative unless it shall have been ratified as an amendment to the Constitution by the legislatures of three-fourths of the several States within seven years from the date of its submission to the States by the Congress. [February 27, 1951]

AMENDMENT XXIII.

Section 1. The District constituting the seat of government of the United States shall appoint in such manner as the Congress may direct:

A number of electors of President and Vice-President equal to the whole number of Senators and Representatives in Congress to which the District would be entitled if it were a State, but in no event more than the least populous State; they shall be in addition to those appointed by the States, but they shall be considered, for the purposes of the election of President and Vice-President, to be electors appointed by a State; and they shall meet in the District and perform such duties as provided by the twelfth article of amendment.

Section 2. The Congress shall have the power to enforce this article by appropriate legislation. [March 29, 1961]

AMENDMENT XXIV.

Section 1. The right of citizens of the United States to vote in any primary or other election for President or Vice President, for electors for President or Vice President, or for Senator or Representative in Congress, shall not be denied or abridged by the United States or any State by reason of failure to pay any poll tax or other tax.

Section 2. The Congress shall have power to enforce this article by appropriate legislation. [January 23, 1964]

AMENDMENT XXV.

Section 1. In case of the removal of the President from office or of his death or resignation, the Vice President shall become President.

Section 2. Whenever there is a vacancy in the office of Vice President, the President shall nominate a Vice President who shall take office upon confirmation by a majority vote of both Houses of Congress.

Section 3. Whenever the President transmits to the President pro tempore of the Senate and the Speaker of the House of Representatives his written declaration that he is unable to discharge the powers and duties of his office, and until he transmits to them a written declaration to the contrary, such powers and duties shall be discharged by the Vice President as Acting President.

Section 4. Whenever the Vice President and a majority of either the principal officers of the executive departments or of such other body as Congress may by law provide, transmit to the President pro tempore of the Senate and the Speaker of the House of Representatives their written declaration that the President is unable to discharge the powers and duties of his office, the Vice President shall immediately assume the powers and duties of the office as Acting President.

Thereafter, when the President transmits to the President pro tempore of the Senate and the Speaker of the House of Representatives his written declaration that no inability exists, he shall resume the powers and duties of his office unless the Vice President and a majority of either the principal officers of the executive departments or of such other body as Congress may by law provide, transmit within four days to the President pro tempore of the Senate and the Speaker of the House of Representatives their written declaration that the President is unable to discharge the powers and duties of his office. Thereupon Congress shall decide the issue, assembling within forty-eight hours for that purpose if not in session. If the Congress, within twenty-one days after receipt of the latter written declaration, or, if Congress is not in session, within twenty-one days after Congress is required to assemble, determines by two-thirds vote of both Houses that the President is unable to discharge the powers and duties of his office, the Vice President shall continue to discharge the same as Acting President; otherwise, the President shall resume the powers and duties of his office. [February 10, 1967]

AMENDMENT XXVI.

Section 1. The right of citizens of the United States, who are eighteen years of age or older, to vote shall not be denied or abridged by the United States or by any State on account of age.

Section 2. The Congress shall have power to enforce this article by appropriate legislation. [June 30, 1971]

AMENDMENT XXVII.

No law, varying the compensation for the services of the Senators and Representatives shall take effect, until an election of Representatives shall have intervened. [May 8, 1992]

FROM GEORGE WASHINGTON'S FAREWELL ADDRESS (1796)

Friends and Citizens:

The period for a new election of a citizen to administer the executive government of the United States being not far distant, and the time actually arrived when your thoughts must be employed in designating the person who is to be clothed with that important trust, it appears to me proper, especially as it may conduce to a more distinct expression of the public voice, that I should now apprise you of the resolution I have formed, to decline being considered among the number of those out of whom a choice is to be made.

★ ★ ★

In looking forward to the moment which is intended to terminate the career of my public life, my feelings do not permit me to suspend the deep acknowledgment of that debt of gratitude which I owe to my beloved country for the many honors it has conferred upon me; still more for the steadfast confidence with which it has supported me; and for the opportunities I have thence enjoyed of manifesting my inviolable attachment, by services faithful and persevering, though in usefulness unequal to my zeal. If benefits have resulted to our country from these services, let it always be remembered to your praise, and as an instructive example in our annals, that under circumstances in which the passions, agitated in every direction, were liable to mislead, amidst appearances sometimes dubious, vicissitudes of fortune often discouraging, in situations in which not unfrequently want of success has countenanced the spirit of criticism, the constancy of your support was the essential prop of the efforts, and a guarantee of the plans by which they were effected. Profoundly penetrated with this idea, I shall carry it with me to my grave, as a strong incitement to unceasing vows that heaven may continue to you the choicest tokens of its beneficence; that your union and brotherly

affection may be perpetual; that the free Constitution, which is the work of your hands, may be sacredly maintained; that its administration in every department may be stamped with wisdom and virtue; that, in fine, the happiness of the people of these States, under the auspices of liberty, may be made complete by so careful a preservation and so prudent a use of this blessing as will acquire to them the glory of recommending it to the applause, the affection, and adoption of every nation which is yet a stranger to it.

Here, perhaps, I ought to stop. But a solicitude for your welfare, which cannot end but with my life, and the apprehension of danger, natural to that solicitude, urge me, on an occasion like the present, to offer to your solemn contemplation, and to recommend to your frequent review, some sentiments which are the result of much reflection, of no inconsiderable observation, and which appear to me all-important to the permanency of your felicity as a people. These will be offered to you with the more freedom, as you can only see in them the disinterested warnings of a parting friend, who can possibly have no personal motive to bias his counsel. Nor can I forget, as an encouragement to it, your indulgent reception of my sentiments on a former and not dissimilar occasion.

Interwoven as is the love of liberty with every ligament of your hearts, no recommendation of mine is necessary to fortify or confirm the attachment.

The unity of government which constitutes you one people is also now dear to you. It is justly so, for it is a main pillar in the edifice of your real independence, the support of your tranquility at home, your peace abroad; of your safety; of your prosperity; of that very liberty which you so highly prize. But as it is easy to foresee that, from different causes and from different quarters, much pains will be taken, many artifices employed to weaken in your minds the conviction of this truth; as this is the point in your political fortress against which the batteries of internal and external enemies will be most constantly and actively (though often covertly and insidiously) directed, it is of infinite moment that you should properly estimate the immense value of your national union to your collective and individual happiness; that you should cherish a cordial, habitual, and immovable attachment to it; accustoming yourselves to think and speak of it as of the palladium of your political safety and prosperity; watching for its preservation with jealous anxiety; discountenancing whatever may suggest even a suspicion that it can in any event be abandoned; and indignantly frowning upon the first dawning of every attempt to alienate any portion of our country from the rest, or to enfeeble the sacred ties which now link together the various parts.

For this you have every inducement of sympathy and interest. Citizens, by birth or choice, of a common country, that country has a right to concentrate your affections. The name of American, which belongs to you in your national capacity, must always exalt the just pride of patriotism more than any appellation derived from local discriminations. With slight shades of difference, you have the same religion, manners, habits, and political principles. You have in a common cause fought and triumphed together; the independence and liberty you possess are the work of joint counsels, and joint efforts of common dangers, sufferings, and successes.

But these considerations, however powerfully they address themselves to your sensibility, are greatly outweighed by those which apply more immediately to your interest. Here every portion of our country finds the most commanding motives for carefully guarding and preserving the union of the whole.

The North, in an unrestrained intercourse with the South, protected by the equal laws of a common government, finds in the productions of the latter great additional resources of maritime and commercial enterprise and precious materials of manufacturing industry. The South, in the same intercourse, benefiting by the agency of the North, sees its agriculture grow and its commerce expand. Turning partly into its own channels the seamen of the North, it finds its particular navigation invigorated; and, while it

contributes, in different ways, to nourish and increase the general mass of the national navigation, it looks forward to the protection of a maritime strength, to which itself is unequally adapted. The East, in a like intercourse with the West, already finds, and in the progressive improvement of interior communications by land and water, will more and more find a valuable vent for the commodities which it brings from abroad, or manufactures at home. The West derives from the East supplies requisite to its growth and comfort, and, what is perhaps of still greater consequence, it must of necessity owe the secure enjoyment of indispensable outlets for its own productions to the weight, influence, and the future maritime strength of the Atlantic side of the Union, directed by an indissoluble community of interest as one nation. Any other tenure by which the West can hold this essential advantage, whether derived from its own separate strength, or from an apostate and unnatural connection with any foreign power, must be intrinsically precarious.

While, then, every part of our country thus feels an immediate and particular interest in union, all the parts combined cannot fail to find in the united mass of means and efforts greater strength, greater resource, proportionably greater security from external danger, a less frequent interruption of their peace by foreign nations; and, what is of inestimable value, they must derive from union an exemption from those broils and wars between themselves, which so frequently afflict neighboring countries not tied together by the same governments, which their own rival ships alone would be sufficient to produce, but which opposite foreign alliances, attachments, and intrigues would stimulate and embitter. Hence, likewise, they will avoid the necessity of those overgrown military establishments which, under any form of government, are inauspicious to liberty, and which are to be regarded as particularly hostile to republican liberty. In this sense it is that your union ought to be considered as a main prop of your liberty, and that the love of the one ought to endear to you the preservation of the other.

These considerations speak a persuasive language to every reflecting and virtuous mind, and exhibit the continuance of the Union as a primary object of patriotic desire. Is there a doubt whether a common government can embrace so large a sphere? Let experience solve it. To listen to mere speculation in such a case were criminal. We are authorized to hope that a proper organization of the whole with the auxiliary agency of governments for the respective subdivisions, will afford a happy issue to the experiment. It is well worth a fair and full experiment. With such powerful and obvious motives to union, affecting all parts of our country, while experience shall not have demonstrated its impracticability, there will always be reason to distrust the patriotism of those who in any quarter may endeavor to weaken its bands.

★ ★ ★

To the efficacy and permanency of your Union, a government for the whole is indispensable. No alliance, however strict, between the parts can be an adequate substitute; they must inevitably experience the infractions and interruptions which all alliances in all times have experienced. Sensible of this momentous truth, you have improved upon your first essay, by the adoption of a constitution of government better calculated than your former for an intimate union, and for the efficacious management of your common concerns. This government, the offspring of our own choice, uninfluenced and unawed, adopted upon full investigation and mature deliberation, completely free in its principles, in the distribution of its powers, uniting security with energy, and containing within itself a provision for its own amendment, has a just claim to your confidence and your support. Respect for its authority, compliance with its laws, acquiescence in its measures, are duties enjoined by the fundamental maxims of true liberty. The basis of our political systems is the right of the people to make and to alter their constitutions of government. But the Constitution which at any time exists, till changed by an explicit and authentic act of the whole people, is sacredly obligatory upon all. The very idea of the power and the right of the people to establish government presupposes the duty of every individual to obey the established government.

★ ★ ★

I have already intimated to you the danger of parties in the State, with particular reference to the founding of them on geographical discriminations. Let me now take a more comprehensive view, and warn you in the most solemn manner against the baneful effects of the spirit of party generally.

This spirit, unfortunately, is inseparable from our nature, having its root in the strongest passions of the human mind. It exists under different shapes in all governments, more or less stifled, controlled, or repressed; but, in those of the popular form, it is seen in its greatest rankness, and is truly their worst enemy.

The alternate domination of one faction over another, sharpened by the spirit of revenge, natural to party dissension, which in different ages and countries has perpetrated the most horrid enormities, is itself a frightful despotism. But this leads at length to a more formal and permanent despotism. The disorders and miseries which result gradually incline the minds of men to seek security and repose in the absolute power of an individual; and sooner or later the chief of some prevailing faction, more able or more fortunate than his competitors, turns this disposition to the purposes of his own elevation, on the ruins of public liberty.

Without looking forward to an extremity of this kind (which nevertheless ought not to be entirely out of sight), the common and continual mischiefs of the spirit of party are sufficient to make it the interest and duty of a wise people to discourage and restrain it.

It serves always to distract the public councils and enfeeble the public administration. It agitates the community with ill-founded jealousies and false alarms, kindles the animosity of one part against another, foments occasionally riot and insurrection. It opens the door to foreign influence and corruption, which finds a facilitated access to the government itself through the channels of party passions. Thus the policy and the will of one country are subjected to the policy and will of another.

There is an opinion that parties in free countries are useful checks upon the administration of the government and serve to keep alive the spirit of liberty. This within certain limits is probably true; and in governments of a monarchical cast, patriotism may look with indulgence, if not with favor, upon the spirit of party. But in those of the popular character, in governments purely elective, it is a spirit not to be encouraged. From their natural tendency, it is certain there will always be enough of that spirit for every salutary purpose. And there being constant danger of excess, the effort ought to be by force of public opinion, to mitigate and assuage it. A fire not to be quenched, it demands a uniform vigilance to prevent its bursting into a flame, lest, instead of warming, it should consume.

It is important, likewise, that the habits of thinking in a free country should inspire caution in those entrusted with its administration, to confine themselves within their respective constitutional spheres, avoiding in the exercise of the powers of one department to encroach upon another. The spirit of encroachment tends to consolidate the powers of all the departments in one, and thus to create, whatever the form of government, a real despotism. A just estimate of that love of power, and proneness to abuse it, which predominates in the human heart, is sufficient to satisfy us of the truth of this position. The necessity of reciprocal checks in the exercise of political power, by dividing and distributing it into different depositaries, and constituting each the guardian of the public weal against invasions by the others, has been evinced by experiments ancient and modern; some of them in our country and under our own eyes. To preserve them must be as necessary as to institute them. If, in the opinion of the people, the distribution or modification of the constitutional powers be in any particular wrong, let it be corrected by an amendment in the way which the Constitution designates. But let there be no change by usurpation; for though this, in one instance, may be the instrument of good, it is the customary weapon by which free governments are destroyed. The precedent must always greatly overbalance in permanent evil any partial or transient benefit, which the use can at any time yield.

★ ★ ★

Observe good faith and justice towards all nations; cultivate peace and harmony with all. Religion and morality enjoin this conduct; and can it be, that good policy does not equally enjoin it? It will be worthy of

a free, enlightened, and at no distant period, a great nation, to give to mankind the magnanimous and too novel example of a people always guided by an exalted justice and benevolence. Who can doubt that, in the course of time and things, the fruits of such a plan would richly repay any temporary advantages which might be lost by a steady adherence to it? Can it be that Providence has not connected the permanent felicity of a nation with its virtue? The experiment, at least, is recommended by every sentiment which ennobles human nature. Alas! is it rendered impossible by its vices?

In the execution of such a plan, nothing is more essential than that permanent, inveterate antipathies against particular nations, and passionate attachments for others, should be excluded; and that, in place of them, just and amicable feelings towards all should be cultivated. The nation which indulges towards another a habitual hatred or a habitual fondness is in some degree a slave. It is a slave to its animosity or to its affection, either of which is sufficient to lead it astray from its duty and its interest. Antipathy in one nation against another disposes each more readily to offer insult and injury, to lay hold of slight causes of umbrage, and to be haughty and intractable, when accidental or trifling occasions of dispute occur. Hence, frequent collisions, obstinate, envenomed, and bloody contests. The nation, prompted by ill-will and resentment, sometimes impels to war the government, contrary to the best calculations of policy. The government sometimes participates in the national propensity, and adopts through passion what reason would reject; at other times it makes the animosity of the nation subservient to projects of hostility instigated by pride, ambition, and other sinister and pernicious motives. The peace often, sometimes perhaps the liberty, of nations, has been the victim.

★ ★ ★

The great rule of conduct for us in regard to foreign nations is in extending our commercial relations, to have with them as little political connection as possible. So far as we have already formed engagements, let them be fulfilled with perfect good faith. Here let us stop. Europe has a set of primary interests which to us have none; or a very remote relation. Hence she must be engaged in frequent controversies, the causes of which are essentially foreign to our concerns. Hence, therefore, it must be unwise in us to implicate ourselves by artificial ties in the ordinary vicissitudes of her politics, or the ordinary combinations and collisions of her friendships or enmities.

Our detached and distant situation invites and enables us to pursue a different course. If we remain one people under an efficient government, the period is not far off when we may defy material injury from external annoyance; when we may take such an attitude as will cause the neutrality we may at any time resolve upon to be scrupulously respected; when belligerent nations, under the impossibility of making acquisitions upon us, will not lightly hazard the giving us provocation; when we may choose peace or war, as our interest, guided by justice, shall counsel.

Why forego the advantages of so peculiar a situation? Why quit our own to stand upon foreign ground? Why, by interweaving our destiny with that of any part of Europe, entangle our peace and prosperity in the toils of European ambition, rivalship, interest, humor or caprice?

It is our true policy to steer clear of permanent alliances with any portion of the foreign world; so far, I mean, as we are now at liberty to do it; for let me not be understood as capable of patronizing infidelity to existing engagements. I hold the maxim no less applicable to public than to private affairs, that honesty is always the best policy. I repeat it, therefore, let those engagements be observed in their genuine sense. But, in my opinion, it is unnecessary and would be unwise to extend them.

Taking care always to keep ourselves by suitable establishments on a respectable defensive posture, we may safely trust to temporary alliances for extraordinary emergencies.

Harmony, liberal intercourse with all nations, are recommended by policy, humanity, and interest. But even our commercial policy should hold an equal and impartial hand; neither seeking nor granting exclusive favors or preferences; consulting the natural course of things; diffusing and diversifying by gentle means the streams of commerce, but forcing nothing; establishing (with powers so disposed, in order to give trade a stable course, to define the rights of our merchants, and to enable the government to support them) conventional rules of intercourse, the best that present circumstances and mutual opinion will permit, but temporary, and liable to be from time to time abandoned or varied, as experience and circumstances shall dictate; constantly keeping in view that it is folly in one nation to look for disinterested favors from another; that it must pay with a portion of its independence for whatever it may accept under that character; that, by such acceptance, it may place itself in the condition of having given equivalents for nominal favors, and yet of being reproached with ingratitude for not giving more.

* * *

Relying on its kindness in this as in other things, and actuated by that fervent love towards it, which is so natural to a man who views in it the native soil of himself and his progenitors for several generations, I anticipate with pleasing expectation that retreat in which I promise myself to realize, without alloy, the sweet enjoyment of partaking, in the midst of my fellow-citizens, the benign influence of good laws under a free government, the ever-favorite object of my heart, and the happy reward, as I trust, of our mutual cares, labors, and dangers.

Geo. Washington

THE SENECA FALLS DECLARATION OF SENTIMENTS AND RESOLUTIONS (1848)

1. DECLARATION OF SENTIMENTS

When, in the course of human events, it becomes necessary for one portion of the family of man to assume among the people of the earth a position different from that which they have hitherto occupied, but one to which the laws of nature and of nature's God entitle them, a decent respect to the opinions of mankind requires that they should declare the causes that impel them to such a course.

We hold these truths to be self-evident: that all men and women are created equal; that they are endowed by their Creator with certain inalienable rights; that among these are life, liberty, and the pursuit of happiness; that to secure these rights governments are instituted, deriving their just powers from the consent of the governed. Whenever any form of government becomes destructive of these ends, it is the right of those who suffer from it to refuse allegiance to it, and to insist upon the institution of a new government, laying its foundation on such principles, and organizing its powers in such form, as to them shall seem most likely to effect their safety and happiness. Prudence, indeed, will dictate that governments long established should not be changed for light and transient causes; and accordingly all experience hath shown that mankind are more disposed to suffer, while evils are sufferable, than to right themselves by abolishing the forms to which they are accustomed. But when a long train of abuses and usurpations, pursuing invariably the same object, evinces a design to reduce them under absolute despotism, it is their duty to throw off such government, and to provide new guards for their future security. Such has been the patient sufferance of the women under this government, and such is now the necessity which constrains them to demand the equal station to which they are entitled. The history of mankind is a history of repeated injuries and usurpations on the part of man toward woman, having in direct object the establishment of an absolute tyranny over her. To prove this, let facts be submitted to a candid world.

He has never permitted her to exercise her inalienable right to the elective franchise.

He has compelled her to submit to laws, in the formation of which she had no voice.

He has withheld from her rights which are given to the most ignorant and degraded men—both natives and foreigners.

Having deprived her of this first right of a citizen, the elective franchise, thereby leaving her without representation in the halls of legislation, he has oppressed her on all sides.

He has made her, if married, in the eye of the law, civilly dead. He has taken from her all right in property, even to the wages she earns.

He has made her, morally, an irresponsible being, as she can commit many crimes with impunity, provided they be done in the presence of her husband.

In the covenant of marriage, she is compelled to promise obedience to her husband, he becoming, to all intents and purposes, her master—the law giving him power to deprive her of her liberty, and to administer chastisement.

He has so framed the laws of divorce, as to what shall be the proper causes, and in case of separation, to whom the guardianship of the children shall be given, as to be wholly regardless of the happiness of women—the law, in all cases, going upon a false supposition of the supremacy of man, and giving all power into his hands.

After depriving her of all rights as a married woman, if single, and the owner of property, he has taxed her to support a government which recognizes her only when her property can be made profitable to it.

He has monopolized nearly all the profitable employments, and from those she is permitted to follow, she receives but a scanty remuneration. He closes against her all the avenues to wealth and distinction which he considers most honorable to himself. As a teacher of theology, medicine, or law, she is not known.

He has denied her the facilities for obtaining a thorough education, all colleges being closed against her.

He allows her in Church, as well as State, but a subordinate position, claiming Apostolic authority for her exclusion from the ministry, and, with some exceptions, from any public participation in the affairs of the Church.

He has created a false public sentiment by giving to the world a different code of morals for men and women, by which moral delinquencies which exclude women from society, are not only tolerated, but deemed of little account in man.

He has usurped the prerogative of Jehovah himself, claiming it as his right to assign for her a sphere of action, when that belongs to her conscience and to her God.

He has endeavored, in every way that he could, to destroy her confidence in her own powers, to lessen her self-respect and to make her willing to lead a dependent and abject life.

Now, in view of this entire disfranchisement of one-half the people of this country, their social and religious degradation—in view of the unjust laws above mentioned, and because women do feel themselves aggrieved, oppressed, and fraudulently deprived of their most sacred rights, we insist that they have immediate admission to all the rights and privileges which belong to them as citizens of the United States.

In entering upon the great work before us, we anticipate no small amount of misconception, misrepresentation, and ridicule; but we shall use every instrumentality within our power to effect our object. We shall employ agents, circulate tracts, petition the State and National legislatures, and endeavor to enlist the pulpit and the press in our behalf. We hope this Convention will be followed by a series of Conventions embracing every part of the country.

2. RESOLUTIONS

WHEREAS, The great precept of nature is conceded to be, that "man shall pursue his own true and substantial happiness." Blackstone in his Commentaries remarks, that this law of Nature being coeval with mankind, and dictated by God himself, is of course superior in obligation to any other. It is binding over all the globe, in all countries and at all times; no human laws are of any validity if contrary to this, and such of them as are valid, derive all their force, and all their validity, and all their authority, mediately and immediately, from this original; therefore,

Resolved, That such laws as conflict, in any way, with the true and substantial happiness of woman, are contrary to the great precept of nature and of no validity, for this is "superior in obligation to any other."

Resolved, That all laws which prevent woman from occupying such a station in society as her conscience shall dictate, or which place her in a position inferior to that of man, are contrary to the great precept of nature, and therefore of no force or authority.

Resolved, That woman is man's equal—was intended to be so by the Creator, and the highest good of the race demands that she should be recognized as such.

Resolved, That the women of this country ought to be enlightened in regard to the laws under which they live, that they may no longer publish their degradation by declaring themselves satisfied with their present position, nor their ignorance, by asserting that they have all the rights they want.

Resolved, That inasmuch as man, while claiming for himself intellectual superiority, does accord to woman moral superiority, it is pre-eminently his duty to encourage her to speak and teach, as she has an opportunity, in all religious assemblies.

Resolved, That the same amount of virtue, delicacy, and refinement of behavior that is required of woman in the social state, should also be required of man, and the same transgressions should be visited with equal severity on both man and woman.

Resolved, That the objection of indelicacy and impropriety, which is so often brought against woman when she addresses a public audience, comes with a very ill-grace from those who encourage, by their attendance, her appearance on the stage, in the concert. Or in feats of the circus.

Resolved, That woman has too long rested satisfied in the circumscribed limits which corrupt customs and a perverted application of the Scriptures have marked out for her, and that it is time she should move in the enlarged sphere which her great Creator has assigned her.

Resolved, That it is the duty of the women of this country to secure to themselves their sacred right to the elective franchise.

Resolved, That the equality of human rights results necessarily from the fact of the identity of the race in capabilities and responsibilities.

Resolved, therefore, That, being invested by the Creator with the same capabilities, and the same consciousness of responsibility for their exercise, it is demonstrably the right and duty of woman, equally with man, to promote every righteous cause by every righteous means; and especially in regard to the great subjects of morals and religion, it is self-evidently her right to participate with her brother in teaching them, both in private and in public, by writing and by speaking, by any instrumentalities proper to be used, and in any assemblies proper to be held; and this being a self-evident truth growing out of the divinely implanted principles of human nature, any custom or authority adverse to it, whether modern or wearing the hoary sanction of antiquity, is to be regarded as a self-evident falsehood, and at war with mankind.

Resolved, That the speedy success of our cause depends upon the zealous and untiring efforts of both men and women, for the overthrow of the monopoly of the pulpit, and for the securing to women an equal participation with men in the various trades, professions, and commerce.

FROM FREDERICK DOUGLASS'S "WHAT, TO THE SLAVE, IS THE FOURTH OF JULY?" SPEECH (1852)

* * *

This, for the purpose of this celebration, is the Fourth of July. It is the birthday of your National Independence, and of your political freedom. This, to you, is what the Passover was to the emancipated people of God. It carries your minds back to the day, and to the act of your great deliverance; and to the signs and to the wonders associated with that act and that day. This celebration also marks the beginning of another year of your national life; and reminds you that the Republic of America is now seventy-six years old. I am glad, fellow citizens, that your nation is so young. Seventy-six years, though a good old age for a man, is but a mere speck in the life of a nation. Three score years and ten is the allotted time for individual men; but nations number their years by thousands. According to this fact, you are, even now, only in the beginning of your national career, still lingering in the period of childhood. I repeat, I am glad this is so. There is hope in the thought, and hope is much needed, under the dark clouds which lower above the horizon. The eye of the reformer is met with angry flashes, portending disastrous times; but his heart may well beat lighter at the thought that America is young, and that she is still in the impressible stage of her existence. May he not hope that high lessons of wisdom, of justice and of truth, will yet give direction to her destiny? Were the nation older, the patriot's heart might be sadder and the reformer's brow heavier. Its future might be shrouded in gloom and the hope of its prophets go out in sorrow. There is consolation in the thought that America is young. Great streams are not easily turned from channels worn deep in the course of ages. They may sometimes rise in quiet and stately majesty, and inundate the land, refreshing and fertilizing the earth with their mysterious properties. They may also rise in wrath and fury, and bear away on their angry waves the accumulated wealth of years of toil and hardship. They, however, gradually flow back to the same old channel and flow on as serenely as ever. But, while the river may not be turned aside, it may dry up and leave nothing behind but the withered branch and the unsightly rock, to howl in the abyss-sweeping wind, the sad tale of departed glory. As with rivers, so with nations.

Fellow citizens, I shall not presume to dwell at length on the associations that cluster about this day. The simple story of it is, that seventy-six years ago the people of this country were British subjects. The style and title of your "sovereign people" (in which you now glory) was not then born. You were under the British Crown. Your fathers esteemed the English government as the home government, and England as the fatherland. This home government, you know, although a considerable distance from your home, did, in the exercise of its parental prerogatives, impose upon its colonial children such restraints, burdens and limitations as, in its mature judgment, it deemed wise, right and proper.

* * *

Feeling themselves harshly and unjustly treated by the home government, your fathers, like men of honesty and men of spirit, earnestly sought redress. They petitioned and remonstrated; they did so in a decorous, respectful and loyal manner. Their conduct was wholly unexceptionable. This, however, did not answer the purpose. They saw themselves treated with sovereign indifference, coldness and scorn. Yet they persevered. They were not the men to look back.

* * *

Citizens, your fathers . . . succeeded; and today you reap the fruits of their success. The freedom gained is yours; and you, therefore, may properly celebrate this anniversary. The Fourth of July is the first great fact in your nation's history—the very ringbolt in the chain of your yet undeveloped destiny.

Pride and patriotism, not less than gratitude, prompt you to celebrate and to hold it in perpetual remembrance. I have said that the Declaration of Independence is the ringbolt to the chain of your nation's destiny; so, indeed, I regard it. The principles contained in that instrument are saving principles. Stand by those principles, be true to them on all occasions, in all places, against all foes, and at whatever cost.

★ ★ ★

[The fathers of this republic] were peace men, but they preferred revolution to peaceful submission to bondage. They were quiet men; but they did not shrink from agitating against oppression. They showed forbearance, but that they knew its limits. They believed in order, but not in the order of tyranny. With them, nothing was "settled" that was not right. With them, justice, liberty and humanity were "final," not slavery and oppression. You may well cherish the memory of such men. They were great in their day and generation. Their solid manhood stands out the more as we contrast it with these degenerate times.

★ ★ ★

Fellow citizens, pardon me, allow me to ask, why am I called upon to speak here today? What have I, or those I represent, to do with your national independence? Are the great principles of political freedom and of natural justice, embodied in that Declaration of Independence, extended to us? and am I, therefore, called upon to bring our humble offering to the national altar and to confess the benefits and express devout gratitude for the blessings resulting from your independence to us?

★ ★ ★

But such is not the state of the case. I say it with a sad sense of the disparity between us. I am not included within the pale of this glorious anniversary! Your high independence only reveals the immeasurable distance between us. The blessings in which you, this day, rejoice, are not enjoyed in common. The rich inheritance of justice, liberty, prosperity and independence, bequeathed by your fathers, is shared by you, not by me. The sunlight that brought light and healing to you, has brought stripes and death to me. This Fourth of July is *yours*, not *mine*. *You* may rejoice, *I* must mourn.

★ ★ ★

Fellow citizens, above your national, tumultuous joy I hear the mournful wail of millions! whose chains, heavy and grievous yesterday, are today rendered more intolerable by the jubilee shouts that reach them. If I do forget, if I do not faithfully remember those bleeding children of sorrow this day, "may my right hand forget her cunning, and may my tongue cleave to the roof of my mouth!" To forget them, to pass lightly over their wrongs and to chime in with the popular theme would be treason most scandalous and shocking and would make me a reproach before God and the world. My subject, then, fellow citizens, is American slavery. I shall see this day and its popular characteristics from the slave's point of view. Standing there identified with the American bondman, making his wrongs mine, I do not hesitate to declare, with all my soul, that the character and conduct of this nation never looked blacker to me than on this Fourth of July. Whether we turn to the declarations of the past or to the professions of the present, the conduct of the nation seems equally hideous and revolting. America is false to the past, false to the present, and solemnly binds herself to be false to the future.

★ ★ ★

For the present, it is enough to affirm the equal manhood of the Negro race. It is not astonishing that, while we are plowing, planting and reaping, using all kinds of mechanical tools, erecting houses, constructing bridges, building ships, working in metals of brass, iron, copper, silver and gold; that, while we are reading, writing and ciphering, acting as clerks, merchants and secretaries, having among us lawyers, doctors, ministers, poets, authors, editors, orators and teachers; that, while we are engaged in all manner of enterprises common to other men, digging gold in California, capturing the whale in the Pacific, feeding sheep and cattle on the hillside, living, moving, acting, thinking, planning, living in families as husbands, wives and children, and, above all, confessing and worshiping the Christian's God and looking hopefully for life and immortality beyond the grave, we are called upon to prove that we are men!

Would you have me argue that man is entitled to liberty? that he is the rightful owner of his own body? You have already declared it. Must I argue the wrongfulness of slavery? Is that a question for republicans? Is it to be settled by the rules of logic and argumentation, as a matter beset with great difficulty, involving a doubtful application of the principle of justice, hard to be understood? How should I look today, in the presence of Americans, dividing and subdividing a discourse, to show that men have a natural right to freedom, speaking of it relatively and positively, negatively and affirmatively? To do so would be to make myself ridiculous and to offer an insult to your understanding. There is not a man beneath the canopy of heaven that does not know that slavery is wrong *for him.*

★ ★ ★

What, to the American slave, is your Fourth of July? I answer: a day that reveals to him, more than all other days in the year, the gross injustice and cruelty to which he is the constant victim. To him, your celebration is a sham; your boasted liberty an unholy license; your national greatness swelling vanity; your sounds of rejoicing are empty and heartless; your denunciation of tyrants brass-fronted impudence; your shouts of liberty and equality hollow mockery; your prayers and hymns, your sermons and thanksgivings, with all your religious parade and solemnity, are to Him mere bom-

bast, fraud, deception, impiety and hypocrisy—a thin veil to cover up crimes which would disgrace a nation of savages. There is not a nation on the earth guilty of practices more shocking and bloody than are the people of the United States at this very hour.

Go where you may, search where you will, roam through all the monarchies and despotisms of the Old World, travel through South America, search out every abuse, and when you have found the last, lay your facts by the side of the everyday practices of this nation, and you will say with me, that, for revolting barbarity and shameless hypocrisy, America reigns without a rival.

★ ★ ★

Americans! your republican politics, not less than your republican religion, are flagrantly inconsistent. You boast of your love of liberty, your superior civilization and your pure Christianity, while the whole political power of the nation (as embodied in the two great political parties) is solemnly pledged to support and perpetuate the enslavement of three millions of your countrymen. You hurl your anathemas at the crowned-headed tyrants of Russia and Austria and pride yourselves on your democratic institutions, while you yourselves consent to be the mere *tools* and *bodyguards* of the tyrants of Virginia and Carolina. You invite to your shores fugitives of oppression from abroad, honor them with banquets, greet them with ovations, cheer them, toast them, salute them, protect them, and pour out your money to them like water; but the fugitives from your own land you advertise, hunt, arrest, shoot and kill. You glory in your refinement and your universal education; yet you maintain a system as barbarous and dreadful as ever stained the character of a nation—a system begun in avarice, supported in pride, and perpetuated in cruelty. You shed tears over fallen Hungary, and make the sad story of her wrongs the theme of your poets, statesmen and orators, till your gallant sons are ready to fly to arms to vindicate her cause against the oppressor; but, in regard to the ten thousand wrongs of the American slave, you would enforce the strictest silence and would hail him as an enemy of the nation who dares to make those wrongs the subject of public discourse! You are all on fire at the mention of liberty for France or for Ireland, but are as cold as an iceberg at the thought of liberty for the enslaved of America. You discourse eloquently on the dignity of labor; yet, you sustain a system which, in its very essence, casts a stigma upon labor. You can bare your bosom to the storm of British artillery to throw off a three-penny tax on tea, and yet wring the last hard-earned farthing from the grasp of the black laborers of your country. You profess to believe "that of one blood God made all nations of men to dwell on the face of all the earth"† and hath commanded all men, everywhere, to love one another; yet you notoriously hate (and glory in your hatred) all men whose skins are not colored like your own. You declare before the world, and are understood by the world to declare, that you *"hold these truths to be self-evident, that all men are created equal; and are endowed by their Creator with certain unalienable rights; and that among these are, life, liberty and the pursuit of happiness"; and yet, you hold securely, in a bondage which, according to your own Thomas Jefferson, "is worse than ages of that which your fathers rose in rebellion to oppose," a seventh part* of the inhabitants of your country.

Fellow citizens, I will not enlarge further on your national inconsistencies. The existence of slavery in this country brands your republicanism as a sham, your humanity as a base pretense, and your Christianity as a lie. It destroys your moral power abroad; it corrupts your politicians at home. It saps the foundation of religion; it makes your name a hissing and a byword to a mocking earth. It is the antagonistic force in your government, the only thing that seriously disturbs and endangers your union. It fetters your progress; it is the enemy of improvement; the deadly foe of education; it fosters pride; it breeds insolence; it promotes vice; it shelters crime; it is a curse to the earth that supports it; and yet you cling to it as if it were the sheet anchor of all your hopes.

★ ★ ★

Allow me to say, in conclusion, notwithstanding the dark picture I have this day presented, of the state of the nation, I do not despair of this country. There are forces in operation which must inevitably work the downfall of slavery.

---

*The fledgling Hungarian republic was invaded by Austria and Russia in 1849.

†Acts 17:26.

THE GETTYSBURG ADDRESS (1863)

Four score and seven years ago our fathers brought forth on this continent, a new nation, conceived in Liberty, and dedicated to the proposition that all men are created equal.

Now we are engaged in a great civil war, testing whether that nation, or any nation so conceived and so dedicated, can long endure. We are met on a great battle field of that war. We have come to dedicate a portion of that field, as a final resting place for those who here gave their lives that that nation might live. It is altogether fitting and proper that we should do this.

But, in a larger sense, we can not dedicate—we can not consecrate—we can not hallow—this ground. The brave men, living and dead, who struggled here, have consecrated it, far above our poor power to add or detract. The world will little note, nor long remember what we say here, but it can never forget what they did here. It is for us the living, rather, to be dedicated here to the unfinished work which they who fought here have thus far so nobly advanced. It is rather for us to be here dedicated to the great task remaining before us—that from these honored dead we take increased devotion to that cause for which they gave the last full measure of devotion—that we here highly resolve that these dead shall not have died in vain—that this nation, under God, shall have a new birth of freedom—and that government of the people, by the people, for the people, shall not perish from the earth.

Abraham Lincoln
November 19, 1863

ABRAHAM LINCOLN'S SECOND INAUGURAL ADDRESS (1865)

Fellow Countrymen:

At this second appearing to take the oath of the presidential office, there is less occasion for an extended address than there was at the first. Then a statement, somewhat in detail, of a course to be pursued, seemed fitting and proper. Now, at the expiration of four years, during which public declarations have been constantly called forth on every point and phase of the great contest which still absorbs the attention, and engrosses the energies of the nation, little that is new could be presented. The progress of our arms, upon which all else chiefly depends, is as well known to the public as to myself; and it is, I trust, reasonably satisfactory and encouraging to all. With high hope for the future, no prediction in regard to it is ventured.

On the occasion corresponding to this four years ago, all thoughts were anxiously directed to an impending civil war. All dreaded it—all sought to avert it. While the inaugural address was being delivered from this place, devoted altogether to *saving* the Union without war, insurgent agents were in the city seeking to *destroy* it without war—seeking to dissolve the Union, and divide effects, by negotiation. Both parties deprecated war; but one of them would *make* war rather than let the nation survive; and the other would *accept* war rather than let it perish. And the war came.

One eighth of the whole population were colored slaves, not distributed generally over the Union, but localized in the southern part of it. These slaves constituted a peculiar and powerful interest. All knew that this interest was, somehow, the cause of the war. To strengthen, perpetuate, and extend this interest was the object for which the insurgents would rend the Union, even by war; while the government claimed no right to do more than to restrict the territorial enlargement of it. Neither party expected for the war, the magnitude, or the duration, which it has already attained. Neither anticipated that the *cause* of the conflict might cease with, or even before, the conflict itself should cease. Each looked for an easier triumph, and a result less fundamental and astounding. Both read the same Bible, and pray to the same God; and each invokes His aid against the other. It may seem strange that any men should dare to ask a just God's assistance in wringing their bread from the sweat of other men's faces; but let us judge not that we be not judged. The prayers of both could not be answered; that of neither has been answered fully. The Almighty has His own purposes. "Woe unto the world because of offences! for it must needs be that offences come; but woe to that man by whom the offence cometh." If we shall suppose that American slavery is one of those offences which, in the providence of God, must needs come, but which, having continued through His appointed time, He now wills to remove, and that He gives to both North and South, this terrible war, as the woe due to those by whom the offence came, shall we discern therein any departure from those divine attributes which the believers in a living God always ascribe to Him? Fondly do we hope, fervently do we pray—that this mighty scourge of war may speedily pass away. Yet, if God wills that it continue until all the wealth piled by the bondsman's two hundred and fifty years of unrequited toil shall be sunk, and until every drop of blood drawn with the lash shall be paid by another drawn with the sword, as was said three thousand years ago, so still it must be said "the judgments of the Lord are true and righteous altogether."

With malice toward none; with charity for all; with firmness in the right as God gives us to see the right, let us strive on to finish the work we are in; to bind up the nation's wounds; to care for him who shall have borne the battle and for his widow and his orphan, to do all which may achieve and cherish a just and a lasting peace, among ourselves and with all nations.

THE POPULIST PLATFORM OF 1892

Assembled upon the 116th anniversary of the Declaration of Independence, the People's Party of America, in their first national convention, invoking upon their action the blessing of Almighty God, puts forth in the name and on behalf of the people of this country, the following preamble and declaration of principles:

PREAMBLE

The conditions which surround us best justify our co-operation; we meet in the midst of a nation brought to the verge of moral, political, and material ruin. Corruption dominates the ballot-box, the Legislatures, the Congress, and touches even the ermine of the bench. The people are demoralized; most of the States have been compelled to isolate the voters at the polling places to prevent universal intimidation and bribery. The newspapers are largely subsidized or muzzled, public opinion silenced, business prostrated, homes covered with mortgages, labor impoverished, and the land concentrating in the hands of the capitalists. The urban workmen are denied the right to organize for self-protection, imported pauperized labor beats down their wages, a hireling standing army, unrecognized by our laws, is established to shoot them down, and they are rapidly degenerating into European conditions. The fruits of the toil of millions are boldly stolen to build up the fortunes for a few, unprecedented in the history of mankind; and the possessors of these, in turn, despise the Republic and endanger liberty. From the same prolific womb of governmental injustice we breed the two great classes—tramps and millionaires.

The national power to create money is appropriated to enrich bondholders; a vast public debt, payable in legal tender currency, has been funded into gold-bearing bonds, thereby adding millions to the burdens of the people. Silver, which has been accepted as coin since the dawn of history, has been demonetized to add to the purchasing power of gold by decreasing the value of all forms of property as well as human labor, and the supply of currency is purposely abridged to fatten usurers, bankrupt enterprise, and enslave industry. A vast conspiracy against mankind has been organized on two continents, and it is rapidly taking possession of the world. If not met and overthrown at once it forebodes terrible social convulsions, the destruction of civilization, or the establishment of an absolute despotism.

We have witnessed for more than a quarter of a century the struggles of the two great political parties for power and plunder, while grievous wrongs have been inflicted upon the suffering people. We charge that the controlling influences dominating both these parties have permitted the existing dreadful conditions to develop without serious effort to prevent or restrain them. Neither do they now promise us any substantial reform. They have agreed together to ignore in the coming campaign every issue but one. They propose to drown the outcries of a plundered people with the uproar of a sham battle over the tariff, so that capitalists, corporations, national banks, rings, trusts, watered stock, the demonetization of silver, and the oppressions of the usurers may all be lost sight of. They propose to sacrifice our homes, lives, and children on the altar of mammon; to destroy the multitude in order to secure corruption funds from the millionaires.

Assembled on the anniversary of the birthday of the nation, and filled with the spirit of the grand general and chief who established our independence, we seek to restore the government of the Republic to the hands of "the plain people," with which class it originated. We assert our purpose to be identical with the purposes of the National Constitution, "to form a more perfect union and establish justice, insure domestic tranquility, provide for the common defense, promote the general welfare, and secure the blessings of liberty for ourselves and our posterity." We declare that this Republic can only endure as a free government while built upon the love of the whole people for each other and for the nation; that it cannot be pinned together by bayonets; that the civil war is over, and that every passion and resentment which grew out of it must die with it; and that we must be in fact, as we are in name, one united brotherhood of free men.

Our country finds itself confronted by conditions for which there is no precedent in the history of the world; our annual agricultural productions amount to billions of dollars in value, which must, within a few weeks or months, be exchanged for billions of dollars of commodities consumed in their production; the existing currency supply is wholly inadequate to make this exchange; the results are falling prices, the formation of combines and rings, the impoverishment of the producing class. We pledge ourselves, if given power, we will labor to correct these evils by wise and reasonable legislation, in accordance with the terms of our platform. We believe that the power of government—in other words, of the people—should be expanded (as in the case of the postal service) as rapidly and as far as the good sense of an intelligent people and the teaching of experience shall justify, to the end that oppression, injustice, and poverty shall eventually cease in the land.

While our sympathies as a party of reform are naturally upon the side of every proposition which will tend to make men intelligent, virtuous, and temperate, we nevertheless regard these questions—important as they are—as secondary to the great issues now pressing for solution, and upon which not only our individual prosperity but the very existence of free institutions depend; and we ask all men to first help us to determine whether we are to have a republic to administer before we differ as to the conditions upon which it is to be administered, believing that the forces of reform this day organized will never cease to move forward until every wrong is remedied, and equal rights and equal privileges securely established for all the men and women of this country.

PLATFORM

We declare, therefore—

First.—That the union of the labor forces of the United States this day consummated shall be permanent and perpetual; may its spirit enter into all hearts for the salvation of the Republic and the uplifting of mankind!

Second.—Wealth belongs to him who creates it, and every dollar taken from industry without an equivalent is robbery. "If any will not work, neither shall he eat." The interests of rural and civic labor are the same; their enemies are identical.

Third.—We believe that the time has come when the railroad corporations will either own the people or the people must own the railroads; and, should the government enter upon the work of owning and managing all railroads, we should favor an amendment to the Constitution by which all persons engaged in the government service shall be placed under a civil-service regulation of the most rigid character, so as to prevent the increase of the power of the national administration by the use of such additional government employees.

FINANCE.—We demand a national currency, safe, sound, and flexible, issued by the general government only, a full legal tender for all debts, public and private, and that without the use of banking corporations, a just, equitable, and efficient means of distribution direct to the people, at a tax not to exceed two per cent per annum, to be provided as set forth in the sub-treasury plan of the Farmers' Alliance, or a better system; also by payments in discharge of its obligations for public improvements.

1. We demand free and unlimited coinage of silver and gold at the present legal ratio of 16 to 1.

2. We demand that the amount of circulating medium be speedily increased to not less than $50 per capita.

3. We demand a graduated income tax.

4. We believe that the money of the country should be kept as much as possible in the hands of the people, and hence we demand that all State and national revenues shall be limited to the necessary expenses of the government, economically and honestly administered.

5. We demand that postal savings banks be established by the government for the safe deposit of the earnings of the people and to facilitate exchange.

TRANSPORTATION.—Transportation being a means of exchange and a public necessity, the government should own and operate the railroads in the interest of the people. The telegraph and telephone, like the post-office system, being a necessity for the transmission of news, should be owned and operated by the government in the interest of the people.

LAND.—The land, including all the natural sources of wealth, is the heritage of the people, and should not be monopolized for speculative purposes, and alien ownership of land should be prohibited. All land now held by railroads and other corporations in excess of their actual needs, and all lands now owned by aliens should be reclaimed by the government and held for actual settlers only.

EXPRESSION OF SENTIMENTS

Your committee on Platform and Resolutions beg leave unanimously to report the following:

Whereas, Other questions have been presented for our consideration, we hereby submit the following, not as a part of the Platform of the People's Party, but as resolutions expressive of the sentiment of this Convention:

1. *Resolved*, That we demand a free ballot and a fair count in all elections, and pledge ourselves to secure it to every legal voter without federal intervention, through the adoption by the States of the unperverted Australian or secret ballot system.

2. *Resolved*, That the revenue derived from a graduated income tax should be applied to the reduction of the burden of taxation now levied upon the domestic industries of this country.

3. *Resolved*, That we pledge our support to fair and liberal pensions to ex-Union soldiers and sailors.

4. *Resolved*, That we condemn the fallacy of protecting American labor under the present system, which opens our ports to the pauper and criminal classes of the world, and crowds out our wage-earners; and we denounce the present ineffective laws against contract labor, and demand the further restriction of undesirable emigration.

5. *Resolved*, that we cordially sympathize with the efforts of organized workingmen to shorten the hours of labor, and demand a rigid enforcement of the existing eight-hour law on Government work, and ask that a penalty clause be added to the said law.

6. *Resolved*, That we regard the maintenance of a large standing army of mercenaries, known as the Pinkerton system, as a menace to our liberties, and we demand its abolition; and we condemn the recent invasion of the Territory of Wyoming by the hired assassins of plutocracy, assisted by federal officers.

7. *Resolved*, That we commend to the favorable consideration of the people and the reform press the legislative system known as the initiative and referendum.

8. *Resolved*, That we favor a constitutional provision limiting the office of President and Vice-President to one term, and providing for the election of Senators of the United States by a direct vote of the people.

9. *Resolved*, That we oppose any subsidy or national aid to any private corporation for any purpose.

10. *Resolved*, That this convention sympathizes with the Knights of Labor and their righteous contest with the tyrannical combine of clothing manufacturers of Rochester, and declare it to be the duty of all who hate tyranny and oppression to refuse to purchase the goods made by the said manufacturers, or to patronize any merchants who sell such goods.

FRANKLIN D. ROOSEVELT'S FIRST INAUGURAL ADDRESS (1933)

I am certain that my fellow Americans expect that on my induction into the Presidency I will address them with a candor and a decision which the present situation of our Nation impels. This is preeminently the time to speak the truth, the whole truth, frankly and boldly. Nor need we shrink from honestly facing conditions in our country today. This great Nation will endure as it has endured, will revive and will prosper. So, first of all, let me assert my firm belief that the only thing we have to fear is fear itself—nameless, unreasoning, unjustified terror which paralyzes needed efforts to convert retreat into advance. In every dark hour of our national life a leadership of frankness and vigor has met with that understanding and support of the people themselves which is essential to victory. I am convinced that you will again give that support to leadership in these critical days.

In such a spirit on my part and on yours we face our common difficulties. They concern, thank God, only material things. Values have shrunken to fantastic levels; taxes have risen; our ability to pay has fallen; government of all kinds is faced by serious curtailment of income; the means of exchange are frozen in the currents of trade; the withered leaves of industrial enterprise lie on every side; farmers find no markets for their produce; the savings of many years in thousands of families are gone.

More important, a host of unemployed citizens face the grim problem of existence, and an equally great number toil with little return. Only a foolish optimist can deny the dark realities of the moment.

Yet our distress comes from no failure of substance. We are stricken by no plague of locusts. Compared with the perils which our forefathers conquered because they believed and were not afraid, we have still much to be thankful for. Nature still offers her bounty and human efforts have multiplied it. Plenty is at our doorstep, but a generous use of it languishes in the very sight of the supply. Primarily this is because the rulers of the exchange of mankind's goods have failed, through their own stubbornness and their own incompetence, have admitted their failure, and abdicated. Practices of the unscrupulous money changers stand indicted in the court of public opinion, rejected by the hearts and minds of men.

True they have tried, but their efforts have been cast in the pattern of an outworn tradition. Faced by failure of credit they have proposed only the lending of more money. Stripped of the lure of profit by which to induce our people to follow their false leadership, they have resorted to exhortations, pleading tearfully for restored confidence. They know only the rules of a generation of self-seekers. They have no vision, and when there is no vision the people perish.

The money changers have fled from their high seats in the temple of our civilization. We may now restore that temple to the ancient truths. The measure of the restoration lies in the extent to which we apply social values more noble than mere monetary profit.

Happiness lies not in the mere possession of money; it lies in the joy of achievement, in the thrill of creative effort. The joy and moral stimulation of work no longer must be forgotten in the mad chase of evanescent profits. These dark days will be worth all they cost us if they teach us that our true destiny is not to be ministered unto but to minister to ourselves and to our fellow men.

Recognition of the falsity of material wealth as the standard of success goes hand in hand with the abandonment of the false belief that public office and high political position are to be valued only by the standards of pride of place and personal profit; and there must be an end to a conduct in banking and in business which too often has given to a sacred trust the likeness of callous and selfish wrongdoing. Small wonder that confidence languishes, for it thrives only on honesty, on honor, on the sacredness of obligations, on faithful protection, on unselfish performance; without them it cannot live.

Restoration calls, however, not for changes in ethics alone. This Nation asks for action, and action now.

Our greatest primary task is to put people to work. This is no unsolvable problem if we face it wisely and courageously. It can be accomplished in part by direct recruiting by the Government itself, treating the task as we would treat the emergency of a war, but at the same time, through this employment, accomplishing greatly needed projects to stimulate and reorganize the use of our natural resources.

Hand in hand with this we must frankly recognize the overbalance of population in our industrial centers and, by engaging on a national scale in a redistribution, endeavor to provide a better use of the land for those best fitted for the land. The task can be helped by definite efforts to raise the values of agricultural products and with this the power to purchase the output of our cities. It can be helped by preventing realistically the tragedy of the growing loss through foreclosure of our small homes and our farms. It can be helped by insistence that the Federal, State, and local governments act forthwith on the demand that their cost be drastically reduced. It can be helped by the unifying of relief activities which today are often scattered, uneconomical, and unequal. It can be helped by national planning for and supervision of all forms of transportation and of communications and other utilities which have a definitely public character. There are many ways in which it can be helped, but it can never be helped merely by talking about it. We must act and act quickly.

Finally, in our progress toward a resumption of work we require two safeguards against a return of the evils of the old order; there must be a strict supervision of all banking and credits and investments; there must be an end to speculation with other people's money, and there must be provision for an adequate but sound currency.

There are the lines of attack. I shall presently urge upon a new Congress, in special session, detailed measures for their fulfillment, and I shall seek the immediate assistance of the several States.

Through this program of action we address ourselves to putting our own national house in order and making income balance outgo. Our international trade relations, though vastly important, are in point of time and necessity secondary to the establishment of a sound national economy. I favor as a practical policy the putting of first things first. I shall spare no effort to restore world trade by international economic readjustment, but the emergency at home cannot wait on that accomplishment.

The basic thought that guides these specific means of national recovery is not narrowly nationalistic. It is the insistence, as a first consideration, upon the interdependence of the various elements in all parts of the United States—a recognition of the old and permanently important manifestation of the American spirit of the pioneer. It is the way to recovery. It is the immediate way. It is the strongest assurance that the recovery will endure.

In the field of world policy I would dedicate this Nation to the policy of the good neighbor—the neighbor who resolutely respects himself and, because he does so, respects the rights of others—the neighbor who respects his obligations and respects the sanctity of his agreements in and with a world of neighbors.

If I read the temper of our people correctly, we now realize as we have never realized before our interdependence on each other; that we cannot merely take but we must give as well; that if we are to go forward, we must move as a trained and loyal army willing to sacrifice for the good of a common discipline, because without such discipline no progress is made, no leadership becomes effective. We are, I know, ready and willing to submit our lives and property to such discipline, because it makes possible a leadership which aims at a larger good. This I propose to offer, pledging that the larger purposes will bind upon us all as a sacred obligation with a unity of duty hitherto evoked only in time of armed strife.

With this pledge taken, I assume unhesitatingly the leadership of this great army of our people dedicated to a disciplined attack upon our common problems.

Action in this image and to this end is feasible under the form of government which we have inherited from our ancestors. Our Constitution is so simple and practical that it is possible always to meet extraordinary needs by changes in emphasis and arrangement without loss of essential form. That is why our constitutional system has proved itself the most superbly enduring political mechanism the modern world has produced. It has met every stress of vast expansion of territory, of foreign wars, of bitter internal strife, of world relations.

It is to be hoped that the normal balance of executive and legislative authority may be wholly adequate to meet the unprecedented task before us. But it may be that an unprecedented demand and need for undelayed action may call for temporary departure from that normal balance of public procedure.

I am prepared under my constitutional duty to recommend the measures that a stricken nation in the midst of a stricken world may require. These measures, or such other measures as the Congress may build out of its experience and wisdom, I shall seek, within my constitutional authority, to bring to speedy adoption.

But in the event that the Congress shall fail to take one of these two courses, and in the event that the national emergency is still critical, I shall not evade the clear course of duty that will then confront me. I shall ask the Congress for the one remaining instrument to meet the crisis—broad Executive power to wage a war against the emergency, as great as the power that would be given to me if we were in fact invaded by a foreign foe.

For the trust reposed in me I will return the courage and the devotion that befit the time. I can do no less.

We face the arduous days that lie before us in the warm courage of national unity; with the clear consciousness of seeking old and precious moral values; with the clean satisfaction that comes from the stern performance of duty by old and young alike. We aim at the assurance of a rounded and permanent national life.

We do not distrust the future of essential democracy. The people of the United States have not failed. In their need they have registered a mandate that they want direct, vigorous action. They have asked for discipline and direction under leadership. They have made me the present instrument of their wishes. In the spirit of the gift I take it.

In this dedication of a Nation we humbly ask the blessing of God. May He protect each and every one of us. May He guide me in the days to come.

FROM THE PROGRAM FOR THE MARCH ON WASHINGTON FOR JOBS AND FREEDOM (1963)

1. Comprehensive and effective *civil rights legislation* from the present Congress—without compromise or filibuster—to guarantee all Americans

> access to all public accommodations
> decent housing
> adequate and integrated education
> the right to vote

2. Withholding of Federal funds from all programs in which discrimination exists.

3. *Desegregation of all school districts in 1963.*

4. Enforcement of the *Fourteenth Amendment*— reducing Congressional representation of states where citizens are disfranchised.

5. A new *Executive Order* banning discrimination in all housing supported by federal funds.

6. Authority for the Attorney General to institute *injunctive suits* when any constitutional right is violated.

7. A massive federal program to train and place all unemployed workers—Negro and white—on meaningful and dignified jobs at decent wages.

8. A national *minimum wage* act that will give all Americans a decent standard of living. (Government surveys show that anything less than $2.00 an hour fails to do this.)

9. A broadened *Fair Labor Standards Act* to include all areas of employment which are presently excluded.

10. A federal *Fair Employment Practices Act* barring discrimination by federal, state, and municipal governments, and by employers, contractors, employment agencies, and trade unions.

*Support of the March does not necessarily indicate endorsement of every demand listed. Some organizations have not had an opportunity to take an official position on all of the demands advocated here.

RONALD REAGAN'S FIRST INAUGURAL ADDRESS (1981)

WEST FRONT OF THE U.S. CAPITOL, JANUARY 20, 1981

Senator Hatfield, Mr. Chief Justice, Mr. President, Vice President Bush, Vice President Mondale, Senator Baker, Speaker O'Neill, Reverend Moomaw, and my fellow citizens:

To a few of us here today this is a solemn and most momentous occasion, and yet in the history of our nation it is a commonplace occurrence. The orderly transfer of authority as called for in the Constitution routinely takes place, as it has for almost two centuries, and few of us stop to think how unique we really are. In the eyes of many in the world, this every-four-year ceremony we accept as normal is nothing less than a miracle.

Mr. President, I want our fellow citizens to know how much you did to carry on this tradition. By your gracious cooperation in the transition process, you have shown a watching world that we are a united people pledged to maintaining a political system which guarantees individual liberty to a greater degree than any other, and I thank you and your people for all your help in maintaining the continuity which is the bulwark of our republic. The business of our nation goes forward. These United States are confronted with an economic affliction of great proportions. We suffer from the longest and one of the worst sustained inflations in our national history. It distorts our economic decisions, penalizes thrift, and crushes the struggling young and the fixed-income elderly alike. It threatens to shatter the lives of millions of our people.

Idle industries have cast workers into unemployment, human misery, and personal indignity. Those who do work are denied a fair return for their labor by a tax system which penalizes successful achievement and keeps us from maintaining full productivity. But great as our tax burden is, it has not kept pace with public spending. For decades we have piled deficit upon deficit, mortgaging our future and our children's future for the temporary convenience of the present.

To continue this long trend is to guarantee tremendous social, cultural, political, and economic upheavals.

You and I, as individuals, can, by borrowing, live beyond our means, but for only a limited period of time. Why, then, should we think that collectively, as a nation, we're not bound by that same limitation? We must act today in order to preserve tomorrow. And let there be no misunderstanding: We are going to begin to act, beginning today. The economic ills we suffer have come upon us over several decades. They will not go away in days, weeks, or months, but they will go away. They will go away because we as Americans have the capacity now, as we've had in the past, to do whatever needs to be done to preserve this last and greatest bastion of freedom.

In this present crisis, government is not the solution to our problem; government is the problem. From time to time we've been tempted to believe that society has become too complex to be managed by self-rule, that government by an elite group is superior to government for, by, and of the people. Well, if no one among us is capable of governing himself, then who among us has the capacity to govern someone else? All of us together, in and out of government, must bear the burden. The solutions we seek must be equitable, with no one group singled out to pay a higher price.

We hear much of special interest groups. Well, our concern must be for a special interest group that has been too long neglected. It knows no sectional boundaries or ethnic and racial divisions, and it crosses political party lines. It is made up of men and women who raise our food, patrol our streets, man our mines and factories, teach our children, keep our homes, and heal us when we're sick—professionals, industrialists, shopkeepers, clerks, cabbies, and truck drivers. They are, in short, "we the people," this breed called Americans.

Well, this administration's objective will be a healthy, vigorous, growing economy that provides equal opportunities for all Americans, with no barriers born of bigotry or discrimination. Putting America back to work means putting all Americans back to work. Ending inflation means freeing all Americans from the terror of runaway living costs. All must share in the productive work of this "new beginning," and all must share in the bounty of a revived economy. With the idealism and fair play which are the core of our system and our strength, we can have a strong and prosperous America, at peace with itself and the world.

So, as we begin, let us take inventory. We are a nation that has a government—not the other way around. And this makes us special among the nations of the Earth. Our government has no power except that granted it by the people. It is time to check and reverse the growth of government, which shows signs of having grown beyond the consent of the governed.

It is my intention to curb the size and influence of the federal establishment and to demand recognition of the distinction between the powers granted to the federal government and those reserved to the states or to the people. All of us need to be reminded that the federal government did not create the states; the states created the federal government.

Now, so there will be no misunderstanding, it's not my intention to do away with government. It is rather to make it work—work with us, not over us; to stand by our side, not ride on our back. Government can and must provide opportunity, not smother it; foster productivity, not stifle it.

If we look to the answer as to why for so many years we achieved so much, prospered as no other people on earth, it was because here in this land we unleashed the energy and individual genius of man to a greater extent than has ever been done before. Freedom and the dignity of the individual have been more available and assured here than in any other place on earth. The price for this freedom at times has been high, but we have never been unwilling to pay the price.

It is no coincidence that our present troubles parallel and are proportionate to the intervention and excessive growth of government. It is time for us to realize that we're too great a nation to limit ourselves to small dreams. We're not, as some would have us believe, doomed to an inevitable decline. I do not believe in a fate that will fall on us no matter what we do. I do believe in a fate that will fall on us if we do nothing. So, with all the creative energy at our command, let us begin an era of national renewal. Let us renew our determination, our courage, and our strength. And let us renew our faith and our hope.

We have every right to dream heroic dreams. Those who say that we're in a time when there are no heroes, they just don't know where to look. You can see heroes every day going in and out of factory gates. Others, a handful in number, produce enough food to feed all of us and then the world beyond. You meet heroes across a counter, and they're on both sides of that counter. There are entrepreneurs with faith in themselves and faith in an idea who create new jobs, new wealth and opportunity. They're individuals and families whose taxes support the government and whose voluntary gifts support church, charity, culture, art, and education. Their patriotism is quiet, but deep. Their values sustain our national life.

Now, I have used the words "they" and "their" in speaking of these heroes. I could say "you" and "your," because I'm addressing the heroes of whom I speak—you, the citizens of this blessed land. Your dreams, your hopes, your goals are going to be the dreams, the hopes, and the goals of this administration, so help me God.

We shall reflect the compassion that is so much a part of your makeup. How can we love our country and not love our countrymen; and loving them, reach out a hand when they fall, heal them when they're sick, and provide opportunity to make them self-sufficient so they will be equal in fact and not just in theory?

Can we solve the problems confronting us? Well, the answer is an unequivocal and emphatic "yes." To paraphrase Winston Churchill, I did not take the oath I've just taken with the intention of presiding over the dissolution of the world's strongest economy.

In the days ahead I will propose removing the roadblocks that have slowed our economy and reduced productivity. Steps will be taken aimed at restoring the balance between the various levels of government. Progress may be slow, measured in inches and feet, not miles, but we will progress. It is time to reawaken this industrial giant, to get government back within its means, and to lighten our punitive tax burden. And these will be our first priorities, and on these principles there will be no compromise.

On the eve of our struggle for independence a man who might have been one of the greatest among the Founding Fathers, Dr. Joseph Warren, president of the Massachusetts Congress, said to his fellow Americans, "Our country is in danger, but not to be despaired of . . . On you depend the fortunes of America. You are to decide the important questions upon which rests the happiness and the liberty of millions yet unborn. Act worthy of yourselves." Well, I believe we, the Americans of today, are ready to act worthy of ourselves, ready to do what must be done to ensure happiness and liberty for ourselves, our children, and our children's children. And as we renew ourselves here in our own land, we will be seen as having greater strength throughout the world. We will again be the exemplar of freedom and a beacon of hope for those who do not now have freedom.

To those neighbors and allies who share our freedom, we will strengthen our historic ties and assure them of our support and firm commitment. We will match loyalty with loyalty. We will strive for mutually beneficial relations. We will not use our friendship to impose on their sovereignty, for our own sovereignty is not for sale. As for the enemies of freedom, those who are potential adversaries, they will be reminded that peace is the highest aspiration of the American people. We will negotiate for it, sacrifice for it; we will not surrender for it, now or ever.

Our forbearance should never be misunderstood. Our reluctance for conflict should not be misjudged as a failure of will. When action is required to preserve our national security, we will act. We will maintain sufficient strength to prevail if need be, knowing that if we do so we have the best chance of never having to use that strength. Above all, we must realize that no arsenal or no weapon in the arsenals of the world is so formidable as the will and moral courage of free men and women. It is a weapon our adversaries in today's world do not have. It is a weapon that we as Americans do have. Let that be understood by those who practice terrorism and prey upon their neighbors. I'm told that tens of thousands of prayer meetings are being held on this day, and for that I'm deeply grateful. We are a nation under God, and I believe God intended for us to be free. It would be fitting and good, I think, if on each Inaugural Day in future years it should be declared a day of prayer.

This is the first time in our history that this ceremony has been held, as you've been told, on the West Front of the Capitol. Standing here, one faces a magnificent vista, opening up on the city's special beauty and history. At the end of this open mall are those shrines to the giants on whose shoulders we stand.

Directly in front of me, the monument to a monumental man, George Washington, father of our country. A man of humility who came to greatness reluctantly. He led Americans out of revolutionary victory into infant nationhood. Off to one side, the stately memorial to Thomas Jefferson. The Declaration of Independence flames with his eloquence. And then, beyond the Reflecting Pool, the dignified columns of the Lincoln Memorial. Whoever would understand in his heart the meaning of America will find it in the life of Abraham Lincoln.

Beyond those monuments to heroism is the Potomac River, and on the far shore the sloping hills of Arlington National Cemetery, with its row upon row of simple white markers bearing crosses and Stars of David. They add up to only a tiny fraction of the price that has been paid for our freedom. Each one of those markers is a monument to the kind of hero I spoke of earlier. Their lives ended in places called Belleau Wood, the Argonne, Omaha Beach, Salerno, and halfway around the world on Guadalcanal, Tarawa, Pork Chop Hill, the Chosin Reservoir, and in a hundred rice paddies and jungles of a place called Vietnam.

Under one such marker lies a young man, Martin Treptow, who left his job in a small town barbershop in 1917 to go to France with the famed Rainbow Division. There, on the western front, he was killed trying to carry a message between battalions under heavy artillery fire.

We're told that on his body was found a diary. On the flyleaf under the heading "My Pledge," he had written these words: "America must win this war. Therefore I will work, I will save, I will sacrifice, I will endure, I will fight cheerfully and do my utmost, as if the issue of the whole struggle depended on me alone."

The crisis we are facing today does not require of us the kind of sacrifice that Martin Treptow and so many thousands of others were called upon to make. It does require, however, our best effort and our willingness to believe in ourselves and to believe in our capacity to perform great deeds, to believe that together with God's help we can and will resolve the problems which now confront us.

And after all, why shouldn't we believe that? We are Americans.

God bless you, and thank you.

BARACK OBAMA'S FIRST INAUGURAL ADDRESS (2009)

My fellow citizens: I stand here today humbled by the task before us, grateful for the trust you've bestowed, mindful of the sacrifices borne by our ancestors.

I thank President Bush for his service to our nation—(*applause*)—as well as the generosity and cooperation he has shown throughout this transition.

Forty-four Americans have now taken the presidential oath. The words have been spoken during rising tides of prosperity and the still waters of peace. Yet, every so often, the oath is taken amidst gathering clouds and raging storms. At these moments, America has carried on not simply because of the skill or vision of those in high office, but because we, the people, have remained faithful to the ideals of our forebears and true to our founding documents.

So it has been: so it must be with this generation of Americans.

That we are in the midst of crisis is now well understood. Our nation is at war against a far-reaching network of violence and hatred. Our economy is badly weakened, a consequence of greed and irresponsibility on the part of some, but also our collective failure to make hard choices and prepare the nation for a new age. Homes have been lost, jobs shed, businesses shuttered. Our health care is too costly, our schools fail too many—and each day brings further evidence that the ways we use energy strengthen our adversaries and threaten our planet.

These are the indicators of crisis, subject to data and statistics. Less measurable, but no less profound, is a sapping of confidence across our land; a nagging fear that America's decline is inevitable, that the next generation must lower its sights.

Today I say to you that the challenges we face are real. They are serious and they are many. They will not be met easily or in a short span of time. But know this America: They will be met. (*Applause*)

On this day, we gather because we have chosen hope over fear, unity of purpose over conflict and discord. On this day, we come to proclaim an end to the petty grievances and false promises, the recriminations and worn-out dogmas that for far too long have strangled our politics. We remain a young nation. But in the words of Scripture, the time has come to set aside childish things. The time has come to reaffirm our enduring spirit; to choose our better history; to carry forward that precious gift, that noble idea passed on from generation to generation; the God-given promise that all are equal, all are free, and all deserve a chance to pursue their full measure of happiness. (*Applause*)

In reaffirming the greatness of our nation we understand that greatness is never a given. It must be earned. Our journey has never been one of short-cuts or settling for less. It has not been the path for the faint-hearted, for those that prefer leisure over work, or seek only the pleasures of riches and fame. Rather, it has been the risk-takers, the doers, the makers of things—some celebrated, but more often men and women obscure in their labor—who have carried us up the long rugged path towards prosperity and freedom.

For us, they packed up their few worldly possessions and traveled across oceans in search of a new life. For us, they toiled in sweatshops, and settled the West, endured the lash of the whip, and plowed the hard earth. For us, they fought and died in places like Concord and Gettysburg, Normandy and Khe Sahn.

Time and again these men and women struggled and sacrificed and worked till their hands were raw so that we might live a better life. They saw America as bigger than the sum of our individual ambitions, greater than all the differences of birth or wealth or faction.

This is the journey we continue today. We remain the most prosperous, powerful nation on Earth. Our workers are no less productive than when this crisis began. Our minds are no less inventive, our goods and services no less needed than they were last week, or last month, or last year. Our capacity remains undiminished. But our time of standing pat, of protecting narrow interests and putting off unpleasant decisions—that time has surely passed. Starting today, we must pick ourselves up, dust ourselves off, and begin again the work of remaking America. (*Applause*)

For everywhere we look, there is work to be done. The state of our economy calls for action, bold and swift. And we will act, not only to create new jobs, but to lay a new foundation for growth. We will build the roads and bridges, the electric grids and digital lines that feed our commerce and bind us together. We'll restore science to its rightful place, and wield technology's wonders to raise health care's quality and lower its cost. We will harness the sun and the winds and the soil to fuel our cars and run our factories. And we will transform our schools and colleges and universities to meet the demands of a new age. All this we can do. All this we will do.

Now, there are some who question the scale of our ambitions, who suggest that our system cannot tolerate too many big plans. Their memories are short, for they have forgotten what this country has already done, what free men and women can achieve when imagination is joined to common purpose, and necessity to courage. What the cynics fail to understand is that the ground has shifted beneath them, that the stale political arguments that have consumed us for so long no longer apply.

The question we ask today is not whether our government is too big or too small, but whether it works—whether it helps families find jobs at a decent wage, care they can afford, a retirement that is dignified. Where the answer is yes, we intend to move forward. Where the answer is no, programs will end. And those of us who manage the public's dollars will be held to account, to spend wisely, reform bad habits, and do our business in the light of day, because only then can we restore the vital trust between a people and their government.

Nor is the question before us whether the market is a force for good or ill. Its power to generate wealth and expand freedom is unmatched. But this crisis has reminded us that without a watchful eye, the market can spin out of control. The nation cannot prosper long when it favors only the prosperous. The success of our economy has always depended not just on the size of our gross domestic product, but on the reach of our prosperity, on the ability to extend opportunity to every willing heart—not out of charity, but because it is the surest route to our common good. (*Applause*)

As for our common defense, we reject as false the choice between our safety and our ideals. Our Founding Fathers—(*Applause*)—our Founding Fathers, faced with perils that we can scarcely imagine, drafted a charter to assure the rule of law and the rights of man—a charter expanded by the blood of generations. Those ideals still light the world, and we will not give them up for expedience sake. (*Applause*)

And so, to all the other peoples and governments who are watching today, from the grandest capitals to the small village where my father was born, know that America is a friend of each nation, and every man, woman and child who seeks a future of peace and dignity. And we are ready to lead once more. (*Applause*)

Recall that earlier generations faced down fascism and communism not just with missiles and tanks, but with the sturdy alliances and enduring convictions. They understood that our power alone cannot protect us, nor does it entitle us to do as we please. Instead they knew that our power grows through its prudent use; our security emanates from the justness of our cause, the force of our example, the tempering qualities of humility and restraint.

We are the keepers of this legacy. Guided by these principles once more we can meet those new threats that demand even greater effort, even greater cooperation and understanding between nations. We will begin to responsibly leave Iraq to its people and forge a hard-earned peace in Afghanistan. With old friends and former foes, we'll work tirelessly to lessen the nuclear threat, and roll back the specter of a warming planet.

We will not apologize for our way of life, nor will we waver in its defense. And for those who seek to advance their aims by inducing terror and slaughtering innocents, we say to you now that our spirit is stronger and cannot be broken—you cannot outlast us, and we will defeat you. (*Applause*)

For we know that our patchwork heritage is a strength, not a weakness. We are a nation of Christians and Muslims, Jews and Hindus, and non-believers. We are shaped by every language and culture, drawn from every end of this Earth: and because we have tasted the bitter swill of civil war and segregation, and emerged from that dark chapter stronger and more united, we cannot help but believe that the old hatreds shall someday pass; that the lines of tribe shall soon dissolve; that as the world grows smaller, our common humanity shall reveal itself; and that America must play its role in ushering in a new era of peace.

To the Muslim world, we seek a new way forward, based on mutual interest and mutual respect. To those leaders around the globe who seek to sow conflict, or blame their society's ills on the West, know that your people will judge you on what you can build, not what you destroy. (*Applause*)

To those who cling to power through corruption and deceit and the silencing of dissent, know that you are on the wrong side of history, but that we will extend a hand if you are willing to unclench your fist. (*Applause*)

To the people of poor nations, we pledge to work alongside you to make your farms flourish and let clean waters flow; to nourish starved bodies and feed hungry minds. And to those nations like ours that enjoy relative plenty, we say we can no longer afford indifference to the suffering outside our borders, nor can we consume the world's resources without regard to effect. For the world has changed, and we must change with it.

As we consider the role that unfolds before us, we remember with humble gratitude those brave Americans who at this very hour patrol far-off deserts and distant mountains. They have something to tell us, just as the fallen heroes who lie in Arlington whisper through the ages.

We honor them not only because they are the guardians of our liberty, but because they embody the spirit of service—a willingness to find meaning in something greater than themselves.

And yet at this moment, a moment that will define a generation, it is precisely this spirit that must inhabit us all. For as much as government can do, and must do, it is ultimately the faith and determination of the American people upon which this nation relies. It is the kindness to take in a stranger when the levees break, the selflessness of workers who would rather cut their hours than see a friend lose their job which sees us through our darkest hours. It is the firefighter's courage to storm a stairway filled with smoke, but also a parent's willingness to nurture a child that finally decides our fate.

Our challenges may be new. The instruments with which we meet them may be new. But those values upon which our success depends—honesty and hard work, courage and fair play, tolerance and curiosity, loyalty and patriotism—these things are old. These things are true. They have been the quiet force of progress throughout our history.

What is demanded, then, is a return to these truths. What is required of us now is a new era of responsibility—a recognition on the part of every American that we have duties to ourselves, our nation and the world; duties that we do not grudgingly accept, but rather seize gladly, firm in the knowledge that there is nothing so satisfying to the spirit, so defining of our character than giving our all to a difficult task.

This is the price and the promise of citizenship. This is the source of our confidence—the knowledge that God calls on us to shape an uncertain destiny. This is the meaning of our liberty and our creed, why men and women and children of every race and every faith can join in celebration across this magnificent mall; and why a man whose father less than 60 years ago might not have been served in a local restaurant can now stand before you to take a most sacred oath. (*Applause*)

So let us mark this day with remembrance of who we are and how far we have traveled. In the year of America's birth, in the coldest of months, a small band of patriots huddled by dying campfires on the shores of an icy river. The capital was abandoned. The enemy was advancing. The snow was stained with blood. At the moment when the outcome of our revolution was most in doubt, the father of our nation ordered these words to be read to the people:

"Let it be told to the future world . . . that in the depth of winter, when nothing but hope and virtue could survive . . . that the city and the country, alarmed at one common danger, came forth to meet [it]."

America: In the face of our common dangers, in this winter of our hardship, let us remember these timeless words. With hope and virtue, let us brave once more the icy currents, and endure what storms may come. Let it be said by our children's children that when we were tested we refused to let this journey end, that we did not turn back nor did we falter; and with eyes fixed on the horizon and God's grace upon us, we carried forth that great gift of freedom and delivered it safely to future generations.

Thank you. God bless you. And God bless the United States of America. (*Applause*)

PRESIDENTIAL ELECTIONS

Year	Number of States	Candidates	Parties	Popular Vote	% of Popular Vote	Electoral Vote	% Voter Participation
1789	11	**GEORGE WASHINGTON**	NO PARTY			69	
		John Adams	DESIGNATIONS			34	
		Other candidates				35	
1792	15	**GEORGE WASHINGTON**	NO PARTY			132	
		John Adams	DESIGNATIONS			77	
		George Clinton				50	
		Other candidates				5	
1796	16	**JOHN ADAMS**	FEDERALIST			71	
		Thomas Jefferson	Republican			68	
		Thomas Pinckney	Federalist			59	
		Aaron Burr	Republican			30	
		Other candidates				48	
1800	16	**THOMAS JEFFERSON**	REPUBLICAN			73	
		Aaron Burr	Republican			73	
		John Adams	Federalist			65	
		Charles C. Pinckney	Federalist			64	
		John Jay	Federalist			1	
1804	17	**THOMAS JEFFERSON**	REPUBLICAN			162	
		Charles C. Pinckney	Federalist			14	
1808	17	**JAMES MADISON**	REPUBLICAN			122	
		Charles C. Pinckney	Federalist			47	
		George Clinton	Republican			6	
1812	18	**JAMES MADISON**	REPUBLICAN			128	
		DeWitt Clinton	Federalist			89	

Year	Number of States	Candidates	Parties	Popular Vote	% of Popular Vote	Electoral Vote	% Voter Participation
1816	19	**JAMES MONROE**	REPUBLICAN			183	
		Rufus King	Federalist			34	
1820	24	**JAMES MONROE**	REPUBLICAN			231	
		John Quincy Adams	Independent			1	
1824	24	**JOHN QUINCY ADAMS**	NO PARTY	108,740	31.0	84	26.9
		Andrew Jackson	DESIGNATIONS	153,544	43.0	99	
		William H. Crawford		46,618	13.0	41	
		Henry Clay		47,136	13.0	37	
1828	24	**ANDREW JACKSON**	DEMOCRAT	647,286	56.0	178	57.6
		John Quincy Adams	National Republican	508,064	44.0	83	
1832	24	**ANDREW JACKSON**	DEMOCRAT	687,502	54.5	219	55.4
		Henry Clay	National Republican	530,189	37.5	49	
		William Wirt	Anti-Masonic	101,051	8.0	7	
		John Floyd	Democrat			11	
1836	26	**MARTIN VAN BUREN**	DEMOCRAT	765,483	51.0	170	57.8
		William H. Harrison	Whig			73	
		Hugh L. White	Whig	739,795	49.0	26	
		Daniel Webster	Whig			14	
		William P. Mangum	Whig			11	
1840	26	**WILLIAM H. HARRISON**	WHIG	1,274,624	53.0	234	80.2
		Martin Van Buren	Democrat	1,127,781	47.0	60	

Year	Number of States	Candidates	Parties	Popular Vote	% of Popular Vote	Electoral Vote	% Voter Participation
1844	26	**JAMES K. POLK**	DEMOCRAT	1,338,464	50.0	170	78.9
		Henry Clay	Whig	1,300,097	48.0	105	
		James G. Birney	Liberty	62,300	2.0		
1848	30	**ZACHARY TAYLOR**	WHIG	1,360,967	47.5	163	72.7
		Lewis Cass	Democrat	1,222,342	42.5	127	
		Martin Van Buren	Free Soil	291,263	10.0		
1852	31	**FRANKLIN PIERCE**	DEMOCRAT	1,601,117	51.0	254	69.6
		Winfield Scott	Whig	1,385,453	44.0	42	
		John P. Hale	Free Soil	155,825	5.0		
1856	31	**JAMES BUCHANAN**	DEMOCRAT	1,832,955	45.0	174	78.9
		John C. Frémont	Republican	1,339,932	33.0	114	
		Millard Fillmore	American	871,731	22.0	8	
1860	33	**ABRAHAM LINCOLN**	REPUBLICAN	1,865,593	40.0	180	81.2
		Stephen A. Douglas	Northern Democrat	1,382,713	29.0	12	
		John C. Breckinridge	Southern Democrat	848,356	18.0	72	
		John Bell	Constitutional Union	592,906	13.0	39	
1864	36	**ABRAHAM LINCOLN**	REPUBLICAN	2,206,938	55.0	212	73.8
		George B. McClellan	Democrat	1,803,787	45.0	21	
1868	37	**ULYSSES S. GRANT**	REPUBLICAN	3,013,421	53.0	214	78.1
		Horatio Seymour	Democrat	2,706,829	47.0	80	

Year	Number of States	Candidates	Parties	Popular Vote	% of Popular Vote	Electoral Vote	% Voter Participation
1872	37	**ULYSSES S. GRANT**	REPUBLICAN	3,596,745	55.6	286	71.3
		Horace Greeley	Democrat	2,843,446	43.9	66	
1876	38	**RUTHERFORD B. HAYES**	REPUBLICAN	4,036,572	48.0	185	81.8
		Samuel J. Tilden	Democrat	4,284,020	51.0	184	
1880	38	**JAMES A. GARFIELD**	REPUBLICAN	4,453,295	48.4	214	79.4
		Winfield S. Hancock	Democrat	4,414,082	48.3	155	
		James B. Weaver	Greenback-Labor	308,578	3.5		
1884	38	**GROVER CLEVELAND**	DEMOCRAT	4,879,507	48.5	219	77.5
		James G. Blaine	Republican	4,850,293	48.2	182	
		Benjamin F. Butler	Greenback-Labor	175,370	1.8		
		John P. St. John	Prohibition	150,369	1.5		
1888	38	**BENJAMIN HARRISON**	REPUBLICAN	5,447,129	47.9	233	79.3
		Grover Cleveland	Democrat	5,537,857	48.6	168	
		Clinton B. Fisk	Prohibition	249,506	2.2		
		Anson J. Streeter	Union Labor	146,935	1.3		
1892	44	**GROVER CLEVELAND**	DEMOCRAT	5,555,426	46.1	277	74.7
		Benjamin Harrison	Republican	5,182,690	43.0	145	
		James B. Weaver	People's	1,029,846	8.5	22	
		John Bidwell	Prohibition	264,133	2.2		
1896	45	**WILLIAM McKINLEY**	REPUBLICAN	7,102,246	51.0	271	79.3
		William J. Bryan	Democrat	6,492,559	47.0	176	

Year	Number of States	Candidates	Parties	Popular Vote	% of Popular Vote	Electoral Vote	% Voter Participation
1900	45	**WILLIAM McKINLEY**	REPUBLICAN	7,218,491	52.0	292	73.2
		William J. Bryan	Democrat; Populist	6,356,734	46.0	155	
		John C. Wooley	Prohibition	208,914	1.5		
1904	45	**THEODORE ROOSEVELT**	REPUBLICAN	7,628,461	56.4	336	65.2
		Alton B. Parker	Democrat	5,084,223	37.6	140	
		Eugene V. Debs	Socialist	402,283	3.0		
		Silas C. Swallow	Prohibition	258,536	1.9		
1908	46	**WILLIAM H. TAFT**	REPUBLICAN	7,675,320	52.0	321	65.4
		William J. Bryan	Democrat	6,412,294	43.4	162	
		Eugene V. Debs	Socialist	420,793	2.8		
		Eugene W. Chafin	Prohibition	253,840	1.7		
1912	48	**WOODROW WILSON**	DEMOCRAT	6,296,547	41.9	435	58.8
		Theodore Roosevelt	Progressive	4,118,571	27.4	88	
		William H. Taft	Republican	3,486,720	23.2	8	
		Eugene V. Debs	Socialist	900,672	6.0		
		Eugene W. Chafin	Prohibition	206,275	1.4		
1916	48	**WOODROW WILSON**	DEMOCRAT	9,127,695	49.4	277	61.6
		Charles E. Hughes	Republican	8,533,507	46.2	254	
		A. L. Benson	Socialist	585,113	3.2		
		J. Frank Hanly	Prohibition	220,506	1.2		
1920	48	**WARREN G. HARDING**	REPUBLICAN	16,153,115	60.6	404	49.2
		James M. Cox	Democrat	9,133,092	34.3	127	
		Eugene V. Debs	Socialist	915,490	3.4		
		P. P. Christensen	Farmer-Labor	265,229	1.0		
1924	48	**CALVIN COOLIDGE**	REPUBLICAN	15,719,921	54.0	382	48.9
		John W. Davis	Democrat	8,386,704	29.0	136	
		Robert M. La Follette	Progressive	4,832,532	16.5	13	

Year	Number of States	Candidates	Parties	Popular Vote	% of Popular Vote	Electoral Vote	% Voter Participation
1928	48	**HERBERT C. HOOVER**	REPUBLICAN	21,437,277	58.2	444	56.9
		Alfred E. Smith	Democrat	15,007,698	40.9	87	
1932	48	**FRANKLIN D. ROOSEVELT**	DEMOCRAT	22,829,501	57.7	472	56.9
		Herbert C. Hoover	Republican	15,760,684	39.8	59	
		Norman Thomas	Socialist	884,649	2.2		
1936	48	**FRANKLIN D. ROOSEVELT**	DEMOCRAT	27,757,333	60.8	523	61.0
		Alfred M. Landon	Republican	16,684,231	36.6	8	
		William Lemke	Union	892,267	2.0		
1940	48	**FRANKLIN D. ROOSEVELT**	DEMOCRAT	27,313,041	54.9	449	62.5
		Wendell L. Willkie	Republican	22,348,480	44.9	82	
1944	48	**FRANKLIN D. ROOSEVELT**	DEMOCRAT	25,612,610	53.5	432	55.9
		Thomas E. Dewey	Republican	22,017,617	46.0	99	
1948	48	**HARRY S. TRUMAN**	DEMOCRAT	24,179,345	49.7	303	53.0
		Thomas E. Dewey	Republican	21,991,291	45.3	189	
		J. Strom Thurmond	States' Rights	1,176,125	2.4	39	
		Henry A. Wallace	Progressive	1,157,326	2.4		
1952	48	**DWIGHT D. EISENHOWER**	REPUBLICAN	33,936,234	55.1	442	63.3
		Adlai E. Stevenson	Democrat	27,314,992	44.4	89	

Year	Number of States	Candidates	Parties	Popular Vote	% of Popular Vote	Electoral Vote	% Voter Participation
1956	48	**DWIGHT D. EISENHOWER**	REPUBLICAN	35,590,472	57.6	457	60.6
		Adlai E. Stevenson	Democrat	26,022,752	42.1	73	
1960	50	**JOHN F. KENNEDY**	DEMOCRAT	34,226,731	49.7	303	62.8
		Richard M. Nixon	Republican	34,108,157	49.6	219	
1964	50	**LYNDON B. JOHNSON**	DEMOCRAT	43,129,566	61.0	486	61.9
		Barry M. Goldwater	Republican	27,178,188	38.4	52	
1968	50	**RICHARD M. NIXON**	REPUBLICAN	31,785,480	43.2	301	60.9
		Hubert H. Humphrey	Democrat	31,275,166	42.6	191	
		George C. Wallace	American Independent	9,906,473	12.9	46	
1972	50	**RICHARD M. NIXON**	REPUBLICAN	47,169,911	60.7	520	55.2
		George S. McGovern	Democrat	29,170,383	37.5	17	
		John G. Schmitz	American	1,099,482	1.4		
1976	50	**JIMMY CARTER**	DEMOCRAT	40,830,763	50.0	297	53.5
		Gerald R. Ford	Republican	39,147,793	48.0	240	
1980	50	**RONALD REAGAN**	REPUBLICAN	43,904,153	50.9	489	52.6
		Jimmy Carter	Democrat	35,483,883	41.1	49	
		John B. Anderson	Independent	5,720,060	6.6		
		Ed Clark	Libertarian	921,299	1.1		

Year	Number of States	Candidates	Parties	Popular Vote	% of Popular Vote	Electoral Vote	% Voter Participation
1984	50	**RONALD REAGAN**	REPUBLICAN	54,455,075	58.8	525	53.1
		Walter F. Mondale	Democrat	37,577,185	40.5	13	
1988	50	**GEORGE H. BUSH**	REPUBLICAN	48,886,097	53.4	426	50.1
		Michael Dukakis	Democrat	41,809,074	45.6	111	
1992	50	**BILL CLINTON**	DEMOCRAT	44,909,326	42.9	370	55.0
		George H. Bush	Republican	39,103,882	37.4	168	
		H. Ross Perot	Independent	19,741,657	18.9		
1996	50	**BILL CLINTON**	DEMOCRAT	47,402,357	49.2	379	49.0
		Bob Dole	Republican	39,198,755	40.7	159	
		H. Ross Perot	Reform Party	8,085,402	8.4		
2000	50	**GEORGE W. BUSH**	REPUBLICAN	50,455,156	47.9	271	50.4
		Albert Gore	Democrat	50,992,335	48.4	266	
		Ralph Nader	Green Party	2,882,738	2.7		
2004	50	**GEORGE W. BUSH**	REPUBLICAN	62,040,610	50.7	286	56.2
		John F. Kerry	Democrat	59,028,111	48.3	251	
2008	50	**BARACK H. OBAMA**	DEMOCRAT	66,882,230	52.9	365	56.8
		John S. McCain	Republican	58,343,671	45.7	173	
2012	50	**BARACK H. OBAMA**	DEMOCRAT	62,611,250	51.1	332	53.6
		W. Mitt Romney	Republican	59,134,475	47.2	206	
2016	50	**DONALD J. TRUMP**	REPUBLICAN	62,475,147	46.4	306	54
		Hillary Clinton	Democrat	64,777,890	48.1	232	

ADMISSION OF STATES

Order of Admission	State	Date of Admission	Order of Admission	State	Date of Admission
1	Delaware	December 7, 1787	26	Michigan	January 26, 1837
2	Pennsylvania	December 12, 1787	27	Florida	March 3, 1845
3	New Jersey	December 18, 1787	28	Texas	December 29, 1845
4	Georgia	January 2, 1788	29	Iowa	December 28, 1846
5	Connecticut	January 9, 1788	30	Wisconsin	May 29, 1848
6	Massachusetts	February 7, 1788	31	California	September 9, 1850
7	Maryland	April 28, 1788	32	Minnesota	May 11, 1858
8	South Carolina	May 23, 1788	33	Oregon	February 14, 1859
9	New Hampshire	June 21, 1788	34	Kansas	January 29, 1861
10	Virginia	June 25, 1788	35	West Virginia	June 30, 1863
11	New York	July 26, 1788	36	Nevada	October 31, 1864
12	North Carolina	November 21, 1789	37	Nebraska	March 1, 1867
13	Rhode Island	May 29, 1790	38	Colorado	August 1, 1876
14	Vermont	March 4, 1791	39	North Dakota	November 2, 1889
15	Kentucky	June 1, 1792	40	South Dakota	November 2, 1889
16	Tennessee	June 1, 1796	41	Montana	November 8, 1889
17	Ohio	March 1, 1803	42	Washington	November 11, 1889
18	Louisiana	April 30, 1812	43	Idaho	July 3, 1890
19	Indiana	December 11, 1816	44	Wyoming	July 10, 1890
20	Mississippi	December 10, 1817	45	Utah	January 4, 1896
21	Illinois	December 3, 1818	46	Oklahoma	November 16, 1907
22	Alabama	December 14, 1819	47	New Mexico	January 6, 1912
23	Maine	March 15, 1820	48	Arizona	February 14, 1912
24	Missouri	August 10, 1821	49	Alaska	January 3, 1959
25	Arkansas	June 15, 1836	50	Hawaii	August 21, 1959

POPULATION OF THE UNITED STATES

Year	Number of States	Population	% Increase	Population per Square Mile
1790	13	3,929,214		4.5
1800	16	5,308,483	35.1	6.1
1810	17	7,239,881	36.4	4.3
1820	23	9,638,453	33.1	5.5
1830	24	12,866,020	33.5	7.4
1840	26	17,069,453	32.7	9.8
1850	31	23,191,876	35.9	7.9
1860	33	31,443,321	35.6	10.6
1870	37	39,818,449	26.6	13.4
1880	38	50,155,783	26.0	16.9
1890	44	62,947,714	25.5	21.1
1900	45	75,994,575	20.7	25.6
1910	46	91,972,266	21.0	31.0
1920	48	105,710,620	14.9	35.6
1930	48	122,775,046	16.1	41.2
1940	48	131,669,275	7.2	44.2
1950	48	150,697,361	14.5	50.7
1960	50	179,323,175	19.0	50.6
1970	50	203,235,298	13.3	57.5
1980	50	226,504,825	11.4	64.0
1985	50	237,839,000	5.0	67.2
1990	50	250,122,000	5.2	70.6
1995	50	263,411,707	5.3	74.4
2000	50	281,421,906	6.8	77.0
2005	50	296,410,404	5.3	81.7
2010	50	308,745,538	4.2	87.4
2015	50	321,418,820	4.1	91.0

LABOR FORCE—SELECTED CHARACTERISTICS EXPRESSED AS A PERCENTAGE OF THE LABOR FORCE, 1800–2010

Year	Agriculture	Manufacturing	Domestic service	Clerical, sales, and service	Professions	Slave	Nonwhite	Foreign-born	Female
1800	74.4	—	2.4	—	—	30.2	32.6	—	21.4
1860	55.8	13.8	5.4	4.8[1]	3.0[1]	21.7	23.6	24.5[1]	19.6
1910	30.7	20.8	5.5	14.1	4.7	—	13.4	22.0	20.8
1950	12.0	26.4	2.5	27.3	8.9	—	10.0	8.7	27.9
2000	2.4	14.7	0.6	38.0[2]	15.6	—	16.5	10.3[2]	46.6
2010	1.6	10.1	1.6	40.2	22.2	—	18.7	15.8	46.7

[1]Values for 1870 are presented here because the available data for 1860 exclude slaves.
[2]1990.
Note: "Clerical, sales, and service" excludes domestic service.

IMMIGRATION, BY ORIGIN (in thousands)

Period	Europe	Americas	Asia
1820–30	106	12	—
1831–40	496	33	—
1841–50	1,597	62	—
1851–60	2,453	75	42
1861–70	2,065	167	65
1871–80	2,272	404	70
1881–90	4,735	427	70
1891–1900	3,555	39	75
1901–10	8,065	362	324
1911–20	4,322	1,144	247
1921–30	2,463	1,517	112
1931–40	348	160	16
1941–50	621	355	32
1951–60	1,326	997	150
1961–70	1,123	1,716	590
1971–80	800	1,983	1,588
1981–90	762	3,616	2,738
1991–2000	1,360	4,487	2,796
2001-10	1,318	4,478	3,621

UNEMPLOYMENT RATE, 1890–2015

UNION MEMBERSHIP AS A PERCENTAGE OF NONAGRICULTURAL EMPLOYMENT, 1880–2015

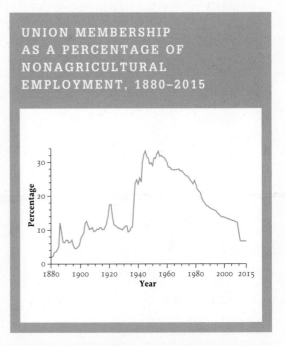

VOTER PARTICIPATION IN PRESIDENTIAL ELECTIONS, 1824–2016

BIRTHRATE, 1820–2015

SUGGESTED READING

CHAPTER 15: "WHAT IS FREEDOM?": RECONSTRUCTION, 1865–1877

Books

Bottoms, D. Michael. *An Aristocracy of Color: Race and Reconstruction in California and the West, 1850–1890* (2013). A study of changing race relations, and definitions of race, in the western states.

Butchart, Ronald E. *Schooling the Freed People: Teaching, Learning, and the Struggle for Black Freedom* (2010). Relates the efforts of black and white teachers to educate the former slaves and some of the conflicts that arose over the purposes of such education.

Downs, Gregory. *Declarations of Dependence: The Long Reconstruction of Popular Politics in the South, 1861–1908* (2011). Traces the changing ways black and white southerners sought aid and protection from the government during and after the Civil War and Reconstruction.

Downs, James. *Sick from Freedom: The Deadly Consequences of Emancipation* (2012). How disease shaped the experience of freedom and how the Freedmen's Bureau and other agencies sought to cope with widespread illness among former slaves.

DuBois, Ellen C. *Feminism and Suffrage: The Emergence of an Independent Women's Movement in America, 1848–1869* (1978). Explores how the split over the exclusion of women from the Fourteenth and Fifteenth Amendments gave rise to a movement for woman suffrage no longer tied to the abolitionist tradition.

Edwards, Laura. *Gendered Strife and Confusion: The Political Culture of Reconstruction* (1997). Considers how issues relating to gender relations affected the course of southern Reconstruction.

Fields, Barbara J. *Slavery and Freedom on the Middle Ground: Maryland during the Nineteenth Century* (1985). A study of slavery and emancipation in a key border state.

Foner, Eric. *Nothing but Freedom: Emancipation and Its Legacy* (1983). Includes a comparison of the emancipation experience in different parts of the Western Hemisphere.

Foner, Eric. *Reconstruction: America's Unfinished Revolution, 1863–1877* (1988). A comprehensive account of the Reconstruction era.

Hahn, Steven. *A Nation under Our Feet: Black Political Struggles in the Rural South from Slavery to the Great Migration* (2003). A detailed study of black political activism, stressing nationalist consciousness and emigration movements.

Hyman, Harold M. *A More Perfect Union: The Impact of the Civil War and Reconstruction on the Constitution* (1973). Analyzes how the laws and constitutional amendments of Reconstruction changed the Constitution and the rights of all Americans.

Jung, Moon-Ho. *Coolies and Cane: Race, Labor, and Sugar in the Age of Emancipation* (2006). Tells the story of Chinese laborers brought to work in the sugar fields after the end of slavery.

Litwack, Leon F. *Been in the Storm So Long: The Aftermath of Slavery* (1979). A detailed look at the immediate aftermath of the end of slavery and the variety of black and white responses to emancipation.

Rable, George C. *But There Was No Peace: The Role of Violence in the Politics of Reconstruction* (1984). The only full-scale study of violence in the Reconstruction South.

Richardson, Heather C. *West from Appomattox* (2007). An account that fully integrates the West into the history of the Reconstruction era.

Rodrigue, John C. *Reconstruction in the Cane Fields: From Slavery to Free Labor in Louisiana's Sugar Parishes, 1862–1880* (2001). A study of how an often-neglected part of the South experienced the aftermath of slavery.

Summers, Mark W. *Railroads, Reconstruction, and the Gospel of Prosperity: Aid under the Radical Republicans, 1865–1877* (1984). A detailed look at southern governments' efforts to promote economic development, and the political corruption that sometimes accompanied it.

Websites

After Slavery: Race, Labor, and Politics in the Post-Emancipation Carolinas: www.afterslavery.com

America's Reconstruction: People and Politics after the Civil War: www.digitalhistory.uh.edu/exhibits/reconstruction /index.html

The Andrew Johnson Impeachment Trial: www.law.umkc.edu/faculty/projects/ftrials/impeach/impeachmt.htm

Freedmen and Southern Society Project: www.history.umd.edu/Freedmen/

Freedmen's Bureau Online: http://www.freedmensbureau.com/

CHAPTER 16: AMERICA'S GILDED AGE, 1870–1890

Books

Bensel, Richard F. *The Political Economy of American Industrialization, 1877–1900* (2000). A study of the policies and political divisions that contributed to and resulted from the second industrial revolution.

Blackhawk, Ned. *Violence Over the Land: Indians and Empires in the Early American West* (2006). A history of the long conflict between Native Americans and the federal government for control of the trans-Mississippi West.

Deutsch, Sarah. *No Separate Refuge: Culture, Class, and Gender on the Anglo-Hispanic Frontier in the American Southwest, 1880–1940* (1987). A careful analysis of the changing experience of people of Hispanic origin in the Southwest during these years.

Fink, Leon. *Workingmen's Democracy: The Knights of Labor and American Politics* (1983). Examines the rise of the Knights of Labor and their forays into local politics in the mid-1880s.

Foster, Gaines. *Moral Reconstruction: Christian Lobbyists and the Federal Legislation of Morality, 1865–1920* (2002). Traces the rise of efforts to use the federal government to promote Protestant notions of moral behavior.

Freeberg, Ernest. *The Age of Edison: Electric Light and the Invention of Modern America* (2013). Explores the numerous ways electricity altered Americans' lives.

Hamalainen, Pekka. *The Comanche Empire* (2008). The rise and fall of Comanche domination over much of the southwestern United States.

Hofstadter, Richard. *Social Darwinism in American Thought* (1944). A classic study of a major tendency in American thought during the Gilded Age.

Jeffrey, Julie R. *Frontier Women: "Civilizing" the West? 1840–1880* (rev. ed., 1998). A study, based on letters and diaries, of the experience of women on the western frontier.

Kasson, Joy S. *Buffalo Bill's Wild West: Celebrity, Memory, and Popular History* (2000). An account of the popular theatrical production that helped to fix an image of the Wild West in the American imagination.

Morgan, H. Wayne. *From Hayes to McKinley: National Party Politics, 1877–1896* (1969). The standard narrative of national politics during these years.

Shannon, Fred A. *The Farmer's Last Frontier: Agriculture 1860–1897* (1945). Remains an excellent introduction to the experience of farmers in the last four decades of the nineteenth century.

Sproat, John G. *"The Best Men": Liberal Reformers in the Gilded Age* (1968). Traces the origins, outlook, and political impact of reformers dissatisfied with the corruption of national politics.

Thomas, John L. *Alternative Americas: Henry George, Edward Bellamy, Henry Demarest Lloyd and the Adversary Tradition* (1983). A thorough exposition of the thought of three critics of Gilded Age society.

Trachtenberg, Alan. *The Incorporation of America: Culture and Society in the Gilded Age* (1982). An influential survey of how economic change affected American life during the Gilded Age.

White, Richard. *Railroaded: The Transcontinentals and the Making of Modern America* (2011). A careful study of the building of the transcontinental railroad and how it epitomized the political corruption and financial mismanagement so widespread in the Gilded Age.

Websites

First-hand Accounts of California 1849–1900: http://memory.loc.gov/ammem/cbhtml/cbhome.html

Indian Peoples of the Northern Great Plains: http://arc.lib.montana.edu/indian-great-plains

The Dramas of Haymarket: www.chicagohistory.org/dramas/overview/over.htm

CHAPTER 17: FREEDOM'S BOUNADRIES, AT HOME AND ABROAD, 1890–1900

Books

Aleinikoff, Alexander. *Semblances of Sovereignty: The Constitution, the State, and American Citizenship* (2002). Includes a careful discussion of the citizenship status of American minorities and residents of overseas possessions.

Blight, David. *Race and Reunion: The Civil War in American Memory* (2001). Examines how a memory of the Civil War that downplayed the issue of slavery played a part in sectional reconciliation and the rise of segregation.

Blum, Edward. *Reforging the White Republic: Race, Religion, and American Nationalism, 1865–1898* (2005). Explores the development of a shared religious culture that united northern and southern Protestants in support of white supremacy and overseas expansion.

Factor, Robert L. *The Black Response to America: Men, Ideals, and Organization from Frederick Douglass to the NAACP* (1970). Discusses black social and political thought, including that of Booker T. Washington and his critics.

Goodwyn, Lawrence. *The Populist Moment: A Short History of the Agrarian Revolt in America* (1978). A sympathetic account of the rise and fall of Populism.

Higginbotham, Evelyn. *Righteous Discontent: The Women's Movement in the Black Baptist Church, 1880–1920* (1993). Explains how black women developed ways of exerting their influence in public life even as black men were losing the right to vote.

Hoganson, Kristin L. *Consumers' Imperium: The Global Production of American Domesticity, 1865–1920* (2007). Shows how the consumer desires of middle-class women helped to spur the consolidation of an American empire.

Hsu, Madeline. *Dreaming of Gold, Dreaming of Home: Transnationalism and Migration between the United States and South China, 1882–1934* (2000). Examines the enduring connections between Chinese immigrants in the United States and their home communities.

Krause, Paul. *The Battle for Homestead, 1880–1892: Politics, Culture, and Steel* (1992). An account of the era's most celebrated conflict between capital and labor.

LaFeber, Walter. *The New Empire: An Interpretation of American Expansion, 1860–1898* (1963). A classic examination of the forces that led the United States to acquire an overseas empire.

Lake, Marilyn, and Henry Reynolds. *Drawing the Global Color Line* (2008). Traces the global transmission of ideas about white supremacy in the late nineteenth century.

Linn, Brian M. *The Philippine War, 1899–1902* (2000). A detailed history of America's "forgotten war."

McClain, Charles J. *In Search of Equality: The Chinese Struggle against Discrimination in Nineteenth-Century America* (1994). Explores how Chinese-Americans worked to combat the discrimination to which they were subjected and to assert their rights.

McMillen, Neil R. *Dark Journey: Black Mississippians in the Age of Jim Crow* (1989). A powerful account of black life in the segregation era and the boundaries within which it operated.

Perez, Louis A. *The War of 1898: The United States and Cuba in History and Historiography* (1998). Presents the Cuban side of the Spanish-American War, including a detailed discussion of the Cuban movement for independence and how American intervention affected it.

Postel, Charles. *The Populist Vision* (2007). A history of the Populist movement that stresses how it anticipated many public policies of the twentieth century.

Sanders, Elizabeth. *Roots of Reform: Farmers, Workers, and the American State, 1877–1917* (1999). Emphasizes the role of farmers' movements in putting forth many of the proposals associated with political reform in the late nineteenth and early twentieth centuries.

Woodward, C. Vann. *Origins of the New South, 1877–1913* (1951). A classic treatment of the New South, emphasizing how its rulers failed to meet the needs of most southerners, white as well as black.

Websites

1896: The Presidential Campaign: http://projects.vassar.edu/1896/1896home.html

The Chinese in California, 1850–1920: http://bancroft.berkeley.edu/collections/chineseinca

The Rise and Fall of Jim Crow: www.pbs.org/wnet/jimcrow

The World of 1898: The Spanish-American War: www.loc.gov/rr/hispanic/1898

CHAPTER 18: THE PROGRESSIVE ERA, 1900–1916

Books

Bodnar, John. *The Transplanted: A History of Immigrants in Urban America* (1985). A comprehensive account of American immigration.

Cott, Nancy F. *The Grounding of Modern Feminism* (1987). A careful study of feminist ideas in the Progressive era.

Dawley, Alan. *Struggles for Justice: Social Responsibility and the Liberal State* (1991). Examines the varieties of Progressive reform and various efforts to use the power of government for social betterment.

Diner, Steven. *A Very Different Age: Americans of the Progressive Era* (1998). A survey of the main trends of the Progressive period.

Glickman, Lawrence B. *A Living Wage: Workers and the Making of American Consumer Society* (1997). Traces the origins and development of the idea that workers are entitled to a "living wage."

Hofstadter, Richard. *The Age of Reform: From Bryan to F.D.R.* (1955). A classic account of the ideas of reformers from Populism to the New Deal.

Johnston, Robert D. *The Radical Middle Class: Populist Democracy and the Question of Capitalism in Progressive Era Portland* (2003). Analyzes how Progressivism operated in one important city.

Lears, Jackson. *Rebirth of a Nation: The Making of Modern America, 1877–1920* (2009). A comprehensive history of the Gilded Age and Progressive era, stressing the extent of social and cultural change.

Montgomery, David. *The Fall of the House of Labor: The Workplace, the State, and American Labor Activism, 1865–1925* (1987). An account of the labor battles of the era and the gradual decline of labor's power, especially at the workplace.

Orsi, Robert A. *The Madonna of 115th Street: Faith and Community in Italian Harlem, 1880–1950* (1985). An influential study of a single immigrant community and the role of religion in binding it together.

Peiss, Kathy. *Cheap Amusements: Working Women and Leisure in Turn-of-the-Century New York* (1986). Explores the rise of mass entertainment and how it affected women's lives in Progressive America.

Recchiuti, John L. *Civic Engagement: Social Science and Progressive-Era Reform in New York City* (2006). Examines the influence of a group of reform-minded scholars on the politics of the Progressive era.

Rodgers, Daniel T. *Atlantic Crossings: Social Politics in a Progressive Age* (1998). A comprehensive study of the flow of Progressive ideas and policies back and forth across the Atlantic.

Stansell, Christine. *American Moderns: Bohemian New York and the Creation of a New Century* (2000). A colorful account of the Greenwich Village radicals who expanded the idea of personal freedom in the Progressive era.

Stromquist, Shelton. *Re-Inventing "The People": The Progressive Movement, the Class Problem, and the Origins of Modern Liberalism* (2006). Discusses how the desire to re-create social harmony in an age of labor conflict shaped Progressivism.

Tichi, Cecelia. *Civic Passions: Seven Who Launched Progressive America* (2009). An exploration of the careers of some of the most prominent leaders of Progressive reform.

Websites

Evolution of the Conservation Movement, 1860–1920: http://lcweb2.loc.gov/ammem/amrvhtml/conshome.html

Immigration to the United States, 1789–1930: http://ocp.hul.harvard.edu/immigration/

Triangle Shirtwaist Factory Fire: www.ilr.cornell.edu/trianglefire/

Urban Experience in Chicago: Hull House and Its Neighborhoods: http://hullhouse.uic.edu/hull/urbanexp

Votes for Women: http://memory.loc.gov/ammem/naw/nawshome.html

CHAPTER 19: SAFE FOR DEMOCRACY: THE UNITED STATES AND WORLD WAR I, 1916–1920

Books

Bederman, Gail. *Manliness and Civilization: A Cultural History of Race and Gender in the United States, 1880–1917* (1995). Explores how ideas concerning civilization and gender affected American foreign policy.

Capozzola, Christopher. *Uncle Sam Wants You: World War I and the Making of the Modern American Citizen* (2008). A careful study of public and private efforts to enforce patriotic ideas and actions during World War I.

Dawley, Alan. *Changing the World: American Progressives in War and Revolution* (2003). Presents the war as a fulfillment and betrayal of the Progressive impulse.

Gilmore, Glenda E. *Gender and Jim Crow: Women and the Politics of White Supremacy in North Carolina, 1896–1920* (1996). A careful study of how black and white women negotiated the boundaries of segregation in a southern state.

Green, Elna C. *Southern Strategies: Southern Women and the Woman Suffrage Question* (1997). Describes how southern women campaigned for the vote without challenging the subordinate status of African-Americans.

Greene, Julie. *The Canal Builders: Making American Empire at the Panama Canal* (2009). Tells the story of the construction of the Panama Canal and the tens of thousands of workers who did the work.

Grossman, James R. *Land of Hope: Chicago, Black Southerners, and the Great Migration* (1989). An in-depth study of the migration of blacks to one American city.

Healy, David. *Drive to Hegemony: The United States in the Caribbean, 1898–1917* (1988). Examines American foreign policy in the Caribbean from McKinley to Wilson.

Jensen, Kimberly. *Mobilizing Minerva: American Women in the First World War* (2008). Examines the participation of women in the war effort and its impact on gender relations.

Kennedy, David M. *Over Here: The First World War and American Society* (1980). A comprehensive account of how the war affected domestic life in the United States.

Manela, Erez. *The Wilsonian Moment* (2007). Details how the Wilsonian ideal of self-determination was received around the world, with results Wilson did not anticipate.

Meier, August. *Negro Thought in America, 1880–1915* (1966). A pioneering study of the ideas of black leaders, including W. E. B. Du Bois.

Mitchell, David J. *1919: Red Mirage* (1970). A global account of the upheavals of 1919.

Preston, William, Jr. *Aliens and Dissenters: Federal Suppression of Radicals, 1903–1933* (1963). An influential study of the federal government's efforts to suppress dissenting ideas, especially during and immediately after World War I.

Renda, Mary A. *Taking Haiti: Military Occupation and the Culture of U.S. Imperialism, 1915–1940* (2001). Examines the causes and consequences of the American occupation of Haiti.

Stein, Judith. *The World of Marcus Garvey: Race and Class in Modern Society* (1986). Places the Garvey movement in an Atlantic perspective linking Africa, the United States, and the West Indies.

Sullivan, Patricia. *Lift Every Voice: The NAACP and the Making of the Civil Rights Movement* (2009). A sweeping history of the country's preeminent civil rights organization, from its founding to the 1950s.

Tuttle, William. *Race Riot: Chicago in the Red Summer of 1919* (1970). A vivid account of the most violent racial upheaval of the era.

Websites

Red Scare: http://newman.baruch.cuny.edu/digital/redscare/

The Bisbee Deportation of 1917: www.library.arizona.edu/exhibits/bisbee/

The U.S.A. and Latin America: www.casahistoria.net/uslatam.htm

CHAPTER 20: FROM BUSINESS CULTURE TO GREAT DEPRESSION: THE TWENTIES, 1920–1932

Books

Boyle, Kevin. *Arc of Justice: A Saga of Race, Civil Rights, and Murder in the Jazz Age* (2004). A history of the Sweet case, placing it in the context of postwar Detroit and the nation.

Cohen, Warren I. *Empire without Tears: America's Foreign Relations, 1921–1933* (1987). A careful examination of American foreign policy between the presidencies of Wilson and Roosevelt.

Dumenil, Lynn. *The Modern Temper: America in the Twenties* (1995). A brief survey of the main political and cultural trends of the decade.

Garraty, John A. *The Great Depression* (1986). Places the Depression in a global context and compares various governments' responses to it.

Gerstle, Gary. *American Crucible: Race and Nation in the Twentieth Century* (2002). A sweeping survey of how changing ideas of race have affected the concept of American nationality, with a strong account of the debates of the 1920s.

Grandin, Greg. *Fordlandia: The Rise and Fall of Henry Ford's Forgotten Jungle City* (2009). Tells the fascinating story of Ford's effort to create a planned community in Brazil's Amazon rain forest.

Higham, John. *Strangers in the Land: Patterns of American Nativism, 1860–1925* (1955). A classic account of American hostility to immigrants, concluding with the immigration restriction of 1924.

Larson, Edward. *Summer for the Gods: The Scopes Trial and America's Continuing Debate over Science and Religion* (1998). A history of the famous trial and the enduring debate over evolution.

Lewis, David L. *When Harlem Was in Vogue* (1981). A lively account of the Harlem Renaissance of the 1920s.

Maclean, Nancy. *Behind the Mask of Chivalry: The Making of the Second Ku Klux Klan* (1994). A careful analysis of the membership and motivations of the Ku Klux Klan of the 1920s.

Marchand, Roland. *Advertising the American Dream: Making Way for Modernity, 1920–1940* (1985). Examines how advertisers responded to and helped to shape changes in American life between the two world wars.

Marsden, George M. *Fundamentalism and American Culture: The Shaping of Twentieth-Century Evangelicism, 1870–1925* (1980). Traces the ups and downs of American fundamentalism, culminating in the Scopes trial.

McGirr, Lisa. *The War on Alcohol: Prohibition and the Rise of the American State* (2015). A penetrating analysis of Prohibition's impact on American society and government.

Murphy, Paul L. *World War I and the Origin of Civil Liberties in the United States* (1979). An analysis of how the repression of free speech during World War I paved the way for a heightened awareness of the importance of civil liberties.

Ngai, Mae. *Impossible Subjects: Illegal Aliens and the Making of Modern America* (2004). An influential examination of immigration policy toward Mexicans and Asians, and the development of the legal category of "illegal alien."

Ross, William G. *Forging New Freedoms: Nativism, Education, and the Constitution, 1917–1927* (1994). Discusses battles over cultural pluralism in the 1920s and how they laid the groundwork for an expanded definition of personal liberty.

Websites

Chicago and the Great Migration: www.loc.gov/exhibits/african/afam011.html

Emergence of Advertising in America: http://library.duke.edu/digitalcollections/eaa/

Prosperity and Thrift: The Coolidge Era and the Consumer Economy: http://memory.loc.gov/ammem/coolhtml /coolhome.html

Scopes Trial: http://law2.umkc.edu/faculty/projects/ftrials/scopes/scopes.htm

CHAPTER 21: THE NEW DEAL, 1932–1940

Books

Blackwelder, Julia Kirk. *Women of the Depression* (1998). Examines how female members of three communities—Anglo, Mexican-American, and black—coped with the Great Depression.

Brinkley, Alan. *Voices of Protest: Huey Long, Father Coughlin, and the Great Depression* (1982). An account of the political careers of two key figures of the New Deal era and their influence on national events.

Carpenter, Joel A. *Revive Us Again: The Reawakening of American Fundamentalism* (1999). Shows how evangelicals adapted to the Depression and used mass communications to spread their message.

Cohen, Lizabeth. *Making a New Deal: Industrial Workers in Chicago, 1919–1939* (1990). Describes how the assimilation of immigrants and their children paved the way for the creation of the New Deal political coalition.

Denning, Michael. *The Cultural Front: The Laboring of American Culture in the Twentieth Century* (1996). A comprehensive account of the rise of cultural activity associated with the political left and the New Deal.

Egan, Timothy. *The Worst Hard Time* (2006). A social history of the Dust Bowl during the Depression, including the stories of victims and survivors.

Katznelson, Ira. *Fear Itself: The New Deal and the Origins of Our Time* (2013). Examines the shaping of New Deal policy and especially the compromises Roosevelt had to make to get measures through a Congress dominated by segregationist members from the South.

Kessler-Harris, Alice. *In Pursuit of Equity: Men, Women, and the Quest for Economic Citizenship in 20th-Century America* (2001). Explores how assumptions regarding the proper roles of men and women helped to shape New Deal measures such as Social Security.

Kirby, Jack T. *Rural Worlds Lost: The American South, 1920–1960* (1987). Traces the transformation of the South in these four decades, with emphasis on how the New Deal affected the southern states.

Leuchtenberg, William E. *Franklin D. Roosevelt and the New Deal, 1932–1940* (1963). Still the standard one-volume account of Roosevelt's first two terms as president.

Naison, Mark. *Communists in Harlem during the Depression* (1983). Examines the rise and decline of the Communist Party in a center of black life, and its impact on the movement for racial justice.

Phillips, Sarah T. *The Land, This Nation: Conservation, Rural America, and the New Deal* (2007). Examines New Deal policies regarding agricultural development, rural conservation, and land use, and its attempt to modernize and uplift rural life.

Sanchez, George. *Becoming Mexican American: Ethnicity, Culture, and Identity in Chicano Los Angeles, 1900–1945* (1995). A careful study of Mexican-Americans in Los Angeles, including their participation in the social unrest of the 1930s and the movement for deporting them during that decade.

Smith, Jason B. *Building New Deal Liberalism: The Political Economy of Public Works* (2006). Places the great construction projects of the 1930s at the center of New Deal economic policy.

Sullivan, Patricia. *Days of Hope: Race and Democracy in the New Deal Era* (1996). Analyzes how the New Deal inspired the emergence of a biracial movement for civil rights in the South.

Williams, Mason B. *City of Ambition: FDR, La Guardia, and the Making of Modern New York* (2014). An illuminating study of the most prominent "little New Deal" and its long-term results.

Zieger, Robert H. *The CIO, 1935–1955* (1995). A comprehensive history of the Congress of Industrial Organizations, the major labor group to emerge during the New Deal.

Websites

America from the Great Depression to World War II: http://memory.loc.gov/ammem/fsowhome.html

FDR Cartoon Archive: www.nisk.k12.ny.us/fdr/FDRcartoons.html

Flint Sit-Down Strike: www.historicalvoices.org/flint/

New Deal Network: http://newdeal.feri.org

CHAPTER 22: FIGHTING FOR THE FOUR FREEDOMS: WORLD WAR II, 1941–1945

Books

Ambrose, Stephen E. *Citizen Soldiers* (1997). Discusses the experience of American soldiers fighting in Europe from D-Day to the end of the war.

Anderson, Karen. *Wartime Women: Sex Roles, Family Relations, and the Status of Women during World War II* (1981). Explores how the experience of World War II opened new opportunities for women and challenged existing gender conventions.

Blum, John M. *V Was for Victory: Politics and American Culture during World War II* (1976). A comprehensive account of the home front during World War II.

Borgwardt, Elizabeth. *A New Deal for the World: America's Vision for Human Rights* (2005). The emergence during the war of the idea of human rights as an international entitlement.

Brinkley, Alan. *The End of Reform: New Deal Liberalism in Recession and War* (1995). Describes how liberals' ideas and policies moved away, during the late New Deal and the war, from combating inequalities of economic power.

Daniels, Rogers. *Prisoners without Trial: Japanese Americans in World War II* (1993). A brief history of the internment of Japanese-Americans during the war.

Dower, John W. *War without Mercy: Race and Power in the Pacific War* (1986). Explores how racial fears and antagonisms motivated both sides in the Pacific theater.

Escobedo, Elizabeth R. *From Coveralls to Zoot Suits: The Lives of Mexican American Women on the World War II Home Front* (2013). Examines how the rise of racial liberalism during World War II and the opening of new jobs affected Mexican-American women.

Frydl, Kathleen. *The G.I. Bill* (2009). How this important piece of legislation changed American society.

Isserman, Maurice. *Which Side Were You On? The American Communist Party during World War II* (1982). Traces the Communist Party's changing political positions during World War II.

Kennedy, David M. *Freedom from Fear: The American People in Depression and War, 1929–1945* (1999). A detailed and lively account of American history from the Great Depression through the end of World War II.

Lichtenstein, Nelson. *Labor's War at Home: The CIO in World War II* (1982). Examines the war's impact on workers and the labor movement.

Rhodes, Richard. *The Making of the Atomic Bomb* (1986). A dramatic account of how the atomic bomb was created.

Von Eschen, Penny. *Race against Empire: Black Americans and Anticolonialism, 1937–1957* (1997). Examines how black Americans responded to the rise of movements for colonial independence overseas during and after World War II.

Zelizer, Julian E. *Arsenal of Democracy: The Politics of National Security—From World War II to the War on Terrorism* (2009). Traces the origins of the national security state from Roosevelt's "arsenal of democracy" speech of 1940 to the present, stressing the tension between the two elements, arsenal and democracy.

Websites

A More Perfect Union: Japanese Americans and the U.S. Constitution: http://amhistory.si.edu/perfectunion/experience/

A People at War: www.archives.gov/exhibits/a_people_at_war/a_people_at_war.html

Bittersweet Harvest: The Bracero Program 1942–1964: http://americanhistory.si.edu/exhibitions/bittersweet-harvest
-bracero-program-1942-1964

Remembering Nagasaki: www.exploratorium.edu/nagasaki/

CHAPTER 23: THE UNITED STATES AND THE COLD WAR, 1945–1953

Books

Biondi, Martha. *To Stand and Fight: The Struggle for Civil Rights in Postwar New York City* (2003). A comprehensive account of the broad coalition that battled for racial justice in New York City, in areas such as jobs, education, and housing.

Canaday, Margot. *The Straight State: Sexuality and Citizenship in Twentieth-Century America* (2009). Details the federal government's efforts to stigmatize and punish homosexuality.

Cullather, Nick. *The Hungry World: America's Cold War Battle Against Poverty in Asia* (2010). Explores how divergent approaches to combating world poverty became a battleground in the Cold War.

Donovan, Robert. *Conflict and Crisis: The Presidency of Harry S. Truman, 1945–1948* (1977). A careful account of Truman's first administration and his surprising election victory in 1948.

Dudziak, Mary L. *Cold War Civil Rights: Race and the Image of American Democracy* (2000). Analyzes how the Cold War influenced and in some ways encouraged the civil rights movement at home.

Gaddis, John. *Strategies of Containment: A Critical Analysis of Postwar American National Security* (1982). An influential analysis of the development of the containment policy central to American foreign policy during the Cold War.

Glendon, Mary Ann. *A World Made New: Eleanor Roosevelt and the Universal Declaration of Human Rights* (2001). Relates the drafting of the Universal Declaration of Human Rights and the response of governments around the world, including the United States.

Hogan, Michael. *The Marhsall Plan* (1987). A detailed look at a pillar of early Cold War policy.

Hunt, Michael. *Ideology and U.S. Foreign Policy* (1987). Discusses how ideas, including the idea of freedom, have shaped America's interactions with the rest of the world.

Leffler, Melvyn P. *A Preponderance of Power: National Security, the Truman Administration, and the Cold War* (1992). An influential account of the origins of the Cold War.

Lipsitz, George. *Rainbow at Midnight: Labor and Culture in the 1940s* (1994). Examines the labor movement and its role in American life in the decade of perhaps its greatest influence.

Saunders, Frances S. *The Cultural Cold War: The CIA and the World of Arts and Letters* (2000). Describes how the CIA and other government agencies secretly funded artists and writers as part of the larger Cold War.

Schrecker, Ellen. *Many Are the Crimes: McCarthyism in America* (1998). A full account of the anticommunist crusade at home and its impact on American intellectual and social life.

Stueck, William. *The Korean War: An International History* (1995). Studies the Korean War in its full global context.

Sugrue, Thomas. *Origins of the Urban Crisis: Race and Inequality in Postwar Detroit* (1996). Explores race relations in a key industrial city after World War II and how they set the stage for the upheavals of the 1960s.

Websites

Cold War International History Project: www.wilsoncenter.org/program/cold-war-international-history-project

The Korean War and its Origins, 1945–1953: www.trumanlibrary.org/korea/

CHAPTER 24: AN AFFLUENT SOCIETY, 1953–1960

Books

Branch, Taylor. *Parting the Waters: America in the King Years, 1954–1963* (1988). A comprehensive account of the civil rights movement from the *Brown* decision to the early 1960s.

Cohen, Lizabeth. *A Consumer's Republic: The Politics of Mass Consumption in Postwar America* (2003). Considers how the glorification of consumer freedom shaped American public policy and the physical landscape.

De Grazia, Victoria. *Irresistible Empire: America's Advance through Twentieth-Century Europe* (2005). An examination of American "soft power" and its triumphant penetration of twentieth-century Europe.

Fones-Wolf, Elizabeth A. *Selling Free Enterprise: The Business Assault on Labor and Liberalism, 1945–1960* (1994). Examines the carefully developed campaign whereby business leaders associated capitalism and a union-free workplace with freedom.

Freeman, Joshua B. *Working-Class New York: Life and Labor since World War II* (2000). An account of the lives of laborers in the nation's largest city, tracing the rise and decline of the labor movement.

Inboden, William. *Religion and American Foreign Policy, 1945–1960: The Soul of Containment* (2008). How religious groups influenced American diplomacy at the height of the Cold War.

Jackson, Kenneth T. *Crabgrass Frontier: The Suburbanization of America* (1985). The standard account of the development of American suburbia.

Jacobs, Meg. *Pocketbook Politics: Economic Citizenship in Twentieth-Century America* (2005). Discusses how consumer freedom became central to Americans' national identity after World War II.

Klarman, Michael J. *From Jim Crow to Civil Rights: The Supreme Court and the Struggle for Racial Equality* (2004). A full study of Supreme Court cases dealing with civil rights, and how they both reflected and helped to stimulate social change.

Klein, Jennifer. *For All These Rights: Business, Labor, and the Shaping of America's Public-Private Welfare State* (2003). Examines the development of the "social contract" of the 1950s whereby many workers received social benefits from their employers rather than the government.

May, Elaine T. *Homeward Bound: American Families in the Cold War Era* (1988). Studies the nuclear family as a bastion of American freedom during the Cold War, at least according to official propaganda.

Nicolaides, Becky M. *My Blue Heaven: Life and Politics in the Working-Class Suburbs of Los Angeles, 1920–1965* (2002). Traces the transformation of Southgate, an industrial neighborhood of Los Angeles, into an all-white suburb, and the political results.

Patterson, James T. *Grand Expectations: The United States, 1945–1974* (1996). A comprehensive account of American history over the three decades following World War II.

Pells, Richard. *The Liberal Mind in a Conservative Age: American Intellectuals in the 1940s and 1950s* (1984). Examines how American writers and artists responded to the Cold War.

Phillips-Fein, Kim. *Invisible Hands: The Making of the Conservative Movement from the New Deal to Reagan* (2009). Relates how a group of economic thinkers and businessmen worked to fashion a conservative movement in an attempt to reverse many of the policies of the New Deal.

Wall, Wendy L. *Inventing the "American Way": The Politics of Consensus from the New Deal to the Civil Rights Movement* (2008). A careful examination of the political and ideological world of the Cold War era.

Westad, Odd Arne. *The Global Cold War* (2005). A wide-ranging analysis of how the Cold War played out in the Third World.

Websites

Brown v. Board of Education: www.lib.umich.edu/brown-versus-board-education/

Herblock's History: Political Cartoons from the Crash to the Millennium: www.loc.gov/rr/print/swann/herblock/

CHAPTER 25: THE SIXTIES, 1960–1968

Books

Anderson, John A., III. *The Other Side of the Sixties: Young Americans for Freedom and the Rise of Conservative Politics* (1997). Considers conservative students of the 1960s and how they laid the groundwork for the later growth of their movement.

Appy, Christian G. *Working-Class War: American Combat Soldiers and Vietnam* (1993). A careful account of how the draft operated to place the burden of fighting on working-class Americans.

Brick, Howard. *Age of Contradiction: American Thought and Culture in the 1960s* (1998). A careful examination of the complex currents of thought that circulated during the decade.

Carson, Clayborne. *In Struggle: SNCC and the Black Awakening of the 1960s* (1981). A study of the Student Nonviolent Coordinating Committee and its impact on the 1960s.

D'Emilio, John. *Sexual Politics, Sexual Communities: The Making of a Homosexual Minority in the United States, 1940–1970* (1983). Explores the status of gay men and lesbians in mid-twentieth-century America and the rise of the gay movement.

Dierenfield, Bruce. *The Battle over School Prayer: How* Engel v. Vitale *Changed America* (2007). One controversial Supreme Court decision of the 1960s and its long-term consequences.

Dittmer, John. *Local People: The Struggle for Civil Rights in Mississippi* (1994). Traces the civil rights movement in one state, looked at from the experience of grassroots activists.

Horwitz, Morton J. *The Warren Court and the Pursuit of Justice* (1998). Analyzes how the Supreme Court redefined the rights of Americans under Chief Justice Earl Warren.

Isserman, Maurice, and Michael Kazin. *America Divided: The Civil War of the 1960s* (2000). A comprehensive account of the social movements and political debates of the 1960s.

Joseph, Peniel E. *Waiting 'Til the Midnight Hour: A Narrative History of Black Power in America* (2007). Demonstrates how the rise of Black Power reconfigured both African-American identity and race relations in the late 1960s.

Logevall, Frederik. *Embers of War: The Fall of an Empire and the Making of America's Vietnam* (2102). An international account of the origins of American military intervention in Vietnam.

McCartin, James P. *Prayers of the Faithful: The Shifting Spiritual Life of American Catholics* (2010). Examines the impact of the 1960s on the Catholic Church.

Rosen, Ruth. *The World Split Open: How the Modern Women's Movement Changed America* (2000). Considers how the "second wave" of feminism transformed the lives of American women and men.

Sale, Kirkpatrick. *The Green Revolution: The American Environmental Movement, 1962–1992* (1993). A brief history of one of the most significant movements to emerge from the 1960s.

Skretny, John. *The Minority Rights Revolution* (2002). An account of the rights revolution and how it affected American society and its understanding of the rights of citizens.

Websites

A Visual Journey: Photographs by Lisa Law, 1965–1971: http://americanhistory.si.edu/lisalaw/1.htm

Free Speech Movement Digital Archive: http://bancroft.berkeley.edu/FSM/

Freedom Now!: http://cds.library.brown.edu/projects/FreedomNow

CHAPTER 26: THE TRIUMPH OF CONSERVATISM, 1969–1988

Books

Adler, William M. *Mollie's Job: A Story of Life and Work on the Global Assembly Line* (2000). Tracks how a manufacturing job moved from the North to the South and eventually out of the country, and what happened to the workers who held it.

Allitt, Patrick. *Religion in America since 1945* (2003). A survey of the main trends of religious development since World War II.

Anderson, Terry H. *The Pursuit of Fairness: A History of Affirmative Action* (2004). A careful study of the origins and development of affirmative action policies.

Busch, Andrew E. *Ronald Reagan and the Politics of Freedom* (2001). Discusses how Ronald Reagan interpreted the idea of freedom and how it influenced his presidency.

Foley, Michael S. *Front Porch Politics: The Forgotten Heyday of American Activism in the 1970s and 1980s* (2013). A lively account of the grassroots movements, of both left and right, that followed the 1960s.

Greenberg, David. *Nixon's Shadow: The History of an Image* (2003). Explores how Nixon's supporters and enemies thought about him during his long political career.

Kruse, Kevin. *White Flight: Atlanta and the Making of Modern Conservatism* (2005). Explores how conservative politics took root in the predominantly white suburbs of Atlanta, with implications for similar communities across the country.

Kutler, Stanley I. *The Wars of Watergate: The Last Crisis of Richard Nixon* (1990). The most thorough analysis of the Watergate scandal that brought down President Nixon.

Luker, Kristin. *Abortion and the Politics of Motherhood* (1984). Describes how the abortion issue affected American politics and the ideas about gender relations that lay behind the debate.

Mathews, Donald G., and Jane S. De Hart. *Sex, Gender, and the Politics of ERA* (1990). An in-depth examination of the debate over the Equal Rights Amendment and why its opponents were successful.

McGirr, Lisa. *Suburban Warriors: The Origins of the New American Right* (2001). An influential study of the rise of conservatism in Orange County, California, once one of its more powerful centers.

Moreton, Bethany. *To Serve God and Wal-Mart: The Making of Christian Free Enterprise* (2009). Explores how the nation's largest employer drew on evangelical Christianity to justify its often-criticized labor policies.

Moyn, Samuel. *The Last Utopia: Human Rights in History* (2010). Traces the development of human rights consciousness, with special emphasis on the 1970s.

Schulman, Bruce J. *The Seventies: The Great Shift in American Culture, Society, and Politics* (2001). A survey of the numerous political, social, and economic changes that took place during the 1970s.

Self, Robert. *All in the Family: The Realignment of American Democracy Since the 1960s* (2013). Identifies changes in the role of women and the structure of the family as key issues in the rise of modern conservative politics.

Stein, Judith. *Pivotal Decade: How the United States Traded Factories for Finance in the Seventies* (2010). A careful analysis of the economic transformations of the 1970s.

Wilentz, Sean. *The Age of Reagan: A History, 1974–2008* (2008). Explores how Ronald Reagan set the terms of public debate during and after his presidency.

Websites

National Security Archive: http://nsarchive.gwu.edu

Watergate: http://watergate.info/

CHAPTER 27: FROM TRIUMPH TO TRAGEDY, 1989–2001

Books

Ash, Timothy Garton. *History of the Present: Essays, Sketches, and Dispatches from Europe in the 1990s* (2009). An account of the decade by a perceptive European commentator.

Brands, H. W. *The Strange Death of American Liberalism* (2001). Explores how liberals' discrediting of the federal government through their criticisms of the Vietnam War and Watergate paved the way for the triumph of antigovernment conservatism.

Cassidy, John. *Dot.con* (2002). Describes the rise and fall of the "new economy."

Christianson, Scott. *With Liberty for Some: 500 Years of Imprisonment in America* (1998). A full-scale study of the history of imprisonment in the United States and its recent dramatic expansion.

Foner, Nancy. *From Ellis Island to JFK: New York's Two Great Waves of Immigration* (2000). Studies the new immigration of the 1980s and 1990s and considers how it does and does not differ from earlier waves of newcomers.

Friedman, Thomas L. *The Lexus and the Olive Tree* (1999). An influential account of globalization and its economic promise.

Hodgson, Godfrey. *More Equal than Others: America from Nixon to the New Century* (2004). A survey of recent American history that identifies growing inequality as a major trend of these years.

Johnson, Haynes. *The Best of Times: America in the Clinton Years* (2001). A sympathetic account of Clinton's presidency.

Katz, Michael B. *The Price of Citizenship: Redefining the American Welfare State* (2001). Presents the history of welfare policy, with attention to the origins and impact of Clinton's welfare reform.

Levitas, Daniel. *The Terrorist Next Door: The Militia Movement and the Radical Right* (2003). A careful study of right-wing extremism of the 1990s.

Lichtenstein, Nelson. *The Retail Revolution: How Wal-Mart Created a Brave New World of Business* (2009). How Wal-Mart became the largest employer in the United States and one of the most profitable.

Phillips, Kevin. *Wealth and Democracy* (2002). A critique of the influence of money on American politics.

Power, Samantha. *A Problem from Hell: America and the Age of Genocide* (2002). Discusses genocides of the 1990s and the problem of the appropriate American response.

Roberts, Sam. *Who We Are Now: The Changing Face of America in the Twenty-First Century* (2004). A social portrait of the American people based on the 2000 Census.

Smelser, Neil J., and Jeffrey C. Alexander. *Diversity and Its Discontents: Cultural Conflict and Common Ground in Contemporary American Society* (1999). Describes the new social diversity of the 1990s and the cultural and political tensions arising from it.

Spence, Michael. *The Next Convergence: The Future of Economic Growth in a Multispeed World* (2011). A Nobel Prize–winning economist examines the impact of globalization on jobs and incomes in the United States.

Websites

The Aids Crisis: http://americanhistory.si.edu/exhibitions/hiv-and-aids-thirty-years-ago

September 11: http://americanhistory.si.edu/exhibitons/september-11-remembrance-and-reflection

Global Exchange: www.globalexchange.org

Making the Macintosh: Technology and Culture in Silicon Valley: http://library.stanford.edu/mac/

CHAPTER 28: A NEW CENTURY AND NEW CRISES

Books

Bacevich, Andrew. *American Empire: The Realities and Consequences of U.S. Diplomacy* (2003). Examines how the idea of an American empire reemerged after September 11, and some of the results.

Brinkley, Douglas. *The Great Deluge: Hurricane Katrina, New Orleans, and the Mississippi Gulf Coast* (2006). A scathing account of how government at all levels failed the people of New Orleans.

Cherlin, Andrew J. *Labor's Love Lost: The Rise and Fall of the Working-Class Family in America* (2015). Studies how class differences affect family life and opportunities for social mobility in today's America.

Cole, David. *Terrorism and the Constitution* (rev. ed., 2006). Explores the constitutional issues raised by the war on terrorism.

Fraser, Steve. *The Age of Acquiescence (2015).* A comparison of the late nineteenth century with the current era, exploring why protest against inequality was stronger in the former.

Gardner, Lloyd C. *The Long Road to Baghdad: A History of U.S. Foreign Policy from the 1970s to the Present* (2008). A careful study of recent American foreign policy and the origins of the Iraq War.

Krugman, Paul. *The Return of Depression Economics and the Crisis of 2008* (2009). A leading economist explains the origins of the Great Recession.

Lakoff, George. *Whose Freedom? The Battle over America's Most Important Idea* (2006). Describes how conservatives and liberals continue to interpret freedom in very different ways.

Lansley, Stewart. *Divided We Stand: Why Inequality Keeps Rising* (2011). A prominent economist explains the reasons for rising economic inequality.

Levitas, Mitchell, ed. *A Nation Challenged: A Visual History of 9/11 and Its Aftermath* (2002). Presents striking photographs of the terrorist attacks and the days that followed.

Little, Douglas. *American Orientalism: The United States and the Middle East since 1945* (2003). A careful study of American relations with a volatile region since World War II.

Nye, Joseph S., Jr. *The Paradox of American Power* (2002). An argument that despite its overwhelming power, the United States cannot do as it pleases in international affairs.

Zakaria, Fareed. *The Future of Freedom: Illiberal Democracy at Home and Abroad* (2003). A foreign policy analyst discusses how the United States should respond to threats to freedom in the world.

Websites

September 11 Digital Archive: http://911digitalarchive.org

The White House: www.whitehouse.gov

GLOSSARY

abolition Social movement of the pre–Civil War era that advocated the immediate emancipation of the slaves and their incorporation into American society as equal citizens.

Act Concerning Religion (or Maryland Toleration Act) 1649 law that granted free exercise of religion to all Christian denominations in colonial Maryland.

Adkins v. Children's Hospital 1923 Supreme Court case that reversed *Muller v. Oregon*, the 1908 case that permitted states to set maximum hours to protect working women. Justices ruled in *Adkins* that women no longer deserved special treatment because they could vote.

affirmative action Policy efforts to promote greater employment opportunities for minorities.

Agricultural Adjustment Act New Deal legislation passed in 1933 that established the Agricultural Adjustment Administration (AAA) to improve agricultural prices by limiting market supplies; declared unconstitutional in *United States v. Butler* (1936).

Albany Plan of Union A failed 1754 proposal by the seven northern colonies in anticipation of the French and Indian War, urging the unification of the colonies under one crown-appointed president.

Alien and Sedition Acts Four measures passed in 1798 during the undeclared war with France that limited the freedoms of speech and press and restricted the liberty of noncitizens.

American Anti-Slavery Society Founded in 1833, the organization that sought an immediate end to slavery and the establishment of equality for black Americans.

It split in 1840 after disputes about the role of women within the organization and other issues.

American Civil Liberties Union Organization founded during World War I to protest the suppression of freedom of expression in wartime; played a major role in court cases that achieved judicial recognition of Americans' civil liberties.

American Colonization Society Organized in 1816 to encourage colonization of free blacks to Africa; West African nation of Liberia founded in 1822 to serve as a homeland for them.

American exceptionalism The belief that the United States has a special mission to serve as a refuge from tyranny, a symbol of freedom, and a model for the rest of the world.

American Federation of Labor A federation of trade unions founded in 1881, composed mostly of skilled, white, native-born workers; its long-term president was Samuel Gompers.

American Indian Movement (AIM) Movement founded in 1963 by Native Americans who were fed up with the poor conditions on Indian reservations and the federal government's unwillingness to help. In 1973, AIM led 200 Sioux in the occupation of Wounded Knee. After a ten-week standoff with the federal authorities, the government agreed to reexamine Indian treaty rights and the occupation ended.

"American standard of living" The Progressive-era idea that American workers were entitled to a wage high enough to allow them full participation in the nation's mass consumption economy.

American System Program of internal improvements and protective tariffs promoted by Speaker of the House Henry Clay in his presidential campaign of 1824; his proposals formed the core of Whig ideology in the 1830s and 1840s.

American system of manufactures A system of production that relied on the mass production of interchangeable parts that could be rapidly assembled into standardized finished products. First perfected in Connecticut by clockmaker Eli Terry and by small-arms producer Eli Whitney in the 1840s and 50s.

Americans with Disabilities Act 1990 law that prohibited the discrimination against persons with disabilities in both hiring and promotion. It also mandated accessible entrances for public buildings.

the *Amistad* Ship that transported slaves from one port in Cuba to another, seized by the slaves in 1839. They made their way northward to the United States, where the status of the slaves became the subject of a celebrated court case; eventually most were able to return to Africa.

Anglican Church The established state church of England, formed by Henry VII after the pope refused to annul his marriage to Catherine of Aragon.

annuity system System of yearly payments to Native American tribes by which the federal government justified and institutionalized its interference in Indian tribal affairs.

Antietam, Battle of One of the bloodiest battles of the Civil War, fought to a standoff on September 17, 1862, in western Maryland.

Anti-Federalists Opponents of the Constitution who saw it as a limitation on individual and states' rights; their demands led to the addition of a Bill of Rights to the document.

Anti-Imperialist League Coalition of anti-imperialist groups united in 1899 to protest American territorial expansion, especially in the Philippine Islands; its membership included prominent politicians, industrialists, labor leaders, and social reformers.

Appomattox Courthouse, Virginia Site of the surrender of Confederate general Robert E. Lee to Union general Ulysses S. Grant on April 9, 1865, marking the end of the Civil War.

Army-McCarthy hearings Televised U.S. Senate hearings in 1954 on Senator Joseph McCarthy's charges of disloyalty in the army; his tactics contributed to his censure by the Senate.

Arnold, Benedict A traitorous American commander who planned to sell out the American garrison at West Point to the British. His plot was discovered before it could be executed and he joined the British army.

Articles of Confederation First frame of government for the United States; in effect from 1781 to 1788, it provided for a weak central authority and was soon replaced by the Constitution.

Atlanta Compromise Speech to the Cotton States and International Exposition in 1895 by educator Booker T. Washington, the leading black spokesman of the day; black scholar W. E. B. Du Bois gave the speech its derisive name and criticized Washington for encouraging blacks to accommodate segregation and disenfranchisement.

Atlantic Charter Agreement issued August 12, 1941, following meetings in Newfoundland between President Franklin D. Roosevelt and British Prime Minister Winston Churchill, that signaled the Allies' cooperation and stated their war aims.

Atlantic slave trade The systematic importation of African slaves from their native continent across the Atlantic Ocean to the New World, largely fueled by rising demand for sugar, rice, coffee, and tobacco.

Attucks, Crispus During the Boston Massacre, the individual who was supposedly at the head of the crowd of hecklers and who baited the British troops. He was killed when the British troops fired on the crowd.

Axis powers In World War II, the nations of Germany, Italy, and Japan.

Aztec Mesoamerican people who were conquered by the Spanish under Hernan Cortes, 1519–1528.

baby boom Markedly higher birthrate in the years following World War II; led to the biggest demographic "bubble" in American history.

backcountry In colonial America, the area stretching from central Pennsylvania southward through the Shenandoah Valley of Virginia and into upland North and South Carolina.

Bacon's Rebellion Unsuccessful 1676 revolt led by planter Nathaniel Bacon against Virginia governor William Berkeley's administration because of governmental corruption and because Berkeley had failed to protect settlers from Indian raids and did not allow them to occupy Indian lands.

Balkan crisis A series of ethnic and political crises that arose following the dissolution of Yugoslavia in the 1990s. Many atrocities were committed during the conflict, and NATO, the United Nations, and the United States intervened several times.

Bank of the United States Proposed by the first secretary of the treasury, Alexander Hamilton, the bank that opened in 1791 and operated until 1811 to issue a uniform currency, make business loans, and collect tax monies. The Second Bank of the United States was chartered in 1816 but President Andrew Jackson vetoed the recharter bill in 1832.

Bank War Political struggle in the early 1830s between President Jackson and financier Nicholas Biddle over the renewing of the Second Bank's charter.

Barbary Wars The first wars fought by the United States, and the nation's first encounter with the Islamic world. The wars were fought from 1801 to 1805 against plundering pirates off the Mediterranean coast of Africa after President Thomas Jefferson's refusal to pay them tribute to protect American ships.

Bargain of 1877 Deal made by a Republican and Democratic special congressional commission to resolve the disputed presidential election of 1876; Republican Rutherford B. Hayes, who had lost the popular vote, was declared the winner in exchange for the withdrawal of federal troops from involvement in politics in the South, marking the end of Reconstruction.

Bay of Pigs invasion U.S. mission in which the CIA, hoping to inspire a revolt against Fidel Castro, sent 1,500 Cuban exiles to invade their homeland on April 17, 1961; the mission was a spectacular failure.

the Beats A term coined by Jack Kerouac for a small group of poets and writers who railed against 1950s mainstream culture.

Bill for Establishing Religious Freedom A Virginia law, drafted by Thomas Jefferson in 1777 and enacted in 1786, that guarantees freedom of, and from, religion.

Bill of Rights First ten amendments to the U.S. Constitution, adopted in 1791 to guarantee individual rights against infringement by the federal government.

birth control movement An offshoot of the early twentieth-century feminist movement that saw access to birth control and "voluntary motherhood" as essential to women's freedom. The birth-control movement was led by Margaret Sanger.

Black Codes Laws passed from 1865 to 1866 in southern states to restrict the rights of former slaves; to nullify the codes, Congress passed the Civil Rights Act of 1866 and the Fourteenth Amendment.

Black Legend Idea that the Spanish New World empire was more oppressive toward the Indians than other European empires; was used as a justification for English imperial expansion.

Black Lives Matter Civil rights movement sparked by a series of incidents of police brutality and lethal force against people of color.

Black Power Post-1966 rallying cry of a more militant civil rights movement.

"Bleeding Kansas" Violence between pro- and antislavery settlers in the Kansas Territory, 1856.

bonanza farms Large farms that covered thousands of acres and employed hundreds of wage laborers in the West in the late nineteenth century.

borderland A place between or near recognized borders where no group of people has complete political control or cultural dominance.

Boston Massacre Clash between British soldiers and a Boston mob, March 5, 1770, in which five colonists were killed.

Boston Tea Party The incident on December 16, 1773, in which the Sons of Liberty, dressed as Indians, dumped hundreds of chests of tea into Boston Harbor to protest the Tea Act of 1773. Under the Tea Act, the British exported to the colonies millions of pounds of cheap—but still taxed—tea, thereby undercutting the price of smuggled tea and forcing payment of the tea duty.

***bracero* program** System agreed to by Mexican and American governments in 1942 under which tens of thousands of Mexicans entered the United States to work temporarily in agricultural jobs in the Southwest; lasted until 1964 and inhibited labor organization among farm workers since *braceros* could be deported at any time.

Brant, Joseph The Mohawk leader who led the Iroquois against the Americans in the Revolutionary War.

Bretton Woods conference International meeting held in the town of Bretton Woods, New Hampshire, in 1944 in which participants agreed that the American dollar would replace the British pound as the most important international currency. The conference also created the World Bank and International Monetary Fund to promote rebuilding after World War II and to ensure that countries did not devalue their currencies.

Brook Farm Transcendentalist commune in West Roxbury, Massachusetts, populated from 1841 to 1847 principally by writers (Nathaniel Hawthorne, for one) and other intellectuals.

Brown v. Board of Education 1954 U.S. Supreme Court decision that struck down racial segregation in public education and declared "separate but equal" unconstitutional.

Bull Run, first Battle of The first land engagement of the Civil War which took place on July 21, 1861, at Manassas Junction, Virginia, and at which Union troops quickly retreated.

Bull Run, second Battle of Civil War engagement that took place one year after the first Battle of Bull Run, on August 29–30, during which Confederates captured the federal supply depot at Manassas Junction, Virginia, and forced Union troops back to Washington.

Bunker Hill, Battle of First major battle of the Revolutionary War; it actually took place at nearby Breed's Hill, Massachusetts, on June 17, 1775.

the Bush Doctrine President George W. Bush's foreign policy principle wherein the United States would launch a war on terrorism.

Bush v. Gore U.S. Supreme Court case that determined the winner of the disputed 2000 presidential election.

busing The means of transporting students via buses to achieve school integration in the 1970s.

Camp David Accords Peace agreement between the leaders of Israel and Egypt, brokered by President Jimmy Carter in 1978.

captivity narratives Accounts written by colonists after their time in Indian captivity, often stressing the captive's religious convictions.

caravel A fifteenth-century European ship capable of long-distance travel.

carpetbaggers Derisive term for northern emigrants who participated in the Republican governments of the Reconstruction South.

checks and balances A systematic balance to prevent any one branch of the national government from dominating the other two.

Chinese Exclusion Act 1882 law that halted Chinese immigration to the United States.

Church of Jesus Christ of Latter-Day Saints Religious sect founded in 1830 by Joseph Smith; it was a product of the intense revivalism of the "burned-over district" of New York. Smith's successor Brigham Young led 15,000 followers to Utah in 1847 to escape persecution.

Civil Rights Act (1964) Law that outlawed discrimination in public accommodations and employment.

Civil Rights Act of 1875 The last piece of Reconstruction legislation, which outlawed racial discrimination in places of public accommodation such as hotels and theaters. Many parts of it were ruled unconstitutional by the Supreme Court in 1883.

Civil Rights Bill of 1866 Along with the Fourteenth Amendment, legislation that guaranteed the rights of citizenship to former slaves.

Civil Service Act of 1883 Law that established the Civil Service Commission and marked the end of the spoils system.

Civilian Conservation Corps (CCC) 1933 New Deal public work relief program that provided outdoor manual work for unemployed men, rebuilding infra-structure and implementing conservation programs. The program cut the unemployment rate, particularly among young men.

Cold War Term for tensions, 1945–1989, between the Soviet Union and the United States, the two major world powers after World War II.

collective bargaining The process of negotiations between an employer and a group of employees to regulate working conditions.

Columbian Exchange The transatlantic flow of goods and people that began with Columbus's voyages in 1492.

Committee of Correspondence Group organized by Samuel Adams in retaliation for the *Gaspée* incident to address American grievances, assert American rights, and form a network of rebellion.

common school Tax-supported state schools of the early nineteenth century open to all children.

Common Sense A pamphlet anonymously written by Thomas Paine in January 1776 that attacked the English principles of hereditary rule and monarchical government.

Commonwealth v. Hunt Landmark 1842 ruling of the Massachusetts Supreme Court establishing the legality of labor unions.

communitarianism Social reform movement of the nineteenth century driven by the belief that by establishing small communities based on common ownership of property, a less competitive and individualistic society could be developed.

Compromise of 1850 Complex compromise devised by Senator Henry Clay that admitted California as a free state, included a stronger fugitive slave law, and delayed determination of the slave status of the New Mexico and Utah territories.

Congress of Industrial Organizations Umbrella organization of semiskilled industrial unions, formed in 1935 as the Committee for Industrial Organization and renamed in 1938.

conquistadores Spanish term for "conquerors," applied to Spanish and Portuguese soldiers who conquered lands held by indigenous peoples in central and southern America as well as the current states of Texas, New Mexico, Arizona, and California.

conservation movement A progressive reform movement focused on the preservation and sustainable management of the nation's natural resources.

Constitutional Convention Meeting in Philadelphia, May 25–September 17, 1787, of representatives from twelve colonies—excepting Rhode Island—to revise the existing Articles of Confederation; the convention soon resolved to produce an entirely new constitution.

containment General U.S. strategy in the Cold War that called for containing Soviet expansion; originally devised by U.S. diplomat George F. Kennan.

Continental army Army authorized by the Continental Congress in 1775 to fight the British; commanded by General George Washington.

Continental Congress First meeting of representatives of the colonies, held in Philadelphia in 1774 to formulate actions against British policies; in the Second Continental Congress (1775–1789), the colonial representatives conducted the war and adopted the Declaration of Independence and the Articles of Confederation.

"the contrabands" Slaves who sought refuge in Union military camps or who lived in areas of the Confederacy under Union control.

Contract with America A list of conservatives' promises in response to the supposed liberalism of the Clinton administration, that was drafted by Speaker of the House Newt Gingrich and other congressional Republicans as the GOP platform for the 1994 midterm elections. It was more a campaign tactic than a practical program; few of its proposed items ever became law.

cotton gin Invented by Eli Whitney in 1793, the machine that separated cotton seed from cotton fiber, speeding cotton processing and making profitable the cultivation of the more hardy, but difficult to clean, short-staple cotton; led directly to the dramatic nineteenth-century expansion of slavery in the South.

"Cotton Is King" Phrase from Senator James Henry Hammond's speech extolling the virtues of cotton, and, implicitly, the slave system of production that led to its bounty for the South. "King Cotton" became a shorthand for Southern political and economic power.

Cotton Kingdom Cotton-producing region, relying predominantly on slave labor, that spanned from North Carolina west to Louisiana and reached as far north as southern Illinois.

counterculture "Hippie" youth culture of the 1960s, which rejected the values of the dominant culture in favor of illicit drugs, communes, free sex, and rock music.

Court packing plan President Franklin D. Roosevelt's failed 1937 attempt to increase the number of U.S. Supreme Court justices from nine to fifteen in order to save his Second New Deal programs from constitutional challenges.

Covenant Chain Alliance formed in the 1670s between the English and the Iroquois nations.

coverture Principle in English and American law that a married woman lost her legal identity, which became "covered" by that of her husband, who therefore controlled her person and the family's economic resources.

Coxey's Army A march on Washington organized by Jacob Coxey, an Ohio member of the People's Party. Coxey believed in abandoning the gold standard and printing enough legal tender to reinvigorate the economy. The marchers demanded that Congress create jobs and pay workers in paper currency not backed by gold.

creoles Persons born in the New World of European ancestry.

crop lien Credit extended by merchants to tenants based on their future crops; under this system, high interest rates and the uncertainties of farming often led to inescapable debts.

Cuban missile crisis Tense confrontation caused when the United States discovered Soviet offensive missile sites in Cuba in October 1962; the U.S.-Soviet confrontation was the Cold War's closest brush with nuclear war.

cult of domesticity The nineteenth-century ideology of "virtue" and "modesty" as the qualities that were essential to proper womanhood.

Culture Wars Battles over moral values that occurred throughout the 1990s. The Culture Wars touched many areas of American life—from popular culture to academia. Flashpoints included the future of the nuclear family and the teaching of evolution.

Dartmouth College v. Woodward 1819 U.S. Supreme Court case in which the Court upheld the original charter of the college against New Hampshire's attempt to alter the board of trustees; set the precedent of support of contracts against state interference.

Dawes Act Law passed in 1887 meant to encourage adoption of white norms among Indians; broke up tribal holdings into small farms for Indian families, with the remainder sold to white purchasers.

D-Day June 6, 1944, when an Allied amphibious assault landed on the Normandy coast and established a foothold in Europe, leading to the liberation of France from German occupation.

Declaration of Independence Document adopted on July 4, 1776, that made the break with Britain official; drafted by a committee of the Second Continental Congress, including principal writer Thomas Jefferson.

decolonization The process by which African and Asian colonies of European empires became independent in the years following World War II.

Defense of Marriage Act 1996 law that barred gay couples from receiving federal benefits. Ruled unconstitutional in 2013.

deindustrialization Term describing decline of manufacturing in old industrial areas in the late twentieth century as companies shifted production to low-wage centers in the South and West or in other countries.

Deism Enlightenment thought applied to religion; emphasized reason, morality, and natural law.

Democracy in America Two works, published in 1835 and 1840, by the French thinker Alexis de Tocqueville on the subject of American democracy. Tocqueville stressed the cultural nature of American democracy, and the importance and prevalence of equality in American life.

Democratic-Republican societies Organizations created in the mid-1790s by opponents of the policies of the Washington administration and supporters of the French Revolution.

Denmark Vesey's conspiracy An 1822 failed slave uprising in Charleston, South Carolina, purported to have been led by Denmark Vesey, a free black man.

deregulation Reagan-Clinton era legislation that removed regulations on many industries, including finance and air travel.

détente Period of improving relations between the United States and Communist nations, particularly China and the Soviet Union, during the Nixon administration.

disenfranchisement To deprive of the right to vote; in the United States, exclusionary policies were used to deny groups, especially African-Americans and women, their voting rights.

Dissenters Protestants who belonged to denominations outside of the established Anglican Church.

division of powers The division of political power between the state and federal governments under the U.S. Constitution (also known as federalism).

Dix, Dorothea An important figure in increasing the public's awareness of the plight of the mentally ill. After a two-year investigation of the treatment of the mentally ill in Massachusetts, she presented her findings and won the support of leading reformers. She eventually convinced twenty states to reform their treatment of the mentally ill.

Dixiecrats Deep South delegates who walked out of the 1948 Democratic National Convention in protest of the party's support for civil rights legislation and later formed the States' Rights Democratic (Dixiecrat) Party, which nominated Strom Thurmond of South Carolina for president.

Dollar Diplomacy A foreign policy initiative under President William Howard Taft that promoted the spread of American influence through loans and economic investments from American banks.

Dominion of New England Consolidation into a single colony of the New England colonies—and later New York and New Jersey—by royal governor Edmund Andros in 1686; dominion reverted to individual colonial governments three years later.

"Don't ask, don't tell" President Clinton's compromise measure that allowed gay people to serve in the military incognito, as officers could no longer seek them out for dismissal but they could not openly express their identity. "Don't ask, don't tell" was ended under the Obama administration, when gay military service was allowed.

the Dorr War A movement in Rhode Island against property qualifications for voting. The movement formed an extralegal constitutional convention for the state and elected Thomas Dorr as a governor, but was quashed by federal troops dispatched by President John Tyler.

double-V Led by *The Pittsburgh Courier*, the movement that pressed for victory over fascism abroad and over racism at home. It argued that since African-Americans were risking their lives abroad, they should receive full civil rights at home.

dower rights In colonial America, the right of a widowed woman to inherit one-third of her deceased husband's property.

Dred Scott v. Sandford 1857 U.S. Supreme Court decision in which Chief Justice Roger B. Taney ruled that Congress could not prohibit slavery in the territories, on the grounds that such a prohibition would violate the Fifth Amendment rights of slaveholders, and that no black person could be a citizen of the United States.

Dust Bowl Great Plains counties where millions of tons of topsoil were blown away from parched farmland in the 1930s; massive migration of farm families followed.

Eighteenth Amendment Prohibition amendment passed in 1919 that made illegal the manufacture, sale, or transportation of alcoholic beverages; repealed in 1933.

Ellis Island Reception center in New York Harbor through which most European immigrants to America were processed from 1892 to 1954.

Emancipation Proclamation Declaration issued by President Abraham Lincoln; the preliminary proclamation on September 22, 1862, freed the slaves in areas under Confederate control as of January 1, 1863, the date of the final proclamation, which also authorized the enrollment of black soldiers into the Union army.

Embargo Act Attempt in 1807 to exert economic pressure by prohibiting all exports from the United States, instead of waging war in reaction to continued British impressment of American sailors; smugglers easily circumvented the embargo, and it was repealed two years later.

Emergency Banking Act Passed in 1933, the First New Deal measure that provided for reopening the banks under strict conditions and took the United States off the gold standard.

empire of liberty The idea, expressed by Jefferson, that the United States would not rule its new territories as colonies, but rather would eventually admit them as full member states.

enclosure movement A legal process that divided large farm fields in England that were previously collectively owned by groups of peasants into smaller, individually owned plots. The enclosure movement took place over several centuries, and resulted in eviction for many peasants.

Enforcement Acts Three laws passed in 1870 and 1871 that tried to eliminate the Ku Klux Klan by outlawing it and other such terrorist societies; the laws allowed the president to deploy the army for that purpose.

English Bill of Rights A series of laws enacted in 1689 that inscribed the rights of Englishmen into law and enumerated parliamentary powers such as taxation.

English liberty The idea that English people were entitled to certain liberties, including trial by jury, habeas corpus, and the right to face one's accuser in court. These rights meant that even the English king was subject to the rule of law.

English Toleration Act A 1690 act of Parliament that allowed all English Protestants to worship freely.

Enlightenment Revolution in thought in the eighteenth century that emphasized reason and science over the authority of traditional religion.

Equal Rights Amendment Amendment to guarantee equal rights for women, introduced in 1923 but not passed by Congress until 1972; it failed to be ratified by the states.

Era of Good Feelings Contemporary characterization of the administration of popular Republican president James Monroe, 1817–1825.

Erie Canal Most important and profitable of the canals of the 1820s and 1830s; stretched from Buffalo to Albany, New York, connecting the Great Lakes to the East Coast and making New York City the nation's largest port.

Espionage Act 1917 law that prohibited spying and interfering with the draft as well as making "false statements" that hurt the war effort.

ethnic cleansing The systematic removal of an ethnic group from a territory through violence or intimidation in order to create a homogeneous society; the term was popularized by the Yugoslav policy brutally targeting Albanian Muslims in Kosovo.

Ex parte Milligan 1866 Supreme Court case that declared it unconstitutional to bring accused persons before military tribunals where civil courts were operating.

Exposition and Protest Document written in 1828 by Vice President John C. Calhoun of South Carolina to protest the so-called Tariff of Abominations, which seemed to favor northern industry; introduced the concept of state interposition and became the basis for South Carolina's Nullification Doctrine of 1833.

Fair Deal Domestic reform proposals of the Truman administration; included civil rights legislation, national health insurance, and repeal of the Taft-Hartley Act, but only extensions of some New Deal programs were enacted.

family values Set of beliefs usually associated with conservatism that stressed the superiority of nuclear family, heterosexual marriage, and traditional gender roles.

family wage Idea that male workers should earn a wage sufficient to enable them to support their entire family without their wives' having to work outside the home.

Federal Housing Administration (FHA) A government agency created during the New Deal to guarantee mortgages, allowing lenders to offer long-term (usually thirty-year) loans with low down payments (usually 10 percent of the asking price). The FHA seldom underwrote loans in racially mixed or minority neighborhoods.

Federal Trade Commission (FTC) Independent agency created by the Wilson administration that replaced the Bureau of Corporations as an even more powerful tool to combat unfair trade practices and monopolies.

federalism A system of government in which power is divided between the central government and the states.

The Federalist Collection of eighty-five essays that appeared in the New York press in 1787–1788 in support of the Constitution; written by Alexander Hamilton, James Madison, and John Jay and published under the pseudonym "Publius."

Federalists and Republicans The two increasingly coherent political parties that appeared in Congress by the mid-1790s. The Federalists, led by George Washington, John Adams, and Alexander Hamilton, favored a strong central government. The Republicans, first identified during the early nineteenth century, supported a strict interpretation of the Constitution, which they believed would safeguard individual freedoms and states' rights from the threats posed by a strong central government.

The Feminine Mystique The book widely credited with sparking second-wave feminism in the United States. Author Betty Friedan focused on college-educated women, arguing that they would find fulfillment by engaging in paid labor outside the home.

feminism Term that entered the lexicon in the early twentieth century to describe the movement for full equality for women, in political, social, and personal life.

Fifteenth Amendment Constitutional amendment ratified in 1870, which prohibited states from discriminating in voting privileges on the basis of race.

flappers Young women of the 1920s whose rebellion against prewar standards of femininity included wearing shorter dresses, bobbing their hair, dancing to jazz music, driving cars, smoking cigarettes, and indulging in illegal drinking and gambling.

Force Act 1833 legislation, sparked by the nullification crisis in South Carolina, that authorized the president's use of the army to compel states to comply with federal law.

Fordism Early twentieth-century term describing the economic system pioneered by Ford Motor Company based on high wages and mass consumption.

Fort McHenry Fort in Baltimore Harbor unsuccessfully bombarded by the British in September 1814; Francis Scott Key, a witness to the battle, was moved to write the words to "The Star-Spangled Banner."

Fort Sumter First battle of the Civil War, in which the federal fort in Charleston (South Carolina) Harbor was captured by the Confederates on April 14, 1861, after two days of shelling.

Four Freedoms Freedom of speech, freedom of worship, freedom from want, and freedom from fear, as described by President Franklin D. Roosevelt during his January 6, 1941, State of the Union Address.

Fourteen Points President Woodrow Wilson's 1918 plan for peace after World War I; at the Versailles peace conference, however, he failed to incorporate all of the points into the treaty.

Fourteenth Amendment 1868 constitutional amendment that guaranteed rights of citizenship to former slaves, in words similar to those of the Civil Rights Act of 1866.

franchise The right to vote.

free blacks African-American persons not held in slavery; immediately before the Civil War, there were nearly a half million in the United States, split almost evenly between North and South.

Free Soil Party Political organization formed in 1848 to oppose slavery in the territory acquired in the Mexican War; nominated Martin Van Buren for president in 1848. By 1854 most of the party's members had joined the Republican Party.

free trade The belief that economic development arises from the exchange of goods between different countries without governmental interference.

the Freedmen's Bureau Reconstruction agency established in 1865 to protect the legal rights of former slaves and to assist with their education, jobs, health care, and landowning.

freedom petitions Arguments for liberty presented to New England's courts and legislatures in the early 1770s by enslaved African-Americans.

Freedom Rides Bus journeys challenging racial segregation in the South in 1961.

French and Indian War The last—and most important—of four colonial wars fought between England and France for control of North America east of the Mississippi River.

Fugitive Slave Act 1850 law that gave the federal government authority in cases involving runaway slaves; aroused considerable opposition in the North.

fugitive slaves Slaves who escaped from their owners.

fundamentalism Anti-modernist Protestant movement started in the early twentieth century that proclaimed the literal truth of the Bible; the name came from *The Fundamentals*, published by conservative leaders.

Gabriel's Rebellion An 1800 uprising planned by Virginian slaves to gain their freedom. The plot was led by a blacksmith named Gabriel, but was discovered and quashed.

Gadsden Purchase Thirty thousand square miles in present-day Arizona and New Mexico bought by Congress from Mexico in 1853 primarily for the Southern Pacific Railroad's transcontinental route.

gag rule Rule adopted by House of Representatives in 1836 prohibiting consideration of abolitionist petitions; opposition, led by former president John Quincy Adams, succeeded in having it repealed in 1844.

Garvey, Marcus The leading spokesman for Negro Nationalism, which exalted blackness, black cultural expression, and black exclusiveness. He called upon African-Americans to liberate themselves from the surrounding white culture and create their own businesses, cultural centers, and newspapers. He was also the founder of the Universal Negro Improvement Association.

Geneva Accords A 1954 document that had promised elections to unify Vietnam and established the Seventeenth Parallel demarcation line which divided North and South Vietnam.

"gentlemen of property and standing" Well-to-do merchants who often had commercial ties to the South and resisted abolitionism, occasionally inciting violence against its adherents.

Gettysburg, Battle of Battle fought in southern Pennsylvania, July 1–3, 1863; the Confederate defeat and the simultaneous loss at Vicksburg marked the military turning point of the Civil War.

Ghost Dance A spiritual and political movement among Native Americans whose followers performed a ceremonial "ghost dance" intended to connect the living with the dead and make the Indians bulletproof in battles intended to restore their homelands.

GI Bill of Rights The 1944 legislation that provided money for education and other benefits to military personnel returning from World War II.

Gibbons v. Ogden 1824 U.S. Supreme Court decision reinforcing the "commerce clause" (the federal government's right to regulate interstate commerce) of the Constitution; Chief Justice John Marshall ruled against the State of New York's granting of steamboat monopolies.

the Gilded Age The popular but derogatory name for the period from the end of the Civil War to the turn of the century, after the title of the 1873 novel by Mark Twain and Charles Dudley Warner.

globalization Term that became prominent in the 1990s to describe the rapid acceleration of international flows of commerce, financial resources, labor, and cultural products.

Glorious Revolution A coup in 1688 engineered by a small group of aristocrats that led to William of Orange taking the British throne in place of James II.

gold rush The massive migration of Americans into California territory in the late 1840s and 1850s in pursuit of gold, which was discovered there in 1848.

gold standard Policy at various points in American history by which the value of a dollar is set at a fixed price in terms of gold (in the post–World War II era, for example, $35 per ounce of gold).

Good Neighbor Policy Policy proclaimed by President Franklin D. Roosevelt in his first inaugural address in 1933 that sought improved diplomatic relations between the United States and its Latin American neighbors.

gradual emancipation A series of acts passed in state legislatures throughout the North in the years following the Revolution that freed slaves after they reached a certain age, following lengthy "apprenticeships."

grandfather clause Loophole created by southern disenfranchising legislatures of the 1890s for illiterate white males whose grandfathers had been eligible to vote before the Civil War.

Great Awakening Fervent religious revival movement in the 1720s through the 1740s that was spread throughout the colonies by ministers like New England Con-

gregationalist Jonathan Edwards and English revivalist George Whitefield.

Great Depression Worst economic depression in American history; it was spurred by the stock market crash of 1929 and lasted until World War II.

Great League of Peace An alliance of the Iroquois tribes, originally formed sometime between 1450 and 1600, that used their combined strength to pressure Europeans to work with them in the fur trade and to wage war across what is today eastern North America.

Great Migration Large-scale migration of southern blacks during and after World War I to the North, where jobs had become available during the labor shortage of the war years.

Great Migration (1630s) The migration of approximately 21,000 English Puritans to the Massachusetts Bay Colony.

Great Railroad Strike A series of demonstrations, some violent, held nationwide in support of striking railroad workers in Martinsburg, West Virginia, who refused to work due to wage cuts.

Great Recession A period of major economic stagnation across the United States and western Europe, characterized by rising unemployment and inflation and a 37 percent decline in the stock market between March and December 1974.

Great Society Term coined by President Lyndon B. Johnson in his 1965 State of the Union address, in which he proposed legislation to address problems of voting rights, poverty, diseases, education, immigration, and the environment.

Griswold v. Connecticut Supreme Court decision that, in overturning Connecticut law prohibiting the use of contraceptives, established a constitutional right to privacy.

Guantánamo Bay A detention center at the American naval base at Guantánamo Bay, Cuba, where beginning in 2002 suspected terrorists and war prisoners were held indefinitely and tried by extrajudicial military tribunals. During his 2008 presidential campaign, Senator Barack Obama pledged to close the prison, but as of 2015 it remained open.

Gulf of Tonkin resolution Legislation passed by Congress in 1964 in reaction to supposedly unprovoked attacks on American warships off the coast of North Vietnam; it gave the president unlimited authority to defend U.S. forces and members of SEATO.

Gulf oil spill Environmental disaster that occurred in 2010 after an explosion on the *Deepwater Horizon* oil rig. Hundreds of millions of gallons of oil were spilled into the Gulf of Mexico, resulting in one of the largest environmental calamities in human history.

Gulf War Military action in 1991 in which an international coalition led by the United States drove Iraq from Kuwait, which it had occupied the previous year.

hacienda Large-scale farm in the Spanish New World empire worked by Indian laborers.

Haitian Revolution A slave uprising that led to the establishment of Haiti as an independent country in 1804.

Half-Way Covenant A 1662 religious compromise that allowed baptism and partial church membership to colonial New Englanders whose parents were not among the Puritan elect.

Harlem Renaissance African-American literary and artistic movement of the 1920s centered in New York City's Harlem neighborhood; writers Langston Hughes, Jean Toomer, Zora Neale Hurston, and Countee Cullen were among those active in the movement.

Harpers Ferry, Virginia Site of abolitionist John Brown's failed raid on the federal arsenal, October 16–17, 1859; Brown became a martyr to his cause after his capture and execution.

Hart-Celler Act 1965 law that eliminated the national origins quota system for immigration established by laws in 1921 and 1924; led to radical change in the origins of immigrants to the United States, with Asians and Latin Americans outnumbering Europeans.

Hartford Convention Meeting of New England Federalists on December 15, 1814, to protest the War of 1812; proposed seven constitutional amendments (limiting embargoes and changing requirements for officeholding, declaration of war, and admission of new states), but the war ended before Congress could respond.

Haymarket Affair Violence during an anarchist protest at Haymarket Square in Chicago on May 4, 1886; the deaths of eight, including seven policemen, led to the trial of eight anarchist leaders for conspiracy to commit murder.

Haynes, Lemuel A black member of the Massachusetts militia and celebrated minister who urged that Americans extend their conception of freedom to enslaved Africans during the Revolutionary Era.

headright system A land-grant policy that promised fifty acres to any colonist who could afford passage to Virginia, as well as fifty more for any accompanying servants. The headright policy was eventually expanded to include any colonists—and was also adopted in other colonies.

Helsinki Accords 1975 agreement between the USSR and the United States that recognized the post–World War II boundaries of Europe and guaranteed the basic liberties of each nation's citizens.

Hessians German soldiers, most from Hesse-Cassel principality (hence, the name), paid to fight for the British in the Revolutionary War.

Hollywood Ten A group called before the House Un-American Activities Committee who refused to speak about their political leanings or "name names"—that is, identify communists in Hollywood. Some were imprisoned as a result.

Holocaust Systematic racist attempt by the Nazis to exterminate the Jews of Europe, resulting in the murder of over 6 million Jews and more than a million other "undesirables."

Homestead Act 1862 law that authorized Congress to grant 160 acres of public land to a western settler, who had to live on the land for five years to establish title.

horizontal expansion The process by which a corporation acquires or merges with its competitors.

House of Burgesses The first elected assembly in colonial America, established in 1619 in Virginia. Only wealthy landowners could vote in its elections.

House Un-American Activities Committee (HUAC) Committee formed in 1938 to investigate subversives in the government and holders of radical ideas more generally; best-known investigations were of Hollywood notables and of former State Department official Alger Hiss, who was accused in 1948 of espionage and Communist Party membership. Abolished in 1975.

Hundred Days Extraordinarily productive first three months of President Franklin D. Roosevelt's administration in which a special session of Congress enacted fifteen of his New Deal proposals.

Hurricane Katrina 2005 hurricane that devastated much of the Gulf Coast, especially New Orleans. The Bush administration's response was widely criticized as inadequate.

illegal alien A new category established by the Immigration Act of 1924 that referred to immigrants crossing U.S. borders in excess of the new immigration quotas.

Immigration Restriction League A political organization founded in 1894 that called for reducing immigration to the United States by requiring a literacy test for immigrants.

impeachment Bringing charges against a public official; for example, the House of Representatives can impeach a president for "treason, bribery, or other high crimes and misdemeanors" by majority vote, and after the trial the Senate can remove the president by a vote of two-thirds. Two presidents, Andrew Johnson and Bill Clinton, have been impeached and tried before the Senate; neither was convicted.

impressment The British navy's practice of using press-gangs to kidnap men in British and colonial ports who were then forced to serve in the British navy.

"In God We Trust" Phrase placed on all new U.S. currency as of 1954.

indentured servants Settlers who signed on for a temporary period of servitude to a master in exchange for passage to the New World; Virginia and Pennsylvania were largely peopled in the seventeenth and eighteenth centuries by English and German indentured servants.

Indian New Deal Phrase that refers to the reforms implemented for Native Americans during the New Deal era. John Collier, the commissioner of the Bureau of Indian Affairs (BIA), increased the access Native Americans had to relief programs and employed more Native Americans at the BIA. He worked to pass the Indian Reorganization Act. However, the version of the act passed by Congress was a much diluted version of Collier's original proposal and did not greatly improve the lives of Native Americans.

Indian Removal Act 1830 law signed by President Andrew Jackson that permitted the negotiation of treaties to obtain the Indians' lands in exchange for their relocation to what would become Oklahoma.

individualism Term that entered the language in the 1820s to describe the increasing emphasis on the pursuit of personal advancement and private fulfillment free of outside interference.

Industrial Workers of the World Radical union organized in Chicago in 1905 and nicknamed the Wobblies; its opposition to World War I led to its destruction by the federal government under the Espionage Act.

inflation An economic condition in which prices rise continuously.

Insular Cases Series of cases between 1901 and 1904 in which the Supreme Court ruled that constitutional protection of individual rights did not fully apply to residents of "insular" territories acquired by the United States in the Spanish-American War, such as Puerto Rico and the Philippines.

Interstate Commerce Commission Organization established by Congress, in reaction to the U.S. Supreme Court's ruling in *Wabash Railroad v. Illinois* (1886), in order to curb abuses in the railroad industry by regulating rates.

interstate highway system National network of interstate superhighways; its construction began in the late 1950s for the purpose of commerce and defense. The interstate highways would enable the rapid movement of military convoys and the evacuation of cities after a nuclear attack.

Intolerable Acts Four parliamentary measures in reaction to the Boston Tea Party that forced payment for the tea, disallowed colonial trials of British soldiers, forced their quartering in private homes, and reduced the number of elected officials in Massachusetts.

Iran-Contra Affair Scandal of the second Reagan administration involving sales of arms to Iran in partial exchange for release of hostages in Lebanon and use of the arms money to aid the Contras in Nicaragua, which had been expressly forbidden by Congress.

Iraq War Military campaign in 2003 in which the United States, unable to gain approval by the United Nations, unilaterally occupied Iraq and removed dictator Saddam Hussein from power.

iron curtain Term coined by Winston Churchill to describe the Cold War divide between western Europe and the Soviet Union's eastern European satellites.

ISIS An insurgency that emerged from the sectarian civil wars that destabilized Syria and post–Saddam Hussein Iraq. Beginning in 2014, ISIS forces attacked towns and cities in Iraq, Syria, and Lybia, systematically murdering members of ethnic and religious minorities.

isolationism The desire to avoid foreign entanglements that dominated the U.S. Congress in the 1930s; beginning in 1935, lawmakers passed a series of Neutrality Acts that banned travel on belligerents' ships and the sale of arms to countries at war.

Japanese-American internment Policy adopted by the Roosevelt administration in 1942 under which 110,000 persons of Japanese descent, most of them American citizens, were removed from the West Coast and forced to spend most of World War II in internment camps; it was the largest violation of American civil liberties in the twentieth century.

Jay's Treaty Treaty with Britain negotiated in 1794 by Chief Justice John Jay; Britain agreed to vacate forts in the Northwest Territories, and festering disagreements (border with Canada, prewar debts, shipping claims) would be settled by commission.

Kansas Exodus A migration in 1879 and 1880 by some 40,000–60,000 blacks to Kansas to escape the oppressive environment of the New South.

Kansas-Nebraska Act 1854 law sponsored by Illinois senator Stephen A. Douglas to allow settlers in newly organized territories north of the Missouri border to decide the slavery issue for themselves; fury over the resulting repeal of the Missouri Compromise of 1820 led to violence in Kansas and to the formation of the Republican Party.

"King Cotton diplomacy" An attempt during the Civil War by the South to encourage British intervention by banning cotton exports.

King Philip's War A multiyear conflict that began in 1675 with an Indian uprising against white colonists. Its end result was broadened freedoms for white New Englanders and the dispossession of the region's Indians.

Knights of Labor Founded in 1869, the first national union; lasted, under the leadership of Terence V. Powderly, only into the 1890s; supplanted by the American Federation of Labor.

Know-Nothing Party Nativist, anti-Catholic third party organized in 1854 in reaction to large-scale German and Irish immigration; the party's only presidential candidate was Millard Fillmore in 1856.

Korean War Conflict touched off in 1950 when Communist North Korea invaded South Korea; fighting, largely by U.S. forces, continued until 1953.

Korematsu v. United States 1944 Supreme Court case that found Executive Order 9066 to be constitutional. Fred Korematsu, an American-born citizen of Japanese descent, defied the military order that banned all persons of Japanese ancestry from designated western coastal areas. The Court upheld Korematsu's arrest and internment.

Ku Klux Klan Group organized in Pulaski, Tennessee, in 1866 to terrorize former slaves who voted and held political offices during Reconstruction; a revived organization in the 1910s and 1920s that stressed white, Anglo-Saxon, fundamentalist Protestant supremacy; revived a third time to fight the civil rights movement of the 1950s and 1960s in the South.

Kyoto Protocol A 1997 international agreement that sought to combat global warming. To great controversy, the Bush administration announced in 2001 that it would not abide by the Kyoto Protocol.

Las Casas, Bartolomé de A Catholic missionary who renounced the Spanish practice of coercively converting Indians and advocated their better treatment. In 1552, he wrote *A Brief Relation of the Destruction of the Indies*, which described the Spanish's cruel treatment of the Indians.

League of Nations Organization of nations to mediate disputes and avoid war established after World War I as part of the Treaty of Versailles; President Woodrow Wilson's "Fourteen Points" speech to Congress in 1918 proposed the formation of the league, which the United States never joined.

League of United Latin American Citizens Often called LULAC, an organization that challenged restrictive housing, employment discrimination, and other inequalities faced by Latino Americans.

Lend-Lease Act 1941 law that permitted the United States to lend or lease arms and other supplies to the Allies, signifying increasing likelihood of American involvement in World War II.

Letters from an American Farmer 1782 book by Hector St. John de Crèvecoeur that popularized the notion that the United States was a "melting pot" while excluding people of color from the process of assimilation.

Levittown Low-cost, mass-produced developments of suburban tract housing built by William Levitt after World War II on Long Island and elsewhere.

Lewis and Clark expedition Led by Meriwether Lewis and William Clark, a mission to the Pacific coast commissioned for the purposes of scientific and geographical exploration.

Lexington and Concord, Battles of The first shots fired in the Revolutionary War, on April 19, 1775, near Boston; approximately 100 minutemen and 250 British soldiers were killed.

liberal internationalism Woodrow Wilson's foreign policy theory, which rested on the idea that economic and political freedom went hand in hand, and encouraged American intervention abroad in order to secure these freedoms globally.

liberalism Originally, political philosophy that emphasized the protection of liberty by limiting the power of government to interfere with the natural rights of citizens; in the twentieth century, belief in an activist government promoting greater social and economic equality.

liberty of contract A judicial concept of the late nineteenth and early twentieth centuries whereby the courts overturned laws regulating labor conditions as violations of the economic freedom of both employers and employees.

Liberty Party Abolitionist political party that nominated James G. Birney for president in 1840 and 1844; merged with the Free Soil Party in 1848.

Lincoln-Douglas debates Series of senatorial campaign debates in 1858 focusing on the issue of slavery in the territories; held in Illinois between Republican Abraham Lincoln, who made a national reputation for himself, and incumbent Democratic senator Stephen A. Douglas, who managed to hold on to his seat.

the Little Bighorn, Battle of Most famous battle of the Great Sioux War; took place in 1876 in the Montana Territory; combined Sioux and Cheyenne warriors massacred a vastly outnumbered U.S. Cavalry commanded by Lieutenant Colonel George Armstrong Custer.

Long Telegram A telegram by American diplomat George Kennan in 1946 outlining his views of the Soviet Union that eventually inspired the policy of containment.

Lord Dunmore's proclamation A proclamation issued in 1775 by the earl of Dunmore, the British governor of Virginia, that offered freedom to any slave who fought for the king against the rebelling colonists.

Lords of Trade An English regulatory board established to oversee colonial affairs in 1675.

the Lost Cause A romanticized view of slavery, the Old South, and the Confederacy that arose in the decades following the Civil War.

Louisiana Purchase President Thomas Jefferson's 1803 purchase from France of the important port of New Orleans and 828,000 square miles west of the Mississippi River to the Rocky Mountains; it more than doubled the territory of the United States at a cost of only $15 million.

Loyalists Colonists who remained loyal to Great Britain during the War of Independence.

Lusitania British passenger liner sunk by a German U-boat, May 7, 1915, creating a diplomatic crisis and public outrage at the loss of 128 Americans (roughly 10 percent of the total aboard); Germany agreed to pay reparations, and the United States waited two more years to enter World War I.

lynching Practice, particularly widespread in the South between 1890 and 1940, in which persons (usually black) accused of a crime were murdered by mobs before standing trial. Lynchings often took place before large crowds, with law enforcement authorities not intervening.

Manhattan Project Secret American program during World War II to develop an atomic bomb; J. Robert Oppenheimer led the team of physicists at Los Alamos, New Mexico.

manifest destiny Phrase first used in 1845 to urge annexation of Texas; used thereafter to encourage American settlement of European colonial and Indian lands in the Great Plains and the West and, more generally, as a justification for American empire.

Marbury v. Madison First U.S. Supreme Court decision to declare a federal law—the Judiciary Act of 1801—unconstitutional.

March on Washington Civil rights demonstration on August 28, 1963, where the Reverend Martin Luther King Jr. gave his "I Have a Dream" speech on the steps of the Lincoln Memorial.

Marshall Plan U.S. program for the reconstruction of post–World War II Europe through massive aid to former enemy nations as well as allies; proposed by General George C. Marshall in 1947.

massive retaliation Strategy that used the threat of nuclear warfare as a means of combating the global spread of communism.

maternalist reforms Progressive-era reforms that sought to encourage women's child-bearing and -rearing abilities and to promote their economic independence.

Mayflower Compact Document signed in 1620 aboard the *Mayflower* before the Pilgrims landed at Plymouth; the document committed the group to majority-rule government.

McCarran-Walter Act Immigration legislation passed in 1952 that allowed the government to deport immigrants who had been identified as communists, regardless of whether or not they were citizens.

McCarthyism Post–World War II Red Scare focused on the fear of Communists in U.S. government positions; peaked during the Korean War; most closely associated with Joseph McCarthy, a major instigator of the hysteria.

McCulloch v. Maryland 1819 U.S. Supreme Court decision in which Chief Justice John Marshall, holding that Maryland could not tax the Second Bank of the United States, supported the authority of the federal government versus the states.

McNary-Haugen bill Vetoed by President Calvin Coolidge in 1927 and 1928, the bill to aid farmers that would have artificially raised agricultural prices by selling surpluses overseas for low prices and selling the reduced supply in the United States for higher prices.

mercantilism Policy of Great Britain and other imperial powers of regulating the economies of colonies to benefit the mother country.

mestizos Spanish word for persons of mixed Native American and European ancestry.

Metacom The chief of the Wampanoags, whom the colonists called King Philip. He resented English efforts to convert Indians to Christianity and waged a war against the English colonists, one in which he was killed.

métis Children of marriages between Indian women and French traders and officials.

Mexican War Controversial war with Mexico for control of California and New Mexico, 1846–1848; the Treaty of Guadalupe Hidalgo fixed the border at the Rio Grande and extended the United States to the Pacific coast, annexing more than a half-million square miles of Mexican territory.

middle ground A borderland between European empires and Indian sovereignty where various native peoples and Europeans lived side by side in relative harmony.

Middle Passage The hellish and often deadly middle leg of the transatlantic "Triangular Trade" in which European ships carried manufactured goods to Africa, then transported enslaved Africans to the Americas and the Caribbean, and finally conveyed American agricultural products back to Europe; from the late sixteenth to the early nineteenth centuries, some 12 million Africans were transported via the Middle Passage, unknown millions more dying en route.

military-industrial complex The concept of "an immense military establishment" combined with a "permanent arms industry," which President Eisenhower warned against in his 1961 Farewell Address.

mill girls Women who worked at textile mills during the Industrial Revolution who enjoyed new freedoms and independence not seen before.

missile gap The claim, raised by John F. Kennedy during his campaign for president in 1960, that the Soviet Union had developed a technological and military advantage during Eisenhower's presidency.

Missouri Compromise Deal proposed by Kentucky senator Henry Clay in 1820 to resolve the slave/free imbalance in Congress that would result from Missouri's admission as a slave state; Maine's admission as a free state offset Missouri, and slavery was prohibited in the remainder of the Louisiana Territory north of the southern border of Missouri.

Monroe Doctrine President James Monroe's declaration to Congress on December 2, 1823, that the American continents would be thenceforth closed to European colonization, and that the United States would not interfere in European affairs.

Montgomery bus boycott Sparked by Rosa Parks's arrest on December 1, 1955, for refusing to surrender her seat to a white passenger, a successful year-long boycott protesting segregation on city buses; led by the Reverend Martin Luther King Jr.

moral imperialism The Wilsonian belief that U.S. foreign policy should be guided by morality, and should teach other peoples about democracy. Wilson used this belief to both repudiate Dollar Diplomacy and justify frequent military interventions in Latin America.

moral suasion The abolitionist strategy that sought to end slavery by persuading both slaveowners and complicit northerners that the institution was evil.

muckraking Writing that exposed corruption and abuses in politics, business, meatpacking, child labor, and more, primarily in the first decade of the twentieth century; included popular books and magazine articles that spurred public interest in reform.

Muller v. Oregon 1908 Supreme Court decision that held that state interest in protecting women could override liberty of contract. Louis D. Brandeis, with help from his sister-in-law Josephine Goldmark of the National Consumers League, filed a brief in *Muller* that used statistics about women's health to argue for their protection.

multiculturalism Term that became prominent in the 1990s to describe a growing emphasis on group racial and ethnic identity and demands that jobs, education, and politics reflect the increasingly diverse nature of American society.

Murray, Judith Sargent A writer and early feminist thinker prominent in the years following the American Revolution.

My Lai massacre Massacre of 347 Vietnamese civilians in the village of My Lai by Lieutenant William Cal-

ley and troops under his command. U.S. army officers covered up the massacre for a year until an investigation uncovered the events. Eventually twenty-five army officers were charged with complicity in the massacre and its cover-up, but only Calley was convicted. He served little time for his crimes.

Nat Turner's Rebellion Most important slave uprising in nineteenth-century America, led by a slave preacher who, with his followers, killed about sixty white persons in Southampton County, Virginia, in 1831.

National Association for the Advancement of Colored People Founded in 1910, the civil rights organization that brought lawsuits against discriminatory practices and published *The Crisis*, a journal edited by African-American scholar W. E. B. Du Bois.

National Defense Education Act 1958 law passed in reaction to America's perceived inferiority in the space race; encouraged education in science and modern languages through student loans, university research grants, and aid to public schools.

National Industrial Recovery Act 1933 law passed on the last of the Hundred Days; it created public-works jobs through the Federal Emergency Relief Administration and established a system of self-regulation for industry through the National Recovery Administration, which was ruled unconstitutional in 1935.

National Organization for Women Organization founded in 1966 by writer Betty Friedan and other feminists; it pushed for abortion rights, nondiscrimination in the workplace, and other forms of equality for women.

National Recovery Administration (NRA) Controversial federal agency created in 1933 that brought together business and labor leaders to create "codes of fair competition" and "fair labor" policies, including a national minimum wage.

nativism Anti-immigrant and anti-Catholic feeling especially prominent in the 1830s through the 1850s; the largest group of its proponents was New York's Order of the Star-Spangled Banner, which expanded into the American (Know-Nothing) Party in 1854.

Navajo's Long Walk The forced removal of 8,000 Navajos from their lands by Union forces to a reservation in the 1860s.

Navigation Act Law passed by the English Parliament to control colonial trade and bolster the mercantile system, 1650–1775; enforcement of the act led to growing resentment by colonists.

neoconservatives The leaders of the conservative insurgency of the early 1980s. Their brand of conservatism was personified in Ronald Reagan, who believed in less government, supply-side economics, and "family values."

Neolin A Native American religious prophet who, by preaching pan-Indian unity and rejection of European technology and commerce, helped inspire Pontiac's Rebellion.

Neutrality Acts Series of laws passed between 1935 and 1939 to keep the United States from becoming involved in war by prohibiting American trade and travel to warring nations.

New Deal Franklin D. Roosevelt's campaign promise, in his speech to the Democratic National Convention of 1932, to combat the Great Depression with a "new deal for the American people"; the phrase became a catchword for his ambitious plan of economic programs.

new feminism A new aspect of the women's rights movement that arose in the early part of the twentieth century. New feminism added a focus on individual and sexual freedom to the movement, and introduced the word "feminism" into American life.

New Freedom Democrat Woodrow Wilson's political slogan in the presidential campaign of 1912; Wilson wanted to improve the banking system, lower tariffs, and, by breaking up monopolies, give small businesses freedom to compete.

New Harmony Community founded in Indiana by British industrialist Robert Owen in 1825; the short-lived New Harmony Community of Equality was one of the few nineteenth-century communal experiments not based on religious ideology.

new immigrants Wave of newcomers from southern and eastern Europe, including many Jews, who became a majority among immigrants to America after 1890.

New Jersey Plan New Jersey's delegation to the Constitutional Convention's plan for one legislative body with equal representation for each state.

New Left Radical youth protest movement of the 1960s, named by leader Tom Hayden to distinguish it from the Old (Marxist-Leninist) Left of the 1930s.

New Nationalism Platform of the Progressive Party and slogan of former president Theodore Roosevelt in the presidential campaign of 1912; stressed government activism, including regulation of trusts, conservation, and recall of state court decisions that had nullified progressive programs.

New Negro Term used in the 1920s, in reference to a slow and steady growth of black political influence that occurred in northern cities, where African-Americans were freer to speak and act. This political activity created a spirit of protest that expressed itself culturally in the Harlem Renaissance and politically in "new Negro" nationalism.

New Orleans, Battle of Last battle of the War of 1812, fought on January 8, 1815, weeks after the peace treaty was signed but prior to the news' reaching America; General Andrew Jackson led the victorious American troops.

New South *Atlanta Constitution* editor Henry W. Grady's 1886 term for the prosperous post–Civil War South he envisioned: democratic, industrial, urban, and free of nostalgia for the defeated plantation South.

new world order President George H. W. Bush's term for the post–Cold War world.

Ninety-Five Theses The list of moral grievances against the Catholic Church by Martin Luther, a German priest, in 1517.

"no taxation without representation" The rallying cry of opponents to the 1765 Stamp Act. The slogan decried the colonists' lack of representation in Parliament.

North American Free Trade Agreement (NAFTA) Approved in 1993, the agreement with Canada and Mexico that allowed goods to travel across their borders free of tariffs. Critics of the agreement argued that American workers would lose their jobs to cheaper Mexican labor.

North Atlantic Treaty Organization (NATO) Alliance founded in 1949 by ten western European nations, the United States, and Canada to deter Soviet expansion in Europe.

Northwest Ordinance of 1787 Law that created the Northwest Territory (area north of the Ohio River and west of Pennsylvania), established conditions for self-government and statehood, included a Bill of Rights, and permanently prohibited slavery.

Notes on the State of Virginia Thomas Jefferson's 1785 book that claimed, among other things, that black people were incapable of becoming citizens and living in harmony alongside white people due to the legacy of slavery and what Jefferson believed were the "real distinctions that nature has made" between races.

NSC-68 Top-secret policy paper approved by President Truman in 1950 that outlined a militaristic approach to combating the spread of global communism.

nullification crisis The 1832 attempt by the State of South Carolina to nullify, or invalidate within its borders, the 1832 federal tariff law. President Jackson responded with the Force Act of 1833.

Obergefell v. Hodges 2015 Supreme Court decision that allowed same-sex couples to marry throughout the United States.

Occupy Wall Street A grassroots movement in 2011 against growing economic inequality, declining opportunity, and the depredations of Wall Street banks.

oil embargo Prohibition on trade in oil declared by the Organization of Petroleum Exporting Countries, dominated by Middle Eastern producers, in October 1973 in response to U.S. and western European support for Israel in the 1973 Yom Kippur War. The rise in gas prices and fuel shortages resulted in a global economic recession and profoundly affected the American economy.

Oneida Utopian community founded in 1848; the Perfectionist religious group practiced "complex marriage" under leader John Humphrey Noyes.

Open Door Policy Demand in 1899 by Secretary of State John Hay, in hopes of protecting the Chinese market for U.S. exports, that Chinese trade be open to all nations.

open immigration American immigration laws under which nearly all white people could immigrate to the United States and become naturalized citizens.

Operation Dixie CIO's largely ineffective post–World War II campaign to unionize southern workers.

Ordinance of 1784 A law drafted by Thomas Jefferson that regulated land ownership and defined the terms by which western land would be marketed and settled; it established stages of self-government for the West. First Congress would govern a territory; then the territory would be admitted to the Union as a full state.

Ordinance of 1785 A law that regulated land sales in the Old Northwest. The land surveyed was divided into 640-acre plots and sold at $1 per acre.

Oslo Accords 1993 roadmap for peace between Israel and the newly created Palestinian Authority, negotiated under the Clinton administration.

Panama Canal Zone The small strip of land on either side of the Panama Canal. The Canal Zone was under U.S. control from 1903 to 1979 as a result of

Theodore Roosevelt's assistance in engineering a coup in Colombia that established Panama's independence.

Panic of 1819 Financial collapse brought on by sharply falling cotton prices, declining demand for American exports, and reckless western land speculation.

Panic of 1837 Beginning of major economic depression lasting about six years; touched off by a British financial crisis and made worse by falling cotton prices, credit and currency problems, and speculation in land, canals, and railroads.

paternalism A moral position developed during the first half of the nineteenth century which claimed that slaves were deprived of liberty for their own "good." Such a rationalization was adopted by some slaveowners to justify slavery.

the "peculiar institution" A phrase used by whites in the antebellum South to refer to slavery without using the word "slavery."

Pentagon Papers Informal name for the Defense Department's secret history of the Vietnam conflict; leaked to the press by former official Daniel Ellsberg and published in the *New York Times* in 1971.

Pequot War An armed conflict in 1637 that led to the destruction of one of New England's most powerful Indian groups.

perfectionism The idea that social ills once considered incurable could in fact be eliminated, popularized by the religious revivalism of the nineteenth century.

Perry, Commodore Matthew U.S. naval officer who negotiated the Treaty of Kanagawa in 1854. That treaty was the first step in starting a political and commercial relationship between the United States and Japan.

pet banks Local banks that received deposits while the charter of the Bank of the United States was about to expire in 1836. The choice of these banks was influenced by political and personal connections.

Philippine War American military campaign that suppressed the movement for Philippine independence after the Spanish-American War; America's death toll was over 4,000 and the Philippines' was far higher.

Pilgrims Puritan separatists who broke completely with the Church of England and sailed to the New World aboard the *Mayflower*, founding Plymouth Colony on Cape Cod in 1620.

plantation An early word for a colony, a settlement "planted" from abroad among an alien population in Ireland or the New World. Later, a large agricultural enterprise that used unfree labor to produce a crop for the world market.

Platt Amendment 1901 amendment to the Cuban constitution that reserved the United States' right to intervene in Cuban affairs and forced newly independent Cuba to host American naval bases on the island.

Plessy v. Ferguson U.S. Supreme Court decision supporting the legality of Jim Crow laws that permitted or required "separate but equal" facilities for blacks and whites.

Pontiac's Rebellion An Indian attack on British forts and settlements after France ceded to the British its territory east of the Mississippi River, as part of the Treaty of Paris in 1763, without consulting France's Indian allies.

Popular Front A period during the mid-1930s when the Communist Party sought to ally itself with socialists and New Dealers in movements for social change, urging reform of the capitalist system rather than revolution.

popular sovereignty Program that allowed settlers in a disputed territory to decide the slavery issue for themselves; most closely associated with Senator Stephen A. Douglas of Illinois.

Populists Founded in 1892, a group that advocated a variety of reform issues, including free coinage of silver, income tax, postal savings, regulation of railroads, and direct election of U.S. senators.

Porkopolis Nickname of Cincinnati, coined in the mid-nineteenth century, after its numerous slaughter houses.

Port Huron Statement A manifesto by Students for a Democratic Society that criticized institutions ranging from political parties to corporations, unions, and the military-industrial complex, while offering a new vision of social change.

Potsdam conference Last meeting of the major Allied powers; the conference that took place outside Berlin from July 17 to August 2, 1945, at which U.S. president Harry Truman, Soviet dictator Joseph Stalin, and British prime minister Clement Attlee finalized plans begun at Yalta.

Proclamation of 1763 Royal directive issued after the French and Indian War prohibiting settlement, surveys, and land grants west of the Appalachian Mountains; caused considerable resentment among colonists hoping to move west.

Progressive Party Political party created when former president Theodore Roosevelt broke away from the Republican Party to run for president again in 1912; the party supported progressive reforms similar to those of the Democrats but stopped short of seeking to eliminate trusts. Also the name of the party backing Robert La Follette for president in 1924.

Progressivism Broad-based reform movement, 1900–1917, that sought governmental action in solving problems in many areas of American life, including education, public health, the economy, the environment, labor, transportation, and politics.

proslavery argument The series of arguments defending the institution of slavery in the South as a positive good, not a necessary evil. The arguments included the racist belief that black people were inherently inferior to white people, as well as the belief that slavery, in creating a permanent underclass of laborers, made freedom possible for whites. Other elements of the argument included biblical citations.

Public Works Administration A New Deal agency that contracted with private construction companies to build roads, bridges, schools, hospitals, and other public facilities.

Pueblo Revolt Uprising in 1680 in which Pueblo Indians temporarily drove Spanish colonists out of modern-day New Mexico.

Pure Food and Drug Act Passed in 1906, the first law to regulate manufacturing of food and medicines; prohibited dangerous additives and inaccurate labeling.

Puritans English religious group that sought to purify the Church of England; founded the Massachusetts Bay Colony under John Winthrop in 1630.

Radical Republicans Group within the Republican Party in the 1850s and 1860s that advocated strong resistance to the expansion of slavery, opposition to compromise with the South in the secession crisis of 1860–1861, emancipation and arming of black soldiers during the Civil War, and equal civil and political rights for blacks during Reconstruction.

Reagan Revolution The rightward turn of American politics following the 1980 election of Ronald Reagan. The Reagan Revolution made individual "freedom" a rallying cry for the right.

Reaganomics Popular name for President Ronald Reagan's philosophy of "supply side" economics, which combined tax cuts with an unregulated marketplace.

reconquista The "reconquest" of Spain from the Moors completed by King Ferdinand and Queen Isabella in 1492.

Reconstruction Act 1867 law that established temporary military governments in ten Confederate states—excepting Tennessee—and required that the states ratify the Fourteenth Amendment and permit freedmen to vote.

Reconstruction Finance Corporation Federal program established in 1932 under President Herbert

Hoover to loan money to banks and other institutions to help them avert bankruptcy.

Red Scare of 1919–1920 Fear among many Americans after World War I of Communists in particular and non-citizens in general, a reaction to the Russian Revolution, mail bombs, strikes, and riots.

Redeemers Post–Civil War Democratic leaders who supposedly saved the South from Yankee domination and preserved the primarily rural economy.

redemptioners Indentured families or persons who received passage to the New World in exchange for a promise to work off their debt in America.

Regulators Groups of backcountry Carolina settlers who protested colonial policies.

repartimiento system Spanish labor system under which Indians were legally free and able to earn wages but were also required to perform a fixed amount of labor yearly. Replaced the *encomienda* system.

republic Representative political system in which citizens govern themselves by electing representatives, or legislators, to make key decisions on the citizens' behalf.

republican motherhood The ideology that emerged as a result of American independence where women played an indispensable role by training future citizens.

republicanism Political theory in eighteenth-century England and America that celebrated active participation in public life by economically independent citizens as central to freedom.

reverse discrimination Belief that affirmative action programs discriminate against white people.

Revolution of 1800 First time that an American political party surrendered power to the opposition party; Jefferson, a Republican, had defeated incumbent Adams, a Federalist, for president.

Roanoke colony English expedition of 117 settlers, including Virginia Dare, the first English child born in the New World; the colony disappeared from Roanoke Island in the Outer Banks sometime between 1587 and 1590.

robber barons Also known as "captains of industry"; Gilded-Age industrial figures who inspired both admiration, for their economic leadership and innovation, and hostility and fear, due to their unscrupulous business methods, repressive labor practices, and unprecedented economic control over entire industries.

Roe v. Wade 1973 U.S. Supreme Court decision requiring states to permit first-trimester abortions.

Roosevelt Corollary 1904 Announcement by President Theodore Roosevelt, essentially a corollary to the Monroe Doctrine, that the United States could intervene militarily to prevent interference from European powers in the Western Hemisphere.

Rwandan genocide 1994 Genocide conducted by the Hutu ethnic group upon the Tutsi minority in Rwanda.

Sacco-Vanzetti case A case held during the 1920s in which two Italian-American anarchists were found guilty and executed for a crime in which there was very little evidence linking them to the particular crime.

Salem witch trials A crisis of trials and executions in Salem, Massachusetts, in 1692 that resulted from anxiety over witchcraft.

salutary neglect Informal British policy during the first half of the eighteenth century that allowed the American colonies considerable freedom to pursue their economic and political interests in exchange for colonial obedience.

Sanitary Fairs Fund-raising bazaars led by women on behalf of Civil War soldiers. The fairs offered items such as uniforms and banners, as well as other emblems of war.

Santa Anna, Antonio López de The military leader who, in 1834, seized political power in Mexico and became a dictator. In 1835, Texans rebelled against him, and he led his army to Texas to crush their rebellion. He captured the missionary called the Alamo and killed all of its defenders, which inspired Texans to continue their resistance and Americans to volunteer to fight for Texas. The Texans captured Santa Anna during a surprise attack, and he bought his freedom by signing a treaty recognizing Texas's independence.

Saratoga, Battle of Major defeat of British general John Burgoyne and more than 5,000 British troops at Saratoga, New York, on October 17, 1777.

scalawags Southern white Republicans—some former Unionists—who supported Reconstruction governments.

Schenck v. United States 1919 U.S. Supreme Court decision upholding the wartime Espionage and Sedition Acts; in the opinion he wrote for the case, Justice Oliver Wendell Holmes set the now-familiar "clear and present danger" standard.

scientific management Management campaign to improve worker efficiency using measurements like "time and motion" studies to achieve greater productivity; introduced by Frederick Winslow Taylor in 1911.

Scopes trial 1925 trial of John Scopes, Tennessee teacher accused of violating state law prohibiting teaching of the theory of evolution; it became a nationally celebrated confrontation between religious fundamentalism and civil liberties.

Scottsboro case Case in which nine black youths were convicted of raping two white women; in overturning the verdicts of this case, the Court established precedents in *Powell v. Alabama* (1932) that adequate counsel must be appointed in capital cases, and in *Norris v. Alabama* (1935) that African-Americans cannot be excluded from juries.

Sea Islands experiment The 1861 pre-Reconstruction social experiment that involved converting slave plantations into places where former slaves could work for wages or own land. Former slaves also received education and access to improved shelter and food.

Second American Revolution The transformation of American government and society brought about by the Civil War.

Second Great Awakening Religious revival movement of the early decades of the nineteenth century, in reaction to the growth of secularism and rationalist religion; began the predominance of the Baptist and Methodist Churches.

second Great Migration The movement of black migrants from the rural South to the cities of the North and West, which occurred from 1941 through World War II, that dwarfed the Great Migration of World War I.

Second Middle Passage The massive trade of slaves from the upper South (Virginia and the Chesapeake) to the lower South (the Gulf states) that took place between 1820 and 1860.

Sedition Act 1918 law that made it a crime to make spoken or printed statements that criticized the U.S. government or encouraged interference with the war effort.

Selective Service Act Law passed in 1917 to quickly increase enlistment in the army for the United States' entry into World War I; required men to register with the draft.

"separate but equal" Principle underlying legal racial segregation, upheld in *Plessy v. Ferguson* (1896) and struck down in *Brown v. Board of Education* (1954).

separation of powers Feature of the U.S. Constitution, sometimes called "checks and balances," in which power is divided between executive, legislative, and judicial branches of the national government so that no one can dominate the other two and endanger citizens' liberties.

Serra, Father Junípero Missionary who began and directed the California mission system in the 1770s and 1780s. Serra presided over the conversion of many Indians to Christianity, but also engaged them in forced labor.

settlement house Late-nineteenth-century movement to offer a broad array of social services in urban immigrant neighborhoods; Chicago's Hull House was one of hundreds of settlement houses that operated by the early twentieth century.

Seven Years' War The last—and most important—of four colonial wars fought between England and France for control of North America east of the Mississippi River.

Seventeenth Amendment Progressive reform passed in 1913 that required U.S. senators to be elected directly by voters; previously, senators were chosen by state legislatures.

Shakers Religious sect founded by Mother Ann Lee in England. The United Society of Believers in Christ's Second Appearing settled in Watervliet, New York, in 1774, and subsequently established eighteen additional communes in the Northeast, Indiana, and Kentucky.

Share Our Wealth movement Program offered by Huey Long as an alternative to the New Deal. The program proposed to confiscate large personal fortunes, which would be used to guarantee every poor family a cash grant of $5,000 and every worker an annual income of $2,500. It also promised to provide pensions, reduce working hours, and pay veterans' bonuses and ensured a college education to every qualified student.

sharecropping Type of farm tenancy that developed after the Civil War in which landless workers—often former slaves—farmed land in exchange for farm supplies and a share of the crop.

Shays's Rebellion Attempt by Massachusetts farmer Daniel Shays and 1,200 compatriots, seeking debt relief through issuance of paper currency and lower taxes, to prevent courts from seizing property from indebted farmers.

Sherman Antitrust Act Passed in 1890, first law to restrict monopolistic trusts and business combinations; extended by the Clayton Antitrust Act of 1914.

Silent Spring A 1962 book by biologist Rachel Carson about the destructive impact of the widely used insecticide DDT that launched the modern environmentalist movement.

single tax Concept of taxing only landowners as a remedy for poverty, promulgated by Henry George in *Progress and Poverty* (1879).

sit-down strike Tactic adopted by labor unions in the mid- and late 1930s, whereby striking workers refused to leave factories, making production impossible; proved highly effective in the organizing drive of the Congress of Industrial Organizations.

sit-in Tactic adopted by young civil rights activists, beginning in 1960, of demanding service at lunch counters or public accommodations and refusing to leave if denied access; marked the beginning of the most militant phase of the civil rights struggle.

Sixteenth Amendment Constitutional amendment passed in 1913 that legalized the federal income tax.

the Slave Power The Republican and abolitionist term for proslavery dominance of southern and national governments.

Smith, John A swashbuckling soldier of fortune with rare powers of leadership and self-promotion who was appointed to the resident council to manage Jamestown.

Smoot-Hawley Tariff 1930 act that raised tariffs to an unprecedented level and worsened the Great Depression by raising prices and discouraging foreign trade.

Snowden, Edward An NSA contractor turned whistleblower, who released classified information relating to the United States' intelligence gathering both at home and abroad.

social contract Agreement hammered out between labor and management in leading industries; called a new "social contract." Unions signed long-term agreements that left decisions regarding capital investment, plant location, and output in management's hands, and they agreed to try to prevent unauthorized "wildcat" strikes.

Social Darwinism Application of Charles Darwin's theory of natural selection to society; used the concept of the "survival of the fittest" to justify class distinctions and to explain poverty.

Social Gospel Ideals preached by liberal Protestant clergymen in the late nineteenth and early twentieth centuries; advocated the application of Christian principles to social problems generated by industrialization.

Social Security Act 1935 law that created the Social Security system with provisions for a retirement pension, unemployment insurance, disability insurance, and public assistance (welfare).

Socialist Party Political party demanding public ownership of major economic enterprises in the United States as well as reforms like recognition of labor unions and women's suffrage; reached peak of influence in 1912 when presidential candidate Eugene V. Debs received over 900,000 votes.

Society of American Indians Organization founded in 1911 that brought together Native American intellectuals of many tribal backgrounds to promote discussion of the plight of Indian peoples.

Society of Friends (Quakers) Religious group in England and America whose members believed all persons possessed the "inner light" or spirit of God; they were early proponents of abolition of slavery and equal rights for women.

soft money and hard money In the 1830s, "soft money" referred to paper currency issued by banks. "Hard money" referred to gold and silver currency—also called specie.

Sons of Liberty Organizations formed by Samuel Adams, John Hancock, and other radicals in response to the Stamp Act.

Sotomayor, Sonia First Supreme Court Justice of Hispanic descent. Justice Sotomayor was appointed by President Barack Obama in 2009.

Southern Christian Leadership Conference (SCLC) Civil rights organization founded in 1957 by the Reverend Martin Luther King Jr. and other civil rights leaders.

Southern Manifesto A document written in 1956 that repudiated the Supreme Court decision in *Brown v. Board of Education* and supported the campaign against racial integration in public places.

spoils system The term meaning the filling of federal government jobs with persons loyal to the party of the president; originated in Andrew Jackson's first term.

Sputnik First artificial satellite to orbit the earth; launched October 4, 1957, by the Soviet Union.

stagflation A combination of stagnant economic growth and high inflation present during the 1970s.

Stamp Act Parliament's 1765 requirement that revenue stamps be affixed to all colonial printed matter, documents, and playing cards; the Stamp Act Congress met to formulate a response, and the act was repealed the following year.

staple crops Important cash crops; for example, cotton or tobacco.

steamboats Paddlewheelers that could travel both up- and down-river in deep or shallow waters; they became commercially viable early in the nineteenth century and soon developed into America's first inland freight and passenger service network.

stock market crash Also known as Black Tuesday, a stock market panic in 1929 that resulted in the loss of more than $10 billion in market value (worth approximately ten times more today). One among many causes of the Great Depression.

Stonewall Inn A gathering place for New York's gay community, the site of the 1969 police raids and resulting riots that launched the modern gay rights movement.

Stono Rebellion A slave uprising in 1739 in South Carolina that led to a severe tightening of the slave code and the temporary imposition of a prohibitive tax on imported slaves.

Strategic Arms Limitation Talks 1972 talks between President Nixon and Secretary Brezhnev that resulted in the Strategic Arms Limitation Treaty (or SALT), which limited the quantity of nuclear warheads each nation could possess, and prohibited the development of missile defense systems.

Student Nonviolent Coordinating Committee (SNCC) Organization founded in 1960 to coordinate civil rights sit-ins and other forms of grassroots protest.

Students for a Democratic Society (SDS) Major organization of the New Left, founded at the University of Michigan in 1960 by Tom Hayden and Al Haber.

suffrage The right to vote.

Sugar Act 1764 decision by Parliament to tax refined sugar and many other colonial products.

Sunbelt The label for an arc that stretched from the Carolinas to California. During the postwar era, much of the urban population growth occurred in this area.

Taft-Hartley Act 1947 law passed over President Harry Truman's veto; the law contained a number of provisions to weaken labor unions, including the banning of closed shops.

tariff of abominations Tariff passed in 1828 by Parliament that taxed imported goods at a very high rate; aroused strong opposition in the South.

tariff of 1816 First true protective tariff, intended to protect certain American goods against foreign competition.

Tea Party A grassroots Republican movement that emerged in 2009 named for the Boston Tea Party of the 1770s. The Tea Party opposed the Obama administration's sweeping legislative enactments and advocated for a more stringent immigration policy.

Teapot Dome Harding administration scandal in which Secretary of the Interior Albert B. Fall profited from secret leasing to private oil companies of government oil reserves at Teapot Dome, Wyoming, and Elk Hills, California.

Tecumseh and Tenskwatawa Tecumseh—a leader of the Shawnee tribe who tried to unite all Indians into a confederation to resist white encroachment on their lands. His beliefs and leadership made him seem dangerous to the American government. He was killed at the Battle of the Thames. His brother, Tenskwatawa—a religious prophet who called for complete separation from whites, the revival of traditional Indian culture, and resistance to federal policies.

Tejanos Texas settlers of Spanish or Mexican descent.

temperance movement A widespread reform movement, led by militant Christians, focused on reducing the use of alcoholic beverages.

Tennessee Valley Authority Administrative body created in 1933 to control flooding in the Tennessee River valley, provide work for the region's unemployed, and produce inexpensive electric power for the region.

Tenochtitlán The capital city of the Aztec Empire. The city was built on marshy islands on the western side of Lake Tetzcoco, which is the site of present-day Mexico City.

Ten-Percent Plan of Reconstruction President Lincoln's proposal for reconstruction, issued in 1863, in which southern states would rejoin the Union if 10 percent of the 1860 electorate signed loyalty pledges, accepted emancipation, and had received presidential pardons.

Tenure of Office Act 1867 law that required the president to obtain Senate approval to remove any official whose appointment had also required Senate approval; President Andrew Johnson's violation of the law by firing Secretary of War Edwin Stanton led to Johnson's impeachment.

Tet offensive Surprise attack by the Viet Cong and North Vietnamese during the Vietnamese New Year of 1968; turned American public opinion strongly against the war in Vietnam.

the Texas Revolt The 1830s rebellion of residents of the territory of Texas—many of them Americans emigrants—against Mexican control of the region.

Thirteenth Amendment Constitutional amendment adopted in 1865 that irrevocably abolished slavery throughout the United States.

Three Mile Island Nuclear power plant near Harrisburg, Pennsylvania, site of 1979 accident that released radioactive steam into the air; public reaction ended the nuclear power industry's expansion.

three-fifths clause A provision signed into the Constitution in 1787 that three-fifths of the slave population would be counted in determining each state's representation in the House of Representatives and its electoral votes for president.

Title IX Part of the Educational Amendments Act of 1972 that banned gender discrimination in higher education.

totalitarianism The term that describes aggressive, ideologically driven states that seek to subdue all of civil society to their control, thus leaving no room for individual rights or alternative values.

Townshend Acts 1767 parliamentary measures (named for the chancellor of the Exchequer) that taxed tea and other commodities, and established a Board of Customs Commissioners and colonial vice-admiralty courts.

Trail of Tears Cherokees' own term for their forced removal, 1838–1839, from the Southeast to Indian lands (later Oklahoma); of 15,000 forced to march, 4,000 died on the way.

transcendentalists Philosophy of a small group of mid-nineteenth-century New England writers and thinkers, including Ralph Waldo Emerson, Henry David Thoreau, and Margaret Fuller; they stressed personal and intellectual self-reliance.

transcontinental railroad First line across the continent from Omaha, Nebraska, to Sacramento, California, established in 1869 with the linkage of the Union Pacific and Central Pacific railroads at Promontory, Utah.

Treaty of Greenville 1795 treaty under which twelve Indian tribes ceded most of Ohio and Indiana to the federal government, and which also established the "annuity" system.

Treaty of Paris Signed on September 3, 1783, the treaty that ended the Revolutionary War, recognized American independence from Britain, established the border between Canada and the United States, fixed the western border at the Mississippi River, and ceded Florida to Spain.

Truman Doctrine President Harry S. Truman's program announced in 1947 of aid to European countries—particularly Greece and Turkey—threatened by communism.

trusts Companies combined to limit competition.

Tubman, Harriet Abolitionist who was born a slave, escaped to the North, and then returned to the South nineteen times and guided 300 slaves to freedom.

Tulsa riot A race riot in 1921—the worst in American history—that occurred in Tulsa, Oklahoma, after a group of black veterans tried to prevent a lynching. Over 300 African- Americans were killed, and 10,000 lost their homes in fires set by white mobs.

Uncle Tom's Cabin Harriet Beecher Stowe's 1852 antislavery novel that popularized the abolitionist position.

Underground Railroad Operating in the decades before the Civil War, a clandestine system of routes and safehouses through which slaves were led to freedom in the North.

United Nations Organization of nations to maintain world peace, established in 1945 and headquartered in New York.

Uprising of 1622 Unsuccessful uprising of Virginia Native Americans that wiped out one-quarter of the settler population, but ultimately led to the settlers gaining supremacy.

urban renewal A series of policies supported by all levels of government that allowed local governments and housing authorities to demolish so-called blighted areas in urban centers to replace them with more valuable real estate usually reserved for white people.

USA Patriot Act A 2001 mammoth bill that conferred unprecedented powers on law-enforcement agencies charged with preventing domestic terrorism, including the power to wiretap, read private messages, and spy on citizens.

U.S.S. *Maine* Battleship that exploded in Havana Harbor on February 15, 1898, resulting in 266 deaths; the American public, assuming that the Spanish had mined the ship, clamored for war, and the Spanish-American War was declared two months later.

utopian communities Ideal communities that offered innovative social and economic relationships to those who were interested in achieving salvation.

V-E Day May 8, 1945, the day World War II officially ended in Europe.

Versailles Treaty The treaty signed at the Versailles peace conference after World War I which established President Woodrow Wilson's vision of an international regulating body, redrew parts of Europe and the Middle East, and assigned economically crippling war repara-tions to Germany, but failed to incorporate all of Wilson's Fourteen Points.

vertical integration Company's avoidance of middle-men by producing its own supplies and providing for distribution of its product.

Vicksburg, Battle of The fall of Vicksburg, Mississippi, to General Ulysses S. Grant's army on July 4, 1863, after two months of siege; a turning point in the war because it gave the Union control of the Mississippi River.

Vietnam Syndrome The belief that the United States should be extremely cautious in deploying its military forces overseas that emerged after the end of the Vietnam War.

Virginia and Kentucky resolutions Legislation passed in 1798 and 1799 by the Virginia and the Kentucky legislatures; written by James Madison and Thomas Jefferson in response to the Alien and Sedition Acts, the resolutions advanced the state-compact theory of the Constitution. Virginia's resolution called on the federal courts to protect free speech. Jefferson's draft for Kentucky stated that a state could nullify federal law, but this was deleted.

Virginia Company A joint-stock enterprise that King James I chartered in 1606. The company was to spread Christianity in the New World as well as find ways to make a profit in it.

Virginia Plan Virginia's delegation to the Constitutional Convention's plan for a strong central government and a two-house legislature apportioned by population.

virtual representation The idea that the American colonies, although they had no actual representative in Parliament, were "virtually" represented by all members of Parliament.

Voting Rights Act Law passed in the wake of Martin Luther King Jr.'s Selma-to-Montgomery March in 1965; it authorized federal protection of the right to vote and permitted federal enforcement of minority voting rights in individual counties, mostly in the South.

Wade-Davis Bill Radical Republicans' 1864 plan for reconstruction that required loyalty oaths, abolition of slavery, repudiation of war debts, and denial of political rights to high-ranking Confederate officials; President Lincoln refused to sign the bill.

Wagner Act (National Labor Relations Act of 1935) Law that established the National Labor Relations Board and facilitated unionization by regulating employment and bargaining practices.

Walking Purchase An infamous 1737 purchase of Indian land in which Pennsylvanian colonists tricked the Lenni Lanape Indians. The Lanape agreed to cede land equivalent to the distance a man could walk in thirty-six hours, but the colonists marked out an area using a team of runners.

war in Afghanistan War fought against the Taliban and Al-Qaeda in Afghanistan following the attacks of September 11, 2001. It remains the longest war in American history.

War Industries Board Board run by financier Bernard Baruch that planned production and allocation of war materiel, supervised purchasing, and fixed prices, 1917–1919.

War of 1812 War fought with Britain, 1812–1814, over issues that included impressment of American sailors, interference with shipping, and collusion with Northwest Territory Indians; settled by the Treaty of Ghent in 1814.

War on Poverty Plan announced by President Lyndon B. Johnson in his 1964 State of the Union address; under the Economic Opportunity Bill signed later that year, Head Start, VISTA, and the Jobs Corps were created, and programs were created for students, farmers, and businesses in efforts to eliminate poverty.

war on terrorism Global crusade to root out anti-American, anti-Western Islamist terrorist cells; launched by President George W. Bush as a response to the 9/11 attacks.

War Powers Act Law passed in 1973, reflecting growing opposition to American involvement in the Vietnam War; required congressional approval before the president sent troops abroad.

Watergate Washington office and apartment complex that lent its name to the 1972–1974 scandal of the Nixon administration; when his knowledge of the break-in at the Watergate and subsequent cover-up were revealed, Nixon resigned the presidency under threat of impeachment.

The Wealth of Nations The 1776 work by economist Adam Smith that argued that the "invisible hand" of the free market directed economic life more effectively and fairly than governmental intervention.

Webster-Hayne debate U.S. Senate debate of January 1830 between Daniel Webster of Massachusetts and Robert Hayne of South Carolina over nullification and states' rights.

welfare state A term that originated in Britain during World War II to refer to a system of income assistance, health coverage, and social services for all citizens.

Whiskey Rebellion Violent protest by western Pennsylvania farmers against the federal excise tax on whiskey, 1794.

Wilmot Proviso Proposal to prohibit slavery in any land acquired in the Mexican War; defeated by southern senators, led by John C. Calhoun of South Carolina, in 1846 and 1847.

Winthrop, John Puritan leader and governor of the Massachusetts Bay Colony who resolved to use the colony as a refuge for persecuted Puritans and as an instrument of building a "wilderness Zion" in America.

woman suffrage Movement to give women the right to vote through a constitutional amendment, spearheaded by Susan B. Anthony and Elizabeth Cady Stanton's National Woman Suffrage Association.

Worcester v. Georgia 1832 Supreme Court case that held that the Indian nations were distinct peoples who could not be dealt with by the states—instead, only the federal government could negotiate with them. President Jackson refused to enforce the ruling.

Works Progress Administration (WPA) Part of the Second New Deal; it provided jobs for millions of the unemployed on construction and arts projects.

Wounded Knee massacre Last incident of the Indian Wars; it took place in 1890 in the Dakota Territory, where the U.S. Cavalry killed over 200 Sioux men, women, and children.

writs of assistance One of the colonies' main complaints against Britain; the writs allowed unlimited search warrants without cause to look for evidence of smuggling.

XYZ affair Affair in which French foreign minister Talleyrand's three anonymous agents demanded payments to stop French plundering of American ships in 1797; refusal to pay the bribe was followed by two years of undeclared sea war with France (1798–1800).

Yalta conference Meeting of Franklin D. Roosevelt, Winston Churchill, and Joseph Stalin at a Crimean resort to discuss the postwar world on February 4–11, 1945; Joseph Stalin claimed large areas in eastern Europe for Soviet domination.

Yamasee uprising Revolt of Yamasee and Creek Indians, aggravated by rising debts and slave traders' raids, against Carolina settlers. Resulted in the expulsion of many Indians to Florida.

yellow press Sensationalism in newspaper publishing that reached a peak in the circulation war between Joseph Pulitzer's *New York World* and William Randolph Hearst's *New York Journal* in the 1890s; the papers' accounts of events in Havana Harbor in 1898 led directly to the Spanish-American War.

yeoman farmers Small landowners (the majority of white families in the Old South) who farmed their own land and usually did not own slaves.

Yorktown, Battle of Last battle of the Revolutionary War; General Lord Charles Cornwallis along with over 7,000 British troops surrendered at Yorktown, Virginia, on October 17, 1781.

Zimmermann Telegram Telegram from the German foreign secretary to the German minister in Mexico, February 1917, instructing the minister to offer to recover Texas, New Mexico, and Arizona for Mexico if it would fight the United States to divert attention from Germany in the event that the United States joined the war.

zoot suit riots 1943 riots in which sailors on leave attacked Mexican-American youths.

CREDITS

PHOTOS

Front Matter: Page i: Library of Congress; **p. ii (top left):** Franklin D. Roosevelt Presidential Library; **(top right):** Granger Collection; **(bottom left):** Abraham Lincoln Presidential Library and Museum; **(bottom right):** Bettmann/Getty Images; **p. v:** Flynn Larsen; **p. vi:** Jewett, William S. (1812-1873) The Promised Land - the Grayson family, 1850. Oil on canvas, 50 3/4 x 64 in. Daniel J. Terra Collection, 1999.79. Terra Foundation for American Art Photo Credit: Terra Foundation for American Art, Chicago / Art Resource, NY; **p. vii:** Adoc-photos / Art Resource, NY; **p. viii:** Roosevelt 560.51 1902-156, Houghton Library, Harvard University; **p. ix:** Library of Congress; **p. x:** Courtesy of The WASP Archive, The TWU Libraries Woman's Collection, Texas Woman's University, Denton, Texas; **p. xi:** American Catholic History Research Center and University Archives, Catholic University of America; **p. xii:** Burt Glinn / Magnum Photos; **p. xiii:** AP Photo/Ira Schwartz; **p. xiv:** Whitney Curtis, The New York Times, Redux; **p. xv:** Official White House Photo by Pete Souza; **p. xviii:** Granger Collection. **Chapter 15: Page 441:** Chicago Historical Society; **p. 443:** Library of Congress; **p. 444 (top):** Photographic History Collection, Division of Information Technology and Communications, National Museum of American History, Smithsonian Institution; **(bottom):** Library of Congress; **p. 445:** Granger Collection; **p. 447:** Smithsonian American Art Museum, Washington, DC / Art Resource, NY; **p. 448:** Library of Congress; **p. 449:** Cook Collection, Valentine Richmond History Center; **p. 453 (top):** Library of Congress; **(bottom):** The Historic New Orleans Collection, Gift of Mr. Harold Schilke and Mr. Boyd Cruise, acc. no. 1953.73; **p. 455:** Library of Congress; **p. 456:** Library of Congress; **p. 457:** Ed Sullivan Collection, Special Collections, University of Hartford; **p. 458:** Library of Congress; **p. 459:** Library of Congress; **p. 462:** Library of Congress;

p. 463 (both): Library of Congress; **p. 464:** Library of Congress; **p. 465:** Library of Congress; **p. 466:** Clements Library Collection, University of Michigan; **p. 467:** Granger Collection; **p. 468:** Wikimedia, public domain; **p. 469:** Library of Congress; **p. 470:** National Archives; **p. 473:** Library of Congress. **Chapter 16: Page 475:** Private Collection / The Bridgeman Art Library; **p. 478:** © The Metropolitan Museum of Art. Image source: Art Resource, NY; **p. 480:** Library of Congress; **p. 481:** Granger Collection; **p. 482 (both):** Library of Congress; **p. 483:** Jacob A. (Jacob August) Riis (1849-1914)/Museum of the City of New York. 90.13.4.111A; **p. 485:** Bullock Texas State History Museum, Austin TX; **p. 486:** Solomon Butcher Collection. Nebraska State Historical Society; **p. 487:** Granger Collection; **p. 489:** Library of Congress; **p. 490 (top):** Courtesy of the Braun Research Library Collection, Autry National Center, Los Angeles; Photo # P.13250; **(bottom):** Image copyright © The Metropolitan Museum of Art / Art Resource, NY; **p. 491:** Image copyright © The Metropolitan Museum of Art. Image source: Art Resource, NY; **p. 492:** Adoc-photos / Art Resource, NY; **p. 493 (top):** Missouri History Museum, St. Louis; **(bottom):** Courtesy of the Museum of the South Dakota State Historical Society, Pierre SD; **p. 497:** Library of Congress; **p. 498:** Library of Congress; **p. 500:** The Ohio State University Billy Ireland Cartoon Library & Museum; **p. 501:** Library of Congress; **p. 505:** bpk, Berlin / Art Resource, NY; **p. 506:** Bettmann/Corbis/Getty Images; **p. 507:** Bettmann/Corbis/Getty Images; **p. 510:** Wisconsin Historical Society, WHS-47662. **Chapter 17: Page 512:** High Museum of Art, Atlanta. Photo by James Schoomaker; **p. 513:** Library of Congress; **p. 515:** Kansas State Historical Society; **p. 517:** The Denver Public Library, Western History Collection, WH2129RMN; **p. 518:** Corbis/Getty Images; **p. 519:** Library of Congress; **p. 521:** Florida State Archives; **p. 522:** Library of Congress; **p. 523:** Library of Congress; **p. 526 (both):** Library of Congress; **p. 527:** Research Divi-

sion of the Oklahoma Historical Society; **p. 528:** Courtesy of the Tennessee State Museum; **p. 529 (top):** Judge Magazine, August 22, 1903; **(bottom):** National Archives; **p. 530 (top):** The Denver Public Library, Western History Collection, X-21518; **(bottom):** University of Washington Libraries, Special Collections, #UW1678; **p. 531:** Library of Congress; **p. 533:** Library of Congress; **p. 535:** Courtesy of the Bernice Pauahi Bishop Museum Archives; **p. 537:** Frederic Remington Art Museum; **p. 538 (top):** Francisco Oller (Puerto Rican, 1833-1917). *Hacienda La Fortuna*, 1885. Oil on canvas, 26 x 40 in. (66 x 101.6 cm). Brooklyn Museum, Gift of Lilla Brown in memory of her husband, John W. Brown, by exchange, 2012.19; **(bottom):** Granger Collection; **p. 539:** National Archives; **p. 543:** Library of Congress; **p. 544:** North Wind Picture Archives / Alamy. **Chapter 18: Page 546:** © 2013 Delaware Art Museum / Artists Rights Society (ARS), New York / The Philadelphia Museum of Art/Art Resource, NY; **p. 549:** Library of Congress; **p. 551:** Library of Congress; **p. 552 (top):** Library of Congress; **(bottom):** Courtesy of the author; **p. 553:** Library of Congress; **p. 554:** Image Courtesy of The Advertising Archives; **p. 555:** Library of Congress; **p. 557:** Brown Brothers; **p. 560:** Library of Congress; **p. 563:** Library of Congress; **p. 564:** Byron Company (New York, N.Y.)/ Museum of the City of New York. 93.1.1.8018; **p. 566:** "Children in Hull-House Court," Hull-House Yearbook, 1913, page 50. University of Illinois at Chicago Library, Special Collections; **p. 567:** Utah State Historical Society; **p. 568:** Minnesota Historical Society; **p. 569:** archive.org. pd; **p. 570:** Courtesy of the Bancroft Library. University of California, Berkeley; **p. 571 (top):** Roosevelt 560.51 1902-156, Houghton Library, Harvard University; **(bottom):** provided courtesy © HarpWeek LLC; **p. 572 (top):** Purchase, Jim and Carol Kautz, class of 1955, in honor of Richard and Ronay Menschel/Francis Lehman Loeb Art Center, Vassar College. **(bottom):** Roosevelt 560.51

1903-115, Houghton Library, Harvard University; p. 574: Fotosearch/Getty Images. **Chapter 19: Page 578:** Imperial War Museum / The Art Archive at Art Resource, NY; **p. 582:** Library of Congress; **p. 585:** Albin Egger-Lienz, Nordfrankreich, 1917/ Photo by Ji-Elle. 2012 http://creativecommons.org/licenses/by-sa/3.0/deed.en; **p. 586 (top):** Private Collection / Chris Deakes/The Art Archive. Art Resource, NY; **(bottom):** Bettmann/Corbis/Getty Images; **p. 589 (top):** Library of Congress; **(bottom):** © Imperial War Museum (Art.IWM PST 6921); **p. 591:** Library of Congress; **p. 594:** Cover of Union Signal, Jan 27, 1916, Frances E. Willard Memorial Library and Archives; **p. 595 (top):** National Archives; **(bottom):** Library of Congress; **p. 596:** Jerry L. Thompson / Art Resource, NY; **p. 597:** Wikimedia, public domain; **p. 599 (top):** Paris Pierce / Alamy Stock Photo; **(bottom):** St. Louis Post-Dispatch, 17 April 1906; **p. 601:** © 2016 The Jacob and Gwendolyn Knight Lawrence Foundation, Seattle / Artist Rights Society (ARS) , New York. Digital Image © The Museum of Modern Art/Licensed by SCALA / Art Resource, NY; **p. 602:** Tulsa Historical Society; **p. 603:** Library of Congress; **p. 605 (top):** Bettmann/Corbis/Getty Images; **(bottom):** National Archives; **p. 609:** Granger Collection. **Chapter 20: Page 612:** The Metropolitan Museum of Art, Gift of AXA Equitable, 2012 (2012.478a-j) © The Metropolitan Museum of Art, Image copyright © The Metropolitan Museum of Art. Image source: Art Resource, NY; **p. 613:** Library of Congress; **p. 615:** Underwood Archives /Getty Images; **p. 616:** kansasmemory.org, Kansas State Historical Society, Copy and Reuse Restrictions Apply; **p. 617:** Minnesota Historical Society; **p. 619:** Honolulu Academy of Arts: Gift of Philip H. Roach, Jr., 2001; **p. 620 (both):** Granger Collection; **p. 621 (top):** The Art Archive / Culver Pictures. Art Resource, NY; **(bottom):** Granger Collection; **p. 622:** Library of Congress; **p. 623:** Bettmann/Corbis/Getty Images; **p. 625:** Paul Avrich Anarchism Collection, Rare Book and Special Collections Division, Library of Congress; **p. 626 (top):** San Diego Museum of Art/Bridgeman Images; **(bottom):** The Denver Public Library, Western History Collection, Rh-1158; **p. 627 (top):** City of Vancouver Archives, Image AM54-S4-I-: CVA 20-2; **(bottom):** Smithsonian Institution Archives,

#2005-26202; **p. 628:** Washington State Historical Society; **p. 629:** Los Angeles Public Library Photo Collection; **p. 631:** Library of Congress; **p. 634:** Photographs and Prints Division, Schomburg Center for Research in Black Culture, The New York Public Library, Astor, Lenox, and Tilden Foundations. Art Resource, NY; **p. 635:** Collection of David J. And Janice L. Frent; **p. 636:** Library of Congress; **p. 637:** Courtesy of author; **p. 638 (top):** National Archives; **(bottom):** Granger Collection; **p. 639:** John Tresilian /NY Daily News Archive via Getty Images; **p. 640:** AP Photo. **Chapter 21: Page 643:** Jeff R. Bridgman American Antiques; **p. 646:** Smithsonian American Art Museum/Art Resource; **p. 647 (top):** Granger Collection; **(bottom):** Bettmann/Corbis/Getty Images; **p. 648:** National Archives; **p. 649:** David Rumsey Map Collection; **p. 651:** Kansas State Historical Society; **p. 652 (top):** Library of Congress; **(bottom):** Punch Limited; **p. 654:** Bettmann/Corbis/Getty Images; **p. 655 (top):** Underwood Archives / Getty Images; **(bottom):** Library of Congress; **p. 656:** Billy Graham Center Archives, Wheaton College, Wheaton, IL; **p. 657 (top):** Library of Congress; **(bottom):** National Archives; **p. 658:** Library of Congress; **p. 659:** Franklin D. Roosevelt Library; **p. 662:** Franklin D. Roosevelt Library; **p. 664:** Bettmann/Corbis/Getty Images; **p. 665 (both):** Library of Congress; **p. 667:** Library of Congress; **p. 668:** Photograph © Morgan and Marvin Smith; **p. 669:** HOLC Residential Security Map, Federal Home Loan Bank Board, Records of the City Survey Program," RG 195, 450/68/03/02, National Archives II, College Park, MD; **p. 670:** Library of Congress; **p. 671:** Franklin D. Roosevelt Presidential Library; **p. 672 (top):** Library of Congress; **(bottom):** Bettmann/Corbis/Getty Images; **p. 673:** © Harvard Art Museum /Art Resource, NY. **Chapter 22: Page 676:** National Archives; **p. 678 (top):** Published with the permission of The Wolfsonian - Florida International University (Miami, Florida); **(bottom):** Library of Congress; **p. 679:** Washington Star; **p. 680:** Andreas Feininger / George Eastman House /Getty Images; **p. 684:** Bettmann/Corbis/Getty Images; **p. 686:** Mariners' Museum; **p. 687:** PhotoQuest / Getty Images; **p. 689 (both):** Library of Congress; **p. 690 (top):** Library of Congress; **(bottom):** Courtesy of The WASP Archive, The TWU Libraries

Woman's Collection, Texas Woman's University, Denton, Texas; **p. 691:** National Archives; **p. 693:** Art © Estate of Ben Shahn/ Licensed by VAGA, New York, NY; Photo: Library of Congress; **p. 694:** National Archives; **p. 695:** Eileen Tweedy / The Art Archive at Art Resource, NY; **p. 698:** National Archives; **p. 700:** Library of Congress/Getty Images; **p. 702:** Library of Congress; **p. 703 (top):** Library of Congress; **(bottom):** National Archives; **p. 705:** Los Alamos Scientific Laboratory, Courtesy of Harry S. Truman Library; **p. 706:** Unidentified Photographer, (Interior damage to steel frame of Honkawa Grammar School Auditorium, Hiroshima), November 8, 1945 International Center Of Photography, Purchase, with funds provided by the ICP Acquisitions Committee, 2006; **p. 707:** Library of Congress. **Chapter 23: Page 711:** American Catholic History Research Center and University Archives, Catholic University of America; p. 713: The Lincoln Highway National Museum & Archives; **p. 715:** Bettmann/Corbis/Getty Images; **p. 716:** Bettmann/Corbis/Getty Images; **p. 717:** Photo Quest /Getty Images; **p. 719: (top):** Bettmann/Corbis/Getty Images; **p. 721:** AP Photo; **p. 722:** Photofest; **p. 723:** © 1998 Kate Rothko & Christopher Rothko / Artist Rights Society (ARS), New York. Mark Rothko, 1903-1970 *Four Darks in Red,* (1958). Oil on canvas, 101 13/16 x 116 3/8in. (258.6 x 295.6 cm) Whitney Museum of American Art, New York; Purchase, with funds from the Friends of the Whitney Museum of American Art, Mr. and Mrs. Eugene M. Schwartz, Mrs. Samuel A. Seaver and Charles Simon 68.9 Digital image © Whitney Museum of American Art, NY; **p. 725:** Bettmann/Corbis/Getty Images; **p. 726 (top):** Library of Congress; **(bottom):** The Hy Peskin Collection, www.HyPeskin .com; **p. 727:** The Jon B. Lovelace Collection of California Photographs in Carol M. Highsmith's America Project, Library of Congress; **p. 728:** Bettmann/Corbis/Getty Images; **p. 729:** Lake County Illinois Discovery Museum, Curt Teich Postcard Archives; **p. 731:** Bettmann/Corbis/Getty Images; **p. 732:** Betttmann/Corbis/Getty Images; **p. 733:** A 1949 Herblock Cartoon, © The Herb Block Foundation. **Chapter 24: Page 740:** Norman Rockwell Artwork courtesy of the Norman Rockwell Family Agency; **p. 741:** Howard Sochurek/Time Life Pictures/Getty

Images; **p. 745 (top):** Hagley Museum & Library, Wilmington, Delaware / Bridgeman Images; **(bottom):** Hulton Archive / Getty Images; **p. 747:** Advertising Archive; **p. 748:** Bettmann/Corbis/Getty Images; **p. 749:** American Economic Foundation, "Man's Belief in God is Personal," CU Libraries Exhibitions, accessed February 22, 2013, https://exhibitions.cul.columbia.edu/items/show2829; **p. 751 (top):** Dwight D. Eisenhower Presidential Library; **(bottom):** Library of Congress; **p. 754:** Bettmann/Corbis/Getty Images; **p. 756:** AP Photo; **p. 757 (top):** Photo Dan Weiner © John Broderick; **(bottom):** Bruce Davidson/Magnum Photos; **p. 758 (top):** Frank Driggs Collection/Jazz at Lincoln Center; **(bottom):** Burt Glinn / Magnum Photos; **p. 760:** Ed Clark / Time Life Pictures/Getty Images; **p. 761:** Carl Wasaki / Time Life Picture s/Getty Images; **p. 762:** AP Photo; **p. 765 (top):** Reprinted with permission of the DC Public Library, Star Collection, © Washington Post; **(bottom):** Bettmann/Corbis/Getty Images; **p. 768:** © Gordon Parks Foundation; **p. 769:** Time & Life Pictures/Getty Images; **p. 770:** Bettmann/Corbis/Getty Images. **Chapter 25: Page 772:** National Archives; **p. 773:** Image courtesy of the Raleigh City Museum; **p. 774:** © Cecil Williams; **p. 775:** Bettmann/Corbis/Getty Images; **p. 776:** © Walter P. Reuther Library, Wayne State University; **p. 779 (top):** Ed Meek/University of Mississippi; **(bottom):** Photo by Carl Mydans/Time Life Pictures/Getty Images; **p. 780:** © United Methodist Board of Global Ministries, Ken Thompson; **p. 783:** Security Pacific National Bank Collection, LA Public Library; **p. 784:** © 1965 Spider Martin; **p. 785:** LBJ Library photo by Cecil Stoughton; **p. 787:** Bettmann/Corbis/Getty Images; **p. 788:** © Gordon Parks Foundation; **p. 789:** Scurlock Studio Records, Archives Center, National Museum of American History, Smithsonian Institution; **p. 790:** Courtesy of the University of Delaware Archives and Records Management; **p. 791:** Lon Wilson/UC Berkeley, University Archives; **p. 794:** Photograph by Yoichi Okamoto, courtesy of the Lyndon Baines Johnson Library; **p. 796:** Archive Photos / Getty Images; **p. 797:** Courtesy Wheaton College Archives and Special Collections; **p. 798:** Ralph Crane/Time Life Pictures/Getty Images; **p. 800:** Boston Globe via Getty Images; **p. 801:** Peter Hujar Archive, Alexander Turbull Library, New Zealand; **p. 802:** AP Photo; **p. 803:** Estate of Karl Hubenthal; **p. 804:** © Grey Villet; **p. 805:** A 1963 Herblock Cartoon, © The Herb Block Foundation; **p. 806:** © Dr. Ernest C. Withers, Sr. courtesy of the WITHERS Family TRUST; **p. 807:** Frederick Douglass mural on the 'Solidarity Wall', Falls Road, Belfast; http://en.wikipedia.org/wiki/GNU_Free_Documentation_License. **Chapter 26: Page 809:** Courtesy Ronald Reagan Library; **p. 811:** National Archives; **p. 812:** Stanleyformanphotos.com Pulitzer Prize 1977; **p. 815:** Photo by Ollie Atkins/Time Life Pictures/Getty Images; **p. 816:** May 4 Collection. Kent State University Libraries. Special Collections and Archives; **p. 817:** Library of Congress; **p. 821 (top):** Bob Kreisel / Alamy; **(bottom):** AP Photo; **p. 822:** Courtesy Gerald R. Ford Library; **p. 824:** Fox Photos/Getty Images; **p. 825:** AP Photo; **p. 826:** Bettmann/Corbis/Getty Images; **p. 830:** Bettmann/Corbis/Getty Images; **p. 831 (both):** Bettmann/Corbis/Getty Images; **p. 834: (top):** Los Angeles Examiner Collection, USC Libraries Special Collections; **(bottom):** Time Life Pictures/Getty Images; **p. 837 (top):** Library of Congress; **(bottom):** © Eli Reed/Magnum Photos; **p. 838 (top):** Ronald Reagan Presidential Library; **(bottom):** Photofest; **p. 840:** AP Photo/Ira Schwartz. **Chapter 27: Page 843:** © Patrick Hagerty; **p. 844:** AP Photo/Thomas Kienzle; **p. 846:** Peter Turnley /Corbis/VCG via Getty Images; **p. 849:** AP Photo/Matt York; **p. 853:** Peter Turnley /Corbis /VCG via Getty Images; **p. 856:** Photo by Joi Ito; http://creativecommons.org/licenses/by/2.0/deed.en; **p. 857:** Reprinted with permission of David Jacobson; **p. 858:** ©Hans Haacke / Artists Rights Society [ARS], New York/ VG Bild-Kunst, Bonn; **p. 859:** AP Photo/Damian Dovarganes; **p. 860:** AP Photo / Steven Senne; **p. 862:** © Catherine Karnow; **p. 864:** Takaaki Iwabu KRT/Newscom; **p. 866:** AP Photo; **p. 867:** Vanessa Vick / Science Source; **p. 868:** Shan Goshorn *Unintended Legacy* Arches paper and archival inks 2014 10 x 9 1/2 x 91/2" Fred Jones Jr. Museum of Art, The University of Oklahoma, Norman; The James T. Bialac Native American Art Collection, 2010; **p. 871:** Ralf-Finn Hestoft/Corbis/Getty Images; **p. 872:** A 1998 Herblock Cartoon, © The Herb Block Foundation; **p. 873:** Reuters; **p. 874:** Steve Ludlum/The New York Times/Redux; **p. 875:** Lionel Hahn/Abaca. **Chapter 28: Page 877:** Ralf-Finn Hestoft/ Corbis/Getty Images; **p. 880 (top):** Owen Freeman; **(bottom):** Serge J-F. Levy; **p. 881:** Steve Benson/Creators Syndicate; **p. 882:** Mario Tama / Getty Images; **p. 883 (top):** AP Photo; **(bottom):** Joe Raedle / Getty Images; **p. 885:** Hank Walker/Getty Images; **p. 887:** Michael Ramirez/Creators Syndicate; **p. 889 (top):** AP Photo; **(bottom):** jr-art.net; **p. 890 (top):** AP Photo/Khampha Bouaphanh; **(bottom):** Wikipedia, public domain; **p. 891:** AP Photo; **p. 894:** Joshua Lott/The New York Times/Redux; **p. 896:** AUTH © 2009 The Philadelphia Inquirer. Reprinted with permission of UNIVERSAL UCLICK. All rights reserved; **p. 897:** © Tribune Media Services, Inc. All Rights Reserved. Reprinted with permission; **p. 898:** AP Photo/Brennan Linsley, Pool, file; **p. 899:** AP Photo; **p. 904:** Spencer Platt/Getty Images; **p. 907:** Whitney Curtis, The New York Times, Redux; **p. 909:** Official White House Photo by Pete Souza; **p. 910:** David Sipress The New Yorker Collection/ The Cartoon Bank; **p. 914:** Alec Soth, Magnum Photos; **p. 915:** © Renee Cox; **p. 916:** Eli Reed / Magnum Photos.

TEXT

Barry Commoner: Excerpts from "Chapter 1: The Environmental Crisis" from *The Closing Circle: Nature, Man, and Technology* by Barry Commoner. Copyright © 1971 by Barry Commoner. Used by permission of Knopf, a division of Random House, Inc. **Global Exchange:** "Declaration for Global Democracy," from Global Exchange, Seattle, December 1999. Reprinted by permission. **Barry Goldwater:** "Acceptance Speech to the Republican National Convention (1964)", from the Barry M. Goldwater Papers, Arizona Historical Foundation Collection, Arizona State University Libraries. Reprinted by permission. **Martin Luther King Jr.:** "Meeting at Holt Street Church", Reprinted by arrangement with The Heirs to the Estate of Martin Luther King Jr., c/o Writers house as agent for the proprietor, New York, NY.Copyright © 1963 Martin Luther King Jr.; Copyright © renewed 1991 Coretta Scott King. **Henry R. Luce:** "The American Century," *Life Magazine*, February 17, 1941, pp. 22-31. Copyright © 1941 Time Inc. Reprinted from LIFE and published with permission of Time Inc. Reproduction in any manner in any language in

TABLES AND FIGURES

INDEX

Page numbers in *italics* refer to illustrations.

AAA, *see* Agricultural Adjustment Act
Abilene, Kans., 487
abolition movement, 531, *807*, 907
Aboriginal peoples, 496, 853
abortion, 813, 814, *831*, 870, 911
   Clinton and, 847
   conservatism and, 830, 831
   feminists and, 800, 831
   religious right and, 830, 838, 869
   Supreme Court and, 805
Abraham Lincoln (aircraft carrier), *883*
Abrams, Jacob (1886–1953), 624, *625*
Abu Ghraib (prison), 886, *886*
abuse, domestic, 566, 594
Acheson, Dean (1893–1971), 737–38
ACLU, *see* American Civil Liberties Union
acquired immunodeficiency syndrome
   (AIDS), 867–68, *867*
Across the Continent (Palmer), *475*
activism, in "The Sixties," 798–807
ACT UP, 868
Adams, Henry (b. 1843), 443
Adams, John (1735–1826), 575
Adamson Act (1916), 575
Addams, Jane (1860–1935), 566–67, *566*
Adenauer, Konrad (1876–1967), 752
Adkins v. Children's Hospital, 621
Adventures of Ozzie and Harriet, The (TV show),
   746
advertising, 553–54, *554*, 615, 620, *620*,
   689–90, *689*, 691, 758
   consumerism and, *553*, *554*, 614, 746
   family life in, 746, *747*
   political, 841
   television and, 746, *746*, 751
   women and, *620*
AFDC, *see* Aid to Families with Dependent
   Children
affirmative action, 787, 812, 813, 833, 847,
   849, 865, 891
Afghanistan, 826, 840, 875, 880, *880*, *883*,
   886, 892, 893, 908, 912, 915
AFL, *see* American Federation of Labor
Africa, 579, 608, 697, 704, 709, 722, 755, 845,
   859, 882, 913
   immigrants from, 865
African-Americans, 509, *521*, 531–32, 544,
   669, 671–72, 673, 709, *728*, 748, 770,
   864–66, 916
   as Afro-Americans, *789*

in arts, 634–35
Birmingham campaign and, 775–76, *775*
and Black Codes, 455–56, 457
black internationalism and, 697, 704
Booker T. Washington and, 531
Carter and, 823
citizenship and, 462, 629
civil rights and, 672, 701–4, *703*, 765,
   773–76, *774*, 779, 786–89
in Clinton administration, 848
as cowboys, 487
as Democrats, 644
education and, 521, 522, 523, *631*
and FDR, 662
feminists and, 619
Freedom Train and, 712
ghetto uprisings and, 786–88
Great Society and, 785–86
Hurricane Katrina and, 889, *889*
IQ tests and, 597
juries and, 672
Knights of Labor and, 505
and Ku Klux Klan, *see* Ku Klux Klan
labor and, 672, 776
LBJ and, 781
loss of voting rights of, 524–25, 565, 602,
   665, 697, 765, 781
March on Washington and, 701, 776
New Deal and, 665–66, *665*, 667–69
Nixon and, 812, 813
northern migration of, 522–23, 601–2, *601*,
   631, *634*, 700–701
Plessy v. Ferguson and, 525
in politics, 464, 523–24
population of, 631
poverty rates of, *905*
prison population of, 866–67
Progressivism and, 598–99
Reagan and, 836
recessions and, 906
in Reconstruction, 453, 456–58, *458*,
   460–66, *463*, 521, 525, 527, 599–600,
   599, 678, 726
and segregation, *see* segregation
Selma campaign and, 759, 783–84, *784*
sit-ins and, *773*, 774
as soldiers in Civil War, *491*
in South, 513, 522, 601–2, 697, 700–701
in suburbs, 747–48, 865
Truman and, 726–29

unemployment and, 667, 787
voting rights of, 783, 912
wages and, 599, 634, 890
welfare and, 811
women, 522, 524, 552, 598, 702, *789*
women's movement neglect of, 599
World War I and, 601–2, *601*
World War II and, 678, 686, 693, 700–
   704, *703*
see also civil rights movement; Great
   Migration; slavery; slaves
African National Congress, 845
Agnew, Spiro T. (1918–1996), 819, 822
Agricultural Adjustment Act (AAA), 650–51,
   652, 669
agriculture, 485–87, *487*, 500, 548, 551, 575,
   667, *667*, 668, 694
   African-Americans and, 666
   bonanza farms and, 486
   Democratic Party and, 636
   Eisenhower and, 752
   and foreclosures, 617, 637
   Great Depression and, 637, 639
   industrial revolution and, 477–78
   migrant workers and, 661, 671, 801
   New Deal and, 650–51, 657, *657*, 659, 662,
   663–64, *665*, 666, 674, 752
   in 1920s, 616–17, *616*, *617*
   Populists and, 513, 514, 516
   post-World War II, 743
   in Progressive era, 550
   railroads and, 514
   Southern expansion of, 521
Aguinaldo, Emilio (1869–1964), 539
AIDS, *see* acquired immunodeficiency
   syndrome
Aid to Families with Dependent Children
   (AFDC), 811, 849–50
aircraft, *see* aviation and aircraft
Air Force, U.S., 701
Akilova, Kamola, *889*
Alabama, 672, 803, 911
   black voting in, 726
Al-Abram (newspaper), 608
Alaska, 794
   corporate mining in, 487
   purchase of, 534
Albania, 852–53
Albuquerque, N.Mex., *745*
Alcatraz Island, 802, *802*

alcohol, banning of, *see* Prohibition
Alcorn, James L. (1816–1894), 465
Alien Act (1798), 594
Allen, Richard, *463*
Allende, Salvador (1908–1973), 815
Allies:
   in World War I, 584, 587, *587*, 603, 608
   in World War II, *678*, 684, 704, 705,
      706–9, 723
Al Qaeda, 875, 882, 886
Altgeld, John Peter (1847–1902), 509
Amalgamated Association, 513
America First Committee, 681
American Century, The (Luce), 691
American Civil Liberties Union (ACLU),
   624, 627
American Communist Party, *711*
American Creed, 703
American Dilemma, An (Myrdal), 703, *703*
American Economic Foundation, *749*
American Enterprise Institute, 827
American Federation of Labor (AFL), 531–32,
   555–57, 588, 589, 604, 653, 725, 753
American Fifth Fleet, 909
American Heritage Foundation, 712
American identity, 596–603
American Indian Movement, 802, 868
American Individualism (Hoover), 635
American International Group (AIG), 894,
   897
Americanism, 628, 670, 671, 784
   vs. racism, 671, 693
Americanization, 628, 632, 633, 747
   Catholics and, 631
   of immigrants, 596–98, 628, 670, 693–94
   see also Americanism; assimilation
*Americanization of the World, The; or, the Trend
   of the Twentieth Century* (Stead), 579
American Jewish Committee, 671
American Jewish Congress, 702
American Liberty League, 659
American Medical Association, 658, 723
American National Exhibition, 741–42, *741*
American Party, *see* Know-Nothing Party
American Protective League (APL), 595
American Railway Union, 518
American Revolution, 502, *713*, 717, 727
American standard of living, 553–54
Americans with Disabilities Act (1990), 867
American Telephone and Telegraph (AT&T),
   814
American Tobacco, 573
American Way, 802
America Today (Benton), *612*
Amnesty International, 824
anarchism, 505, 509, 595, 613
Ancona, Victor, *702*
Anderson, John (1922–), 834
Anderson, Marian (1897–1993), 668

Andersonville, Ga., Confederate prison at,
   456
And Not This Man (Nast), *469*
Andrews, Sidney (1837–1880), 446
Angel Island, 550
Anglo-Iranian Oil Company, 755
Ann Arbor, Mich., Beats in, 759
Anniston, Ala., 774
Anthony, Susan B. (1820–1906), 462, *462*
Anti-Ballistic Missile Treaty (1972), 815, 838
anti-Catholicism, 769, *769*
Anti-Defamation League of B'nai B'rith, 631
Anti-Imperialist League, 544
anti-Semitism, 631, 656, 694, 810, 870
   see also Jews
antiwar movement, Vietnam era, 772, 796,
   796, 805, 806, 816–17, *816*, 888
apartheid, 845
Appalachia, 785, *785*
   poverty rates in, *905*
Appeal to Reason, 556
appeasement, 679
Apple Computers, *856*
appliances, household, *see* consumerism,
   and household appliances; *specific
   appliances*
Appomattox Courthouse, 454
Arabs, 608, 821
   nationalism and, 756
Arbenz Guzmán, Jacobo (1913–1971), 755, 756
Argentina, 486, 824
Arizona, 617, *894*
   agriculture in, 548
Arkansas, 524, 847
armed forces, U.S., *see* military, U.S.
armistice, Korean War, 721
Armstrong, Louis, 760
Armstrong, Samuel (1839–1893), 531
Army, U.S., *493*, 704
   desegregation in, 703
   Japanese-Americans in, 700
Army-McCarthy hearings, 732, 733, 746
art, freedom and, 723
Arthur Andersen, 857
artisans:
   Second New Deal and, 657
Artists for Victory, 678
arts:
   African-Americans in, 634–35
   during Cold War, 722
   Second New Deal and, 657–58, *657*
Aryan Nation, 870
Aryans, 630
   as "master race," 693
Ashcan School, *546*
Asia, 538, 579, 608, 697, 713, 722, 756, 855,
   859, 913
   pre-World War II, 679
Asian-Americans, voting by, 912

Asian immigrants, 550, 598, 694, 784,
   864–65, *864*, 865
   affirmative action and, 813
   World War II and, 698–700
assembly lines, 553, *615*, 653, 688
assimilation, 631, 670, 693–94
associational action, 635–36, 640
Association of Unemployed Single Women,
   665
asylums, 598
AT&T (American Telephone and Telegraph),
   814, 910
Atlanta Cotton Exposition, 531, 533, 540
Atlantic, Battle of the, 682
Atlantic and Pacific Tea Company, 479
Atlantic cable, 480
Atlantic City, N.J., 781
atomic bomb, 705–7, *706*, 709, 713, *729*, 731,
   732, 753–54
   of Soviet Union, 717, 719
   see also hydrogen bomb; nuclear weapons
Atomic Energy Commission, 715
Attlee, Clement (1883–1967), 707
Aurora, Colo., 914
Austin, Tex., 856, *899*
Australia, 486, 496, 608
   in World War II, 682
Austria, 606, 679
Austro-Hungarian Empire, 584, *606*, 852
   immigrants from, 528, 549
automobiles, 554, 614–15, *615*, 616, 619, 637,
   687, *687*, 741, 743, 744–45, 746
   Ford and, 553
   highways and, 752
   Japanese production of, 821
   in Los Angeles, 617
   pollution and, 770, 811
Avenger Field, *690*
aviation and aircraft, 615–16, 617, 687,
   687, 690, *690*, 701, 730, 742, 743,
   823, *824*
Axis of Evil, 881
Axis powers, 680, 682, 684, 695
Azikiwe, Nnamdi (1904–1996), 704

baby boom, 743, 747, *747*
Bacall, Lauren (1924–), *731*
Bachelor Girls Social Club, 552
Baghdad, 883
Bailey v. Alabama, 600
Bain Capital, 911
Baker, Ella (1903–1986), 774
Baker v. Carr, 804
Baldwin, James (1924–1987), 773, 790
Balkans, 852
"Ballad for Americans," 671
Ballinger, Richard A. (1858–1922), 573
Baltimore, Md., *751*, 907
Bank of America, 897

banks, 500, 514, 519, 576, *581*, 583, 616, 656, 738, 837, 857–58
  British, 579
  failure of, 637, 646
  in financial crisis of 2008, 858, 893–94, 895, 896–97, 901
  and foreclosures, 617, 637, 641, 651
  in Great Depression, 637, 639, 641, 646–47, *647*, 651
  New Deal and, 674
  regulation reforms of 2010 and, 900, 901
  Socialist party and, 573
  in Soviet Union, 603
  suburbs and, 747–48
"Banned in Boston," 623
Baptists, 528, 763, 823
Barbados, 582
Barbie doll, *858*
Barbie's Liberty (Haacke), *858*
Bargain of 1877, 471–72
Barnett, Ross (1898–1987), 775
Barrow plantation, maps of, *446*
Baruch, Bernard (1870–1965), 589
Bataan, 682, *698*
Batista, Fulgencio (1901–1973), 678, 777
Baxter Street Court, *483*
Bay of Pigs invasion, 777
Beats, *758*, *759*, 798
Begin, Menachem (1913–1992), *825*
Beijing, 815, 844, *846*
Belfast, 603, *807*
Belgium, 584, 680
Bellamy, Edward (1850–1898), 506, 507, *507*, 562
Belle Plaine, Minn., *914*
Bellows, George (1882–1925), *626*
Benedict, Ruth (1887–1948), 694
Ben-Hur (movie), 749
Benson, Steve, *881*
Berger, Victor (1860–1929), 605
Berlin:
  airlift, 717
  blockade, 717
  occupation of, 717
Berlin Wall, 777–78, 844, *844*
Bernays, Edward (1891–1995), 620
Bethlehem Steel, *837*
Bethune, Mary McLeod (1875–1955), 668
Between Two Worlds (Wohaw), *493*
Beverly Hills, Calif., *862*
Bible, *519*, 625, *627*, 764, 804
  interpretation of, *627*, *627*
Bible Belt, 508
Biden, Joe (1942–), *909*
Bierstadt, Albert, *490*
Bill of Rights (American), 458, 461, *673*, 688–89, *689*, 804, 892
"Bill of Rights for the Disadvantaged," 787

bin Laden, Osama (1957–2011), 875, 880, *909*
  death of, 908
Birmingham, Ala., 712, 759
  church bombing in, 775
  civil rights campaign in, 775–76, *775*
  Freedom Rides in, 774
  manufacturing in, 521, 725
birth control, 561, *561*, 619, 798, 804, 805, 814
Birth of a Nation (Griffith), 599, *599*
birthrate:
  decline in U.S., 639
  infant mortality and, 914
  in Mexico, 862
  minority, 865
Black, Hugo (1886–1971), 700
black Americans, *see* African-Americans
Blackbirds (Broadway show), 634–35
Blackboard Jungle (movie), 758
Black Codes, 455–56, *455*, 457
Black Hills, 492
black internationalism, 697, 704
blacklisting:
  in Hollywood, 731
  of union organizers, 658
Black Lives Matter, 907
Black Muslims, 788
Black Panther Party, 789
Black Power, 782, 788–89, 790, 801, 816
Black Sea, 714
Black Sunday, *651*
Black Tuesday, 636
Blaine, James G. (1830–1893), 499, *500*, 529, 534
Blair, Francis P., Jr. (1821–1875), 460
Blakemore, Richard E., 829
blitzkrieg, 680, *680*
Block, Herbert (1909–2001), *733*, *805*, *872*
Bock, Vera (1905–), *657*
Boesky, Ivan (1937–), 836–37
Bogart, Humphrey (1899–1957), *731*
bohemians, 796
bomb shelters, 754, *754*
bonanza farms, 486
bonus marchers, 639
Boone, Pat, *783*
bootleggers, 627
Border Patrol, U.S., 629, *629*, 695, 889
Bosch, Juan (1909–2001), 794
Bosnia-Herzegovina, 584
Bosses of the Senate, The, *498*
Boston, Mass., *860*
  integration in, *812*, 813
Boston Globe, 897
Boston Marathon, *800*
Boston Tea Party, *899*, 910
Boumediene v. Bush, 892
Bourke-White, Margaret (1906–1971), 617

Bourne, Randolph (1886–1918), 596–97
Boutwell, George S. (1818–1905), 544
Bow, Clara (1905–1965), 619
Bowers v. Hardwick, 838, 892
boycotts, 762–63, 764, 801
Boy Scouts, *689*
bracero program, 694–95
Bradwell, Myra (1831–1894), 462
"brains trust," 646
Brandeis, Louis D. (1856–1941), 555, 568–69, 574, 625, 646
Brazil, 514
Brentwood, Calif., *667*
Bretton Woods, N.H., conference at, 708, 820
Brewer, David J. (1837–1910), 530
Breyer, Stephen (1938–), 848
Brezhnev, Leonid (1906–1982), 815
Bridges, Harry (1901–1990), 653
Bridges, Ruby, *740*
Britain, Battle of, 680
British-Americans:
  World War I and, 585
British Empire, 533, 579, 603, 608, 684, 714, 722
Broadway theatre, 634
Brooklyn, N.Y., 561, 652
Brooklyn Dodgers, 727
Brown, Linda, *761*
Brown, Matt, 449
Brown, Michael, 907
Brown, Oliver (1918–1961), 761
Brown, Olympia, 461
Brown, William Wells, *463*
Brown v. Board of Education, 461, 761–62, *761*, 764–65, 767, 768
Bruce, Blanche K. (1841–1898), 464
Bryan, William Jennings (1860–1925), 519, *519*, *520*, 544, 572, 583, 585–86, 627, *627*
  "cross of gold" speech of, 519, *519*
Bryn Mawr, 814
Buchanan, James (1791–1868), 489
Buchanan, Pat (1938–), 847
Buckley, William F. (1925–), 782
Buck v. Bell, 598
Buddhism, Buddhists, 798
  as immigrants, 860
  in Vietnam, 791
buffalo, 493
  hunting of, 490–91, 492, *497*
Buffalo, N.Y., 252, 570
Buffalo Bill's Wild West Show, *497*, *497*
Bulgaria, 714
Bulge, Battle of the, 704
Bureau of Indian Affairs, U.S., 492, 562
Bureau of Labor Statistics, Mass., 502
Burger, Warren (1907–1995), 812
Burger Court, 812–13
Burma, 682

Bush, George H. W. (1924–), 841, 845, 854, 855, 882
  in election of 1992, 847
  Gulf War and, 846
  NAFTA and, 848
Bush, George W. (1946–), 869, 878–85, 887–88, 891, 898, *898, 899*
  civil liberties and, 885–87
  debates with Gore, 874
  economy under, 887, 893–97
  in election of 2000, 872–73
  foreign policy of, 879, 880–81, 882–85, 887, 893
  and Hurricane Katrina, 888, 893
  Iraq War and, 882–83, *883*, 893
  and Supreme Court, 892–93
  unemployment and, 887
Bush, Jeb (1953–), 873
Bush (George W.) administration, 875, 879–81, *880*, 885, 886, 887, 888–89, 892, 893, 897, 899, 910
  2008 financial crisis and, 858
Bush Doctrine, 880–81
Bush v. Gore, 873
business:
  and government, 620–23, 691
  rise of, 480–83
  vertically integrated, 481, 482
  see also corporations
busing, desegregation of schools and, 812–13, *812*, 833

California, 486, 487, *487*, 550, 563, 564, 567, *572*, 629, *629*, 637, 667, *667*, 687, 743, 745–46, 862
  agriculture in, 548, 743
  Asian-Americans in, 598, 864
  boycott of grapes from, 801
  immigrants in, 869
  Japanese-Americans in, 698
  migration to, 617, 832, *861*
  1934 election in, 655
  1964 election in, 782
  population of, 488
  Reagan as governor of, 834
  suburbs in, 746
  tax law in, 832
  woman suffrage in, 517
California, University of:
  at Berkeley, 790–91, *791*
  at Davis, 813
California Supreme Court, 530
  segregation and, 761
California Trail, 490
Call, The, 561
Calley, William (1943–), 817
Cambodia, 816, 864
  immigrants from, 860
Cambridge, Mass., *605*

camera, handheld, 480
Camp David, 825
Canada, 543, 629, 644, 850, *859, 914*
  border with United States, *890*
  D-Day and, 684
  draft dodgers' flight to, 796
  NAFTA and, 848
Canadians, Canadian immigrants, 486
Canal Zone, 580–82
capitalism, 645, 691, 693, 749
  free market, 755
  "golden age" of, 742–50
  industrial, 554
  international, 844, 854
  labor vs., 502, 505–8
  modern, 741
  revolution vs. reform of, 670
  Ronald Reagan and, 834
  Socialist Party vs., 573, 670
  as "welfare capitalism," 618
"captains of industry," 482
Caribbean, *536, 581,* 704, 784, 838, *839*
  immigrants from, 859, 862, 865
  U.S. troops in, 580
  see also West Indies
Carmichael, Stokely (1941–1998), 788
Carnegie, Andrew (1835–1919), 481, 482, 513, *513*
carpetbaggers, 464–65
Carranza, Venustiano, 584
Carson, Rachel (1907–1964), 790, 802
Carswell, G. Harold (1920–1992), 812
Carter, Jimmy (1924–), 582, 823, *825,* 827, 833, 852
  economic crisis and, 823–24
  in election of 1980, 834
  human rights and, 824–25, 839
  Iran hostage crisis and, 825–26
Carter administration, 823, *826,* 827, 833, 839
Carter Doctrine, 826
Caruso, Enrico (1873–1921), 615
Casey, William (1913–1987), 840
Casey v. Planned Parenthood of Pennsylvania, 870
Casino Grounds, *482*
casinos, gambling, Native Americans and, 868–69
Castillo Armas, Carlos (1914–1957), *756*
Castro, Fidel (1926–), 777
Catholics, Catholicism, 499, 508, 625, 636, 662, 711, 806, *807,* 911
  and abortion, 800, 831
  and Americanization, 631
  anticommunism of, 736, 748–49, 891
  counterculture and, 798
  in FDR administration, 669
  JFK as, 768–70, *769,* 888
  John Kerry as, 888
  Ku Klux Klan and, 628

  in 1960 campaign, 768–70, *769*
  prejudice against, 631
Catt, Carrie Chapman (1859–1947), 533
cattle drives, 487
CCC (Civilian Conservation Corps), 648–49, *648,* 665
censorship, 625
  anticommunism and, 733
  Hollywood and, 624
  sex and, 624
census, federal, 865, *865,* 868
Census Bureau, 478
Central America, *839,* 840
  immigrants from, 860, 865
  Theodore Roosevelt's policies in, 580–83
Central High School, Ark., segregation at, 768
Central Intelligence Agency (CIA), 715, 755, *756,* 815, 819, 875, 886
  Bay of Pigs Invasion and, 777
  support of arts by, 722
Central Powers (World War I), 584
Cermak, Anton (1873–1933), 638–39
Chambers, Whittaker (1901–1961), 731
Chaney, James (1943–1964), 781
Changing West (Benton), *612*
Chaplin, Charlie (1889–1977), 615
Charge of the Rough Riders at San Juan Hill (Remington), *537*
Charleston, S.C., 903, 914
Chavez, César (1927–1993), 801, 864
Cheney, Dick (1941–), 846, 872, 881
Chevrolet Corvair, 803
Cheyennes, 491, *491*
Chicago, Ill., 566–67, *634,* 757, 822, *877, 878, 891*
  alleged voter fraud in, 770
  in Great Depression, 638–39, *638*
  Haymarket affair in, 509
  manufacturing in, 478
  1968 Democratic convention in, 806
  population of, 478
  race riot in, 602
  World's Fair in, *481*
Chicago Freedom Movement, 787
Chicago Gospel Tabernacle, *656*
Chicago Tribune, 609
Chicanos, 801
  see also Latinos
child labor, 549, *549,* 564, 565, 566, 575, 619, 621, 663
children, poverty rates of, 905
Chile, 815, 839
Chillin' with Liberty (Cox), *915*
China, 538, 679, 717–19, 794, 810, 815, *815, 817,* 864, 894, 915
  human rights and, 909
  Iran nuclear program and, 908
  Iraq War and, 882

jobs exported to, 887
Korean War and, 719–21
Lend-Lease and, 681
loss of U.S. jobs to, 887
market reforms in, 844–45
rise of communists in, 717–19
Tiananmen Square protest in, 844, *846*
in U.N., 708
Chinese, Chinese immigrants, 453, 484, 495,
    526, 529–31, *530*, 543, 544, 550
in Hawaii, 535
in IWW, 557
in West, 487–89
World War II and, 698
see also Asian immigrants
Chinese Exclusion Act (1882), 529–30
Christ, Jesus, *see* Jesus
Christian Coalition, 869
Christianity, 507–8, 534, 614, 748–49, 750,
    763, 827–30, 859
    "Christian patriots" and, 870
    evangelical, 832, 911
    fundamentalism and, 625–27, 827–30
    modernism in, 625–27
    in movies, 749
    and Republican Party (modern), 810
    see also specific denominations
Christian lobby, 507–8
Christian Right, 833, 838
    see also religious right
Chrysler, 616
Chu, Judy, 530
Church, Frank (1924–1984), 819
church and state:
    separation of, 627, 804, *805*
Church Committee, 819
Churchill, Winston (1874–1965), 635, 683–
    84, 707–8, *707*, 714, 751
Church of Jesus Christ of Latter-day Saints,
    see Mormons
CIA, *see* Central Intelligence Agency
cigarettes, marketing to women of, 619, *620*
CIO, *see* Congress of Industrial
    Organizations
Citibank, 896
Citigroup, 857, 897
citizenship, 457–58, 460–61, 462, 539–43,
    667, *860*
    of African-Americans, 462, 629, 645
    Chinese immigrants and, 530
    Fourteenth Amendment and, 462
    Hawaii and, 543
    Native Americans and, 493
    Puerto Rico and, 543
    second-class, *see* segregation
    voting rights and, 565
    welfare state and, 569
Citizens United v. Federal Elections Commission,
    913

Civilian Conservation Corps (CCC), 648–49,
    648, 665
Civil Liberties Bureau, *see* American Civil
    Liberties Union
Civil Rights Act (1875), *441*, 470, 525
Civil Rights Act (1964), 776, 780, 781, 799
civil rights and liberties, 594–96, 605, 623–
    25, 641, 672–73, 712, 737–38, 759–68,
    885–87
    Adlai Stevenson and, 737–38
    A. Mitchell Palmer and, 605
    anticommunism and, 736
    Baldwin on, 773
    Bush administration and, 885–87, 892–93
    Cold War and, 737–38
    domestic surveillance and, 910
    Eleanor Roosevelt and, 664
    FDR and, 668
    in Great Depression, 641, 670
    Japanese-American internment and,
        698–700
    labor and, 560, 672–73
    legislation on, 465
    New Deal and, 672–73
    new movements in, 798–807
    post–World War II, 726–29, *726*, *728*
    revolution in, 803–4
    Scottsboro case and, 672
    September 11 terrorist attacks and, 885–87
    in Soviet Union, 723, 724
    suspension of, 892
    Truman and, 726–29
    Woodrow Wilson and, 595
    World War II and, 678, 694–95, 762
    see also Bill of Rights (American); civil
        rights movement; constitutional
        amendments, U.S.; freedom;
        McCarthy era; women's rights
Civil Rights Bill (1866), 456–57
Civil Rights Cases, 525
Civil Rights Memorial, *916*
civil rights movement, 759–68, *765*, 786–89,
    827, 878
    backlash against, 782, 833
    Birmingham campaign and, 775–76, *775*
    birth of, 701–4, *703*
    FBI and, 819
    freedom and, 763–64
    JFK and, 778–79
    LBJ and, 779
    March on Washington and, 776
    Montgomery bus boycott and, 762–63,
        764
    1964 election and, 781–82
    radicalization of, 788–89
    Selma campaign and, 783–84, *784*
    in South, 773–76
    television and, 775, *775*, 783
    women and, 799–800

Civil Service Act (1883), 500
Civil War, U.S., 442, *443*, 490, 491, 494, 499,
    501, 502, 509, 514, 527–28, 584, 589,
    594, 712
    black soldiers in, *491*
    casualties in, 446
Civil Works Administration (CWA), 649
Clarendon County, S.C., 761
Clark, William (1770–1838), 491
*Clash of Civilizations and the Remaking of the
    World Order, The* (Huntington), 891
class:
    in American Society, 502
    see also middle class
Clayton Act (1914), 575
Clean Air Act (1970), 803, 811, 833
Clean Water Act (1972), 803
Clemenceau, Georges (1841–1929), 605
Cleveland, Grover (1837–1908), 518, 519, 529,
    535, 640
Clinton, Bill (1946–), 666, *740*, 841, 847–53,
    854, 857, 871–72, *872*, 897
    Balkan crisis and, 852
    budget and, 855
    in election of 1992, 847–48
    foreign policy of, 852–53
    impeachment of, 872
    national health care plan of, 848, 849
    sexual misconduct and, 872
    Whitewater and, 872
Clinton, Hillary Rodham (1947–), 848, 898,
    909
    in election of 2008, 878
    as feminist, 871
Clinton administration, 847–53, 897, 900
    women in, 848
Closing Circle, The (Commoner), 828
Cloud, N. B. (1809–1875), *468*
coal, 522, 725, 879
    mining, *522*, *664*
Coast Guard, U.S., *676*
Coca-Cola, 615
code-breakers, in World War II, 682–83
"code-talkers," 695
Cody, William "Buffalo Bill," 497, *497*
Cold War, 709, 711–39, *711*, *718*, 796, 799, 815,
    819, 820, 825, 826, *838*, *839*, 875, 881,
    891, 908, 909, 915, 916
    anticommunism during, 748, *749*
    Beats and, 759
    Berlin blockade in, 717
    big business and, 749
    Carter and, 824–25
    consumerism and, 741, 743
    cultural, 722
    Eisenhower and, 753–54
    end of, 844, *845*, 846, 852, 859
    freedom and, 721, 722–24, 730, 733, 749,
        756

Cold War (*continued*)
  highways and, 730, 752
  human rights and, 723
  Iran and, 714
  JFK and, 777
  Khrushchev and, 754
  Korean War and, 719–21
  and Middle East oil, 714, 715
  "missile gap," 769
  national exhibitions and, 741–42
  in 1960 election, 769
  organized labor and, 737
  origins of, 713–22
  political debate and, 756
  Reagan and, 838–40
  in Third World, 755–56
Colfax, La., massacre in, 468, 470
Collier, John (1789–1883), 666
Colombia, 581
colonialization:
  decolonization and, 755
  international, 533
Colorado, 651
  woman suffrage in, 517, 567
Colorado River, *646*
Colored Rule in a Reconstructed (?) State (Nast),
  469
Columbia, S.C., *864*
Columbia College, 878
Columbia River, 644, *646*
Columbia University, 646
Columbine High School, 914
Columbus, N.Mex., 584
Commissioner of Indian Affairs, 666
Commission on Civil Rights, 727
Committee on Public Information (CPI),
  589–90
Commoner, Barry (1917–2012), 828
communism, 573, 628, 653, 670, 673, 679,
  702, 707, *711*, 713, 714, 715, 716, 717–19,
  718, 723, 726, 729–38, *731*, 734, 755,
  756, 757, 782, *783*, 806, 815, 816, 817,
  823, 824, 839, 852
  capitalism vs., 755
  in China, 717–19
  collapse of, *844*, 854
  crusade against, 729–38, *732*, *733*, 748–49,
    749, 751, 791, 803
  flag of, 595
  Henry Wallace and, 728
  refugees from, 730
  religion v., 748–49, *749*, 750
  rise of, 587
  in Soviet Union, 741
  Truman Doctrine and, 715
  in Vietnam, 791
Communist Party, *605*, 639–40, *639*, 655,
  670, 671, *711*, 728, 733, 789
  in China, 844

Communist Party Congress, 754
company unions, 618
computers, 687, 730, 855–56, *856*
  see also Internet
concentration camps, 679, 686, 694
  see also Japanese immigrants, Japanese
    Americans, World War II
    internment of
Coney Island, *757*
Confederate States of America, 490, 509
Congress, U.S., *470*, 499–500, 536, 592, *594*,
  646–47, 658, 692, *715*, 751, 812, 818–19,
  831, 885, 886, 893
  African-Americans in, 523
  anticommunism and, 736
  apologizes for Japanese-American
    internment, 700
  Civil Rights Act (1964) and, 776
  civil rights and, 765
  Clinton and, 857
  domestic surveillance and, 910
  in elections of 1946, 725
  Equal Pay Act and, 799
  FDR and, 663
  federal bailouts and, 897
  health care bill passed by, 900
  immigration and, 495
  immigration restriction and, 529, 629, 698
  isolationism and, 680
  and League of Nations, 609–10
  and Native American treaty system, 492
  New Deal and, 646–47, 648, 692
  presidential veto and, 457, 725, 736
  Reagan's defiance of, 840
  Reconstruction policies of, 454
  Resolution of Regret passed by, 530
  "stimulus" package passed by, 899
  Truman Doctrine and, 715
  Voting Rights Act passed by, 783
  World War II and, 682
  see also House of Representatives, U.S.;
    Senate, U.S.
Congressional Medal of Honor, 599
Congressional Record, 734
Congress of Industrial Organizations (CIO),
  653–54, 655, 670, 672, 702, 725, 753
Congress of Racial Equality (CORE), 702,
  774, 789
Connor, Eugene "Bull" (1897–1973), 775, 827
conservationism, 571–72, *572*, 802, 830–31
conservatism, 693, 749–50, 782–83, 803,
  809–42, *809*, 860, 869–70, 891, 898,
  911
  abortion and, 830, 831
  anti-Semitism and, 810
  Clinton and, 847
  libertarians and, 749–50
  neoconservatism and, 827
  New Deal and, 691

  Nixon and, 810, 811
  radical, 782, 792, 870
  Reagan and, 838
  rising tide of, 826–34
Constitution, U.S., 560, 593, 594, 619, 632,
  633, 712, 735, 767, 805, 872, 891–92,
  899
  African-Americans and, 442, 461
  and territories acquired, 543
  women's rights and, 461, 462
constitutional amendments, U.S.:
  First, 624, 731, 803, 804
  Second, 914
  Thirteenth, 485, 712
  Fourteenth, 457–58, 461–62, 470, 525, *526*,
    530, 600, 631, 633, 712, 762, 767, 873,
    892, 902
  Fifteenth, 460, 461–62, 524, 600, 619, 712
  Sixteenth, 573
  Seventeenth, 565
  Eighteenth, 594
  Nineteenth, 591
  Twentieth, 662
  Twenty-first, 651
  Twenty-fourth, 783–84
Constitution Hall, 668
consumerism, 551, 620–21, *745*
  advertising and, *553*, *554*, 614, 746
  in American National Exhibition, 741–42
  economy and, 615–16
  and household appliances, 615, *615*, 741,
    742, 743, 887
  television and, 746
  unionization and, 554
  wages and, 552, 553
Consumer Protection Agency, 900
containment, 713–15, 716, 717, 754, 755
contracts, labor, 503–4
  "yellow dog," 504
contracts, "liberty of contract" doctrine and,
  568–69
"Contract with America," 849
Contras, 840
Coolidge, Calvin (1872–1933), 614, 621, *621*,
  622, 629, 636
Coolidge administration, 621
Cooper, Gary (1901–1961), 731
Cooperative Commonwealth, The (Gronlund),
  506–7
Cooper Union, 560
copper, *482*
Coral Sea, Battle of, 682–83, *683*
CORE (Congress of Racial Equality), 702,
  774, 789
corporations, 531, 563, 564, 570, 646, 743,
  749, 856–57, 887
  absentee, 539
  Bush era scandals in, 895–96
  and conformity, 757–58

economic control of countries by, 755–56

farms owned by, 770

Federal Trade Commission and, 576

free enterprise and, 749

multinational, 854

"new despotism" of, 662

in 1920s, 617–18

power and, 565, 755–56

and profits, 616, 656, 674, 687, 688, 821–22, 832, 836–37

and public relations, 618

and rise of West, 498

Social Darwinist view of, 503

taxes on, 656

Theodore Roosevelt and, 571

and white collar jobs, 743

in World War II, 687–88

see also specific corporations

corruption, of politics, 498–99

Cortez, Gregorio, 497

Cosmopolitan, 800

cost of living wage increases, 737, 753

cotton, 449, *453*, 514, 515, 521, 669, *716*, 743

plantations, *see* planters, plantations, cotton

Cotton Belt, 449

Couch, W. T. (1901–1988), 697

Coughlin, Charles E. (1891–1979), 656, 681

counterculture, 772, 796–97, *796*, 813–14

Buddhism and, 798

Catholicism and, 798

and faith, 797–98, *798*

gurus and, 798

and Jesus People, *797*, 798

yoga and, 798, *798*

"court packing," *662*, 663

cowboys, 487, 497

Cox, Archibald (1912–2004), 818

Cox, James (1870–1957), 645

Cox, Renée, *915*

Coxey, Jacob (1854–1951), 518

Coxey's Army, 518

crack cocaine, 866, 867

Crazy Horse (1842?–1877), 492

creationism, 627, 869

see also fundamentalism

Crédit Mobilier, 499

Creel, George (1876–1953), 590

crime, 866–67

Crisis, The, 601

Croatia, *853*

Croly, Herbert (1869–1930), 570

crop lien system, 449–52

"cross of gold" speech, 519, *519*

Cruikshank, U.S. v., 470

Cuba, 533–38, *537*, *543*, 678, *885*

Bay of Pigs invasion in, 777

diplomatic relations resumed with, 908

Guantánamo Bay, 885–86, *885*, 886, 892, 899, 908

immigrants from, 862

Missile Crisis in, 777–78

U.S. intervention in, 582–83

Cullen, Countee (1903?–1946), 634

cultural pluralism, 631

Culture Wars, 869

currency, 500, 519

Federal Reserve System and, 576

for international trade, 708

reform, 505

Currier, Nathaniel (1813–1888), *457*

Curtis, Charles (1860–1936), *635*

Custer, George A. (1839–1876), 491

Custer's Last Stand, 497

Customs Service, 623

CWA (Civil Works Administration), 649

Czakalinski, Steve, *745*

Czechoslovakia, 606, 609, 679, 806

breakup of, *845*

Czolgosz, Leon (1873–1901), 570

Dakota Territory, 492

gold in, 487

Daley, Richard J. (1902–1976), 787–88

Dallas, Tex., 745, 779

dams, 667, 745

Columbia River, 644, *646*

Darrow, Clarence (1857–1938), 627, *627*

Darwin, Charles (1809–1882), 503, 627, 869

Darwinism, *see* evolution

Daugherty, Harry (1860–1941), 622

Daughters of the American Revolution, 668

Davis, James J. (1873–1947), 629–30

Davis, John W. (1873–1955), 622

Davis, Sammy, Jr. (1925–1990), 760

Davis Dam, *646*

Dawes, Henry L. (1816–1903), 492

Dawes Act (1887), 492–93, 666–67

D-Day, 408, 684, *684*

DDT, 802

Dean, James (1931–1955), 758

Dearborn, Mich., *615*

Death and Life of Great American Cities, The (Jacobs), 790

Debs, Eugene V. (1855–1926), 518, 573, *574*, 593, 595, 624

Declaration for Global Democracy, 851

Declaration of Conscience, 733, 735

Declaration of Independence (1776), 542, 559, 712, 721

Dedham, Mass., *613*

Deep South, 522, 653, 729, 774, 775, 781, 782

Defense Department, U.S., 770, *794*, 817, 872, 886

McCarthy and, 732

Office of Public Information, *717*

deficit, federal, *see* national debt

de Gaulle, Charles (1890–1970), 752

Delany, Martin, 704

Delaware, University of, *790*

Delegation of Advocates of Women's Suffrage Addressing the House Judiciary Committee, A, *462*

Delta Council, 738

demobilization, of U.S. military, 724

Democratic Party, 499, 517, 519, 520, 632, 636, 655, 662, 688, 738, 751, 753, 781, 782, 785, 796, 805, 823, 832, 834, 835, 841, 849, 854, 860, 887–88, 893, 898, 910–11

African-Americans and, 668

in campaign of 1960, 768, 770

civil rights movement and, 781

decolonization and, 722

economic policies of, 692

1860 convention of, 394–95

in election of 1900, 544

in election of 1920, 645

in election of 1924, 622

in election of 1928, 636

in election of 1932, 645

in election of 1946, 725

in election of 1948, 727–29, *728*

in election of 1952, 751, *751*

in election of 1954, 751

in election of 1972, 818

in election of 1992, 847

in election of 2000, 872–73

in election of 2008, 878

FDR's transformation of, 644

Fifteenth amendment and, 460

Great Society and, 785

high tariff opposed by, 500

HUAC and, 673

left wing of, 674

and New Deal coalition, 662, 811, 827

1964 national convention of, 781

Nixon and, 810, 811

in Reconstruction, *458*, 466–67, 469, 470–72

South and, 524, 665, 674

Truman Doctrine and, 715

welfare and, 849

see also specific elections and campaigns

Dempsey, Jack (1895–1983), 615

Denmark, 579

Denver, Colo., *489*, 745

depression, economic, 912

agricultural, 617–18

of 1873, 470, 480, 481, 483, 503

of 1893, 480, 483, 503, 517, 519, 535

of 1929, *see* Great Depression

deregulation, 823, *824*, 832, 837, 849, 857–58

and financial crisis of 2008, 896, *896*

derivatives, 900

Deseret, Mormon empire of, 489

détente, 814–15, *817*, 822–23
Detroit, Mich., 563, 701, *703*, 822, *830*
   breadlines in, 638
   riot in, 787
Dewey, George (1837–1917), 536, 539
Dewey, John (1859–1952), 563, 588
Dewey, Thomas E. (1902–1917), 705, 728
Díaz, Porfirio (1830–1915), 583
dictators, dictatorships, 678–79, 777, 815, 824
   FDR and, 678–79
   U.S. support of, 839–40
   see also Hitler, Adolf; Mussolini, Benito;
     Saddam Hussein; Stalin, Joseph;
     totalitarianism
Dictionary of Races of People, 596
Dingley Tariff (1897), 520
diseases:
disenfranchisement, 525
Disney, Walt (1901–1966), 731
diversity, 631, 670, 671, 693, *695*, 860, 862–
   65, *864*, 869, 872
   see also pluralism
divorce, *560*, 814, 870
Divorce the Lesser Evil, *560*
Dixiecrats, 728–29
Dixie to Broadway (Broadway show), 634
Dixon, Frank (1892–1965), 702
Dodge City, Kans., 487
Dole, Bob (1923–), 852
Dollar Diplomacy, 583
domestic abuse, 566, 594
domestic surveillance, 910
Dominican Republic, 582, 583, 678, 794
   immigrants from, 862
Donnelly, Ignatius (1831–1901), 516
"don't ask, don't tell" policy, 848
"Don't Buy Where You Can't Work"
   campaign, 668, *668*
dot coms, 856
double-V, 702
Douglas, Helen Gahagan (1900–1980), 751
Douglas, Stephen A. (1813–1861), 381–82, 387,
   388–92, *389*, 394–96
Douglas, William O. (1898–1980), 804–5
Douglass, Frederick (1817–1895), *463*, *465*,
   703–4, 764, *807*
   on abolition, 444
   death of, 531, 540
Dow Jones Industrial Average, 895
draft:
   in Vietnam War, 796, 816, 825
   in World War I, 589, 595
   in World War II, 686
Dred Scott case, 504
Dreiser, Theodore (1871–1945), 624
Dresden, 706–7
Drew, Charles, 700
drugs, 759, 796, 798, 866, 867
   and "Just Say No" campaign, *838*

Noriega and, 846
   Vietnam War and, 816
   see also crack cocaine
Du Bois, W. E. B. (1868–1963), 541, 599–600,
   603, 608, 703–4, 737
Dukakis, Michael (1933–), 841
Dulles, John Foster (1888–1959), 754
Dumbarton Oaks, conference at, 708
Duncan, Isadora (1877?–1927), 561, *561*
DuPont, *745*
Dust Bowl, 651, *651*, *652*
Dutch East Indies, 682, 722
   see also Indonesia
Dylan, Bob (1941–), 796

Earned Income Tax Credit (EITC), 848
Earth Day, 803
Eastern Band Cherokees, *868*
East Germany:
   absorption of, 844
   creation of, 717
East Harlem, *748*
East St. Louis, Ill., race riot in, 602, 603
Economic Bill of Rights, 692
economy:
   Clinton and, 855
   financial crisis of 2008 and, 893–97, *895*,
     896, 901
   growth of, 500, 614–15
   G. W. Bush and, 887, 893–97
   housing bubble crisis and, 893–94, *894*
   indicators of change in, *477*
   rise of corporations in, 480–83
   U.S. and new, 855–59
   see also depression, economic; market
     economy; recessions
Economy Act (1932), 665
Edison, Thomas A. (1847–1931), 480, 636
Edisto Island, S.C., 450
education:
   civil rights and, 774–75, *779*, 785
   of freed slaves, 444, *444*, *446*, 447, 448
   higher, 730, 753, 790, 799, 814, 860
   Native Americans and, 802
   public, *463*, 465, *466*, *467*, 501, 525, 526,
     555, 567, 628, 655, 673, 692–93, 724,
     727, 742, 743, 784, 866, 869, 899
   women and, 566, 569, 590, 870
Egger-Lienz, Albin, *585*
Egypt, 514, 608, 609, 821, 825, *825*, 909
   in Suez fiasco, 756
Ehrlichman, John (1925–1999), 819
Eickemeyer, Rudolph (1831–1895), *444*
Eiffel Tower, *719*
Eighteenth Amendment, 594
Einstein, Albert (1879–1955), 705
Eisenhower, Dwight D. (1890–1960), 756,
   757, 761, 768, 811, 852
   atomic bomb and, 707

   civil rights and, 760, 765–68
   Cold War and, 753–54
   D-Day and, 684
   Farewell Address of, 770
   Little Rock and, 768
   "military-industrial complex" and, 677
   Modern Republicanism and, 752–53
   1952 campaign and, 751–52, *751*
   Suez fiasco and, 756
Eisenhower administration, 750, *756*, 760,
   762, 791
   and Cuba, 777
   Native Americans and, 801
EITC, *see* Earned Income Tax Credit
Electioneering in the South, *463*
elections and campaigns:
   of 1868, 459–60, *459*, *460*, 499
   of 1872, 469
   of 1876, 471–72, *472*, 499
   of 1888, 499, *501*
   of 1892, 499, *516*
   of 1896, 520, *520*
   of 1900, 544
   of 1912, 573–74, *574*, *576*, 646
   of 1916, 586, *586*
   of 1920, 645
   of 1924, *622*
   of 1928, 635–36, *635*, *636*
   of 1932, 645, *645*
   of 1934, 655
   of 1936, 662
   of 1940, 681
   of 1944, 692, 705
   of 1946, 725
   of 1948, 727–29, *728*, *729*
   of 1952, 751–52, *752*
   of 1960, 768–70, *769*, 810
   of 1964, 781–82, *782*, 810
   of 1968, 807
   of 1972, *817*
   of 1976, 823
   of 1980, 833–34, *833*
   of 1984, 837
   of 1988, 841
   of 1992, 847–48
   of 1996, 852
   of 2000, 872–73, *873*, 874
   of 2004, 887–88
   of 2006, 893
   of 2008, *877*, *878*, 897–98
   of 2012, 911–13, *912*
Electoral College, 499, 586, 834, 873, 888
Electoral Commission (1877), 472
electrical industry, 554
electricity, 480, 644, 674, 857
Electricity Building at the Chicago World's Fair of
   1893, The (Hassam), *481*
Elliott, Robert B. (1842–1884), *441*
Ellis Island, 550

El Mozote, El Salvador, massacre in, 840
El Salvador, 825, 839–40, 890
e-mail, 856
Emancipation Proclamation (1862), 450, 712
Emanuel African Methodist Episcopal
    Church, mass shooting in, 903, 914
Emergency Banking Act (1933), 647
empire, U.S., 537–39, 542–44, 542
Endangered Species Act (1973), 803, 811
End Poverty in California, 655
Enforcement Acts (1870–71), 468, 470
England, see British Empire; Great Britain
Engle v. Vitole, 804
English, as official language, 869
Enron, 857, 857
environmentalism, 790, 802–3, 823, 828,
    829, 832, 833, 835, 848, 849, 849, 854,
    879, 879, 908–9
    see also pollution
Environmental Protection Agency, 811
Episcopalians, 827
Equal Employment Opportunity
    Commission, 784, 799
Equal Pay Act (1963), 799
Equal Rights Amendment (ERA), 618–19,
    830–31, 833
Espionage Act (1917), 593, 594–95, 624, 625
Estonia, 606, 707
Ethiopia, 679, 909
ethnic cleansing, 852, 853
eugenics, 596
Europe, European powers, 605–8, 606, 607,
    635, 713, 716, 717, 719
    immigration from, 784, 859, 863
    pre-World War II, 679
    see also specific countries
European Union, Iran nuclear program
    and, 908
evangelical Christians, 832, 911
Evers, Medgar (1925–1963), 775
evolution, 503, 627–28, 869
Executive Order 8802, 701
Executive Order 9066, 698
Exodus, book of, 328, 523
Expansionist, The (Millet), 512

factories, 551, 552, 555, 614, 854
    automobile, 614
    pollution and, 811
    in Soviet Exhibition, 741
    during World War II, 687
factory farms, 617
Fairbanks, Douglas (1883–1939), 595
Fair Deal, 724–25
Fair Employment Practices Commission
    (FEPC), 695, 701–2
Fair Labor Standards Act (1938), 640,
    668–69
Fair Labor Standards Bill, 663

Fall, Albert (1861–1944), 622
Fall In!, 662
Falwell, Jerry (1933–2007), 827
Family Assistance Plan, 811
family life, 800
    "family values" and, 833, 834, 869, 870
    and nuclear family, 869
Family Record, 443
Farmers' Alliance, 514
farms, see agriculture
Farm Security Administration, 665, 667
fascism, 656, 679, 693, 723
    Mussolini as founder of, 679
"Father Was Killed by a Pinkerton Man"
    (song), 513
"Fat Man" atomic bomb, 705
Faubus, Orval (1910–1994), 768
FBI, see Federal Bureau of Investigation
FCC, see Federal Communications
    Commission
FDIC, see Federal Deposit Insurance
    Corporation
Federal Art Project, 657, 671
federal bailout, of banks, 897, 901
Federal Bureau of Investigation (FBI), 711,
    713, 736, 789, 819, 886
Federal Communications Commission
    (FCC), 651–52
Federal Deposit Insurance Corporation
    (FDIC), 647
Federal Emergency Management Agency
    (FEMA), 889
Federal Emergency Relief Administration,
    648
Federal Home Loan Bank System, 641
Federal Home Loan Mortgage Corporation
    (Freddie Mac), 897
Federal Housing Administration (FHA), 651,
    669, 669
Federal Land Policy Management Act (1976),
    829
Federal National Mortgage Association
    (Fannie Mae), 897
Federal Reserve Bank, 893, 894
Federal Reserve System, 576
Federal Savings and Loan Insurance
    Corporation, 837
Federal Trade Commission, 576
FEMA, see Federal Emergency Management
    Agency
Feminine Mystique, The (Friedan), 799
feminism, 736, 747, 774, 798–800, 800,
    847, 871
    African-Americans and, 619
    Hillary Clinton and, 871
    in middle class, 799
    new, 560–61
    radical, 800
    reproductive rights and, 800

second-wave, 793, 830
    see also gender relations; women; women's
        rights
Fenway Park, 860
FEPC, see Fair Employment Practices
    Commission
Ferguson, Mo., 907, 907
Ferraro, Geraldine (1935–), 837
FHA, see Federal Housing Administration
Fifth Freedom, 689–90
Fifteenth Amendment, 460, 461–62, 524,
    600, 619, 712
Filipinos, 539, 682, 743
    see also Philippines
financial crisis of 2008, 893–97, 895, 896,
    898, 901
Finland, 606
Fire Next Time, The (Baldwin), 790
fireside chats, 659, 659, 660
    on radio, 659, 660
Firestone, 836
First African Church, The, 445
First Amendment, 624, 731, 803, 804
    Holmes doctrine and, 624
First Vote, The, 464
Fisher, Sidney George, 461
Fisher Body Plant, 654
Fishman, Simon, 616
Fisk University, 444, 600
Fitzgerald, F. Scott (1896–1940), 624
Five Generations of a Black Family, 444
flappers, 614, 619
Flint, Michigan, 654, 654
Florida, 637, 726, 898, 904, 906
    in election of 2000, 872–73, 873
    prison labor and, 521
FOIA (Freedom of Information Act) (1966),
    819
Fong Yue Ting v. United States, 530–31
Food Administration, 589, 594
food stamps, 785, 811
Foraker Act (1900), 543
Ford, Gerald (1913–2006), 822–23, 822,
    827, 831
    Nixon pardoned by, 822
Ford, Henry (1863–1947), 553, 614, 617, 636,
    680, 681
Ford administration, 848
Fordism, 553
Ford Motor Company, 553, 614, 615, 616,
    687, 858
    assembly lines and, 553
Fordney-McCumber Tariff (1922), 623
Forest Service, U.S., 572, 833
Forging the Shaft (Weir), 478
Forman, Stanley, 812
Fort Hood, 727
Fort Marion, Fla., 493
Fortune, 689

"47 percent" remark by Romney, 912

Four Freedoms, 677–78, *678*, 688–89, 693, 697, 709, 712, 723, 727

Fourteen Points, 587–88, 605–6, *606*, 608, 609

Fourteenth Amendment, 457–58, 461–62, 470, 525, *526*, 530, 600, 631, 633, 712, 762, 767, 873, 892, 902

Foxwoods casino, 868–69

France, 476, *578*, 623, 679, 680, 704, 709, *716*, 717, 752, 756, 914
  communist party in, 716
  declares war on Germany, 680
  German occupation of, 684
  in Great Depression, 637
  industry in, 478
  Iraq War and, 883
  male suffrage in, 498
  1968 strike in, 806
  occupation of Germany by, 717
  Progressivism in, 562
  in Suez fiasco, 756
  in U.N., 708
  in World War I, 584
  see also French Empire

Frank, Leo (1884–1915), 628

Frank Leslie's Illustrated Newspaper, 455, 462, *506*

Franklin, Benjamin (1706–1790), 593

Franz Ferdinand, archduke of Austria (1863–1914), 584

Frazier, Garrison (b. 1797), 442

Freedman's Savings and Trust, *470*

Freedmen's Bureau, 444, 447–48, 457, *458*, 491

Freedmen's Bureau, The, 448

Freedmen's Bureau Bill (1866), 457

freedom, 544, 554–55, 703, 712–13, 723, 804, 885, 893, 899, 902, 909, 914, *915*, 916
  American National Exhibition and, 741
  of assembly, 672
  Bellamy's view of, 503
  Chief Joseph on, 491
  civil rights movement and, 737, 738, 759–68, *765*
  Cold War and, 719, 721, 722–24, 730, 756, 774
  conservatism and, 750
  consumerism and, 551, 745
  counterculture and, 796–97, 798
  Debs's view of, 519
  degradation of, 624–25
  employer vs. employee, 513
  of expression, 560, 593, 594, 595, 623–25, 627, 672, 677, 697, 723, 731, 749, 791, 880
  FDR and, 659, 660
  in Gilded Age, 502–4
  in Great Depression, 641
  Great Society and, 785–86
  immigration and, 550
  Indians and, 491–93
  Iraq War and, 885, 888
  left wing groups and, 670
  Marshall Plan and, 716
  New Deal and, 648, 659
  New Left's definition of, 789
  in 1964 election, 810
  post–World War II, 691–93
  of the press, 593, 625, 803, 817
  Prohibition and, 626
  Reagan and, 834–35
  in Reconstruction, 442, 443–54
  Red Scare and, 613
  religious, *see* religious freedom
  Social Darwinists view of, 503
  of speech, *see* freedom, of expression
  Statue of Liberty and, 476
  Thurmond and, 729
  Truman Doctrine and, 715
  U.S. foreign policy and, 580
  war on terror and, 879, 880
  women and, 552, 558, 619–20, *620*, 690, *691*, 799–800
  of workers, 483–84
  World War I and, 590, 594, 596
  World War II and, 678, *678*, 688–89, *691*, 709
  see also Four Freedoms; religious freedom

Freedom Award, 782

freedom from want, 689

Freedom in the Modern World, 641

Freedom of Information Act (FOIA) (1966), 819

Freedom Revolution, 849

Freedom Rides, 774

Freedom Schools, *780*

Freedom Summer, 780–81

Freedom Train, 712–13, *713*

free enterprise, *689*, 690, 721, 749

free labor, 447

Freeman, Owen, *879*

Free Speech Movement, 791, *791*

free trade, 623, 846, 848, 850, 852, 857
  see also NAFTA (North American Free Trade Agreement)

Free World, 722, 749, 750
  U.S. president as leader of, 715

Free World Association, 691

French Empire, 533, 579, 608
  Vietnam and, 756

French Indochina, 722, 791

Frick, Henry Clay (1849–1919), 513

Friedan, Betty (1921–2006), 793, 799

From the Plantation to the Senate, 463

Fuel Agency, 589

Fulton, Mo., "iron curtain" speech at, 714

fundamentalism, 625–27, 826, 859
  Islamic, 826, 845, 859, 875, 882, 890–91
  religious freedom vs., 627
  Saddam Hussein and, 882
  see also creationism

Gabbard, Tulsi (1981–), 913

Gaddafi, Muammar (1942–2011), 908

Gaffney, Mary (b. 1846), 449

Gaines, Lloyd (1913?–1939), 761

Galesburg, Ill., Maytag factory in, 887

Gandhi, Mohandas (Mahatma; 1869–1948), 709, 764

Garfield, James A. (1831–1881), 443
  assassination of, 500

Garner, Eric, 906–7

Garner, John Nance (1868–1967), 691

Garrison, William Lloyd (1805–1879), 460, 593

Garvey, Marcus (1887–1940), 603, *603*

Garveyism, 603

Garvey movement, 635

gas, poison, 584

Gassed (Sargent), *578*

Gates, Bill (1955–), *856*, 858

GATT, *see* General Agreement on Tariffs and Trade

Gay Liberation Front, *801*

Gay Men's Health Crisis, 868

gay rights, 561, 774, 800–801, *801*, 814, 838, 847, 867–68, 869, 872
  military and, 847
  see also homosexuals, homosexuality

GE, *see* General Electric

gender relations:
  World War II and, 678
  see also women; women's rights

General Agreement on Tariffs and Trade (GATT), 716

General Assembly, U.N., 708, 723

General Electric (GE), 615, 834, *834*

General Motors, 616, 637, 654–55, *654*, *687*, 752, 803, 859

General Slocum, 547

General Theory of Employment, Interest, and Money (Keynes), 663

Geneva:
  summit conference in, 754
  Vietnam peace conference in, 756

Geneva Conventions, 886
  First, 892

Gentlemen's Agreement (1907), 598

George, Henry (1839–1897), 506, 510, 562, 563

Georgia, 450, 522, 823, 892
  Ku Klux Klan in, 628
  Mexican immigrants in, 862

German-Americans, 486, 528, 631
  Prohibition and, 594
  World War I and, 585, 597
  World War II and, 680, 698
Germany, 606-8, *606*, 609, *685*, 707, *707*,
    723, 820, 823, 896, 914
  aggression by, 679, *680*
  as Axis power, 680
  D-Day and, 684, *684*
  declaration of war against U.S. of, 682
  division of, 714, 717
  empire of, 579
  in Great Depression, 637
  industry in, 478
  invasion of Poland by, 680
  invasion of Soviet Union by, 681, 713
  Iraq War and, 882-83
  occupation of, 717
  post-Cold War, 844
  Progressivism in, 562
  rise of Hitler in, 679, 680
  Soviet Union invasion of, 704
  submarine war and, 684
  in World War I, 584-86
  in World War II, 679-81, *684*, 698, 704,
    707
  see also East Germany; West Germany
Gettysburg Address, The, *498*, 712
Ghana, 755
Ghost Dance, 492-93
GI Bill of Rights (1944), 692, 695, 701, 724,
    725
Gilded Age, 475-510, *482*, 555, 563
  corruption of politics in, 498
  courts in, 504
  economy in, 500, 502
  elections in, 499-500, *499*
  freedom in, 502-4
  labor in, 505-10, *506*
  liberty of contract in, 503-4
  political parties in, 499-500
  politics in, 497-502
  Social Darwinism, 502-3
  state governments in, 501-2
Gilded Age, The (Twain and Warner), 497
Gilman, Charlotte Perkins (1860-1935),
    558, 589
Gingrich, Newt (1943-), 849
Ginsberg, Allen (1926-1997), 759
Ginsburg, Ruth Bader (1933-), 848
Gladden, Washington (1836-1918), 508
Glasgow, 603
glasnost, 840
Glass-Steagall Act (1932), 647, 857
globalization, 850, 851, 854-59, 860
global warming, 879, *879*, 901, 909
GNP, *see* gross national product
Goddess of Democracy and Freedom, 844,
    846

Godkin, E. L. (1831-1902), 469
gold, 820
  in California gold rush, 484, 487
  Chinese immigrants and, 530
  corporate mining of, 487
Gold Coast, 722, 755
Golden Anniversary of the Festival of Lights,
    636
"golden door," 628-29
Goldman, Emma (1869-1940), 561, *561*, 595,
    605
Goldman Sachs, 896
gold rush, California, 484
gold standard, 500, 519, 520, 820
Gold Standard Act (1900), 520
Goldwater, Barry (1909-1998), 781-82, 792,
    810, 834
Gompers, Samuel (1850-1924), 532, 557, 588
Goodman, Andrew (1949-1964), 781
Good Neighbor Policy, 678
Gorbachev, Mikhail (1931-), 840, *840*, 844
Gore, Albert (1907-1998), 765
Gore, Albert, Jr. (1948-), 872-73, 874
Goshorn, Shan, *868*
government, U.S.:
  business and, 620-23, 691
  corruption in, 621-22
  debt of, *see* national debt
  employment discrimination, 668
  housing discrimination by, 669, *669*
  labor and, 517-18
  regulatory powers of, 571, 621, 646-47,
    663, 674, 785, 786
  in Second New Deal, 659
  workforce size of, 500
  see also specific branches
Grady, Henry (1850-1889), 521
Graham, Billy (1918-), 749
"Grand Alliance," in World War II, 683-84
Grand Coulee Dam, 644, *646*
grandfather clause, voting rights and, 524
Grange, 501
Grant, Ulysses S. (1822-1885), 468, 469, 499
  in election of 1868, 459-60, *459*
  Indian policy of, 490
  Ku Klux Klan and, 468
  scandals under, 467
  Southern violence and, 470
Grapes of Wrath, The (Steinbeck), 661
Great Awakening, Third, 827
Great Britain, 623, 658, 679, 680, 697, 714,
    752, 768, 806, 914
  D-Day and, 684
  declares war on Germany, 680
  in Great Depression, 637
  immigrants from, 486
  industry in, 478
  Iraq War and, 883
  Lend-Lease and, 681

occupation of Germany by, 717
  Progressivism in, 562
  submarine war and, 684
  in Suez fiasco, 756
  suffrage in, 498, 591
  and Third World, 755
  in U.N., 708, 709
  in World War I, 584-86
  see also British Empire; England
Great Depression, 635-41, *638*, *640*, 644-45,
    646, *646*, *651*, 655, 656, 661, 687, 689,
    690, 708, 820, 832, 856-57, 893, 895,
    912
  Dust Bowl and, 651
  Eisenhower and, *751*
  homelessness and, 638, *638*, 661
  housing and, 651
  minorities and, 665-66
  radio and, 656
  wages in, 637
  women and, 664
  World War II and, 674, 677, *686*
  see also New Deal
Greatest Department Store on Earth, The, 480
Great Labor Parade of September 1, 506
Great Migration, 601-2, *601*, 631, *634*,
    700-701
Great Plains, 484, 486, 487, 548, *616*, 617
  women in, 486
Great Railroad Strike of 1877, 505, *505*
Great Society, 447, 669, 784-85, 796, 807,
    811, 848, 852, 899, 901
  see also Johnson, Lyndon
Great Steel Strike, 654
Great War, *see* World War I
Greece, rebellion in, 715
Greeley, Horace (1811-1872), 469
Green, James K. (1823-1891), 463
Greenglass, David (1922-), 731-32
Greensboro, N.C., 773
  sit-in at, 773
Greenwich Village, N.Y., Stonewall Inn raid
    in, 800-801
Grenada, 838
gridlock, political, 912
Griffith, D. W. (1875-1948), 599
Griswold v. Connecticut, 804-5
Gromyko, Andrey (1909-1989), 823
Gronlund, Laurence (1846-1899), 506-7
Gropper, William, *646*
gross national product (GNP), 677, 682, 687,
    742, *742*
Gruening, Ernest (1887-1974), 794
Guadalcanal, 683
Guam, 538, 543
  in World War II, 682
Guantánamo Bay, 538, 885-86, *885*, 886, 892,
    899, 908
Guatemala, 755, *756*, 825, 839, 890

Gulf Coast:
    Hurricane Katrina and, 888–89
Gulf of Tonkin resolution, 749
Gulf War, 846, 847, 875, 881
guns:
    murder rate and, 914
    school shootings and, 914
    and Second Amendment, 214, 914
gurus, 798
Guthrie, Tex., *453*
Gypsies, Nazi extermination of, 686

Haacke, Hans (1936–), *858*
Haas, Ernst (1921–1986), *745*
Hacienda La Fortuna (Oller), *538*
Haiti, 583
    immigrants from, 860
Haldeman, H. R. (1926–1993), 819
Hamer, Fannie Lou (1917–1977), 781
Hampton, Wade (1818–1902), 471
Hampton Institute, 531
Hampton University, 444
Hanna, Mark (1837–1904), 520
Hanna, Tom, 509–10
Harding, Warren G. (1865–1923), 595, 610,
    621–22, *621*
    death of, 614
Harlan, John Marshall (1833–1911), 525
Harlem, N.Y., 631–34, 667–68, *668*, 671,
    788
    race riots in, 786
Harlem Renaissance, 634–35
Harper's Weekly, *445*, 448, *463*, *464*, *469*, *473*
Harrington, Michael (1928–1989), 785, 790
Harrison, Benjamin (1833–1901), *501*,
    534–35
Harrison administration, 535
Hart, Gary (1936–), 841
Hart-Celler Act (1965), 784
Harvard Law School, 878
Harvard University, 600
    Marshall Plan announced at, 715
Harvest Gypsies, The: On the Road to the Grapes of
    Wrath (Steinbeck), 661
Hassam, Childe, *481*
Havana Harbor, 535
Havemeyer, Louisine (1855–1929), *569*
Havens, Richie (1941–), 797
Hawaii, 543, 550, 631
    acquisition of, 535, *535*, 538
Hay, John (1838–1905), 536, 538
Hayashida, Fumiko (1901–1977), *700*
Hayek, Friedrich A. (1899–1992), 693
Hayes, Rutherford B. (1822–1893), 471–72,
    491, 494
Haymarket affair, 509
Haynsworth, Clement (1912–1989), 812
Hays code, 624
Head Start, 785

health care, national, 692, 723, 725, 737, 848,
    900, 901
    attacked, 912
Health Maintenance Organizations (HMOs),
    848
Hearst, William Randolph (1863–1951),
    535, *537*
Helsinki Accords, 822–23
Hemingway, Ernest (1899–1961), 624
Henderson, Alex, *745*
Hepburn Act (1906), 571
Heritage Foundation, 827
Hersey, John (1914–1993), 707
Hewitt, Abram (1822–1903), 510
Hidden Persuaders, The (Packard), 758
Highland Park, Mich., Ford plant at, 553
highways, 745, 746
    building of, 730, *744*, 752
Hilton, David, *486*
Hindus, 859, 913
    as immigrants, 860
Hine, Lewis (1874–1940), 522, 549, *549*, 617
Hirono, Mazie K. (1947–), 913
Hiroshima:
    atomic bombing of, 705, *706*, 754
    population of, 705
Hiroshima (Hersey), 707
Hispanics, *see* Latinos
Hiss, Alger (1904–1996), 731
History of Southern Illinois, *671*
Hitler, Adolf (1889–1945), 609, 679–81, *680*,
    704, 712, 713
    "final solution" of, 686, 694
    and nonaggression pact, 680, 681
    Soviet Union invaded by, 684
HMOs, *see* Health Maintenance
    Organizations
Ho Chi Minh (1890–1969), 609, 756
Hoffman, Abbie (1936–1989), 797
Holland, *see* Netherlands
Holland, François (1954–), 910
Hollywood, 617, 624
    blacklisting in, 731
    communism and, 722, *722*, 731, *731*, *838*
    racism and, 722
    rise of, 615
    sexually charged films from, 619
    World War II and, 690
    see also motion pictures
Hollywood Ten, 731
Holmes, Oliver Wendell (1841–1935), 598,
    624–25
Holocaust, 686, 694
Homeland Security Department, U.S., 879
homelessness, *837*
    Great Depression and, 638, *638*, 661
home ownership, 865, *865*, 895
    middle class and, 662
    post–World War II, 692–93, 724

Home Owners' Loan Corporation, 651, *669*
Home Protection movement, 532
Homer, Winslow (1836–1910), *447*
Homestead, Pa., Carnegie's factories in, 481,
    513, 531, 654
Homestead Act (1862), 485, 548
homosexuals, homosexuality, 561, 736, 774,
    800–801, *801*, 814, 838, 869
    and AIDS, 867–68
    Nazi extermination of, 686
    see also gay rights
Honduras, 890
"Honor America," *811*
Hoover, Herbert (1874–1964), 617, 635–36,
    635, 645, *647*, 678
    background of, 635
    Depression and, 640–41
    in election of 1928, 635–36
    as Secretary of Commerce, 622
Hoover, J. Edgar (1895–1972), *711*, 736
Hoovervilles, 638, *638*
Hopkins, Harry (1890–1946), 646
Horne, Lena (1917–2010), 760
horses, 490
Horton, Willie, 841
Hose, Sam (d. 1899), 527
House of Representatives, U.S., 499, 519, 632,
    767, 849, 885, 893, 898, 911
    African-Americans in, 464
    Clinton's impeachment and, 872
    immigration and, 890
    Johnson's impeachment and, 459–60
    Judiciary Committee of, 819
    Un-American Activities Committee
        (HUAC) of, 673, 730–31, *731*, 733, 803
    World War I and, 586
housing bubble, 893–94, *894*, 906
Houston, Charles Hamilton, 761
Houston, Tex., *726*, 745
Howard, Mary W., *567*
Howard, O. O. (1830–1909), 447, 450, 491
Howard University, 444, *789*
Howl (Ginsberg), 759
How the Other Half Lives (Riis), 484
HUAC, *see* House of Representatives,
    Un-American Activities Committee of
Hubenthal, Karl (1917–1998), *803*
Hudson-Bank Gymnasium, *564*
Huerta, Victoriano (1854–1916), 583–84
Hughes, Charles Evans (1862–1948), 586, 622
Hughes, Langston (1902–1967), 634, 712, 916
Hull House, 566–67, *566*, 646
human rights, 839, 852, 853
    ambiguities of, 724
    Carter and, 824–25
    Obama and, 909
    rise of, 723, 728
Humphrey, Hubert (1911–1978), 727–28, 768,
    781, 806

Hundred Days, 647, 648, 649
Hungary, 606, 754
Huntington, Samuel P. (1927–2008), 891
hydrogen bomb, 753–54
   see also atomic bomb; nuclear weapons

ICBMs, *see* intercontinental ballistic missiles
Ickes, Harold (1874–1952), 646, 649, 668
Idaho, 491, 819
   corporate mining in, 489
   woman suffrage in, 517, 567
"If We Must Die" (McKay), 635
"I Have a Dream" (King), 764
Illegal Act, The, 652
illegal alien, Immigration Act and, 629
Illinois, 745, 878
   woman suffrage in, 567
Illinois, University of, 748
Illinois Central Railroad, *518*
Illinois Federal Art Project, *671*
Illinois Supreme Court, 504
I Married a Communist (movie), 722
immigrants, immigration, 476, 478, 484,
      487, 496, 513–14, 526, 535, 543, 548,
      550, 555, *566*, 596–98, 661, 669, 693–94,
      747, 859–65, *859*, *860*, *861*, *863*, *864*,
      869, 879, 889–90, *889*
   AFL and, 532
   from Africa, 865
   Americanization and, 596–98, 628, 670,
      693–94
   Asian, 550, 598, 617, 629, 694, 784, 864–
      65, *864*, 865
   from China, 487, 529–31, *530*, 543
   to cities, 549–51
   Cold War and, 730
   Congress and, 736
   freedom and, 550–51, 552
   global, 549–51
   "golden door" and, 628–29
   illegal, 889, 890, *890*, 901
   from India, 860, 864
   IQ tests and, 597
   from Japan, 487
   Jews and, *551*
   Ku Klux Klan and, 628
   from Latin America, 784, 859, *859*, 860–
      65, *862*, 865
   from Mexico, 484, 487, 617, 629, *629*, 667,
      694–95, 784, 860–65, 889, 890, 911
   to New York, 549, *564*
   prejudice and, 613
   Progressivism and, 566
   quotas, 784
   reform of 1965, 784
   religion and, 625
   Republicans and, 912
   Republicans as anti-immigration, 869,
      912

   restrictions on, 528–31, *529*, 597–98, *597*,
      628–29, *630*, 631, 670, 694, 698
   rights, 890, *891*
   from Russia, 585
   volume of, 549–51, *550*
   wages and, 551
   and West, 484, 485
   from Western Hemisphere, 629
   women and, 552, 860, *862*
   World War I and, 601
   World War II and, 677–78
   see also specific nationalities
Immigration Act (1924), 629–30, *629*
Immigration Commission, U.S., 596
Immigration Restriction League, 528
impeachment:
   of Andrew Johnson, 459–60
   of Clinton, 872
imperialism, 697
   decolonization and, 721–22, 755
   international, 533–34
   moral, 583
   as "New Imperialism," 533
   U.S., 533–44, 691
Inchon, South Korea, 719, *720*
income taxes, *see* taxes, income
Independent Monitor, *468*
India, 514, 603, 608, 708, 709, 755, 798, 859
   immigrants from, 860, 864
   jobs exported to, 887
   loss of U.S. jobs to, 887
Indiana, 898
   anticommunist law in, 733
   blacks barred from, 275
   Ku Klux Klan, 628
Indian New Deal, 666
Indian radicalism, 562
Indian removal, 485
   see also Native Americans
Indian Reorganization Act (1934), 666
"Indians of All Tribes," 802, *802*
individualism, 507, 554, 749
Indonesia, 755
industrial revolution:
   "second," 476–84
Industrial Workers of the World (IWW),
      556–57, 560, 589, 595, 604, 605, 653,
      654
industry, 693, 695
   African-Americans in, 672, 701–2
   in California, 617
   child labor and, 549
   decline in, 821–22
   Fordism and, 553
   freedom and, 554–55
   New Deal and, 674
   Populists and, 519
   post–World War I, 604
   post–World War II, 743

   in Progressive era, 549, 550, 562
   rise of, 579
   scientific management in, 554–55
   in South, 521, 688
   in West, *488*
   women in, 690–91, *690*
   World War II and, 686–88, *686*, *687*,
      690–91
   see also manufacturing; *specific industries*
infant mortality, 914
inflation, 716, 725, 812, 820, *820*, 821, 822,
      822, 823, 835, 836
Influence of Sea Power Upon History, The
      (McMahon), 534
influenza, 604
Ingersoll, Robert G. (1833–1899), *500*
"In God We Trust," on paper money, 749
innovations, technological, 480
In re Debs, 518
Insular Cases, 543
insurance:
   national health, 658, 674, 692, 723, 725,
      737, 785, 848, 900, 901
   unemployment, 658, 665, 668, 752, 897
   unions and, 737, 753
integration, labor and, 505, 522
intercontinental ballistic missiles (ICBMs),
      769
Interior Department, U.S., *646*, 649
International Business Machines (IBM), 615
International Convention Against Torture,
      886
International Harvester, 481
internationalism, black, 697, 704
International Labor Defense, 671
International League for Human Rights, 824
International Longshoremen's Association,
      653
International Monetary Fund, 708, 855
International Telephone and Telegraph, 615
Internet, 854, 856, 878, 904, 910
Interrupting the Ceremony, *609*
Interstate Commerce Commission (ICC), 501,
      571, 774
interstate highway system, *744*, 752
intervention, era of U.S., 580–84
Iowa, 635, 888
IQ tests, 597
Iran, 714, 755, 756, 815, 821, 825–26, 840,
      881
   American hostages in, 825–26, *826*
   nuclear program of, 908
   television and American hostages in, *826*
Iran-Contra affair, 840
Iraq, 608, 840, 881–82, 886, 887, 915
   economic sanctions on, 845
   in Gulf War, 846
   ISIS in, 909
   militias in, 883

Iraq War, 878, 879, *881*, 882–85, *883*, 887,
  888, 893, 898, 908
  casualties in, *883*, 908
  protests against, *882*
Ireland, 608, 609, 806, *807*
Irish, Irish immigrants, 499, 509, 528, 585
  integration and, 813
  World War II and, 680
Irish Free State, 608
"iron curtain," 714
iron industry, 487, 521
Iroquois:
  in World War II, 695
irrigation, 617
Isato, Sono, 700
ISIS (Islamic State), 909–10
Islam:
  Egypt and, 909
  and fundamentalism, 859, 875, 882,
    890–91
  Gulf War and, 846
  Iran and, 826
  Middle East, 840
  Nation of, 788
  radicals and, 756
  Saudi Arabia and, 788
Islamic State (ISIS), 909–10
isolationism, 622, 679–80, 751
Israel, 756, 821, 825, *825*, 838, 859, 875, 915
issei, 698
Is This a Republican Form of Government? (Nast),
  473
Is This the End? (Freeman), *879*
Italians, Italian-Americans, 528, 549, 551,
  596, 613
  in East Harlem, *748*
  World War II and, 680, 698
Italy, 623, 680, 698, 723, 914
  as Axis power, 680
  communist party in, 716
  liberation of, 684
  rise of Mussolini in, 679
Ives, James (1824–1895), *457*
Ivory Soap, 479
IWW, *see* Industrial Workers of the World

Jackson, Robert H., 700
Jackson, Thomas "Stonewall" (1824–1863),
  528
Jackson State University, 816
Jacobs, Jane, 790
Jacobson, David, *857*
Jamaica, 582, 634
Japan, 538, *582*, 598, 608, 623, 629, 680,
  683, 687, 705–7, 708, 719, 820, 821,
  896, 914
  as Axis power, 680
  economic reconstruction of, 716–17
  expulsion from Vietnam of, 756

immigrants from, 487, 550
invasion of Manchuria by, 679
trade with, 680, 681
U.S. declaration of war against, 682
U.S. oil and, 680, 681
in World War I, 584
in World War II, 679–80, 681–83, 698,
  702, 705–6, *706*
World War II surrender of, 705
Japanese immigrants, Japanese-Americans,
  698–700, 864
  in Hawaii, 535
  World War II internment of, 678, 698–
    700, *699*, *700*, 761
jazz, 634, 722
Jazz Age, 614
Jefferson, Thomas (1743–1826), 593
Jefferson Davis Highway, *784*
Jesus, 798
Jesus People, *797*, 798
Jews, 555, 596, 608, 625, 628, 630, *646*, 662,
  694, 709, 731–32, 859, 872
  in FDR administration, 669
  in flight from Russia, 551
  Holocaust and, 686, 694
  as immigrants, *551*
  Ku Klux Klan and, 628
  lynching of, 628
  in movies, 749
  in Nazi Germany, 679
  prejudice against, 630, 631
  World War I and, 585
  see also anti-Semitism
Jim Crow, 712, 760, 762, 764, 776, 803, 836
Jobs, Steve (1955–), *856*
Johnson, Andrew (1808–1875), 450
  background of, 454
  emancipation and, 454
  impeachment of, 459–60
  Reconstruction policies of, 448, 450,
    454–57, *457*, 458–59
  veto power and, 457
Johnson, Hiram (1866–1945), 563, 564
Johnson, Hugh S. (1871–1938), 648
Johnson, Lyndon (1908–1973), 765, 779–86,
  785, 792, 805
  in campaign of 1960, 768
  civil rights and, 779–80, 786, 787
  Dominican Republic and, 794
  in election of 1964, 781
  Great Society and, 784–85
  Native Americans and, 801
  Vietnam and, 791–94
Joint Chiefs of Staff, 846
Jones, Mary "Mother" (1830–1930), 560
Jones, Paula (1966–), 872
Joseph, Chief (1840–1904), 491, *492*, 494
Joyce, James (1882–1941), 623, 625
J.P. Morgan Chase, 857, 896

JR, *889*
Judaism:
  in movies, 749
  see also Jews
Judge, 519, *529*, 582
Jungle, The (Sinclair), 549
juries, African-Americans and, 672
Justice Department, U.S., 595, 712, 886, 906
  Civil Liberties Unit, 672
"Just Say No" campaign, *838*
juvenile delinquency, 758

Kagan, Elena, 899
Kallen, Horace (1882–1974), 641
Kanab, Utah, *567*
Kansas, 485, *616*
  black migration to, 522–23, *523*
  in Dust Bowl, 651, *651*
  Mexican immigrants in, 862
  Populist Party in, *515*
  woman suffrage in, 517
Kansas City, Mo., 509
Kansas Pacific Railroad, 487
Katrina, Hurricane, 888–89, *889*, 893
  and African-Americans, 889, *889*
  death toll from, 889
Kaufman, Irving (1910–1992), 732
Kaufmann, Theodore (1814–1896), *465*
Keating-Owen Act (1916), 575
Kefauver, Estes (1903–1963), 765
Kelley, Florence (1859–1932), 567, 589
Kennan, George (1904–2005), 714
Kennedy, Anthony (1936–), 892–93, 902
Kennedy, Jacqueline (1929–1994), 770, *770*
Kennedy, John F. (1917–1963), 770, 776–79,
  785, *794*, 888
  assassination of, *778*, 779, 794
  in campaign of 1960, 768–70, *769*, 810
  civil rights and, 778–79
  Cuban Missile Crisis and, 777–78
  in debates with Nixon, 770, 874
  desegregation and, 775
  inaugural address of, 777
  Native Americans and, 801
  space race and, 769
  Vietnam and, 791
Kennedy, Robert F. (1925–1968),
  assassination of, 806
Kennedy administration, 775, 776–79
Kent State University, 816, *816*
Kenya, 755
Kenyatta, Jomo (1894–1978), 704
Kerner, Otto (1908–1976), 787
Kerner Report, 787
Kerry, John (1943–), 888
Keynes, John Maynard (1883–1946), 663
Keynesian economics, 663–64
Khmer Rouge, 816
Khomeini, Ayatollah (1900–1989), 756, 826

Khrushchev, Nikita (1894–1971), 741–42, *741*, 754, 778
King, Martin Luther, Jr. (1929–1968), 517, 759, 763–64, 766, 787, 796, 801, 823, 899, 907
  assassination of, 805, *806*
  Birmingham campaign and, 775–76
  March on Washington and, 776
  Montgomery boycott and, 763–64
  Poor People's March and, 805
  Selma campaign of, 783
King, Rodney (1965–), 867
Kiowas, *493*
Kipling, Rudyard (1865–1936), 539, *544*
Kirkpatrick, Jeane (1926–2006), 839
Kissinger, Henry (1923–), 814, 815, 823
kitchen debate, 741–42, *741*
Kiyoshi, Kobayakawa, *619*
Knights of Labor, 505–6, 510, 531
Koehler, Karl, *702*
Koran, 891
Korea, 608, 719–21
  immigrants from, 698, 864, *864*
  see also North Korea; South Korea
Korean War, *717*, 719–21, *720*, *721*, 727, 732, 751, 756
  armistice in, 753, 754
  casualties in, 721
Korematsu, Fred (1919–2005), 700
Korematsu v. United States, 700
Kosovo, 852–53
Kroc, Ray (1902–1984), 745
Ku Klux Klan, 468, *468*, 509, 599, *599*, *628*, 631, 727, 774
  reemergence of, 628
Kuwait, 846
Kyoto Protocol (1997), 879
Kyrgyzstan, *845*

labor, 505–10, *510*, 652–55, *657*, 712, 753
  African-Americans and, 672, 776
  agricultural, 667, *667*
  capital vs., 502, 505–8
  civil liberties and, 560, 672–73
  contracts, 503–4, 753
  "cross of gold" speech and, 519
  decline of, 618
  Fordism and, 553
  in Gilded Age, 505–10, *506*
  globalization and, 860
  government and, 517–18
  New Deal and, 648, 691
  and politics, 654–55
  Populist Party and, 516
  prisoners as, 521, *521*
  and Prohibition, 591
  racially integrated, 505, *522*
  radicals, 670, 673
  railroads and, 518

  Reagan and, 835–36
  reform, 575
  rioting and, 509
  Roosevelt and, *643*
  segregation and, 522, 531
  unemployment and, 574, 575, 616, 638, *640*, 648, 654, 656, 658, 659, 663–64, *663*, 665, 667, 668, 673, 742, 787, 821, 887, 895
  women and, 505, 532, 564, 568, 677, 870, *871*, 895
  and work hours, 501–2, 504, 551, 564, 568–69, 589, 653, 663
  working conditions and, 555, 567, 568, 589, 618
  workmen's compensation and, 569
  and World War II, *686*, 687, 688
  see also child labor; unions
Labor Department, U.S., 664, 812
labor movement, 555
  decline of, 836
  rise of AFL in, 531–32
  World War I and, 585
  see also unions
Laboulaye, Édouard de (1811–1883), 476
Labour Party (Great Britain), 707
Lackawanna, N.Y., *837*
La Follette, Robert M. (1855–1925), 563, 564, 565–66, 622, *622*
laissez-faire economics, 693
Lakin, A. S. (1810–1890), *468*
Lakota Sioux, 155, *493*
Land Commission, 465
Landon, Alfred (1887–1987), 662
Lange, Dorothea (1895–1965), *667*, *670*, 671, *672*
Lansing, Robert (1864–1928), 608
Lardner, Ring, Jr. (1915–2000), 731
Las Vegas, Nev.:
  nuclear tests in, *729*
  segregation in, 760
Latin America, 623, 678, 714, 824, 825, 845, 855, 883
Latinos, *695*, 743, 748, 836, 862, 864, 867, 899
  activism among, 801
  affirmative action and, 813
  immigrant rights movement and, 889–90
  as immigrants, 784, 859, 862–65, *862*, 865
  poverty rates of, *905*
  in suburbs, 860
  and voting, 912
Latvia, 606, 707
Laurens, Henry (1724–1792), 712
Lawrence, Jacob, *601*
Lawrence, Mass., strike in, 557–60
Lawrence v. Texas, 892
Lay, Kenneth (1942–2006), 857

Lazarus, Emma (1849–1887), 476
League for Industrial Democracy, 790
League of Nations, 588, 606, 608, 609–10, *609*, 623, 708
  Congress and, 609–10
League of United Latin American Citizens (LULAC), 696, 760
Lease, Mary Elizabeth (1853–1933), 517
Leave It to Beaver (TV show), 746
Lebanon, 608, 838
Lee, Robert E. (1807–1870), 528, *528*
Le Havre, *716*
Lehman Brothers, 895, 897
Lend-Lease Act (1941), 681
Lenin, Vladimir I. (1870–1924), 587, 603
Leo XIII, Pope (1810–1903), 554
"Letter from Birmingham Jail" (King), 775
Levitt, Alfred (1912–1966), 744
Levitt, William (1907–1994), 744, 748
Levittown, N.Y., 744
Lewelling, Lorenzo, 517
Lewinsky, Monica (1973–), 872
Lewis, John L. (1880–1969), 653, 776
Lewis, Meriwether (1774–1809), 491
liberalism, 641, 644, 671, 691, 692, 702, 725, 749, 781, 807, 827, 831, 835, 841
  Clinton and, 847, 849
  FDR and, 659
  New Deal and, 728
  New Left and, 789
  1968 election and, 807
  Watergate and, 819
Liberal Republican Party, 468–69
Liberia, 615
libertarianism, 749–50, 834
Liberty Bonds, 589, 590, *595*, 604
Liberty Enlightening the World, 476
Liberty Island, 476
Liberty Motors and Engineering Corporation, *689*
liberty of contract, 568–69, 652, 659
Libya, 908, 909
Lieberman, Joseph (1942–), 872
Liebowitz, Samuel (1893–1978), 672
Life, *620*, 749, 757, *760*
light bulb, 636
Liliuokalani, queen of Hawaii (1838–1917), 535
Lincoln, Abraham (1809–1865), 454, 476, *498*, 593, 660, 668, *693*
  see also Emancipation Proclamation
Lincoln Memorial, 668, 796
  King's speech in front of, 776
Lindbergh, Charles (1902–1974), 616, 681
Lippmann, Walter (1889–1974), 791
  on Cold War, 721
Lithuania, 606, 707
Little, Malcolm, *see* Malcolm X
Little Bighorn, Battle of, 491

Little Rock, Ark., integration in, 759, *765*, 768
Living Wage, A (Ryan), 554
Lloyd, Henry Demarest (1847–1903), 482
Lloyd George, David (1863–1945), 605, 607
lobbies:
    business, 621
    special interest, 498
Lochner v. New York, 504, 568
Locke, Alain (1885–1954), 602
London, 704
London, Meyer (1871–1926), 555
Lonely Crowd, The (Riesman), 757–58
Long, Huey (1893–1935), 655, *655*, 656
Long Island, N.Y., 744, 748
Long Telegram, 714
Looking Backward (Bellamy), 506, 507, *507*
Los Alamos, N.Mex., 732
Los Angeles, Calif., 671, 746, *783*, 904
    Mexicans in, 862
    1992 riots in, 867
    pollution in, 770
    population of, 617
    Watts riot in, 786, *787*
    zoot suit riots in, 695
Los Angeles Herald-Examiner, 803
Lost Cause, 527–28, *528*
Lost Generation, 624
Louisiana, 655, *655*
    Gulf Coast of, 888–89
    illiteracy in, 521
    Plessy v. Ferguson and, 525
    voting rights in, 524
Loving, Richard and Mildred, 804, *804*
Loving v. Virginia, 803–4
Loyal Publication Society, 589
loyalty:
    oaths, 595, 700, 733
    program (review system), 730–31, 736
Luce, Henry (1898–1967), 691–92
LULAC (League of United Latin American
    Citizens), 760
LULAC News, 696
lumber, 498, 564, 571
Lusitania, 585–86, *586*
Lybia, ISIS in, 909
lynchings, 526–27, *526*, 527, 599, *599*, 600,
    602, 628, 668, 702, *702*, 726
    antilynching legislation and, 668, 701, 727
    of Jews, 628
    of Mexican-Americans, 598
Lynd, Helen (1896–1982), 620
Lynd, Robert (1892–1970), 620

MacArthur, Douglas (1880–1964), 716, 719,
    720, 750
MAD (mutual assured destruction), 754
Madero, Francisco (1873–1913), 583
Madison, Wis., Beats in, 759
Madoff, Bernard (1938–), 896

Magazine of Wall Street, The, 637
Mahan, Alfred T. (1840–1914), 534
Maine, 732
Maine, USS, 535
Malaya, 722
Malaysia, 755
Malcolm X (1925–1965), 788, *788*
Manchuria, 679, 705
Mandela, Nelson (1918–), 845
Manhattan Project, 705
manifest destiny, *512*
Manila Bay, 535, 536
Mann Act (1910), 508
manufacturing, 743, 785, 821–22, 854, 860,
    887
    decline of, 819–21, 835, 836, *837*, 841, 858,
        858, 887, 894
    in Mexico, 858
    unions and, 835
    see also industry
Mao Zedong (1893–1976), 717
March on Washington, 701, 776, *776*
Marine Corps, U.S., *676*
Marion, Fort, *493*
market economy:
    capitalism and, 854
    and "captains of industry," 482
    competition in, 480–83
    expansion of, 478–79
    rich and poor in, 483–84
    workers' freedom and, 483–84
market fundamentalism, 896
marriage, 814, *814*, *869*, 870, *870*
    interracial, *804*, 878
    same-sex, 892, 902
    see also divorce
Marshall, George C. (1880–1959), 715
Marshall, Thurgood (1908–1993), 761–62
Marshall Plan, 715–16, *716*, 717
Martin, James "Spider," *784*
Martin, Trayvon, 906
Marx, Karl (1818–1883), 507, 585
Maryland, 819
Massachusetts, 622, 818
Masses, The, 552
"massive retaliation," 754
"master race," 693
maternalist reform, 567–69, 658
maternity leave, paid, 915
May Day, 509, *673*
Mayflower Compact (1620), 712
Maytag, 887
McCain, John (1936–), 897
McCarran Internal Security Act (1950), 736
McCarran Internal Security Bill, 736
McCarran-Walter Act (1952), 736
McCarthy, Eugene (1916–2005), 805
McCarthy, Joseph R. (1908–1957), 730,
    732–33, *732*, 734, 735

McCarthy era, 594, 730–31, 732–33, 737, 757,
    759, 803
McCarthyism, 730–31, 732–33, 734, 737,
    757, 759
McDonald's, 745, 901–4
McGovern, George (1922–), 818
McKay, Claude (1890–1948), 634, 635
McKinley, William (1843–1901), 520, *520*,
    535–36, *535*, 544
    assassination of, 570
    Philippines and, 537, 539
McKinley Tariff (1890), 520
McNamara, Robert (1916–), *794*, 817
McPherson, Aimee Semple (1890–1944), 656
McReynolds, James C. (1862–1946), 633
McVeigh, Timothy (1968–2001), 871
Meat Inspection Act (1906), 549
Mecca, 788
Medicaid, 784, 831, 838
Medicare, 784, 838, 849, 901, 912
Mediterranean Sea, 714
Mellon, Andrew (1855–1937), 640
Melting Pot, The (Zangwill), 596
"melting pot," U.S. as, 596, 694
Memphis, Tenn., 712, 774, 805, *806*
    Reconstruction riot in, 459
Memphis Free Press, 527
Mendez v. Westminster, 761
Meredith, James (1933–), 774, *779*
Merkel, Angela (1954–), 910
Methodists, Methodism, 528, 537
    African-American, 444
Meuse-Argonne campaign, 588
Mexican-Americans, 497
Mexicans, Mexican immigrants, 484, 487,
    526, 550, 551, 598, 629, *629*, 696, 779,
    784, 860–65, *863*, 890, 911
    activism among, 801
    as cowboys, 487
    New Deal and, 667
    Operation Wetback and, 736
    and wages, 801, 890
    World War II and, 694–95
Mexican War, 583–84, 586, 593, 688
Mexico, 586, 629, *629*, 667, 694–95, *859*,
    889, 890
    jobs exported to, 887
    loss of U.S. jobs to, 887
    NAFTA and, 848, 850, 858, 859
    Wilson and, 583–84
Mexico City, Mexico:
    Olympics at, 806
Meyer v. Nebraska, 631, 633
MFDP, *see* Mississippi Freedom Democratic
    Party
Miami, Fla., *883*
Michigan, 553, 687
Michigan, University of, affirmative action
    and, 891

microchip, 855
Microsoft, 854, *856*, 858
Middle Border, 485
middle class, 746, 747, 836, 850, 858, 901,
    906
  feminism in, 799
  home ownership and, 662
  materialism of, 759
  reformers, 508
  socialism and, 507
Middle East, 584, *606*, 609, 714, 715, 756, 821,
    826, 859, 879, 882, *884*, 885, 915
  Islam and, 840
  2011 uprisings in, 909
  U.S. presence in, 884, *884*
  see also Gulf War; Iraq War; Israel
Middletown (Lynd and Lynd), 620
Midway Island, Battle of, 682–83, *683*
migrant farm workers, 661, 671, 743, 801,
    890
Migration Series, The (Lawrence), *601*
military, U.S.:
  desegregation of, 727
  gays in, 847
  and Operation Wetback, 736
  post-World War II demobilization of,
    724
  prisons, *885*, *886*, 887, 892, 899
  Reagan and build-up of, 838–39
  segregation in, 601, 701
  spending on, 752, 837
  tribunals, 892
  see also Army, U.S.; Navy, U.S.
military-industrial complex, 677, 687,
    729–30, 770, 820
militias:
  in Iraq, 883
  New York and, *409*
  radical conservative, 870
Millet, Francis Davis, *512*
Milliken v. Bradley, 813
Millionaire's Row, 549
Mills, C. Wright (1916–1962), 757
Mills, Florence (1895–1927), 635
Milošević, Slobodan (1941–2006), 853
minimum wage, 569, 574, 589, 621, 663, 668,
    725, 753, 776, 859, 904–5
mining, 487, 551, 575
  coal, *522*, *664*
  in national parks, 572, 573
  strikes and, 518–19
  United Mine Workers and, 559
Minneapolis, Minn., *568*
Minnesota, 485, *617*, 805, 837
  Mexican immigrants in, 862
Miranda v. Arizona, 804
misery index, *820*, 821
Miss America pageant, protest at, 799–800
missiles, 838, 840

and Cold War "missile gap," 769
and Cuba, 777–78
Jupiter, 778
  see also nuclear weapons
missionaries, 534
  in Hawaii, 543
Mississippi, 738, *740*, 788
  black voting in, 726
  Freedom School in, *780*
  "freedom schools" in, 763
  Gulf Coast of, 888–89
  voter registration drive in, 780–81
Mississippi, University of, 774–75, 778,
    779
Mississippi Freedom Democratic Party
    (MFDP), 781
Mississippi River, 888
Missouri, University of, segregation at, 761
Mitchell, John N. (1913–1988), 819
Mitchell, John P. (1870–1919), 504–5, 559
Mobile, Ala., 768
Model T, 553
modernism, 625–26
Modern Republicanism, 752–53
moga, 619
Mondale, Walter (1928–), 837
monopolies, 483, *498*, 509
  Federal Trade Commission and, 576
  "natural," 563
  Theodore Roosevelt and, 571
  see also trusts, business
Monroe Doctrine, 534, 580, 582
Montezuma, Carlos, 562
Montgomery, Ala., *762*, 766, *916*
  bus boycott in, 759, 762–63, 764, 766
  Civil Rights Memorial in, *916*
Montgomery Ward, 479, 688
Moody, Dwight, 534
moon landing, 777
Moral Majority, 830
moral suasion, 508
Morgan, J. P. (1837–1913), 481, 549, 571
Mormons, 489–90, 891
  Brigham Young and, 489
  and Deseret empire, 489
  James Buchanan and, 489
  Mitt Romney as, 911
  Mountain Meadows Massacre and, 489
  polygamy and, 489
  in Salt Lake City, 489
  see also Christianity
Morrill Land Grand Act, 485
Morse, Wayne (1900–1974), 794
Moscow, 723, 754, 755, 817, 826, *840*
  Nixon and Khrushchev in, 741–42, *741*
Mossadegh, Mohammed (1882–1967), 755,
    756
*Mother and Daughter Reading, Mt. Meigs,
    Alabama* (Eickemeyer), *444*

motion pictures, 551, 579, 614, 615, 617, 624,
    671
  family life in, 747
  religion celebrated in, 749
  see also Hollywood
Mountain Meadows Massacre, 489
Mr. Deeds Goes to Town (movie), 671
Mr. Smith Goes to Washington (movie), 671
Mubarak, Hosni (1928–), 909
Muck, Karl, 597
muckrakers, 549
Muir, John (1838–1914), 571–72
Muller v. Oregon, 568, 621
multiculturalism, 869–70
  see also diversity; pluralism
Muncie, Ind., 620–21
Munich conference, 680
murder, mass, 903, 914
Murphy, Frank (1890–1949), 672
music, *551*, 671
Muslim Brotherhood, 909
Muslims, 755, 826, 838, 859, 883, 899, 909
  in Afghanistan, 826, 875
  Black, 788
  fundamentalism and, 826, 846
  Gulf War and, 846
  as immigrants, 860
  Malcolm X and, 788
  Shiite, 883
  Sunni, 883
Mussolini, Benito (1883–1945), 679, 684
mutual assured destruction (MAD), 754
Myanmar, *see* Burma
My Lai massacre, 816–17
Myrdal, Gunnar, 703–4, *703*

NAACP, *see* National Association for the
    Advancement of Colored People
Nabisco, 836
Nader, Ralph (1934–), 803
NAFTA (North American Free Trade
    Agreement), 848, 850, 858, 859
Nagasaki, atomic bombing of, 705, *705*, 754
Nanjing, 679
napalm, 794
NASDAQ, 856–57
Nasser, Gamal Abdel (1918–1970), 756
Nast, Thomas (1840–1902), 469, *473*
Nation, The, 469, 692
National American Woman Suffrage
    Association, 533, 567
National Archives, 712
National Association for the Advancement
    of Colored People (NAACP), 600–601,
    666, 668, 702, 724, *726*, 737, 759,
    760–61, 763, 775
National Association of Colored Women,
    The, 524
National Association of Manufacturers, 690

National Catholic Welfare Council, 631
National Committee for a Sane Nuclear
    Policy, 754
National Conference of Christians and Jews,
    671
National Consumer's League, 567
national debt, 500, 838, 847
National Defense Education Act, 753
National Endowment for the Arts, 785
National Endowment for the Humanities,
    784
National Environmental Protection Act
    (1970), 829
National Farmer's Holiday Association, 639
National Forest Management Act (1976), 829
National Guard, 602, 768, 786, 816, *816*, 907
National Industrial Recovery Act (1935), 647
nationalists, nationalism, 859
    Arab, 755
    and "New Nationalism," 574–75, 576
    of R.F.K. assassin, 806
    socialism as, 507
    World War I and, 585
National Labor Relations Board, 658
National Liberation Front, 756
National Organization for Women (NOW),
    793, 799
national parks, 571–72, *572*
National Police Gazette, 533
National Recovery Administration (NRA),
    647–48, 652, *652*
National Reform Association, 508
National Resources Planning Board (NRPB),
    692
National Rifle Association (NRA), 914
National Security Agency (NSA), *910*
    domestic surveillance by, 910
National Security Council, 715, 719, 794, 840
National Transportation Safety Board, 811
National War Labor Board, 703
National Women's Party, 590–91, 619
Nation of Islam, 788
Native Americans, 490–93, 544, 868–69, *868*
    affirmative action and, 813
    buffalo and, 484, 492
    as casino operators, 868–69
    citizenship (U.S.) and, 493, 868
    civil rights movement and, 801–2, *802*
    government treatment of, 491–93
    New Deal and, 666–67
    poverty and, 869, *905*
    Progressivism and, 562
    Puritans and, 868
    removal of, 477, 722
    slavery and, 868
    "termination" and, 801
    treaty system and, 492
    tribalism attacked, 492
    in West, *490*

westward expansion of U.S. and, 484–85
    World War II and, 694, 695
    see also Indian removal
Native Americans, population of, 484, 493
nativism, 528–29, 630, 636, 694, 911
NATO, *see* North Atlantic Treaty
    Organization
Navajos:
    "code-talkers" of, 695
Naval Academy, U.S., 823
Navy, U.S., *676, 682,* 909
    African-Americans in, 703
    segregation, 601, 701
Nazi Party, 645, 679, 680, 684, 693, *693,* 694,
    700, *702,* 704, 707, 709, 723
Nebraska, 485, *486,* 631, 633
Negro Leagues, 727
Nelson, Laura, *527*
Nelson, L. D., *527*
neoconservatives, 827
Netherlands, 680
Neutrality Acts, 680
Nevada, 730, 829, 833
Newark, N.J., riot in, 787
New Deal, 447, 519, 569, 643–75, *643, 652,*
    678, 681, 691, 692, 693, 728, 752, 789,
    824, 857, 899
    African-Americans and, 665–66, 667–69
    agriculture and, 650–51, 666, 667, *667,*
        668
    Eisenhower and, 752, 753, 811, 852
    end of, 673–74
    Father Coughlin and, 656
    First, 645–52
    Goldwater and, 781
    housing and, 651
    Johnson and, 779
    legacy of, 644–45, 674
    libertarians and, 749–50
    Mexican immigrants and, 667
    Popular Front and, 670, 671
    Reagan and, 834
    roads in, 648, 649, *649*
    Second, 655, 656–59, 663
    in South, 665–66
    Supreme Court and, 652, *652,* 662–63
    Truman and, 725, 737
    wages and, 655
    West and, 651, 667
    women and, 664–65, *665*
    work projects in, 644, *646,* 648–49, *649,*
        674
"New Deal coalition," 662, 811, 827
New England:
    deindustrialization in, 616
    Puritan emigration to, 868
    strikes in, 653
New Federalism, 811
New Freedom, 574–75, 576

New Hampshire, 805, 888
New Left, 774, 789–90, 796, 798
New Mexico, 617, 705, 888
New Nationalism, 574–75, 576
"New Negro," 635
New Negro, The (Locke), 602
New Orleans, La., 465, *740*
    and Hurricane Katrina, 888–89, *889*
    population of, 889
    Reconstruction riot in, 459
Newport, R.I., *482*
New Republic, 570
New School for Social Research, 641
New South, 521
newspapers, *see* press
Newsweek, 741
Newtown, Conn., 914
New York, *563,* 744, 746, 800, 878, 904
    Al Smith as governor of, 636
    Theodore Roosevelt as governor of, 537
New York, N.Y., *483,* 510, *546, 555,* 569, 619,
    639, 647, 649, *649,* 657, 665, 673, *680,*
    778, 864, 868, *882, 889,* 906–7
    African-Americans in, 631–34
    antiwar demonstration in, 812
    Beats in, *758,* 759
    draft riots in, 867
    garment strike in, *557*
    immigration to, 555
    population of, 548
    September 11 attacks in, 874
    socialism and, 555
    Statue of Liberty in, 476
    World Trade Center in, *821,* 822
New York Consumers' League, 646
New York Court of Appeals, 504
New Yorker, 910
New York Journal, 535, *537*
New York Stock Exchange, 639, 797
    explosion at, 605
New York Times, 662, 816–17
New York Times v. Sullivan, 803
New York Tribune, 469
New York World, 535
Next!, 482
Nez Percés, 491, *492,* 494
Ngo Dinh Diem (1901–1963), 756–57, 791
Nguyen That Thanh (1890–1969), 608, 609
    see also Ho Chi Minh
Niagara Falls, 600
Nicaragua, 583, 623, *623,* 679, 840
Nicodemus, Kans., *523*
Nigeria, 722, 755
Nineteenth Amendment, 591
nisei, 698
Nixon, E. D. (1899–1987), 763
Nixon, Richard (1913–1994), 731, 802, 810–
    19, *811,* 827, 832, 833, 840, 852, 898
    African-Americans and, 812

in China, 815, *815*
in debates with JFK, 770, 874
détente and, 814–15, *817*, 822
in election of 1968, 807
in Moscow, 741–42, *741*
New Federalism of, 811
in 1952 campaign, 751
in 1960 campaign, 768–70, 810
pardoned by Ford, 822
Pentagon Papers and, 817
resignation of, 819
Supreme Court and, 812–13
Vietnam War and, 815, 816–17
Watergate scandal and, 818
welfare and, 810
Nixon administration, 810–12
Nkrumah, Kwame (1909–1972), 704
Nobel Peace Prize, 580
nonaggression pact, 680
Noriega, Manuel Antonio (1934–), 846
Normandy, France, 684
North, Oliver (1943–), 840
North Africa, 680
Allied invasion of, 684
North American Free Trade Agreement
    (NAFTA), 848, 850, 858
North Atlantic Treaty Organization (NATO),
    717, *719*, 853, 908
North Carolina, 726, 813, 898
North Carolina Agricultural and Technical
    State University, 773
North Dakota, 485, 486
Northern Ireland, 609, 806, *807*
Northern Pacific Railroad, 571
Northern Securities Company, 571
North Korea, 719, 881
creation of, 719
North Vietnam, 794, 805, 815, 816, 817
NOW, *see* National Organization for Women
NRA, *see* National Recovery Administration
NRPB, *see* National Resources Planning Board
NSC-68, 719
nuclear energy, 824
nuclear weapons, 753–54, 813, 825, 840,
    881, 882
cessation of tests of, 754, 778
Iran and, 908
proposed international control of, 728
tests of, *729*, 730
U.S. arsenal of, 754
U.S.-Soviet treaty on, 778
see also atomic bomb; hydrogen bomb;
    missiles
Nuremberg, Nazi trials at, 723

Oakland, Calif., *703*, 789
Oakley, Annie, 497
Obama, Barack (1961–), 898–901, *899*,
    900–904, *909*

in election of 2008, *877*, 878, 897–98, *898*
foreign policy of, 908–10
Obama administration, 889, 899–901, 908,
    909
2008 financial crisis and, 858
Obergfell v. Hodges, 892, 902
Occupational Safety and Health
    Administration, 811
Occupy (Wall Street) Movement, 904, *904*
O'Connor, Sandra Day (1930–), 838, 891
Office of Price Administration, 687
Office of Public Information, *717*
Office of War Information (OWI), *678, 695*
"Of Mr. Booker T. Washington and Others"
    (Du Bois), 541
oil, 482–83, 575, 614, 615, 617, 655, 682, 745,
    821, 824, 836, 879
Arab embargo on, 821, *821*
Cold War and, 714, 715
Gulf War and, 846
highways and, 752
in Iran, 755
Iraq War and, 885
Japan and U.S., 680, 681
-producing regions, *884*
and Teapot Dome scandal, 622
see also Standard Oil Company
Okemah, Okla., lynching in, *527*
Oklahoma, 492, 493
in Dust Bowl, 651
Indians removed to, 491
Oklahoma City, Okla., terrorist attack in,
    605, 871, *871*
Old Faithful geyser, *572*
Old Left, 789–90
Oller, Francisco, *538*
Olney, Richard (1835–1917), 518
Olympic Games, 806, 826
"one percent, the" (wealthiest Americans),
    904
On the Origin of Species (Darwin), 503
On the Town, 700
Open Door policy, 538
Operation Desert Storm, 846
Operation Dixie, 725
Operation Iraqi Freedom, 883
    see also Iraq War
Operation Wetback, 736
Orangeburg, S.C., *774*
Orange County, Calif., 761, 782, 860
oranges, 743
Oregon, 491, 563, 628, 633, 644, 794
women's rights in, 568
Oregon System, 563–64
Oregon Trail, 490
Organization Man, The (Whyte), 758
Organization of Afro-American Unity, 788
Oswald, Lee Harvey (1939–1963), 779
Other America, The (Harrington), 785, 790

Ottoman Empire, in World War I, 584, *606*,
    608
Outdoor Recreation League, *564*
outsourcing of jobs, 858
Overseas Highway, 649
overtime pay, 663
Oxford, Miss., 775

Pacific islands, 730
Pacific Northwest, 644
Pacific Ocean, *536*
Packard, Vance (1914–1996), 758
PACs (political action committees), 913
Padmore, George (1903–1959), 704
Paine, Thomas (1737–1809), 593
Pakistan, 755, 909
raid into, 908
Palestine, 608, 806, 875
Palin, Sarah (1964–), 898
Palmer, A. Mitchell (1872–1936), 604, 605
Palmer, Francis F. (1812–1876), *475*
Palmer Raids, 605
Palmolive soap, *554*
Pan-African Congress, 608
Panama, 581–82, 846
Panama Canal, 579, 580–82, 825
construction of, 581–82
Pan-American Exposition, 570
Paris, *719*, 806
German occupation of, 680
liberation of, 684
2015 terrorist attacks in, 909
Vietnam peace agreement in, 817
Park Forest, Ill., *757*
Parks, Gordon, *768*
Parks, Rosa (1913–2005), 762–63, *762*, 766,
    897
Parrish, Lucian W., 632
Parsons, Albert (1849–1887), 509
PATCO, 835
patriotism, 595–96
Patrons of Husbandry, 501
    see also Grange
Patten, Simon (1852–1922), 528
Paul, Alice (1885–1977), 591, 619, 830
Peabody Conservatory of Music, *631*
Peace Corps, 777, 785
Pearson, Levi, 761
Pelosi, Nancy, 893
Pennsylvania, 498, 824, 904
Pentagon, *772*, 796
September 11 attack on, 874
Pentagon Papers, 817
"peonage" laws, 600
People's Party, *see* Populist Party
Pequot Indians, 868
perestroika, 840

Perkins, Frances (1882–1965), 646, 664, 682
Perot, Ross (1930–), 847
Pershing, John J. (1860–1948), 584, 588
Persian Gulf, 846
   Carter Doctrine and, 826
Philadelphia, Miss., 781, 833
Philadelphia, Pa., 6, *669*
   Freedom Train in, 712
Philadelphia Plan, 812
Philippines, 536, 543, 815, 825
   immigrants from, 487, 535, 698
   U.S. acquisition of, 514, 537–39, 579
   in World War II, 682, *698*
   see also Filipinos
Philippine War, *538*, 539, *539*, 544, 595
Phillips, Wendell (1811–1884), 593
Phoenix, Ariz., 746
phonograph, 615
photography:
   in Great Depression, *670*, 671
Pike, James S. (1811–1882), 469
Pinchot, Gifford (1865–1946), 572, 573
Pinckney, Clementa, 903
Pingree, Hazen (1840–1901), 563
Pinkerton Detective Agency, 513
Pinochet, Augusto (1915–2006), 815
Pittsburgh, Pa., *643*
   manufacturing in, 478
   September 11 terrorist attack in, 874
Pittsburgh Courier, 666, 702
Plains Indians, 490–91
plantations, sugar, *538*
planters, plantations, 465, 521
   in California, 486–87
   in Caribbean, *538*, 539
   cotton, *463*
   emancipated slaves and, *446*
   in Hawaii, 543
   post-Civil War, 446–47, 448, 449
   sugar, 550
Platt, Orville H. (1827–1905), 538
Platt Amendment (1901), 538
Playboy, 800
Pledge of Allegiance, 535, 748
Plessy v. Ferguson, 525, *526*, 761, 767
pluralism, 670, 671, 693, 695
   see also diversity
poison gas, 584
Poland, 606, 707, 714
   German invasion of, 680
police:
   militarization of, 907
   racial bias by, 906–7
Polish-Americans, 551, 604, 736
political action committees (PACs), 913
pollution, 770, 811, 828
   see also environmentalism
Pontchartrain, Lake, 888
Ponzi schemes, 896

Poolesville, Md., *765*
Poor People's March, 805
"popery," *see* Catholics, Catholicism
Popular Front, 670, 671
population:
   of African-Americans, 631
   of buffalo, 491
   of California, 488
   of Chicago, 478
   of Hiroshima, 705
   of Los Angeles, 617
   of Middle Border, 485
   of Native Americans, *see* Native
      Americans, population of
   of New Orleans, 889
   rise of, 548
   of United States, 747, *747*, 748
Populism, 832
Populist movement, 514–20, 639
   agriculture and, 513, 514
Populist (People's) Party, 515–19, *515*, *516*,
   524, 563, 575
   Bryan in, 519
   depression of 1893 and, 518
   election of 1892 and, *516*
   election of 1896 and, 520
   industrial workers and, 515, 518
   labor and, 516
   platform of 1892 of, 516
   Pullman strike and, 518
   racial alliances of, 517
   supporters of, 515
   and woman suffrage, *517*
   women in, 517
Port Huron, Mich., 790
Port Huron Statement, 782, 790
Portland, Oreg., 687
Posse Comitatus, 870
Postal Service, U.S., 623
Potomac River, 796
Potsdam conference, 707, 754
poultry, 743
poverty rate, 742, *786*, 901, 905, *905*, 906
   of Native Americans, 869
Powderly, Terence V. (1849–1924), 505
Powell, Adam Clayton (1908–1972), *668*
Powell, Colin (1937–), 846–47, 882
Powell, Lewis F. (1907–1998), 813
Poyntz, Juliet Stuart (1886–1937?), 619
Presbyterians, 827
Presidential Citizens Medal, *740*
Presidential Reconstruction, 454–55
presidents, presidency, U.S.:
   expansion of powers of, 651–52, 886
   as "Free World" leader, 715
   veto power of, 457, 725, 736
   see also specific presidents
Presley, Elvis (1935–1977), *758*, 759
press, 689, 690, 702, 803, 841

African-American, 600, 666, 702
   in election of 1928, 636
   in election of 1936, 662
   Espionage Act and, 594
   Iraq War and, 882
   during Reconstruction, 469, 470
   Republican (modern), 509
   Underground, 797
   in World War I, 590
   as "yellow press," 535, 537
   see also freedom, of the press
"Price of Free World Victory, The" (Wallace),
   691
Prince Edwards County, Va., desegregation
   in, 765
prisons, 866–67, *866*
   African-Americans in, 866–67
   incarceration rates for, 915
   labor from, 521, *521*
   population of, 866
privacy, right to, 624, 627, 804–5
Problem We All Live With, The (Rockwell), *740*
profits, *see* corporations, and profits
Progress and Poverty (George), 506
Progressive era, 546–76, *564*
   in the West, 563–65
   women in, 590–91
Progressive Optimism, 622
Progressive Party, 564–65, 573–75, 622,
   658, 728
   social agenda of, 575
Progressivism, 547–48, 641, 823, 835
   ACLU and, 624
   and African-Americans, 598–99
   Alfred Landon and, 662
   civil liberties and, 594–96
   consumerism and, 551
   disintegration of, 621
   FDR and, 646
   Harding and, 610, 621–22
   Herbert Hoover and, 635
   immigration and, 548, 549–50, 596–97, 630
   as international movement, 562–63
   Native Americans and, 562
   politics in, 562–69
   presidents in, 570–76
   Prohibition and, 591–94, *594*
   race and, 596–97
   socialism and, 555–56
   varieties of, 554–62
   women's rights in, 561
   World War I and, 588, 610, 623
Prohibition, 508, *533*, 591–94, *594*, 614, 615,
   626, *626*, 631, 636, 645, 651
   see also temperance
propaganda:
   in World War I, 589–90, *589*
   in World War II, *698*
Proposition 13 (California), 832

Proposition 187 (California), 869
Prospective Scene in the City of Oaks, A, 468
Prostrate State, The (Pike), 470
Protestants, 508, 597, 628, 662, 731, 769, 831
    and Al Smith, 636
    as anticommunists, 748–49
    evangelical, 827, 831
    fundamentalist, 625–27
    modernism and, 625–27
    moral reform and, 507–8
    Prohibition and, 508, 594
    see also Christianity; *specific denominations*
public opinion, opinion polls, 729, 830, 872,
    885, 893, 895
    public relations and, 702
public relations, 618
    and public opinion, 702
    see also Bernays, Edward
Public Utilities Act (California), 564
Public Works Administration (PWA),
    649–50, *649*
Puck, 480, 482, 498, 535, 560
Puerto Rico, 536, 538, 539, 543
    migration from, 748, *748*, 862
    U.S. acquisition of, 514, 535, *538*, 579
Pulitzer, Joseph (1847–1911), 535
Pulitzer Prize, *812*
Pullman, Ill., strike in, 518, *518*, 531
Pure Food and Drug Act (1906), 549, 571
Puritans, Puritanism:
    Indians and, 868
    slavery and, 868
Putting the Screws on Him, 571
PWA, *see* Public Works Administration

Quaker Oats Company, 479
Quayle, Dan (1947–), 841

Rabelais, François (ca. 1494–1553?), 623
race, racism, *631*, 671, 694, 701, 702–3, 704,
    722, 724, 730, *775*, 776, 784, 799, 841,
    870
    Americanism vs., 670, 693, 786
    Andrew Johnson and, 454
    Hollywood and, 722
    and Japanese-Americans, 698
    law and, 629–30
    marriage and, *804*
    Nixon and, 812, 813
    among police, 906–7
    and post–World War II civil rights, 726
    Progressivism and, 596–97
    as "race problem," 596–97
    Reconstruction and, 467, 470
    riots and, *530*, *602*, 701, 786–88, *787*, 867
    social construction of, 630
    in South Africa, 722
    by U.S. government, 669
    see also segregation

Races and Racism (Benedict), 694
radar, 687, 743
radiation, 705, *729*, 730, 754
Radical Reconstruction, 454–57
Radical Republicans, 456, *456*, 459
radio, 614, 615, *656*, 690
    FDR's fireside chats on, *659*, 660
    Great Depression and, 656
    religion and, 656
Railroad Administration, 589
railroads, 449, 478–79, 484–85, 498, 525, 551,
    553, 555, 563, 564, 573, 575, 622
    agriculture and, 487, 514
    Great Depression and, 641
    labor and, 518
    land granted to, 477, 485, *485*
    lobbyists of, 498
    network of, 479
    Populists and, 514, 516
    prison labor and, 521
    protests against, 501
    rates regulated, 571
    in Reconstruction, 466
    segregation and, 525
    Socialist party and, 573
    strikes, 505, *505*, 518
    transcontinental, 478–79, 490
    trusts, 481
Rainey, Joseph H., *463*
Raleigh, N.C., *773*, 774
Randolph, A. Philip (1889–1979), 701, *728*
Rankin, Jeanette (1880–1973), 590, 682
Rauschenbusch, Walter (1861–1918), 508
RCA Victor, 615
Reagan, Nancy (1921–2016), *783*, *838*
Reagan, Ronald (1911–2004), 731, *783*, *809*,
    833, 834–41, *834*, 848, 855, 879, 880,
    897, 899
    background of, 834
    Cold War and, 838–40
    conservatives and, 838
    in election of 1980, 833–34
    Gorbachev and, 840, *840*
    inequality under, 836
    Iran-Contra affair and, 840
    labor and, 835–36
    legacy of, 841
Reaganomics, 835–36
Reagan Revolution, 834–41
real estate:
    deals, 837
    speculation, 836
Rebel without a Cause (movie), 758
recessions, 856–57
    of 1974–75, 823
    of 1991, 847
    of 2001, 887
    of 2007, 893, 894–95
    of 2008, 879

African-Americans and, 906
    Reaganomics and, 836
Reconstruction, 441–74, *471*
    African-Americans in, *441*, 453, 456–58,
        458, 460–62, *464*, 521, 522, 523, 524,
        525, 527, 599–600, 678, 726
    battle over, 454–55
    black officeholders during, 464
    Chinese laborers during, 453
    Johnson's policies in, 448, 454–57, *457*,
        458–59
    Ku Klux Klan in, 599, 628, *628*
    overthrow of, 466–73, *473*
    public schools in, 465, *466*, *467*
    radical, 454–57
    railroads built in, 466
    Redeemers and, 521
    segregation in, 526
    violence in, 467–68
    white farmers in, 449–52
    women's rights and, 461–62
    see also Presidential Reconstruction;
        Radical Reconstruction; Second
        Reconstruction
Reconstruction Act (1867), 458–59, 462
Reconstruction Finance Corporation, 641
Red Cross, 700
Red Dawn (movie), *838*
Redeemers, 470, 521
redlining, *669*
Red Menace, The (movie), 722, *722*
Red Power, 801–2
Red Scare, 604–5, 613, 636
Red Square, *840*
Reedy, William M., 561
reform, 563–67, 575, 673
    in Gilded Age, 500–501
    maternalist, 567–69, 658
    middle class and, 506–7
    and Prohibition, 591–94, *594*
    segregation and, 599–600
    sexual freedom and, 619
Reform Act (British) (1884), 498
Reform Bureau, 508
Refregier, Anton, *727*
Regents of the University of California v. Bakke,
    813, 891
regulatory power, 621
    rise of U.S. government, 571, 646–47, 663,
        674, 785
religion, 579, 869, 914
    of African-Americans, rise in, 444, *446*
    communism vs., 748–49, *749*, 750
    counterculture and, 797
    fundamentalist, 625–27
    and Prohibition, 594
    radio and, 656
    social reform and, 507–8
    see also specific denominations

religious freedom, 697
  Four Freedoms and, 677
  Fourteenth Amendment and, 631
  fundamentalism vs., 627
  September 11 terrorist attacks and, 880
  Universal Declaration of Human Rights
    and, 723
  see also diversity; pluralism
religious right, 827–30, 833
  see also Christian Right
Remington, Frederic (1861–1909), 537
Reno, Janet (1938–), 847
Reno, Milo, 639
"Report on Economic Conditions in the
  South," 673
reproductive rights, 561, 800, 804, 805, 899
Republican Party (modern), 499, *501*, 510,
    517, 519, 520, 564, 620, 671, 681, 688,
    728–29, 735, 750, 752–53, 780, 782,
    792, 794, 811, 832, 841, 849, 854, 857,
    888, 893, 897–98, *899*, 900
  as anti-immigrant, 869
  black members of, 524
  black voters and, 462–63
  in campaign of 1960, 768, 769
  Christianity aligned with, 810
  Clinton and, 847
  Contract with America, 849
  Eisenhower and, 750–51
  in election of 1896, 520, *520*
  in election of 1916, 586
  in election of 1928, *635*, 636
  in election of 1946, 725–26
  in election of 1952, 751, *751*
  in election of 1968, 807
  in election of 1972, 818
  in election of 1992, 847
  in election of 2000, 872–73
  and Equal Rights Amendment, 833
  high tariff supported by, 500, *500*
  immigration and, 912
  Johnson's impeachment and, 459–60
  Ku Klux Klan and, 628
  Liberal, 468–69
  nativism and, 911
  in 1920s, 621
  1964 convention of, 781, 834
  1984 convention of, *809*, 834
  1992 convention of, 847
  press of, 509
  in Reconstruction, 447, 454–60, 462–63,
    465, 467, 468–69, 470, 471–72
  South and, 524
  Soviet Union and, 678
  and Supreme Court, 652
  Taft and, 573
  Truman Doctrine and, 715
  2010 revival of, 910–11
  YAF and, 782

  see also Radical Republicans; *specific
    elections and campaigns*
Rerum Novarum, 554
reservations, Indian, *496*, 562, 667, 695, 801
Resettlement Administration, *652*
Resolution of Regret (2012), 530
Return from Toil, The (Sloan), *552*
Revels, Hiram (1827–1901), *463*, 464, *465*
Revere, Paul (1735–1818), *713*
Rhineland, 679
Rhine River, 704
rice, 521
Richardson, Elliot (1920–1999), 818
Richmond Times-Dispatch, 662
Rickey, Branch (1881–1965), 727
Riesman, David (1909–2002), 757–58
Riis, Jacob (1849–1914), *483*, 484
Rincon Center, 727
riots:
  draft, 867
  labor, 509
  race, *530*, 602, *602*, 701, 786–88, *787*, 867
  Reconstruction, 459
  zoot suit, 695
River Rouge auto plant, *615*
R.J. Reynolds Tobacco Company, 836
roads, 648, 649, *649*, 655
Road to Serfdom, The (Hayek), 693
Roaring Twenties, 614
robber barons, 482, 749
Robertson, Pat (1930–), 869
Robeson, Paul (1898–1976), 671, *703*, 704,
  737
Robin Hood, 733
Robinson, Bill, 635
Robinson, Earl (1910–1991), 671
Robinson, Jackie (1919–1972), *726*, 727
rock-and-roll, 758–59
Rockefeller, John D. (1839–1937), 481–83,
  534, 572–73
Rockefeller, Nelson (1908–1979), 822
Rockefeller family, 637
Rockwell, Norman (1894–1978), 677, *678*,
  690, 727, *740*
Rocky Mountains, Lander's Peak (Bierstadt), *490*
Roe v. Wade, 805, 831, *831*
Rogers, Will (1879–1935), 622
Romania, 714
Romney, Mitt (1947–), 911–13
  Bain Capital and, 911
  conservatives and, 911
  "47 percent" remark by, 912
  Massachusetts health care plan and, 911
Roosevelt, Eleanor (1884–1962), 664, *664*,
  668, 723
Roosevelt, Franklin D. (1882–1945), 522, *643*,
  647, 657, *659*, 660, 665, 669, 678–79,
  682, 683–84, 687, 701, 707, *707*, 714,
  810, 835, 852, 872, 880

antilynching law and, 668
background of, 645
black voters and, 662
"court packing" by, 662–63, *662*
death of, 705
Economic Bill of Rights and, 692
First New Deal and, 645–52, *652*
Four Freedoms and, 677, *678*, 689, 709, 712
freedom and, 659, 660, 677, 712
Hitler and, 679, 681, 694
on housing, 651
Japanese American internment and, 698
and polio, 645
Second New Deal and, 656–59
on Social Security, 658
and South, 673
and West, 644
see also New Deal
Roosevelt, Theodore (1858–1919), 510, 549,
  571, *582*, 645, 662, 847
  African-Americans and, 599
  Asian-Americans and, 598
  as conservationist, 571–72, *572*, 573
  and corporations, 571
  Panama Canal and, 580–82
  as Progressive candidate, 573–75, 646
  as Progressive president, 570–72
  as Rough Rider, 537, *537*
  U.S. government regulatory power and,
    571
Roosevelt Corollary, 582–83
Rosenberg, Ethel (1915–1953), 731–32
Rosenberg, Julius (1918–1953), 731–32
Rosie the Riveter, 690
"Rosita the Riveter," 695
Ross, Thomas J., 451
Rothko, Mark, 723
Rough Riders, 537
Royal Air Force, 680
rubber, 532, 614, 615, 687
Ruins of the Pittsburgh Round House, 505
Rumsfeld, Donald, 881
Rural Electrification Agency, 656
Russia, 551, *606*, 915–16
  Iran nuclear program and, 908
  Iraq War and, 882
  in World War I, 585
  see also Soviet Union
Russian immigrants, 528, 549
Russian Revolution, 587, 603, 605, 624, *625*
Russo-Japanese War, 580
Ruth, Babe (1895–1948), 615
Rwanda, genocide in, 852
Ryan, John A. (1869–1945), 554
Ryan, Paul D. (1970–), 911
  as Catholic, 911

Sacco, Nicola (1891–1927), 613, *613*
Sadat, Anwar (1918–1981), *825*

Saddam Hussein (1937–2006), 846, 881–82, 883, 885
  and weapons of mass destruction, 882, 885
Sagebrush Rebellion, 829, 833
Sailing of Old Glory, The (Forman), *812*
St. Louis, Mo., 837
St. Louis Post-Dispatch, *599*
St. Paul, Minn., *568*
SALT (Strategic Arms Limitations Talks), 815
Salt Lake City, Utah:
  Mormons in, 489
San Bernardino, Calif, terrorist attack in, 909–10
San Diego, Calif., *859*
Sandinistas, *623*, 840
Sandino, Augusto César (1895–1934), 623, *623*
Sandy Hook Elementary School, 914
San Francisco, Calif., 564, *655*, 687, 727, 800, 856, 868
  Beats in, 759
  immigration to, 550
  strike in, 653
  U.N. conference in, 708
San Francisco Bay, 802, *802*
Sanger, Margaret (1883–1966), 561
San Juan, Calif., *490*
San Juan Hill, 537
Santiago, Cuba, 536
Sarajevo, Bosnia and Herzegovina, 584
Sargent, John Singer (1856–1925), *578*
Saturday Night Massacre, 818
Saudi Arabia, 788, 846, 875, 892, 909
Saum Song Bo, 495
Savings and Loans Associations, 837
Savio, Mario (1942–1996), *791*
scabs, *555*
scalawags, 464–65
Scandinavia, 680
Scandinavian immigrants, 486, 528
Schechter Poultry Company, 652
Schenck, Charles T., 624
school integration, *740*, 759, *765*, 768, *812*, 813
school shootings, 914, *914*
Schultz, George (1920–), 812
Schurz, Carl (1829–1906), 460
Schwerner, Michael (1939–1964), 780–81
Scopes, John (1900–1970), 627
Scopes Trial, 627–28, *627*
Scottsboro, Ala., trial in, 671–72, *672*, 763
Scowcroft, Brent (1925–), 882
Screen Actors Guild, 834
Scribner's Magazine, *505*
SDS, *see* Students for a Democratic Society
Sea Islands, South Carolina, 448
  Special Field Order 15 and, 442
Sears, Roebuck & Co., 479

Seattle, Wash., *638*, 687, 851, 856, 904
  anti-Chinese riot in, *530*
  government contracts and, 743
  Hooverville in, *638*
  Ku Klux Klan in, *628*
  WTO meeting in, *843*, 854, 855
Seattle Post-Intelligencer, *700*
Second Amendment, 914
"second industrial revolution," *see* industrial revolution, "second"
Second New Deal, *see* New Deal, Second
Second Reconstruction, 533
  civil rights movement as, 473
Second Vatican Council (1962–1965), 798
Securities and Exchange Commission, 652, 896
Security Council, U.N., 708, 719
Sedition Act (1798), 594
Sedition Act (1918), 594–95
segregation, 465, 525–26, 543, 544, 601, 668, *669*, 694, 697, 701–2, 703, 712, 727–29, 730, 738, 759–61, *760*, *761*, 767, 774–76, *779*, 787, 813, 865, 866
  Birmingham campaign and, 775–76
  Booker T. Washington on, 531
  courts and, 760–61, 764–65, 767, 768
  dismantling of, 761–62, 764–65, 767, 768, 786, 813
  education and, 531, 813
  federal government and, 776
  in federal housing, 669, *669*
  in Greensboro, N.C., 773
  JFK and, 777
  labor and, 522, 531–32
  laws, 525–26
  railroads and, 525
  reformers and, 599–600
  "separate but equal" principle and, 525, 761–62, 767
  in South, *670*
  South and, 521–28, *526*
  in Southwest, 598
  suburbia and, 747–48
  unions and, 522
  in U.S. military, 601, 701
  see also race; racism; South, segregation in
Selective Service Act (1917), 589
Selling a Freeman to Pay His Fine at Monticello, Florida, 455
Selma, Ala., 759, 783, *784*
Senate, U.S., 499, 535, 655, 708, 767, 873, 878, 885, 887, 888, 898, 899, 911
  African-Americans in, 464
  and Johnson's impeachment, 459–60
  McCarthy and, 732–33
  popular vote and, 565
  Versailles Treaty debate in, 609–10, *609*
  World War I and, 586
Senate Indian Affairs Committee, 492

Seoul, South Korea, *721*
"separate but equal" principle, 525, *526*, 761–62, 767
September 11, 2001, terrorist attacks of, 594, 822, 874–75, 879, 881, 882, 885, 889, 890–91, 915
Serbia, 852–53, *853*
Servicemen's Readjustment Act, 692
settlement houses, 566, *566*, 575
Seventeenth Amendment, 565
Seward, William H. (1801–1872), 534
sex:
  Beats and, 759
  censorship and, 623
  and public officials, 872
  women's rights and, 560–61, 619, 798, 800
sexual harassment, 872
sexual politics, 800
sexual revolution, 798, 805, 813–14, 827, 869
Seymour, Horatio (1810–1886), 460
Shackle Broken—by the Genius of Freedom, The (Elliott), *441*
Shahn, Ben, *652*
Shahn, Bernarda, *652*
Shame of the Cities, The (Steffens), 549
sharecropping, 449, 451, *452*, 466, 514, *665*, 669, 671, *672*, 740, 743, *784*
Share Our Wealth, 655, *656*
sharia law, 891
Sharon, Conn., 782
Sharon Statement, 782
Sheeler, Charles (1883–1965), 617
Sheen, Fulton J. (1895–1979), 749
Sheppard-Towner Act (1921), 619
Sheridan, Philip H. (1831–1888), 490–91
Sherman, William T. (1820–1891), 442, 447–48, 776
Sherman Antitrust Act (1890), 501, 504, 571, 573
  see also monopolies; trusts, business
Shiite Muslims, 883
shipbuilding:
  in South, 743
  in World War II, 690
shopping, 746
Siam, *see* Thailand
Sicily, invasion of, 684
Sierra Club, 571, 802
Silent Protest Parade, 603
Silent Spring (Carson), 790, 802
Silicon Valley, 856
silver:
  corporate mining of, 487
  as currency, 519
Sinclair, Upton (1878–1968), 549, 588, 624, 655
Singer Sewing Machines, 534
Singleton, Benjamin "Pap" (1809–1892), 523

Sioux, 491–92, *493*
Sirica, John J. (1904–1992), 818
sit-ins, 773, 774, 777
Sitting Bull (ca. 1831–1890), 492
Sixteenth Amendment, 573
Sixth Avenue and Thirtieth Street (Sloan), *546*
"Sixties, The," 790, 802, 805, 813
    activism in, 798–807
    legacy of, 807
Skilling, Jeffrey, 857
slacker raids, 595
Slaughterhouse Cases (1873), 470
Slave Power, *506*
slavery, 527–28, 865
    arguments in favor of, 502
    Indians and, 868
    in West, 484
    see also abolition movement
slaves, emancipated, 443, *444*
    Andrew Johnson and, 454
    Second New Deal and, 658
    suffrage and, 442, 444, 460–62
Slavs, Nazi extermination of, 686
Sloan, John (1871–1951), *546, 552*
Smith, Adam (1723–1790), 895
Smith, Alfred E. (1873–1974), 636
    Protestants and, 636
Smith, Margaret Chase, 732–33, 735
Smith Act (1940), 673
Smithfield, R.I., *849*
Smith v. Allwright, 703
Smoot-Hawley Tariff (1930), 640–41
SNCC, *see* Student Non-Violent Coordinating
    Committee
Snowden, Edward, 910
Social Darwinism, 502–3, 507
Social Gospel, 508, 519
socialism, 555–56, 560, 588, 645, 653, 724,
    736, 790, 806
    capitalism vs., 573, 670
    in Chicago, 509
    Communist Party and, 670
    Espionage Act and, 595
    European vs. American view of, 507
    Friedrich Hayek and, 693
    in Gilded Age, 505, 506
    Henry Wallace and, 728
    middle class and, 507
    as nationalism, 507
    woman suffrage and, 567
    World War I and, 584
Socialist Party, 555, *556*, 573–74, *574*, 589,
    593, 605
    capitalism vs., 573, 670
social realism, *646*
Social Security, *658*, 662, 663, 665, 674, 781,
    811, 838, 912
    African-Americans and, 666, 668
    creation of, 658

Eisenhower and, 752
FDR on, 658
freedom and, 664
NRPB and, 692
taxes support for, 665
Truman and, 725, 737
Social Security Act (1935), 644, 658, 666,
    667
Social Security Bill, 658
Society of American Indians, 562
Solomon Islands, 683
Somoza, Anastasio (1925–1980), 623, *623*,
    678, 840
Sons of Italy, 613
Sotomayor, Sonia (1954–), 899
Souls of Black Folk, The (Du Bois), 541, 600
Souter, David (1939–), 899
South, 499, 500, 601–2, 616, 677, 774–76,
    779, 810, 818, 898
    African-Americans in, 522, 601–2, 619,
      631, *634*, 635, 694, 697, 700, 738,
      781–82, 786
    agriculture in, 743
    black migration from, 748
    Democratic Party and, 636
    desegregation in, 703, 761, 763, 764–65,
      767, 768, 786
    in election of 1948, 728–29
    in election of 1964, 781–82
    Freedom Rides in, 774
    fundamentalists in, 627
    industry in, 688, 743
    Jim Crow and, 760
    libertarianism in, 750
    New, *see* New South
    New Deal and, 665–66
    Nixon and, 813
    Operation Dixie in, 725
    People's Party in, 515
    poverty in, 673
    secession of, 397
    segregation in, 513, 521–28, *526*, *670*, 694,
      697, *760*, 773, 774–76, *779*, 813
    sit-ins in, 773
    strikes in, 653
    urban areas of, 452
    voting in, 620, 726, 780–81
    see also Confederate States of America
South Africa, 543, 608, 722, 815, 839, 845
    immigrants from, 860, 865
South Braintree, Mass., Sacco and Vanzetti
    in, 613
South Carolina, *441*, 450, 522
    Reconstruction in, 465, 470
South Dakota, 485
    corporate mining in, 487
    Wounded Knee massacre in, 493
Southern Christian Leadership Conference,
    764

Southern Conference for Human Welfare,
    673
Southern Manifesto, 765, 767
Southern Pacific Railroad, 487, 564
South Gate, Calif., 836
South Korea, 820, 825
    creation of, 719
    immigrants from, 860
South Vietnam, 791–94, 805, 816
Soviet Exhibition, 741
Soviet Union, 603, 639, 678, 679, 680, 686,
    706, 707, *711*, 713–22, 723, 724, 728,
    731, 737, 750, 789, 810, 815, *817*, 822–
    23, 826, 840, 859
    Afghanistan invasion by, 826
    American National Exhibition and,
      741–42, *741*
    atomic bomb of, 717, 719
    Berlin occupation by, 717
    breakup of, 844, *845*, 847
    Cold War and, 721
    collapse of communism in, 844, 847
    Cuban Missile Crisis and, 777–78
    Czechoslovakia invasion by, 806
    Eastern Europe occupation by, 707, 709,
      713, 716, 717
    Eisenhower and, 754–55
    European empires and, 755
    German invasion of, 681, 684, *685*, 713
    hydrogen bomb and, 754
    invaded by Hitler, 684
    invasion of Germany by, 704
    Korean War and, 719–21
    Lend-Lease and, 681
    Manchuria invasion by, 705
    Reagan and, 838
    space exploration and, 752–53, 769, 777
    spying of, 733
    in U.N., 708
    Universal Declaration of Human Rights
      and, 724
    Vietnam and, 815
    see also Cold War
soybean, 743
Spain, 535–37, *536*, 539, 603
Spanish-American War, *512*, 535, *536, 537*,
    538, *538*, 542, *542*, 543
    acquisition of empire and, 514, 579
    Battle of San Juan Hill in, 537
    casualties in, 536
    causes of, 535–36
    effects of, 539
    naval battle at Manila Bay in, 536
    see also Philippine War
Sparkman, John (1899–1985), 738
speakeasies, 614, 626, 634
Special Field Order 442
special interests, 572
    lobbying by, 498, 621

Springfield, Mo., 599, *599*, 600
Sputnik, 752–53, 769
Square Deal, 571
stagflation, 821, 832, 833
Stalin, Joseph (1879–1953), 680, 683–84, 707, *707*, 713, 714, 717, 721, 728, 754
　death of, 754
　and nonaggression pact, 680
Stalingrad, 684
Standard Oil Company, 481, 482–83, *482*, 534, 571, 572–73
Stanford University, 597
Stanton, Edwin M. (1814–1869), 442, 459
Stanton, Elizabeth Cady (1815–1902), 462, *462*, 593
Starr, Kenneth (1947–), 872
"Star-Spangled Banner, The" (Key), 535
state-church separation, 627, 804, *805*
State Department, U.S., 731, 734, 754, 791, 823, 840, 882, 883
　McCarthy and, 732
Statement of Purpose (NOW), 793
State of the Union Address (1941), 677
State of the Union Address (1996), 849
State of the Union Address (2002), 881
states' rights, 728, 832, 833
　Andrew Johnson's views of, 455
States' Rights Democratic Party, 728, 729
Statue of Liberty, 476, 495, 509, 510, 553, *553*, *589*, 599, *599*, *689*, *733*, *783*, *803*, 844, *846*, *858*, *915*
Stead, W. T. (1849–1912), 579
steel industry, 481, *482*, 483, 513, 521, 532, 553, 554, 604, 605, 614, 653–54, 725, 753, 835, *837*
Steel Workers Organizing Committee, 654
Steffens, Lincoln (1866–1936), 549
Stein, Gertrude (1874–1946), 624
Steinbeck, John (1902–1968), 661
Stennis, John C. (1901–1995), 818
sterilization, involuntary, 597–98
Stettheimer, Florine, *596*
Stevens, Thaddeus (1792–1868), 456, *456*
Stevenson, Adlai (1900–1965), 738, 751, *751*
Stimson, Henry (1867–1950), 705
stimulus package, 899
stock market, 614, 618, 636–37, *637*, 646, 647, 836, 856–57, 895–96, 901
Stonewall Inn, police raid on, 800–801
Strategic Arms Limitations Talks (SALT), 815
Strategic Bombing Survey, *706*
Strategic Defense Initiative, 838
strikes, 505, 509, 557–60, 603–4, 618, 725–26, 805, *806*, 835
　of air traffic controllers, 835
　in Boston, Mass., 622
　in colleges, 816
　in Depression, 653, *654*, *655*

in Detroit, Mich., 701
in France, 806
in Homestead, Pa., 513, 531
in Lawrence, Mass., 557–60
mining and, 519
in New York, N.Y., *557*
in 1934, 653
Pullman, 518, 531
railroad, 505, *505*, 518
rights and, 575
scabs and, *555*
steel, 604, 605, 753
in World War II, 688
Student Non-Violent Coordinating Committee (SNCC), 774, 776, 788, 789, 799
students, as activists, 773, 774, *779*
Students for a Democratic Society (SDS), 782, 790, *790*, 796, 799
Student Volunteer Movement for Foreign Missions, 534
submarines, 592
　in World War I, 584, 585–86, *586*
　in World War II, 684
"subprime" mortgages, 894
subtreasury plan, 514, 519
suburbs, 757, 758, 770, 799, 813, 827, 834, 860, 898
　African-Americans in, 865
　highways and, *744*, 752
　Latinos in, 860
　rise of, 743–45, *744*, 746
　as segregated, 747–48, 760
Sudetenland, 679
Suez Canal, 756
suffrage, *see* voting rights
sugar, *538*
　in Caribbean, 580
　in Cuba, 777
　in Hawaii, 535
　plantations, *see* planters, plantations, sugar
　in Puerto Rico, 748
suicide rate, Great Depression and, 639
Sullivan, Timothy "Big Tim," *563*
Sumner, Charles (1811–1874), 456, 461, 593
Sumner, William Graham (1840–1910), 503
Sunday, Billy (1862–1935), 625, *626*
Sunni Muslims, 883
Sun Yat-Sen, 562
supply and demand, law of, 502
supply-side economics, 835, 837, 879
Supreme Court, U.S., 461, 462, 470, 472, 504, 518, 524, 530, 543, 555, 568–69, 571, 572–73, 621, 624–25, 630, 631, 633, 818, 891–92
　abortion and, 805, 831, *831*, 870
　affirmative action and, 813
　African-American rights and, 600, 703

Brown v. Board of Education and, 761–62, *761*, 764–65, 767
civil liberties and, 624, 672, 764
civil rights and, 803–4, 813
Clinton's appointments to, 848
"court packing" and, *662*, 663
FDR and, 646, 662–63, *662*
G. W. Bush and, 892–93
homosexuals and, 838
housing segregation and, 747
Japanese-American internment and, 700
New Deal and, 652, *652*
Obama and, 899
Obamacare and, 900
Plessy v. Ferguson and, 525, *526*, 761, 767
political contribution restrictions and, 913
right to privacy and, 804–5
same-sex marriage and, 902
sanctions involuntary sterilization, 598
Scottsboro case and, 672
"separate but equal" ruling of, 525, *526*
and 2000 election, 873, *873*
Voting Rights Act invalidated by, 906
see also Burger Court; Warren Court
surveillance, domestic, 910
Swann v. Charlotte-Mecklenburg Board of Education, 813
sweatshops, 547
Sweatt, Heman (1912–1982), 761
Sweetwater, Tex., *690*
Switzer, Katherine, *800*
Switzerland, male suffrage in, 498
Syria, 608, 821
　ISIS in, 909

Taft, Robert (1889–1953), 750
Taft, William Howard (1857–1930), 570, 572–73, 621
　Latin America and, 583
Taft-Hartley Act (1947), 726, 753
Tahrir Square, 909
Taiwan, 719, 815, 820
Tajikistan, *845*
Taliban, 826, 880
tanks (military), 687, *687*
Tanzania, 755
Tape, Joseph and Mary, 530
Tape v. Hurley, 530
tariffs, 477, 500, *500*, *501*, 519, 520, 535, 573, 575, 621, 623, 640–41
taxes, 575, 622, 655, 725, 826, 835, 837, 848, 866, *899*, 910
　corporate, 564
　on corporations, 656
　demands for lowering, 832
　Gingrich and, 849
　Great Depression and, 641
　G. W. Bush's cuts in, 879, 893, 899

taxes (*continued*)
  income, 516, 571, 573, 575, 589, 621, 687, 785
  inheritance, 571
  New Deal and, 665
  poll, 524, 599, 727, 784
  property, 563
  single, 506
  Social Security, 665
  World War I and, 589
  World War II and, 687
Tax Reform Act (1986), 835
Taylor, Frederick W. (1856–1915), 554–55
Teacher, Frank, Jr., *643*
"tea parties," *899*
Tea Party, 910, 911
  Paul D. Ryan and, 911
Teapot Dome scandal, 622
technology:
  in agriculture, *616*, 617
  innovations in, 480
  in World War I, 584
teenagers, 757, 758, *758*
Tehran, 707, *707*, 826
telegraph:
  transatlantic, 480
telephones, 480, 615
television, 741, 742, 743, 746, *746*, 840
  civil rights movement and, 775, *775*, 783
  family life on, 746
  Iran hostage crisis and, *826*
  in 1960 campaign, 770
  politics and, 751, 841
  religious programing and, 827
  Vietnam War and, 805
Teller, Henry (1830–1914), 536
Teller Amendment, 536
temperance, 532, *533*
  see also Prohibition
Ten Commandments, The (film), 749
Tennessee, 524
  Ku Klux Klan founded in, 468
  Scopes trial in, 627–28, *627*
Tennessee River, 650
Tennessee Valley Authority (TVA), 649–50, *650*
Tenure of Office Act (1867), 459
Terman, Lewis (1877–1956), 597
"termination," and Native Americans, 801
terrorism, 874–75, 908, 909–10
  in Oklahoma City, 605, 871, *871*
  September 11 attacks, 594, 822, 874, 879, 881, 882, 885, 889, 890–91, 915
  war on, *539*, 879–81, 885–87, 889, 892
Tet offensive, 805
Texas, 514, 617, 632, *690*, 726, *834*, 862, 904
  in Dust Bowl, 651
  Hurricane Katrina victims and, 889
Texas, University of, segregation at, 761

Texas Minutemen, *890*
textile industry:
  plant closings in, 887
  strikes in, 618, 653, 725
Thailand, 682
Theory of the Leisure Class, The (Veblen), 483
Thind, Bhagat Singh (1892–1967), 630
Third Great Awakening, 827
Third World, 755–56, 791, 814, 825, 839
  Cold War in, 755–56
Thirteenth Amendment, 485, 712
This Godless Communism, 711
This Is America, 694
This Is the Enemy (Ancona and Koehler), 702
Thoreau, Henry David (1817–1862), 572, 764
Three Mile Island, 824
Thurmond, Strom (1902–2003), 728–29, *728*, 782
Tiananmen Square, protests in, 844, *846*
Tibet, 798
Tilden, Samuel J. (1814–1886), 471
Time, 731, 762
Times Square, *680*
"Times They Are A-Changin', The" (Dylan), 796
Tipsy (Kiyoshi), *619*
Title IX, 814
tobacco, 449, 521
Tobacco Belt, 449
Tokyo, Japan, 707
"too big to fail" rationale, 897
Topeka, Kans., *761*
torture, 886–87, 899
  water-boarding as, *886*
To Secure These Rights, 727
totalitarianism, 722–23, 839
  see also dictators, dictatorships
Townsend, Francis (1867–1960), 655, 656
trade:
  in World War II, 680, 681, 689
  see also free trade
transcendentalism, 572
"Trans-National America" (Bourne), 596–97
transportation, 563
  public, 746
  see also railroads
Treasure Chest, 711
Treaty of Amity and Commerce (1778), 717
treaty system:
  elimination of, 492
Triangle Shirtwaist Company, fire at, 547, 552
tribalism, attack on Native American, 492
Triborough Bridge, 649, *649*
trickle-down economics, *see* supply-side economics
Troubles, The, 806
Trujillo Molina, Rafael (1891–1961), 678

Truman, Harry S. (1884–1972), 692, 704–5, 707, 712, 713, 714–15, *715*, 723, 849, 880
  African-Americans and, 726–29
  anticommunism and, 736
  Berlin airlift and, 717
  in campaign of 1948, 727–29
  civil rights and, 726–29
  communist China and, 717
  decolonization and, 722
  Fair Deal and, 724–25
  Korean War and, 719
  presidency of, 724–29
  strikes and, 725
  Vietnam and, 756
Truman administration, 712, 714–15, 717, 722, 724–29, 736–37, 738, 752, 791
  Native Americans and, 801
Truman Doctrine, 714–15, *715*, 730, 737
Trumbo, Dalton (1905–1976), 731
Trumbull, Lyman (1813–1896), 457, 468
trusts, business, 481, 571, *571*, 575
  and antitrust laws, 575
  see also monopolies; Sherman Antitrust Act (1890)
Tulsa, Okla., race riot in, 602, *602*
Tunisia, 909
Turkey, 584, 714, 778
  missiles removed from, 778
Turner, Benjamin S., *463*
Tuskegee Institute, 531
TVA, *see* Tennessee Valley Authority
TV dinner, 746
Twain, Mark (1835–1910), 497
Tweed, "Boss" William M. (1823–1878), 498–99
Tweed Ring, 467, 498–99
Twentieth Amendment, 662
Twenty-first Amendment, 651
Twenty-fourth Amendment, 783–84
typewriter, 480

U-2 spy plane, 755
UAW, *see* United Auto Workers
UFW, *see* United Farm Workers
Ukraine, 916
Ulysses (Joyce), 625
Uncle Sam, *480*, *529*, *538*, *652*, *679*, *689*, *717*
Underground newspapers, 797
Underwood Tariff (1913), 575
unemployment, 574, 575, 616, 663, 665, 677, 687, 742, 776, *820*, 821, 822, 823, 836, 858, 895, 898, 901
  African-Americans and, 667, 787
  Great Depression and, 637–39, 648, 655, 660
  insurance, 658, 665, 668, 897
  in 1990s, 855
  public spending to combat, 663–64
  Second New Deal and, 656, 659, 673, 674
  in 2001, 887

Unintended Legacy (Goshorn), *868*
Union League, 462, 464, 589
Union of Soviet Socialist Republics, *see* Soviet Union
Union Pacific Railroad, 499
unions, 510, 513, 519, 532, 557–60, 604, 618, 621, 639, 653–55, 670, 672, 712, 736, 737, 743, 750, 822, 835–36, 901, 914
    African-Americans and, 599, 602, 672, 702, 759, 776
    blacklisting organizers of, 658
    Brandeis and, 555
    Clinton and, 852
    company unions vs., 618
    consumerism and, 554
    in election of 1936, 662
    in Great Depression, 652–55
    highways and, 752
    Homestead strike and, 513
    industrialism and, 482, 483
    Ku Klux Klan and, 628
    Latinos and, 801
    membership in, 654, 688, *688*
    NAFTA and, 848
    New Deal and, 648, 673
    in 1950s, 753
    Nixon and, 812
    open shop policies and, 648
    Operation Dixie and, 725
    Reagan and, 834, 835–36
    scabs and, *555*
    segregation and, 522
    supported by left, 670
    Supreme Court and, 504
    Taft-Hartley Act and, 726
    Wal-Mart and, 859
    War Labor Board and, 589
    women and, 690–91
    in World War II, 688
    see also labor; labor movement; *specific unions*
United Auto Workers (UAW), 654–55, 690
United Electric Worker's, 799
United Farm Workers (UFW), 801, 864
United Fruit Company, 755
United Labor Party, 510
United Mine Workers of America, 559, *643*, 653
United Nations, 719, 723, 724, 815, 823, 846, 853, 881
    in Balkans, 853
    Charter of, 755
    creation of, 708
    Iraq War and, 881, 883
    see also General Assembly, U.N.; Security Council, U.N.
United States Housing Act, 663
United States v. Butler, 652
United States v. Cruikshank, 470

United States v. E. C. Knight Co., 504
United States v. Wong Kim Ark, 530
United Steelworkers of America, 654
United Textile Workers, 653
Universal Declaration of Human Rights, 723, 724
Universal Negro Improvement Association, 603
University of North Carolina Press, 697
Unsafe at Any Speed (Nader), 803
urbanization, 548–54
    rise of cities, *549*
Urban League, 666
urban renewal, 748
U'Ren, William, 563–64
USA Patriot Act, 885, 908
U.S. Steel, 481, 571, 637, 654
U.S. v. Abrams, 625
Utah:
    woman suffrage in, 567
utilities, 564
Uzbekistan, *889*

Valentino, Rudolph (1895–1926), 619
Vance, Cyrus (1917–2002), *794*
Vanderberg, Arthur (1884–1951), 715
Vanzetti, Bartolomeo (1888–1927), 613, *613*
vaudeville, 551
Veblen, Thorstein (1857–1929), 483
V-E Day, 704
velvet revolution, 844
Venezuela, 615
Veracruz, Mexico, 583–84
Verdun, Battle of, 584
Verizon, 910
Vermont, 677
Versailles Treaty, 606–7, *606*, 608, 609, *609*
    Senate debate on, 609–10
vertical integration, 481, 482
Veterans' Administration, 651
Veterans' Administration Medical Center, *864*
veto, presidential, 457, 725, 736
Viet Cong, 794, 805, 817
Vietnam, 608, 609, 864, 883
    see also North Vietnam; South Vietnam
Vietnamization, 816
Vietnam syndrome, 838
Vietnam War, 590, 686, 770, 789–98, *794*, *795*, 823, 888
    and antiwar movement, 772, 796, *796*, 805, 806, 816–17, *816*
    casualties in, 817
    draft resisters of, 796, 825
    My Lai massacre in, 816–17
    Nixon and, 815, 816–17
    origins of, 756–57, 791–94
    Paris peace agreement and, 817
    protests against, 772, 796, 810

    television and, 805
    Tet offensive in, 805
    troop numbers in, 794
Villa, Francisco "Pancho" (1878–1923), 584
Villet, Grey (1927–2000), *804*
Vindication of the Rights of Woman, A (Wollstonecraft), 230
Vinson, Fred (1890–1953), 761
Virginia, 804, *804*, 898
    desegregation in, 765
Virginia Tech University, 914
Virgin Islands, 579
Visit from the Old Mistress, A (Homer), *447*
VISTA, 785
Voice of America, McCarthy and, 732
Volga River, 684
voting rights, 565, 763
    African-American loss of, 524–25, 565, 602, 665, 697, 765, 781
    for African-Americans, 460–62, *464*
    citizenship and, 565
    emancipated slaves and, 442, 444, 460–62, *464*
    grandfather clause and, 524
    for Japanese women, 716
    literacy tests and, 524, 565
    registration and black, 524–25, 565
    Voting Rights Act and, 783
    for women, 460, 461–62, *462*, 517, 532–33, 548, 564, 565, 567, *568*, *569*, *570*, 575, 586, 590–91, *591*, 618, 620
Voting Rights Act (1965), 783–84, 786
    invalidated by Supreme Court, 905

wages, 604
    African-Americans and, 599, 634, 890
    agricultural work for, 486
    consumerism and, 552, 553, 567
    cost of living increases in, 737, 753
    cowboys and, 487
    decline in real, 822, *822*, *836*, 841, 858
    equal pay for equal work and, *830*
    Fordism and, 553
    Great Depression and, 637
    hourly, 859
    immigrants and, 551
    inflation and increasing, 616
    international standards for, 855
    "living," 553
    "living wage" and, 575, 590, 659
    and Mexican immigrants, 801, 890
    migrant farm workers and, 801, 890
    minimum, 569, 574, 621, 663, 753, 859, 904–5
    New Deal and, 655
    overtime and, 663
    real, 742
    rising, 742, 743
    Social Security tax on, 665

wages (continued)
  in South, 616
  stagnation of, 890, 901
  strike for higher, 487
  women and, 532, 690, 799, 830, 870
  in World War I, 589
  in World War II, 687, 688, 690
Wagner Act (1935), 658, 663, 667, 712
Waite, Davis (1825–1901), 518
Walker, David, 704
Wallace, George (1919–1998), 781, 783, 807, 811, 827
Wallace, Henry (1888–1965), 691–92, 728–29
Wall Street, 618, 622, 656, 681, 894, 896, 901
  in depression, 639
Wal-Mart, 859, 901–4
War Advertising Council, 689
war bonds, 595, 687, 689
Warehouse Act (1916), 575
War Industries Board, 589, 648
War Labor Board, 589
War Manpower Commission, 687
War Message to Congress (Wilson), 592
Warner, Charles Dudley (1829–1900), 497
War of 1812, 593, 682
War of Independence, see American Revolution
War on Poverty, 785, 785, 789, 801
War on Terrorism, 539, 879–81, 885–87, 889, 892
War Powers Act (1973), 817
War Production Board, 687
Warren, Earl (1891–1974), 761, 762, 803–4, 812
Warren Court, 762, 803–4, 807
Warsaw Pact, 717
washing machines, 615
Washington, 564, 644
Washington, Booker T. (1856?–1915), 531, 531, 533, 540, 541, 599, 600
Washington, D.C., 668, 789, 793, 805–6, 831, 837, 867, 880, 899
  march on, 776, 776
  segregation in, 761
  September 11 attacks on, 874
  Vietnam protests in, 796
Washington, George (1732–1799), 593, 681, 770
Washington Naval Arms Conference, 622–23
Washington Navy Yard, 914
Washington Post, 687, 818
WASPs (Women Airforce Service Pilots), 690
Wassaja newspaper, 562
Watch and Ward Committee, 623–24
waterboarding, 539, 886
Watergate scandal, 818, 822
  Saturday Night Massacre and, 818
Waters, Ethel (1896–1977), 635
Watson, Tom (1854–1934), 517
Watterson, Henry, 534

Watts, Calif., riot in, 786, 787
Wayne State University, 748
WCTU, see Woman's Christian Temperance Union
Wealth Against Commonwealth (Lloyd), 482
Wealth of Nations, The (Smith), 895
weapons of mass destruction, 881
  long-range bombers and, 754
  Saddam Hussein and, 882, 885
  tests of, 729, 730, 778
Weaver, James B. (1833–1912), 517
Webster, Daniel (1782–1852), 593
Weir, Ferguson (1841–1926), 478
Welch, Joseph (1805–1891), 732, 733
welfare, 569, 575, 658–59, 662, 665, 666, 669, 674, 728, 737, 781, 783, 838, 847, 849–52, 869, 897, 914
  expansion of, 692
  Nixon and, 811–12
  Reagan and, 833, 835, 838
  stigma of, 666
"welfare capitalism," 618
Wells, Ida B. (1862–1931), 527
Wells, Josiah T., 463
"We Shall Overcome," 783
Wesley, Charles H., 697
West, 487, 500, 501, 514, 677, 690, 810
  African-Americans in, 700
  cattle drives in, 487
  economic development of, 651
  environmentalism in, 829, 833
  fundamentalists in, 628
  government contracts and, 743
  growth of, 745–46
  immigrants and, 484, 485
  industry in, 488
  libertarianism in, 750
  Native Americans in, 490
  New Deal and, 651, 667
  People's Party in, 515
  political corruption in, 498–99
  Progressive era and, 563–65
  romanticized as "Wild West," 497, 497
  slavery in, 484
  transformation of, 498
  war production in, 687
  woman suffrage in, 591
West Germany, 719, 752
  creation of, 717
West Indies, 634
West Memphis, Ark., 760
West Virginia, 664
Wharton, Edith (1862–1937), 561
"What Every Girl Should Know," 561
"What Freedom Means to Us" (Nixon), 741
What the Negro Wants, 697
wheat, 485, 487
Wheeling, W.Va., McCarthy speech at, 732–33, 734

Whig Party, 469
Whiskey Ring, 467
White, John (1585–1593), 594–95
White, Theodore (1915–1986), 810
white-collar jobs:
  corporations and, 743
  minorities and, 748
"white man's burden," 539, 543, 544
white supremacists, 903
Whitewater, 872
Whitman, Walt (1819–1892), 484
Whitney, Richard (1888–1974), 639
Whyte, William (1917–1999), 758
Wichita, Kans., 487
Wild and Scenic Rivers Act (1968), 829
Wilderness Act (1964), 829
Wilhelm II, emperor of Germany (1859–1941), 588
Willard, Frances (1839–1898), 532–33
Willkie, Wendell (1892–1944), 681
Willow Run factory, 687
Wilson, Charles (1890–1961), 752
Wilson, Edith (1872–1961), 610
Wilson, Henry, 459
Wilson, Woodrow (1856–1924), 555, 570, 573–76, 583–84, 586, 604, 605, 607–10, 622, 646, 684
  African-Americans and, 599, 601
  civil liberties and, 595
  Debs and, 595
  first term of, 575–76
  foreign policy of, 580, 583–84
  Fourteen Points and, 587–88
  and League of Nations, 609–10
  Mexican policy of, 583–84
  New Freedom of, 574
  stroke of, 610
  at Versailles, 605–7
  woman suffrage and, 590–91
  World War I and, 585–86, 587–88, 592
Wilson administration, 589, 591, 595, 601
Wilsonism, 610
Winnipeg, 603
Wirz, Henry (1823–1865), 456
Wisconsin, 563, 564, 622, 730, 732
Wisconsin, University of, 565
Wisconsin Idea, 564
Wohaw (Kiowa warrior), 493
Wolfowitz, Paul D. (1943–), 881
Woman Rebel, 561
Woman's Christian Temperance Union (WCTU), 508, 532, 594
  Home Protection movement of, 532
women, 547, 870
  advertising and, 620, 691
  African-American, 522, 524, 552, 598, 702
  changing role of, 552, 552, 619–20, 690–91, 691

and Civil War, 590
in Clinton administration, 848
education and, 566, 569, 591, 870
freedom and, 552, 558, 619–20, *620*, 690
in Great Plains, 486
Great Society and, 669
as immigrants, 860, *862*
in kitchen debate, 742
Knights of Labor and, 505
labor and, 505, 532, 568
maternalist reform and, 567–69, 658
minimum wage and, 621
New Deal and, 664–65, *665*
politics and, 566–67
in Progressive era, 590–91
right to vote for Japanese, 716
rise of feminism and, 532–33
Supreme Court and, 870
and traditional homemaker role, 742,
    746–47, *747*, 770, 830, *869*
and wages, 532, 690, 799, 870
in the work force, 505, 552, *552*, *553*, 558,
    564, 567, 677, 690–91, *690*, 746–47,
    814, 838, 870, *871*, 895
working hours and, 568–69
and World War II, 677, 678, 690–91
see also gender relations; women's rights
Women and Economics (Perkins), 558
Women's Party, 830
women's rights, 524, 532–33, 564–65,
    618–20, 628, 716, 774, 799–800, *800*,
    899, 913
and education, 566, 569
post–World War II, 746–47
in Progressive era, 560–61, 567
Prohibition and, 594, *594*
Reconstruction and, 460, 461–62
sex and, 560–61, 619
and suffrage, 460, 461–62, *462*, 513, *513*,
    532–33, 548, 564, 565, 567, *568*, *569*,
    570, 575, 586, 590–91, *591*, 618, 620
see also abortion; gender relations; women
Woodstock, *796*, 797
Woolworth's, sit-in at, 773
*Workingman's Conception of Industrial Liberty,
    The* (J.P. Mitchell), 559
workmen's compensation, 569

Works Progress Administration (WPA), *646*,
    657–58, *657*, 663
World Bank, 708, 855
World's Constable, The, 582
World's Fair, *481*
World Trade Center, *821*, 822, 874, 875
World Trade Organization (WTO), *843*, 851,
    854, 855
World War I, *578*, 584–96, *585*, *606*, 623, 624,
    631, 632, 648, 680
    African-Americans and, 601–2, *601*
    agriculture in, 616
    casualties in, 584, 588
    causes of, 584
    divisiveness of, 688
    effects of, 609, 610, 623, 692
    freedom and, 590, 594, 596
    Hoover's relief program in, 635
    immigration and, 601, 677–78, 694
    Jeanette Rankin and, 590, 682
    Meuse-Argonne campaign in, 588
    mobilization in, 677
    patriotism in, 595–96
    Progressives and, 588
    propaganda in, 589–90, *589*
    revolutions and, 603
    technology in, 584
    U.S. view of, 585
    western front, *587*
    woman suffrage and, 590–91
World War II, 645, 676–710, *676*, *678*, 750,
    855, *881*, *884*, *904*
    African-Americans and, 678, 693, 700–
    704, *703*
    British welfare state and, 658
    casualties in, 682, 686, 704, 705–7, 713
    causes of, 679
    civil rights and, 678, 762
    draft in, 686
    effects of, 708–9, 713
    end of, 704–9
    European theater of, 683–86, *685*
    freedom and, 678, *678*, 688–90, *691*, 709
    as Good War, 688
    "Grand Alliance" of, 683–84
    Great Depression and, 674, 677
    home front during, 686–89

industry and, 686–88, *687*, 690–91
    Japanese-Americans and, 678, 698–700,
        699, *700*, 761
    Pearl Harbor and, 681–82
    and post-war freedom, 691–93
    propaganda in, *698*
    Rosenbergs and, 731
    unions in, 688
    U.S. entry into, 674, 682
    women and, 678, 690–91
    see also Four Freedoms
"World War II and Mexican Americans," 696
Wounded Knee Creek, Indian massacre
    at, 493
Wright, Jonathan (1840–1887), 464
WTO, *see* World Trade Organization
Wyoming:
    woman suffrage in, 567
    Yellowstone in, 571

YAF, *see* Young Americans for Freedom
Yalta, conference at, 707–8
Yazoo-Mississippi Delta, 781
yellow press, 535, 537
Yellowstone National Park, 571, *572*
Yes Sir, He's My Baby, 621
yippies, 797
yoga, counterculture and, *798*, *798*
Yoga Journal, *798*
Yosemite National Park, *648*
Young, Andrew (1932–), 823
Young, Brigham (1801–1877), 489
Young Americans for Freedom (YAF), 782
Youth International Party, 797
Yugoslavia, 606, 609, 852–53, *853*
    breakup of, *845*
yuppies, 837

Zangwill, Israel, 596
Zapata, Emiliano, 584
Zhou Enlai (1898–1976), *815*
Zimmerman, George, 906
Zimmermann, Arthur (1864–1940), 586
Zimmermann Telegram, 586
"zoot suit" riots, 695
Zuccotti Park, Occupy Movement in, 904
Zulu, 484